Speaking of Sexuality

Interdisciplinary Readings

Second Edition

J. Kenneth Davidson, Sr.
University of Wisconsin, Eau Claire

Nelwyn B. Moore
Texas State University, San Marcos

Preface by
Pepper Schwartz
University of Washington

Foreword by
John D. DeLamater
University of Wisconsin–Madison

Instructor's Manual/Testing Program Available

Roxbury Publishing Company
Los Angeles, California

Library of Congress Cataloging-in-Publication Data

Speaking of sexuality: interdisciplinary readings / [edited by] J. Kenneth Davidson, Sr., Nelwyn B. Moore; preface by Pepper Schwartz; foreword by John D. DeLamater.—2nd ed.
    p.   cm.
Includes bibliographical references.
ISBN 1-931719-38-1
    1. Sex. 2. Sex (Psychology) 3. Hygiene, Sexual. 4. Interpersonal relations. I. Davidson, Sr., J. Kenneth. II. Moore, Nelwyn B.

HQ21.S6244 2005
306.7--dc22

2004042835
CIP

SPEAKING OF SEXUALITY: INTERDISCIPLINARY READINGS, SECOND EDITION

Publisher: Claude Teweles
Managing Editor: Dawn VanDercreek
Production Editor: Carla Plucknett
Production Assistant: Erin Record-Clemons
Copy Editor: Ann West
Proofreader: Arlyne Lazerson
Typography: Abe Hendin
Cover Design: Marnie Kenney

Printed on acid-free paper in the United States of America. This book meets the standards for recycling of the Environmental Protection Agency.

ISBN 1-931719-38-1

ROXBURY PUBLISHING COMPANY
P.O. Box 491044
Los Angeles, California 90049-9044
Voice: (310) 473-3312 • Fax: (310) 473-4490
E-mail: roxbury@roxbury.net
Website: www.roxbury.net

*We dedicate this book to the countless thousands of
students who have touched our lives in more
years than we care to count . . .*

*And to our professional colleagues
with whom we share both a common
passion for teaching, and a common illusion . . .
the belief that we know more about the subject
of sexuality than do the students.*

—J. Kenneth Davidson, Sr.
Nelwyn B. Moore

Contents

Part I ✦ Historical, Theoretical, and Research Perspectives on Sexuality

Ira L. Reiss and Harriet M. Reiss

The authors delineate the reasons for the emergence of two sexual revolutions in the late twentieth century, and propose a pluralistic approach to sexuality: individual choices guided by the values of honesty, equality, and responsibility (HER).

Vern L. Bullough

Bullough chronicles the life and career of Alfred Kinsey, from biologist to renowned sex researcher, and offers numerous insights into why his work continues to be controversial.

Vern L. Bullough

This brief history of Masters and Johnson's research documents their clinical measurements of physiological sexual response that led to their often-cited, arbitrary four-stage division of the sexual response.

Edward O. Laumann, John H. Gagnon, Robert T. Michael, and Stuart Michaels

A noted research team describes the underlying theoretical basis for conducting their landmark survey of sexual behavior and attitudes in the United States.

Joseph Adelson

In a well-written commentary, the author argues that Laumann and colleagues' study represents an accurate appraisal of sexual behavior in American society, that is, "everyone is not playing around."

Part II ✦ Sexuality and the Life Cycle: Childhood and Adolescence

Part III ✦ Sexuality and the Life Cycle: Young Adulthood

* Denotes a chapter new to this edition.

Part IV ✦ Sexuality and the Life Cycle: Middle and Later Adulthood

---

* Denotes a chapter new to this edition.

Part V ✦ Sexual Desire and Gender

Part VI ✦ Sexually Transmitted Diseases and Abortion

---

* Denotes a chapter new to this edition.

Part VII ✦ Sexual Orientation

* Denotes a chapter new to this edition.

Part VIII ✦ Sexual Victimization and Compulsion

Part IX ✦ Sexuality and Society: Law, Economics, Religion, and Education

* Denotes a chapter new to this edition.

---

* Denotes a chapter new to this edition.

Preface

Each time authors create a new edition of a book of readings, the process is almost like creating a whole new book. Previously selected articles have to vie with new nominees, and choices have to be made. Times change, and issues that may have seemed necessary before bow to new cultural debates or fresh research material. Even with all this addition and subtraction, it is, sad to say, impossible to include every important aspect of sexuality or stay current with a sudden galvanization over a sexual issue (such as gay marriage having moved to front and center of American politics in the early months of 2004).

Given that all Tables of Contents have their limitations, we can assume that different academic disciplines would have made different choices. The vision of what are central observations and issues in society might be substantially different if this book were on the medical aspects of sexuality or the psychology of sexuality. Still, I think this volume has taken into account what many disciplines consider cutting-edge issues in an attempt to give you, the reader, the widest possible view of the most important ways sexuality touches our lives. More interdisciplinary than most, but still using a sociological lens, these authors focus on sexuality by using comparative and interdisciplinary materials. In other words, one of the beauties of *Speaking of Sexuality* is that sociology will illuminate how human interaction and social groups affect our sexuality—but you will have the benefit of historical, medical, legal, psychological, and therapeutic materials to help you understand each issue. (As a major bonus, most of the articles were also chosen for their readability so that the book won't seem like medicine: good for you, but hard going down.)

What do I like about the book? Why do I use it in my class (an intimate lecture hall of over 700 students . . .)? I like the organization of the book, and I like specific articles for the "Ah Ha!" factor of personally important and often surprising information. The first section of the book gives students a "framework," a way of seeing how history influences which questions on sexuality are asked, how sexual issues and "crises" are influenced by the cultural moment (and sometimes the authors' own background), and why we need to pay attention to the differences between people of different gender, race, class, age, sexual orientation, and marital status. Once we understand the need to pay attention to these social factors, we can and should address sexuality as we progress through the life cycle, since the life cycle orders much of the variation in sexuality we observe. Certainly children have different sexual issues based on their level of physiological development, but they also need to be examined separately from teenagers or adults because the younger they are, the more they are constrained by adult values and at the mercy of parental beliefs and fears, and treated differently from adults by legal systems and other institutions. Consequently, we can understand that sexuality will have different effects and different consequences on children than adolescents—and that first acts will be different than similar later acts in how they are experienced or remembered.

This is, of course, also true for adolescence, which is why it is given a section of its own. Adolescence seems to have lengthened into what might have been called early adulthood in other periods of history; but that caveat not withstanding, we need to look at those pivotal moments of first intercourse, the meaning of virginity (and "experience"), and how young people learn how to talk about what they want. The truth is, as many of you know, that talking about sex is often a lot harder to do than just having sex. When people are learning about themselves at the same time as they are falling in love (or lust), clear expression of needs, and wants (and "don't wants") are extremely difficult. Yet, while communication is at the center of an ability to conduct a satisfying and safe sexual relationship, most people negotiate sexual desire awkwardly and sometimes downright disastrously. This may sound familiar: Many, perhaps most, college students are still inexperienced when it comes to expressing their sexual thoughts and desires to a partner; which is why putting in articles on sexuality and communication seems like critical content to me.

This doesn't mean, of course, that communication and honesty cease to be a challenge after adolescence. The section in this book on young adulthood indicates how important these issues continue to be in the maintenance of longer-term relationships. One of the things I like about this section is that the authors show that problems, such as infidelity or communicating honestly about what is really happening during sex, are not uncommon issues that many relationships have to face. In fact, as Part IV shows us, creating and keeping desire in relationships cannot be taken for granted; nor, because issues vary from one race, gender, class, or age group to another, can one answer be assumed to be relevant for all populations.

Finally, the last third of the book pays attention to sexual problems and policy issues. Although the first part of the book is about how sexuality works in "ordinary" situations (if any situations are ever ordinary!), the last sections make us face up to aspects of sexuality that can prove painful, or even fatal, if not understood and attended to. Unplanned and unwanted pregnancies happen to millions of women every year, and choices must be made about what to do about them (and how to do what you want to do). The specter of AIDS and even nonlethal STDs changes the values, feelings, and procedures of contemporary men and women. Differential risk for these diseases (for example, gay men versus lesbians) may mean different emotions or differential risk taking, but no one in the world is untouched by the fear of catching a terrible disease—much less the stigma, pain, and psychic distress of having to manage a life-threatening or painful physical disability that has been transmitted through sexual conduct.

Other challenges also exist because of differential exposure to stigmatization or victimization. No book on sexuality can ignore the fact that the right to sexual consent is often abused and that we as citizens need to know who is at risk and how to protect ourselves and our children. As sociologists, however, we know that consent to engage in sexual activity is often ambiguous and that gender norms may make it more than less likely for one person to feel violated while the other feels betrayed and mystified. Good research in this area has created articles that every person needs to read, to help understand how interpretation of what just happened can be so different between two people.

Cultural battles over sexuality are going on now, and perhaps they will always be going on. Sexuality education itself, the very process you are voluntarily entering into, is quite controversial and a battleground in many school districts. Sexual social policy is fought over in the schools, courts, legislatures, and religious institutions. This is perhaps most vividly played out in the current debate over how homosexuality shall be regarded in Western culture. Though gay men and lesbians are far more open and integrated into general society than ever before in the United States, this is not true in some areas of the country and in many parts of the world (where an openly homosexual man or woman might justly fear for his or her life). Homophobia (loathing for and aversion to homosexuals) exists, and debates rage about whether homosexuality should be accepted because it is a biological inheritance involving no choice or an option for an individual or whether it is a "lifestyle," able to be contained if it is denied ratification. Polls indicate split opinions about acceptance of homosexual civil rights. Some of these disagreements have erupted in the recent battle in the United States (and in some European countries) over whether or not gays and lesbians have the right to marry. People feel strongly about this issue, lawsuits have been filed; and civil disobedience is evident in some parts of the United States (for example, the mayor of San Francisco allows marriages to be performed in City Hall while the Governor and Attorney General of California call for all such marriages to stop and be declared illegal). Legislatures throughout the country heatedly debate gay marriage, coming to different conclusions about whether or not gay marriages are allowed under their state constitutions. (Massachusetts says yes, Illinois and many other states say no . . .). As this book goes to press, the President of the United States has called for a constitutional amendment to "protect marriage" by defining it as being only between a man and a woman. A hot debate has ensued over whether or not civil union is an acceptable "middle ground" by which same-sex couple rights can be preserved but marriage as an institution would remain heterosexual.

So gay marriage was the galvanizing issue at the time this edition was published, but certainly others will emerge. These battles over sexual morality and practice occur because we all hold deeply held beliefs about sexuality and we are all affected by what laws and social policies are made. This book is so constructed as to give you solid research on which to test your beliefs, add information to your decision making on personal issues, and become an informed citizen as you vote on issues that will affect your sexual life, your personal happiness, and, perhaps, the health, welfare, and safety of your friends and fellow citizens. Enjoy the readings, examine your assumptions, and profit from the thoughtful and provocative moments that this book will encourage.

Pepper Schwartz
University of Washington

Foreword

A visitor to the United States would probably conclude that it is a completely open society with regard to sexuality. Every one of us is surrounded by sexual materials and information. On network television, sexual behavior and relationships are portrayed in prime-time programs and soap operas; on cable television, explicit sexual interactions are increasingly frequent. "News stories" about sexual topics fill our daily papers, news magazines, and TV news. Feature films display and provide scripts for a wide range of sexual behaviors and lifestyles. Advertisers use images of sexually attractive women and men to sell us everything from cosmetics and clothing, to beer and wine, automobiles and vacations. And then there is explicit pornography, available on cable television, in magazines, at your local video rental outlet, and on the Internet, where it is the largest single category.

Unfortunately, the young man or woman who attempts to fashion his or her sexual expression and lifestyle using these media depictions is not likely to find sexual fulfillment or lasting relationships. The portrayals we see on television and in films are unrealistic; they feature young, attractive people who are often not in long-term relationships, and these people do not worry about pregnancy or sexually transmitted diseases and infections. The portrayals in pornography are not realistic either; they feature people who are very attractive, have large breasts or penises, and who engage in a wide variety of sexual acts with abandon. Either type of portrayal is difficult for most people in the United States to identify with. On the other hand, the plots of soap operas and news stories often focus on the dangers associated with sexuality, such as rape, unwanted pregnancy, and STDs.

Fortunately, we have much better sources of information available to us. Scientific research on human sexuality dates back at least to the 1890s and the pioneering work of Sigmund Freud. Over the years, many biological, behavioral, and social scientists have contributed to our contemporary understanding of sexuality. Since the 1970s, textbooks written by knowledgeable scientists and educators and anthologies of professional readings have become increasingly accessible to students and the general public. The Davidson and Moore collection of articles and chapters is designed to introduce sexuality research and writings by biological scientists, psychologists, social psychologists, and sociologists. The Volume Editors have carefully selected these readings to reflect the diversity of materials published in this field. They have also edited the original readings to make them more concise and informative.

This is the Second Edition of this volume. Based on feedback from students and faculty, the Editors have deleted some of the original chapters and added new ones. I used the First Edition as an assigned reader for several semesters. I used it because I want my students to have access to original articles, to see and appreciate the complexity of a research project or a theoretical argument. Many of my students spontaneously commented on how interesting or important they found the material in some of these articles to be. My students also appreciated the introductory paragraphs written by the Editors; these paragraphs both provide a context for and summarize the themes of each chapter.

The selections will introduce you to important influences on your sexual thoughts, emotions, and behavior. Biological development and aging, parents, friends, lovers, sexuality education, religion, and culture all affect sexuality throughout a person's life. Such complex influences can lead to emotionally and sexually satisfying relationships and behavior. They can also lead to frustrating and painful outcomes, such as loneliness, problems in sexual functioning, STDs, and forms of sexual victimization. Reading the articles in this book, you can learn about the influences on your sexuality and gain a sense of agency and control, enabling you to avoid undesirable outcomes and increasing your chances of creating positive ones.

As you read, consider whether and how the content of an article relates to you and your relationships. For example, if the article discusses communication in relationships, consider whether you can improve communication with your partner(s) based on what you read. If you find a particular article especially interesting or thought-provoking and want more information, consult the sources listed in the references, or the relevant sections in your textbook.

I have been teaching human sexuality for twenty-eight years. Many of my students have told me that it was the single most important course that they took, because they gained a greater understanding of their sexuality and of our society. I hope these readings contribute to your own achievement of this understanding.

John D. DeLamater
University of Wisconsin, Madison

About This Edition

Overview

No aspect of human life seethes with so many un-exorcised demons as does sex. No human activity is so hexed by superstition, so haunted by residual tribal lore, and so harassed by socially induced fear.

—Harvey Cox

The captivating words by noted theologian Harvey Cox alluding to the unstateable state of the subject of this anthology, sexuality, are less than rhetorical. They portend that all is not well in the real world of sexuality. We agree. But neither is all lost. This latter belief is the basis of the paradigm for this work.

By choosing to reframe many of today's considered-to-be sexuality issues, we hope to dispel a number of sexual myths that have been formed from society's free-floating sexual anxieties. To accomplish this feat, we called upon academicians—women and men of letters in the fields of medicine, theology, sexology, sociology, marriage and family therapy, psychology, social work, psychiatry, and family studies. Most have spoken with empirical authority, based on their own research. Some few by virtue of the respect gained over a lifetime of work in the field of sexology were selected for their accumulated acumen. For balance, a number of challenging selections were included from authors whose writings appear in popular sources, such as *Forbes, Harper's, Newsweek, The New York Times Magazine,* and award-winning books.

English educator Robert Grimm once said that if you want to know what individuals are really like at their very core, look at the way they use their sexuality. If, for you, this book has a voice, you may well hear it ask, "How are we, as a part of humankind, collectively using our sexuality?" We invite you to accompany us into the pages of this book that we may all more authoritatively answer this question.

About the Anthology

Speaking of Sexuality (SOS) is the alternative for instructors of human sexuality courses who prefer a student-friendly, yet more rigorous, less sensationalized, book of readings than any currently on the market. No other sexuality reader has both comprehensive Part Openers, with absorbing discussions of each Chapter Topic, and insightful Chapter Lead-Ins that encourage students to think critically about the subject as they read.

Combining the best of "the old with the new," this edition has retained the same distinctive features that made the First Edition of *SOS* the leading sexuality reader in its class. Presenting an array of personal and societal sexuality issues at a scholarly level that other works have failed to achieve, it also uniquely addresses the subject of human sexuality from a personal perspective of strength, one that is sex-positive but realistic. The framework for this anthology, as in the first edition, is lifetime sexual health, an organizing principle based on two assumptions: Sexuality is an inseparable part of an individual's persona and sexuality spans the life cycle from birth to death. The core belief that a healthy sexual script is a realistic goal for every person is the book's bottom-line rationale.

To enable the reader to encounter leading sexuality authorities, past and present, seminal works in sexuality research and theory are included here. The balance achieved by also offering articles that reveal popular treatment of today's timely topics enables students to become more discriminating consumers of sexuality materials in the mass media, a skill we believe to be essential in a sex-saturated society.

Respect for the integrity of the professor and the student has guided this professional endeavor. Because we believe that professors bring their own personality to the process of facilitating learning and that students are both interested in and capable of learning, the narrative in this anthology is purposefully classic in format, challenging in content, and devoid of jargon.

Instructors using the First Edition of *SOS* (2001) cited the following benefits to students and themselves:

- High readability and style;
- Blending of contemporary and classic works in research and theory;
- Multidisciplinary approach to studying sexuality;
- Balance of the physical, psychological, and sociological aspects of sexuality;
- Timely and interesting coverage of topics students most want to know about;
- Eclectic mix of articles from scholarly and popular sources;
- Extensive, absorbing discussion of each topic in Part Openers;
- Strong introductory lead-ins for each chapter that promote critical thinking;
- Coverage of the historical and political contexts of sexuality;
- Theme of health promotion and the life cycle as organizing principles;
- Rationale for critiquing the various forms of sexuality-related media; and
- Easy application to a variety of teaching methods.

We have listened to our respected colleagues who reviewed the First Edition of *SOS*, many of whom had "hands on" experience using it in their own courses. As a result, seventeen new selections have been added. Users will find that topical areas have been expanded so that each Part has one or more new Chapters. This Second Edition of *SOS* contains many timely and thought-provoking topics not featured in other sexuality readers: a meta-analysis of sexuality research in the 1990s; the "primal scene" and children; RU-486; cybersex addiction and its effect on families; religion and erotic development in children; pretending orgasm; race, class, and gender in adult sexual scripts; sexual scripting and token resistance; estrogen and sexual desire; college virgins; sexuality and religiosity; sexuality laws; economics of pornography; philosophies of sexuality education; and the Catholic Church, child sexual abuse, and legal greed.

In weaving together the Second Edition of *SOS*, the following unique selections were added:

- An exposé from Judith Levine's controversial book, *Harmful to Minors: The Perils of Protecting Children from Sex*, laying bare the "politics of fear" in the war against AIDS;

- "Venus in Furs," a fascinating chapter from Pulitzer prize-winning writer Natalie Angier's book, *Woman: An Intimate Geography*, revealing a scientific fantasia of womanhood;
- From Pepper Schwartz and Virginia E. Rutter's book, *The Gender of Sexuality*, persuasive arguments calling for an end to polemics that distort the opposing views of gender and sexual desire;
- An original treatise exploring philosophies and practices of sexuality education from Terrance D. Olson, a veteran in the field;
- An odyssey of the life stages of sexual development that shapes a person's sexual identity, attitudes, and behavior by John D. DeLamater and William N. Friedrich; and
- A decade-long review of theoretical and methodological advancements in sexuality research in the 1990s by F. Scott Christopher and Susan Sprecher.

With every product, there is a parallel process story. In this case, negotiating the sometimes slippery slope between a sociologist/researcher and a family scientist/family therapist was not always an easy task. However, we feel the results are considerably stronger because of our team efforts. Together, we have interwoven complex phenomena from fields known for their diversity of theories, concepts, and issues. The final product is an anthology with professional integrity and pragmatic pedagogical purposes. If we provoke critical thinking about today's timely topics surrounding sexuality and motivate students to continue their efforts to learn about sexuality after their course has ended, we will have achieved our combined purposes in this edition of *SOS*.

Instructor's Manual/Testing Program

A full-scale *Instructor's Manual* is available to provide assistance when integrating the anthology material into sexuality courses and when evaluating student achievement. The components for each entry include general summarizing statements, key points, and general conclusions. Additionally, there are multiple choice, true-false, and essay questions for student evaluation. Finally, the following pedagogical tools are provided: a Topical Matrix, based on current sexuality texts; an Article Review Form, a one-page document that can be reproduced as needed; and Web site addresses, which focus on sexuality and sexual health issues and topics.

J. Kenneth Davidson, Sr.
Nelwyn B. Moore

About the Contributors

Paul R. Abramson, Professor of Psychology at the University of California, Los Angeles (UCLA), has research interests in the epidemiology of HIV and sex and the law. His recent books include *A House Divided: Suspicions of Mother-Daughter Incest* (2000) and *With Pleasure: Thoughts on the Nature of Human Sexuality*(1995).

Joseph Adelson is a retired professor of psychology at the University of Michigan.

Peter B. Anderson, Professor of Health Performance and Health Promotion and Women's Studies at the University of New Orleans, conducts research on women as sexual aggressors and AIDS. He has coauthored/coedited *Sexually Aggressive Women: Current Perspectives and Controversies* (1998) and *Does Anyone Remember When Sex Was Fun? Positive Sexuality in the Age of AIDS* (1996).

Natalie Angier, author and science writer for the *New York Times*, received a Pulitzer Prize in 1991 for a 10-article series on scientific topics that included the biology of scorpions, disputes over the Human Genome Project, and the ubiquitousness of philandering in the animal kingdom. Her books include *Woman: An Intimate Geography* (2000); *The Beauty of the Beastly* (1995); and *Natural Obsessions* (1988).

J. Michael Bailey, Professor of Psychology at Northwestern University, focuses his research activities on sexual orientation.

Leah Beardsley holds an appointment in the Department of Epidemiology and Social Medicine at the Albert Einstein College of Medicine.

Robert Bierman works in the Rutgers University Student Health Service.

Kimberly Black serves as a counselor at Safe Place: Domestic Violence and Sexual Assault Survival Center, in Austin, Texas, directing her primary attention to the sexuality issues of spinal-cord injured women and sexual assault victims.

Vern L. Bullough is Distinguished Professor Emeritus at the State University of New York at Buffalo. A prolific writer, he has authored, co-authored, or coedited thirty (30) books on sexual topics, including *Before Stonewall: Trail Blazers and Founders of the Gay and Lesbian Movement* (2002); *Prostitutes, Pimps, and Whores* (1998); and *Science in the Bedroom: A History of Sex Research* (1994).

Robert D. Burk, Professor of Pediatrics at Albert Einstein College of Medicine, has primary research interests in the genital human papillomavirus infection (HPV), especially in young women.

William M. Byne holds an appointment as Assistant Professor of Psychiatry in the Mt. Sinai School of Medicine and has primary research interests in sexual orientation.

F. Scott Christopher, Professor of Family Studies in the Department of Family and Human Development of Arizona State University, maintains research interests in sexuality in relationships and sexual aggression. He is the author of *To Dance the Dance: A Symbolic Exploration of Premarital Sexuality* (2001).

Daniel Daley is a contributing editor at the Sexuality Information and Education Council of the United States (SIECUS).

J. Kenneth Davidson, Sr. is Professor of Sociology and Coordinator of Family Studies at the University of Wisconsin-Eau Claire. His research interests include sexual attitudes and behavior of college students, the Grafenburg spot and female ejaculation, sexual fantasies, and the orgasmic response in women. He is coauthor of *Marriage and Family: Change and Continuity* (1996) and *Marriage and Family* (1992) and coeditor of *Speaking of Sexuality* (2001) and *Cultural Diversity and Families* (1992).

John D. DeLamater is Professor of Sociology at the University of Wisconsin-Madison, with primary research interests in sexuality and the life cycle. He is coauthor of *Understanding Sexuality*, 8th edition (2003); *Social Psychology* (2003); and *Premarital Sexuality* (1974).

Emme Edmunds is a Certified Nurse-Midwife and Women's Health Nurse at the Planned Parenthood Clinic in Binghamton, New York, and the Tiogo County Family Planning Clinic in Owego, New York.

Julia A. Ericksen, Professor of Sociology at Temple University, concentrates her research on sexuality and gender, with a current focus on the study of breasts and breast cancer. She is coauthor of *Kiss and Tell: Surveying Sex in the Twentieth Century* (1999).

Pamela I. Erickson, Associate Professor of Anthropology at the University of Connecticut, has research interests in adolescent sexual and reproductive behavior. She is author of *Latina Adolescent Childbearing in East Los Angeles* (1998).

Stephen L. Fielding, sociologist and Research Assistant Professor of Family Medicine at the University of Rochester, maintains research interests in the social history of abortion and contraception and the well-being of women with unintended pregnancy. He has coauthored *Practice of Uncertainty: Voices of Physicians and Patients in Medical Malpractice Claims* (1999).

David Finkelhor, Research Professor of Sociology and Director of the Crimes Against Children Research Center at the University of New Hampshire, continues his research interests in family violence, sexual behavior, and victimology. He is author of *Sexually Victimized Children* (1979) and coauthor of *Theory-Based Assessment, Treatment, and Prevention of Sexual Aggression* (1996).

Robert T. Francoeur, Professor Emeritus of Biology and Psychology at Fairleigh Dickinson University, has written extensively about cross-cultural sexual attitudes, values, and behavior. He has coauthored, edited, and coedited over thirty (30) books, including *Scent of Eros: Mysteries of Odor in Human Sexuality* (2002); *Sex, Love, and Marriage in the Twenty-First Century* (1999); *Sexuality in America* (1998); *The International Encyclopedia of Sexuality* (1997), and *Becoming a Sexual Person* (1984).

William N. Friedrich is a psychologist in the Department of Psychiatry and Psychology at the Mayo Clinic in Rochester, Minnesota.

John H. Gagnon is Professor of Sociology at the State University of New York at Stony Brook and a past president of the International Academy of Sex Research. His coauthored books, which reflect his research interests in sexual conduct, include *The Social Organization of Sexuality* (1994); *Sex in America* (1994); *Conceiving Sexuality* (1994); and *Sexual Conduct* (1973).

Deirdre Giesen is a statistical researcher at Statistics Netherlands, in Voorburg, Netherlands.

Susan E. Golombok is Professor of Psychology at City University, London, with research interests in gender development and lesbian-mother families. She is author of *Parenting: What Really Counts* (2000) and coauthor of *Growing Up in a Lesbian Family: Effects on Child Development* (1997); *Gender Development* (1996); and *Bottling It Up* (1985).

Gordon C. Nagayama Hall has an appointment as Professor of Psychology at Pennsylvania State University, and a special interest in sexual aggression. He is coauthor of *Theory-Based Assessment, Treatment, and Prevention of Sexual Aggression* (1996).

Gloria Y. F. Ho is affiliated with the Department of Microbiology and Immunology at the Albert Einstein College of Medicine.

Gerald Hotaling is a professor in the Department of Criminal Justice at the University of Massachusetts at Lowell.

Sheryl A. Kingsberg, Associate Professor of Reproductive Biology in the Department of Reproductive Biology and Staff Psychologist in the Department of Obstetrics and Gynecology at Case Western University School of Medicine, maintains research interests on the psychological aspects of infertility, menopause, and female sexuality, including sexual dysfunction and aging.

Lewis H. Lapham works as a staff writer for *Harper's Magazine*.

Edward O. Laumann, George Herbert Mead Distinguished Service Professor, is Chairman of the Department of Sociology and Director of the Ogburn Stouffer Center for Population and Social Organization at the University of Chicago, where his major research interests include social stratification and sociology of human sexuality. He has authored or coauthored fourteen (14) books, including *The Sexual Organization of the City* (2004); *Sex, Love, and Health in America: Public Choices and Public Policy* (2001); *The Social Organization of Sexuality* (1994); and *Sex in America* (1994).

Michele Lempa is affiliated with the Rutgers University Student Health Service.

Judith Levine, a writer who explores the influence of history, culture, and politics on intimate life, including sexuality, is a contributor to *New York Times, Harper's, Philadelphia Inquirer, Glamour,* and *Village Voice*. She has authored *Do You Remember Me? A Father, a Daughter, and a Search for the Self* (2004); *Harmful to Minors: The Perils of Protecting Children From Sex* (2002), which won the *Los Angeles Book* Prize; and *My Enemy, My Love: Women, Masculinity, and the Dilemmas* (1992).

I. A. Lewis conducted polls as a staff member for the *Los Angeles Times*.

Daniel Lyons, Senior Editor at *Forbes*, covers major financial issues and their implications for American society. He has published a novel, *Dog Days* (1998).

Jenna Mahay is a postdoctoral fellow at the Population Research Center at the University of Chicago, working on the Chicago Health and Social Life Survey Project.

Gloria Gia Maramba is affiliated with Kent State University.

Barry W. McCarthy, whose writing interests are related to sexual dysfunction, serves as Professor of Psychology at American University and is coauthor of *Couple Sexual Awareness* (1998).

Robert T. Michael serves as Eliakim Hastings More Distinguished Service Professor of Public Policy Studies at the University of Chicago. He has coauthored *Sex, Love, and Health in America* (2001); *Sex in America* (1994); and *The Social Organization of Sexuality* (1994).

Stuart Michaels, a researcher at the University of Chicago, was Project Manager for the National Health and Social Life Survey (NHSLS), which led to the publication of *The Social Organization of Sexuality* (1994) and *Sex in America* (1994).

Nelwyn B. Moore is Professor Emerita of Family and Child Studies at Texas State University–San Marcos and a certified marriage and family therapist. Her research interests include sexual attitudes and behavior, teen pregnancy, adoption, and cross-cultural sexuality education. She is coauthor of *Marriage and Family: Change and Continuity* (1996) and *Marriage and Family* (1992), and coeditor of *Speaking of Sexuality* (2001) and *Cultural Diversity and Families* (1992).

Charlene L. Muehlenhard is Professor of Psychology and Women's Studies at the University of Kansas, with research interests in rape and other forms of sexual coercion, sexual consent, and communication and miscommunication about sexuality issues.

Paul Okami, a postdoctoral scholar in psychology at the University of California, Los Angeles (UCLA), has research interests in sex differences in behavior, childhood sexuality, and the evolution of sexuality.

Richard Olmstead, Assistant Research Psychologist at the University of California, Los Angeles (UCLA), conducts research on addiction from a bio-behavioral perspective.

Terrance D. Olson, Professor of Family Science in the School of Family Life at Brigham Young University, focuses his research interests on character, citizenship, familial, and moral issues related to adolescent sexuality.

Susie Orenstein works as a contributing author for the Sexuality Information and Education Council of the United States (SIECUS).

Laura Pendleton is a graduate student in the Department of Psychology at the University of California, Los Angeles (UCLA).

Michael Peters works in the Rutgers University Student Health Service.

Richard C. Pillard, Professor of Psychology at Boston University, has primary research interests in sexual orientation.

Pamela C. Regan, Professor of Psychology and Director of the Social Relations Laboratory at California State University at Los Angeles, has research interests in sexual attraction and interpersonal rela-

tionships. She is coauthor of *Lust: What We Know About Human Sexual Desire* (1999).

Harriet M. Reiss is a retired social worker, with research and writing interests in premarital sexuality.

Ira L. Reiss, Professor Emeritus at the University of Minnesota, has authored numerous publications on sexuality, gender, and the family as well as fourteen (14) books, including *At the Dawn of the Sexual Revolution* (2002); *Solving America's Sexual Crisis* (1997); *The Social Context of Premarital Sexual Permissiveness* (1967); and *Premarital Sexual Standards in America* (1960).

Frank Rich, Associate Editor at the *New York Times*, pursues and contributes stories of major societal and national importance. His books include *Ghost Light: A Memoir* (2000) and *Hot Seat: Theatre Criticism for the New York Times, 1980–1993* (1998).

Carie S. Rodgers holds an appointment as a post-doctoral fellow in clinical psychology at the University of California, San Diego, and the San Diego Veterans Administration Medical Center. She has research interests in the psychology of women, gender-role development, and treatment of sexual trauma.

Virginia E. Rutter, a sociologist at the Battelle Research Institute in Seattle, Washington, concentrates her research interests in the areas of gender, female sexuality, and contraceptive choices. She is coauthor of *The Love Test: Romance and Relationship Self-Quizzes Developed by Psychologists and Sociologists* (1998) and *The Gender of Sexuality* (1998).

Ritch C. Savin-Williams is Professor of Developmental and Clinical Psychology at Cornell University, with primary research interests in same-sex attractions, behavior, and identity. He is the author of *Mom, Dad. I'm Gay: How Families Negotiate Coming Out* (2001) and *"And I Became Gay": Young Men's Stories* (1998).

Eric A. Schaff, Professor of Family Medicine and Director of the Reproductive Health Program at the University of Rochester, directs his research interests toward clinical abortion training.

David M. Schnarch, a certified sex therapist and clinical member of the American Association of Marriage and Family Therapists, is Director of the Marriage and Family Health Center in Evergreen, Colorado, where he focuses on the treatment of sexual desire problems. He is the author of *Passionate Marriage* (1997) and *Constructing the Sexual Crucible* (1991).

Jennifer P. Schneider, is board certified in internal medicine and holds a Ph.D. in genetics. She practices medicine with the Arizona Community Physicians Group in Tucson, Arizona where she specializes in pain management and addiction medicine. Her primary research interests are sexual addiction and compulsivity, and her books include *Disclosing Secrets: When, How Much, and to Whom to Reveal Addiction* (2002); *Cybersex Exposed: Simple Fantasy or Obsession* (2001); and *Back From Betrayal: Recovering From His Affairs* (2001).

Pepper Schwartz, Professor of Sociology at the University of Washington, focuses her research interests in the areas of sexual and marital relationships. She is the author and coauthor of numerous books, including *201 Questions Parents Should Ask Children/201 Questions Kids Should Ask Parents* (2000); *What I Have Learned About Sex: Leading Sex Educators, Therapists, and Researchers Share Their Secrets* (1998); *The Gender of Sexuality* (1998); *American Couples: Money, Work, and Sex* (1983); and *Women at Yale: An Examination of Male and Female Roles* (1971).

Marca L. Sipski, Associate Professor of Neurologic Surgery in the University of Miami School of Medicine, specializes in the sexual functioning of spinal-cord injured women. She is coeditor of *Sexual Function in People With Disability and Chronic Illness* (1997).

Christine Smith is a staff member of Abt Associates, Cambridge, Massachusetts.

Susan Sprecher, Professor of Sociology at Illinois State University, has primary research interests in the sexual attitudes and behavior of college students and sexual intimacy in close relationships. She is coauthor of *Handbook of Sexuality in Close Relationships* (in press); *Sexuality* (1993); and *Mirror, Mirror . . .: The Importance of Looks in Everyday Life* (1986) and coeditor of *Sexuality in Close Relationships* (1993).

Sally A. Steffen, an associate in the law firm Ballard, Spahr, Andrews, and Ingersoll, LLP, is coauthor of *Kiss and Tell: Surveying Sex in the Twentieth Century.*

Ron Stodghill, II serves as a contributing correspondent for *Time* magazine.

Susanne S. Strauss works as a social worker in the Department of Physical Medicine and Rehabilitation at the New Jersey Medical School.

Cindy J. Struckman-Johnson, Professor of Psychology at the University of South Dakota, specializes in research on the sexual coercion of women and men on college campuses and in prison set-tings. She is coeditor of *Sexually Aggressive Women: Current Perspectives and Controversies* (1998).

David L. Struckman-Johnson, Professor of Computer Science at the University of South Dakota, has research interests in prison sexual assault and sexually aggressive women.

Nova D. Sweet is a graduate student in the Department of Justice Administration at the University of Louisville.

Fiona L. Tasker is Senior Lecturer at Birkbeck College, University of London, with major research interests in lesbian-mother families, gay-father families, and family therapy of sexual identity. She is coauthor of *Growing Up in a Lesbian Family* (1997).

Richard Tewksbury, Professor of Criminal Justice Administration at the University of Louisville, maintains research interests in sex work and men's sexuality. He is the coeditor of *Sexual Deviance* (2003) and *Gender Sexualities* (2002).

Evan W. Thomas, Assistant Managing Editor of *Newsweek*, contributes news stories of significant national interest.

Judith Treas is Professor of Sociology at the University of California, Irvine, with primary research interests in attitudes toward nonmarital sex.

Kristen Marie Ullstrup is a family therapist at RSA, Inc. in Lakewood, Colorado. Her research interests have been focused on teenage pregnancy and unsafe sexual behavior.

Michael W. Wiederman, Associate Professor of Psychology at Columbia College, focuses his research interests on extradyadic sex, gender differences, and jealousy and is author of *Understanding Sexuality Research* (2001).

Amy K. Windover is affiliated with Kent State University.

Vivian Wong serves as a contributing author for the Sexuality Information and Education Council of the United States (SIECUS).

Lore K. Wright holds an appointment as Professor and Department Chair of Nursing at the Medical College of Georgia and has research interests in aging and sexuality. She is the author of *Alzheimer's Disease and Marriage* (1993). ✦

About the Editors

J. *Kenneth Davidson, Sr.,* Professor of Sociology at the University of Wisconsin–Eau Claire and a nationally recognized authority in the field of human sexuality, has taught a course in the sociology of human sexuality for the past twenty-nine (29) years. His selected teaching materials appear in *The Sociology of Sexuality and Sexual Orientation: Syllabi and Teaching Materials* (2002), published by the American Sociological Association. He was co-recipient of the 2003 Ernest G. Osborne Award for Excellence in Teaching Family Studies conferred by the National Council on Family Relations. Davidson is also one of the most widely published researchers in the area of human sexuality, with numerous papers in professional journals concerning premarital sexual attitudes and behavior of college women and men, the female sexual response and sexual satisfaction, the Grafenberg spot and female ejaculation, sexual fantasies, and adoption. In addition, he is coauthor of *Marriage and Family: Change and Continuity* (1996) and *Marriage and Family* (1992), and coeditor of *Speaking of Sexuality* (2001) and *Cultural Diversity and Families* (1992).

For both editions of *Speaking of Sexuality,* Davidson primarily assumed management and production responsibilities including literature searches, article selection, editorial suggestions, and proofreading.

Nelwyn B. Moore, Professor Emerita of Family and Child Studies at Texas State University–San Marcos, taught courses in family and child development for thirty-seven (37) years. She was corecipient of the National Council on Family Relations 2003 Ernest G. Osborne Award for Excellence in Teaching Family Studies. Moore is a certified Marriage and Family Therapist (AAMFT), a licensed Marriage and Family Therapist, a licensed Professional Counselor, and Certified Family Life Educator, with professional training in the area of human sexuality. She is recognized for her contributions to sexuality education as well as her publications in professional journals on sexual attitudes and behavior of college women and men, adoption, teen pregnancy, family life education, child development and guidance, curriculum design, and family and interpersonal relations. Moore is coauthor of *Marriage and Family: Change and Continuity* (1996) and *Marriage and Family* (1992) and coeditor of *Speaking of Sexuality* (2001) and *Cultural Diversity and Families* (1992).

For both editions of *Speaking of Sexuality,* Moore primarily assumed literary responsibilities including article selection and the writing of the Part Openers and Chapter Lead-Ins. ✦

Acknowledgments

First among persons acknowledged for contributions to this book must be those thousands who shall remain nameless: students who over many years of teaching have taught us far more valuable lessons about life and humanity than we ourselves have taught. And, the many family professionals along the way who have served as mentors may be unaware of their influence in our lives, but it is present just the same. Some are names instantly recognizable, such as Gerald R. Leslie (JKD), Felix M. Berardo (JKD), Azalete Little (NBM), and James Leslie McCary (NBM), but not all. Some are no longer with us, some are retired, while still others remain in our current networks of professional colleagues. Many of those who have touched our lives significantly and kept us true to our purpose are today's promising young scholars.

Our faith in the review process has been strengthened by the significant contributions made by our colleagues who served as reviewers for this work. We express sincere appreciation to these consummate professionals, without whose numerous comments and recommendations this anthology would not be as pragmatic, student friendly, or interesting. They are Carol V. Apt, South Carolina State University; Rebecca Bach, Duke University; Phillip G. Batten, Wake Forest University; John D. DeLamater, University of Wisconsin, Madison; Lori C. Ebert, University of New Mexico; Jeffrey E. Hall, University of Alabama, Birmingham; Christina R. McKittrick, Drew University; Sandra Shroer, Western Michigan University; and Thomas L. Walton, Warner Southern College.

We are indebted to Claude Teweles, Publisher, Roxbury Publishing Company, without whose persistence, perseverance, and patience the second edition of this sexuality anthology would never have come to fruition. In addition, we want to acknowledge the numerous helpful suggestions, cordial assistance, and understanding provided by Carla Plucknett at Roxbury. Further, we thank Ann West for her expert copyediting, which has made our second edition a more concise and tightly written work.

Without the capable support of research assistants, this work would not have been developed and brought to completion. Ilsa A. Hillert helped to compile the large pool of resources from which these selections were made and conducted a detailed analysis of the reviewers' comments. Lisa M. Nackers made invaluable contributions with her scanning of articles, typing, and editorial suggestions. Amanda E. Matzek deserves special recognition for her myriad contributions to this project. She spent many hours typing, revising, and proofreading numerous drafts; conducting library research; setting up and managing the word processing files and the contributor files; and providing editorial suggestions. And, we also greatly appreciate the many efforts of Cynthia J. Mudrak, Department Program Assistant, in obtaining copyright permissions for this edition.

Finally, this second edition would not have been possible without the loving support of our families: Jo, sons John and Stephen, and John's wife Lisa and their children John III and William (JKD); Jerry, son Jay and daughter Amy and her children Madeleine and Max (NBM). They have understood and supported our passion for completing what has proven to be an infinitely more complex and time-consuming task than we originally perceived. And the paw prints that have warmed these words belong to G. B., who has walked across these pages of our lives time and time again.

J. Kenneth Davidson, Sr.
Nelwyn B. Moore

Part I

Historical, Theoretical, and Research Perspectives on Sexuality

As the most ambitious of the offerings in this anthology, Part I almost assumes a life of its own. Most of the selections were purposely chosen because they reflect seminal works in the field of sexuality research. Names like Kinsey, Masters and Johnson, Lauman, Gagnon, and Reiss are instantly recognizable as standard-bearers in the field of sexuality research, yesterday and today. Although most students may not be primarily interested in the theory and history of sexuality research, they will be fascinated with the insights furnished by the authors.

The selections in Part I introduce readers to highly detailed portraits of American sexuality—who does what, with whom, how, and how many times—a feat certainly more easily accomplished with the click of a mouse to browse the Internet. But the difference between Internet browsing and mining the minds of the last century's giants in the field of sexuality research is immeasurable. Applying their scientific orientation to the study of sexual behavior and attitudes, each of the authors here helps students reframe the issues to fit into broader social contexts. The picture that emerges for avid readers is a sum that is truly greater than the individual parts.

As a young professional, Ira Reiss was one of the first observers on the American scene to predict the sexual revolution of the 1960s. Here, with Harriet Reiss, he presents a logical argument that another sexual revolution is needed, one that supports pluralism of sexual morality. After a careful review of this entry, students may be better prepared to formulate their own opinions about troubling issues in American society. Why, for example, as the Reisses point out, does the United States, a leader in the Western world, remain the nation with the highest rates of virtually every sexual problem: teen pregnancy, rape, child sexual abuse, and AIDS? Perhaps, students reading about previous sexual revolutions will be motivated to become twenty-first century sexuality researchers and help resolve this apparent national paradox.

Historian Vern Bullough not only records interesting facts, but also reveals the colorful personalities of three key players—Kinsey and Masters and Johnson. This prolific writer's unbiased treatment of the life and work of these giants in the field of sexuality research documents their singular, rare contributions, while also acknowledging their shortcomings as researchers.

Born on the cusp of the last century in 1894, Alfred Kinsey entered the field of sexuality research at a time when two circumstances occurred simultaneously: a growing awareness of the importance of sexuality and an increasing volume of studies about human sexuality. His study of human males, published in 1948, and his study of females, published in 1952, were hailed as benchmarks for changes in American society. Perhaps best known for his distinctive interviewing techniques, Kinsey's most valuable contribution is said to be his success in treating the study of sexuality as a scientific discipline.

Although Kinsey pioneered the use of case histories to study human sexuality, Masters and Johnson were the first to use clinical techniques of observing, measuring, and recording actual sexual behaviors in a laboratory setting. Technological advances made after the Kinsey data were collected, such as the development of an artificial coital device with a miniature camera and intrauterine electrodes, enabled the latter research team to achieve its goal of replacing many "phallic fallacies" with facts. Vern Bullough carefully details the unprecedented clinical research conducted by the Masters and Johnson team.

The Laumann et al. selection and the Adelson selection stand alone, but students will miss an interesting exercise in analyzing and synthesizing if they fail to read both. Hailed by *Time* (Elmer-Dewitt 1994) as probably the "First truly scientific study of sexuality in America," the Laumann team's study, published as *The Social Organization of Sexuality,* (1994) exploded many sexuality myths. Whether the findings were received as reassuring or alarming depended upon one's personal agenda. The first chapter is included here as a significant piece of work in that it clarifies the rationale and theoretical base of the study.

Joseph Adelson's treatment of the Laumann et al. data in "Sex Among the Americans" is at once compelling and practical. Students will enjoy the fast read with its astonishing facts, guaranteed to shatter at least some myths about Americans and sexuality. Adelson's critique points to the authors' avoidance of a value construct and their questionable choice of social networks and the sexual marketplace as theoretical structures. He is troubled by the authors' lack of consideration of the "inner world," the motives and character that influence sexual behavior and attitudes. He does conclude, however, that the data have great value. This offering, more than most, will motivate students to move closer to their own position statement about sexuality in America.

Julia Ericksen and Sally Steffen's provocative history of sex surveys in the United States is a revealing account of the social construction of sexuality and scientific knowledge. The author's excellent discussion of how a researcher's "agenda" may influence the choice and wording of questions helps to explain some of the nonrepresentative, biased data and even "incorrect" findings that may surface in researchland. For example, she clearly delineates how men studying female sexuality can derive incorrect conclusions, due to male assumptions about gendered sexuality. Various aspects of gendered sexuality are a common thread woven throughout the history of sexuality research. A *New York Times* (Kolata 1998) feature, titled "Women and Sex: On This Topic, Science Blushes," serves to illustrate this point. Do women become sexually excited by talk of love and romance or are they turned on by explicit talk of sexual activity itself? This interesting question was posed by Julia Heiman (1975), a psychologist who directs the Reproductive and Sexual Medicine Clinic at the University of Washington. To discover answers, she asked college women to wear a tampon-like device that detects blood flow to the vagina while alternately listening to romantic tape recordings and erotic ones. The results indicated that, if blood flow to the vagina is an accurate measure of sexual excitement, women, like men, are sexually excited by erotic talk, not romance.

What makes this study unique? It occurred in the early 1970s, and, for all of the medical advances in the past 30 years, Heiman's study still represents the state of the art. When the recent Viagra rush occurred for men, drug-company scientists asked academic scientists what was known about women's sexual responses; not much, came the reply. Although every survey invariably finds that many more women than men complain of sexual difficulties, the dearth of female sexuality research suggests a resistance by researchers, most of whom are men, to understanding women's sexual responses.

A natural closure for Part I, the decade review by Scott Christopher and Susan Sprecher, highlights the research advances made during the 1990s in the study of sexuality in close relationships. The authors critically review the major empirical data, beginning with a discussion of theoretical and methodological issues. Other than the increase in the numbers of scholars who employed an evolutionary perspective, they found that the theoretical advancements in sexuality research were somewhat limited in the decade of the 1990s. Questioning this atheoretical stance, Christopher and Sprecher note at least six (6) theories applicable to sexuality that were featured in the February 1998 special issue of *The Journal of Sex Research,* which was devoted to theory.

A number of topics were covered in this review: sexual activity and satisfaction in marriages and committed gay and lesbian relationships, premarital sexual involvement, sexual assault, sexual coercion, and extramarital sex. The concluding recommendations for the study of sexuality in the 2000 decade are noteworthy, particularly because both authors are professors who are known for their prolific sexuality research and publications. This chapter, as a fitting framework for the readings that follow, is a must read for both the serious and the not-so-serious consumer of the sexuality literature.

References

Elmer-Dewitt, P. (1994, October 17). "Now for the Truth About Americans and Sex." *Time,* pp. 62–66, 68, 70.

Heiman, J. R. (1975). "The Physiology of Erotica: Women's Sexual Arousal." *Psychology Today,* 8, 90–94.

Kolata, G. (1998, June 21). "Women and Sex: On This Topic, Science Blushes." *New York Times,* p. A3. ✦

Chapter 1

The Stalled Sexual Revolutions of This Century

Ira L. Reiss

Harriet M. Reiss

In a professional lifetime devoted to the study of sexuality, sociologist Ira Reiss has long evoked reason in the often murky waters of emotion surrounding the subject of sexuality. As one of the few voices predicting the second sexual revolution of the twentieth century that occurred in the 1960s, Reiss seems eminently qualified to analyze the unfolding of twentieth-century sexuality in America. Drawing upon the parallels that propelled the sexual revolutions of the 1920s and the 1960s, he uses words such as intolerance, inequity, *and* dogmatism *to argue convincingly for far more complex causes of these grassroots uprisings than merely the revolutionary power of the pill or of women in the workforce.*

"Shaping Our Next Sexual Revolution" is a fitting subtitle to the book An End to Shame, *in which a pluralistic approach to sexuality is proposed: individual choices, guided by the values of honesty, equality, and responsibility (HER). Against a backdrop of twentieth-century sexuality, readers are left to ponder a number of salient points raised by Reiss: Are we, as fellow travelers with women and men of the Western world, really traveling in the same direction in our move toward gender equality and sexual permissiveness? Is the price to pay for every societal arrangement always self-evident? If social customs are not built on principles of fairness, what are their basic premises? What should they be? If the homosexual revolution that began in 1969 led to more tolerance for gays and lesbians, why does American society, in general, continue to engage in repression of homosexuality? And, finally, if as suggested, the two sexual revolutions of the last century were only stalled, partial revolutions, what might the sexual script be like for a successful twenty-first century sexual revolution?*

Readers will undoubtedly gain an important historical perspective from this work. More personally, such insight may spark a reassessment of their own sexual script. If so, pluralism will, it is hoped, be the criterion of choice.

Revolutions: One Isn't Enough

One day back in 1973 historian Carl Degler was sifting through the materials in the archives of Stanford University's library. To his surprise he found a manuscript by a medical doctor who had started a study of the sexual lives of married women in the year 1892! The author was Clelia Duel Mosher, M.D., born in 1863. She began her research as a student of biology at the University of Wisconsin and finished it at Stanford University. She never published her story and just tucked it away in Stanford University's archives at the end of her life in 1940. When it was discovered thirty-three years later, it was indeed like an archaeological find—the oldest recorded study of sexual practices in America, gathering dust in the archives at Stanford!

Most of the forty-five women Mosher interviewed were, like herself, born before 1870. They were highly educated women for their times; over three quarters of them had been to college or normal school. When Stanford historian Carl Degler read Dr. Mosher's findings, he was taken aback by the strength of the sexual interests of these Victorian women. Over 40 percent of these wives reported that they usually or always had orgasm in sexual intercourse and only one-third reported that they rarely or never had orgasm during sexual intercourse. Their rate of sexual intercourse was five times a month—not so low even by today's averages of almost seven times a month.[1] There were clear signs that, at least for these women, Victorian restraints were not fully dominating their sexuality. They were, of course, more sexually constrained than we are today, but they also showed that even a century ago sexual intercourse in marriage was for many women far more than just a "wifely duty."

Later in her career, when she was sixty-three years old, Dr. Mosher taught a class in Personal Hygiene at Stanford University. It was the 1920s and "the times they were a-changin'." The premarital sexual escapades of this generation far exceeded the moderate pursuit of marital sexual pleasure by her nineteenth-century sample of women. This new generation was born in the first decade of the twentieth century and came to maturity in the 1920s.[2] Dr. Mosher was lecturing to the "flaming youth" of the 1920s. This century's first sexual revolution was in progress. According to the data gathered by

Kinsey, the percentage of women born between 1900 and 1909 who had intercourse before marriage doubled from 25 percent to 50 percent! The premarital nonvirginity rate for men in that same birth cohort held relatively stable at about 80 percent.[3] It may shock today's baby boomers to realize that these were their grandparents!

Still, despite some sensationalized reporting, the 1920s were not a time of orgiastic sexuality. Most of the increased sexuality occurred in stable, affectionate relationships. Men moved more toward intercourse with women for whom they cared rather than with prostitutes or casual sexual partners. During the 1920s, these young revolutionaries fashioned a more egalitarian version of courtship and sexuality—one that continued to evolve during the rest of the century.[4]

The 1920s were a turning point in our society. As University of California historian Paula Fass sees it: "The twenties [were] a critical juncture between the strict double standard of the age of Victoria and the permissive sexuality of the age of Freud."[5] Fass describes the overall spirit of the 1920s:

> Did the young use sex and morals as a basis for conscious generational revolt? On the whole the answer would appear to be no, although their sexual attitudes and practices did distinguish them from their elders and made them appear rebellious. They welcomed the lingering naughtiness of which they were accused, but more in the spirit of play than with any serious display of anger. As eager capitalists, the young were anything but rebellious in social and political questions.[6]

There are some remarkable similarities in the social forces that propelled the sexual revolution of the 1920s and those involved in the second sexual revolution which began in the late 1960s. Both revolutions involved a major war, a dramatic rise in divorce, and increased equality between men and women.

World War I ended in 1918. It was the first war in which American troops had been sent to Europe. The war provided a more panoramic view of the world to millions of American men and women. "How you gonna keep 'em down on the farm after they've seen Paree" was not just a line from a World War I song. It reflected the realization that the war had enlarged our awareness of possible lifestyles and that the nineteenth-century wall of Victorianism had started to crumble.

The Vietnam war, starting in the mid-1960s, helped to propel us into the *second* sexual revolution of this century. That war produced a profound disruption of our customary ways of viewing the world. It was the most unpopular war in our history, and young people felt justified in criticizing our in-

volvement. Anyone over thirty can recall the scores of protests, often followed by violent confrontations with police and national guardsmen. The tragedy at Kent State epitomized the public turmoil in that war:

> On April 30, 1970, President Nixon announced that American and South Vietnamese forces were moving against enemy sanctuaries in Cambodia. Minutes after this announcement, student-organized protest demonstrations were under way.... On May 2, the ROTC building at Kent State was set afire. On May 4, Kent State students congregated on the University Commons and defied an order by the Guard to disperse. Guardsmen proceeded to disperse the crowd. The students then began to taunt Guard units and to throw rocks . . . the three ranking officers on the hill all said no order to fire was given. . . . Twenty-eight guardsmen have acknowledged firing from Blanket Hill . . . the firing . . . lasted approximately 13 seconds. The time of the shooting was approximately 12:25 p.m. Four persons were killed and nine were wounded.[7]

The Vietnam war increased our willingness to criticize our society. Our view of what was right and wrong was changing. Many people reasoned that if our country could be wrong about Vietnam, then it could be wrong about other things like family, religion, and certainly sexuality. This critical stance helped prepare the fertile soil in which the second and much more angry sexual revolution was starting to grow.

The 1920s' sexual revolution set the direction of change, which during the next few decades transformed the public view of sexuality, and helped to clear the path for the sexual revolution of the late 1960s. But as I have noted, there were significant differences in the tone of these two sexual revolutions. One shorthand way to grasp the difference is to listen to the popular music of each time period. For example, the lyrics of Cole Porter's 1928 hit "Let's Do It (Let's Fall in Love)" portray the jocular sexual atmosphere of the 1920s in comments about the birds and the bees and springtime. Contrast that with the Beatles hit of 1968 "Why Don't We Do It in the Road."[8] The Beatles were not talking about birds or bees or springtime. They were directly talking about "doing it." The mood and type of emotion involved in these two revolutions are revealingly written into these contrasting popular tunes of the two eras.

In both the 1920s' and the 1960s' sexual revolutions, there was a move toward greater equality between men and women. In 1920 the Nineteenth Amendment enfranchised women after more than seventy years of political struggle. Women were entering the labor force in growing numbers and their incomes slowly began to increase their social power. In addition, women were going to college in greater numbers than ever before, and that, too, was destined to increase their influence and change the image of the "gentler sex." Most of us have forgotten that it was during the 1920s that feminists made their first unsuccessful attempt to pass an Equal Rights Amendment granting legal equality to women. By the end of the 1920s the feminist movement declined somewhat in influence. But it was only a pause, not an ending. The rush into the labor force by women, which started in World War II and continued into the 1960s, reignited the drive for greater female power and aided the revival of the feminist movement in this country. The 1960s, like the 1920s, also showed a sharp rise in the percentage of women in our colleges. The expectations men and women held for each other continued to alter in accordance with the new opportunities to meet and to get to know one another on the campuses and in the workplaces in our country.

Gender Equality: The Mother of Change

Each sexual revolution moved us closer to an egalitarian relationship between men and women in all spheres of life. Still we must admit that even in the late 1990s we've got a long way to go before even coming into sight of full equality between the genders. Evidence of this is that women in 1997, in the last few years of the twentieth century, comprise only 11 percent of Congress and at work earn 30 percent less pay than men do; furthermore, there are very few female rabbis or ministers and there are no female priests. Finally, even in nurturing institutions like the family, men still dominate.

But we have made some progress in gender equality. As an example of political changes in gender attitudes, in 1972 only 74 percent of a national sample representative of the country said they would vote for a woman president. But by 1996 that percentage had risen to 93 percent. All these findings document the fact that sizable changes in attitudes have occurred and these trends seem to be continuing at the present time.[9]

When male and female roles change rapidly, there is always a price to pay. Major changes in the divorce rate are almost always an unambiguous sign of rapid social change. In both sexual revolutions, the divorce rate soared skywards. Between 1915 and 1920 our divorce rate increased 50 percent. That is a relatively moderate increase compared to what has happened recently—between 1963 and 1979 our divorce rate more than doubled![10] When there are extensive changes in the way

men and women relate in the workplace, the schools, and elsewhere, they can no longer depend on conventional ways of interacting with each other in marriage. Each couple must privately negotiate new ways of getting along. That process is often accompanied by conflict, and more than occasionally it breaks down and ends in divorce.

Divorce rates have been stable or slightly down during the entire decade of the 1980s and in the 1990s have dropped a bit more. Maybe we are getting better at our new marital negotiations and expectations. But new problems have arisen. As sociologist Lenore Weitzman has pointed out in her award-winning book *The Divorce Revolution*, the new "no fault" divorce laws did not take into account the sacrifices made by wives for their husbands' careers.[11] After a divorce, a husband still has his career, but his wife often has a house that she can no longer afford to keep. This situation has pressured women to prepare better for their economic futures just in case a divorce does occur. Seeking economic independence has an impact on many parts of the female role—including the sexual. Economic autonomy reduces dependence on others and makes sexual assertiveness a much less risky procedure.

The family may still be the number one priority for most women, but the ability to earn money is running a close second. Given the poor record of child-support payments, being employable becomes essential. One divorced wife in California described her economic plight to sociologist Lenore Weitzman this way: "There is no way I can make up for twenty-five years out of the labor force. . . . No one wants to make me president of the company just because I was president of the PTA."[12]

High divorce rates have given many people more years during which they are not married and thus more time to rethink their sexual standards. And thought is the enemy of habitual ways of behaving in sex and everything else. Divorced people are more open in acknowledging their sexual interests and are more aware of what they do and don't like in dating. Sexual standards often change after a divorce. For both men and women it is common after a divorce to have a period of time during which sex takes over center stage.

Sociologist Robert Weiss studied the transition to being single again. He reports what one of his divorced men told him:

> At first I went around screwing everything I could get my hands on. You go through that stage. And then you ask yourself why you did that. And then you realize that sex isn't all you want out of a relationship. And then you can start having normal relationships with people. But it took me a year, a year and a half.[13]

Divorce adds a variety of new family forms—single parents, stepparents, and even parents who marry each other a second time. About half of today's children will at some time in their lives live with only one parent. These experiences change our conception of marriage and the family. People are more likely to think about the possibility of having more than one marriage, for they know that half of those who marry today will divorce.

About 10 percent of our young people will never marry—most of them by choice. Another 10 percent will most likely never have children—some by choice and some due to repeated postponements that exceeded the time on the biological clock. The average age at first marriage has increased from twenty for women and twenty-three for men in the early 1960s to over twenty-four for women and twenty-six for men in 1996—the oldest age at marriage in the twentieth century!

All these changes do not mean that young people don't want to marry, that they don't want to have children, or that they don't value marriage. What the sexual revolutions did was increase the value of other choices and legitimize a wider range of choices relating to marriage. But almost all young people continue to expect to marry someday and have children someday.

Nevertheless, there is more than one script to read from today. Young people can now think about whether they want to marry, have children, remarry, live together, focus on a career, or just put off deciding anything. The age of pluralism is arriving in our gender roles. It makes life more interesting and exciting but also less secure and less predictable. Choices increase the ability to find a rewarding fit between lifestyle and personal values, but they also increase the need for awareness, understanding, and hopefully a bit of luck in making those choices. Sexual practices have also become more pluralistic. One prime example is cohabitation. Young people now feel they have the right to live together without being married if they so choose. In the late 1960s there were about five hundred thousand unmarried couples living together in America. By the mid-1990s that number had reached three and a half million.

Premarital sexual intercourse changed dramatically during the last sexual revolution. During the 1970s the percentage of women having intercourse before they married rose sharply from the 50 percent level that had been reached in the 1920s' sexual revolution. Since the late 1970s the percentage of women having premarital intercourse has surpassed the 80 percent mark and is now approaching 90 percent. For men, over 90 percent had premarital intercourse, only a small rise from the 80 percent figure prevalent in the 1920s.[14] In addition, women were starting to have intercourse at much earlier ages.

Sexual attitudes, too, had changed a great deal. In a national study I conducted in 1963, only 23 percent of Americans accepted premarital intercourse under some conditions, but by 1975 that percentage had risen to over 70 percent and in 1996 it was 76 percent.[15] Choice had become legitimate in the area of premarital sexual intercourse. Sexual attitudes on extramarital sexuality change much more slowly, but here too there seems to have been some change: more people feel that if a married couple is in the process of divorcing or if they have an agreement to accept affairs, then extramarital sexuality may not always be wrong.[16]

During most of this century, the entire Western world has been moving in the same direction toward gender equality and sexual permissiveness. The greatest amount of equality has occurred in Sweden and Denmark and the least in Spain and Ireland. We [fall] somewhere in between in our degree of progress toward overall sexual and gender equality. But we are all together, traveling in the same direction; only the speed of movement varies.

The Leadership Role of the Baby Boomers

The pacesetters of the sexual revolution of the late 1960s were the so-called baby boomers. They are the progeny of the millions of men and women who after World War II produced large families so quickly that startlingly high birth rates resulted. Our families had been getting smaller for over one hundred years, but from 1946 to 1964 American women gave birth to an average of four million babies a year. That amounts to almost twice as many babies for each woman of childbearing age as are born today. This dramatic rise in birth rate is what has come to be known as the baby boom. There are seventy-six million baby boomers, and if you were born between 1946 and 1964, you are one of them.

When the massive baby-boomer cohorts began to reach adolescence in the 1960s, they changed our outlook on youth. Politicians very quickly recognized a large potential constituency and in 1971 passed the Twenty-Sixth Amendment to the Constitution dropping the voting age to eighteen. These early baby boomers were joined year after year by more fellow baby boomers like wave after wave, crashing against the shore of conventions until they permanently transformed the shape of our lifestyles.

The mothers of these baby boomers were themselves changing in ways that helped prepare their children for their future revolutionary role. During the 1950s and especially the 1960s, the mothers of the baby boomers joined the labor force in unprecedented numbers.[17] There were many reasons for this change—money for their larger families, interests in the world outside the home, the desire to be more economically independent, the desire to have a higher standard of living, and the availability of jobs in our expanding economy—all were motivations for change. Day care centers began to grow all over the country and grandparents filled in when needed. It is remarkable that in 1950 just 12 percent of the mothers of preschoolers were employed, whereas today the figure is about 60 percent. The employment of mothers of preschoolers indicates there has been a significant change in the way people conceive of a woman's role. It shows that motherhood, though still of primary importance, can be modified because of the desire to work outside the home. That alteration decreased the difference between men and women. Men have long been allowed both family and employment as acceptable parts of their gender role.

The Victorian family with its dominant husband and full-time housewife had ironically been dealt a lethal blow at the very time that we were glorifying parenthood in the baby-boom years. It certainly isn't easy for women to combine parenthood and full-time employment, but neither was it easy to meet the demand that every woman be a full-time mother regardless of her ability or interest in doing so and despite whatever career interests she might have. Of course, pluralism would allow a woman to choose for herself to be a full-time housewife or any other lifestyle. There is a price to pay for every societal arrangement, but at least now a woman has more choice in her lifestyle.

The employed mother played a key role in the sexual revolution that began in the late 1960s. For one thing, her employment meant that her child probably had a greater variety of role models. Children were exposed to other adults who gave them choices that parents alone might not. Accordingly, such children were likely to become more autonomous—more desirous of running their own lives. In particular, those children had a more varied model of the role of mothers. That more flexible view of mothers expanded the acceptance by both boys and girls of female autonomy—the freedom of women to choose what they wish to do with their lives. Now, despite Sigmund Freud, autonomy rather than anatomy was becoming destiny for women!

The increased autonomy of baby boomers themselves meant that they did not simply pass on the traditions of their parents but were more likely to be innovative and to scrutinize their traditions carefully. They experimented with new sexual scripts—

some wisely and some not so wisely—but they strove for a much higher degree of overall equality between men and women. The baby boomers were the generation for which our second sexual revolution was waiting. They took another giant step away from our Victorian traditions. But they were a charismatic generation that established changes for younger and older Americans and energized our entire society. They redesigned our concepts of sexuality and gender equality in their own image. But, unfortunately they never really finished the job. They left us as "liberated Victorians"—not fully able to enjoy our liberation or to escape our Victorianism. But they set the stage for the third sexual revolution.

The Mythical Place of the Pill in the 1960s Revolution

The media and even many experts have spread the word and convinced many people that changes in gender equality and the autonomy that those changes brought were not the key causes of our sexual revolution. Here are the words of historian Bradley Smith:

> The event that was to have the greatest effect upon sexuality in the United States and, ultimately, in the world was the release of the birth control pill. . . . Young women who would never before take a chance on sex with their boyfriends for fear of pregnancy . . . adopted new attitudes towards sex. . . . The resulting freedom changed the sex habits of the nation.[18]

Smith is thus arguing that gender equality and autonomy were themselves the consequences of the development of the contraceptive pill. In this view, the pill is seen as the central force that produced the sexual revolution and the related changes in our society. The reasoning is that with the pill available the main reason blocking women from sexual equality was removed. We have also had support for this view from the famous sex therapists Masters, Johnson, and Kolodny:

> The pill made premarital sex considerably safer and permitted millions to think of sex as relational or recreational rather than procreative . . . the availability of the pill provided a sense of freedom for many women and probably contributed more to changing sexual behavior than has generally been imagined.[19]

Lots of people believe this explanation and it sounds persuasive. But let me indicate why it's really not a very accurate picture of what happened.

Those who believe in the revolutionary power of the pill are presuming that before the sexual revolution of the 1960s women were ready and willing to have intercourse if only their worries about pregnancy were alleviated. That makes female sexual motivations much like a car with an engine running but blocked from movement by one obstacle, fear of pregnancy. Just remove that road block and it will surely push forward. But the major block for women was not their fear of pregnancy. Women throughout this century have been subjected to a restrictive sexual upbringing. Accordingly, they have been programmed by society to start premarital sexuality, if at all, cautiously and only with the justification of serious emotional commitment. The evidence indicates that this upbringing and not the fear of pregnancy is the basic cause of female sexual resistance.

The Kinsey data gathered mostly in the 1940s supports my perspective. In the Kinsey sample the primary reason for women restricting premarital coitus was "moral objections." That was cited as a "definite reason" by 80 percent of his sample, whereas fear of pregnancy was cited as such by only 21 percent of his sample. I should add that 32 percent of the women said that lack of sexual responsiveness was a reason for restricting coitus.[20] This lack of primary emphasis upon pregnancy doesn't mean that it was not a concern and unimportant. But for most women, whether virginal or not, moral objections drilled into them by our society were by far the more important reasons for their reluctance to have sex.

Another way to see the flaws in the "powerful pill" view of our last sexual revolution is to ask, what if the pill did launch the last sexual revolution? If so, then today, thirty years later, we should surely find that most women starting to have premarital coitus would be on the pill. But if that were the case, we wouldn't have the Western world's highest rate of unwanted pregnancy. There is far from universal use even today. The latest data from the National Survey of Family Growth (1995) showed that only 15 percent of the women having first sexual intercourse in the 1990s were on the pill.[21]

Reluctance to have uncommitted premarital intercourse was instilled in women throughout this century by their parents and by our patriarchal traditions. In a formal sense both men and women were supposed to be abstinent before marriage, but in reality the harsher restraints and punishments were imposed upon women. Limiting the sexual experience of women gave husbands more confidence that their wives and girlfriends would be loyal and faithful to them. In effect this was an expression of the power of men over women. Of course, wives in our male-dominant society would not have the power to insist on equivalent behavior from their husbands.

But insisting that women be chaste doesn't stop men from having sex. Men would simply persuade some women to violate their standards and then blame the women for the transgression. That practice is the heart of the ancient double standard. The sexual revolution of the 1960s did somewhat mute the difference in sexual restrictions between men and women, but the difference is still very real even for young women in the 1990s. Unfair? Of course, but social customs are not built on the principle of fairness—they are based far more on who has power. Just ask Blacks, Jews, Hispanics, Catholics, or any other minority group about that.

Women even today feel that they cannot be as free as men for they must avoid the appearance of being too cavalier about sex. We don't live in isolation from our fellow humans. Their opinions of us and especially the wishes of those close to us influence us more than does a new contraceptive advance. A changed attitude of acceptance of sexuality among the key people in one's life makes it far easier to accept sex than does the advent of a new contraceptive technique. The revolutionaries of the 1920s and the 1960s did not have to wait for effective contraceptive methods. If they wanted to use them, they were already here. What they needed in order to be sexually freer was a change in the equality and autonomy our basic social institutions granted to women. Accompanying such egalitarian changes is the acceptance by one's friends and family of the right to have sex. That group support is the vital element needed for any lasting change in sexual behavior.

'Swept Away': The Escape from 'Being Used'

Even today women don't fully accept their right to have sex. Dr. Carol Cassell, a well-known sex educator, has written in depth about the ways in which women in our society have been trained to feel the need to be "swept away" by passionate, romantic feelings in order not to feel "used" and to justify their sexual interests. That need was built into women by our society. I call our society's approach the "dirty glass of water" view of sexuality. Sexuality is perceived as too dirty for women to ingest unless they add a magical elixir that will purify it. The magical potion that can make the sexual water digestible is called passionate romantic love. It is mainly women who are seen as needing this special purification. In accord with my own views, Cassell describes the sexual plight of all too many women even today:

Despite the sexual revolution, the pill, slogans of sisterhood, and media assurance that "we've come a long way," we are still not sexually free or emotionally satisfied. . . . Swept Away is a sexual strategy, a coping mechanism, which allows women to be sexual in a society that is, at best, still ambivalent about, and at worst, condemnatory of female sexuality. It is a tactic, employed unconsciously by women to get what they want—a man, sexual pleasure—without having to pay the price of being labeled wanton or promiscuous. Swept Away is, consequently, a counterfeit emotion, a fraud, a disguise of our true erotic feelings which we've been socialized to describe as romance.[22]

The persistence of the "swept away" phenomenon tells us that equality in sexuality is very hard to achieve in a society where the power of men and women is still unequal.[23] To be sure, we have moved somewhat toward greater overall gender equality and accordingly there are more women today who feel that they do not need to be swept away in order to justify their sexuality. They may require love or friendship or just physical attraction, but in all these cases they take responsibility for their choices and do not feel the need for the excuse that they were emotionally swept away.

Surely many more women would pursue sexual pleasures if they were treated as equals by men and therefore did not have to be concerned so much about whether their sexual behaviors might alienate some men. However, women would still have their requirements for a good sexual relationship beyond the physical. We all want women and men to act responsibly and honestly with each other. But if we want to achieve that important goal, we will have to equalize the distribution of power between men and women. That involves far more than simply giving women greater rights to have sex. Many women have learned that they can be free sexually but will still not be treated equally by men. Several feminist writers have noted the clash between sexual equality and inequality in social power:

> For women, sexual equality with men has become a concrete possibility, while economic and social parity remains elusive. We believe it is this fact, beyond all others, that has shaped the possibilities and polities of women's sexual liberation.[24]

As long as women have less power they will feel the need somehow to please and attach themselves to these more powerful creatures called men, and sex will serve as a commodity in that pursuit. Inequality can easily lead to distrust, force, and manipulation between men and women. Women will see sex as a service to men as long as they are doing sex "his way and for him." When they have the feeling of power

to pursue sex for their own satisfaction and not just for their partner's satisfactions, then the concept of sex as a service and being used will become rarities.

Some readers, no doubt, may still be skeptical and think that sexual differences between men and women are just "natural." Well, come with me on an imaginary journey to a mythical society and I think I'll convince you otherwise. Picture yourself in a society called *Matriarchia* in which women dominate in every major institution—they hold the top political offices; they are the religious leaders; they are the leaders in the economy; they even are expected to lead in their marriages. Men are raised knowing that they have less power than the women with whom they will eventually mate. Women are the initiators in sex just as they are in every area because they are the most powerful group.

How many men reading this account would like to live in this type of society? The mirror image of that society is the heritage of women in most cultures in the world. It is not the "nature" of women to be less sexually assertive. Rather, it is the nature of human beings with little social power to be generally less assertive.

If we want women and men to have equal rights to sexual expression, then we must work to create equality in the overall society between women and men. Gender equality can bring into being the values that should go with sexuality: honesty, equality, and responsibility.

The Homosexual Revolution: Out of the Closet and into the Streets

Contrary to what many people think, we did not have only a heterosexual revolution in the late 1960s. There was also a very important revolution involving homosexual men and women. There were some moderate gay right movements in the 1950s and 1960s, but they only laid the foundation for what was to come. The significant gay liberation revolt began with the Stonewall riot in New York City in 1969. At that time it was routine to harass the patrons in gay bars, but something different happened that summer night in Greenwich Village. As historian John D'Emilio describes it:

> On Friday, June 27, 1969, shortly before midnight, two detectives from Manhattan's Sixth Precinct set off with a few other officers to raid the Stonewall Inn, a gay bar on Christopher Street in the heart of Greenwich Village. . . . Patrons of the Stonewall tended to be young and nonwhite. Many were drag queens and many came from the burgeoning ghetto of runaways living across town in the East Village. As the police released them one by one from inside the

bar, a crowd accumulated on the street. Jeers and catcalls arose from the onlookers when a paddy wagon departed with the bartender, the Stonewall's bouncer, and three drag queens. A few minutes later, the scene became explosive. Almost by signal the crowd erupted into cobblestone and bottle heaving. . . . From nowhere came an uprooted parking meter used as a battering ram on the Stonewall door. I heard several cries of "Let's get some gas," but the blaze of flame which soon appeared in the window of the Stonewall was still a shock. . . . Rioting continued far into the night, with Puerto Rican transvestites and young street people leading charges against rows of uniformed police officers and then withdrawing to regroup in Village alleys and side streets. By the following night, graffiti calling for "Gay Power" had appeared along Christopher Street. . . . After the second night of disturbances, the anger that had erupted into street fighting was channeled into intense discussion of what many had begun to memorialize as the first gay riot in history. . . . Before the end of July, women and men in New York had formed the Gay Liberation Front. . . . Word of the Stonewall riot and GLF spread rapidly among the networks of young radicals scattered across the county and within a year liberation groups had sprung into existence on college campuses and in cities around the nation.[25]

The gay liberation movement built up the identification of gays with one another. The conflict unified homosexuals, gave them a sense of belonging, and thereby a sense of common identity. Historian John D'Emilio summed it up by noting that: "Gay liberation transformed homosexuality from a stigma that one kept carefully hidden into an identity that signified membership in a community organizing for freedom."[26]

In the 1970s thousands of young gay men and lesbian women left their small towns and headed for the cities. Pulitzer Prize–winning author Frances FitzGerald described the changing scene, particularly in San Francisco, in this way:

The gay liberationists called upon homosexuals to make an open avowal of their sexual identity. "Coming out" symbolized the shedding of self-hatred, but it was also a political act directed toward the society as a whole. . . . "We're the *first* generation to live openly as homosexuals," Randy Shilts said. "We have no role models. We have to find new ways to live."[27]

Gay organizations and publications grew in many cities, but nowhere did they flourish as in San Francisco. In the 1970s gay men by the tens of thousands migrated to the city by the bay. It is estimated today that about a third of the adult men in San Francisco are gay. When the AIDS epidemic hit, San Francisco had a politically powerful gay community that fought its way through the conflicts of those early epidemic years and came out with an organized way of coping. In contrast, cities like New York with larger gay populations but with less open gay identity were much less effective in the early handling of the AIDS crisis.[28]

It is important to note that it was not until the late nineteenth century that the term homosexual was applied as a label for a "type of person." Until then homosexual behavior was simply an act that violated Christian teaching—similar to adultery, masturbation, or fornication. It was not believed that it took a special type of person to do any of those acts. We need to regain that belief because there is no one type of homosexual person. A homosexual orientation, important as it may be, is but a part of a person's makeup. The same is, of course, true of heterosexuals. One doesn't really learn very much about a person by being told that he or she is a heterosexual. Things like our social class, politics, religion, job, and basic values determine much more about what kind of person we are than whether we are heterosexual or homosexual.

In homosexuality, as in heterosexuality, our society's gender roles are a powerful determinant of behavior. Many gay males tend to orient themselves to sexuality just as heterosexual men do—emphasizing physical pleasure—whereas a great many lesbians approach sexuality like heterosexual women do—emphasizing emotional involvement with each other. But, especially during the last ten years gay males have radically changed their behaviors and lesbian females today do not fit so neatly into any one "feminine" pattern. Therapist Margaret Nichols notes:

Tastes in erotica became more varied and not limited to "warm" sex and many women began to prefer sex that included activities heretofore considered to be outside the boundaries of "normal" female sexuality: rough sex, "dirty" sex, role-polarized sex, "promiscuity," anonymous sex, sex without love, and sadomasochistic sex. By the mid-1980s, some women were producing pornographic magazines for lesbians such as *On Our Backs* (a takeoff on a well-known feminist newspaper called *Off Our Backs*).[29]

For lesbians the broader societal influence was visible in the fusion for many women of lesbian identity with feminism. Sisterhood was often more important than erotic pleasures, and the bond to women and the freedom from men was primary. Lesbianism, in this sense, developed the "male-free" potential of women. In contrast, the middle-class, college-educated women who founded the National

Organization for Women (NOW) in 1966 were mostly heterosexually oriented feminists. Most feminists are not lesbians, but a great many lesbians do identify as feminists.

The lesbian feminist position is well put by Lillian Faderman:

> There is a good deal on which lesbian-feminists disagree. . . . But they all agree that men have waged constant battle against women, committed atrocities or at best injustices against them, reduced them to grown-up children, and . . . a feminist ought not to sleep in the enemy camp.[30]

Lesbian feminists want to see a dramatic change in men's treatment of women before they will be willing to sanction heterosexuality. Many other feminists believe that "sleeping in the enemy camp" is an advantage that can encourage change toward greater gender equality.

It seems that just as straight women sought equality in the heterosexual revolution, the goal of the homosexual revolution was for homosexuality to be recognized as a legitimate option and for homosexuals to be treated as equals rather than as inferiors. In this sense, for both homosexuals and heterosexuals, the last sexual revolution was a movement toward greater social equality with sexuality serving as one of the lead vehicles in that pursuit.

The Deadly Mixture of Victorianism and Liberation

The rapidity of change during the sexual revolutions of this century left many with the illusion of being sexually liberated from the past. After this roller-coaster ride of social upheaval, we might well feel that everything has indeed changed. In reality the sexual revolutions of the 1920s and 1960s, instead of destroying our Victorian heritage, suppressed large segments of it in our collective psyche. The two revolutions were partial revolutions—what one might call "stalled revolutions" waiting to be finished. Without a doubt, there was considerable change, but much remains the same. The excitement of increased sexual liberation has blinded us to the sex-negative Victorian feelings residing within us. By and large, we have retained our dogmatic stance against gender equality, homosexuality, and teenage sexuality, and we continue to harbor remnants of an overall degrading and fearful view of sexuality.[31]

Each new sexual problem that arises, like teen pregnancy or date rape, breathes new life into those Victorian feelings about the degrading, demeaning, and dehumanizing qualities of sexuality. As a result instead of a reasoned response, each new crisis panics millions of Americans into emotionally running away from their newly won sexual freedoms. We have become a nation of fair-weather sexual liberals. At the first sign of a sexual storm we retreat to a more traditional position. Victorianism, though weakened, is far from dead in America. Why else would so many Americans at the end of the 1990s still think that homosexuality is immoral and so many women feel the need to justify their sexuality by being "swept away"?

Changes in sexual behavior and attitudes take time to be fully digested and to become a natural part of our lives. It is one thing to accept a new behavior intellectually and quite another to accept it emotionally. The forty years between our two sexual revolutions were a time for consolidation of our thinking, feeling, and acting in the sexual realm.[32] The dramatic changes of the last sexual revolution left us with a new consolidation problem. The sexual revolution ended in the late 1970s and only moderate changes have occurred in sexual behavior or attitudes during the decade of the 1980s. Both the remnants of our Victorianism and the societal inequalities between men and women have blocked our making further progress toward the goal of pluralism.

The Victorian sexual philosophy in America is part of a traditional approach to life in which male dominance is accepted and the inequality between men and women is considered proper. One basic reason why Victorianism is so difficult to eradicate is that it has the support of those who endorse the traditional philosophy in our country. But, the 1990s offered a major opportunity for promoting a more gender-equal lifestyle and strengthening our new sexual philosophy of pluralism. The widely shared values of HER (honesty, equality, and responsibility) can guide our sexual acts in this pluralistic context.

Many Americans have allegiances to both our traditional *and* our pluralistic sexual philosophies. Because of this internal conflict we have fallen behind most other Western nations in gaining control over our sexual problems. One thing is clear: we need a more pluralistic view of sexuality. We need to broaden, not narrow, our sexual choices and we need to empower, not restrict, ourselves. Our freedom to make wise choices depends on our moving in this direction. Despite our two sexual revolutions, many Americans are still uncomfortable in dealing with their sexuality. We are in a sense "liberated Victorians." In today's world that can be a fatal mixture.

Notes

1. Edward Laumann, John Gagnon, Robert Michael, and Stuart Michaels, *The Social Organization of Sexuality* (Chicago: University of Chicago Press, 1994), p. 98.

2. Clelia Duel Mosher, *The Mosher Survey: Sexual attitudes of 45 Victorian Women* (New York: Arno Press, 1980), p. xviii.

3. See Alfred C. Kinsey, W. Pomeroy, C. Martin, and P. Gebhard, *Sexual Behavior in the Human Female* (Philadelphia: Saunders, 1952), Ch. 8, and Alfred C. Kinsey, W. Pomeroy, and C. Martin, *Sexual Behavior in the Human Male* (Philadelphia: Saunders, 1948), Ch. 8.

4. See Ira L. Reiss, *Premarital Sexual Standards in America* (New York: The Free Press of Macmillan, 1960), and *The Social Context of Premarital Sexual Permissiveness* (New York: Holt, Rinehart and Winston, Inc., 1967).

5. Paula Fass, *The Damned and the Beautiful: American Youth in the 1920's* (New York: Oxford University Press, 1977), p. 260.

6. Ibid., p. 326.

7. William A. Williams, T. McCormick, L. Gardner, and W. LaFeber (eds.), *America in Vietnam: A Documentary History* (New York: Anchor Books, 1985), pp. 288–289.

8. Cole Porter, "Let's Do It (Let's Fall in Love)," copyright 1928 by Harms, Inc. John Lennon and Paul McCartney, "Why Don't We Do It in the Road," by The Beatles, Apple Records, copyright 1968 Northern Songs, BMI.

9. Arland Thornton, "Changing Attitudes Toward Family Issues in the United States," *Journal of Marriage and the Family* 51 (November 1989): 873–93, Table 1; National Opinion Research Center, *General Social Surveys, 1972–1996* (Chicago: NORC, 1996), p. 204.

10. Ira L. Reiss and Gary R. Lee, *Family Systems in America*, 4th ed. (New York: Holt, Rinehart and Winston, Inc., 1988), Chs. 7 and 12.

11. Lenore J. Weitzman, *The Divorce Revolution: The Unexpected Social and Economic Consequences for Women and Children in America* (New York: The Free Press of Macmillan, 1985), especially Ch. 11.

12. Ibid., p. 209.

13. Robert S. Weiss, *Marital Separation: Coping with the End of a Marriage and the Transition to Being Single Again* (New York: Basic Books, 1975), p. 288.

14. The 1995 National Survey of Family Growth reported 89 percent of unmarried women aged twenty-five to twenty-nine had experienced intercourse.

15. National Opinion Research Center, *General Social Survey, 1972–1996*, p. 215.

16. See Ira L. Reiss, "Sexual Behavior," pp. 828–30, in George T. Kurian and Graham T. T. Molitor, eds., *Encyclopedia of the Future*, Vol. 2 (New York: Macmillan Publishers, 1996). On extramarital sexual attitudes and behavior see Edward Laumann, John Gagnon, Robert Michael, and Stuart Michaels, *The Social Organization of Sexuality* (Chicago: University of Chicago Press, 1994), p. 216. See also Philip Blumstein and Pepper Schwartz, *American Couples* (New York: William Morrow, 1983), pp. 289 and 585.

17. Steven D. McLaughlin et al., *The Changing Lives of American Women* (Chapel Hill: The University of North Carolina Press, 1988), Ch. 6.

18. Bradley Smith, *The American Way of Sex: An Informal Illustrated History* (New York: Two Continents Publishing Company, 1978), p. 232.

19. William H. Masters, Virginia E. Johnson, and Robert C. Kolodny, *Masters and Johnson on Sex and Human Loving* (Boston: Little, Brown and Company, 1986), pp. 22–23.

20. The choices add to more than 100 percent because respondents were permitted to check more than one choice. See Kinsey et al., *Sexual Behavior in the Human Female*, p. 344. See Donn Byrne and William A. Fisher, *Adolescents, Sex, and Contraception* (Hillsdale, NJ: Lawrence, Erlbaun Assoc., 1983), p. 181.

21. National Center for Health Statistics, "Fertility, Family Planning and Women's Health: New Data from the 1995 National Survey of Family Growth," *Vital Health Statistics* 23, No. 19 (May 1997).

22. Carol Cassell, *Swept Away: Why Women Fear Their Own Sexuality* (New York: Simon and Schuster, 1984), pp. 20, 24.

23. In my book, *Journey into Sexuality: An Exploratory Voyage*, I examined the close relationship of power and sexuality not only in Western societies but in 186 non-Western cultures.

24. Barbara Ehrenreich, Elizabeth Hess, and Gloria Jacobs, *Re-making Love: The Feminization of Sex* (Garden City, New York: Anchor Books, 1987), p. 9.

25. John D'Emilio, *Sexual Politics, Sexual Communities: The Making of a Homosexual Minority in the United States, 1940–1970* (Chicago: University of Chicago, 1983), pp. 231–33.

26. Ibid., p. 247.

27. Frances FitzGerald, *Cities on a Hill: A Journey Through Contemporary American Cultures* (New York: Simon and Schuster, 1986), pp. 42, 47. See Jeffrey Weeks, *Invented Moralities: Sexual Values in an Age of Uncertainty* (New York: Columbia University Press, 1995). See also Jeffrey Weeks, *Sexuality and Its Discontents: Meanings, Myths, and Modern Sexualities* (London: Routledge and Kegan Paul, 1985).

28. See Randy Shilts, *And the Band Played On: Politics, People, and the AIDS Epidemic* (New York: St. Martin's Press, 1987).

29. Margaret Nichols, "Sex Therapy with Lesbians, Gay Men, and Bisexuals," in Sandra Leiblum and Raymond Rosen, *Principles and Practice of Sex Therapy*, 2d ed. (New York: The Guilford Press, 1989), p. 276.

30. Lillian Faderman, *Surpassing the Love of Men: Romantic Friendship and Love Between Women from the Renaissance to the Present* (New York: William Morrow, 1981), p. 413. See also Lillian Faderman,

Odd Girls and Twilight Lovers: A History of Lesbian Life in 20th Century America (New York: Penguin Books, 1991).

31. Albert D. Klassen, Colin J. Williams, and Eugene E. Levitt, *Sex and Morality in the United States: An Empirical Enquiry Under the Auspices of the Kinsey Institute* (Middletown, Conn.: Wesleyan University Press, 1989).

32. John Modell, *Into One's Own: From Youth to Adulthood in the United States 1920–1975* (Berkeley and Los Angeles: University of California Press, 1989).

Chapter 2
Alfred Kinsey

Vern L. Bullough

"...*The most influential American sex researcher of the twentieth century.*" *Readers do not have to be experts in the area of sex research to recognize that this quote refers to Alfred Kinsey. A biologist turned sexologist, Kinsey is portrayed in the literature as both a colorful character and a consummate researcher. Kinsey's advocates and adversaries alike agree that his controversial life's work sparked a revolution in sexuality research. But there has long been disagreement about the nature of his influence. Was the greatest significance of Kinsey's work that it was a marker of changes occurring at that time as claimed by one historian? Or, as suggested by others, was his work seminal because it was instrumental in bringing about the changes? Noted therapist David Mace, who defined the sexual revolution of the 1960s as a grassroots uprising against organized religion's teachings about sexuality, alluded to the latter position when he identified Kinsey along with Sigmund Freud and Albert Ellis as the three most influential forces in the sexual revolution. Mace believed their contributions to the knowledge about human sexuality was unparalleled.*

Regardless of how one views the influence of Kinsey's work, facts cannot be ignored. The radical changes in public attitudes that followed his first published report on male sexuality in 1948 foreshadowed a new discipline of sexology, a new profession of sex therapy, and new materials and methodology for sexuality education. Nevertheless, Kinsey today is still a controversial figure, attracting both detractors who would defame him and advocates who would vindicate him.

Kinsey has been criticized by many professionals in the field, including the recent Director of the Kinsey Institute. Critics point to problems such as the following:

- *His difficulties with sampling and survey research, illustrated by the fact that he confused, in some cases, the concepts of random sampling and representativeness.*

- *His infamous seventeen-hour interview with a pedophile that admittedly was the basis for much*

of his data about the onset of childhood sexual activity.

- *His use of data collected from an Indiana State Prison for the bulk of his male study.*

Kinsey, however, has been recognized, even by his detractors for the following singular contributions made to sexuality research:

- *His Seven-point scale, which placed persons along a continuum of sexual activity from exclusively heterosexual to exclusively homosexual and is still in use today.*

- *His objectifying the existence of homosexuality and his conclusion that one or a few homosexual experiences do not classify a person as homosexual.*

- *His reported data on the percentage of the population that is exclusively homosexual are amazingly consistent with national probability samples today.*

- *His early data reporting multiple orgasms among women, which are still cited today.*

- *His landmark federal court case (1957) decided after his death, which resulted in scientists and scholars being treated as a "community"; therefore, they can possess obscene materials for scientific purposes. Today, the Kinsey Institute at Indiana University has the largest collection of pornography in the world.*

After reading Vern Bullough's treatment of the life of Alfred Kinsey, on which side of the Kinsey controversy do you find yourself? What factors most influenced your position either as an advocate or an adversary?

It was in a setting of a growing awareness of the importance of sexuality and an ever-increasing volume of studies on human sexuality that Alfred Kinsey began to do his research. Kinsey was born in 1894 in Hoboken, New Jersey; he was at the height of his career in 1938 when he shifted from the study of gall wasps to the study of human sexuality. He probably also was going through what might be called a midlife crisis, hunting for new fields to conquer. In the summer of that year, Indiana University began to teach a course in marriage, one of the many colleges and universities to venture into this new area. Because no professor on the faculty was considered qualified to teach it singlehandedly, teachers (all men) were gathered together from the departments of law, economics, sociology, philosophy, medicine, and biology to do so. Kinsey ended up as coordinator of the course.

To add to his own knowledge, he soon began taking histories of the students, many of whom came to him for counseling. He sought information on age at first premarital intercourse, the frequency of sexual activity, the number of partners, and similar data. Gradually, he amplified his search for information by including questions about prostitutes, the age of the partner with whom the subject had his or her first intercourse, the percentage of partners who were married, and so forth. Kinsey, a compulsive data gatherer, began an extensive reading program into all aspects of sexual behavior. This led him to build up a personal library, since serious studies on sex were difficult to find in most public or university libraries. To extend his collection of data beyond the classroom, Kinsey took a field trip to Chicago in June 1939 to conduct interviews. About this time, he also began working with inmates at the Indiana State Penal Farm and their families, compiling their sexual histories. All of this he did in consultation with the university officials, who had ruled that the histories were to be kept completely confidential. His students apparently trusted him, and many of them who had taken the class continued to write Kinsey about their sexual problems long after they had graduated.

Kinsey's expanding research into human sexuality was not without controversy, and one of his most persistent critics was Thurman Rice, a bacteriology professor at the university who had written extensively on sex, primarily from the point of view of eugenics. Rice had long given the sex lecture that was part of a required course in hygiene at the university and for which males were separated from females. Rice was typical of an earlier generation of sex experts, in that he considered moral education a part of sex education. He believed masturbation was harmful, condemned premarital intercourse, and was fearful that Kinsey's course on marriage was a perversion of academic standards. He charged Kinsey with, among other things, asking some of the women students about the length of their clitorises, and then demanded the names of students in the class so he could verify such classroom voyeurism. Rice totally opposed Kinsey's questioning in general, because he believed that sexual behavior could not be analyzed by scientific methods as it was a moral subject, not a scientific one. Some parents also objected to the specific sexual data given in the course, and university president Herman Wells, a personal friend of Kinsey, offered him the alternative of either continuing to teach the course or to conduct his sex research.[1] In any case, Kinsey would continue to teach in the biology department. He elected to do the research and dropped his participation in the marriage course.

Kinsey was not only interested but well prepared. As a bench scientist, he felt the researcher had to be directly involved in the project. He was somewhat disdainful of the work of most of his predecessors in sex research. He was appalled at how Freud and the early analysts, still under the influence of Krafft-Ebing, had looked on masturbation as a sickness. He was also concerned that Freud relied on subjective impressions and did not test them. Similarly, he disagreed with Stekel and, ultimately, with the whole psychoanalytic approach. He had no use for Krafft-Ebing's unscientific cataloging of sexual behavior. Kinsey believed that American psychologists and American followers of Freud were not objective scientists and were too highly influenced by traditional moral codes. Though he had good words to say about Ellis, his esteem dwindled when he learned that the British researcher was so timid about his work that he could not talk to his subjects face to face and depended entirely on letters written to him. Kinsey was also offended by Hirschfeld's open proclamation of his own homosexuality, which led him to regard Hirschfeld as a special pleader and not an objective scientist. Similarly, he was disdainful of Malinowski because in his mind Malinowski was not only afraid of sex but had been taken in by the islanders. He and Mead disagreed publicly, because Mead accused him of talking only about sex per se and not about such things as maternal behavior. Kinsey thought they were different things and said he wanted to study sex, not love. Obviously, Kinsey was a strong-minded individual— some might call him arrogant; he was critical of most of his predecessors, although he was always careful to cite them in his work if they had broken new ground. Moreover, in spite of his criticism, he recognized that some, particularly Freud and Ellis, had made important contributions for their time. They just fell short of what Kinsey felt was necessary, namely the study of human sexual activity in as detached and scientific a way as possible. He had the commitment and the temperament to do so, since he thought he had to be rigorously neutral and nonjudgmental and let his data speak for him.[2]

In short, after years of skirting around the subject of human sexuality, the CRPS (Committee for Research in the Problems of Sex) jumped in with full support for Kinsey. The result was a revolution in sex research. Aiding this revolution was what for a time was believed to be the elimination of the threat of venereal diseases, or as the Centers for Disease Control began to call them, sexually transmitted diseases.[3]

The first big step in this direction was the discovery of sulfa drugs in 1935, and this was followed by the development of a commercial process for making penicillin during World War II. Sulfa proved effective against gonorrhea, while penicillin was effective against both gonorrhea and syphilis. Other new antibiotics soon appeared in the postwar period, and for a time at least, the fear of sexually transmitted diseases was no longer an issue and, more important, no longer an inhibitor, in sexual relations. In sum, Americans, who had been among the most sexually inhibited, proved to be a receptive audience for the new findings about human sexuality.

The two decades following the appearance of the first Kinsey report in 1948 saw a radical change in public attitudes about sexuality spurred both by the development of the oral contraceptive and by new studies in human sexuality, including additional ones by Kinsey and his team and by William Masters and Virginia Johnson. The results of these studies included the establishment of a new discipline, sexology; the emergence of a new helping profession, sex therapist; and a reorientation of the way sex was taught. Individually and collectively, there was also a changing attitude, more positive if you will, toward sexuality.

Kinsey's Research

Kinsey is a good marker of these changes because, unlike almost all previous American sex researchers, Kinsey emphasized the sex part of sex research and held that sex was as legitimate a subject to study as any other. He recognized the many facets of sexual behavior from biology to history and gathered together one of the great resource libraries of the world devoted entirely to sex. He openly challenged the traditional medical dominance of sexual topics and, in the process, opened up the field to many other disciplines. Though some of his statistics can be challenged, it was the combination of all his contributions that make him the most influential American sex researcher of the twentieth century.

His two major works, the male study in 1948 and the female study in 1952, serve as effective indicators of the change taking place in American society.[4] Though Kinsey is known for his diligent interviewing and summation of data, his work is most significant because of his attempt to treat the study of sex as a scientific discipline, compiling and examining the data and drawing conclusions from them without moralizing.

The Kinsey Interview

The key to Kinsey's studies was the interview, since Kinsey was convinced that it was only through this means that accurate data could be compiled.

His interview technique included a number of checks for consistency, and if inconsistencies appeared, either from attempts to deceive or from faulty memory, the interviewer probed deeper until the apparent disagreement could be explained or eliminated. Kinsey strongly believed he could detect fraudulent answers, and certainly his ingenious coding system was designed to detect the most obvious ones.

Exaggeration proved almost impossible in the system in which questions were asked rapidly and in detail, because few subjects could give consistent answers. Though he recognized that some subjects might not remember accurately, he felt errors resulting from false memories would be offset by errors other subjects made in an opposite direction. A deliberate cover-up was a more serious problem, but he felt his numerous cross-checks made it difficult. If histories were taken of a husband and wife, the two were cross-checked to see how they conformed; some retakes were conducted after a minimum interval of two years and an average interval of four years to see if people would give the same basic answers.

Kinsey was also concerned with potential bias by the interviewer, and he sought to overcome this by limiting the number of interviewers to four: himself, Wardell Pomeroy, Clyde Martin, and eventually Paul Gebhard. These men engaged in discussion sessions after a series of interviews to see if they agreed on the coding of certain kinds of responses. Collaboratively, the four interviewed some eighteen thousand individuals: eight thousand each by Kinsey and Pomeroy and two thousand by Martin and Gebhard.[5] Kinsey actually hoped to get one hundred thousand sexual histories, but his death ended this long-term plan.

The interview covered a basic minimum of about 350 items, and these items remained almost unchanged throughout all the interviews. A maximum history covered 521 items, and whenever there was any indication of sexual activity beyond what the basic questions covered, the interviewer could go as far as he thought necessary to get the material. All the questions had been memorized by the interviewers, and there was no referral to any question sheet. Questions were asked directly and without apology, and the interviewer waited for a response from the subject. Initial questions were simply informational ones about the informant's age, birthplace, educational experience, marital status, and children. These were followed by questions on religion, personal health, hobbies, special interests, and so on. It was not until 20 minutes into the interview that sex questions appeared, and these started with sex education, proceeded to ages when a person first became aware of where babies came from, and then on to menstruation and growth of pubic hair and various anatomical changes. From here, the questions went on to early sex experiences, including age at first masturbation. Techniques of masturbation were investigated for both men and women. There were questions on erotic fantasies during masturbation and about erotic responses, and next was a series of questions about actual sex practices. The answers to the basic 350 questions could be coded on one page; Pomeroy estimated that the code sheet provided information equivalent to twenty-five typewritten pages.[6]

Before any specific questions about homosexuality were asked, twelve preliminary inquiries were scattered throughout the early questions, the answers to which would give the interviewer hints about the subject's sexual preference in partners. If the interviewer thought the subject was not being honest, he told the person so and generally refused to finish the interview. In some cases, the interview continued, but at the end the interviewer then told the subject that he wanted to go through some questions again, so that the subject could answer accurately questions that he or she had not been honest about the first time. In general, the interview ran from 1.5 hours to 2 hours. Children were also interviewed, but a different approach was used and at least one parent was always present.

Some individuals were interviewed for much longer periods of time. For example, those individuals who had extensive homosexual experiences were asked more questions than those who did not; subjects who had engaged in prostitution were also asked more questions. The longest interview was of a pedophile. It took some 17 hours and involved both Pomeroy and Kinsey. This man was sought out because he was known to have kept accurate written records of his sexual activity, a not uncommon occurrence among pedophiles. The man had sexual relations with six hundred preadolescent males and two hundred preadolescent females, as well as intercourse with countless adults of both sexes and with animals of many species. He had developed elaborate techniques of masturbation and reported that his grandmother had introduced him to heterosexual intercourse and that his first homosexual experience was with his father.

His notes on his sexual relations with preadolescents furnished much of the information on childhood activity that Kinsey reported, since it included the length of time it took the child to be aroused, the child's response, and other such data. Kinsey's use of these data has been much criticized,[7] in part because Kinsey did not report his subject to the authorities. During the interview, the man was boastful about his ability to masturbate to ejaculation in 10 seconds from a flaccid start, and

when Kinsey and Pomeroy openly expressed their disbelief at such a statement, the man effectively demonstrated his ability to them then and there. Pomeroy added that this was the only sexual demonstration that took place during the eighteen thousand interview sessions.[8] There were, however, laboratory observations from which data were derived, but these were separate from the interview and did not necessarily include the same individuals.

Kinsey and Statistics

One of the major criticisms of Kinsey was the way in which he drew his sample. Two difficulties were at the heart of the criticism: (1) it was not random, and (2) it depended on volunteers. His critics urged him to undertake at least a small interviewing project on randomly selected individuals to test the validity of his findings,[9] but he refused. His reason for the refusal is that he believed some of those chosen randomly would not consent to answering the questions, and thus he argued it would no longer be a random sample. Though sampling techniques when Kinsey began in the 1930s were not as advanced as they later became, the issue of Kinsey's sampling concerned the Committee for Research in the Problems of Sex very early in their support. They had concluded, however, that the cluster method he advocated was as good as could be expected.[10] After the first Kinsey volume was published, Kinsey took greater care to explain his sampling method in his second book, and also eliminated some of the more controversial data gathered from interviews with prisoners.[11]

Kinsey's sample is clearly overrepresented in some areas; for example, there are too many midwesterners, particularly from Indiana, and in the male study there is a disproportionate number of prison inmates and perhaps also of homosexuals.[12] Critics also charged that those who volunteered for the project were among the less inhibited members of society, and this gave an erroneous picture of the American public. There probably is some truth in this charge, but Kinsey tried to guard against it through what he called 100 percent sampling. When he turned to organized groups to obtain subjects, all members had to agree to be interviewed about their sexual histories, whether the group was a college fraternity, a woman's club, or the residents of a particular building. About a quarter of his sample was picked this way, and since he found few significant differences between the reports of those who belonged to groups and those he contacted in other ways, he felt he was able to establish the representativeness of his sample. Though this was an ingenious resolution to the problem, his sample was, by any definition, not a cross-sample of the total population.[13]

One of the problems with any statistical summary of sex life is what is reported and how it is reported. Kinsey, for example, put sexual activity on a 7-point continuum that ranged from 0 to 6; exclusively heterosexual behavior was on one end (0) and exclusively homosexual or lesbian behavior was on the other (6). The effect of this was to emphasize the variety of sexual activity and to demonstrate that homosexuality and lesbianism were more or less a natural aspect of human behavior. This was a partial solution to an impossible question: What is homosexuality, or for that matter what is heterosexuality? Kinsey avoided these questions by defining sex in terms of outlet, any activity that resulted in orgasm. This was something that could be measured with his 7-point bipolar scale.

At the time Kinsey began his research, 5-, 6-, and 7-point scales seem to have been the most popular, and he probably adopted such a scale for this reason. Although the Kinsey scale can be improved on and although it does not measure all the things that many researchers would now want to measure, it did two things of great importance. It offered comfort to both homosexuals and heterosexuals. Kinsey, in effect, demonstrated that homosexual activity was widespread in the American population: 37 percent of his American male sample had at least one homosexual experience to orgasm sometime between adolescence and old age.[14] This statistic gave assurance to many worried heterosexuals who had experimented briefly with same-sex activities that they were not homosexuals and could relax in their normality.

Homosexuals, on the other hand, found that they were more numerous than the general public (and perhaps they themselves) realized and that many heterosexuals had experimented with homosexuality. It also led many writers on homosexuality to claim a higher percentage of homosexuals in society than probably existed. Reports of the proportion of gays in the population ranged from one person in twenty to one person in ten to even higher ratios, depending on which Kinsey statistic was used.[15] However, only 4 percent of Kinsey's subjects could be labeled as exclusively homosexual; this percentage is close to what has been found in more recent studies. Kinsey noted that the proportion of women engaging in same-sex activity was less than half that of the men.

Kinsey's Definitions and Homosexuality

Kinsey's insistence on a behavioral definition of homosexuality has led to speculation about his own potential homosexuality,[16] a question that seems to arise about almost every investigator of homosexuality. There is no evidence for this, but Kinsey did not condemn homosexuality, which might have been the basis for the charge. He also rejected the popular stereotype of the homosexual as effeminate, temperamental, and artistic; instead, he held there were wide variations among homosexuals. To gauge this he turned to measuring sexual activity. He did, however, believe that homosexual relations were characterized by promiscuity and instability, a statement somewhat contrary to his own data, as homosexual contacts accounted for only 6 to 7 percent of all male orgasms.[17]

Undoubtedly, Kinsey's findings and the publicity about homosexuality were valuable in assuring many a parent and many a client that one experience does not a homosexual make. On the other hand, his conclusion that a significant percentage of his sample was exclusively homosexual or almost exclusively homosexual allowed American society to come to terms with the facts of life and to recognize the widespread existence of this phenomenon. These are extremely important contributions, and the modern gay movement would probably not have come into being without them, at least at the time it did. Kinsey, in effect, accepted the bisexual potential of humans as a reality and this in itself was a major challenge to existing concepts in the psychoanalytic community, which tended to argue that bisexuals were really homosexuals trying to adjust to societal norms.[18] Kinsey's emphasis on outlet and his bipolar scale not only challenged traditional attitudes about sex but undermined them.

Other Findings

Kinsey was also important in emphasizing that there are class distinctions in sexual practices, that highly educated individuals have a different history of sexual activity than do the less educated, and the affluent have patterns that are different from the poor. This finding basically challenged the validity of most of the studies that had gone before his, which for the most part were based on college-educated or upper-middle-class samples. He also found that the younger generation in his male study was less likely to visit prostitutes than the older, suggesting not only that there was a generational change, but that age cohorts also must be taken into account. Kinsey was not the first to recognize generational change; it had been much commented on by others, including Terman, even though the phenomenon had not been measured effectively by his predecessors.

Kinsey challenged all sorts of myths about sexuality. One such challenge had to do with female frigidity, or what is now called anorgasmia. A total of 49 percent of the females he studied had experienced orgasm within the first month of marriage, 67 percent by the first six months, and 75 percent by the end of the first year. More remarkable was the fact that nearly 25 percent of the women in the sample recalled experiencing orgasm by the age of fifteen, and more than 50 percent by the age of twenty and 64 percent before marriage. The orgasms occurred through masturbation (40 percent), through heterosexual petting without penetration (24 percent), and through premarital coitus (10 percent). For 3 percent it was through a homosexual experience.[19]

Women varied enormously in the frequency of their orgasmic responses, with some reporting only one or two orgasms during their entire lives, while some 40 to 50 percent responded being orgasmic almost every time they had coitus. Still, 10 percent of his sample who had been married at least fifteen years had never had an orgasm. He also reported cases in which women failed to reach orgasm until after twenty years of marital intercourse. He also documented (as had others) the female ability to achieve multiple orgasm. Some 14 percent of the females in his sample responded that they had multiple orgasms. Several managed to have a dozen or more orgasms while their husbands ejaculated only once.[20] He concluded from his data that the human female, like the human male, is an "orgasm experiencing animal."[21]

Sometimes Kinsey seemed deliberately to flaunt the differences between widely held beliefs about traditional conduct and reality. He showed that fewer than half of the orgasms achieved by American males were derived from intercourse with their wives, which meant, he said, that more than half were derived from sources that were "socially disapproved and in large part illegal and punishable under the criminal codes."[22] He seemed to imply that premarital abstinence was unnatural and argued that nearly all cultures other than those in the Judeo-Christian tradition made allowance for sexual intercourse before marriage.[23] Similarly, he found that nearly 50 percent of the women in his sample had coitus before they were married, although in a "considerable portion" it had been confined to their fiancé and had taken place within one or two years preceding marriage.[24] He also argued that his data did not justify the general opinion then existing that premarital coitus was of necessity "more hurried and consequently less satisfactory than coitus usually is in marriage."[25] Kinsey, in effect, ended up defending premarital intercourse just as he had masturbation and petting, arguing

that premarital experience contributed to sexual success in marriage.[26]

The two reports hit different emotional responses in the American public. For the male study it was the incidence of homosexuality that received much of the headlines, while for the female study it was the generalized premarital and even extramarital activity of the women. Some 26 percent of the women had engaged in extramarital coitus,[27] and about 50 percent of the married male population had.[28] Still, it was the case of the women "adulteress" that roused public opinion.

Kinsey reported that 50 percent of the males who remained single until age thirty-five had overt homosexual experiences, and some 13 percent of his sample had more homosexual than heterosexual experiences between the ages of sixteen and fifty-five, and Kinsey noted that between 4 and 5 percent of the male population were exclusively homosexual.[29] This figure corresponds to some of Hirschfeld's figures and, as indicated, tends to be supported by more recent data. Women in his sample reported considerably fewer homosexual contacts than the men. Some 28 percent had reported homosexual arousal by age forty-five, but only 13 percent had actually reached orgasm.[30] The homosexual pattern, however, differed between men and women by social class. Among men it was the lower socioeconomic class that had more homosexual experiences, whereas among women, it was the upper class, better-educated group that had more homosexual activity.[31] He did not really explain this difference, which might well have been due to the ability of the upper-class women to have more choices in their partners and the economic capability to be independent of a man.

Kinsey openly and willingly challenged many basic societal beliefs. Though there is considerable evidence of Kinsey's commitment to marriage, and he demanded that his interviewers be happily married,[32] his data seemed to many to undermine the belief in marriage and traditional family. Kinsey had questioned the assumption that extramarital intercourse always undermined the stability of marriage and held that the full story was more complex than the most highly publicized cases led one to assume. He seemed to feel that the most appropriate extramarital affair, from the standpoint of preserving a marriage, was an alliance in which neither party became overly involved emotionally. He was, however, more cautious in the female book and conceded that extramarital affairs probably contributed to divorces in more ways and to "a greater extent than the subjects themselves realized."[33] Inevitably, his ideas came under attack, because he seemed to be assaulting traditional religious teachings.[34]

Interestingly, Kinsey ignored what might be called sexual adventure, paying almost no attention to swinging, group sex, and alternate lifestyles as well as such phenomena as sadism, masochism, transvestism, voyeurism, and exhibitionism. He justified this neglect by arguing that such practices were statistically insignificant. But the real answer is probably that Kinsey was not interested in them. He was also not particularly interested in pregnancy[35] or sexually transmitted diseases. What he did, however, was to demystify discussions of sex as much as it was possible to do so. Sex, to him, became just another aspect of human behavior, albeit an important part. He made Americans and the world at large aware of just how big a part human sexuality played in the life cycle of the individual and how widespread many kinds of heterosexual and homosexual activity were.

Criticism

Though the general public accepted the importance of the study,[36] many people attacked it, including Harold W. Dodds, president of Princeton University, and the Reverend Henry P. Van Dusen, president of Union Theological Seminary as well as a member of the Rockefeller Foundation.[37] While a significant proportion of the more serious criticisms was based on the sampling method and the statistical reliability of the data, the vast majority of criticism was based on what can only be called moralism and prudery. Kinsey was surprised and upset by the criticism, but since he basically had challenged much of psychoanalytic thinking, disagreed with and criticized the findings of many of his predecessors in the social sciences, and stated that much of Western moral teaching ignored reality, it is difficult to understand why he did not expect severe criticism. Moreover, as Lionel Trilling reported, in spite of Kinsey's scientific stance, his book was "full of assumptions and conclusions; it makes very positive statements on highly debatable matters, and it editorializes very freely."[38] This made criticism easier than it might have been if he had not, either consciously or unconsciously, engaged in editorializing.

Though in terms of serious criticism, he had as many defenders as he did hostile critics, most of his defenders also had some criticism not only of his results but of his plans.[39] Despite the criticisms of the first report, the CRPS continued to fund Kinsey. Because the response to the first volume had made it a best-seller, the press had eagerly anticipated the publication of the second volume on the female. By the time the book was ready to appear, the advance interest was so great that Kinsey and co-workers were literally besieged by the press, which was engaging in what has since come to be called a frenzy. The center of the assault on the female volume was essentially by the moralists, particularly by the clergy, who seemed to feel that Kinsey had undermined the virginal status of American womanhood. Some who had supported the first study, such as Karl Menninger, joined in the denunciation of the second. In part, some of the criticism was a turf war. For example, Menninger said, "Kinsey's compulsion to force human sexual behavior into a zoological frame of reference leads him to repudiate or neglect human psychology, and to see normality as that which is natural in the sense that it is what is practiced by animals."[40]

For public relations purposes, it was announced that Kinsey's support was not renewed because he had failed to request support, but there is ample evidence in the Rockefeller Archives that he did. Some of the slack in funding for Kinsey was taken up by Indiana University through the effort of its president, Wells. The scope of the project, however, was severely curtailed. Kinsey continued to try to gain funding from the Rockefeller Foundation. He continued to pursue his research and tried desperately to raise more funds, up until his death on August 25, 1956. In spite of the trauma of his last years and the serious and legitimate criticism of his studies, he was probably the major figure in transforming American public attitudes about sex, helping Americans to come to terms with the existence of real sexual behaviors that had been previously ignored.[41]

Kinsey and Censorship

Kinsey also broke new legal ground in disseminating information about sex. This was because he was nothing if not thorough, and typical of his research was his attempt to survey exhaustively the literature about human sexuality. This, among other things, involved collecting materials from all over the world. Inevitably, he ran into difficulty with postal and customs officials. Alden H. Baker, Collector of Customs at Indianapolis, called some of the incoming materials, "Damned dirty stuff," and held in 1950 it was inadmissible. Kinsey believed that the law specifically granted exceptions to scientists and medical individuals in matters dealing with possible obscenity, and he argued, it was under this category that the materials should be admitted. Washington, D.C. customs officials said there was nothing in the materials that was of intrinsic value or that made it valuable to scientists. Rather than destroy the material outright, as they held was their right, they agreed to wait for final court adjudication.[42] The case, *U.S. v. 31 Photo-*

graphs, was finally decided after Kinsey's death in the Federal Court of New York.[43] Judge Edmund L. Palmieri, ruling in Kinsey's favor, stated that there was no warrant for either custom officials or the court to sit in review of the decisions of scholars as to the bypaths of learning on which they would tread. The legal question was narrowly defined, whether among those persons who sought to see the material, there was a reasonable probability that it would appeal to prurient interest.[44] In this case, Palmieri decided it would not. The important aspect of the case was that the court, in determining community standards for defining whether a material was obscene, recognized those scientists and scholars interested in studying human sexuality as a community when it could be shown that this was the audience for which the material was intended. Customs decided not to appeal the ruling, and this has allowed various institutions and professionals to collect materials essential for sex research.

Kinsey was determined to make the study of sex a science and had projected a number of projects and book-length reports. Though some of these studies on which data had been collected were brought to fruition by his successors in Indiana and other new projects were initiated, Kinsey's death led to a greater dispersion of sex research across the United States than might have been the case had he lived.

A good example is the study of the biological factors involved in sexual behavior, for which Kinsey had been gathering data. At his death, his collection included, among other things, more than four thousand sets of measurements of penises made by subjects who gave their case histories, and another twelve thousand measurements made by a person who turned his records over to Kinsey. In the Kinsey files, the longest authenticated measurement of a penis was 10.5 inches in erection, although there were unofficial reports of longer ones. The average length was nearly 6.5 inches.

Kinsey had also attempted to measure clitorises, but this was more complicated because the amount of fleshy material and the position of the material in the prepuce. Still, clitorises that measured as long as 3 inches were reported (primarily in black women), and Kinsey noted that peep shows had exhibited women with 4-inch clitorises. Kinsey also turned to gynecologists to determine the extent to which women were aware of tactile and heavier stimulation in every part of the genitalia. He thought that clitoral stimulation was the key to female orgasm.[45] Kinsey, ever the entrepreneur, had grand plans to do much more in this area and had requested funds for a physiologist, a neurologist, and a specialist in the sexual behavior of lower animals, but nothing had come of these requests. In-stead, William Masters and Virginia Johnson were the pioneers in this area.

Notes

1. Wardell B. Pomeroy, *Dr. Kinsey and the Institute for Sex Research* (New York: Harper & Row, 1972). Judith Reisman has charged that Kinsey was not simply chosen for the university's new marriage course but that he had maneuvered for many years to gain approval for the course and to be able to direct it. See Judith A. Reisman and Edward W. Eichel, *Kinsey, Sex and Fraud: The Indoctrination of a People* (Lafayette, LA.: Lochinvar-Huntington House, 1990).
2. George W. Corner, *The Seven Ages of a Medical Scientist* (Philadelphia: University of Pennsylvania Press, 1981), 314.
3. Ibid., 268.
4. Alfred Kinsey, Wardell Pomeroy, and Clyde Martin, *Sexual Behavior in the Human Male* (Philadelphia: Saunders, 1948); and Alfred Kinsey, Wardell Pomeroy, Clyde Martin, and Paul Gebhard, *Sexual Behavior in the Human Female* (Philadelphia: Saunders, 1953).
5. Wardell B. Pomeroy, *Dr. Kinsey and the Institute for Sex Research* (New York: Harper & Row, 1972).
6. Ibid., 121; and Wardell Pomeroy, personal communication.
7. See Judith A. Reisman and Edward W. Eichel, in *Kinsey, Sex, and Fraud*, ed. J. Gordon Muir and John H. Court (Lafayette, LA.: Lochinvar-Huntington House, 1990). This is a badly written and poorly edited book, in which Kinsey is described as unscientific for relying on either the memory of older subjects or data gathered from a pedophile. See the reply from Gebhard, "Dr. Paul Gebhard's Letter to Dr. Judith Reisman Regarding Kinsey Research Subjects and Data" (March 11, 1981) [Appendix B], in *Kinsey, Sex, and Fraud*, 223.
8. Ibid., 122–3.
9. William G. Cochran, Frederick Mosteller, and John W. Tukey, *Statistical Problems of the Kinsey Report* (Washington, D.C.: American Statistical Association, 1954), 23.
10. See "Report" Foundation 1, Ser. 200, Box 41, Rockefeller Foundation Archives, Pocantico Hills, North Tarrytown, New York.
11. George W. Corner, *The Seven Ages of a Medical Scientist: An Autobiography* (Philadelphia: University of Pennsylvania Press, 1981), 315–6.
12. Pomeroy, *Dr. Kinsey*, 464.
13. See Kinsey et al., *Sexual Behavior in the Human Female*, 28–31.
14. Kinsey et al., *Sexual Behavior in the Human Male*, 161, 610–50.
15. See Vern L. Bullough, "The Kinsey Scale in Historical Perspective," in *Homosexuality/Heterosexuality: Concepts of Sexual Orientation*, ed. David P. McWhirter, Stephanie A. Sanders, and June

Machover Reinisch (New York: Oxford University Press, 1990), 3–14.

16. See Pomeroy, *Dr. Kinsey*, 46; and Paul Robinson, "Dr. Kinsey and the Institute for Sex Research," *Atlantic* 229 (May 1972): 99–102.

17. Kinsey et al., *Sexual Behavior in the Human Male*, 610, 633–6. This is the explanation advanced by Paul Robinson, *The Modernization of Sex* (New York: Harper & Row, 1976), 70–71.

18. See Kenneth Lewes, *The Psychoanalytic Theory of Male Homosexuality* (New York: Simon & Schuster, 1988).

19. Kinsey et al., *Sexual Behavior in the Human Female*, 375–408.

20. Ibid., 377, 383.

21. Edward M. Brecher, *The Sex Researchers* (Boston: Little, Brown, 1969), 124.

22. Ibid., 568.

23. Ibid., 547, 549, 559; and Kinsey et al., *Sexual Behavior in the Human Female*, 284.

24. Ibid., 186.

25. Ibid., 311.

26. Ibid., 328.

27. Ibid., 416.

28. Kinsey et al., *Sexual Behavior in the Human Male*, 585.

29. Ibid., 650–1.

30. Kinsey et al., *Sexual Behavior in the Human Female*, 450–1.

31. Ibid., 460.

32. Pomeroy, *Dr. Kinsey*, 101.

33. Kinsey et al., *Sexual Behavior in the Human Female*, 435–6.

34. See Reinhold Niebuhr, "Kinsey and the Moral Problems of Man's Sexual Life," in *An Analysis of the Kinsey Reports*, ed. Donald Porter Geddes (New York: New American Library, 1954), 62–70.

35. Actually, he had collected data on pregnancy, birth, and abortion, which appeared in Paul H. Gebhard, Wardell B. Pomeroy, Clyde E. Martin, and Cornelia V. Christenson, *Pregnancy, Birth, and Abortion* (New York: Harper, 1958).

36. A Gallup poll following the book's publication found that 58 percent of the men and 55 percent of the women thought Kinsey's research was a good thing; only 10 and 14 percent, respectively, thought it a bad thing. See Pomeroy, *Dr. Kinsey*, 283–4.

37. Dodds went so far as to meet with officials of the Rockefeller Foundation to express his unhappiness and that of Van Dusen. See Memo of June 28, 1948, Foundation Ser. 200, Box 40, Rockefeller Foundation Archives.

38. Lionel Trilling, *The Liberal Imagination* (1950; reprint, New York: Viking, 1957), 218.

39. Pomeroy, *Dr. Kinsey*, 298–9.

40. Quoted in Ibid., 367.

41. Corner, *Seven Ages of a Medical Scientist*, 316–7.

42. *The New York Times,* "U.S. Customs Refuses to Pass Obscene European Photos," November 18, 1950, n18, 9:5, and in *Indianapolis Star-News*, December 8, 1950. See Foundation Records [National Research Council] Ser. 200, Box 41, 463, Rockefeller Foundation Archives.

43. *United States v. 31 Photographs*, 156 F. Supp. 350 (S.D.N.Y., 1957).

44. Morris L. Ernst and Alan U. Schwartz, *Censorship: The Search for the Obscene* (New York: Macmillan, 1964), 125.

45. Pomeroy, *Dr. Kinsey*, 317–9.

Chapter 3
Masters and Johnson

Vern L. Bullough

Building on a baseline of Alfred Kinsey's sociological data about patterns of sexual behavior, Masters and Johnson emphasized the application of clinical scientific methods in studying the physiology of sexual response in women and men. Through such methods, they clearly delineated varied physiological responses to sexual stimulation in women and, to a lesser degree, in men. For example, they clinically documented multiple orgasms in women and discovered the source of vaginal lubrication during sexual arousal to be the walls of the vagina, rather than the Glands of Bartholin as previously believed. Even though they clinically verified Kinsey's findings concerning the similarity of the anatomy and physiology of the sexual response in females and males, they rejected his claim that the differences were centered in the brain's capacity to respond to psychological stimuli. Masters and Johnson are perhaps best recognized for their arbitrary four-stage division of the sexual response cycle still in use today: the excitement, plateau, orgasmic, and resolution stages.

The Masters and Johnson team was the first to challenge the assumption that psychiatry and psychoanalysis should be the sole providers of the treatment for sexual dysfunction. By moving the focus to the medical model, they expanded treatment options to include obstetrics and gynecology, urology, and, later, sex therapy. Today, medical and behavioral professionals across many disciplines can more competently address the problems of sexual dysfunction because of the remarkable work of this research team.

A careful reading of Vern Bullough's Kinsey and Masters and Johnson chapters will enable you to establish an imaginary time line of sexuality advances in the mid-twentieth century. It would be interesting to consider who in your family tree was your present age in 1954, when the Masters and Johnson laboratory program for the investigation of the human sexual response began. Based on your knowledge of this ancestor, do you think she or he would have volunteered to be an experimental subject using miniature cameras and electronic devices? Would you do so

today? These questions may border on the ridiculous, but they highlight the significance of an era that fostered not only the principal players in this chapter, but also other contemporary characters in sexuality advances, such as Alan Guttmacher and Mary Calderone.

William Masters and Virginia Johnson from the first were much more practice oriented than Kinsey. Masters was a physician who was concerned with helping his patients overcome their problems. Together, Masters and Johnson thought of themselves as therapists, which meant they accepted the world as they saw it existing and wanted to help their clients adjust to it. Kinsey, on the other hand, was a scientist, describing the world as it existed but also emphasizing the contradictions between actuality and accepted standards. Masters and Johnson conducted their research for a reason that was entirely different from Kinsey's.

When the laboratory program for the investigation in human sexual functioning was designed in 1954, the greatest handicap to successful treatment of sexual inadequacy was a lack of reliable physiological information in the area of human sexual response. It was presumed that definitive laboratory effort would develop material of clinical consequence that could be used by professionals in the field to improve methodology of therapeutic approach to sexual inadequacy.[1]

Just as Kinsey had challenged, sometimes with considerable hostility, the psychiatric monopoly on sexual treatment and research, Masters and Johnson offered whole new areas for the gynecologist, urologist, and other medical specialists to extend their services. Ultimately, Masters and Johnson also helped establish a whole new profession, the sex therapist, which was no longer restricted to the psychiatrist but included nurses, psychologists, social workers, and counselors. It should be added, however, that the initial promise of nonevasive therapeutic techniques for problems of sexual inadequacy was oversold by some therapists and that, as the years passed, the balance between medical intervention and nonintrusive therapy changed. The basic teaching techniques pioneered by Masters and Johnson and their contemporaries, however, still remain important.

Masters was a native of Cleveland and was born to a well-to-do family in 1915. He attended Lawrenceville Prep School and went on to Hamilton College, where he received his bachelor's degree in 1938. He then entered the University of Rochester School of Medicine and Dentistry, where he worked in Corner's laboratory. Interestingly, Corner had three of the leaders in what he called "the practical application of scientific thought to problems of human sex behavior" as students: Guttmacher, who became internationally prominent in the family planning movement; Mary Steichen Calderone, co-founder of the Sex Information and Educational Council of the United States (SIECUS); and Masters.[2]

Masters, who had always been more interested in medical research than in the practice of medicine, decided he would like to do sex research when he completed his degree, and went to Corner for advice. Corner essentially gave him three general principles to follow in pursuing sex research: (1) he should establish a scientific reputation in some other scientific field first, (2) he should secure the sponsorship of a major medical school or university, and (3) he should be at least forty years of age.[3]

Masters followed the advice almost to the letter, although he did start his research into sexuality at the age of thirty-eight. After graduation from medical school, he accepted a position at Washington University in St. Louis. Willard Allen, another of Corner's students and an active researcher in endocrinology, helped Masters get the appointment as an intern in obstetrics and gynecology. Masters moved up the ladder through resident to assistant professor and associate professor. He married and had two children. Masters also published a number of papers covering a variety of obstetrical and gynecological topics, although the majority dealt with hormone-replacement therapy for aging and aged women, a treatment that he strongly advocated[4] and that is widely used today.

The Beginnings

Gradually, Masters turned to studying the sexual act itself. The pioneer in this respect had been the French physician Félix Roubaud, who had published his account of the female response cycle in 1855.[5] Kinsey had called Roubaud's description unsurpassed,[6] even though the Frenchman had been mistaken on two points, namely the claim that there was direct frictional contact between the penis and the clitoris, and that the semen was sucked up through the cervix.

Just as Masters was actively beginning to plan his own program, G. Klumbies and H. Kleinsorge, two physicians at the University Clinic in Jena, Germany reported on a patient who was capable of fantasizing to orgasm, a fact that made it possible to distinguish the direct effects of orgasm from the muscular exertion that ordinarily preceded it or accompanied it. With the aid of an electrocardiograph and a blood pressure recorder, Klumbies and Kleinsorge recorded physiological changes, including pulse rate, systolic and diastolic blood pressure, rhythm of heart chamber contractions, respiratory volume, and muscle irritability. The woman identified some of her orgasms as more intense than others, and Klumbies and Kleinsorge noted that the intensity of the orgasm as subjectively reported showed a close relation to the acuteness of the blood pressure peak.[7] Another investigator, Abraham Mosovich, recorded electroencephalograms (brain wave patterns) during sexual arousal and orgasm.[8]

The best and most complete observations made before Masters and Johnson's studies were Kinsey's. He reported that he had access to a considerable body "of observed data on the involvement of the entire body in the spasms following orgasm."[9] Actually, most of the observations had been made on volunteers by Kinsey or his staff, independent of the interview portion of his research.

When Masters began his studies in 1954, he interviewed at length and in depth 118 female and 37 male prostitutes. Of these, 8 of the women and 3 of the men then participated as experimental subjects in a preliminary series of laboratory studies. Suggestions of this select group of techniques for support and control of the human male and female in situations of direct sexual response proved invaluable. They described many methods for elevating or controlling sexual tensions and demonstrated innumerable variations in stimulative technique. Ultimately many of these techniques have been found to have direct application in therapy of male and female sexual inadequacy and have been integrated into the clinical programs.[10]

Ultimately, however, the experimental results derived from the prostitute population were not included in the final published results, because Masters and Johnson wanted a baseline of what they regarded as "anatomic normalcy." To get this, they turned to patient populations and volunteers for data. It was during this phase that Virginia Johnson joined Masters's team, because Masters strongly believed that a woman should be involved in his research. Born Virginia Eshelman in Missouri in 1925, she had studied music at Drury College and later attended the University of Missouri. In 1950, Johnson married and had a son and daughter before separating from her husband in the late 1950s. Masters was seeking a woman to assist in research interviewing and had specified that he wanted a woman who had experience and interest in working with people. The Bureau sent Johnson, and she was hired. The two later married, but were divorced in 1992.

Johnson's work was particularly important in the first two books but played a lesser part in later studies. The fact that Masters and Johnson were a male-female team separates them from Kinsey. Though Kinsey had added a woman to his team shortly before he died, he seems to have not felt it necessary to do so before. Masters, in general, gave more emphasis to the female than to the male not only in his team but in his studies. In the discussion of physiology, for example, the female is mentioned first. Masters seems to have emphasized that the female is not just an inferior imitation of the male, an attitude widely prevalent even at the time of his research.

Sexual Response Cycle

Masters and Johnson held that the sexual response cycle involved much more than a penis and vagina, and they sought to measure heart rate, respiratory functions, muscle tension, breast response, and any other physiological measurement they could think of. A key element in the ability of Masters and Johnson to break new ground was technological. Advances in the miniaturization of cameras and electronic devices meant that they could be used inside of a plastic phallus. This allowed Masters and Johnson to record what took place inside the vagina during orgasm, and they could observe the phenomena in some detail. This new technology permitted them to give definitive answers to some of the questions about which there had been arguments or on which there had only been subjective data. It allowed Masters and Johnson to determine that there was a moistening of the vaginal lining with lubricating fluid within 10 to 30 seconds of the onset of erotic stimulation and to note that this fluid came from the coalescence of a "sweating" of the vagina's walls. They emphasized that neither the Bartholin's glands nor the cervix, previously believed to be the source of the lubrication, contributed to the fluid. Rather the sweating resulted from the increased blood supply and the engorgement of vaginal tissues.[11]

Masters and Johnson also noted a lengthening and distension of the vaginal walls, while the cervix and the uterus are pulled slowly back and up into the false pelvis (the part of the pelvis above the hip joint). The vagina's walls also undergo a distinct coloration change, from purplish red to a darker purple, as a result of vasocongestion, and the wrinkled or corrugated aspects of the vaginal wall (technically called the rugal pattern) are flattened. Gradually, the outer third of the vagina becomes grossly distended with venous blood, and the vasocongestion is so marked that the central lumen (interior) of the outer third of the vaginal barrel wall is reduced by a least a third. All this takes place during what

Masters and Johnson called the plateau phase, or second phase of the sexual response cycle.

This is followed by the orgasmic phase, during which much of physiologic activity is confined to what Masters and Johnson called the orgasm platform in the upper third of the vagina. Here there are strong contractions at 0.8 second intervals, which recur within a normal range of three to five and up to ten to fifteen times per individual orgasm. The uterus elevates and contracts rhythmically with each contraction, beginning at the upper end of the uterus and moving like a wave through the midzone and down to the lower or cervical end. These uterine contractions had been long associated with the idea that the cervix sucks up sperm. Masters and Johnson, however, theorized that contractions in such a direction would, if anything, expel sperm. They then proceeded to demonstrate the uterine contractions could not possibly lead to a sucking up of the sperm into the uterus. They prepared a tight-fitting cervical cup that they filled with a semen-like liquid in a radiopaque base. Masters and Johnson then made radiograms during the orgasmic experience and found no such sucking action.[12]

To describe what took place during intercourse, Masters and Johnson developed a four-phase description: (1) excitement, (2) plateau, (3) orgasm, and (4) resolution. They found that men responded in terms of basic physiological changes along the same lines as women; in both sexes, there was an increase in heart rate, blood pressure, and muscle tension, and in the majority of both men and women a "sex flush" (a rosy measlelike rash over the chest, neck, face, shoulders, arms, and thighs) is observable. At orgasm the heart and respiratory rates are at a maximum and the sex flush at its peak, although the male has what are called ejaculatory contractions during the orgasm. The orgasm phase is followed by the resolution phase in which there is a return to conditions as they were before the sexual excitement phase began. Women were found to have a wider variety of orgasmic responses and many could have multiple orgasms.

Masters and Johnson criticized what they called the "phallic fallacy" of comparing the clitoris with the penis. They emphasized that even though the clitoris might be the anatomical analogue of the penis, it reacts to sexual stimulation in a manner quite different from the penis. It does not become erect during arousal but instead withdraws beneath its protective foreskin, and in fact, its length is reduced by at least half as orgasm approaches. When it is retracted, however, it responds to generalized pressure on the labial hood.[13]

Patient concerns were always present in Masters and Johnson's minds. For example, they reported that the average flaccid measurement of a penis was

7.5 centimeters (about 3 inches) and during erection the penis more than doubled in length. However, they recognized that not all men had the same size penis.[14] To allay the qualms of their readers, they emphasized that the vagina was a "potential rather than an actual space," and was "infinitely distensible."[15] Interestingly, however, there is no evidence that they ever asked any of their female subjects whether penis size made a difference, or if they did, the answer was not recorded.

Sample

All told, 694 individuals, including 276 married couples, participated in the Masters and Johnson laboratory program. Of these, 142 were unmarried but 44 had been previously married. The men ranged in age from twenty-one to eighty-nine and the women, from eighteen to seventy-eight. Volunteers for the laboratory research program were involved in masturbation by hand, fingers, or a mechanical vibrator; in sexual intercourse with the woman on her back, with the male on his back; and in artificial coition with a transparent probe. Also studied were the anatomy and physiology of the aging male and aging female, although the data were not as complete as for the younger ages. Masters and Johnson emphasized, however, that if opportunity for regularity of coitus exists, the elderly woman will retain a far higher capacity for sexual performance than her female counterpart who does not have similar coital opportunity. They reported that even though the postmenopausal woman has lost some of her hormone output, the psyche is as important, if not more important, in determining the sex drive.[16] Similarly, while in the aging male the entire ejaculatory process undergoes a reduction in physiological efficiency, the sexual response remains. Masters and Johnson concluded,

> There is every reason to believe that maintained regularity of sexual expression coupled with adequate physical well-being and healthy mental orientation to the aging process will combine to provide a sexually stimulative climate within a marriage. This climate will, in turn, improve sexual tension and provide a capacity for sexual performance that frequently may extend to and beyond the 80-year level.[17]

Sexual Dysfunction

A natural follow-up to the physiological studies of the human sexual response was treatment for dysfunctional clients. For this purpose, Masters and Johnson developed a sex therapy team (a woman and a man) and a methodology through which they said they were treating the "marriage," since the basic foundation of their treatment was that both the husband and wife in a sexually dysfunctional marriage be treated.[18] Such a statement emphasizes Masters and Johnson's marital orientation, something that probably contributed to their widespread acceptance on the American scene. Although a significant proportion of their clients were unmarried, most came to therapy accompanied by a partner.

Because Masters and Johnson always emphasized the therapeutic nature of their research, their aim in effect had always been the development of treatment modalities. In their treatment, they concentrated on specific symptoms rather than generalized disorders. In a way, they adopted some of the concepts of the behavioral psychologists who had begun treating sexual problems in the 1950s,[19] but in the process, they popularized sex therapy and systematized it on a physiological base.

One result was the development of a new specialty in the helping professions, that of sex therapist. Before their entrance on the scene, the predominant treatment of sexual dysfunction, at least in the United States, was through psychoanalysis. What Masters and Johnson essentially did was challenge perhaps the final bastion of the control that psychiatry, and particularly psychoanalysis, had over the sex field. Kinsey had basically undermined many of the assumptions that psychiatry had made about sexual behavior and furnished a new kind of database. With Masters and Johnson, even the treatment option, which psychiatry had dominated, was now redirected to other specialists, many of whom were not physicians. The result was to increase the number of individuals who were not only professionally but economically interested in sex. Kinsey, in effect, had reestablished the concept of sexology. Although sexological research was a somewhat limited field, the rise of sex therapy gave sexology enough other professionals to justify separate sexological societies and journals.

Masters and Johnson were also important because they, although in a much gentler form than Kinsey, emphasized the importance of sex education. For example, in their discussion of the anorgasmic female, they stated that women in general were victims of the double standard, because they more than men had been taught to repress their sexual feelings. Masters and Johnson concluded that repression, in the form of historical and psychological experience, was the most important factor in the development of frigidity.[20] Ignorance and superstition about sex were and remain the major problems in an inadequate sexual response, and when the sexual partners manage to have their prejudices, misconceptions, and misunderstandings of natural sexual functioning exposed, then and only then can "a firm basis for mutual security in sexual expression" be established.[21] In short, for marriage to reach its full potential, and Masters and Johnson were always concerned with marriage, knowledge of sex was essential. This message was seized on not only by a new generation of sex educators to bring about reforms in sex education but by the public in general, who seemed to grow ever more interested in how to have a better marriage, which they believed was highly dependent on sexual performance.

The largest component of the expanding group of sex professionals in the 1960s was the sex therapist, the number of which grew rapidly. Masters and Johnson had established a two-week basic program that involved a male and female sex therapist and a client couple; this program served as the initial model. Masters and Johnson reported that the two-week session eliminated sexual difficulties for 80 percent of their clients. Not content with these immediate results, they followed up these studies five years later and stated that of those they were able to recontact, only 7 percent reported recurrence of the dysfunctions for which they originally had sought treatment.[22] The result of such claims was a demand by the public for help with sexual problems and an awareness by the various kinds of professionals that they could expand their client base if they could gain some expertise in sex.

Many would-be sex therapists went to St. Louis to take special training sessions with Masters and Johnson. Professionals who entered sex therapy from a slightly different background also offered special seminars. On the West Coast, for example, William Hartman and Marilyn Fithian, who had included sexual therapy as part of their marriage and family counseling, had begun to carry out their own set of experiments on the sexual response in their Long Beach, California, center. As the demand for sex therapists grew, Hartman and Fithian conducted training seminars not only in Long Beach but all over the country, introducing would-be professionals to new trends in sex therapy.

Another important early sex therapist was Helen Singer Kaplan, who tried to combine some of the insights and techniques of psychoanalysis with behavioral methods. She questioned Masters and Johnson's use of two therapists and felt that one therapist of either sex would be sufficient,[23] a finding made by others.[24] Kaplan agreed that many sexual difficulties stemmed from superficial causes, but she believed that when unconscious conflict was at the heart of the problem and involved deep-seated emotional problems the therapist should use more analytic approaches. As a result, her approach is designated as psychosexual therapy to distinguish it from sex therapy, and her entry into the field emphasizes how psychoanalysts themselves gradually adjusted to the new sex therapy techniques.

In the afterglow of success, the sex therapy originally presented by Masters and Johnson did not seem to hold true for a growing number of therapists as the field rapidly expanded. This was perhaps because of not only the existence of deep-seated emotional problems in some clients, as Kaplan had pointed out, but the presence of basic physiological problems such as diabetes. The result was an attack on the success claims of Masters and Johnson, as an increasing number of studies reported much higher failure rates.[25]

The difference in success rates, however, is probably the result of both the changing nature of clients and the differing methods of client selection. Many of the original problems presented by the early clients of Masters and Johnson resulted from a lack of knowledge of basic sexual activity, something that was comparatively easy to overcome. The very success of the books by Masters and Johnson made such clients increasingly less likely to seek the help of a therapist, since they could read about the sources of human sexual inadequacy and adjust their own practices. On the other hand, the physical exam required by Masters and Johnson for their patients undoubtedly eliminated many of those with physiological difficulties that other, less knowledgeable therapists attempted to treat and failed to help. The major result of the criticism of Masters and Johnson was to emphasize that sex therapy at its best involved a team, not only of therapists but of medical professionals, particularly the urologist and gynecologist.

Notes

1. William H. Masters and Virginia E. Johnson, *Human Sexual Inadequacy* (Boston: Little, Brown, 1970), 1. The therapeutic intent is not emphasized in their first study, William H. Masters and Virginia E. Johnson, *Human Sexual Response* (Boston: Little, Brown, 1966).

2. George W. Corner, *The Seven Ages of a Medical Scientist* (Philadelphia: University of Pennsylvania Press, 1981), 212.

3. Corner, *The Seven Ages of a Medical Scientist*, 213.

4. Among his articles are W. H. Masters, "Long Range Sex Steroid Replacement: Target Organ Regeneration," *Journal of Gerontology* 8 (1953): 33–39; W. H. Masters, "Endocrine Therapy in the Aging Individual," *Obstetrics and Gynecology* 8 (1956): 61–67; and W. H. Masters, "Sex Steroid Influence on the Aging Process," *American Journal of Obstetrics and Gynecology* 74 (1957): 733–46.

5. Félix Roubaud, *Trait de l'Impuissance et de la Sterilité chez l'Homme et chez la Femme* (1855; reprint, Paris: Baillière, 1876).

6. Alfred E. Kinsey, Wardell B. Pomeroy, and Clyde Martin, *Sexual Behavior in the Human Female* (Philadelphia: Saunders, 1953).

7. G. Klumbies and H. Kleinsorge, "Das Herz in Orgasmus," *Medizinische Klinik* 45 (1950): 952–8; and G. Klumbies and H. Kleinsorge, "Circulatory Dangers and Prophylaxis During Orgasm," *International Journal of Sexology* 4 (1950): 61–66.

8. Kinsey et al., *Sexual Behavior in the Human Female*, 630, fig. 140.

9. Ibid., 631, n. 46.

10. Masters and Johnson, *Human Sexual Response*, 10.

11. Ibid., 300.

12. Ibid., 124.

13. Ibid., 57–61.

14. Ibid., 192.

15. Ibid., 194–5.

16. Ibid., 242.

17. Ibid., 270.

18. Masters and Johnson, *Human Sexual Inadequacy*, 3.

19. Joseph Wolpe, *Psychotherapy by Reciprocal Inhibition* (Stanford, Calif.: Stanford University Press, 1958).

20. Ibid., 214–8, 222–6.

21. Ibid., 62.

22. Masters and Johnson, *Human Sexual Inadequacy*, 366, tab. 11 B.

23. Helen Singer Kaplan, *The New Sex Therapy* (New York: Brunner/Mazel, 1974).

24. Joseph LoPiccolo, J. R. Heiman, D. R. Hogan, and C. W. Roberts, "Effectiveness of Single Therapists Versus Cotherapy Teams in Sex Therapy," *Journal of Counsulting and Clinical Psychology* 53 (1985): 287–94.

25. S. Schumacher and C. W. Lloyd, "Physiology and Psychological Factors in Impotence," *Journal of Sex Research* 17 (1981): 40–53; and B. Zilbergeld and M. Evans, "The Inadequacy of Masters and Johnson," *Psychology Today* 14 (1980): 29–43.

Chapter 4
The Social Organization of Sexuality

Edward O. Laumann
John H. Gagnon
Robert T. Michael
Stuart Michaels

Following the work of Kinsey and of Masters and Johnson, little sexuality research was conducted in the United States from the mid-1950s to the mid-1960s. And even in the period of permissiveness that evolved during the sexual revolution, most of the survey research was retrieved on samples from college students. By the early 1970s, it was evident that significant changes were occurring in sexual behavior and attitudes: rising percentages of young people were having premarital sexual intercourse, and the gay/lesbian movement and the feminist movement were in full swing.

Sex became a household word as the mass media contributed to the widespread belief that everyone, youth and adult, was actively involved in premarital sex and postmarital sexual affairs. Publications such as Playboy and Redbook disseminated information from reader surveys of sexual behavior via "tear out and mail in" questionnaires. Shere Hite reported, in her controversial bestseller, The Hite Report, that 70 percent of married persons were having extramarital affairs within the first five years of marriage. Her claim was based on a survey of 100,000 women, which had a return rate of 3 percent. Her somewhat politicized sample included members of the National Organization for Women (NOW), the American Association of University Women (AAUW), and abortion rights groups. Scholars, lamenting that bad data are worse than no data, concluded that the ability of mass media to produce their own facts is a fact of life that even researchers must learn to live with. By the 1980s, it became apparent that not only were people looking at bad data, they also were looking backward at old data for answers.

It was into such a world in the late 1980s that Laumann, Gagnon, Michael, and Michaels, a research team from the University of Chicago and the State University of New York at Stony Brook, launched their National Health and Social Life Survey, the goal of which was to develop a social scientific theory of sexual conduct. The $1.7 million study was financed in 1992 by eight private foundations after conservative senators had killed federal funding of the research project in 1991.

Although studies in the previous decades had chronicled changes in sexual behavior, the researchers of earlier periods had neglected the construction of theories to explain human sexual behavior. Because sexual behavior is social, the theorists proposed that it must be studied within relationships to explain it as a social phenomenon. Psychological studies invariably center on an individualistic approach to the study of sexuality, but sociological studies focus on the social, the external, the relational, and the public dimensions. Thus, social logic was suggested to be a missing variable in the study of sexuality and, therefore, chosen as a theoretical framework for the National Health and Social Life Survey.

The nation's most comprehensive, representative survey of sexual behavior in the general population to date, the Laumann et al. study utilized face-to-face, 90-minute interviews with subjects from a randomly selected sample of 3,432 American women and men between the ages of 18 and 59. The results of the survey led to a better understanding of how sexual behavior is organized in American society and its broad-ranging public policy implications. Two books were published with the findings: The Social Organization of Sexuality: Sexual Practices in the United States, which included extensive statistical analyses for academic readers, and Sex Practices in America: A Definitive Work, intended for general readership.

As chapter 1 from their scholarly book shows, the theoretical background for this study is carefully constructed from three theories: scripting theory to explain sexual conduct; choice theory to explain sexual decision making; and network theory to explain the sexual dyad. Together, they form at least a middle-range theoretical basis for construction of a social-scientific approach to sexuality. With a careful review of the following selection, readers may gain insight into the Laumann et al. study. More significantly, they can broaden their awareness of theory construction and its importance in survey research.

Human sexual behavior is a diverse phenomenon. It occurs in different physical locations and social contexts, consists of a wide range of specific activities, and is perceived differently by different

29

people. An individual engages in sexual activity on the basis of a complex set of motivations and organizes that activity on the basis of numerous external factors and influences. Thus, it is unlikely that the tools and concepts from any single scientific discipline will suffice to answer all or even most of the questions one might ask about sexual behavior. This [narrative] introduces the several approaches that we have found especially helpful in formulating what we hope will prove to be a more comprehensive social scientific understanding of sexuality.

A Social Scientific Approach to Sexuality

Much of the previous scientific research on sexuality has been conducted by biologists and psychologists and has thus focused on sexual behavior purely as an "individual level" phenomenon. Thus, such research has defined sexual activity to be the physical actions that a person performs (or the thoughts and feelings that a person experiences) and has sought to explain individual variation in these actions in terms of processes endogenous to the individual. A good example of this approach is the study of sexual "drives" or "instincts." In drive theories, people are assumed to experience a buildup of "sexual tension" or "sexual need" during periods of deprivation or during particularly erotic environmental stimulation. When sexual activity is experienced, the drive is satiated and the need reduced. Such cycles of increased drive and its resultant satiation are often used to explain hunger and thirst and, by analogy, sexual conduct. Differences in drives across individuals are generally assumed to result from underlying biological or psychological differences in those individuals.

The major shortcoming of such studiously individualistic approaches is that they are able (at most) to explain only a very small part of the story. This is because, unlike the sexual behavior of certain animal species (e.g., salmon, who are genetically programmed to swim upstream at the appropriate time to spawn), human sexual behavior is only partly determined by factors originating within the individual. In addition, a person's socialization into a particular culture, his or her interaction with sex partners, and the constraints imposed on him or her become extremely important in determining his or her other sexual activities. This observation is perhaps obvious, yet research on social processes represents a disproportionately small amount of the extant scientific literature on human sexuality.

This does not mean that there have been no social scientific studies of sexual behavior. One prominent researcher, Ira Reiss (1990), recently enumerated more than a dozen national surveys of sexual attitudes and practices since Kinsey and his associates' work appeared in the late 1940s. Previous national studies of sexual behavior have targeted specific subpopulations or have focused on a relatively narrow range of sexual conduct. For example, Zelnik and Kantner (1972; 1980) conducted three national studies of pregnancy-related behavior among adolescents. Subsequently, Sonenstein, Pleck, and Ku (1991) conducted a more comprehensive study of sexual practices among adolescent males, and the CDC (1992) reported on a limited number of sexual behaviors among a national sample of high school students.

With regard to adults, the first nationally representative data were collected by Reiss in 1963. Later, Klassen, Williams, and Levitt (1989) conducted a study of adults age twenty-one and older (the data were collected in 1970) that focused primarily on sexual attitudes. In addition, the National Survey of Family Growth (Mosher and McNally 1991) asked its fifteen- to forty-four-year-old female respondents a limited number of questions about sexual behavior, and Tanfer's study of twenty- to twenty-nine-year-old women (Tanfer 1992) focused on a much broader range of sexual behaviors, relationships, and attitudes. These studies were followed in 1991 by a well-publicized study conducted by the Batelle Institute of twenty- to thirty-nine-year-old men that collected data on a wide range of sexual conduct (Billy et al. 1993). Finally, the National AIDS Behavioral Surveys (Peterson et al. 1993) collected behavioral data relevant to the transmission of AIDS from respondents in twenty-three "high-risk" U.S. cities. While these studies provide information on several important issues, few have attended seriously to the fact that sexual activity occurs in the context of a relationship (Blumstein and Schwartz 1983) or the epidemiological consequences of the structure of sexual networks.

We thus have in hand a number of important indications of where to look for the effects that social factors have on sexual behavior. One example is the persistent finding that a person's social class ("working" vs. "middle") is correlated with certain aspects of sexual behavior (Weinberg and Williams 1980), although there is some evidence that the strength of this association is diminishing with time (DeLamater 1981). Another persistent finding comes from the relatively large literature on adolescent sexuality (Brookman 1990).

Sociologists have found that adolescents involved in religious activities tend to delay first intercourse longer than those who are not (DeLamater and MacCorquodale 1979). These and other essentially descriptive findings are certainly interesting, yet, without a systematic theoretical framework within which to interpret them, they cannot help us understand how and why specific social processes or circumstances affect sexual behavior.

Biological and psychological studies of sexual behavior focus solely on the individual as the relevant "unit of analysis." That is, the objective of such research is to answer questions about why an individual exhibits certain sexual behaviors. But this line of inquiry can reveal only part of the story. Most sexual behavior is not performed by an individual alone and in the absence of others. Instead, sexual behavior is social in the sense that it involves two people (or more). Sex involves negotiation and interplay, the expectation and experience of compromise. There is competition; there is cooperation. The relationships between the partners and between their mutual actions make the sexual partnership or dyad an essential analytic unit in the study of sexuality. This focus on the social, the external, the relational, and the public dimensions is what distinguishes our inquiry from the psychological and biological orientations that have characterized much sex research in the past.

Although little progress has been made in the social sciences toward developing systematic theories about the social processes involved in sexual behavior, social psychology, sociology, and economics have each developed persuasive theories explaining other spheres of social behavior. Therefore, it seems sensible to draw on such theories in attempting to formulate a social scientific theory of sexual conduct. We have begun with three theoretical traditions—scripting theory, choice theory, and social network theory—each addressing certain aspects of sexual behavior.

Scripting Theory: Explaining Sexual Content

Previous researchers have generally adopted the perspective that there is an inevitable negative conflict between the biological nature of human beings and the cultures in which they are reared. With regard to sexual behavior, this implies that social factors function solely to inhibit or constrain people's intrinsic sexual desires and urges. For example, it is assumed that biologically mature adolescents will naturally have intercourse (that they both want to and have the opportunity to do so) and that those who do not are simply better at "controlling their urges." We reject this perspective, not because it allows for the influence of biological effects on sexual behavior, but because it takes a narrow view of the role of social processes as merely constraining sexual conduct. We argue that sociocultural processes

play a fundamental role in determining what we perceive to be "sexual" and how we construct and interpret our sexual fantasies and thoughts. Thus, although biological factors may indeed affect sexual behavior, they play at most a small role in determining what those specific behaviors will be and how they will be interpreted.

Scripting theories of sexual conduct address exactly these types of questions. The starting point for these theories can be expressed in terms of several assumptions about the ways in which specific sexual patterns are acquired and expressed. First, they assume that patterns of sexual conduct in a culture are locally derived (i.e., that what is sexual and what sex means differ in different cultures). Second, they assume either that human beings possess no biological instincts about how to act sexually or that the effects of such instincts are minor in comparison with the effects of an individual's socially determined scripts for conduct. People may vary biologically in activity level and temperament, but there are no direct links between this variation and what they will do sexually as adults. Third, they assume that, through a process of acculturation lasting from birth to death, individuals acquire patterns of sexual conduct that are appropriate to their culture (including those patterns that are thought to deviate from the norms of the culture). Fourth, they assume that people may not enact the scripts provided by their culture exactly but instead may make minor adaptations to suit their own needs. In complex and contradictory cultures, such individual adaptations will be very diverse.

On the basis of these four principles, sexual scripts specify with whom people have sex, when and where they should have sex, what they should do sexually, and why they should do sexual things. These scripts embody what the intersubjective culture treats as sexuality (cultural scenarios) and what the individual believes to be the domain of sexuality. Individuals improvise on the basis of the cultural scenarios and in the process change the sexual culture of the society. In this way, individual sexual actors as well as those who create representations of sexual life (e.g., the mass media, religious leaders, educators, and researchers) are constantly reproducing and transforming sexual life in a society. For example, introducing condoms into sexual activity as part of an AIDS education and prevention program requires changing scripts for sexual conduct on the part of individuals. If large numbers of individuals adopt this new script, they will change the effects that sexual activity has on health by reducing unwanted pregnancies, abortions, and the spread of sexually transmitted diseases.

The scripting perspective distinguishes between cultural scenarios (the instructions for sexual and other conduct that are embedded in the cultural narratives that are provided as guides or instructions for all conduct), interpersonal scripts (the structured patterns of interaction in which individuals as actors engage in everyday interpersonal conduct), and intrapsychic scripts (the plans and fantasies by which individuals guide and reflect on their past, current, or future conduct) (Gagnon and Simon 1987; Gagnon 1991).

Several studies provide evidence for the importance of sexual scripts in shaping both perception and behavior (Geer and Brussard 1990; Castillo and Geer 1993). For example, in one study, male subjects listened to one of two different narratives, during which time their level of sexual arousal was monitored. Both narratives began with identical stories describing a young woman getting into her car and driving to a building, where she goes into a room, closes the door, and removes her clothes. At this point, a man enters the room; he is identified in the first narrative as the woman's gynecologist, in the second as her boyfriend. Predictably, subjects hearing the first narrative experienced significantly less arousal than those who heard the second, despite the similarity of the two narratives. Since the physician was not part of the subjects' sexual scripts, they had to reevaluate their perceptions of the situation.

With regard to the effects of scripts on actual behavior, research among adolescents has repeatedly demonstrated the existence of a general pattern of activities that young people follow as they acquire sexual experience (DeLamater and MacCorquodale 1979). The pattern begins with kissing, proceeding first to necking and then to the male fondling the female's breast (first over the clothing, then underneath). Next occurs fondling of each other's genitals, first by the male, then by the female. This is followed by genital-genital contact and then by vaginal intercourse. Only after intercourse do adolescents go on to try oral sex, again first by the male, then by the female. What this means is that those who have had vaginal intercourse are also likely to have engaged in kissing, necking, fondling, and apposition. Similarly, those who have not yet engaged in "heavy petting" are unlikely to move directly to intercourse. Of course, not all adolescents complete the entire program or, to use the especially apt euphemism, "go all the way." Moreover, any single interaction is subject to practical considerations (such as being restricted to the backseat of a car) that may result in temporary deviations from the script.

Choice Theory: Sexual Decision Making

While scripting theories are useful in explaining the range of activities (or scripts) available to an individual, they tell us little about how the individual chooses among these various possibilities. For example, an individual may have different scripts for how to act toward different partners (e.g., a new partner, a "one-night stand," and a spouse) and in different situations; however, the content of these scripts alone tells us little about why that individual may choose to pursue certain types of relationships to the exclusion of others. In order to address this important issue, we turn to an economic approach to decision making. Essentially, economic choice theory is concerned with how people utilize the resources available to them in the pursuit of one or more specific goals. Since one's resources are generally limited, choices arise regarding how these resources should be apportioned among various activities leading to one or another goal. Were there no scarcity of the necessary resources, there would be no constraint on the achievement of one's goals and no need for choices to be made. However, the necessary resources (i.e., time, money, emotional and physical energy, personal reputation) required to engage in sexual behavior are limited, and choices must therefore be made.

It is important to recognize that an economic approach presumes the existence of a goal or a set of goals. Thus, in order to utilize this approach, we must first identify what those goals (or at least some of them) are. For example, the goals of sexual behavior may include sexual pleasure itself, the emotional satisfaction that results from being intimately involved with someone toward whom one feels affection, having children, and acquiring a "good reputation" among one's friends. So we have listed four goals that may motivate a person to use his or her limited money, time, and energy to achieve one or another of these goals.

People differ in the importance that they accord these various goals and in their capacities to achieve them. Choice theory focuses on how these goals and capacities influence behavior. Invariably, the efforts of one person to achieve his or her goals affect the efforts of others. That is what makes this a social science—people's efforts do not take place in isolation. When it comes to selecting a sex partner, for example, if one person succeeds in attracting a partner, that person is "taken," or "spoken for," and is no longer available to anyone else. This social dimension of sexual behavior is less obvious but no less real when it comes to most other activities, from using contraception to selecting a "sexy" outfit to wear to a party.

In order to make our discussion more concrete, suppose that we are interested in explaining why people have the number of sex partners that they do. Our research shows that 71 percent of adults (aged eighteen to fifty-nine) report having only one sex partner during the previous year and that 53 percent report having only one sex partner over the previous five years. These data suggest that most people change sex partners relatively infrequently, choosing instead to remain in long-term, sexually exclusive relationships. As we stated above, we will assume that most people desire some amount of sexual stimulation and that this, together with other goals, leads them to pursue sexual relationships with one or more partners. Yet securing partners is not without cost; one must expend time, money, emotional energy, and social resources in order to meet people and negotiate a sexual relationship. Solely on the basis of this consideration, it would seem to be more cost effective to fulfill one's sexual needs by remaining in a long-term relationship than by constantly searching for new partners. One might "look around" and perhaps even fantasize about potential partners, but the costs involved in actually pursuing them relative to simply maintaining one's current relationship may be too high. Only those whose objectives explicitly include having sex with many partners (perhaps because of the excitement and uncertainty) will frequently choose to incur such costs.

In this example, an individual spends resources and engages in activities for the purpose of achieving sexual pleasure, in much the same way as an industrial firm manufactures a product in order to make a profit; both may be described as productive activities. And, like most productive activities, both can involve the creation of unintended by-products, desirable and undesirable. In the case of having sex with a partner, an unwanted pregnancy, a sexually transmitted infection or disease, a happier, more pleasant personality, and a greater ability to concentrate are examples of possible by-products.

These decisions are often made in the face of uncertainty: about detection, about the nature of the new partnership, and about the risk of disease, pregnancy, and harm. The more information one has about the outcome of a choice, the wiser will be the choice, of course, but then there is the decision about how much information to acquire before making the choice.

Like so many choices we make, choices regarding sexual behavior are often made under uncertainty. It is the case that people have different attitudes toward risk; some enjoy taking risks, while others prefer to avoid risk. One reason that couples discuss their views and their prior sexual histories is to share information about the probabilities of good and bad eventualities from having sex together. Similarly, people use contraception to avoid pregnancy and disease, travel to distant places to carry on affairs in order to avoid detection, and generally treat their decisions about sexual behavior with some degree of strategy and purpose that characterizes their choices in other domains.

While formal models of behavior often assume that risks are perceived accurately, research in psychology has shown that people do a rather poor job of estimating not only the absolute sizes but even the relative sizes of the risks that they encounter. For example, in a study of possible determinants of self-perceived risk for AIDS, Prohaska et al. (1990) found that respondents in those demographic subgroups with the highest prevalence of HIV infection (singles, males, Blacks, and Hispanics) were not more likely to perceive themselves as at risk than other respondents. The study did, however, show higher perceptions of risk among respondents with multiple partners during the past five years as well as among those who knew little or nothing about the previous sexual behavior of their partners. Finally, respondents who reported that they would be ashamed if they contracted AIDS were less likely to perceive themselves as being at risk. Although it is difficult to interpret this last finding, it suggests the possibility that people's emotional and moral reactions to the disease—factors that may have nothing to do with objective risk—may affect their subjective risk assessment.

In addition to risk management, another conceptual tool from economics that can be useful in understanding sexual behavior is that of human capital. Individuals invest in education and skills in order to achieve their objectives. This is obvious in the case of people preparing to enter or reenter the job market. However, there are also types of human capital that facilitate the pursuit of sexual objectives. One example is the skills necessary to attract potential sex partners. These might include a healthy and attractive appearance, good conversational skills, and the like. Clearly, such human capital is most valuable to those who are actively searching for a partner, so these people should be expected to invest more highly in these skills than others who are involved in long-term monogamous relationships. Since skills tend to deteriorate with disuse, people who have been out of the market for a period of time are likely to find their skills rusty on returning. Moreover, new expectations and protocols in dating may require learning the new "rules of the game."

Another type of human capital used to secure sexual activity is the skills necessary for maintaining an existing relationship. These might include the ability to satisfy one's partner physically as well as the ability to accommodate his or her personality and interests, to get along with his or her family and friends, and so forth. Such skills have been the focus of studies that seek to understand why married couples choose to remain married or to divorce. In a marriage (or in any long-term sexual relationship), each partner acquires specific skills that are beneficial in the couple's interactions. Yet these skills are valuable only as long as the couple remains together. This loss of value associated with dissolution provides incentive for couples to remain together.

Thus far, our discussion about choice theory has been oriented around an individual decision maker. However, the decisions of one person (or institution) often impinge on others through the marketplace in which people acquire the resources to achieve their goals. The key factor in determining an item's value in the market is desirability relative to scarcity. Value is determined by the competitive forces of demand (reflecting desirability) and supply (reflecting availability), while it is measured by the commodity's unit price relative to other goods.

Perhaps the most obvious example of a market in the context of sexual behavior is the market for sex partners. In most cases, this market does not involve a product being exchanged for money but consists instead of a barter exchange in which each person both seeks (i.e., demands) a sex partner and offers (i.e., supplies) himself or herself as a partner in exchange. Each prospective partner offers his or her own physical attributes, personality, skills, etc., in exchange for those of a partner of interest to him or her. This exchange is made explicit in advertisements that appear in the personals column of the newspaper, such as "SWM gd looking, seeks F undr 30 for fun/companionship."

Anyone who has participated in the market for sex partners knows that those possessing more of the traits most valued in a particular culture have more opportunities for exchange than those possessing fewer. The majority of these opportunities are likely to involve similarly or less attractive potential partners, from among whom each individual is expected to choose the "best deal" that he or she can get. If there is a disparity between the numbers of males and females on the market, those who are least desirable are likely to be left without a partner altogether. An example of this is the often talked about "marriage squeeze" in which middle-aged and older women lose out to younger women in the competition for an insufficient number of eligible men.

An important aspect of selecting a sex partner is that it involves little prior knowledge of the other's sexual competence. Like many other "products" acquired in the marketplace, one does not know all about the partner's sexual interests, capabilities, and limitations before a match is made. That, of course, is true of the car you buy or the job you accept. Consequently, one relies on reputation, on what you can tell from looking and talking, on the reliability of the broker or grocer. Buyers invest in information about the product, while sellers invest in presentation and persuasion.

In a day when one shunned sexual contact before marriage, the information that partners had about their sexual compatibility was probably far less at the time of the wedding than is the case in a day when most couples have sex with each other before they form marriage bonds. You would think that this more "intensive searching" would lead to more compatible matches and thus lower divorce rates, but that surely has not been the case in the United States over the past three decades.

In the marketplace for sex partners, there is a time of considerable searching and exploring and a time after a selection is made and a partnership formed when the searching stops or is at least greatly diminished. Interest in a new sex partner can be renewed when divorce or separation occurs, and it is during these times of more extensive searching that additional sex partners are more likely to be acquired. Over the lifetime of an individual we should expect to see certain periods of relatively extensive exploration of the sex partner marketplace and other times with little involvement in that marketplace.

When we think about the market for sex partners, despite the strangeness of the concept to some, there are many parallels to other, more familiar marketplaces. We noted above that individuals surely differ in their goals or objectives as they choose a sex partner—recreational sex, an intense companionship, a partner for raising children, for example. Not surprisingly, then, those active in the market will surely place different values on different attributes in prospective partners—some men might value companionship more than physical attractiveness, while others might value earning power or a strong sense of family loyalty in a prospective sex and marriage partner more than any other attribute.

Another aspect of markets is that they have physical dimensions. Geographic distance adds costs to matching just as much as acquiring information does. Most people search in local markets, and the partitioning of the market into the sex partners in the local community—even in the local social networks in which a person is active—reflects the cost-liness of searching more widely. That, like the fact that information about options is costly, is a reality in most markets.

As individuals, most of us are accustomed to thinking of sexuality in highly personal terms, consisting of our own thoughts and what we do with our partners. For this reason, our choices about which sexual activities to pursue are based on our personal assessments of the benefits and costs involved. However, the private choices that we make about sexual behaviors and attitudes can also have consequences at a collective or societal level. There can be both benefits and costs to society as a whole that are not immediately visible to the individual. Such benefits or costs are called externalities.

In the United States, an externality resulting from fertility, many would argue, is the burden on the welfare system of children whose parents are either unable or unwilling to support them financially. While many couples determine how many children they can afford to support and plan their fertility accordingly, other couples bear children they did not plan or plan children they subsequently cannot afford. Child welfare programs in effect lower the cost of raising a child to the natural or custodial parents and impose these costs on the taxpayer.

Another externality associated with sexual behavior is the possible transmission of diseases such as gonorrhea, chlamydia, and HIV. Such diseases not only threaten an individual's health but also contribute to collective costs such as the provision of subsidized medical care and research and the increased risk of being exposed to the infection as it becomes more widespread.

The choices that individuals make about sexual behavior that exposes them to the risk of unwanted pregnancy or disease are made in the context of the costs of avoiding these outcomes. Since there are negative externalities associated with these outcomes, it seems a sensible strategy to subsidize the costs of avoiding them. That is one rationale for government support of programs that distribute contraceptives and information about how to avoid pregnancy and sexually transmitted disease or infection.

Note how a brief discussion of externalities can quickly become a discussion of government policy or an advocacy of collective action. Choice theory promotes discussion of this nature since it facilitates an articulation of the relation between private choices and public repercussions between individual and collective action.

Network Theory: The Sexual Dyad

So far, we have said little about how the sexual partnership (or dyad) is theoretically significant. Both scripting and choice theories focus on what individuals do, explaining it on the basis of the experiences, circumstances, and decisions of those individuals. However, sexual activity is fundamentally social in that it involves two or more persons either explicitly or implicitly (as in the case of sexual fantasy and masturbation). This simple fact has three important implications. First, since sexual partnerships are a special case of social relationships we may expect these partnerships to conform to certain regularities that have been observed regarding social relationships more generally. This provides a theoretical framework within which to study the dynamics of sexual parnerships—who becomes partners with whom, how these partnerships are maintained, and why some of them eventually dissolve. Second, since sexual activity is negotiated within the context of a social relationship, the features of the relationship itself become important in determining what activities will occur. This may seem obvious at first; however, such thinking represents a subtle major departure from previous research on sexuality (Sprecher and McKinney 1993). Finally, sexual dyads do not exist in a vacuum but are instead embedded within larger networks of social relationships. Thus, individual dyads are affected by the social networks surrounding them, and this in turn influences the sexual activity of their members. We now turn to a more detailed discussion of each of these implications.

One of the most persistent empirical regularities that has been observed among social relationships is the tendency toward equal status contact, meaning that people tend to initiate and maintain relationships with others who have the same or similar social characteristics as they themselves do. This general pattern of same-status contact has been observed in studies of friendship (Laumann 1966, 1973; Hallinan and Williams 1989), professional relationships (Heinz and Laumann 1982), and relationships among discussion partners (Marsden 1988). Specifically, these studies have shown that such relationships are more likely to exist among persons of the same gender, age, race, education, and religion. Several factors account for these findings, including the fact that our society is geographically and socially segregated in ways that greatly reduce an individual's opportunities to interact with people unlike himself or herself. In addition, some authors have suggested that people prefer to interact with similar others in order to reinforce their own self-identity, to validate their own behaviors and attitudes and, most obviously, because they are more likely to share common interests with such people. Finally, a person's family, friends, and other associates maintain control over the kinds of people with whom that person forms relationships, often decreasing the likelihood that he or she will interact with dissimilar others.

For similar reasons, we also expect sexual relationships to occur more frequently between people with the same or similar characteristics. Research on similarity among married couples seems to confirm this general hypothesis, identifying large amounts of both educational (Mare 1991) and religious (Kalmijn 1991) homogamy (in other words, marriage partners share similar characteristics). More recently, the same has also been found among cohabiting couples (Schoen and Weinick 1993).

Just as the nature of asymmetries has changed over time, we also expect them to differ across different types of sexual relationships. More specifically, we expect the patterns of racial, age, educational, and religious similarity that have been observed in marital relationships to be different in noncohabitational sexual partnerships. An individual interested in pursuing an extramarital relationship, for example, might intentionally locate a socially dissimilar person in order to minimize the possibility of being discovered by his or her spouse, family, and friends.

In sum, sexual relationships differ markedly from other types of relationships with respect to the types of exchanges that occur within them, and these differences lead to different predictions about the occurrence of sexual relationships between persons with different social characteristics. Moreover, we expect the pattern of sex partner choice to differ across the different types of sexual relationships.

The social composition of sexual relationships also affects the type of behavior that occurs within them. These effects are distinct from those that are due to the individual characteristics of the partners; hence, they can be examined only by studying the dyad as whole. For example, we show that oral sex is a largely reciprocated activity, which implies that it is more likely to occur in those relationships where both parties are willing to perform the act.

In addition, other characteristics of respondents' sexual partnerships are likely to affect whether they engage in oral sex. Thus, while more educated people are more likely to have oral sex, it may also be the case that there is something about the types of sexual relationships that these more highly educated respondents have that increases the likelihood that oral sex will occur within them.

There are several elements of sexual relationships that might plausibly affect which sexual behaviors occur within them. We have already identified one of these as being related to the characteristics of the partners involved. This is the nature of the exchange between the two partners. Relationships that, in addition to sexual interaction, involve the exchange of items, such as economic resources, companionship, and other types of support, may place certain constraints on the types of sexual services that one partner can (or is willing to) extract from the other. For example, if a woman perceives that she is getting more from her partner than she is giving, she may feel obligated to correct this imbalance by performing sexual activities that her partner enjoys. Similarly, if a man perceives himself to be dependent on his partner, he might be willing to forgo his own sexual interests in order to please his partner (Emerson 1981). Conversely, people who perceive themselves as giving more than they receive or as being less dependent on their relationships than their partners might be more likely to ask their partners to perform certain activities or refuse to comply with their partner's wishes.

The exchanges that occur within a relationship are not the only features of that relationship that can affect sexual behavior. Another important feature is the way in which the relationship is socially defined and perceived by the participants. Some common examples of socially defined sexual relationships are "high school sweethearts," "lovers," "boyfriend and girlfriend," "husband and wife," and "one-night stand." Clearly, these may be interpreted differently by different people, and it is also possible that culturally distinct subgroups use a different set of definitions. Consequently, we learn and make decisions about what is and is not appropriate sexual behavior within the context of a specific type of relationship, rather than solely in terms of the individual performing the behavior. Thus, some men force their wives to have sex with them because they believe that, within marriage, a husband is owed sex by his wife whenever and however he wants it, even though the same man might consider the exact same behavior directed toward a stranger or even a girlfriend to be rape.

Both scripting and choice theories combine with a network approach to generate more comprehensive explanations of sexual conduct. Although the network approach emphasizes the properties of relationships rather than persons, it cannot by itself be used to explain what goes on within a specific relationship. This requires an understanding of what motivates the individuals in that relationship, such as that provided by scripting and choice theory. Understandings about what is appropriate within the context of a specific relationship are nothing other than scripts—scripts that are specific not only to the persons involved but also to the relationship between those two people. Similarly, exchanges between partners result from the strategically motivated interests of both partners, implying that, if a relationship costs a partner more than it benefits him or her, he or she will withdraw from the exchange. Nevertheless, regardless of people's cultural understandings and their motivations, sexual activity can occur only when two people come together in a relationship. The fundamental contribution of the network approach is in showing how the social networks in which people are embedded affect whether two people will get together to form a sexual relationship and, if they do, which cultural understandings and economic motivations they will bring to that relationship.

Sexual scripts are learned through interaction with others, and this interaction is clearly shaped by the networks in which we are embedded. Most research on this subject has focused on the sexual behavior of adolescents and has generally found that sexually active adolescents tend to have friends who are also sexually active (Billy, Rodgers, and Udry 1984), although it is unclear which causes which. Similarly, the legitimacy of oral sex in youthful sexual relationships is dependent on gendered support networks that supply different legitimations for these forms of conduct to both male and female adolescents (Gagnon and Simon 1987). Another less common but still convincing illustration of the role of networks is provided by reports among young boys of "circle jerks," an activity in which a group will masturbate to orgasm, often in some competitive fashion (to see who will ejaculate the soonest, who has the largest penis, or how far the semen travels on ejaculation).

We also expect social networks to be important in determining the sexual behavior of adults. To understand these influences, we must specify the interests that third parties have in the occurrence (or nonoccurrence) of certain activities within specific types of partnerships. By third parties we mean people connected to either or both members of a focal sexual dyad by one or more types of social relationship. Thus, parents have interests in the sexual experiences of their children, such as wanting them to refrain from sexual activity until they are "ready," wanting them not to date people whom they consider to be "poor" influences, etc. Similarly, children of divorced parents also have interests in the sexual relationships of their parents since these can claim part of the parent's attention and lead to remarriage. Third-party interests are not limited to relatives; friends too can be interested in each other's happiness in a relationship and be wary of

the threat that that relationship might pose for the stability of the friendship.

Probably the best organized of all groups that have an interest in sexuality are stakeholders in reproductive activity. They range from individual parents to large-scale organizations such as Planned Parenthood that supply services, participate in political lobbying, and seek private and government resources and support for their programs. Control of reproduction involves the control of sexual activity, necessarily a complicated relationship. Morally conservative stakeholders attempt to control both sexuality and reproduction through moral instruction, policing the content of school curriculum and of the media, limiting information about contraception and the availability of contraceptive devices, limiting the access of the potentially sexually active to services for the prevention of sexually transmitted infection and disease (including HIV), and so forth. In contrast, liberal stakeholders seek to provide most of these services while remaining (somewhat) indifferent to the sexual expressions of consenting adults over the age of sixteen.

Other highly organized and politically active stakeholders are those who seek either to facilitate or to limit the acceptance of same-gender sexual relationships and the legal provision of the same rights and privileges for these couples as are enjoyed by heterosexual couples (e.g., allowing them to raise children, to show affection in public, etc.). Friends, relatives, and even parents often admonish or outright reject gay individuals because they do not know how to behave or are uncomfortable around them and, more important, because they are forced to justify or deny the individual's behavior in front of their own friends and associates. In fact, intolerance of homosexuality is so ubiquitous in this country that many homosexuals are forced either to conceal their sexual preference or to move to one of the few social environments where being gay is accepted.

An example of a less organized but still powerful third-party interest is that in maintaining exclusivity in established sexual partnerships, especially marriages. Part of this interest stems from the belief that extramarital sex is morally wrong, a belief that is almost universally accepted (roughly 90 percent of adults believe that extramarital sex is either "always wrong" or "almost always wrong"). In keeping with this attitude, our data suggest that the annual incidence of extramarital sexual activity is modest. Although we do not deny the fact that one's own moral and religious beliefs strongly influence the decision to limit oneself to a single partner at a time, we do argue that these beliefs are legitimated and reinforced through interaction with others who share such beliefs and who have concrete interests in the couple's sexual exclusivity. For example, in their attempts to support one spouse, the relatives and friends of that person are likely to regard any extramarital activity on the part of the other spouse as unjustifiable.

To acknowledge the potential for extramarital activity, even if only by discussing it with a friend, risks both personal temptation and the possibility of being labeled by others as a potential "cheater." This fact increases people's reluctance to address the topic in conversation, thus decreasing the possibility of locating potential partners or social approval for the behavior.

Opportunities to pursue extramarital sexual activity are also limited by the very large proportion of individuals in the society who are already in relationships. Especially after age thirty, the number of uncoupled individuals is small. This is exacerbated by the fact that marriage accustoms a couple to the conversations and activities of the other married couples to whom they usually restrict their associations. Presumably, some fraction of these married individuals might be willing to engage in extramarital sex; however, this number is almost certainly quite small and, more important, very difficult to identify for the reasons discussed above.

Sexual activity is not unique in being motivated and constrained by the interests of third parties. However, unlike other spheres of activity, sexual activity almost always occurs in private and is usually talked about in highly routine and nonrevealing ways. This fact makes the surveillance of the sexual dyad by outsiders remarkably difficult—third parties are privy only to the testimony of the individuals themselves about what happened. This has both positive and negative social consequences—sexual encounters may be conducted entirely by trial and error and independently of regulation, leading to sexual experimentation, or they may be occasions on which the participants deliberately or ignorantly exploit or violate each other.

Interrelations Among the Theories

As we have indicated, each of these three theories is intended to answer different types of questions about sexual activity. However, since these questions are interrelated, so are the theories used to explain them. In most cases, these interrelations take the form of consistent or complementary predictions by the different theories. For example, we have already shown how both scripting and choice theories may be used to explain what occurs within specific relationships identified by the network approach. Occasionally, however, there are inconsistencies in what the theoretical approaches would

predict and no clear way of reconciling these differences on the basis of theoretical arguments alone.

The sharpest inconsistency among the three approaches is between scripting and choice theories. As we have already noted, a fundamental assumption in choice theory is that individuals act strategically or rationally in the pursuit of goals. In contrast, scripting theory suggests that individuals model their actions on the basis of a predetermined (although somewhat flexible) set of cultural scenarios. Given the small number of scenarios relative to the number of different circumstances that people encounter, it is likely that certain people will be unable to locate a scenario that represents what would be considered "rational behavior" in their particular case. In such instances, the predictions of the two theories would conflict. Yet there is a more fundamental difference between scripting and choice theories than the existence of discrepant predictions. The two theories assume very different mechanisms underlying people's behavior. Choice theory assumes that individuals are constantly evaluating their situations and making choices, whereas scripting theory assumes that individuals are constrained by a script that they learned from those around them.

At this point, the reader might be wondering how these general theoretical approaches can be used to inform and interpret analyses of the actual data collected in this study. After all, using a survey instrument limits the researcher to asking only those questions that are easy to understand and to answer. Thus, for example, we were unable to measure sex scripts directly since doing so would require a complicated series of questions about numerous specific activities and the order in which they occurred. More important, the fact that ours was a national survey prohibited us from tailoring certain questions to particular locations or subpopulations. This meant that much fine-grained cultural (and, to some extent, regional) variation in these scripts was beyond our grasp. Similarly, our ability to measure people's networks was also quite limited; we could not ask them about specific places or events where they socialized, nor could we ask them about their relationships with specific persons other than their sex partners. For example, it would be very useful to know something about the larger network structures in which respondents are embedded since these structures certainly affect the structure of their sexual networks. Since such structures are unique to particular locations, however, they are beyond the scope of this type of study. Finally, the methods used to study rational decision making also require an intensive set of questions (such as those designed to determine an individual's preference ordering) targeted to a specific situation. These limitations are important ones, forcing us to relegate focused examinations of specific issues to future projects. However, a national study such as this one is a necessary precursor to more specialized work.

References

Billy, John O. G., Joseph Lee Rodgers, and J. Richard Udry. 1984. Adolescent sexual behavior and friendship choice. *Social Forces*, 62:653–78.

Billy, John O. G., Koray Tanfer, William R. Grady, and Daniel H. Klepenger. 1993. The sexual behavior of men in the United States. *Family Planning Perspectives* 25, no. 2:52–60.

Blumstein, Philip, and Pepper Schwartz. 1983. *American Couples*. New York: Morrow.

Brookman, Richard R. 1990. Adolescent sexual behavior. In *Sexually Transmitted Diseases*, eds. King K. Holmes et al. New York: McGraw-Hill.

Castillo, C. O., and J. H. Geer. 1993. Ambiguous stimuli: Sex in the eye of the beholder. *Archives of Sexual Behavior* 22:131–43.

Centers for Disease Control (CDC). 1992. *STD/HIV Prevention 1991 Annual Report*. Atlanta.

DeLamater, John. 1981. The social control of sexuality. *Annual Review of Sociology* 7:263–90.

DeLamater, John, and Patricia MacCorquodale. 1979. *Premarital Sexuality: Attitudes, Relationships, Behavior*. Madison: University of Wisconsin.

Emerson, Richard M. 1981. Social exchange theory. In *Social Psychology: Sociological Perspective*, eds. M. Rosenberg and R. H. Turner. New York: Basic Books.

Gagnon, John H. 1991. The implicit and explicit use of scripts in sex research. In *The Annual Review of Sex Research*, ed. John Bancroft, Clive Davis, and Deborah Weinstein. Mt. Vernon, Iowa: Society for the Scientific Study of Sex.

Gagnon, John H., and William Simon. 1987. The scripting of oral-genital sexual conduct. *Archives of Sexual Behavior* 16, no. 1:1–25.

Geer, J. H., and D. B. Brussard. 1990. Scaling sex behavior and arousal: Consistency and sex differences. *Journal of Personality and Social Psychology* 58:644–71.

Hallinan, Maureen T., and Richard A. Williams. 1989. Interracial freindship choices in secondary schools. *American Sociological Review* 54:67–78.

Heinz, John P., and Edward O. Laumann. 1982. *Chicago Lawyers: The Social Structure of the Bar*. Chicago: Russell Sage Foundation and American Bar Foundation.

Kalick, S. Michael, and Thomas E. Hamilton III. 1986. The matching hypothesis reexamined. *Journal of Personality and Social Psychology* 51, no. 4:673–82.

Kalmijn, Matthijs. 1991. Shifting boundaries: Trends in religious and educational homogany. *American Sociological Review* 57:706–800.

Klassen, A. D., C. J. Williams, and E. E. Levitt. 1989. In *Sex and Morality in the U.S.*, ed. H. J. O'Gorman. Middletown, Conn.: Wesleyan University Press.

Laumann, Edward O. 1966. *Prestige and Association in an Urban Community*. New York: Bobbs-Merrill.

———. 1973. *Bonds of Pluralism: The Form and Substance of Urban Social Networks*. New York: Wiley.

Mare, Robert D. 1991. Five decades of educational assortative mating. *American Sociological Review* 56:15–32.

Marsden, Peter V. 1988. Homogeneity in confiding relations. *Social Networks* 10:57–76.

Mosher, William D., and James W. McNally. 1991. Contraceptive use at first premarital intercourse: United States, 1965–1988. *Family Planning Perspectives* 23, no. 3:108–16.

Peterson, John L., Joseph A. Catania, M. Margaret Dolcini, and Bonnie Faigeles. 1993. Multiple sexual partners among blacks in high risk cities. *Family Planning Perspectives* 25:263–67.

Prohaska, Thomas R., Gay Albrecht, Judith A. Levy, Noreen Sugrue, and Joung-Hwa Kim. 1990. Determinants of self-perceived risk for AIDS. *Journal of Health and Social Behavior* 31:384–94.

Reiss, Ira L. 1990. *An End to Shame: Shaping Our Next Sexual Revolution*. New York: Prometheus Books.

Schoen, Robert, and Robin M. Weinick. 1993. Partner choice in marriages and cohabitations. *Journal of Marriage and Family* 55: 408–14.

Sonenstein, F. L., J. H. Pleck, and L. C. Ku. 1991. Levels of sexual activity among adolescent males in the United States. *Family Planning Perspectives* 23, no. 4:162–67.

Sprecher, Susan, and Kathleen McKinney. 1993. *Sexuality*. London: Sage Publications.

Tanfer, Koray. 1992. Coital frequency among single women: Normative constraints and situational opportunities. *Journal of Sex Research* 29:221–50.

Weinberg, Martin S., and Colin J. Williams. 1980. Sexual embourgeoisment? Social class and sexual activity: 1938–1970. *American Sociological Review* 45, no. 1:33–48.

Zelnick, Melvin, and John F. Kantner. 1972. Sexuality, contraception, and pregnancy among young unwed females in the U.S. In *Demographic and Social Aspects of Population Growth*, eds. Charles F. Westoff and R. Parke. Washington, D.C.: U.S. Government Printing Office.

———. 1980. Sexual activity, contraceptive use and pregnancy among metropolitan-area teenagers: 1971–1979. *Family Planning Perspectives* 12:230–37.

Chapter 5

Sex Among the Americans

Joseph Adelson

Juxtaposing the sexually inhibited and the sexually liberated, Joseph Adelson mines the fields of facts generated by the research of Laumann et al. with a 1990s survey that shocked Americans. The cover of Time *(October 17, 1994) announced the news: "Sex in America: Surprising News From the Most Important Survey Since the Kinsey Report!" As the news hit the airwaves and the press, Americans were surprised to learn that the hotbed of sex in the '90s was the marriage bed.*

Although media "sexperts," such as Cosmopolitan *editor Helen Gurley Brown; Hugh Hefner, founder of* Playboy; *and Bob Guccione, publisher of* Penthouse, *were uttering words like "outrageous," "stupid," "ridiculous," and "come on now," Europeans seemed less surprised by the findings. They were, in fact, parallel with studies in England and France that also had found low rates of homosexuality and high rates of marital fidelity.*

Critics abounded! They decried the absence of women among the study's directors, asking if this could have skewed the questions. Doubts were also raised about whether personal interviews could elicit truly candid answers to intimate questions, for example, about masturbation, or whether the sample was too small to generalize about some groups, like homosexuals. Adelson himself is less than ebullient about some of the interpretations, given the findings by the researchers and the choice of the theories used as a framework for the study. He does, however, praise its technical competence and its findings, which "carry us beyond, and largely discredit, the data of earlier studies." Among those who praised the survey, Ira Reiss, sexuality scholar from the University of Minnesota, declared that of the major sex surveys to date, the Laumann et al. study was probably the best thought out and had the broadest coverage.

As readers today take a retrospective look at the findings that Adelson presents from the Laumann et al. survey, they can add their own cacophony of beliefs and disbeliefs. After all, their ideas will be no less reflective of their own experiential findings than were those of Brown, Hefner, and Guccione.

I teach a seminar for first-year undergraduates on the troubles of adolescence. During a discussion of teenage illegitimacy not too long ago, I mentioned in passing a surprising datum I had just come across: the average American woman, during her lifetime, has two sex partners. The reaction in my classroom was electric—amazement, disbelief. That can't be! It's more than that! They must be lying!

These are youngsters, mind, who can absorb the most horrendous social statistics—that the killing of adolescents has increased fourfold in the last decade, that two-thirds of all black children are born out of wedlock—without batting an eye. They may or may not find such data troubling (it is often hard to tell), but they do not find them shocking. What shocked them was the *not*-shocking—news of modesty, decorum, restraint.

After class, a young man came up to me who wanted to know the data for homosexuality in the source I had referred to. Well, I replied, if self-definition is the criterion, the figures are a bit under 3 percent for males, and between 1 and 2 percent for females. He was furious. I know that literature in detail, he told me. We're studying it in philosophy (!) class; those numbers are not only false but probably falsified, and I'm sure they're being circulated to discourage the gay community, which in fact is growing by leaps and bounds.

Later in the week, thinking these inflamed responses might reflect the passions of youth, I asked several friends and colleagues—each and every one of them (it goes without saying) wise and worldly-wise—to estimate the number of partners American women have over a lifetime. Their guesses ranged from a low of six to a high of twenty. When apprised of the figure I had come across, they, too, reacted with disbelief, in some cases mixed with heavy sarcasm about the pretensions of survey research and what one of them termed "social so-called science."

Where, then, did I get the numbers I had so innocently broadcast? From a recent sociological study, *Sex in America: A Definitive Survey*,[1] published in both a popular and scholarly edition, the latter under the appropriately academic title, *The Social Organization of Sexuality*.[2] This, the publishers tell us, is the "only comprehensive and methodologically sound survey of America's sexual practices and beliefs."

They were drawn to it, they tell us, by dissatisfaction with prior studies of American sexual behavior. At their best, earlier surveys like the famous one done by Alfred Kinsey and his associates in 1948 were well-intentioned but flawed, the most common problem being a reliance on catch-as-catch-can methods of recruiting interviewees. These studies also lacked any means for checking the truthfulness of the responses given, and the worst of them, like the egregious *Hite Report* on female sexuality of 1976, solicited responses from selected and sometimes highly politicized groups. In the case of the *Hite Report* that meant that the data were drawn from members of the National Organization for Women, abortion-rights advocates, and the like; even so, *Hite* managed but a 3-percent response rate, making it certain that the respondents bore little likeness to American women in general.

The authors of *Sex in America* set out to do things right by sampling accurately our adult population (aged 18–60); preparing a carefully pre-tested questionnaire; training their interviewers rigorously; and introducing several methods of checking the veracity of the responses obtained. One may have some serious reservations, as I do, about what went into the questionnaire as well as what was left out, and about the interpretations offered; but the sampling itself is state-of-the-art, and the authors are right to be pleased with themselves. Carrying out a national survey of this scope is extremely expensive ($450 per interview) and requires great technical expertise and a high level of patience and compulsiveness.

As a culture—and my students beautifully represent that culture—we have come to believe that the degree of individual sexual pleasure can be placed on a linear chart extending from "inhibited" at one end to "liberated" at the other. The sexually free are unattached and unencumbered. They have been everywhere and done everything, and are ready for more—more positions, more variations, more partners, more often. At the other extreme are those who have sex only within marriage and then only infrequently, who employ the missionary position, perform the act rapidly, and achieve shallow orgasms or none at all.

Though we might not say so openly, many of us also tend to believe that blacks are more active sexually than whites, and that those belonging to conservative religious denominations are bound to be more inhibited than those without any religious affiliation. And we may also believe that, sooner or later, sex with the same person becomes too familiar and boring, leading us to seek adventure elsewhere. After all, a cardinal rule in matters sexual is that we are drawn to those unlike us, to what is alien or taboo: opposites attract.

What the research gathered in *Sex in America* tells us is that none of the above is true. In fact, American sexuality is marked by moderation and fidelity. Husbands and wives are faithful to each other, and so are those living together though unmarried. Even the unattached rarely wander, and are certainly not promiscuous. As I had accurately reported to my students, one-half of all Americans of both sexes have three or fewer partners in a lifetime; as one might expect, men are more active sexually, but not by a wide margin. (And lest one protest that all this is the baleful legacy of American Puritanism, parallel studies throughout the Western world, in countries Catholic as well as Protestant, yield essentially the same findings.)

American sexual practices are, similarly, conventional. Vaginal intercourse is by far the most appealing mode, almost universally judged exciting and pleasurable. It is followed, at a distance, by the mild voyeurism of "watching partners undress," and then by oral sex. All other sexual practices—group sex, anal sex in its several variations, sadomasochism, the use of sexual toys and devices, homosexuality, sex with strangers, watching strangers have sex—all these are deemed unappealing, in most cases very unappealing, and by all segments of the population, men and women, young and old.

Sex in America (as I told my young student of philosophy) comes up with a dramatically lower figure for homosexual identity and practice. Until quite recently, the standard number was 10 percent, and when cited it was often preceded by the phrase "at least," suggesting that the true figure was higher and was being suppressed either by caution or by shame. Many psychologists and psychiatrists had their doubts about this, believing the true figure to be 5 to 6 percent for men, and half that for women; but for the most part these doubts went unvoiced. We now learn that even the reduced number was too high. Fewer than 3 percent of men identify themselves as homosexual; more inclusive criteria give us no more than 5 percent. Lesbianism is about half as common. European studies provide similar data.

Among the most interesting findings in *Sex in America* are what one might call the absent findings: in particular, the absence of expected variations associated with race, ethnicity, education, religion, and the like. Both the popular and the scholarly editions of this study are glutted with charts and tables illustrating these modest or nonexistent differences. How frequently do men achieve orgasm with their "primary partners"? About three-quarters of men say "always," no matter what their age, marital status, education, or race. Between a quarter to a third of women say the same, again regardless of age, marital status, education, or race. "How many times do you have sex each month?" Again, little variation: almost always six to seven times a month, for men and women, well-educated or not, of all religious affiliations; the only blip is that those over fifty report a slightly lower rate (four or five times monthly).

To whom do we become attached? Here we come to a central emphasis of this study: we become dear to those who are near, that is, those who are like us and whom we come to know in the daily routines and venues of our lives. Sexual behavior, the authors tell us time and again, is shaped by the social networks we occupy. We choose (and are chosen by) those within our network, those like us in almost all respects—race, religion, education, class. We rarely venture out of these boundaries, and should we try to, those within them signal their disapproval.

If you enjoy wallowing in numbers, the tables in *Sex in America* provide what seem to be small surprises now and again. For example: more conservative Protestant women report always having orgasms than do women of any other religion. Really? Yes, really; but also not really—they do outpace others in the "always" category, but that aside, there are no other important differences by religion. Nor do the occasional variations by race and education add up to a consistent pattern. Blacks, for example, are high on a few measures, but average or low on others.

Still, that figure about conservative Protestant women and their orgasms does point to what is the real bombshell in this study. Not only does it turn out that, in the war between the prudes and the libertines, Americans in general have continued to hold fast on the side of the prudes. It also turns out—horror!—that the prudes are having much more fun.

This study, in fact, is a paean to sexual bonding, to marriage or its near-equivalents. Intimate, exclusive relationships between spouses or committed partners provide, by far, the greatest degree of sexual gratification. More: in a finding that turns the standard scenario of pornography on its head, these books reveal that those without committed partners are far less likely to engage in casual sex during a given period than to do without sex altogether. Twenty-three percent of unattached men report having had no sex, as opposed to less than 1 percent of those married or living with someone; among women, the figures are 32 percent compared to 2 percent. At the other extreme, attached men and women are twice as likely as unattached to have sex two or more times a week. In the pleasure sweepstakes, monogamy counts.

And we are not done. Perhaps the most astonishing single datum reported in these books has to do with those conducting extramarital affairs: they report that they are more gratified sexually by their spouses than by their lovers. To add insult to injury, they also have sex less often than those faithfully married. Among the unmarried, those who have at least two sexual partners are less pleased with their sex lives, emotionally and physically, than those married or living together. For women in particular, a close attachment is essentially a necessity for a gratifying sex life.

Let me sum up, in the authors' own words, the key findings of this research. Whether you count by "adult lifetime or in the past year," nearly all Americans have "a very modest number of partners." This number "varies little with education, race, or religion." Rather, it is determined by marital status or by whether a couple is living together. Once married, people tend to have one and only one partner, and those who are married and living together are almost as likely to be faithful. Sexual practices, moreover, are highly conventional. Only vaginal intercourse is universally attractive, while almost all the *outre* variations are disliked. Finally, when it comes to sexual pleasure, liberation carries a palpable cost, fidelity its own very great reward.

Which leads to a question: if all this is essentially correct, why are my students and my friends and all the rest of us so mistaken? Why do we think of ourselves as a society which has happily (or, for those scandalized by it, sinfully) thrown off most of the constraints of the past, a society in which more and more of us are sexually adventurous both before and during marriage, and are willing and even eager to try out exotic sexual combinations and practices?

Well, for one thing we believe what "empirical science" has taught us to believe. The Kinsey data, initially so shocking, were rather quickly absorbed into the conventional wisdom. The 10-percent "datum" for homosexuality, for example, had its origins in the Kinsey findings. That statistic and others like it were not superseded by more accurate ones, in large part because subsequent studies made the same sorts of sampling error. Kinseyesque findings were thus presumably confirmed and became accepted even by those distressed by what they implied morally. In this connection, it is ironically pertinent that the research in *Sex in America* failed to win federal support because of the opposition of conservative legislators who expected that it would show a high level of deviant behavior.

This in itself tells us that sexual information is not ideologically neutral. Sexuality is important terrain in the cultural wars that divide us, and what we believe to be true about it is conditioned by a larger set of assumptions and expectations about human nature and the social order. In particular, when we read about sex, or see it portrayed in films or on television, we do not see its mundane, quotidian side; we see persons taking dangerous risks to achieve pleasure, or struggling to realize their true selves by means of erotic liberation.

Robert Lichter of the Media Research Center reports that seven out of eight sexual encounters in television dramas involve extramarital relations. No surprise there—the illicit is all but a *sine qua non* of the dramatic. Yet this same partiality is found throughout the public culture. As I write, my local newspaper—small-city, staid, sober in most respects—has helpfully brought us a report of a bright new development in erotic practice called playful sadomasochism, wherein the gestures and rituals of the real thing are mimicked without serious pain being inflicted. My favorite national newspaper, the *Wall Street Journal*, recently ran a front-page story on another bright new trend, this one among women: serial bisexuality, or going back and forth between male and female partners. These accounts have in common the tone and feel of fashion reporting, complete with the tacit assurance to the shy that, however odd it may appear at the moment, this is indeed the coming style.

Missing in all these savvy, wide-eyed reports is any sense of the everyday torments free-lance sexuality imposes on ordinary and (as we glean from *Sex in America*) even not-so-ordinary people. Will he (she) like it? Will she (he) have an orgasm? Is my body attractive? Do I smell badly? Can I keep going long enough? Will he (she) *really* like it? Am I better than he (she) has had before? Am I being too rough? Not rough enough? Too responsive? Not responsive enough? And on, and on. Not everyone is quite so anxious, but as any psychotherapist can testify, a great many are.

Nor does one need therapeutic testimony to confirm the part played in sexual life by self-doubt, shame, and narcissistic injury. Simply visit any good bookstore to find a substantial array of titles offering advice, instruction, encouragement, and spiritual uplift designed to calm your fears, assuage your guilt, overcome your embarrassment, and protect you against humiliation, thus making the sexual act enjoyable, or in some cases simply possible. Media sex, with its incessant stress on triumph and variety, is blind to this side of sexual feeling; one might say it represents a manic defense against it, if not a denial of its existence.

And this leads us to yet another answer to the question of why we were all so mistaken. Those who construct the public image of sexuality in our country—journalists, dramatists, pundits, professors, etc.—occupy quite a special sociological niche within the population at large, and their constructions to a greater or lesser degree tend to mirror their own attitudes and practices. Significantly, only a quarter of the overall survey sample in *Sex in America*—those whom the authors term "recreationals"—see sex in terms of pleasure alone, removed from obligation, devotion, or moral concern, and these same "recreationals" are four to five times more likely to have committed adultery, and two to three times more likely to have engaged in deviant sex. We learn from the sociological charts provided by the authors that—surprise—these same "recreationals" tend to be without religious affiliation. In which academic and professional precincts they live, and what they do for a living, it is not hard to guess.

As opposed to the "recreationals," a substantial majority of those surveyed in *Sex in America* report that they are guided in their sexual practices by their religious beliefs, or link sex to marriage or a loving attachment. Here we begin to see most clearly how differences in moral outlook play out in behavior. And here, too, we edge close to the realm of values. This is a realm which our authors, for their part, sedulously strive to avoid.

They, after all, are sociologists (with the exception of Gina Kolata, a science journalist), and they bring to their enterprise a fierce belief in the heuristic powers of their discipline. Thus, they inform us quite solemnly that they have employed the "advanced and sophisticated methods of social-science research," the same ones that have worked so well in the study of such topics as "labor-force participation . . . or migration behavior." In analyzing their findings, they rely almost entirely on two quintessentially social-scientific concepts: social networks and the (sexual) marketplace.

They seem unable, however, to grasp how little these concepts explain. In a long discussion of racial barriers, for instance, the authors succeed in demonstrating that only rarely do American blacks and whites become sexual or marital partners. They cite this finding to support their emphasis on the general explanatory power of social networks as cementers of sexual bonds. But whatever the figures may be for whites and blacks, marriages between whites and Asian-Americans have now become commonplace. If race is so important, how did that happen, and why?

Nor do we hear anything from the authors about the Jews, whose rates of intermarriage are now high enough to threaten the group's survival. When I was a boy, one did not marry outside the faith because doing so would mortify one's family. Needless to say, that pattern changed, and rather quickly. Why? Is religion a less powerful barrier than race? Is family less powerful than class or peer group?

In illustrating the efficacy of social networks, the authors provide a fairly long discussion of how the sexes were kept apart on campuses during the 1950s and early 1960s, when colleges acted *in loco parentis* as guardians of sexual boundaries. Then, in the late 60s, they tell us, due to the pressures of the youth movement, these rules disappeared "virtually overnight," and the era of sexual liberation was unloosed. But no matter what was, or was not, happening in the dormitories between one moment and the next, the same tired notion of a social network is brought in to explain it. How can this be? A social network that stops on a dime, completely reverses direction, and still performs the same function, has no value as an explanatory concept. It is simply a piece of jargon.

Consider, finally, the concept of the sexual marketplace, which the authors invoke to explain how people choose mates. Each person in a pair—so the reasoning goes—trades his or her assets to make the most advantageous match available. Among the examples given are those of Ross Perot and Henry Kissinger, both of whom, the second time around, found women younger and more attractive than themselves, trading money and power for youth and beauty. The authors believe that all such calculations are unconscious; "certainly most people are not consciously aware" of them.

To the contrary, most of us are very much aware of them, and some of us can think of nothing else. My Aunt Sadie's truisms on marriage were largely devoted to such observations: "He didn't marry her for her looks, but her father has a nice business." Come to think of it, so are the truisms of Aunt Jane Austen, Uncle Anthony Trollope, and most of the other greats and not-so-greats who have written about what goes into the formation of domestic arrangements.

The concepts of "network" and "marketplace," in other words, allow us to fashion explanations after the fact—*post hoc ergo propter hoc*. They are a capacious umbrella under which we can place everything we already know—but little else. Why are a given network's boundaries sometimes permeable and sometimes not? How does a group's history influence its members? Which networks evolve in expectable directions, and which do not, and why? These questions are never asked by our authors because they cannot be answered with the equipment they have assembled.

Even more troubling is the avoidance of any consideration of the inner world—the world of motives and character—which influences sexual and mental behavior. Some of the findings simply cry out for the insights of sociobiology, a discipline mentioned briefly only to be firmly dismissed. And when it comes to the psychological sources of behavior, the authors are singularly myopic.

A small but revealing example can be found in the index; for the category "shame," the entry reads, "see guilt." But guilt and shame are very different emotions, different not only subjectively but also in origin and effect. Another small example: general

happiness, the authors discover, is correlated with a good sex life—but which comes first? Amazingly, they confess to not having a clue.

The most revealing instance of such myopia concerns the treatment of forced sex. The authors find that about one-fifth of women report having been coerced sexually at some time. The coercers are not, as one might assume, strangers or casual pickups; most of them are husbands or loved ones. And it is usually not clear just what the coercion consists of, though it seems not to be physical assault or rape. Now, these same women also report having many problems in sexual response—pains, difficulty in lubricating, lack of pleasure. It would appear they are inhibited about sex, and would prefer to avoid it. But then we also learn that they have many more sexual partners, and engage in more deviant activities. Finally, sex aside, they are unhappy in general.

What does it all mean? The authors dance around, unable to venture a coherent explanation. It is a case of political correctness—a fear of blaming the victim—joined to a *deformation professionelle*, the limitations produced by vocational bias: in this case, an aversion to psychological inferences. They cannot, in short, bring themselves to state the obvious: these are troubled women whose troubles are almost certainly rooted in personality. Here, as elsewhere throughout their study, the authors have built a conceptual cage and locked themselves in.

But I do not want to end on a wholly critical note. Many of the reviews of this study have been negative, at times scathingly so, the burden of complaint being close to that voiced by my first-year undergraduates—that you cannot trust what people tell you in an interview on sex; that the researchers are self-deceived to think otherwise; that we need some objective, independent measures of the truth, otherwise we are at the mercy of those who lie, or fudge, or misremember, or leave things out.

Most psychological research, Freud's included, depends on self-reporting to some degree. It can rarely do independent checks on veracity, and hence it cannot fully guarantee the probity of its findings. This is an old problem—and those who do survey research are, most of them, especially aware of it. They do what can be done, practically speaking, and present their data honestly and modestly. What other choices do we have? Do we declare some topics off-limits to research? If so, we will soon enough substitute our own experience, writ large, or our own imaginings, or our stern beliefs about what ought to be.

That is just what we have done to sexuality—as this study, despite its flaws, allows us to see. Its strength rests on its technical competence and its findings, which carry us beyond, and largely discredit, the data of earlier studies. That is a lot. The rest, which has to do with human happiness and how it is won and lost, lies in the domain of subtler doctors of the soul than sociologists.

But is it not wonderful enough to learn, through graphs, charts, tables, and survey data, that many of the secrets of such human happiness, no matter how obscure they may be to undergraduates and their professors, have not altogether been lost to most men and women?

Notes

1. Robert T. Michael, John H. Gagnon, Edward O. Laumann, and Gina Kolata. Little, Brown, 300 pp.
2. Edward O. Laumann, John H Gagnon, Robert T. Michael, and Stuart Michaels. University of Chicago Press, 718 pp.

From Joseph Adelson, "Sex Among the Americans." *Commentary,* July 1995, pp. 26–30. Reprinted by permission. All rights reserved. ✦

Chapter 6
Kiss and Tell: Surveying Sex in the Twentieth Century

Julia A. Ericksen
with
Sally A. Steffen

"Kiss and Tell" is an apt title for this carefully choreographed description of the history of sexuality research: a dance including researchers, respondents, funders, and recipients. Although not an exposé of sensationalism as the title might suggest, the treatise challenges readers to define and perhaps refine their own biases relative to sexuality research.

The rationale for this work is based on the authors' core beliefs that the assumptions driving sexuality research help to create the sexuality that the research reveals. This is hardly an arguable premise. In reality, the relationship between assumptions and outcomes may have been best illustrated by the "media myths" created in the last presidential election. Consider the polarities exemplified in two national news personalities, Rush Limbaugh and Dan Rather. Following the authors' line of reasoning, the assumptions driving Limbaugh and Rather in gathering and reporting political news helped to create the very attitudes in their listeners that their news revealed. Marshall McLuhan popularized this phenomenon more than 30 years ago with his slogan, "The media is the message."

Ericksen and Steffen point to the polarities underlying assumptions in sexuality research. They contend that the bulk of sexuality research to date has been based on the assumption that sexuality is innate, while the flip side of the coin, that sexuality is socially created, has only recently been emphasized in the research arena. Readers are reminded that most researchers' assumptions are the products of the larger society, of the positions within that society, and of the findings of their predecessors. Ericksen and Steffen claim that, because over time, social or profes-sional positions about sexuality have changed little, two factors have remained constant in sexuality research: the belief in innate differences between women and men and the fact that most researchers have been men who viewed the world through the eyes of male privilege.

As readers contemplate the significance of such influential perspectives in guiding research outcomes, they may better understand the challenges in defining their own premises about sexuality and underscore the importance of doing so. This thought-provoking treatise encourages readers to think for themselves, a timely virtue in an era characterized by choices.

It is both surprising and disturbing how empirically ill informed we as a nation are about important aspects of sexual behavior.

—Edward Laumann, John Gagnon,
Robert Michael, and Stuart Michaels, 1994

In 1977, after reanalyzing findings from the Kinsey Reports of thirty years earlier, Bruce Voeller, the Chair of the National Gay Task Force, declared that 10 percent of the U.S. population was gay.[1] The media accepted and promoted this as fact until the late 1980s, when the figure was challenged by conservative groups as inflated and self-serving, indeed as "Exhibit A in any discussion of media myths created by scientific research."[2] At a gay rights march in Washington, D.C., the Lesbian Avengers and Act Up, two politically militant groups, chanted "10 percent is not enough, Recruit! Recruit!" while Bob Knight of the conservative Family Research Council insisted that 10 percent was a gross exaggeration. Knight and other conservatives cast aspersions on a proposed national survey of sexual behavior designed to supply updated and more reliable data. They described this proposal as the result of pressure by "the homosexual activist community" to "gather evidence to buttress up the old claim; if not 10 percent, something close to it."

The controversy flared further when researchers at a Seattle-based think tank, the Battelle Research Center, concluded on the basis of a 1991 survey that only 1 percent of men were gay, a figure the press quoted widely.[3] This new finding stunned both gays and conservatives and became a new rallying point. Gay groups were concerned at the depletion of their numbers and suspicious of the survey's methodology; the sample was too small and the questions too few for an accurate measure. Conservatives were jubilant that gays were less than 10 percent of the population, but such a severely diminished adversary might compromise their anti-gay agenda altogether. Only forty years earlier McCarthyite senators had used Kinsey data to argue that the "homosexual menace" was considerably more serious than previously understood.[4]

To most observers, this disagreement about numbers could be easily resolved by a larger, more rigorous, and more comprehensive survey. Or could it? While "facts" appeared to be the basis of the conflict between the National Gay Task Force and the Family Research Council, the fight went far beyond the data. It was a fight over the nature and validity of social science and over the role of surveys in establishing accurate information about sexual behavior. And it quickly became a political battle over the right to define normal behavior and the nature of the evidence to be used in such definitions.

Sexual behavior is a volatile and sensitive topic, and surveys designed to reveal it have both great power and great limits. By revealing the private behavior of others, they provide a way for people to evaluate their own behavior and even the meaning of information the surveys produce. And they provide experts with information they urgently seek to understand society and develop social policy. Social scientists often view surveys as providing hard facts about behavior, yet results are limited by researchers' often unrecognized preconceptions about what the important questions are and also by respondents' ability and willingness to reveal what they have done. Surveyors frequently assume that the facts are ahistorical realities to be tapped by experts rather than transitory events that are open to interpretation. And the "truths" surveys reveal have enormous implications.

As Voeller understood from the first, 10 percent was large enough to represent an attack on heterosexuality as the accepted norm and indeed on the conventional meaning of gender. It implied that at least one gay person existed in almost every extended family in America. It challenged the underlying principle of family life: the "natural" sexual attraction between men and women. No wonder the leaders of the Family Research Council expended enormous energy in challenging this figure at every possible opportunity. The size of the gay population was critical for determining whether being gay constituted a normal identity. Those who believed the answer to be affirmative knew that a large gay population would strengthen demands for social inclusion, while conservatives seeking exclusion strove to prevent "deviants" from claiming normality.

For most of Western history, religion decreed appropriate standards for sexual and social behavior. By the twentieth century, however, secular social scientists had become the experts. Even conservatives like Knight, who want to espouse the cause of religious fundamentalism, defend their arguments not with theology but with statistical data and other scientific evidence. In deciding what is normal, experts have viewed private behavior, particularly sexual behavior, as an important indicator of personal stability and well-being. They have regarded their assessments as scientific but have based them on assumptions about gender, assumptions promoted by biologists as scientific fact.

Biologists have viewed men's and women's different reproductive systems as inevitable sources of difference in all aspects of their lives, making men and women not only different but complementary, in need of each other to be fulfilled.[5] In this view, fundamental gender distinctions find particular expression in sexual activity between men and women, whose intense natural physical attraction to each other is the centerpiece of their relationship and of the societal ideal of the couple. Individuals may deviate widely from this norm, but such assumptions provide powerful incentives toward conformity. To be normal sexually means to do what is natural, that is, heterosexual. If gay sex is shown to be widespread in the population, it challenges the assumption that men and women are natural sexual partners. . . .

The French intellectual Michel Foucault argued that with the development of the modern nation-state sexual identity became a central component of Western identity.[6] This emphasis on sexual identity, he explained, arose as a mechanism for monitoring individual behavior in a world where external authority had declined. . . . If social order was to remain in this new world, people must assume responsibility for their own behavior. . . .

In such a world, Foucault argued, citizens learned to control their own behavior by checking on the normality of their acts. Private behavior became especially vulnerable to personal scrutiny, since its very nature makes it difficult for others to police. As science replaced religion as the source of advice, biology became the basis for determining what constituted normal sexual behavior. Experts deciphered sexual activities, evaluated their normality, and gave advice to potential practitioners. While Foucault wrote little about gender, those influenced by his work have noted that this normal sexual behavior was gendered. As sexologists catalogued sexual types, they described men and women as having fundamentally different sexual desires, responses, and roles to play in their relationships with each other.

Foucault took issue with the twentieth-century view that the nineteenth century was a period when human sexuality was subjected to a repressed silence. The Victorians, he argued, discussed sexuality obsessively, since they viewed out-of-control sexuality as a threat to social order. In doing so, they created new sexual identities through which to catalogue sexual acts: for example, the child who masturbated or the sexual deviate whose behavior could be interpreted only by experts. The most famous of the early experts, Richard von Krafft-Ebing, classified a huge array of sexual types, providing detailed descriptions of the personalities of those who engaged in various behaviors or displayed various tastes.[7] . . . In this view, sexuality and society were at odds with each other, and social order faced constant threats from an out-of-control sexuality.

. . . Although governments could attempt to legislate morality and police private lives, the cities, in particular, afforded sexual marketplaces with a broad spectrum of flourishing sexual activity. Such an atmosphere occasioned great anxiety about sex and its practice among the general population.[8]

The citizens of villages and towns in earlier times could scrutinize their neighbors' lives more easily. Proximity made shame a potent force for the regulation and repression of illicit sexual activity. Once people could keep aspects of their lives hidden from families and friends, preventing transgressions became a personal rather than a collective responsibility. Guilt, not shame, ensured conformity. Guilt was especially powerful in a country where immigrants from all over the world flaunted different and sometimes frightening behaviors. Concerns about others' most intimate acts exacerbated fears about moral taint and threats to health.

Turn-of-the-century writers still viewed sexuality as in conflict with society rather than as a product of it, but they were more sympathetic to sexual variety. Sigmund Freud was convinced that the normal path to sexual maturity lay in heterosexuality. Yet he assumed that everyone had to repress a variety of other sexual desires in order to achieve this, and he was tolerant of those who took a different path. Freud's contemporary Havelock Ellis went a step further by describing sexual variety itself as part of the natural order of things. Ellis thought scientific sexology would liberate individuals from the constraints of a repressive social system.[9] But even Freud and Ellis helped increase the pervasive sense that the sexual world held dark secrets. The existence of sexology created the possibility of watching for signs of deviant behavior and rooting it out.

During the twentieth century, experts following in the footsteps of Freud and Ellis espoused increasingly liberal views of sexuality and, like Ellis, sought to liberate sexuality from societal repression. . . . Individuals and institutions concerned with the general welfare, including the government, public health officials, the media, and social scientists, continued to worry that private acts threatened public safety.

All those providing sexual advice viewed the family as the bedrock of social stability and the gendered couple as its foundation. For them, women and men occupied separate spheres of control. Men's assertive personalities, symbolized in their role in sexual intercourse, were ideally suited to run public life, while women were keepers of the private sphere who provided sustenance, sexual and otherwise, to those who ran the world. Over the century, despite significant modifications of these assumptions, the gendered nature of private sexual behavior remained central. Likewise, a pervasive sense that sexuality is so inherently unstable and irrational that society must be ever vigilant kept experts busy proffering advice. This fear that private behavior could affect public well-being fed repeated panics about such issues as venereal disease, teenage pregnancy, and indiscriminate sex, while it fostered an interest in expert counsel.

The first sexologists relied on their own insights supplemented by clinical records to document the dangers of sexual excess. In the twentieth century this task fell to social scientists. Since the Progressive era, American social scientists have viewed their disciplines as capable of furthering human progress by alleviating such panic. They approached this task using scientific methods, in particular statistical methods. In each time of sexual crisis they perceived an urgent need for information. Yet they did not collect data with the scientific disinterest they imagined. Instead, their assumption that men and women differed from each other sexually dictated the form of their questions about the nation's social and sexual health. Believing that solutions start with the facts, the experts produced their urgently needed data through a filter of gendered sexuality.

Given the long-standing American belief that numbers provide factual representations of the world, surveys are an obvious source of information.[10] Since sex is an arena in which what others do is unclear, actual information about sexual behavior had two ready-made audiences: experts concerned that private behavior had a negative impact on public order, and individuals anxious to use hard evidence to evaluate and regulate their own behavior. Since 1892, when the biology student Clelia Mosher started asking upper-middle-class married women whether they liked intercourse, how often they had intercourse, and how often they wanted to have intercourse[11]—information she never had the courage to publish—researchers have asked hundreds of thousands of people about their sexual behavior and *have* published their findings for others to read.

This intense scrutiny created a window into the sexual lives of ordinary women and men that exposed private behavior to professional interpretation. Experts relayed this information to the public in reports and press releases. They evaluated the meaning of the data for what men and women should do, what they should like to do, and what they should fear doing. They not only reported what they believed to be the facts but helped create these facts in line with their own ideological positions, particularly their beliefs about gender. These facts, in turn, helped create sexual practices in two ways. First, reports about what others were doing suggested to readers that they should model their behavior on those who appeared to represent them. Second, surveys evaluated the behavior of those in the surveys, and this also provided lessons to readers. Thus even reports that accurately described aspects of the behavior of a particular group at a particular time created behavior by acting as guides or warnings to others. Since the most consistent assumption on which the surveys rested was of a gendered sexuality, albeit a changing one, surveys helped sustain a vision of sexuality as innately contained within masculinity and femininity.

The potential impact of such revelations is the reason those who disagree with results find it necessary to discredit them. Since the meanings attributed to the data have political implications beyond the facts, those who conduct sex surveys feel pressure to meet certain social needs. Investigators do not operate in a cultural vacuum. They approach their research holding beliefs about what is normal and what they expect to find, beliefs shaped by their personal experiences and desires, by their social circumstances, and by the findings of earlier researchers. Furthermore, when survey results become public, readers may change their sexual behavior as a result of finding out what others "like them" do, and researchers find themselves influencing what they had merely hoped to record.

Survey researchers, sensitive to charges of subjectivity, claim that as scientists using modern survey methods they can eliminate the effects of the expectations and biases they bring to their research. They concede that, without the advantage of modern techniques, early researchers were less objective, but they insist that today's methodology can take care of such problems. Asking questions of persons one at a time and aggregating the answers appears to reveal reality. Such scientific surveys seem the perfect way to amass information about a variety of social problems—venereal disease, divorce, teen pregnancy, for example—in order to develop informed public policies aimed at alleviating their ill effects.

Modern survey practice evolved throughout the twentieth century but came into its own after the Second World War.[12] Nowadays, letting prior hypotheses influence outcomes is decried as poor technique and a betrayal of the fundamental principles of science. Researchers view the scientific method as demanding hypotheses, or at least research questions, which they test in ways that do not influence the outcome. Although there has been little acknowledgment that the choice of research topic inevitably represents a point of view, four phases of the survey process have been the subjects of methodological studies intended to achieve this goal of objectivity. These are decisions about whom to interview; methods of data collection, including interviewer training; content and structure of the interview schedule; and the analysis of data.

Early researchers did not understand either the importance of interviewing all segments of the target population or that researchers who chose which respondents to interview might influence the results. They consciously surveyed "the better part of the middle class," or those who were "not pathological mentally or physically," in order to present the best possible case for their arguments.[13] The use of random sampling in surveys, a technique that ensures that each person in the target population has an equal, or a known, probability of being selected, developed in the 1930s. In this method, researchers completely remove themselves from decisions about which persons to interview.[14] . . .

While sampling techniques changed survey research, sex researchers were slow to adopt these superior methods. Alfred Kinsey, who undertook his survey when modern sampling was in its infancy, did not believe random sampling was possible in sex surveys, and many subsequent sex surveyors followed his example. Kinsey believed that people contacted at random would refuse to answer personal questions. Unlike his predecessors, Kinsey understood that all segments of the population should be included, so he went to great lengths to represent all sexual tastes. Unfortunately, in his determination to be inclusive, he most likely overestimated less common sexual activities such as same-gender sexual behavior.

Since the 1980s this avoidance of random sampling has ended. A number of recent sexual behavior surveys, for example the Battelle survey, have successfully used random sampling techniques to select respondents. While a 100 percent response rate is unlikely in a random sample, and nonrespondents can bias the results, the use of this method of selecting respondents has improved the reliability of the data immeasurably.

The history of interviewing in sex surveys is more complex, and many issues remain unresolved. From the beginning some researchers insisted on using face-to-face interviews on the grounds that this would create the intimacy and trust necessary for respondents to reveal their sexual secrets. But they did not understand the problems involved when researchers personally conducted the interviews. Gilbert Hamilton, who surveyed the sexual adjustment of married couples in New York in the late 1920s, did all the interviewing himself and imposed his own notions of intimacy and trust idiosyncratically. Commenting that his interviewing technique produced frequent "weeping and trips to the toilet," he maintained scientific objectivity by noting all such occurrences and by tying "the subject's chair to the wall in order to forestall the tendency that most persons have to draw closer to the recipient of confidences as these become more intimate."[15] Kinsey also was too early to understand the importance of using professional interviewers, of keeping the hypotheses from interviewers, and of training interviewers to ask sensitive questions.

By 1955, when the sociologist Ronald Freedman conducted the first national survey of married women's contraceptive practices, he and his colleagues used properly trained and monitored interviewers; and techniques have further improved since then.[16] Today investigators make well-informed decisions on whether to have interviewers ask the questions or to ask them in other ways, such as by computer. Interviewers receive extensive training and are held to rigorous standards. . . . From the beginning some researchers avoided interviews. Instead, they designed self-administered questionnaires for respondents to fill out and return. This method assures respondents of confidentiality and increases their willingness to disclose sexual secrets. But it produces lower response rates and creates problems for respondents who have difficulty reading.

All surveys, regardless of interview method, require some type of questionnaire. Because the researcher holding the hypothesis selects, words, and orders the questions, questionnaire design is particularly vulnerable to researcher bias. In the early years of sex surveys, surveyors did not understand the problem, and, in order to protect themselves from respondent outrage, wrote reassurances that the sexual acts respondents were being asked to describe were normal. Katharine Davis' 1920 mail-in survey of the sexual experiences of middle-class women included a long prefatory statement to her questions on masturbation communicating the opinion—shared by other progressive thinkers in her day—that, in spite of condemnation, masturbation was not harmful for women. Indeed, some experts, she said, maintained that it was "a normal stage in the development of the sex nature and must be passed through if sexual development is to be complete."[17]

Davis expected to find that many women masturbated, and not surprisingly she found this. In modern questionnaires, such reassurance—which may push a respondent in the direction of a particular response—rarely appears. Before the survey takes place, pretesting helps achieve clear, nondirective questions. Careful wording and ordering of questions produce more accurate responses. It is more difficult to examine the effect of turning abstract concepts into terms that respondents can understand, or to ascertain what a respondent might reasonably remember. Even here, however, research has made progress. For example, one source of variation in estimates of the size of the gay population is the questions asked. Not only does asking the gender of respondents' sexual partners produce different results than asking respondents if they are homosexual, bisexual, or heterosexual, but the specific wording of the question makes a difference. It is hard to compare the findings of the Battelle researchers with those of Kinsey because of the differences in the questions.

During the final phase, data analysis, bias was endemic but often unrecognized in early surveys. Indeed, obtaining impartial data and analyzing them in a manner unfettered by the investigator's agenda was not always the aim. Max Exner, who in 1913 embarked on one of the earliest sex surveys, stated that "we are in urgent need of facts which would enable us to speak with reasonable definiteness" about the need for sex education as a way of curbing young men's excessive sexual desires.[18] Although draped in scientific garb, Exner's questions and analysis reveal that for him the survey was not a tool to discover information. He used it to support his preexisting "knowledge" that learning about sex from the street led to unhygienic sexual practices.

Over time, with increasingly rigorous survey methods, such obviously prejudiced practices ceased. Researchers even began to realize that their unconscious biases could influence the outcome. With more sophisticated data analysis techniques, researchers could be more certain of their conclusions and less able to shape them to satisfy an agenda. Yet they remained largely oblivious of the fact that the questions they ask of the data reveal a point of view. The Battelle researchers insisted that the furor over their reported incidence of male homosexuality was misplaced. This, they said, was not the main target of their research, and they did not have sufficient data for accuracy. But they revealed this result in a carefully orchestrated manner that seemed designed to maximize publicity.

Throughout the century, survey researchers interested in sexual behavior viewed their results as improvements on earlier findings. Indeed, this brief description of survey practice suggests that a history of surveys of sexual behavior should be a history of the growing sophistication of researchers and the increasing certainty of their conclusions. In order for this to be the case, two conditions would have to hold. First, researchers would have to be neutral observers of sexual behavior, an unlikely proposition in a world where no one escapes pressure to monitor personal sexual standards and desires. Second, sexual behavior would have to be independent of history and culture. In such a case, questions such as the proportion of gays in the population would be technical, not political or historically specific questions.

In fact, while survey improvements have produced more accurate reflections of historical moments, surveys do not divulge universal truths, only those relative to their time and place. Furthermore, even with the best intentions, researchers have managed their surveys in such a way as to produce findings reflecting their own beliefs about gender and normality and their concerns about the dangers of sex research. Responsible researchers adopted techniques to neutralize the effect of their biases, but their very choice of research topics assumed a certain view of sexuality. When, in 1992, the research team quoted in the epigraph to this [work] finally received funds for a large national survey of American adults, they used the latest survey techniques. Yet they conducted their research in a climate in which sexual coupling, especially with strangers, was perceived as potentially fatal. Their concern over "promiscuity" colored all aspects of the survey.[19]

In addition to researchers and respondents, two other groups had an impact on what information surveys revealed: those who funded surveys and those who interpreted the results for larger audiences. At first sex surveys were commissioned by private organizations interested in promoting a particular point of view. In later years the federal government took over much of the funding. Those who dispensed federal dollars also had a point of view to promote, although they did so in a less directive manner.

In the early years, researchers not only controlled who respondents were and what their answers meant; they also controlled the dissemination of results to other experts and the general public.... Once the media began reporting the results of surveys, their goals differed widely from those of the researchers, who often found their results presented in a distorted manner. The Battelle researchers experienced this. They used the media to promote their survey, but they quickly lost control of the debate. As discussion raged over the percentage of men who were gay, the rest of the results, including those of most interest to the researchers, almost disappeared from view.

Do these limits and problems mean we can learn little from surveys of sexual behavior? On the contrary, such surveys teach us a great deal about sexuality in America, about the beliefs that have shaped sexual behavior, and about the concerns that have driven researchers to ask questions. They show the changes in these concerns and in assumptions about sexuality. Tracing these changes reveals the history of sexuality in the twentieth century. Furthermore, as survey practice improved, the ensuing descriptions of sexual practice not only provided a behavioral control but provided comfort and encouraged people to act on their desires.

We tell this story in the belief that sexuality is not a trait with which individuals are born but a crucial aspect of identity that is socially created. Researchers often assumed that sexuality was innate and that their task was to reveal what already existed. In contrast, we believe that the assumptions driving the research helped create the sexuality the research revealed. Researchers' assumptions were the product of the larger society, of the researchers' positions within that society, and of the findings of their predecessors. While the culture changed over time and researchers did not occupy identical social or professional positions, two factors remained almost constant. First, researchers shared general beliefs in the existence of innate differences between men and women and viewed such differences as the basis of sexual attraction. Second, most researchers were men and viewed the world through the eyes of male privilege. They assumed a straightforward male sexuality while puzzling over "the problem of female sexuality." In this, their major concern was that women should satisfy men's needs. Female sexual pleasure was increasingly viewed as a way to make men happy and families secure. It was not until the 1980s, when women began to undertake sex surveys, that the focus began shifting to female pleasure as a woman's concern.

Researchers believed that women become aroused slowly and through love, while men experience constant arousal. These beliefs influenced surveys and were so powerful that researchers did not always know how to handle contrary findings. For example, the few women surveyors in the early decades described a strong female sex drive, more similar to than different from men's.[20] Yet even as male experts reported these women's results they ignored the voices behind them, choosing instead to reinterpret findings to fit conventional assumptions. Furthermore, these assumptions about gender and sexuality differed according to respondents' race, class, and age. Middle-class adults received the most attention because of beliefs that only they had the time or education to achieve sexual bliss. Only during periods of crisis when sexuality became a symbol for concern about other social changes did groups other than the white middle class become the targets of sex research.

Part of the reason for caution over whom to interview involved researchers' need to justify sex surveys while protecting themselves from charges of prurience. Those undertaking sex surveys found them to be a dangerous enterprise. Sex talk, with its forbidden overtones, was often embarrassing because it was exciting. Doing the research involved invading a private sphere. This affected the nature of the research questions and the explanations given for asking them. Surveyors rarely justified sex surveys on the grounds of interest. Instead, they used the urgent social problems of the day as an explanation for their questions. Their justifications had implications for the collection of data, for the questions asked, and for what constituted knowledge. Discomfort over sex talk, even in scientific guise, made sex surveys more vulnerable to personal pressures at every stage of the survey process.

Researchers in many areas claim their results are definitive, but these claims have a particular cast in sex research because worries about criticism often lead to overstatement of the reliability of conclusions. In reaction to the claims of conservative opponents like Senator Jesse Helms that "most Americans resent even being asked to answer questions about how often they engage in sex, with whom, their preferences for sexual partners, and which sex act they prefer,"[21] researchers tended to downplay the methodological and theoretical challenges of their research. In such a climate they were loath to consider the impact of their research on behavior. They tried to convince skeptical audiences that asking questions about sex was easy and the results were trustworthy. Paradoxically, this need for certainty created resistance to research on the methodology of sex surveys, since such research requires an acknowledgment of uncertainty. It also made researchers hesitant to share their experiences with other researchers, which, in turn, slowed the accumulation of knowledge on which to build. This made researchers vulnerable to attack on methodological grounds even from those whose objections were actually political.

Nevertheless, the history of sexual behavior surveys remains a history of the optimism of researchers and of the enlightenment of readers. Living in a culture in which no topic has been considered too difficult or too private for scientific inquiry, and believing that knowledge would further human progress, surveyors saw themselves as pioneers venturing where others dared not go and doing so without fear of personal consequences. Their goal was to delve into the most secret and shame-laden human behavior, and to reveal it for all to see in the hope that the truth would liberate people from ignorance and stigma. In recent years many writers about sexuality have agreed with Foucault's argument that talk about sex does not liberate sex but is merely another way of controlling it. Researchers had a limited understanding of how they shaped the results of surveys. But they showed courage in following their beliefs that social stability is best served by exposing practice rather than by hiding it. Their work reveals an important thread of cultural and sexual history in the twentieth century.

Notes

1. Bruce Voeller, "Some Uses and Abuses of the Kinsey Scale," in David P. McWhirter, Stephanie A. Sanders, and June Machover Reinisch, eds., *Homosexuality/Heterosexuality* (New York: Oxford University Press, 1990).
2. Interview with Robert Knight, May 24, 1993.
3. John O. G. Billy et al., "The Sexual Behavior of Men in the United States," *Family Planning Perspectives* 25, no. 2 (March/April 1993).
4. John D'Emilio, *Sexual Politics, Sexual Communities* (Chicago: University of Chicago Press, 1983).
5. Thomas Laqueur, *Making Sex* (Cambridge, Mass.: Harvard University Press, 1990).
6. Michel Foucault, *The History of Sexuality*, vol. 1 (New York: Random House, 1978).
7. Richard von Krafft-Ebing, *Psychopathia Sexualis* (New York: Physicians and Surgeons Book Co., 1931).
8. John D'Emilio and Estelle B. Freedman, *Intimate Matters: A History of Sexuality in America* (New York: Harper and Row, 1988).
9. Havelock Ellis, *Studies in the Psychology of Sex* (1899; New York: Random House, 1942).
10. Patricia Cline Cohen, *A Calculating People* (Chicago: University of Chicago Press, 1982).
11. James MaHood and Kristine Wenburg, *The Mosher Survey* (New York: Arno, 1980).
12. Bernard Lecuyer and Anthony R. Oberschall, "The Early History of Social Research: Postscript: Research in the United States at the Turn of the Century," in *International Encyclopedia of Statistics*, eds. William H. Kruskal and Judith M. Tanur (New York: Free Press, 1978).
13. Walter F. Robie, *Rational Sex Ethics* (Boston: Richard G. Badger, 1916), 30; Katharine Bement Davis, *Factors in the Sex Lives of Twenty-Two Hundred Women* (New York: Harper and Row, 1929), x.
14. Morris H. Hansen, William Hurwitz, and William G. Madow, *Sample Survey Methods and Theory*, vol. 1(New York: Wiley, 1953).
15. Gilbert V. Hamilton, *A Research in Marriage* (New York: A. C. Boni, 1929), 17–18.

16. Ronald Freedman, Pascal K. Whelpton, and Arthur A. Campbell, *Family Planning, Sterility and Population Growth* (New York: McGraw-Hill, 1959).

17. Davis, *Factors in the Sex Lives*, 96.

18. Max J. Exner, *Problems and Principles of Sex Education* (New York: Association Press, 1915), 3.

19. Edward O. Laumann et al., *The Social Organization of Sexuality* (Chicago: University of Chicago Press, 1994).

20. Davis, *Factors in the Sex Lives;* Dorothy Dunbar Bromley and Florence Haxton Britten, *Youth and Sex* (New York: Harper, 1938).

21. Jesse Helms, "Debate on Amendment no. 1757 to the 1992 NIH Revitalization Act," *Congressional Record* (April 2, 1992), S4738.

Chapter 7
Sexuality in Marriage, Dating, and Other Relationships
A Decade Review

F. Scott Christopher
Susan Sprecher

Before reading this chapter, consider first the good news and then the bad! That relationship variables such as attraction, satisfaction, intimacy, equity, love, communication, and stability are receiving increasing emphasis in the science of interpersonal relationships is certainly good news. Because scholars in the field are examining the relationship of sexuality to these phenomena, you as a university student can anticipate scholarly answers to some of the more pressing issues of your time. The bad news, however, reflects the general lack of government funding for research on intimate relationships, especially sexually intimate relationships. This circumstance means that most investigations are limited to smaller convenience samples, that is, university students, family planning clinics, and the readership of popular magazines.

Given this scenario, how would you, as a consumer of sexuality research, assess the major effects of such sample limitations? Other than sample limitations, what other negative effects may derive from using convenience samples? From your perspective, what should be the role of government in funding research? As a voter, how could your opinion be expressed? After reading the reviews of the impressive array of sexuality research that was done in the previous decade, what would you, as a sexuality researcher, be most interested in pursuing? Such questions posed here may seem irrelevant to you now as a student. But, as lifetime consumers of scientific discoveries, we all have a part to play in the enactment of reason.

Sexuality is woven into the fabric of many close relationships. It is sanctioned in marriage; it is often explored in dating; and it is an intricate part of other committed romantic relationships. The past decade saw a marked increase in scholarly interest in sexuality within a relational context. This increased interest posed a challenge for us as we developed the foci of this review. In deciding what areas of research to review, we considered the interests of family scientists balanced with the sexual phenomena explored by scholars from a variety of disciplines, including but not limited to family studies, sociology, psychology, communication, public health, and women's studies. More specifically, the purpose of our review was to identify, summarize, and critique theoretical, methodological, and empirical breakthroughs in sexuality research from the 1990s as they relate to marriage and other relationships that occur prior to or outside of marriage.

We open by identifying major theoretical and methodological advancements in sexuality research of the 1990s that have relevance to marriage, dating, and committed relationships. In the second section, we review the empirical literature from the 1990s on sexuality in marriage and other committed relationships. In the third section, we review the past decade's literature on sexuality in dating (premarital) relationships. Although most of our review concentrates on sexuality's positive aspects, sexuality also has a "dark side" involving sexual coercion and assault. Hence, our review of the literatures on marital and dating sexuality includes findings on this aspect of sexuality. We end the review with recommendations for research on sexuality for the coming decade.

Because of page limits, we could not review all topics relevant to sexuality. For example, we did not include a review of adolescent sexuality, contraceptive use, or teenage pregnancy (for reviews see Gullotta, Adams, & Montemayor, 1993; Moore, Miller, Glei, & Morrison, 1995). Furthermore, although the 1990s saw an increase in research on risk behaviors and individual and family outcomes related to AIDS, these topics are also beyond the scope of this review (see Kelly, 1995, for a review). Moreover, the topics we were able to cover were limited primarily to research conducted in North America, although advances were also made in sexuality research in other countries and cross-culturally.

Advancements in the 1990s

We wish to identify several advancements in sexuality research in the 1990s that have relevance to family science. These can be aggregated broadly into two areas: (1) advancements in conceptualization and theory involving sexuality-related phenomena and (2) advancements in methodology.

The 1990s witnessed an increased focus on sexuality within a relational context, which broadened the concepts, topics, and theories linked to sexuality (e.g., McKinney & Sprecher, 1991). The science of interpersonal relationships is one of the most rapidly growing areas in behavioral sciences (Berscheid & Reis, 1998), and it is now chronicled in two multidisciplinary journals (*Journal of Social and Personal Relationships* and *Personal Relationships*) that have published several articles on sexuality. Scholars from the close relationships field have examined how sexuality is related to such relationship phenomena as attraction, satisfaction, intimacy, equity, love, communication, and stability. Reflecting the general lack of government funding for research on intimate relationships, most of these investigations are based on smaller convenience samples (Gierveld, 1995). However, because the issues examined by relationship scholars have not, in general, also been examined in the larger, national studies, we highlight some of their findings in this review because of their insights and heuristic promise.

Overall, theoretical advancements in sexuality research were somewhat limited during this past decade. However, there was an increase in the number of scholars who employed an evolutionary perspective, either as an explanation for their findings or to test *a priori* hypotheses derived from this perspective. Evolutionary approaches focus on distal causes of sexual behavior and argue that current patterns of sexual behavior, including gender differences in these behaviors, exist because they have been associated with reproductive success in our ancestral past. According to this perspective, current gender differences in a variety of sexual behaviors can be traced to the smaller investment that men, relative to women, need to make in order to create offspring, balanced against women's more limited access to resources needed to ensure their offsprings' survival. In particular, evolutionary perspectives were used to explain gender differences in extramarital behavior, jealousy reactions to extradyadic affairs, sexual conflict in marriage, and choice of sexual influence tactics in dating. Despite the increase in evolutionary-based research, more of the research on sexuality in the 1990s was atheoretical than theoretical (see discussion by Weis, 1998). There is little reason for this to continue. Near the end of the decade, *The Journal of Sex Research* devoted a special issue to theory, which included reviews and critiques of social constructionism (DeLamater & Hyde, 1998), sexual strategy theory (Buss, 1998), social exchange (Sprecher, 1998); symbolic interactionism (Longmore, 1998), social learning theory (Hogben & Byrne,1998), and systems theory (Jurich & Myers-Bowman, 1998) as they apply to sexuality. This collected work provides a solid reference for informing sexual research in the coming decade.

A number of methodological advances were worthy of recognition. First, there was an increased availability of large-scale national studies that included sexuality data. Knowledge of patterns of sexual behavior was increased significantly with the publication of data from the National Health and Social Life Survey (NHSLS; Laumann, Gagnon, Michael, & Michaels, 1994; Michael, Gagnon, Laumann, & Kolata, 1994). For this study, a probability sample of 3,432 Americans, aged 18 to 59, was interviewed, and respondents completed a brief questionnaire with more sensitive questions about sexuality. Approximately 54 percent of the sample were married, and another 7 percent were in cohabiting relationships. Several other ongoing and first-time large-scale probability studies provided data about adult or adolescent sexuality in the 1990s (e.g., General Social Survey—GSS, The National Survey of Men—NSM, The National Study of Adolescent Health—Add Health). In general, it became more legitimate to ask about sexual behaviors and attitudes in national studies because information on sexual patterns was relevant to the AIDS crisis. More government and private funding was placed into this type of research.

Another methodological advancement was the maturation of several longitudinal studies conducted with married or committed couples. Researchers who began longitudinal studies in the 1980s continued to follow the couples over several years and multiple waves, which allowed them to examine, when sexuality data were available, how sexual phenomena change over time, and how the sexual health of the relationship at one time might be related to a future outcome of the relationship. Two longitudinal studies in particular have included measures of sexuality over time: The Early Years of Marriage Project, based on a sample of Black and White married couples in the Detroit area (e.g., Oggins, Leber, & Veroff, 1993); and the Marital Instability over the Life-course Project, which was based on a national sample of married individuals obtained through random digit dialing (e.g., Edwards & Booth, 1994).

A final methodological advancement we want to note is an increase in the sophistication and accessibility of information on particular methods and measurement. For example, a recent issue of *The Journal of Sex Research* was devoted to methodological advances (Catania, 1999a). Several of the works will likely prove valuable to family scientists into the next decade. Gribble, Miller, Rogers, and Turner (1999) reviewed the advantages of incorporating new technologies into survey work, including computer-assisted personal and telephone interviewing. These are technologies that, when compared to traditional survey and interview methods, appear to increase respondents' reports of engaging in sensitive sexual practices. Morrison, Leigh, and Gillmore (1999) provided a useful comparison of three different methods of daily data collection: individual-initiated phone calls, investigator-initiated phone calls, and self-administered questionnaires. Wiederman (1999) identified volunteer biases among college students who typically participate in sexuality research. Catania (1999b) provided a thoughtful analysis of the origins of reporting biases in interviews. Finally, Binik, Mah, and Kiesler (1999) examined ethical issues connected with conducting research using the Internet, a practice that will likely increase in the coming decade. In addition, several methodological issues were discussed in an edited volume sponsored by the Kinsey Institute (Bancroft, 1997). Furthermore, Davis, Yarber, Bauserman, Schreer, and Davis (1998) published a handbook of over 200 sexuality measures, including information on their reliability and validity. The advances in methodology, coupled with an increased accessibility of measures of sexuality-related variables, will likely increase the volume of research conducted on sexuality in the next decade.

In addition to advances in conceptualizations, theory, and methods, scholars' empirical investigations revealed new insights into the sexuality of adults in relationships. We begin our review of these findings by examining sexuality in marriage and other committed romantic relationships.

Sex In (and Outside of) Marriage and Other Committed Relationships

The most socially approved context for sexual activity is the marital relationship. Because sex and marriage are legally and morally linked, marital sex is generally not viewed as a social problem or as a phenomenon likely to lead to negative outcomes. As a result, marital sex has not been the central focus of much research in the past decade. This scarcity of research on marital sex has also been noted in previous decades (Greenblat, 1983). Nonetheless, several studies were conducted in the 1990s that included data on sexuality in marriage or other committed relationships, as described below.

Descriptive Information about Sexual Activity

One issue that received research attention, before and during the 1990s, is the frequency of couples' sexual activity. Scientific interest in frequency of marital sex is based in part on its association with both fertility and quality of marriage. Although data collected on this topic prior to 1990 were based on nonprobability samples (e.g., Blumstein & Schwartz, 1983; Kinsey, Pomeroy, & Martin, 1948; Kinsey, Pomeroy, Martin, & Gebhard, 1953), this past decade yielded data on sexual frequency from national probability samples.

Because the national samples included respondents from across the life-span, how sexual frequency is associated with marital duration or age, two passage-of-time variables that are highly confounded, was examined. The National Survey of Families and Households (NSFH), based on interviews conducted in 1987–1988 (Wave 1) with a randomly selected sample of over 13,000 Americans, included a question on frequency of sexual intercourse in the self-administered questionnaire completed by the respondents. Call, Sprecher, and Schwartz (1995) reported that the NSFH Wave 1 married respondents had an overall mean frequency of sex of 6.3 times per month. Couples under the age of 24 had a mean frequency of 11.7, but the frequency declined with each subsequent age group. For example, in the 75 and older age group, the mean frequency was slightly less than once per month. Call, Sprecher, and Schwartz (1996) reported a similar negative association of sexual frequency with age at Wave 2 (1992–1994) of the NSFH. With slightly different foci and subsamples from the NSFH Wave 1 data, Rao and DeMaris (1995), Marsiglio and Donnelly (1991), and Donnelly (1993) published similar findings about marital sexual frequency. The decline in sexual frequency seems to be due to both psychological and biological factors associated with the aging process. Any decreases due to habituation resulting from being with the same partner seem to occur early in the marriage (Call et al., 1995). A habituation perspective can also explain the finding from NSFH (Call et al., 1996) that a remarriage was associated with an increase in marital sex, controlling for other factors including age.

Measures of sexual frequency were included in the National Health and Social Life Survey [NHSLS] (Laumann et al., 1994; Michael et al., 1994), the large-scale national study referred to earlier. The researchers provided data on the sample members' frequency of sexual activity in various ways, but, for our interests, reported a mean frequency of sexual activity per month of 6.9 for married men and 6.5 for married women. The cohabitors had a higher level of sexual activity (which was also found in the NSFH data; e.g., Call et al., 1995; Rao & DeMaris, 1995), whereas the single individuals had the lowest level of sexual activity. Laumann and colleagues (1994) also reported the ubiquitous decrease in sexual frequency with age, although the data were presented for the entire sample, married and unmarried.

The General Social Survey (GSS), an interview study on a variety of attitudes and experiences conducted biennially by the National Opinion Research Center with probability samples of Americans, also contains data on sexual frequency. As reported in Smith (1994b, based on 1993 GSS data), married respondents engaged in sexual intercourse an average of 67 times per year, or slightly over once a week. The frequency rates were highest among the young and those married less than 3 years.

Only a few longitudinal studies were conducted in the 1990s that included information on sexual frequency, but their findings confirm a decrease in sexual frequency with marital duration. In a longitudinal study of newly married couples selected randomly from central Pennsylvania, Huston and Vangelisti (1991) found that a decrease in sexual activity and interest began in the first 2 years of marriage. Preliminary analyses based on both waves of the NSFH data (Call et al., 1996) indicated that the younger couples in the original sample experienced a decrease in sexual frequency between Waves 1 and 2. In a four-wave longitudinal study conducted with 570 pregnant women and their husbands or partners, Hyde, DeLamater, Plant, and Byrd (1996) found that the respondents reported having sex 4–5 times per month during pregnancy, had almost no sex in the first month post-partum, said they resumed sexual intercourse approximately 7 weeks postpartum, and had a sexual frequency rate at 4 and 12 months postpartum that was similar to the rate during pregnancy (4–5 times per month). More long-term longitudinal studies are needed to examine the pattern of sexual activity with the passage of time and with other family transitions, including the launching of children and retirement.

The rates of marital sexual activity found in the national probability samples of the 1990s appear to be similar to, and in some cases slightly lower than, those reported in nonprobability samples conducted in previous decades. The major advancement in the 1990s on this topic was the examination of a wide range of possible predictors of sexual frequency through multivariate analyses. Passage of time (i.e., age, duration of marriage) was found to have the strongest (negative) association with frequency of marital sex, although marital satisfaction also had a unique and strong (positive) association with sexual frequency (e.g., Call et al., 1995; Smith,

1994b). Social and background characteristics, such as race, social status, and religion, were generally unrelated to marital sexual frequency, with the exception of a few modest associations, such as a Catholic background being associated with a lower frequency (Call et al., 1995). The multivariate results conducted in the 1990s on predictors of sexual frequency indicated only a modest amount of variance in marital sexual frequency explained, despite a notable number of predictor variables (e.g., 20 percent was explained in Call et al. [1995], using the NSFH data and 18 predictors), suggesting that future research needs to broaden the type of predictors considered.

There was very little discussion in the 1990s of measurement issues associated with sexual frequency. The sexual frequency question varied slightly in format across the studies described above. For example, the question in the NSFH referred to "sexual intercourse" and was open-ended, whereas the NHSLS asked about "sex" and elicited closed-ended responses. Responses might vary in systematic ways as a function of the format of the item, although we suspect not by much. The NHHLS study further explored what couples do when they have sex and found that almost all of the married men and women (95 percent) had vaginal intercourse in their last sex act. Although a majority of the respondents had engaged in oral sex in their lifetime, less than one-fourth of the married respondents reported having oral sex during their last sex act. Anal sex was even less common, 1–2 percent reported having had it during their last episode, although 9.7 percent of married men and 7.3 percent of married women reported engaging in anal sex during the past year. Oral and anal sex were more common among the more highly educated and the White respondents.

A continued focus on documenting frequency of marital sex and its predictors might not be as fruitful as examining other issues about sexual frequency, including how married respondents believe their frequency compares to that of other couples and to what they desire or expect, and the implications of these comparisons. In addition, we suggest that the focus of research move from how often couples have sex overall (e.g., each week on average) to the degree of variation, week to week, both in frequency of sexual activity and in the specific behaviors engaged in and the length of time sex lasts. This intracouple variation (over time) is likely to be linked in complex ways to relationship phenomena, including balance of power, conflict, and communication. We encourage research on this issue, possibly through daily diaries kept by married individuals, a method used infrequently in the 1990s.

Sexual Satisfaction

Married individuals' assessments of the quality of their sexual relationship also received research attention in the 1990s. Consistent with findings from previous decades (e.g., Blumstein & Schwartz, 1983), married couples were generally sexually satisfied. For example, Laumann and colleagues (1994), in the NHSLS, found that 88 percent of the married individuals in the sample were either extremely or very physically pleased in their relationship. When asked about the specific feelings they experienced after having sex, a majority of the participants reported positive feelings (i.e., felt "loved," "thrilled and excited") and only a small minority reported any negative feelings (e.g., "anxious and worried"). Married respondents, particularly if they were monogamous, reported the highest level of sexual satisfaction; cohabiting and single (i.e., dating) respondents had slightly lower levels of sexual satisfaction. Greeley (1991) also found high sexual satisfaction among his married respondents, obtained from the 1988 and 1989 GSS and from telephone interviews conducted by the Gallup Organization using a national probability sample of married couples. High levels of marital sexual satisfaction were reported in several other studies as well (e.g., Edwards & Booth, 1994; Lawrance & Byers, 1995; Oggins et al., 1993). Couples who become sexually dissatisfied, however, might be less likely to be in these studies because of their greater risk of having divorced early in marriage.

Less consistent information is available on how sexual satisfaction might change with marital duration or age, although the accumulating evidence suggests that it does not decline as rapidly or as dramatically as does frequency of sex. For example, Laumann and colleagues (1994) reported that most of their respondents, regardless of age, were happy with their partnered sex. Although physical pleasure was found to be lower for women over the age of 40 than for women under 40, their analyses were based on all respondents, married and unmarried. Men did not experience the same drop in physical pleasure with age, which, as explained by the authors, might be due to divorced and widowed men's greater likelihood of obtaining new and younger sex partners, relative to their female counterparts. Edwards and. Booth (1994), in their national sample of married individuals, found no differences in sexual happiness as a function of age, although wives in their late middle years (48–60) were more likely than younger wives to say that loss of interest in sex was a problem in their relationship (nonetheless, only a small minority had this view). Men and women tended to agree that it was the wife who was more likely to lose interest. Their longitudinal analyses revealed a significant decrease in happiness with sex and a significant increase in loss of interest in sex in the sample over 9 years of marriage. Greeley (1991), in a cross-sectional analysis based on a national sample of married couples, also found a decline in sexual satisfaction with age (and therefore marital duration).

Not surprisingly, sexual satisfaction is associated with sexual frequency. Couples who have the most frequent sex are the most sexually satisfied (Greeley, 1991; Laumann et al., 1994). This past decade, however, did not yield any findings of import about this association. For example, no significant knowledge was gained about how the quantity and quality of sexual activity influence each other over time (is one more likely to lead to the other?), the specific processes that might mediate the association, and the degree to which the strength of the association differs based on other characteristics of the couple such as their ages and relationship duration. That sexual frequency appears to decline more rapidly than sexual satisfaction with age (and marital duration) suggests that the association between the quantity and quality of sex might change with the passage of time. These are issues that need more investigation in the next decade.

In the previous section, we reported that social and demographic characteristics are generally unrelated to frequency of sex. Research conducted in the 1990s indicated that social and demographic variables also are generally unrelated to the degree of sexual satisfaction (e.g., Davidson, Darling, & Norton, 1995; Henderson-King & Veroff, 1994; Laumann et al., 1994). An exception is that at Wave 1 of the Early Years of Marriage Project, Black spouses reported more sexual enjoyment than White spouses, controlling for other demographic variables, including income (Henderson-King & Veroff, 1994; Oggins et al., 1993). These researchers also found that higher household income was associated with less sexual satisfaction for women and speculated that higher family income is associated with one or both partners working longer hours or having more work stress, which might be detrimental to women's sexual satisfaction. However, with a national sample, Greeley (1991) reported that after controlling for age there was no association between the wife working and sexual satisfaction in marriage. Another work variable, working different shifts, was found to be associated with sexual problems or sexual dissatisfaction in a national sample of married individuals (White & Keith, 1990).

Investigations designed to identify predictors of sexual satisfaction have been generally atheoretical and focused on personality attributes (as noted by Lawrance & Byers, 1995); these studies are beyond the scope of this review. More relevant to this review, however, are investigations that have focused on how sexual satisfaction might be predicted by behavior and affect in sexual and nonsexual aspects of the relationship. Lawrance and Byers (1995) developed a model of sexual satisfaction that focuses on the interpersonal context and is based on exchange theory. Their Interpersonal Exchange Model of Sexual Satisfaction states that sexual satisfaction is affected by rewards, costs, comparison level, comparison level for alternatives, and equality within the sexual area of the relationship, as well as by relationship satisfaction. Evidence for components of this model was found in a study of married and cohabiting men and women (Lawrance & Byers, 1995), a study of daters (Byers, Demmons, & Lawrance, 1998), and a study of Chinese married men and women (Renaud, Byers, & Pan, 1997). Sexual satisfaction also has been found to be associated with other aspects, of the interpersonal environment, including quality of sexual communication (Cupach & Comstock, 1990), sexual self-disclosure as mediated by relationship satisfaction (Byers & Demmons, 1999), and equity (Henderson-King & Veroff, 1994).

Investigations in the 1990s that focused on predictors of sexual satisfaction most often were based on smaller, geographically limited samples, although their strength was the frequent use of either multi-item scales with known reliability and validity, multidimensional measures, or both (e.g., Lawrance & Byers, 1995; Oggins et al., 1993), in contrast to the use of single-item global measures of sexual satisfaction typical of national studies. Ideally, research in the future will combine good sampling techniques with sophisticated measures of sexual satisfaction. In addition, more theoretically driven research is needed to identify how factors associated with the individual, the relationship, and "the environment" might interact to affect sexual satisfaction.

In the next section, we discuss how sexual satisfaction, as well as level of sexual activity, are related to overall relationship satisfaction and other relationship outcome variables.

The Association Between Sexual Dimensions of the Relationship and Relationship Quality

In our discussion of findings from the 1990s on sexual frequency, we noted that sexual frequency was found to be associated positively with general relationship satisfaction in married couples (e.g., Call et al., 1995; Smith, 1994b). What appears to be a more important predictor of marital satisfaction, however, is sexual satisfaction or other feelings about sex (Greeley, 1991). Several studies conducted in the past decade have demonstrated that

sexual satisfaction is associated with higher marital satisfaction (Cupach & Comstock, 1990; Edwards & Booth, 1994; Haavio-Mannila & Kontula, 1997; Henderson-King & Veroff, 1994; Kurdek, 1991). The quality and quantity of sex also appear to be associated with feelings of love for one's spouse or partner, especially a passionate or erotic type of love (e.g., Marston, Hecht, Manke, McDaniel, & Reeder, 1998; Sprecher & Regan, 1998). Sexual intimacy, however, has been found to be a weaker predictor of love or of general relationship quality than have other forms of intimacy, including degree of affection expressed (Huston & Vangelisti, 1991) and supportive communication (Sprecher, Metts, Burleson, Hatfield, & Thompson, 1995).

In the examination of how a sexuality variable (e.g., sexual satisfaction) is associated with a general relationship construct (e.g., relationship satisfaction), caution must be exercised so that the two variables do not overlap in measurement content (e.g., Fincham & Bradbury, 1987). For example, several marital satisfaction scales (e.g., Roach, Frazier, & Bowden, 1981; Spanier, 1976) include an item or two about sexual activity. Measures of other relationship dimensions, including intimacy, love, interdependence, maintenance strategies, and exchange, have also included elements referring to sexuality (for a discussion, see Sprecher & McKinney, 1993). One solution has been to delete from the scale measuring the general relationship construct any items that refer to sexuality (e.g., Kurdek, 1991).

On a broader conceptual level, researchers must determine whether the sexuality variable is the independent or dependent variable. One's theoretical framework guides the determination of the specific causal connections between partners' feelings about the sexual relationship and the overall evaluation of the relationship. In most research, the focus has been on a sexuality variable as the predictor and on a general relationship quality measure as the variable to be explained, often within a multivariate framework (e.g., Edwards & Booth, 1994). However, the reverse causal direction is proposed in some models, such as the interpersonal Exchange Model of Sexual Satisfaction described earlier (e.g., Lawrance & Byers, 1995). Furthermore, Henderson-King and Veroff (1994), among others, have speculated that marital well-being and sexual feelings are reciprocal and that both causal directions operate over time. More multiple-wave, longitudinal investigations are needed to adequately address the possible reciprocal relation between these variables over time.

Research in the 1990s also examined whether sexual satisfaction predicts marital stability versus dissolution. Oggins et al. (1993), using data from the Early Years of Marriage Project, reported that sexual dissatisfaction at Year 1 predicted marital dissolution by Year 4 of marriage. Based on later analyses, however, Veroff, Douvan, and Hatchett (1995) found that sexual (dis)satisfaction measured in the 3rd year of marriage was not a significant predictor of later relationship dissolution. In their longitudinal study of married individuals, Edwards and Booth (1994) found that a decline in sexual satisfaction over time was associated with the increased likelihood of divorce. Furthermore, in a national study of married individuals (White & Keith, 1990), a measure of sexual problems or dissatisfaction at Time 1 was associated positively with the likelihood of divorce by Time 2, controlling for general marital happiness and other variables. Thus, these limited findings suggest that sexual satisfaction contributes to marital stability. To our knowledge, however, no research has examined the effects of frequency of sexual activity on the likelihood that marriages dissolve over time.

In the next section, we discuss extramarital sex, which has also been found to be associated with negative outcomes for the relationship.

Extramarital Sex

Although sex in marriage is the most socially approved form of sexual outlet, sex by married persons with someone other than their spouse is one of the most stigmatized. The GSS has included an attitudinal question on extramarital sexuality, and, consistently through the years, 70–80 percent of Americans express complete disapproval of a married person having sex with someone other than his or her spouse, and most others express at least some disapproval (e.g., Smith, 1994a). The NHSLS (Laumann et al., 1994) included a similar attitudinal question and found that 77 percent of participants said extramarital sex was always wrong. Considerable research has been done to examine predictors of attitudes about extramarital sex, although most of this research was conducted in the decades prior to 1990 (for reviews, see Glass & Wright, 1992; Sponaugle, 1989). Among the variables that have been found to be associated with permissive attitudes toward extramarital sex are: premarital sexual permissiveness, high education, low religiosity, and being male.

Research conducted in the past decade on the incidence of extramarital sex has yielded rates lower than those reported in earlier studies based on nonprobability samples (for a review of the earlier research, see Thompson, 1983). In the NHSLS study (Laumann et al., 1994), approximately 25 percent of married men and 15 percent of married women reported having engaged in extramarital

sex at least once. Less than 4 percent of married respondents reported having engaged in sex with someone other than their spouse in the prior year. Similar low rates have been found in other national studies, including the GSS (e.g., Smith, 1994b; Wiederman, 1997), the 1991 National Survey of Men (Billy, Tanfer, Grady, & Klepinger, 1993), the 1991 National Survey of Women (Forste & Tanfer, 1996), and a national sample based on the National AIDS Behavioral Study (Choi, Catania, & Dolcini, 1994). Nonetheless, these percentages translate into a significant number of Americans who have experienced sex with someone other than their spouse at least once. Furthermore, individuals who divorce are less represented in married samples but perhaps more likely to have experienced sex with someone other than their spouse.

Cohabitors have a higher rate of nonmonogamy than do married couples (Forste & Tanfer, 1996). In addition, a higher lifetime incidence of extramarital sex is found among men, Blacks, remarried individuals, those in the lowest and highest education categories, those in urban areas, and those low in religiosity (e.g., Laumann et al., 1994; Wiederman, 1997).

Perhaps because of the relatively low incidence of extramarital sex, few studies in the past decade have focused on its association with marital satisfaction. There are two major issues that can be examined, however, about this association: First, does marital dissatisfaction lead to extramarital sex? Second, what are the effects of a partner's infidelity on one's marital satisfaction?

The limited research from the 1990s on the first issue suggests that marital dissatisfaction might play only a small role in married individuals' decision to engage in extramarital sex. For example, Greeley (1991) reported that marital dissatisfaction has only an indirect influence on the likelihood of extramarital sex, mediated by such factors as premarital sexual permissiveness and a lower value placed on fidelity. However, several studies prior to 1990 (reviewed in Bringle & Buunk, 1991, and in Edwards & Booth, 1994) did show an association between extramarital sex and marital dissatisfaction, especially for women. Opportunity and having a reference group that supports nonmonogamy also seem to be important factors leading to the behavior.

Concerning the second issue, research suggests that spouses become upset with a partner's infidelity. Not all spouses find out about a partner's infidelity, but those who do tend to have negative reactions (e.g., Bringle & Buunk, 1991) or say they would if it were to happen (Shackelford & Buss, 1997). Gender differences in negative reactions to partner's real, or hypothetical infidelity have been a focus of several studies conducted in the 1990s. This research suggests that men become more upset by the sexual aspect of a partner's infidelity, whereas women become more upset by the emotional aspect. These gender differences are explained most frequently from an evolutionary perspective (e.g., Buunk, Angleitner, Oubaid, & Buss, 1996). In the aggregate, however, it appears that marital satisfaction is rarely affected by the threat of extramarital sex. For example, in their national study of married individuals, Edwards and Booth (1994) reported that only about 5 percent of the sample reported that extramarital sex caused a problem in their marriage. However, those who perceived it as a problem were more likely to be dissatisfied in their marriage.

Although laypersons and family scholars alike might not agree on the extent to which extramarital sex is a social problem, most can agree that forced sex in marriage or other committed relationships is indeed a problem and a dark side to human sexuality. We discuss sexual assault and coercion in marriage next.

Husbands' Sexual Assault and Coercion of Wives

In spite of important foundational studies in the 1980s (e.g. Finkelhor & Yllo, 1985; Russell, 1982), husbands' sexual assault and coercion of their wives remains one of the most understudied areas of marriage and sexuality. Perhaps this reflects society's struggle with accepting that sexual assault in marriage actually occurs. The American Law Institute's Model Penal Code recommends exempting spouses from sexual assault laws (Poser & Silbaugh, 1996). Four states follow this recommendation by exempting spouses from sexual assault statutes if a married couple co-resides. In addition, many states' statutes allow spouses partial exemptions from their sexual assault laws when a spouse is mentally incapacitated or disabled or, in one state, no penetration occurs.

Knowledge about the exact prevalence of marital sexual assault and coercion remains elusive. Laumann et al. (1994), in their national survey, asked women whether they had been "forced to do something sexual they did not want to" (p. 334). Twenty-two percent of the women had been sexually forced by a man and in 9 percent of these cases the women referred to a spouse. Extrapolating from these percentages suggests a rate of 2 percent for married women, although the wording of this item is at best a rough indicator of sexual assault, a problem readily acknowledged by the investigators. The 2 percent rate is notably lower than the marital rape rates of 10 percent (Finkelhor & Yllo, 1985) and 14 percent (Russell, 1982) found in earlier investigations that used area-probability samples and more exact measures.

Knowledge about the marital dynamics associated with sexual coercion and assault in marriage remained equally elusive. Using the first wave of NSFH data, DeMaris (1997) found that the monthly sexual frequency of couples with violent husbands was 2.5 times higher than that for couples with nonviolent husbands, when controlling for other factors. Based on previous findings of an overlap between husbands' physical and sexual abuse of their wives, DeMaris hypothesized that violent husbands sexually coerced their wives into this higher frequency of sexual activity. Unfortunately, the data set contained no direct measures of sexual coercion, although indirect measures provided some support for his hypothesis. Additional work with Swinford (DeMaris & Swinford, 1996) using the National Family Violence Survey also provided partial support for the hypothesis. DeMaris and Swinford's analyses revealed that husbands' previous attempted or completed rapes of their spouses significantly predicted wives' fear of being hit. Hence, husbands' sexual and physical violence co-occur in some marriages. DeMaris (1997) provides insights into these wives' mental states; couples' coital frequency was positively related to wives' depression if husbands were violent, or, in instances where both spouses were violent, if wives but not husbands suffered physical injuries.

The lack of empirical and theoretical attention to sexual assault and coercion in marriage in the 1990s is striking. Work in the 1980s that combined qualitative and quantitative methods painted compelling and vivid pictures of patriarchal terrorism (see Johnson, 1995, for a definition) and of the long-term effects of these women's experiences (e.g., Finkelhor & Yllo, 1985; Russell, 1982). The role of social, familial, couple, and individual factors in sexual coercion and assault in marriage is unclear at this time. Moreover, investigations have centered primarily on wives and have excluded husbands' reports. We echo the call of others in noting the great need for scholarly attention to this area.

Research also documents that forced sex occurs in other committed relationships, including gay and lesbian relationships (e.g., Waldner-Haugrud & Gratch, 1997). The more positive aspects of sex in gay and lesbian relationships, however, will be discussed next.

Sex in Gay and Lesbian Committed Relationships

Although considerable research was done in the past decade on the sexual behavior of homosexuals, particularly gay men, the focus of most of this research was on risky versus safe-sex behavior (e.g., Barrett, Bolan, & Douglas, 1998). Very little research focused on sexuality in committed, long-term homosexual relationships. Furthermore, the national probability studies conducted on sexuality (e.g., Laumann et al.'s [1994] NHSLS) did not include enough homosexual participants to systematically analyze their results separately. Thus, the Blumstein and Schwartz (1983) study from the 1980s continues to be the most extensive study on the sexuality of gay and lesbian couples to date.

The research that did include gay and lesbian samples and a focus on sex in a relational context (e.g., Deenen, Gijs, & van Naerssen, 1994; Kurdek, 1991; Lever, 1995) suggests that sexuality in committed lesbian and gay relationships is similar to sexuality in heterosexual married couples. For example, Kurdek (1991) found no differences in sexual satisfaction across four types of couples: gay, lesbian, heterosexual cohabiting, and heterosexual married. He also found that in all four couple types, sexual satisfaction was associated with general relationship satisfaction. Lesbian couples might have sex slightly less often than women in heterosexual marriages (Lever, 1995), and gay couples might have sex slightly more often than other couples, at least early in the relationship. However, sexual frequency declines with relationship duration in lesbian and gay relationships, just as it does among heterosexual married couples. One characteristic that continues to distinguish gay male couples from both heterosexual married couples and lesbian couples is their higher rates and acceptance of nonmonogamy (Kurdek, 1991).

The reliance on volunteer samples, including magazine surveys (e.g., Lever, 1995), for data on sexuality in committed gay and lesbian couples is problematic because sexuality in couples open about their sexual orientation might differ from those who are less public. National probability samples have oversampled for other groups in society with small populations (e.g., Blacks, Hispanics, certain religious groups) and then allowed for a weight adjustment based on probability of selection when the data are analyzed in the aggregate; future national studies could also oversample homosexual couples. In addition, studies of married couples should not automatically exclude committed gay and lesbian couples simply because they do not have a legal tie. Realistically, however, it can be expected that most of the research on sex in gay and lesbian relationships will continue to rely on nonprobability samples. We encourage such research because it is through the accumulation of such findings that we can build a knowledge base about the role of sexuality in committed gay and lesbian relationships.

Sexuality in Dating Relationships

General Trends in Sexual Behavior and Attitudes in Dating

Then-current and representative studies in the 1990s attested to a striking shift in coital incidence of adolescents during this decade. Four cross-sectional, national probability samples of high school students from the Youth Risk Behavior Survey, collected between 1991 and 1997, showed an 11 percent increase in the incidence of virgin adolescents (Centers for Disease Control and Prevention, 1998). Change was not uniform; male but not female youths, and White and Black but not Hispanic youths contributed to this increase. This represents a significant reversal from the higher incidence of nonvirginity among adolescents during the 1970s and 1980s.

Such decreases in coital experiences were not evident for the single adult population. Analysis of the National Survey of Men ages 20–39 indicated that 88 percent of never-married men were coitally experienced (Billy et al., 1993). When investigators asked about the previous 1.5 years, most of these men had a single coital partner, but 18.3 percent had four or more partners. Laumann and colleagues (1994) reported similar findings. When they queried never-married men ages 18–29 about the previous 12 months, they found that 40.7 percent had one partner, 30.5 percent had two to four partners, and 14.2 percent had five or more.

Comparable findings were reported for women. Tanfer and Cubbins' (1992) use of the National Survey of Unwed Women (NSUW) ages 20–29 showed that 80.75 percent were nonvirgins. Seidman, Mosher, and Aral's (1992) examination of the 1988–1996 GSS data indicated that 7.9 percent of never-married women ages 15–44 had two or more partners over a 3-month period. Using a 12-month period, Laumann and colleagues (1994) reported that 56.6 percent of never-married women ages 18–29 had one partner, 24.2 percent had two to four partners, and 6.2 percent had five or more. Taken together, these findings from multiple sources suggest that young, single, adult men and women continue to be sexually active. Possibly this is an outgrowth of the delay in marriage that characterizes this age cohort (U.S. Bureau of the Census, 1988), combined with the overall acceptance of engaging in sex before marriage (Smith, 1994a).

In light of this coital activity, some scholars have investigated predictors of having multiple intercourse partners. Bogaert and Fisher's (1995) smaller scale study suggests age, hypermasculinity, sensation seeking, and testosterone levels are associated positively with men's experiences of high numbers of coital partners. Youthful coital experiences and low levels of religiosity predicted number of partners for Black and White women, and living in a major city was an additional and positive predictor for Whites (Seidman et al., 1992).

Other scholars have examined predictors of coital frequency among unmarried young adults. Analysis of the 1983 NSUW data demonstrated that single Black and White women engaged in coitus more frequently if they experienced early onset of coitus, were in a relationship, and were protected from pregnancy (Tanfer & Cubbins, 1992). Living independently, not being religious, and being in the early stages of dating additionally predicted coital frequency for White women. Comparable analyses were unavailable for single men and represent a well-defined gap in our knowledge.

As in much research from previous decades, a general correspondence continued to be found between the coital activity of singles and societal attitudes about sex before marriage (Roche & Ramsbey, 1993; Smith, 1994b). Using data from the 1972–1991 GSS, Smith (1994b) notes fewer respondents have rated sexual relations before marriage as always wrong, and more have rated them as not wrong at all, in recent as compared to earlier years. Smith interpreted these changes as a shift towards being morally neutral about engaging in coitus prior to marriage. Nonetheless, Smith demonstrated that societal approval of premarital sexual relationships has generally remained stable since 1982. Since 1982, roughly 38 percent of respondents have rated sex before marriage as not wrong at all, with an approximate 23 percent seeing it as only sometimes wrong. Smith found that predictors of such sexual permissiveness paralleled pre-1990s findings. Multivariate tests revealed that greater acceptance corresponded most strongly with low religiosity, with not having teens in the household, and with being young, politically liberal, Black, male, single (Smith, 1994b). Roche and Ramsbey's (1993) more limited study does show, however, that young adults' sexual permissiveness for dating varies with the commitment level of those involved; higher levels of dating commitment coincide with greater approval for engaging in sexual intercourse. Sprecher and Hatfield (1996) found similar results.

Although these findings collectively demonstrate that most never-married young adults accepted premarital coitus and were sexually active, they concurrently demonstrate that some young adults remain virgins. There are at least four groups of reasons, derived from factor analysis, for this choice (Sprecher & Regan, 1996): (1) not experiencing enough love, (2) feeling fearful (of AIDS, STDs, pregnancy), (3) holding beliefs supportive of virginity, and (4) feeling inadequate or insecure. Women

rate the first three of these as more important than men do; the reverse holds for the final group of reasons.

Empirically scrutinizing the general trends in singles' coital behavior and sexual attitudes highlighted in this section continues to be important in light of these variables' association with the increased incidence of STDs such as chlamydia and AIDS among single heterosexuals. Aside from this compelling need, however, this research additionally points to ethnic differences that are not well understood. Researchers typically investigate ethnicity either by making comparisons across ethnic groups or by calculating separate models for each ethnic group. Although these practices increase our knowledge about the similarities among ethnic groups and uniqueness within them, scholars have yet to grapple with the larger question of why ethnic subcultures approach sexuality before marriage uniquely. Measuring ethnicity by using categorical variables fails to capture the richness and complexity that is inherent in ethnicity as a variable. The time is ripe for scholars to take a more comprehensive, possibly qualitative look at the relationship between ethnicity and sexuality, rather than simply to continue documenting commonalties and differences.

Besides ethnic influences, investigations in the last decade revealed that relationship and sexual experiences are often interrelated. We review the findings in this area in the next section.

Sexuality and Dating Relationship Experiences

The 1990s witnessed scholars' increased recognition that sexual and relational experiences covary in myriad ways. This recognition translated into different empirical foci. Issues of sexual influence and consent, including initiating sexual involvement, sexual resistance, and complying with a partner's sexual wishes, constituted one empirical focus. For instance, Greer and Buss (1994) identified sexual initiation tactics that men and women perceived were effective and were commonly used. There was considerable overlap in the tactics men and women used and had used on them, including the tactics of implying commitment, increasing attention, and displaying status cues. Men initiated sexual activity more frequently than women, although no gender difference appeared to exist in how frequently men and women considered initiating sex (O'Sullivan & Byers, 1992). There were more frequent sexual initiations in steady as compared to less committed dating relationships, and these initiations involved both indirect verbal messages and nonverbal behaviors for both men and women.

Some investigations of sexual compliance focused on singles who consent to unwanted sexual acts without sexual coercion or aggression. Women most often comply unwillingly with partners' sexual wishes as a form of relationship maintenance (O'Sullivan & Gaines, 1998). In later dating stages, compliant women did not want to disappoint their partners or risk damaging the relationship. Men resist their partners' sexual initiations at times. In fact, examinations of women's attempts to influence reluctant male partners found these to be common experiences, especially in steady dating relationships (O'Sullivan & Byers, 1993). In such instances, men more than women offered the inappropriateness of the relationship as the reason for their reluctance, whereas women more than men identified problems with the time or place.

Scholars have additionally focused on token resistance, as when individuals say "no" but mean "yes" to intercourse. Sprecher, Hatfield, Cortese, Potapova, and Levitskaya (1994) sampled college students in the United States, Russia, and Japan and found that the U.S. samples had the lowest incidence of token resistance among nonvirgins. Gender comparisons that included virgins and nonvirgins revealed that more men than women engaged in token resistance; comparisons within nonvirgins only revealed no gender differences. O'Sullivan and Allgeier (1994) asked singles why they used token resistance, and found that the most frequently offered reasons reflected emotional, relational, and practical concerns. Only a small minority of individuals offered control or game-playing reasons for their actions. Token resistance might also be a sign of ambiguity in coital decision making. Shotland and Hunter (1995) revealed that the use of token resistance was more prevalent among women who had previously engaged in co-. itus with their partners and might have involved women changing their coital intentions from "no" to "yes" over the course of a date. Such ambivalence about engaging in coitus is often associated with more general concerns about the relationship (O'Sullivan & Gaines, 1998).

This collection of studies demonstrates that issues of influence and sexual consent are complex. Although the use of force by a dyad partner is a clear index of sexual aggression, it is not always clear whether the lack of forceful influence by one dating partner corresponds with the other partner's willing consent to engage in sexual activity. Given that initiations and consent usually involve nonverbal signals, opportunities for miscommunication that can affect the relationship exist. Hence, it is important to continue this line of research into the next decade. Operationalizing variables of influence and consent, however, must be done carefully. For instance, Muehlenhard and Rogers' (1998) recent work demonstrates the need to provide respondents with multiple memory cues, such as asking about incidents with current and past partners, when measuring token resistance. Similarly, O'Sullivan and Allgeier's (1998) careful conceptualization and operationalization of sexual consent demonstrates the importance of differentiating undesired from nonconsensual sexual involvement.

Another research focus during the 1990s centered on motivations, and beliefs about motivations, for sexual expression for singles. Hill and Preston's (1996) examination of motivations for engaging in coitus revealed that feeling nurturing towards one's partner, emotionally valuing one's partner, and experiencing pleasure all predicted individuals' engagement in vaginal, oral, and anal intercourse. Emotionally valuing a partner, however, motivated women more than men to engage in coitus. Women's sexual motivations might be important for predicting sexual involvement for dating couples. Cohen and Shotland (1996) found the concordance between individuals' sexual expectations and actual experiences holds more strongly for women than for men. Thus women's desire to pair emotional and sexual experiences played a more direct role in couples' sexual interactions. Research has consistently shown such a gender difference across pre-1990s studies, so it is not surprising that Oliver and Hyde's (1993) meta-analysis found women less accepting of casual sex than men.

Findings that women link their relationship experiences with their sexual expression resonates with young adults' belief that single women's sexual desire is keyed by professing love and that women's sexuality is strongly related to their relationship experiences (Regan, 1997; Regan & Berscheid, 1995). Women's sexuality, however, might actually be more complicated than this. In a series of studies, Cyranowski and Andersen (1998; Andersen & Cyranowski, 1994) showed that young women's sexual schemas, or self views, include not only estimations of how romantic and passionate they are—clear indicants of relational experiences—but also self judgments about how sexually open and direct or how embarrassed and sexually conservative they are.

Additional work points to a range of relationship properties that are related to different facets of couples' sexuality. Regan and Berscheid (1999) combined previous conceptualizations of love with empirical evidence to argue that sexual desire is a component of romantic love and that sexual desire is popularly perceived to be part of the experience of being in love. Long, Cate, Fehsenfeld, and Williams

(1996) found sexual conflict related negatively to sexual and relationship satisfaction and positively to dyadic conflict and feelings of obligation to engage in intercourse. Byers and colleagues (1998) found dating individuals' sexual satisfaction strongly related to their relationship satisfaction, as was perceived equality of sexual costs and comparisons of sexual rewards to such costs. Lally and Maddock (1994) proposed that the meaning couples assign to their sexual involvement (i.e., affection, communication, recreation or play) is important. They showed that engaged couples were more apt to develop a joint meaning when those couples cohabited, had attained higher education levels, had the same religious affiliation, and agreed on family planning options.

Although the above investigations focused on relationship experiences that either preceded or were concurrent with sexual involvement, other investigations during this decade explored the effects of sexual involvement on short- and long-term relationship outcomes. For instance, Cate, Long, Angera, and Draper (1993) examined the impact of first coitus in a dating relationship on later relational development. Relationships improved for men and women when relationship quality played a role in coital decision making and when they were sexually satisfied. Being sexually permissive was an additional predictor of improved relationship quality for men. Other investigators looked beyond dating to consider outcomes of sexuality in family and marriage. Using data on women from the 1982 National Survey of Family Growth (NSFG), Miller and Heaton (1991) examined the relationship between age at first coitus and the later timing of marriage and childbirth. They showed that after controlling for other factors, early onset of coitus among adolescents corresponded with earlier age at forming a family and with an increased probability that the family would begin with childbirth—as opposed to marriage. Finally, Kahn and London (1991) queried whether engaging in premarital sexual intercourse would put women at risk for divorce. Using White respondents from the 1988 NSFG data, and controlling for other factors, they revealed that women who were virgins at marriage were less likely to be separated or divorced than nonvirgins 10 years into marriage. This difference disappeared when potential differences between virgins and nonvirgins were taken into account (mother's education, strictness of rules, and religiosity at age 14). Kahn and London speculated that women who are virgins at marriage might find divorce less acceptable than would women who are nonvirgins, although this hypothesis could not be directly tested with the data.

These findings extend the previous body of research in this area (see Sprecher & McKinney, 1993, for a review) by illustrating different ways in which sexuality is intertwined with relational experiences for singles and ways in which premarital sexual experiences potentially influence marital and familial experiences. For instance, these studies reveal that singles' relationship satisfaction is associated with a number of sexually related variables. There is a need, however, to develop theory-based models for how sexual cognitions, evaluations, and interactions are intertwined with the relationship dynamics for dating individuals. Byers and colleagues (1998) take important steps in this direction with their use of social-exchange theory, but more comprehensive models are needed.

Sexual Coercion and Aggression in Dating

Scholarly interest in sexual coercion and aggression in dating flourished during the 1990s. The corpus of work developed to the point where a number of general reviews and critiques were written (i.e. Koss & Cleveland, 1997; Marx, Van We, & Gross, 1996), and midlevel theoretical models were proposed (Byers, 1996; Malamuth, 1998; Thornhill & Thornhill, 1992). Space limitations prevent us from reviewing all advances in this area. Instead, we highlight new research directions generally not included in previous reviews.

The first of these areas reflects early experiences with and influences on sexual coercion. Evidence continued to accumulate that some adolescents fall victim to sexual coercion (Erickson & Rapkin, 1991; Jordan, Price, Telljohann, & Chesney, 1998). Sexually coerced teens were more sexually active, had poorer peer relationships, and had more same-sex friends who also were sexually active than those who had not suffered coercion (Vicary, Klingaman, & Harkness, 1995). Those who experienced unwanted coitus also were older, experienced less parental monitoring and more parental sexual abuse, and conformed more to peers (Small & Kerns, 1993). A number of investigations pointed to the role that early developmental influences play in later acts of sexual coercion. These include experiences of family violence (Dean & Malamuth, 1997), early history of behavior problems (Lalumiere & Quinsey, 1996), and delinquency (Calhoun, Bernat, Clum, & Frame, 1997).

A second new area of research further illuminated the role that dating experiences play in men's sexual coercion. Sexually coercive men, when compared to noncoercive men, were more apt to endorse a Ludic love style—a style characterized by a noncommittal, manipulative, game-playing approach to love (Kalichman at al., 1993). They experienced conflict and ambivalence with their coerced partners; experiences that directly predicted their acts of sexual coercion (Christopher, Madura, & Weaver, 1998; Christopher, Owens, & Stecker, 1993a). Such men might also lack skills for communicating well in a relationship. Based on responses to videotapes in which women respond in a variety of ways to a man's sexual advances, Malmuth and Brown (1994) suggest that sexually coercive men use cognitive schemas that discount the truthfulness of women's rejection messages. Hence, sexually coercive men might have a propensity to inaccurately decode women's sexual rejections.

Research evidence also reveals that sexually coercive men are different from noncoercive men in their approach to relationships and sexuality. They date more frequently (Byers & Eno, 1991), begin sexual activity at an early age (Malamuth et al., 1995), and have high numbers of sexual partners (Christopher et al., 1993a, 1993b; Lalumiere, Chalmers, Quinsey, & Seto, 1996), especially in uncommitted dating relationships (Lalumeire & Quinsey, 1996). They also prefer novel and casual sexual encounters (Lalumeire et al., 1996). Koss and Cleveland (1997), in reviewing such findings, speculate that sexually coercive men take a predatory approach to their sexual interactions with women.

Finally, a limited number of investigators in the 1990s focused on female-initiated sexual coercion. Studies comparing single women's and single men's coercion experiences reveal that fewer women are sexually coercive; and when women are coercive, they use less forceful techniques (Christopher et al., 1998). Moreover, when men are victims of coercion, they experience less and shorter term emotional upset as a consequence of their experiences, than women (O'Sullivan, Byers, & Finkelman, 1998). These results must be interpreted carefully, because few men in these studies experienced violent sexual aggression. Comparing men who experienced no coercion to those who experienced pressure or violence reveals that men who experienced violent sexual coercion were angrier and more depressed than men in the other two groups (Zweig, Barber, & Eccles, 1997). Examination of the sexual outcomes of coercive acts showed that men's experiences with being coerced most often do not advance beyond kissing or fondling whereas women's experiences most often result in intercourse (Waldner-Haugrud & Magruder, 1995).

Attempts to identify correlates of female-initiated sexual coercion revealed that women who use coercion see themselves as more open, and rate themselves higher in self-esteem and in relation-

ship satisfaction, than female victims of coercion (Busby & Compton, 1997). They also feel hostile towards men, possess a brooding anger, have a history of being sexually coercive, and experience relational conflict with and ambivalence about their coerced partners (Christopher et al., 1993b; Christopher et al., 1998).

Of the new research directions we have highlighted, two are particularly noteworthy. First, the corpus of our knowledge about sexual coercion and aggression in dating relationships is largely limited to what occurs among college students. Sampling from early- and middle-adolescent populations represents an important first step in breaking out of this limitation. The next decade should see an expansion of investigations into the more general single adult population. Second, research to date has focused primarily on individual-level predictors of sexual aggression. We are encouraged that investigators have tested models that additionally included relational (e.g., conflict) and social (e.g., peer association) variables (Christopher et al., 1998). Such integrated approaches will likely continue to prove useful in advancing our understanding of this phenomenon.

Future Directions

Throughout this review, we have suggested possible areas for research in the coming decade. In closing, we want to highlight three directions that hold heuristic promise and represent important next steps in the study of sexuality.

We identified new and noteworthy findings about marital sexuality in this review. More is known about sexuality in marriage at this time than has ever been true in the past. Yet we still have only a limited view of how sexuality is integrated into the normal flow of married life—how it influences and is influenced by other marital phenomena. Thus there exist several viable research questions for the coming decade. Does sexuality play a role in maintaining marital relationships? Does it contribute to couples' commitment or to family cohesion? How is sexuality related to dyadic conflict? How do married couples communicate about their sexuality, and does this communication play a role in relationship functioning? Addressing these and similar questions will provide a better understanding of sexual expression in its most socially approved context.

This review additionally attests that research that includes close relationship and sexuality constructs provides useful insights into sexual phenomena. Sexual interaction takes place in a dyadic context, so it should not be surprising that relational and sexual variables co-vary. To date, however, this developing literature suffers limitations common to many fields, including small samples that disproportionately represent college students, cross-sectional designs, and a high number of atheoretical investigations. Nonetheless, the findings generated from these empirical efforts are intriguing and should be investigated further, albeit with better designed investigations. We encourage sexuality researchers in the coming decade to include relational constructs in their investigations while simultaneously addressing current shortcomings.

Finally, the 1990s saw theoretical and methodological advances in the study of sexuality. Although the advances in theory were moderate, important foundational and exemplary work now exists (Weis, 1998). Methodological advances were more robust and included insights into survey design and the increased use of national data sets. We end our review with the perennial but necessary comment of other reviewers of social science advances. We encourage sexuality researchers to build from these advances. We encourage the increased use of theory, probability sampling, and longitudinal designs. Incorporating these advances into new research in the coming decade will allow researchers to test causal models that more accurately reflect complex influences on sexual expression and will thereby extend our understanding of sexuality in close relationships.

References

Andersen, B. L., & Cryanowski, J. M. (1994). Women's sexual self-schema. *Journal of Personality and Social Psychology, 67,* 1079–1100.

Bancroft, J. (Ed.) (1997). *Researching sexual behavior: Methodological issues.* Bloomington, IN: Indiana University Press.

Barrett, D. C., Bolan, G., & Douglas, J. M., Jr. (1998). Redefining gay male anal intercourse behaviors: Implications for HIV prevention and research. *The Journal of Sex Research, 35,* 381–389.

Berscheid, E., & Reiss, H. T. (1998). Attraction and close relationships. In D. R. Gilbert, S. T. Fisk, & G. Lindzey (Eds.), *The handbook of social psychology* (Vol. 2, 4th ed., pp. 196–281). New York: McGrawHill.

Billy, J. O. G., Tanfer, K., Grady, W. R., & Klepinger, D. H. (1993). The sexual behavior of men in the United States. *Family Planning Perspectives, 25,* 52–60.

Binik, Y. M., Mah, K., & Kiesler, S. (1999). Ethical issues in conducting sex research on the internet. *The Journal of Sex Research, 26,* 82–90.

Blumstein, P., & Schwartz, P. (1983). *American couples.* New York: William Morrow.

Bogaert, A. F., & Fisher, W. A. (1995). Predictors of university men's number of sexual partners. *The Journal of Sex Research, 32,* 119–130.

Bringle, R. G., & Buunk, B. E. (1991). Extradyadic relationships and sexual jealousy. In K. McKinney & S. Sprecher (Eds.), *Sexuality in close relationships* (pp. 135–153). Hillsdale, NJ: Erlbaum.

Busby, D. M., & Compton, S. V. (1997). Patterns of sexual coercion in adult heterosexual relationships: An exploration of male victimization. *Family Process, 36,* 81–94.

Buss, D. M. (1998). Sexual strategies theory: Historical origins and current status. *The Journal of Sex Research, 35,* 19–31.

Buss, D. M., Larsen, R., Westen, D., & Semmelroth, J. (1992). Sex differences in jealousy: Evolution, physiology, and psychology. *Psychological Science, 3,* 251–255.

Buunk, B., Angleitner, A., Oubaid, V., & Buss, D. (1996). Sex differences in jealousy in evolutionary and cultural perspectives: Tests from the Netherlands, Germany, and the United States. *Psychological Science, 7,* 359–363.

Byers, E. S. (1996). How well does the traditional sexual script explain sexual coercion? Review of a program of research. *Journal of Psychology & Human Sexuality, 8,* 7–25.

Byers, E. S., & Demmons, S. (1999). Sexual satisfaction and sexual self-disclosure within dating relationships. *The Journal of Sex Research, 36,* 180–189.

Byers, E. S., Demmons, S., & Lawrance, K. (1998). Sexual satisfaction within dating relationships: A test of the interpersonal exchange model of sexual satisfaction. *Journal of Social and Personal Relationships, 15,* 257–267.

Byers, E. S., & Eno, R. J. (1991). Predicting men's sexual coercion and aggression from attitudes, dating history, and sexual response. *Journal of Psychology and Human Sexuality, 4,* 55–70.

Calhoun, K. S., Bernat, J. A., Clum, G. A., & Frame, C. L. (1997). Sexual coercion and attraction to sexual aggression in a community sample of young men. *Journal of Interpersonal Violence, 12,* 392–406.

Call, V., Sprecher, S., & Schwartz, P. (1995). The incidence and frequency of marital sex in a national sample. *Journal of Marriage and the Family, 57,* 639–650.

——. (1996, November). Changes over time in the incidence and frequency of marital sex: Longitudinal data from a U.S. National Sample. Paper presented at the National Council on Family Relations. Portland, OR.

Catania, J. A. (1999a). A comment on advancing the frontiers of sexological methods. *The Journal of Sex Research, 36,* 1–2.

——. (1999b). A framework for conceptualizing reporting bias and its antecendents in interviews assessing human sexuality. *The Journal of Sex Research, 36,* 25–38.

Cate, R. M., Long, E., Angera, J. J., & Draper, K. K. (1993). Sexual intercourse and relationship development. *Family Relations, 42,* 158–164.

Centers for Disease Control and Prevention. (1998, September 18). Trends in sexual risk behaviors among high school students—United States, 1991–1997. *Morbidity and Mortality Weekly Report [Online] 47*, 749–751. Available: http://www.cdc.gov/epo/mmwr/preview/mmwrhtml/00054814.htm

Choi, K., Catania, J. A., & Dolcini, M. M. (1994). Extramarital sex and HIV risk behavior among US adults: Results from the national AIDS behavioral survey. *American Journal of Public Health, 84*, 2003–2007.

Christopher, F. S., Madura, M., & Weaver, L. (1998). Premarital sexual aggressors: A multivariate analysis of social, relational, and individual variables. *Journal of Marriage and the Family, 60*, 56–69.

Christopher, F. S., Owens, L. A., & Stecker, H. L. (1993a). Exploring the dark side of courtship: A test model of male premarital sexual aggressiveness. *Journal of Marriage and the Family, 55*, 469–479.

Cohen, L. L., & Shotland, R. L. (1996). Timing of first sexual intercourse in a relationship: Expectations, experiences, and perceptions of others. *The Journal of Sex Research, 33*, 291–299.

Cupach, W. R., & Comstock, J. (1990). Satisfaction with sexual communication in marriage. Links to sexual satisfaction and dyadic adjustment. *Journal of Social and Personal Relationships, 7*, 179–186.

Cyranowski, J. M., & Andersen, B. L. (1998). Schemas, sexuality, and romantic attachment. *Journal of Personality and Social Psychology, 74*, 1364–1379.

Davidson, J. K., Sr., Darling, C. A., & Norton, L. (1995). Religiosity and the sexuality of women: Sexual behavior and sexual satisfaction revisited. *The Journal of Sex Research, 32*, 235–243.

Davis, C. M., Yarber, W. L., Bauserman, R., Schreer, G., & Davis, S. L. (Eds.) (1998). *Handbook of sexuality-related measures.* Thousand Oaks, CA: Sage.

Dean, K. E., & Malamuth, N. M. (1997). Characteristics of men who aggress sexually and of men who imagine aggressing: Risk and moderating variables. *Journal of Personality and Social Psychology, 72*, 449–455.

Deenen, A. A., Gijs, L., & van Naerssen, A. X. (1994). Intimacy and sexuality in gay male couples. *Archives of Sexual Behavior, 23*, 421–431.

DeLamater, J. D., & Hyde, J. S. (1998). Essential versus social constructionism in the study of human sexuality. *The Journal of Sex Research, 35*, 10–18.

DeMaris, A. (1997). Elevated sexual activity in violent marriages: Hypersexuality or sexual extortion? *The Journal of Sex Research, 34*, 361–373.

DeMaris, A., & Swinford, S. (1996). Female victims of spousal violence: Factors influencing their level of fearfulness. *Family Relations, 45*, 98–106.

Donnelly, D. A. (1993). Sexually inactive marriages. *The Journal of Sex Research, 30*, 171–179.

Edwards, J. N., & Booth, A. (1994). Sexuality, marriage, and well-being: The middle years. In A. S. Rossi (Ed.), *Sexuality across the life course* (pp. 233–259). Chicago: University of Chicago Press.

Erickson, P. I., & Rapkin, A. (1991). Unwanted sexual experiences among middle and high school youth. *Journal of Adolescent Health, 12*, 319–325.

Fincham, E D., & Bradbury, T. N. (1987). The assessment of marital quality: A reevaluation. *Journal of Marriage and the Family, 49*, 797–809.

Finkelhor, D., & Yllo, K. (1985). *License to rape: Sexual abuse of wives.* New York: Holt, Rinehard & Winston.

Forste, R., & Tanfer, K. (1996). Sexual exclusivity among dating, cohabiting, and married women. *Journal of Marriage and the Family, 58*, 33–47.

Gierveld, J. J. (1995). Research into relationship designs: Personal relationships under the microscope. *Journal of Social and Personal Relationships, 12*, 583–588.

Glass, S. P., & Wright, T. L. (1992). Justifications for extramarital relationships: The association between attitudes, behaviors, and gender. *The Journal of Sex Research, 29*, 361–387.

Greeley, A. M. (1991). *Faithful attraction: Discovering intimacy, love, and fidelity in American marriage.* New York: Doherty.

Greenblat, C. S. (1983). The salience of sexuality in the early years of marriage. *Journal of Marriage and the Family, 45*, 289–299.

Greer, A. E., & Buss, D. M. (1994). Tactics for promoting sexual encounters. *The Journal of Sex Research, 31*, 185–201.

Gribble, J. N., Miller, H. G., Rogers, S. M., & Turner, C. F. (1999). Interview mode and measurement of sexual behaviors: Methodological issues. *The Journal of Sex Research, 36*, 16–24.

Gullotta, T. P., Adams, G. R., & Montemayor, R. (Eds.) (1993). *Adolescent sexuality.* Newbury Park, CA: Sage.

Haavio-Mannila, E., & Kontula, O. (1997). Correlates of increased sexual satisfaction. *Archives of Sexual Behavior, 26*, 399–419.

Henderson-King, D. H., & Veroff, J. (1994). Sexual satisfaction and marital well-being in the first years of marriages. *Journal of Social and Personal Relationships, 11*, 509–534.

Hill, C. A., & Preston, L. K. (1996). Individual differences in the experience of sexual motivation: Theory and measurement of dispositional sexual motives. *The Journal of Sex Research, 33*, 27–45.

Hogben, M., & Byrne, D. (1998): Using social learning theory to explain individual differences in human sexuality. *The Journal of Sex Research, 35*, 58–71.

Huston, T. L., & Vangelisti, A. L. (1991). Socioemotional behavior and satisfaction in marital relationships: A longitudinal study. *Journal of Personality and Social Psychology, 61*, 721–733.

Hyde, J. S., DeLamater, J. D., Plant, E. A., & Byrd, J. M. (1996). Sexuality during pregnancy and the year postpartum. *The Journal of Sex Research, 33*, 143–151.

Johnson, M. P. (1995). Patriarchal terrorism and common couple violence: Two forms of violence against women. *Journal of Marriage and the Family, 57*, 283–294.

Jordan, T. R., Price, J. H., Telljohann, S. K., & Chesney, B. K. (1998). Junior high school students' perceptions regarding nonconsensual sexual behavior. *Journal of School Health, 68*, 289–300.

Jurich, J. A., & Myers-Bowman, K. S. (1998). Systems theory and its application to research on human sexuality. *The Journal of Sex Research, 35,* 72–87.

Kahn, J. R., & London, K. A. (1991). Premarital sex and the risk of divorce. *Journal of Marriage and the Family, 53,* 845–855.

Kalichman, S. C., Sarwer, D. B., Johnson, J. R., Ali, S. A., Early, J., & Tuten, J. T. (1993). Sexually coercive behavior and love styles: A replication and extension. *Journal of Psychology & Human Sexuality, 6,* 93–106.

Kelly, J. A. (1995). Advances in HIV/ADDS education and prevention. *Family Relations, 44,* 345–353.

Kinsey, A. C., Pomeroy, W. B., & Martin, C. E. (1948). *Sexual behavior in the human male.* Philadelphia: Saunders.

Kinsey, A. C., Pomeroy, W. B., Martin, C. E., & Gebhard, P. H. (1953). *Sexual behavior in the human female.* Philadelphia: Saunders.

Koss, M. P., & Cleveland, H. H. (1997). Stepping on toes: Social roots of date rape lead to intractability and politicization. In M. D. Schwartz (Ed.), *Researching sexual violence against women: Methodological and personal perspectives* (pp. 4–21). Thousand Oaks, CA: Sage.

Kurdek, L. A. (1991). Sexuality in homosexual and heterosexual couples. In K. McKinney & S. Sprecher (Eds.), *Sexuality in close relationships* (pp. 177–191). Hillsdale, NJ: Erlbaum.

Lally, C. E., & Maddock, J. W. (1994). Sexual meaning systems of engaged couples. *Family Relations, 43,* 53–60.

Lalumiere, M. L., Chalmers, L. J., Quinsey, V. L., & Seto, M. C. (1996). A test of the mate deprivation hypothesis of sexual coercion. *Ethology and Sociobiology, 17,* 299–318.

Lalumiere, M. L., & Quinsey, V. L. (1996). Sexual deviance, antisociality, mating effort, and the use of sexually coercive behaviors. *Personality and Individual Differences, 21,* 34–48.

Laumann, E. O., Gagnon, J. H., Michael, R. T., & Michaels, S. (1994). *The social organization of sexuality: Sexual practices in the United States.* Chicago: University of Chicago Press.

Lawrance, K., & Byers, E. S. (1995). Sexual satisfaction in long-term heterosexual relationships: The interpersonal exchange model of sexual satisfaction. *Personal Relationships, 2,* 267–285.

Lever, J. (1995, August 22). Lesbian sex survey. *The Advocate,* 21–30.

Long, E. C. J., Cate, R. M., Fehsenfeld, D. A., & Williams, K. M. (1996). A longitudinal assessment of a measure of premarital sexual conflict. *Family Relations, 45,* 302–308.

Longmore, M. A. (1998). Symbolic interactionism and the study of sexuality. *The Journal of Sex Research, 35,* 44–57.

Malamuth, N. M. (1998). The confluence model as an organizing framework for research on sexually aggressive men: Risk moderators, imagined aggression, and pornography consumption. In R. G. Geen & E. Donnerstein (Eds.), *Human aggression: Theories, research, and implications for social policy* (pp. 227–245). San Diego, CA: Academic Press.

Malamuth, N. M., & Brown, L. M. (1994). Sexually aggressive men's perceptions of women's communications: Testing three explanations. *Journal of Personality and Social Psychology, 67,* 699–712.

Malamuth, N. M., Lintz, D., Heavey, C. L., Barnes, G., & Acker, M. (1995). Using the confluence model of sexual aggression to predict men's conflict with women: A 10-year follow-up study. *Journal of Personality and Social Psychology, 69,* 353–369.

Marsiglio, W., & Donnelly, D. (1991). Sexual intercourse in later life: A national study of married persons. *Journal of Gerontology, 46,* 338–344.

Marston, P. J., Hecht, M. L., Manke, M. L., McDaniel, S., & Reeder, H. (1998). The subjective experience of intimacy, passion, and commitment in heterosexual loving relationships. *Personal Relationships, 5,* 15–30.

Marx, B. P, Van Wie, V., & Gross, A. M. (1996). Date rape risk factors: A review and methodological critique of the literature. *Aggression and Violent Behavior, 1,* 27–45.

McKinney, K., & Sprecher, S. (Eds.). (1991). *Sexuality in close relationships.* Hillsdale, NJ: Erlbaum.

Michael, R. T., Gagnon, J. H., Laumann, E. O., & Kolata, G. (1994). *Sex in America: A definitive survey.* Boston: Little, Brown.

Miller, B. C., & Heaton, T. B. (1991). Age at first sexual intercourse and the timing of marriage and childbirth. *Journal of Marriage and the Family, 53,* 719–732.

Moore, K. A., Miller, B. C., Glei, D., & Morrison, D. R. (1995). Adolescent sex, contraception, and childbearing: A review of recent research. Washington, DC: *Child Trends.*

Morrison, D. M., Leigh, B. C., & Gillmore, M. R. (1999). Daily data collection: A comparison of three methods. *The Journal of Sex Research, 36,* 76–81.

Muehlenhard, C. L., & Rodgers, C. S. (1998). Token resistance to sex. *Psychology of Women Quarterly, 22,* 443–463.

Oggins, J., Leber, D., & Veroff, J. (1993). Race and gender differences in black and white newlyweds' perceptions of sexual and marital relationships. *The Journal of Sex Research, 30,* 152–160.

Oliver, M. B., & Hyde, J. S. (1993). Gender differences in sexuality: A meta-analysis. *Psychological Bulletin, 114,* 29–51.

O'Sullivan, L. F., & Allgeier, E. R. (1994). Disassembling a stereotype: Gender differences in the use of token resistance. *Journal of Applied Social Psychology, 24,* 1035–1055.

———. (1998). Feigning sexual desire: Consenting to unwanted sexual activity in heterosexual dating relationships. *The Journal of Sex Research, 35,* 234–243.

O'Sullivan, L. F., & Byers, E. S. (1992). College students' incorporation of initiator and restrictor roles in sexual dating interactions. *The Journal of Sex Research, 29,* 435–446.

——. (1993). Eroding stereotypes: College women's attempts to influence reluctant male sexual partners. *The Journal of Sex Research, 30,* 270–282.

O'Sullivan, L. F., Byers, E. S., & Finkelman, L. (1998). A comparison of male and female college students' experiences of sexual coercion. *Psychology of Women Quarterly, 22,* 177–195.

O'Sullivan L. F., & Gaines, M. E. (1998). Decision-making in college students' heterosexual dating relationships: Ambivalence about engaging in sexual activity. *Journal of Social and Personal Relationships, 15,* 347–363.

Posner, R. A., & Silbaugh, K. B. (1996). *A guide to America's sex laws.* Chicago: University of Chicago Press.

Rao, K. V., & DeMaris, A. (1995). Coital frequency among married and cohabiting couples in the U.S. *Journal of Biosocial Science, 27,* 135–150.

Regan, P. C. (1997). The impact of male sexual request style on perceptions of sexual interactions: The mediational role of beliefs about female sexual desire. *Basic and Applied Social Psychology, 19,* 519–532.

Regan, P. C., & Berscheid, E. (1995). Gender differences in beliefs about the causes of male and female sexual desire. *Personal Relationships, 2,* 345–358.

Regan, P. C., & Berscheid, E. (1999). *Lust: What we know about human sexual desire.* Thousand Oaks, CA: Sage.

Renaud, C., Byers, E. S., & Pan, S. (1997). Sexual and relationship satisfaction in mainland China. *The Journal of Sex Research, 34,* 1–12.

Roach, A. J., Frazier, L. P., & Bowden, S. R. (1981). The marital satisfaction scale. *Journal of Marriage and the Family, 40,* 537–546.

Roche, J. P., & Ramsbey, T. W. (1993). Premarital sexuality: A five-year follow-up study of attitudes and behavior by dating stage. *Adolescence, 28,* 67–80.

Russell, D. E. H. (1982). *Rape in marriage.* Bloomington, IN: Indiana University Press.

Seidman, S. N., Mosher, W. D., & Aral, S. O. (1992). Women with multiple sexual partners: United States, 1988. *American Journal of Public Health, 82,* 1388–1394.

Shackelford, T. K., & Buss, D. M. (1997). Anticipation of marital dissolution as a consequence of spousal infidelity. *Journal of Social and Personal Relationships, 14,* 793–808.

Shotland, R. L., & Hunter, B. A. (1995). Women's "token resistant" and compliant sexual behaviors are related to uncertain sexual intentions and rape. *Personality and Social Psychology Bulletin, 21,* 226–236.

Small, S. A., & Kerns, D. (1993). Unwanted sexual activity among peers during early and middle adolescence: Incidence and risk factors. *Journal of Marriage and the Family, 55,* 941–952.

Smith, T. W. (1994a). Attitudes toward sexual permissiveness: Trends, correlates, and behavioral connections. In Rossi, A. S. (Ed.), *Sexuality across the life course* (pp. 63–97). Chicago: University of Chicago Press.

Smith, T. W. (1994b). *The demography of sexual behavior.* Menlo Park, CA: Kaiser Family Foundation.

Spanier, G. B. (1976). Measuring dyadic adjustment. *Journal of Marriage and the Family, 38,* 15–28.

Sponaugle, G. C. (1989). Attitudes toward extramarital relations. In K. McKinney & S. Sprecher (Eds.), *Human sexuality: The societal and interpersonal context* (pp. 187–209). Norwood, NJ: Ablex.

Sprecher, S. (1998). Social exchange theories and sexuality. *The Journal of Sex Research, 35,* 32–43.

Sprecher, S., & Hatfield, E. (1996). Premarital sexual standards among U.S. college students: Comparison with Russian and Japanese students. *Archives of Sexual Behavior, 25,* 261–288.

Sprecher, S., Hatfield, E., Cortese, A., Potapova, E., & Levitskaya, A. (1994). Token resistance to sexual intercourse and consent to unwanted sexual intercourse: College students' dating experiences in three countries. *The Journal of Sex Research, 31,* 125–132.

Sprecher, S., & McKinney, K. (1993). *Sexuality.* Newbury Park, CA: Sage.

Sprecher, S., Metts, S., Burleson, B., Hatfield, E., & Thompson, A. (1995). Domains of expressive interaction in intimate relationships: Associations with satisfaction and commitment. *Family Relations, 44,* 203–210.

Sprecher, S., & Regan, P. C. (1996). College virgins: How men and women perceive their sexual status. *The Journal of Sex Research, 33,* 3–15.

——. (1998). Passionate and companionate love in courting and young married couples. *Sociological Inquiry, 68,* 163–185.

Tanfer, K., & Cubbins, L. A. (1992). Coital frequency among single women: Normative constraints and situational opportunities. *The Journal of Sex Research, 29,* 221–250.

Thompson, A. (1983). Extramarital sex: A review of the research literature. *The Journal of Sex Research, 19,* 1–22.

Thornhill, R., & Thornhill, N. W. (1992). The evolutionary psychology of men's coercive sexuality. *Behavioral and Brain Sciences, 15,* 363–421.

U.S. Bureau of the Census. (1988). Households, families, marital status, and living arrangements: March, 1988 [Advance Report] (Current Population Reports, Series P-20, No. 432). Washington, DC: Governnment Printing Office.

Veroff, J., Douvan, E., & Hatchett, S. J. (1995). *Marital instability: A social and behavioral study of the early years.* Westport, CT: Praeger.

Vicary, J. R., Klingaman, L. R., & Harkness, W. L. (1995). Risk factors associated with date rape and sexual assault of adolescent girls. *Journal of Adolescence, 18,* 289–306.

Waldner-Haugrud, L. K., & Gratch, L. V. (1997). Sexual coercion in gay/lesbian relationships: Descriptives and gender differences. *Violence and Victims, 12,* 87–98.

Waldner-Haugrud, L. K., & Magruder, B. (1995). Male and female sexual victimization in dating relationships: Gender differences in coercion techniques and outcomes. *Violence and Victims, 10,* 203–215.

Weis, D. L. (1998). The use of theory in sexuality research. *The Journal of Sex Research, 35,* 1–9.

White, L., & Keith, B. (1990). The effect of shift work on the quality and stability of marital relations. *Journal of Marriage and the Family, 52,* 453–462.

Wiederman, M. W. (1997). Extramarital sex: Prevalence and correlates in a national survey. *The Journal of Sex Research, 34,* 167–174.

——. (1999). Volunteer bias in sexuality research using college student participants. *The Journal of Sex Research, 36,* 59–66.

Zweig, J. M., Barber, B. L., & Eccles, J. S. (1997). Sexual coercion and well-being in young adulthood. *Journal of Interpersonal Violence, 12,* 291–308.

Part II

Sexuality and the Life Cycle: Childhood and Adolescence

All the world's a stage and all the men and women merely players; They have their exits and their entrances; And one man in his time plays many parts, His acts being seven ages.

—*William Shakespeare*

William Shakespeare is one among many poets, prophets, and priests who have long proclaimed that the essence of life lies in its progression; that as individuals struggle to balance the inevitable intricacies of change and continuity, life is expressed. It was not until the latter part of the twentieth century that the multidisciplinary field of life-span development emerged from the disciplines of child development and developmental psychology. The study of the journey in human sexuality over the life span is the touchstone personally and professionally for those who seek a holistic understanding of sexuality.

Especially for the young, a life-cycle perspective of sexuality can lend continuity in a day characterized by disconnects. When using a life span focus to understand the development of their psychosexual scripts, students may ask different questions that have somewhat surprising answers. For example, they may wonder, Is it possible to predict with whom I will have my longest sexual affair? Without referring to a crystal ball, scientists can answer this question. They can state the following fact with great accuracy: Your longest sexual affair will be with yourself. And, it will last a lifetime.

John DeLamater, a professor of sociology, and William Friedrich, a psychologist, team together to succinctly trace the tempestuous journey of human sexual development in the lead article of Part II. To do this in a coherent way, they divide the sexual life cycle into childhood (birth to 7 years); preadolescence (8 to 12 years); adolescence (13 to 19 years); adulthood; and the period of aging, when adulthood fades into the latter part of life. This last stage occurs anywhere from age 40 to 60 when the periods of menopause for females and andropause for males signal that a fully evident aging process has begun. Because of their professional backgrounds, DeLamater and Friedrich are uniquely qualified to summarize the empirical research about the biological, sociological, and behavioral factors that impact human sexual development throughout life. Information in this chapter provides a needed overview for students of sexuality who are interested in relationships, sexuality, and the life cycle—all issues that are raised in the readings that follow in Parts II, III, and IV.

Robert Francoeur begins with the headwaters of life, the childhood and adolescent years that are significant in the development of psychosexual scripts. As such, they offer watershed opportunities for promoting healthy attitudes and behaviors about sexuality, a central core that touches every aspect of a person's being. But, conversely, when the headwaters are troubled, it is difficult to calm the downstream flow. For this reason, family life-cycle and developmental theorists focus on the importance of the formative years in their efforts to understand human behavior. Defining childhood operationally as any time between infancy and the point at which the individual becomes a sexually mature adult, Francoeur broadens his topic beyond the years that are typically considered to be the childhood years.

His thesis that normative religious doctrines—the attitudes, values, and doctrines endorsed by a culture, society, and parents—are central factors in the psychosexual development throughout one's formative years is hardly debatable. However, what he so richly portrays about this topic will leave readers with an informed awareness of the lack of childhood sexual ethics in most religious traditions.

A neglected research arena is highlighted with an important study by Paul Okami, Richard Olmstead, Paul Abramson, and Laura Pendleton about the long-term effects of early childhood exposure to parental nudity and to the "primal scene." The authors tap into 18 years of longitudinal data from the UCLA Family Lifestyles Project to clarify what some clinicians and child development experts have postulated to be potentially harmful experiences in childhood. A major contribution of this important study is the review of the research literature that reveals a lack of empirical support for such claims.

Particularly those students who bring an awareness of family systems theory to the Okami et al. reading may be puzzled by the authors' assertion that their specific findings were not predicted by any theory with which they were familiar. Nevertheless, readers who understand developmental theory and psychosexual development throughout the formative years, emphasized in the beginning selections, may be better able to formulate questions for future research because of this study. Further, the results of this research may quiet alarmists whose references to phrases like "the emotional incest syndrome," "maternal seductress," and "sexualized attention" feed the paperback tradition of empirically unsubstantiated theories that abound in the popular genre. Then again, perhaps, it will not.

The reporting of research in Pamela Erickson's chapter about Latino adolescent mothers differs significantly from what Journal Editor James Walters has called "endless statistics which accompany endless articles about endless teenage pregnancies." This selection should be of substantial interest to readers specifically because it is a different approach to gathering data; it is based on case studies of life-history interviews with 40 young Latino adolescent mothers and their partners. Such qualitative data in the literature are rare for several reasons. First, interviews are much more time consuming than are other methods of data collection, such as surveys. Second, the paucity of qualitative data in the literature is related to their analysis problems.

Reviewers and editors often claim that "lack of rigor" produces results "too soft" to merit their inclusion in professional journals, an argument that rephrased means there are no "endless statistics" with which to formulate results and conclusions. Although all professionals in the research arena have a responsibility to maintain the highest standards of excellence for self and others in the discipline, students must learn that differences in research methods are not to be mistaken for deficiencies. Instead, embracing the diversity in methods of research so aptly demonstrated by Erickson in this chapter affirms the mutual quest for excellence, an important lesson for future researchers as well as those who are consumers of research. ✦

Chapter 8
Human Sexual Development

John D. DeLamater
William N. Friedrich

Have you checked your sexual health today? The issue of sexual health just might be the unspoken agenda of this selection by DeLamater and Friedrich, an important work that describes the stages in the human sexual development process. In the absence of an instant sexual-health meter, we are left to our own devices in assessing how we are doing on this front. In actuality, a thorough check-up would follow a somewhat circuitous route that along the way must consider our sexual gender, sexual identity, sexual attitudes, and sexual behavior. Not only are all of these factors shaping forces, but more important, our subjective feelings about them may be the most significant markers of our sexual health.

By university age, most peoples' gender and sexual identities are fully formed and, thus, can be more objectively observed than can their sexual attitudes and behavior be assessed. As you read the developmental tasks that are to be achieved in childhood, preadolescence, adolescence, adulthood, and later life, ask yourself How am I doing thus far? In reading about the childhood years, for example, several questions may occur to you. At what childhood age did I become aware that cultural norms prohibited freedom of sexual play? Who was important to me in the formation of my gender identity, or in my sense of femaleness or maleness? At what age did I begin to be socialized to the gender-role norms of society, learning how females and males are expected to behave? Are there specific sexual experiences from my childhood that are guilt-inducing? And if so, how have they influenced my adult life? Certainly, a thorough reading of this article will contribute to your understanding of human sexual development. But, on a more personal note, it could also lead to insight that would illuminate one of the most important journeys you will ever take with yourself: enhanced sexual health.

Empirical research by scholars from several disciplines provides the basis for an outline of the process of sexual development. The process of achieving sexual maturity begins at conception and ends at death. It is influenced by biological maturation/aging, by progression through the socially-defined stages of childhood, adolescence, adulthood, and later life, and by the person's relationships with others, including family members, intimate partners, and friends. These forces shape the person's gender and sexual identities, sexual attitudes, and sexual behavior. Adults display their sexuality in a variety of lifestyles, with heterosexual marriage being the most common. This diversity contributes to the vitality of society. Although changes in sexual functioning in later life are common, sexual interest and desire may continue until death.

Human beings are sexual beings throughout their entire lives. At certain points in life, sexuality may manifest itself in different ways. Each life stage brings with it pressures for change and sexual development milestones to be achieved if sexual health is to be attained or maintained. The stages of sexual development are a human developmental process involving biological and behavioral components.

CHILDHOOD
(BIRTH TO 7 YEARS)

The capacity for a sexual response is present from birth. Male infants, for example, get erections, and vaginal lubrication has been found in female infants in the 24 hours after birth (Masters, Johnson, & Kolodny, 1982). Infants have been observed fondling their genitals. The rhythmic manipulation associated with adult masturbation appears at ages 2 1/2 to 3 (Martinson, 1994). This is a natural form of sexual expression (Friedrich, Fisher, Broughton, Houston, & Shafran, 1998). Children engage in a variety of sexual play experiences while very young; this play becomes increasingly covert as the child ages (ages 6 to 9) and becomes aware of cultural norms (Reynolds, Herbenick, & Bancroft, in press). Infants and young children have many other sensual experiences, including sucking on their fingers and toes, and being rocked and cuddled. These experiences may establish preferences for certain kinds of stimulation that persist throughout life.

The quality of relationships with parents is also very important to the child's capacity for sexual and emotional relationships later in life. Typically, an attachment or bond forms between the infant and parent(s) (Bowlby, 1965). It is facilitated by positive physical contact. If this attachment is stable, secure, and satisfying, positive emotional attachments in adulthood are more likely (Goldberg, Muir, Kerr, 1995).

Early childhood is also the period during which each child forms a gender identity, a sense of maleness or femaleness. This identity is typically formed by age 3. The child is simultaneously being socialized according to the gender-role norms of the society, learning how males and females are expected to behave (Bussey & Bandura, 1999).

Between the ages of 3 and 7, there is a marked increase in sexual interest and activity. Children form a concept of marriage or long-term relationships; they practice adult roles as they "play house." They also learn that there are genital differences between males and females (Goldman & Goldman, 1982), and show interest in the genitals of other children and adults as part of their natural curiosity about the world. Children may engage in heterosexual play, including "playing doctor." There is little impact of childhood sex play on sexual adjustment at ages 17 and 18 (Okami, Olmstead, & Abramson, 1997). In response to such play, some parents teach children not to touch the bodies of others, and restrict conversation about sex. As a result, children turn to their peers for information about sex (Martinson, 1994).

PREADOLESCENCE
(8 TO 12 YEARS)

In this period, children have a social organization that is homosocial; that is, the social division of males and females into separate groups (Thorne, 1993). One result of this is that sexual exploration and learning at this stage is likely to involve persons of the same gender.

During this period, more children gain experience with masturbation. About 40 percent of the women and 38 percent of the men in a sample of college students recall masturbating before puberty (Bancroft, Herbenick, & Reynolds, in press). Adolescents report that their first experience of sexual attraction occurred at age 10 to 12 (Bancroft et al., in press; Rosario et al., 1996), with first experience of sexual fantasies occurring several months to 1 year later.

Group dating and heterosexual parties emerge at the end of this period. These experiences begin the process of developing the capacity to sustain intimate relationships.

ADOLESCENCE
(13 TO 19 YEARS)

Biological Development

The biological changes associated with puberty, the time during which there is sudden enlargement and maturation of the gonads, other genitalia, and secondary sex characteristics (Tanner, 1967), lead to a surge of sexual interest. These changes begin as early as 10 years of age to as late as 14 years of age, and include rises in levels of sex hormones, which may produce sexual attraction and fantasies. Bodily changes include physical growth, growth in genitals and girls' breasts, and development of facial and pubic hair. These changes signal to the youth and to others that she or he is becoming sexually mature.

Whereas biological changes, especially increases in testosterone levels, create the possibility of adult sexual interactions, social factors interact with them, either facilitating or inhibiting sexual expression (Udry, 1988). Permissive attitudes regarding sexual behavior and father absence for girls are associated with increased masturbation and heterosexual intercourse, whereas church attendance and long-range educational and career plans are associated with lower levels of sexual activity. Many males begin masturbating between ages 13 and 15, whereas the onset among females is more gradual (Bancroft et al., in press).

Sexual Behavior

Toward the middle and end of adolescence, more young people engage in heterosexual intercourse: In 1999, 48 percent of females and 52 percent of males in grades 9 to 12 reported engaging in intercourse (CDC, 2000). Women today are engaging in intercourse for the first time at younger ages, compared with young women 30 years ago (Trussell & Vaughn, 1991). Patterns of premarital intercourse vary by ethnic group. African Americans have sex for the first time, on average, at 15.5 years; Cuban Americans and Puerto Ricans at 16.6 years, and Mexican Americans and Whites at 17 years; in each group, men begin having intercourse at younger ages than women (Day, 1992). These variations reflect differences between these groups in family structure (intact family), church attendance, and socioeconomic opportunities (parents' education, neighborhood employment rates).

These rates of premarital heterosexual intercourse are connected to two long-term trends. First, the age of menarche has been falling steadily since the beginning of the twentieth century. The average age today is 12.5 years for Blacks and 12.7 years for Whites (Hofferth, 1990). Second, the age of first marriage has been rising—in 1960, first marriages occurred at age 20.8 for women and 22.8 for men; in 1998, it was 25 for women and 26.7 for men (U.S. Bureau of the Census, 1999). The effect is a substantial lengthening of the time between biological readiness and marriage; the gap is typically 12 to 14 years today. Thus, many more young people are having sex before they get married than in 1960. Since many do not consistently use birth control, there was a corresponding rise in the rate of pregnancy among single adolescents from the 1970s to 1991; however, from 1991 to 1997 the rate of teen pregnancy declined 18 percent. This decline reflects increased attention in society to the importance of pregnancy prevention, increased access for teens to birth control, and increased economic opportunities for teenagers (Ventura, Mosher, Curtin, Abma, & Henshaw, 1998).

Between 5 percent and 10 percent of adolescent males report having sexual experiences with someone of the same gender, compared with 6 percent of adolescent females (Bancroft et al., in press; Turner et al., 1998). These adolescents usually report that their first experience was with another adolescent. In some cases the person has only one or a few such experiences, partly out of curiosity, and the behavior is discontinued.

Developmental Tasks

Several psychosocial developmental tasks face adolescents. One is resolving the conflict between identity and role confusion, developing a stable sense of who one is in the midst of conflicting social influences (Erikson, 1968). Gender identity is a very important aspect of identity; in later adolescence, the young person may emerge with a stable, self-confident sense of manhood or womanhood, or alternatively, may feel in conflict about gender roles. A sexual identity also emerges—a sense that one is heterosexual, homosexual, or bisexual, and a sense of one's attractiveness to others.

Another task of adolescence is learning how to manage physical and emotional intimacy in relationships with others (Collins & Sroufe, 1999). Youth ages 10 to 15 most frequently name the mass media, including movies, TV, magazines, and music, as their source of information about sex and intimacy. Smaller percentages name parents, peers, sexuality education programs, and professionals as sources (Kaiser Family Foundation, 1997).

ADULTHOOD

The process of achieving sexual maturity continues in adulthood. One task in this life stage is learning to communicate effectively with partners in intimate relationships; this is difficult for many persons, in part because there are few role models in our society showing us how to engage in direct, honest communication in such relationships. A second task is developing the ability to make informed decisions about reproduction and prevention of sexually transmitted infections, including HIV infection.

Sexual Lifestyle Options

Adults have several options with regard to sexual lifestyle. Some plan to remain single. They may remain celibate, participate in one long-term monogamous relationship, participate in sexual relationships with several persons, or engage in serial monogamy—a series of two or more relationships involving fidelity to the partner for the duration of each relationship. Among single persons, 26 percent of the men and 22 percent of the women report having sexual intercourse two or more times per week; 22 percent of the men and 30 percent of the women report not having sex in the preceding year (Laumann, Gagnon, Michael, & Michaels, 1994). Black men and women are more likely to remain single than their White counterparts; in 1999, 41 percent of Black men and 38 percent of Black women were never married, compared with 20 percent of White men and 16 percent of White women (U.S. Bureau of the Census, 2000). In part this reflects choice, but it also reflects the economic position of Blacks in American society. It is difficult for many Black men to find a job that provides the wages and benefits needed to support a family. Among Hispanics, 33 percent of men and 25 percent of women are never married (U.S. Bureau of the Census, 2000).

Living together is an option chosen by increasing numbers of couples. It is an important step in development not only because it represents commitment but because it is a public declaration of a sexual relationship. For some couples, cohabitation is an alternative to marriage. In 1999, 7 percent of all women were cohabiting (U.S. Bureau of the Census, 1999). These relationships tend to be short-lived; one third last less than 1 year, and only 1 out of 10 lasts 5 years (Bumpass et al., 1991).

Marriage is the most common sexual lifestyle in the United States. In 1999, 73 percent of men and 80 percent of women had been married at least once; by age 45, 95 percent of all women have married at least once (U.S. Bureau of the Census, 1999). Marriage is the social context in which sexual expression is thought to be most legitimate. The average couple engages in sexual intercourse 2 or 3 times per week (Laumann et al., 1994). At the same time, there is great variability in frequency. For example,

7 percent of couples report that they have not had coitus in the preceding year (Smith, 1994). Sexual frequency in marriage reflects the joint influence of biological and social factors. There is a decline in the frequency of intercourse with age (Smith, 1994). Biological factors include physical changes that affect sexual frequency, and chronic illnesses. Social factors include habituation to sex with the partner, and unhappiness with the relationship (Call, Sprecher, & Schwartz, 1995).

Couples report engaging in a variety of sexual activities in addition to vaginal intercourse, including oral-genital sexuality (70 percent of married men and 74 percent of married women), anal intercourse (27 percent and 21 percent), and hand-genital stimulation. Many adults continue to masturbate even though they are in a long-term relationship; 17 percent of married men and 5 percent of married women masturbate at least once a week (Laumann et al., 1994).

Sexual satisfaction with one's sexual relationship is an important component of sexual health. While many factors may contribute to satisfaction, three that differentiate people who are happy from those who are not are (a) accepting one's own sexuality, (b) listening to one's partner and being aware of the partner's likes and dislikes, and (c) talking openly and honestly (Maurer, 1994). In other words, successfully completing the developmental tasks of adolescence and young adulthood are keys to sexual health.

Most couples will experience fundamental changes in their sexual experience at least once over the course of the relationship. The change may result from developing greater understanding of oneself or partner, changes in communication patterns, accidents or illnesses that interfere with one's sexual responsiveness, or major stressors associated with family or career. Some couples will need professional support to enable them to successfully cope with these forces. Some relationships will not survive.

Extramarital sexual activity is reported by 25 percent of married men and 15 percent of married women (Laumann et al., 1994). Many of these persons will only engage in this activity once while they are married. The incidence varies by ethnicity; 27 percent of Blacks report extramarital sexual activity, compared with 14 percent of Whites (Smith, 1994). Hispanics have the same incidence as Whites (Laumann et al., 1994). Several reasons have been suggested for extramarital relationships, including dissatisfaction with marital sexuality, dissatisfaction with or conflicts in the marriage, and placing greater emphasis on personal growth and pleasure than on fidelity (Lawson, 1988).

Persons who lose their partner through divorce or death have the option of postmarital sexual relationships. Most divorced women, but fewer widows, develop an active sex life; 28 percent of divorced women and 81 percent of the widowed reported being sexually abstinent in the preceding year (Smith, 1994). By gender, 46 percent of divorced and widowed men and 58 percent of divorced and widowed women reported engaging in sexual intercourse a few times or not at all in the preceding year (Laumann et al., 1994). There is a higher probability of being sexually active postmaritally for those who are under 35 and those who have no children in the home (Stack & Gundlach, 1992).

Divorced persons, especially women, face complex problems of adjustment. These problems may include reduced income, lower perceived standard of living, the demands of single parenthood, and reduced availability of social support (Amato, 2001). These problems may increase the motivation to quickly reestablish a relationship with a partner.

Some adults engage in sexual activities that involve risks to their physical health, such as STIs and HIV infection. Examples of such activities include engaging in vaginal or anal intercourse without using condoms, engaging in sexual activity with casual partners, and engaging in sex with multiple partners. Since 1985 there has been substantial publicity about these risks. Have adults changed their sexual behavior to reduce their risk? Between 1981 and 1991, men who have sex with men reported reducing the number of partners, having fewer anonymous encounters, and engaging less often in anal intercourse or using condoms consistently (Ehrhardt, Yingling, & Warne, 1991). Among heterosexuals, the number of single adults who report having multiple partners has declined (Smith, 1991), and condom use by men and women at risk has increased (Catania, Canchola, Binson, Dolcini, & Paul, 2001).

SEXUALITY AND AGING

Biological Changes

Biology, a major influence in childhood and adolescence, again becomes a significant influence on sexual health at midlife.

In women, menopause—the cessation of menstruation—is associated with a decline in the production of estrogen; this occurs, on the average, over a 2-year period beginning around age 50 (it can begin at any age from 40 to 60). The decline in estrogen is associated with several changes in the sexual organs. The walls of the vagina become thin and inelastic. Further, the vagina shrinks in both width and length. These changes may make penile insertion more difficult, and intercourse uncomfortable. By 5 years after menopause, the amount of vaginal lubrication often decreases noticeably. Intercourse may become more difficult and painful. There are a number of ways to deal with these changes successfully, including estrogen-replacement therapy, supplemental testosterone, and use of a sterile lubricant.

As they age, men experience andropause (Lamberts, van den Beld, & van der Lely, 1997) or ADAM—androgen decline in the aging male (Morales, Heaton, & Carson, 2000), a gradual decline in the production of testosterone; this may begin as early as age 40. Erections occur more slowly. The refractory period, the period following orgasm during which the person cannot be sexually aroused, lengthens. These changes may be experienced as problems; on the other hand, they may be experienced as allowing the man greater control over orgasm.

These biological changes in women and men do not preclude satisfying sexual activity. Among older people who are healthy and active and have regular opportunities for sexual expression, sexual activity in all forms including masturbation and same-gender behavior-continues past 74 years of age (AARP, 1999).

Social Influences

An important influence on sexuality is the attitudes of others, especially those attitudes that define specific behaviors as acceptable or unacceptable. This is especially evident with regard to older persons. American society has a negative attitude toward sexual expression among the elderly. It seems inappropriate for two 75-year-old people to engage in intercourse, and especially inappropriate for persons of that age to masturbate. These negative attitudes are particularly obvious in nursing homes and care facilities where rules prohibit or staff members frown upon sexual activity among the residents. These attitudes affect the way the elderly are treated, and the elderly may hold such attitudes themselves. These attitudes may be a more important reason why many elderly people are not sexually active than the biological changes they experience.

Summary

Human sexual development is a process that begins at conception and ends at death. The principal forces are biological maturation/aging; progression through the socially defined stages of childhood, adolescence, adulthood, and later life; and one's social relationships during each of these stages. These forces interact to influence the person's sexual identity, sexual attitudes, and sexual behavior. While similarities can be identified in the lives and sexual expression of many people, there is wide variation in sexual attitudes, behaviors, and lifestyles. This diversity contributes to the vitality of society.

References

Amato, P. (2001). The consequences of divorce for children and adults. In R. Milardo (Ed.), *Understanding families into the new millennium: A decade in review* (pp. 433–465). Minneapolis, MN: National Council on Family Relations.

American Association of Retired Persons. (1999). *AARP/ Modern Maturity sexuality study*. Atlanta, GA: NFO Research, Inc.

Bancroft, J., Herbenick, D., & Reynolds, M. (In press). *Masturbation as a marker of sexual development In J. Bancroft (Ed.), Sexual development*. Bloomington, IN: Indiana University Press.

Bowlby, J. (1965). Maternal care and mental health. In J. Bowlby (Ed.), *Child care and the growth of love*. London: Penguin.

Bumpass, L. L., Sweet, J. A., & Cherlin, A. (1991). The role of cohabitation in declining rates of marriage. *Journal of Marriage and the Family, 53*, 913–927.

Bussey, K., & Bandura, A. (1999). Social cognitive theory of gender development and differentiation. *Psychological Review, 106*, 676–713.

Call, V., Sprecher, S., & Schwartz, P. (1995). The incidence and frequency of marital sex in a national sample. *Journal of Marriage and the Family, 57*, 639–652.

Catania, J. A., Canchola, J., Binson, D., Dolcini, M. M., & Paul, J. P. (2001). National trends in condom use among at-risk heterosexuals in the United States. *Journal of Acquired Immune Deficiency Syndromes, 27*, 176–182.

Centers for Disease Control and Prevention. (2000). Youth risk behavior surveillance-United States, 1999. *Morbidity and Mortality Weekly Report, 49*, SS–5.

Collins, W. A., & Sroufe, L. A. (1999). Capacity for intimate relationships: A developmental construction. In W. Furman, B. B. Brown, & C. Feiring (Eds.), *The development of romantic relationships in adolescence* (pp. 125–147). Cambridge, UK: Cambridge University Press.

Day, R. (1992). The transition to first intercourse among racially and culturally diverse youth. *Journal of Marriage and the Family, 54*, 749–762.

Ehrhardt, A. A., Yingling, S., & Warne, P. A. (1991). Sexual behavior in the era of AIDS: What has changed in the United States? *Annual Review of Sex Research, 2*, 25–48.

Erikson, E. H. (1968). *Identity: Youth and crisis*. New York: Norton.

Friedrich, W. N., Fisher, J., Broughton, D., Houston, M., & Shafran, C. R. (1998). Normative sexual behavior in children: A contemporary sample. *Pediatrics, 101*, e9.

Goldberg, S., Muir, R., & Kerr, J. (1995). *Attachment theory: Social, developmental, and clinical perspectives*. Hillsdale, NJ: Analytic Press.

Goldman, R. J., & Goldman, J. D. G. (1982). *Children's sexual thinking*. London: Routledge and Kegan Paul.

Hofferth, S. L. (1990). Trends in adolescent sexual activity, contraception, and pregnancy in the United States. In J. Bancroft & J. Reinisch (Eds.), *Adolescence and puberty* (pp. 217–233). New York: Oxford University Press.

Kaiser Family Foundation. (1997.) *Talking with kids about tough issues*. Menlo Park, CA: Author.

Lamberts, S. W. J., van den Beld, A., & van der Lely, A. J. (1997). The endocrinology of aging. *Science, 278,* 419–424.

Laumann, E. O., Gagnon, J. H., Michael, R. T., & Michaels, S. (1994). *The social organization of sexuality: Sexual practices in the United States*. Chicago: The University of Chicago Press.

Lawson, A. (1988). *Adultery: An analysis of love and betrayal*. New York: Basic Books.

Martinson, F. M. (1994). *The sexual life of children*. Westport CT: Bergin and Garvey.

Masters, W. H., Johnson, V. E., & Kolodny, R. C. (1982). *Human sexuality*. Boston: Little, Brown

Maurer, H. (1994). *Sex: Real people talk about what they really do*. New York: Penguin Books.

Morales, A., Heaton, J. P. W., & Carson, C. C. (2000). Andropause: A misnomer for a true clinical entity. *Journal of Urology, 163,* 705–712.

Okami, P., Olmstead, R., & Abramson, P. (1997). Sexual experiences in early childhood: 18-year longitudinal data from the UCLA Family Lifestyles Project. *The Journal of Sex Research, 34,* 339–347.

Reynolds, M., Herbenick, D., & Bancroft, J. (in press). The nature of childhood sexual experience: Two studies 50 years apart. In J. Bancroft (Ed.), *Sexual development*. Bloomington, IN: Indiana University Press.

Rosario, M., Meyer-Bahlburg, H., Hunter, J., Exner, T., Swadz, M., & Keller, A. (1996). The psychosexual development of urban lesbian, gay and bisexual youths. *The Journal of Sex Research, 33,* 113–126.

Smith, T. W. (1991). Adult sexual behavior in 1989: Number of partners, frequency of intercourse, and risk of AIDS. *Family Planning Perspectives, 23*(3), 102-107.

Smith, T. W. (1994). The demography of sexual behavior. Menlo Park, CA: Kaiser Family Foundation.

Stack, S., & Gundlach, J. H. (1992). Divorce and sex. *Archives of Sexual Behavior, 21,* 359–368.

Tanner, J. M. (1967). Puberty. In A. McLaren (Ed.), *Advances in reproductive physiology* (Vol. Il). New York: Academic Press.

Turner, C. F., Ku, L., Rogers, S. M., Lindberg, L. D., Pleck, J. H., & Sonenstein, F. L. (1998). Adolescent sexual behavior, drug use, and violence: Increased reporting with computer survey technology. *Science, 280,* 867–8.

Thorne, B. (1993). *Gender play: Girls and boys in school*. New Brunswick, NJ: Rutgers University Press.

Trussell, J., & Vaughn, B. (1991). *Selected results concerning sexual behavior and contraceptive use from the 1988 National Survey of Family Growth and the 1988 National Survey of Adolescent Males*. (Working Paper 91–12). Princeton, NJ: Office of Population Research.

Udry, J. R. (1988). Biological predispositions and social control in adolescent sexual behavior. *American Sociological Review, 53,* 709–722.

U.S. Bureau of the Census. (1999). *Statistical abstract of the United States, 1999*. Washington, DC: Author.

U.S. Bureau of the Census. (2000). *Statistical abstract of the United States, 2000*. Washington, DC: Author.

Ventura, S. J., Mosher, W. D., Curtin, S. A, Abma, J. C., & Henshaw, S. (2001). Trends in pregnancy rates for the United States, 1976–97. *National Vital Statistics Reports, 49*(4).

Chapter 9

Current Religious Doctrines of Sexual and Erotic Development in Childhood

Robert T. Francoeur

Students who wish to be informed about either religion and sexuality or childhood and sexuality will find Robert Francoeur's combination of the two concepts intriguing. The author, a university teacher of human sexuality with degrees in embryology, theology, and biology, is uniquely qualified to explore the relationship between religious doctrines and childhood sexuality. From his thorough literary review, he synthesizes current knowledge concerning the influence of religious doctrines as they relate to the sexual development of children. In so doing, he cuts a wide path through the doctrines of the major religious traditions in Western societies as they intersect with sexuality and childhood. Those whose interest extends to the Latino cultures of Latin America, the Islamic culture of the Middle East, or the Hindu, Buddhist, and Confucian Taoist cultures of the Far East are referred to the full text of his chapter.

Major points of interest are the various religious views toward sexual behaviors, such as masturbation, premarital sexual intimacy, and homosexuality. But perhaps of more importance to readers, the information may prompt an assessment of their own experiential data, gleaned from "childhood sexuality lessons" via parents and religious leaders. Although a sample of one is admittedly less than scientific, each person is acutely aware of the significance of his/her own experiences in sexual scripting. Extrapolating from the broader context of adult beliefs and values as a model, Francoeur weaves plausible explanations of this scripting. For example, he postulates that parental efforts to prohibit, prevent, or punish natural sexual behavior in childhood and adolescence may vandalize the formation of normophilic lovemaps and

promote the formation of paraphilic lovemaps. The review of Money's concept of the crucial periods of psychosexual development, through which the child passes in the preparation of her/his individual lovemap aids such an introspective journey.

Students may especially resonate to the carefully crafted thesis that as sexually mature single persons today, they are a new human subspecies. It is true that young adults today can claim that they had no ancestors to model appropriate sexual behaviors because the day in which they live is so uniquely characterized by socially prolonged adolescence and later marriages.

Though theoretical in nature, much of this information will be perceived as pragmatic, with tables particularly contributing to this end. The range of sexual moralities in different religious traditions, as related to their basic worldviews, are revealed in Table 9.1. In Table 9.2, the dichotomous "Hot and Cool Sex" paradigm, influenced by Western sexual values and behaviors, may strike a familiar chord with the parents of today's college students. Francoeur's earlier work (1974) furnishes a down-to-earth touch to an at times weighty offering. This treasury which traces independently developed paradigms from a variety of religious philosophies is a must-read for serious students of sexuality.

Objective, Definitions, and Premises

The purpose of this work is to summarize the relatively little information available on religious doctrines as they relate to and affect the sexual and erotic development of children in various contemporary cultures. The cultures surveyed are the Judaic, Christian (both Protestant and Catholic) and humanist traditions in Western societies.

Within this purview, certain premises need to be spelled out.

The child. The status of child is operationally and dynamically defined as including those phases of psychosexual development which occur between infancy and that point, somewhere after puberty, when the individual is socially recognized as a sexually mature adult.

Normative religious doctrines. This work assumes that the religious attitudes, values and doctrines endorsed by a culture, society and parents are a central factor in the psychosexual development of the child. Religious values and doctrines, both directly and indirectly, provide major affective and cognitive sources for establishing standards of acceptable and accepted behavior. Even when an individual, parent or society does not adhere to what would be termed a religious value system, as in the humanist tradition, the normative doctrines endorsed are usually articulated against the backdrop of a prevailing religious tradition.

Moreover, there is good evidence, both historical and contemporary, that in times of political and economic upheaval, societies commonly enlist religious doctrines, even to the point of creating new interpretations and rules, as a means of shoring up the status quo (1).

The dearth and derivative character of childhood sexual ethics. Religious traditions have seldom dealt with the sexual and erotic development of children as something of value in its own right. Childhood sexuality is seldom mentioned, let alone discussed in any detail, in religious studies and secular histories of sexuality.

Moreover, whatever is said about childhood sexuality in religious doctrines is, invariably, subordinate to and derived from the broader context of adult beliefs and values which focus on the pivotal adult sexual relationship, marriage. As the concept of marriage has changed in Europe and North America so have the doctrines about childhood sexuality derived from this adult model. When marriage was based on dynastic or political concerns, adolescent sexual relations were judged in terms of paternal property rights, the legitimacy of offspring and the avoidance of sexual behaviors that would complicate social organization. Premarital and extramarital erotic experiences may have been allowed, or even expected in this context. As the procreative function of marital sex decreased and dynastic/political concerns yielded increasingly to a norm of exclusive emotional and romantic bonding within marriage, so did the acceptability of extramarital erotic fulfillment wane (2–4).

The role of adult religious beliefs in sexual scripting. While Money has detailed the crucial periods or "gates" of psychosexual development through which the child passes after birth, a brief recapitulation here will situate our exploration of the role of parental religious beliefs in the psychosexual development of the child.

When parents first observe the sexual anatomy of their newborn infant and respond by assigning it a gender, as boy or girl, that gender of assignment triggers a sexually dimorphic scripting of the infant for masculine or feminine roles which, in part, reflects the religious beliefs and values of the parents and their adult society.

Infants quickly and spontaneously discover the sensuousness of their genitals. They explore their own bodies. They respond to the rhythmic pressure, squeezing, rubbing and touching that bring pleasurable sensations. In the process, many males and fewer females learn to masturbate. Young males

also experience episodic nocturnal penile tumescence (NPT) on average three times per night, for a total duration of two to three hours. Later, during puberty, NPT will be enriched and associated with erotic dreams. Casual genital fondling and masturbatory activities are natural and common between ages three and five. Equally natural and common, when not inhibited or repressed by adults, is the tendency of young children to engage in flirtatious rehearsal play with a parent or other older children of the opposite sex.

About age five, as the child's social context enlarges with the beginning of formal schooling, flirtatious play expands to incorporate boyfriend-girlfriend playmate romance. This is also the age when pelvic rocking or thrusting movements against the body of a partner while lying side by side gives way to the rehearsal play of coitus (5). In our repressed society, positioning rehearsal for coitus is frequently reduced to playing doctor and nurse.

In late childhood, prenatally encoded neural pathway tendencies are elaborated on by an unknown and variable combination of childhood and adolescent sexual fantasies, experiences and scriptings to determine the child's sexual orientation (status) and uniquely personal lovemap. At around age eight, pairbonding in a love affair may occur in a type of prepubertal mating rehearsal. Finally, with puberty, secondary sex characteristics make obvious the physical maturation of the child and its new sexual potential.

Parents are frequently oblivious of the many natural and spontaneous experiences of childhood psychosexual development. When, however, these spontaneous explorations are observed, the parents become mentors and scriptors for what they consider sexually appropriate for children. Given the strong antisexual biases of Western societies, these natural explorations, sexual responses and masturbatory activity are frequently short-circuited because the parental religious beliefs judge these activities sinful and forbidden.

Parental efforts to prohibit, prevent or punish this natural behavior may well vandalize the formation of normophilic lovemaps and promote the formation of paraphilic lovemaps in early childhood and preadolescence, when nurturance or the lack of it elaborates on and reinforces neural templates laid down in the brain before birth (6).

A new human subspecies. In non-technological societies, the physical maturation of puberty is commonly marked with a rite of passage to adulthood which confers and celebrates all the sexual rights and responsibilities that status carries in a particular society. In the technological West, this concurrence has been radically disassociated by socioeconomic changes. In the days of Romeo and

Juliet, marriages were arranged by the parents before their children entered sexual maturity, which came in the late teens. In this context, the prolonged period of adolescence we know today did not exist. Thus, adolescent sexual relations, premarital sex, were of minor concern to religious thinkers.

As the Industrial Revolution progressed, the length of adolescence was extended and children no longer married in their early teens. From the late nineteenth century on, the growing emphasis on public education reinforced the social prolongation of adolescence and later marriages. In the mid-twentieth century, the advent of effective and convenient contraceptives culminated in the emergence of a new human subspecies, the sexually mature single person. Unfortunately, religious rites of passage which traditionally acknowledged adult status and responsibilities at puberty, Jewish bar (bat) mitzvah and Christian confirmation, remained devoid of any recognition of this new separation of sexual maturation and marriage.

The period of adolescence is a Western phenomenon. In it, the young person is sexuoerotically capable but socially prohibited from entering the marital state where he/she could legitimately express sexual drives and needs. This new subspecies, the sexually mature single and legally dependent adolescent, has created new questions of sexual morality with which religious groups are only just beginning to deal (7–8). The advent of sexuoerotic drives and interests at puberty and the postponement of adult status leaves the adolescent in a state of limbo. The adolescent's growing need for self-actualizing independence, erotic and romantic fantasies, erotic drives and early erotic experiences with self and others is immediate and real.

The tensions of this transition are evident in Piaget's model of moral development as the child moves from a heteronomous stage based on total acceptance of a morality imposed by others to an autonomous stage in which sexual and other norms are internalized in a morality of cooperation. Kohlberg has proposed a similar, more detailed model with a transition from a conventional morality based on conformity to societal and parental norms to the social contract and universal ethical principles of a postconventional morality (9–11). An application of these models to religious institutions appears at the end of the next section.

The Value Spectrum Within Religious Denominational Doctrines

Although religious value systems are quite varied, their doctrines and norms focus primarily on the adult and adult relationships in marriage, the family and the world outside. Children are addressed mainly in terms of initiation rituals such as baptism and their education for adult responsibilities. Because of this, any discussion of religious doctrines related to childhood sexuality must begin with an analysis of adult religious doctrines.

Recent efforts to analyze doctrinal systems have revealed two distinct world philosophies (weltanschauungs) tenuously coexisting for centuries within the Judaic, Christian, Islamic and Hindu traditions. This author is not aware of evidence of a similar coexistent dualism of world views in the other religious traditions examined here, but the conclusion of Mayr is that no greater revolution has occurred in the history of human thought than the radical shift from a fixed cosmology rooted in unchanging archetypes to a dynamic, evolving cosmogenic world view based on populations and individuals (12). While the process or evolutionary world view may be gaining dominance in Western cultures and religious traditions, the Moral Majority and religious New Right in the United States, and the growing vitality of orthodox Judaism provide ample evidence that the fixed world view still has a clear influence in moderating human behavior (13–15).

Ideologically, the fixed and process world views are at the two ends of a continuum or spectrum that includes a wide range of approaches to moral and sexual issues. While individuals often take a fixed position on one issue and a process position on a second issue, these general categories are instructive when examining the impact of religious doctrines on childhood sexuality because individuals generally tend to adopt one or the other approach and maintain a fairly consistent set of intertwined religious values and attitudes.

Religious doctrines, and their adherents, can be divided by the weltanschauung which underlies their religious beliefs and doctrines. Either the world is a completely finished universe in which human nature was created by some supreme being, perfect, complete and unchanging in essence from the beginning, or the world is a universe characterized by continual change with human nature constantly evolving as it struggles to reach its fuller potential or what it is called upon to become by the deity. Either one believes that the first human beings were created by God as unchanging archetypes, thus determining standards of human behavior for all time, or one believes that human nature, behavior and moral standards have been evolving since the beginning of the human race. In the former view, a supreme being created human nature; in the latter view, the deity is creating human nature with human collaboration.

Deriving from these two views of the world and human nature, one finds two distinct views of the origins of evil and sexuality. If one believes that human nature, the purposes of sexuality and the nature of sexual relations were established in the beginning, then one also finds it congenial to believe that evil results from some original sin, a primeval fall of the first humans from a state of perfection and grace. If, on the other hand, one believes in an evolving human nature, then physical and moral evils are viewed as the inevitable, natural growth pains that come as humans struggle toward the fullness of their creation (16).

Divergent world views and sexual value systems in the Roman Catholic, Protestant, Judaic, Islamic, and Humanist religious traditions are illustrated in Table 9.1.

This general dichotomy of world views comes through with a powerful consistency in an analysis of traditional and contemporary Western sexual values, as Table 9.2 shows (17).

The convergence of independently developed value paradigms from a variety of different disciplines confirms the importance and necessity of ascertaining the weltanschauung that supports any religious doctrinal system and its sexual values. Once these premises are understood, the type of influence a particular religious doctrinal system is likely to have on children can be projected with some degree of accuracy. Since so little is available in terms of specific doctrines or moral precepts for childhood sexual development, this insight, however limited, is valuable as a starting point from which one can appreciate better the divergence of sexual values, for both adults and children.

In an adaptation of the moral development models of Piaget, Kohlberg and Gilligan to American religious institutions, Stayton (Ref. 8, p. 134) sees three institutional types. Corresponding to stage one in moral development are System A religious institutions, which focus on acts of masturbation, homosexuality, abortion or premarital sex. The act is either right or wrong. Absolute obedience to the authority is expected. At the other end of the spectrum are System C religious institutions, for whom acts are neither evil nor good in themselves and the focus is on the nature of relationships and individual responsibilities, as in stages five or six of the moral development models. System B religious institutions are more complex because they can reflect any of stages two to four, and individuals often fluctuate between stages depending on the extent of their personal involvement in a particular issue of sexuality. As Stayton notes,

> The dilemma for many adolescents is that they may be further along in their moral development than the religious institutions to which they belong. The Judaeo-Christian traditions have almost exclusively interpreted sexual morality from a System A or absolutist position, although most religious groups have modified their positions slightly in the direction of increased sexual liberality, and a few rabbis, priests, and ministers have become considerably more modern in their views. (Ref. 8, p. 134)

Table 9.1

A Spectrum of Ethical Systems with Typical Adherents in Different Traditions

Tradition Source	A Spectrum	
	Fixed Philosophy of Nature	**Process Philosophy of Nature**
Roman Catholic natural law tradition	Act-oriented natural law/divine order ethics expressed in formal Vatican pronouncements	Person-oriented, evolving ethics expressed by many contemporary theologians
Protestant Nominalism	Fundamentalism based on a literal interpretation of the Bible, as endorsed by the Moral Majority and the religious New Right: Seventh Day Adventists, Jehovah's Witnesses, Church of the Latter Day Saints	An ethic based on the covenant between Jesus and humankind; examples in the 1970 United Presbyterian document on Sexuality and the Human Community
Humanism	Stoicism and epicurean asceticism	Situation ethics, e.g., the 1976 American Humanist Association: A New Bill of Sexual Rights and Responsibilities
Judaism	Orthodox and Hassidic concern for strict observation of the Torah and Talmudic prescriptions	Liberal and reformed application of moral principles to today's situations

Table 9.2
A Dichotomous Paradigm Based on Western Sexual Values and Behavior

Hot Sex	Cool Sex
Definitions	
Reduction of genital sex.	Sexuality coextensive with personality.
Genitally focused feelings.	Diffused sensuality/sexuality.
Time and place arrangements.	Spontaneous.
Value System	
Patriarchal.	Egalitarian.
Male dominance by aggression.	Equal partnership as friends.
Double moral standard.	Single moral standard.
Behavioral Structures	
Closed possessiveness.	Open inclusiveness.
Casual, impersonal.	Involved, intimate.
Physical sex segregated from life, emotions and responsibility.	Sex integrated in whole framework of life.
Concerns	
Orgasm obsessed.	Engaging, pleasuring communications.
Extramarital relations as escape.	Comarital relations a growth of primary bond.
Fear of emotions and senses.	Embracing of emotions and senses.

Judaic Doctrines of Childhood Sexuality

Judaism exhibits a clear doctrinal range within the fixed/process philosophies spectrum (Table 9.1). On the fixed world view end, Orthodox Judaism and its most conservative sect, Hassidic Judaism, claim to be most faithful to traditional religious principles, beliefs and rituals. On the liberal side of the spectrum, Reformed and humanistic Judaism are the most open and adaptable to insights from modern developmental psychology and sexology. Conservative Judaism represents the middle of the spectrum.

In general, the Jewish tradition has escaped the antisexualism of the neoplatonic dualism of body/soul that has been so influential in Christian thought. The Judaic tradition affirms sexuality as a blessing, a gift from God which grounds and stabilizes the family. Centuries of persecution and enforced emigration, coupled with a strong biblical tradition, have made the patriarchal family central in the Jewish experience. It is assumed that every Jewish man and woman will marry and have children. The first commandment of the Torah is "You

shall be fruitful and multiply." Hence, there is no place for asceticism, sexual or otherwise. Celibacy is condemned and there is little tolerance or understanding of the single life (18).

Male-female dualism is, however, deeply rooted in the Jewish patriarchal family. Particularly in the orthodox sects, women are peripheral Jews. They are excluded from circumcision, the primary sign of Yahweh's covenant with his chosen people, from study of the Torah, and from ritual service as rabbis. Jewish women are honored as devoted wives and play a powerful role as mothers of the family. In orthodoxy, the sexes are segregated in ritual and much of daily life. There is a fear of female sexuality and the power of women to lure men into lascivious thoughts or untoward behavior that distract them from study of the Torah. "Family purity" is a significant concern for both men and women. At their wedding, Hassidic and orthodox women are given manuals providing meticulous directions about menstruation and its consequences. A woman is ritually unclean during menstruation and forbidden to have sexual intercourse or physical contact of any kind with her husband or any male until the evening of the seventh day after the last sign of vaginal discharge, when she immerses herself in a mikveh, or ritual bath (19–20). Most conservative and reformed Jews no longer adhere to the laws of niddah or menstruation and ritual purity.

As might be expected, Orthodox Judaism has made little if any accommodation to the new discoveries in sexology and child development because all that can be said about these issues has been set down in an unchanging tradition centuries ago. Orthodox Judaism adheres to a strict historical and legalistic interpretation of the Torah which views the pleasures of sexual relations as a mutual right and blessing exchanged between husband and wife. Since marriage and procreation are the most important responsibilities, contraception, masturbation, premarital sexual relations, adultery and homosexuality are all rigorously condemned. Single people are expected to avoid masturbation and premarital sex. In this respect, orthodox Judaism has much in common with the sexual restrictions of formal Catholic doctrine and fundamentalist Protestantism. Reformed Jews, and to a lesser extent Conservative Jews, are more flexible, maintaining a loyalty to tradition while emphasizing themes that allow adherents to adapt to new scientific developments and social exigencies.

Christian Doctrines of Childhood Sexuality

A Historical Overview

Underlying the whole of Christian doctrine is the struggle to overcome the consequences of original sin. In attempting to differentiate themselves from the Jews, the early Christians unfortunately lost the positive Judaic view of sexuality. In its place, under the influence of Paul, Jerome, the Desert Fathers, and especially Augustine in the third century, Christianity adopted a pagan dualism from Hellenic and neoplatonic philosophy that has permeated Christian thinking about sexuality until the present. Linked with Judaic patriarchal dualism, this pagan body-versus-soul dualism created a strongly antisexual ethic. Men were portrayed as rational, spiritual and good, provided they avoided the contaminating touch of women. Women, for their part, were passionate, earthly, and "the outpost of hell, the gateway of the devil." They could, however, achieve salvation, preferably in virginity, but also through childbearing. A strong ascetic tradition exalted martyrdom, virginity and celibacy.

Early and medieval Christianity was dominated by a sexual morality based on a selective interpretation of the natural order and purpose of things. Marriage and sexual intercourse could be tolerated but only if they were used exclusively for continuation of the human race. Sex for pleasure was not allowed. The result, in medieval Christianity, was a complete catalog of sexual practices based on natural acts which were procreative (marital intercourse, fornication and rape) and those which were unnatural (masturbation, contraceptive intercourse and sodomy). Sex was licit only between husband and wife, and natural only when it was not enjoyed and nothing was done to interfere with its procreative purpose. For centuries, Christianity has struggled with a radical inability to cope theologically and ethically with the issues of self-love, pleasure and play. Spiritual love, agape, was the ideal and physical love, eros, a sinful indulgence in passion (21–22).

Recently, the analysis of Christian sexual ethics has moved beyond this obvious antisexual posture. Gardella (2) argues convincingly that the contemporary American ethic of sexual pleasure resulted in large part from the struggle of Protestants and Catholics to overcome original sin, gain freedom from guilt and find innocent ecstasy. Without the interplay of Catholic and Protestant sexual moralists in the past two centuries, the contemporary American ethic of sexual pleasure and ecstasy would not be what it is. This more positive interpretation, however, does not alter the fact that with rare exception Christian ethics has been quite uncomfortable with sexual pleasure and sexuality, especially outside the marital and heterosexual realms.

From the early Victorian era to the present, Christian morality in America has maintained two contradictory images of the child and its psychosexual development. In one view, the child, though conceived in original sin, enjoyed a period of sublime innocence which the sexual awakening of puberty shattered. Freud's belief in a period of preadolescent sexual latency reinforced this view.

In the second view, the doctrine of original sin emphasized the innate inclinations to evil and depravity in every child. Since original sin was frequently associated with sex, the parents' role was to watch over each child constantly and eradicate any sign of depraved activity, especially any hint of the vile practice of "self-pollution." Despite their seeming difference, the outcome of both religious views was the prohibition and punishment of any and all expressions of the psychosexual rehearsal behaviors natural to childhood. The Victorian hysteria over masturbation, which lasted well into this century, has been well documented (23).

Contemporary Doctrines

In Catholicism, formal statements from the Vatican continue adhering to the natural law interpretation of sexuality, focusing on acts, and concluding that any sexual activity outside heterosexual marital procreative sex is a gravely sinful, intrinsically evil and disordered act. This view has been balanced in the past decade by the vast majority of contemporary Catholic moralists who have shifted to a person-oriented, process-based moral thinking. On the subject of masturbation, this person-oriented view ranges from statements that "not every deliberately willed act of masturbation necessarily constitutes the grave matter required for mortal sin" to Catholic moralists who maintain that "it must be said once and for all that the masturbation of the child and of the adolescent is a normal act which has no unfavorable consequences, either physical or moral, as long as one does not make the mistake of placing these acts on a moral plane, with which they have nothing to do" (24).

Despite the disagreements of different sects within mainstream Protestant Christianity, sexuality is affirmed as a good gift of the Creator which has been marred and distorted by human sin and alienation. Unlike Catholicism, Protestantism early on abandoned procreation as the primary purpose of marriage and sexual expression. It has also been more open to new empirical knowledge about sex and more willing to move from categories of acts to an interpersonal focus on the meanings of sexual expression (Ref. 25, pp. 364–392). The United Presbyterian Workstudy document of 1970, for instance, clearly states that morally good and evil sexual actions "are not susceptible of being catalogued" (26). This person-oriented approach is evident in a variety of denominational statements compiled by Genne (27). Typical is the following statement from the United Presbyterian Church:

> Since masturbation is often one of the earliest pleasurable sexual experiences which is identifiably genital, we consider it essential that the church, through its teachings and through the attitudes it encourages in Christian homes, contribute to a healthy understanding of this experience which will be free of guilt and shame. The ethical significance of masturbation depends entirely on the context in which it takes place. Therefore, we can see no objection to it when it occurs as a normal developmental experience or as a deliberately chosen alternative to inappropriate heterosexual activity. (Ref. 26, pp. 14–15)

On issues of adolescent sexual relations, premarital sexual intercourse and homosexuality, the mainstream Protestant churches have been more cautious in breaking with the traditional heterosexual marital ethics, asking questions rather than taking definitive positions:

> In a society where the sexes are moving more and more toward equal status and away from double standards, is it the responsibility of the Church to examine her traditional standards of sexuality for single adults and ask what values would be best to help single men and women to be themselves as whole human beings? (28)

> Sexual union as a communicative act has increasingly become associated with the showing of affection both within and without the institution of marriage and herein lies the problem. If we as a church have and do condone sexual union as a communicative act, can we and should we condone it only within the institution of marriage? (29)

> Sexual intercourse outside marriage is a growing reality in our time. To state categorically that it is wrong is to come at it legalistically rather than contextually. (30)

The ordination of acknowledged gay men and lesbian women to the ministry by the Episcopal Church and United Church of Christ (Congregational) and debates over this possibility in other Protestant denominations are indicative of a similar shift in sexual values which will inevitably affect childhood sexuality. John Boswell has noted that homosexually oriented children suffer a unique problem because of their "lack of social category" (1). Both secular and religious cultures ignore gay children as non-existent. Gay children fall off the map of human society. It is to be hoped that, as the mainstream Protestant Churches and process-oriented Catholic moralists adjust more to the realities of modern life, this destructive situation will change for the better.

In 1968, an interfaith statement developed by the National Council of Churches, the Synagogue Council of America and the U.S. Catholic Conference called for tolerance and acceptance of differences in school sexuality programs, informed and dignified discussion on all sides of moral questions, and promotion of our potential as human beings (8).

It is obvious from any cursory reading of religious doctrines based on the fixed world view that the conservative judgments of Orthodox Jews, Eastern Orthodox Christians, the Vatican, Jehovah's Witnesses (31–32), the Seventh Day Adventists, the Church of the Latter Day Saints (Mormons) and fundamentalist Moral Majority Protestant groups will remain unalterably opposed to any acceptance of masturbation, homosexual relations and heterosexual expressions of any kind for the unmarried, adolescents, or especially children. As mentioned earlier, Stayton suggests that most institutions within the Judaeo-Christian tradition, particularly recent pronouncements from the Vatican, reflect a moral development which has been arrested at stage one (Ref. 8, p. 134).

A 1987 report prepared by The Task Force on Changing Patterns of Sexuality and Family Life for Study by the Episcopal Diocese of Newark, New Jersey, is the most advanced and liberal document to be issued by any mainstream Christian church. In essence, this document would provide for gay unions "the same recognition and affirmation which nurtures and sustains heterosexual couples in their relationships, including, where appropriate, liturgies which recognize and bless such relationships." While this report calls for "maintaining the sacredness of the marital relationship in the sacrament of Holy Matrimony," it also calls for recognition and acceptance of young adults who choose to engage in premarital sexual relations or nonmarital cohabitation. Moral criteria urged by the report include: "life-enhancing for both partners and exploitative of neither . . . grounded in sexual fidelity and not involving promiscuity . . . founded on love and valued for the strengthening, joy, support and benefit of the couple and those to whom they are related." Recognition of premarital sex should create a most positive and responsible atmosphere for teenagers (33).

The Society of Friends (Quakers) and the Unitarian/Universalist Church have moved beyond stage-one morality, and have openly acknowledged and dealt positively with issues of sexuality in childhood and adolescence (34). In 1971, a nationwide controversy erupted with the release of a very explicit student-centered experiential program sponsored by the Unitarian/Universalist Church, in which sexually explicit filmstrips, student manuals and parent guides, "About Your Sexuality," dealt with a range of topics no church document had previously dared touch (35). For some, it may have been acceptable for a program for adolescents to deal with male and female sexual anatomy and physiology, dating, partner choice, conception and childbirth, but the inclusion of explicit filmstrips and texts dealing with sexual intercourse, same sex behaviors, masturbation, contraception and sexual diseases was unheard of. In some states, criminal prosecutions were threatened against the main author, Derek Calderwood, and local Unitarian/Universalist Churches which used this program. Fifteen years later, the third updating of "About Your Sexuality" is still too controversial for use in many Christian churches although its preeminent position is widely recognized.

Humanist Doctrines

Drawing on input from 35 leading sexologists, Lester Kirkendall drafted "A New Bill of Sexual Rights and Responsibilities" for the American Humanist Association. Among the nine main points proposed in this statement was one related specifically to children:

> Individuals are able to respond positively and affirmatively to sexuality throughout life; this must be acknowledged and accepted. Childhood sexuality is expressed through genital awareness and exploration. This involves self-touching, caressing parts of the body, including the sexual organs. These are learned experiences that help the individual understand his or her body and incorporate sexuality as an integral part of his or her personality. Masturbation is a viable mode of satisfaction for many individuals, young and old, and should be fully accepted. Just as repressive attitudes have prevented us from recognizing the value of childhood sexual response, so have they prevented us from seeing the value of sexuality in the middle and later years . . . (36)

In Christianity and especially in Roman Catholicism, the patriarchal, marital, reproductive symbols of sexuality have dominated, often reinforced by a competitive or dichotomous dualism of body versus soul, a concept of an "original sin" linked in the common mind with sexual sin, and a redemption achieved by subordination and denial of the body with its passions and emotions. In Western sexual archetypes, the male is active and dominant, the female passive. The rational male is clearly superior to the emotional and passionate female. The world view of the early Persian philosopher Zoroaster split the world into a realm of light, goodness and spirit on one side and a world of darkness, evil and body on the other side. This dichotomy flourished in the West, especially in Roman Catholicism (37).

While the doctrines and symbols of the great religions of the world undoubtedly play a substantial normative role in guiding the sexual lives of adults, only scant indirect and inferential conclusions can be made about their impact on childhood sexual development. In the more dualistic Christian tradition, more can be concluded because of the pervading religious concerns expressed about controlling and regulating sexual expression for those who are not married and ready to have a family. Much more research is needed to answer the question of to what extent dysfunctional and paraphilic lovemaps can be traced to which religious doctrines.

Notes

1. Boswell J. (1980) *Christianity, Social Tolerance and Homosexuality*. University of Chicago Press, Chicago.
2. Gardella P. (1985) *Innocent Ecstasy: How Christianity Gave America an Ethic of Sexual Pleasure*. Oxford University Press, New York.
3. Bullough V.L. (1976) *Sexual Variance in Society and History*. Wiley, New York.
4. Brinton C. (1959) *A History of Western Morals*. Harcourt Brace and Co., New York.
5. Money J., Cawte J.E., Bianchi G.N., Nurcombe B. (1970) Sex training and traditions in Arnhem Land. *Br. J. Med. Psychol*, 43, 383.
6. Money J. (1986) *Lovemaps: Clinical Concepts of Sexual/Erotic Health and Pathology, Paraphilia, and Gender Transposition in Childhood, Adolescence, and Maturity*, pp. xvi and 18. Irvington Press, New York.
7. Francoeur R.T. (1972) *Eve's New Rib: 20 Faces of Sex, Marriage and Family*, pp. 43–64. Harcourt Brace Jovanovich, New York.
8. Stayton W.R. (1985) Religion and adolescent sexuality. *Semin. Adolescent Med.*, 1, 131–137.
9. Piaget J. (1965) *The Moral Judgment of the Child*. Free Press, New York.
10. Hersh R.D., Paolitto D., Reimer J. (1979) *Promoting Moral Growth: From Piaget to Kohlberg*. Longmans, New York.
11. Gilligan C., Kohlberg L. (1974) Moral reasoning and value formation. In Calderone M.S. (Ed), *Sexuality and Human Values*. Association Press, New York.
12. Mayr E. (1963) *Animal Species and Evolution*, p. 5. Harvard University Press, Cambridge, MA.
13. Francoeur R.T. (1965) *Perspectives in Evolution*. Helicon Press, Baltimore.
14. Francoeur R.T. (1970) *Evolving World Converging Man*. Holt Rinehart Winston, New York.
15. Francoeur R.T. (1984) Moral concepts in the year 2020: The individual, the family, and society. In Kirkendall L.A., Gravatt A.E. (Eds), *Marriage and the Family in the Year 2020*. Prometheus Press, Buffalo, NY.
16. Francoeur R.T. (1982) *Becoming a Sexual Person*, Ch. 14. John Wiley, New York.
17. Francoeur A.K., Francoeur R.T. (1974) *Hot and Cool Sex: Cultures in Conflict*. Harcourt Brace Jovanovich, New York.
18. Nelson J.B. (1983) *Between Two Gardens: Reflections on Sexuality and Religious Experience*, pp. 56–59. Pilgrim Press, New York.
19. Schneid H. (1973) *Marriage* (Popular Judaica Library). Keter Books, Jerusalem.
20. Blasz E. (1967) *Code of Jewish Family Purity: A Condensation of the Nidah Laws Committee for the Preservation of Jewish Family Purity*. Brooklyn, NY.
21. Bullough V.L., Brundage J. (1982) *Sexual Practices and the Medieval Church*, pp. 1–12. Prometheus Press, Buffalo, NY.
22. Bullough V.L., Bullough B. (1977) *Sin, Sickness, and Sanity*, Ch. 2. New American Library Meridian, New York.
23. Phipps W.E. (1977) Masturbation: Vice or virtue? *J. Relig. Health*, 16(3), 183.
24. Kosnik A., Carroll W., Cunningham A., Modras R., Schulte J. (1977) *Human Sexuality: New Directions in American Catholic Thought*. A Study Commissioned by The Catholic Theological Society of America, pp. 219–229. Paulist Press, New York.
25. Herz F.M., Rosen E.J. (1982) Jewish families. In McGoldrick M., Pearce J.K., Giordano J. (Eds), *Ethnicity and Family Therapy*, pp. 364–392. Guilford Press, New York.
26. United Presbyterian Church of the U.S. (1977) *Sexuality and the Human Community*, p. 11. U.P.C.U.S.A., Philadelphia.
27. Genne W. H. (Ed) (1970) *A Synoptic of Recent Denominational Statements on Sexuality*. National Council of Churches, New York.
28. *Christianity and Human Sexuality* (No date) p. 50. The Executive Council of the Episcopal Church.
29. A Staff Report of the Work of the Task Force on Sex Ethics (1969) p. 10. The United Church of Christ, Division of Christian Education, Philadelphia.
30. *Sex, Marriage, and Family: A Contemporary Christian Perspective* (1970) p. 67. Board of Social Ministry of the Lutheran Church in America, New York.
31. Watch Tower Bible and Tract Society of New York (1978) *Making Your Family Life Happy*. Watch Tower Bible and Tract Society of New York, Inc., New York.
32. Watch Tower Bible and Tract Society of New York (1976) *Your Youth: Getting the Best Out of It*. Watch Tower Bible and Tract Society of New York, Inc., New York.
33. Thayer N.S.T. (1987) (March) Report of the Task Force on Changing Patterns of Sexuality and Family Life. Episcopal Diocese, Newark, NJ.
34. Friends (1966) *Towards a Quaker View of Sex*. Friends Home Service Committee, London.
35. Calderwood D. (1971) *About Your Sexuality*. Beacon Press, Boston.
36. Kirkendall L.A. (1976) A new bill of sexual rights and responsibilities. *The Humanist*, 36(1), 4–6.
37. Cousins E.H. (1987) Male-female aspects of the Trinity in Christian Mysticism. In Gupta B. (Ed), *Sexual Archetypes, East and West*, pp. 45–49. Paragon House, New York.

Chapter 10

Early Childhood Exposure to Parental Nudity and Scenes of Parental Sexuality

Paul Okami

Richard Olmstead

Paul R. Abramson

Laura Pendleton

Is exposure of a child to parental nudity or scenes of parental sexual activity a subtle form of sexual abuse as suggested by some researchers and clinicians? According to Okami et al., empirical data on the long-term outcomes of such scenarios are scant, although seemingly authoritative statements alluding to this fact frequently appear in the popular literature. Thus, the authors' investigation of this subject is a welcome addition to the research literature.

Sigmund Freud coined the term "primal scene" to refer to visual or auditory exposure of children to parental sexual intercourse. Psychoanalysts have long related such exposure to mental health problems of children. The researchers conducting this study reasoned that any such harm from exposure to these events would result from interactions with specific ecological variables, such as age or sex of the child. They framed their study with a number of important outcome measures chosen to reflect long-term adjustment in areas of concern to clinicians.

Readers should be aware of some methodological limitations of the Okami et al. study: the sample was not from "average" U.S. families; the sample was limited in size; a non-random sample was used; and there were some problems of measurement. Nevertheless, this study is an important effort among the few other empirical studies that do exist, and readers will

be better positioned to discriminate between myth and fact about this controversial topic.

Introduction

Increasing numbers of academic researchers and clinicians have suggested that behaviors such as exposure of a child to parental nudity or scenes of parental sexuality ("primal scenes") constitute subtle forms of sexual abuse that previously have gone unrecognized (Haynes-Seman and Krugman, 1989; Kritsberg, 1993; Krug, 1989). Such subtle sexual abuse—referred to as syndromes like "maternal seductiveness," "emotional incest syndrome," "emotional sexual abuse," "covert sexual abuse," and "sexualized attention"—may also include less easily defined behaviors such as parent "flirtatiousness," or inappropriate and excessive displays of physical affection (Sroufe and Fleeson, 1986).

As Okami (1995) suggested, however, such concern is not new. That is, although these "syndromes" have recently entered the discourse on sexual abuse, some of the behaviors that constitute them have long held positions in the pantheon of improper parenting practices. For example, Esman (1973) observed that just one of these practices—exposure of the child to primal scenes—has been indicted in 75 years of psychoanalytic, psychiatric, and psychological literature as the primary etiologic agent in virtually every form of child and adult pathology. However, Esman concluded that, "One is moved to wonder whether we are here confronted with one of those situations in which a theory, by explaining everything, succeeds in explaining nothing" (pp. 64–65). In the present article we report results of the first longitudinal investigation of long-term correlates of exposure to parental nudity and primal scenes.

Exposure to Parental Nudity

Only three empirical articles have addressed the issue of childhood exposure to parent and other adult nudity: Lewis and Janda (1988); Oleinick et al. (1966); and Story (1979). In several other cases, descriptive, self-report studies of social nudist or other groups practicing casual nudity have been conducted without comparison groups (Berger, 1977; Hartman et al., 1991; Smith and Sparks, 1986). In general, the tone of all of this work is antialarmist, representing childhood exposure to nudity as benign.

Apart from these tentative attempts to collect data, writings on this topic consist of theory-driven clinical opinion and commentaries by child rearing specialists. Clinical writings typically reflect the notion that exposure to nudity may be traumatic as a result of (i) premature and excessive stimulation in a manner controlled by the adult, leaving the child feeling powerless; (ii) the child's unfavorable comparison between his or her own anatomy and the adult's; or (iii) the intensification of Oedipal desires and consequent anxiety (DeCecco and Shively, 1977; Justice and Justice, 1979).

Given the vehemence with which clinicians and child-rearing specialists often condemn childhood exposure to parental nudity, it is paradoxical that their dire predictions are not supported by the (scant) empirical work that does exist. Findings are at worst neutral, or ambiguous as to interpretation, and there is even the implication of possible positive benefits in these studies (particularly for boys) in domains such as self-reported comfort with physical affection (Lewis and Janda, 1988) and positive "body self-concept" (Story, 1979). Although these investigations are methodologically limited, their results are consistent with the view of a smaller group of child-rearing specialists and other commentators who have stressed the potential benefits to children of exposure to nudity in the home, in areas such as later sexual functioning, and capacity for affection and intimacy (Goodson, 1991; Martinson, 1977). Although some of these writers make reference to the cross-cultural ubiquity of childhood exposure to parental nudity—although objecting to alarmist positions taken by Western commentators who fail to provide supportive data—the cross-cultural record is not generally explicit on the question of actual exposure of children to parental nudity. It does, however, present a strong case for the universality of parent-child cosleeping or room sharing (Caudill and Plath, 1966; Lozoff et al., 1984; Morelli et al., 1992). It may tentatively be inferred that under such conditions large numbers of the world's population of children are exposed to parental nudity. Finally, a third group of writers stress the importance of the context in which childhood exposure to nudity takes place, insisting that outcomes are mediated by such contextual variations as gender of child, age of child, family climate, cultural beliefs, and so on (Okami, 1995; Okami et al., 1997).

Exposure to Scenes of Parental Sexuality (Primal Scenes)

Freud and his followers chose the term "primal scenes" to refer to visual or auditory exposure of children to parental intercourse, and subsequent fantasy elaborations on the event (Dahl, 1982). Despite the identification of such exposure by psychoanalysts and others as uniquely dangerous to the mental health of children, there are, once again,

scant empirical data bearing on effects of primal scene exposure. We could locate only one prevalence study (Rosenfeld et al., 1980) and two studies of initial response and subsequent adult functioning (Hoyt, 1979, 1979). Of course, numbers of case studies exist, including a very rich psychoanalytic literature describing putative consequences of exposure to primal scenes. These writers have explained the traumatagenic issues by referring to "a) the erotically charged character of the exposure, resulting in undischarged libidinal energy and concomitant anxiety; b) the sadomasochistic content of fantasy misinterpretation of the event; and c) the exacerbation of oedipal desires and resultant castration anxiety or other fears of retaliation" (Okami, 1995, p. 56).

Again, however, the few attempts to validate these notions empirically do not support predictions of harm. For example, Rosenfeld et al. (1980) concluded that the extent of psychological damage has been exaggerated. These investigators arrived at their conclusion by two routes: First, exposure to primal scenes appeared to be rather prevalent, with the most conservative estimates as high as 41 percent. Rosenfeld et al. suggested that given this frequency of occurrence, factors other than the primal scene qua primal scene must be responsible for trauma when it occurs. Second, parents reported largely neutral and noncomprehending responses from their small children (ages 4–6). On the other hand, some children appeared to respond with amusement, giggling, and clear comprehension. Thus, the rather sinister portrait emerging from psychoanalytic literature was largely absent from these parent reports.

Hoyt (1978) queried college students about their childhood exposure to scenes of parental sexuality. He found that although these students reported that their exposure had resulted in largely negative emotional responses at the time, the exposed group did not differ from the nonexposed group on self-report ratings of "current happiness" or frequency of and satisfaction with current sexual relations. Moreover, these subjects recalled exposure primarily at prepubescent and pubertal ages. Given that the mean ages for first exposure reported by parents in the Rosenfeld et al. (1980) studies were between 4 and 6, it is conceivable that subjects in Hoyt's investigations were not reporting their first actual exposure to scenes of parental sexuality. Therefore, findings of exposure at peripubertal ages are of limited value in assessing outcome of exposure to primal scenes generally, because with a few exceptions, primal scenes have been defined in the literature as events of early childhood. That is, responses such as "castration anxiety" and "Oedipal desires" are said to be of most critical importance in the lives of very young children.

The Present Study

Despite the lack of empirical support, psychoanalytic and family systems theorists continue to stress the potential for harm in exposure to parental nudity and primal scenes. Therefore, longitudinal outcome data are important in beginning to resolve this question. In the present exploratory study, 204 families were enlisted during the mid-1970s as part of a multidisciplinary investigation of emergent family life-styles, UCLA Family Lifestyles Project. Children were followed from birth to the current wave of data collection at ages 17–18. Because there was no indication in the literature that either of the target behaviors is harmful, we hypothesized no deleterious effects of early childhood exposure either to nudity or primal scenes.

Theories based in evolutionary biology, cognitive science, and ethology predict sex differences in psychological mechanisms mediating sexual behavior in humans (Abramson and Pinkerton, 1995; Buss, 1994, 1995). Although most evolutionary theorizing about human sex differences in sexuality has focused on reproductively mature individuals, sex differences in sexuality-related psychological response also have been found among children and early adolescents (Gold and Gold, 1991; Knoth et al., 1988). In their study of adolescents ages 12–18 who were asked to recall their earliest sexual arousal and sexual feelings, Knoth et al., (1988) reported outcomes markedly congruent with evolutionary theory. Specifically, these investigators found that girls, as compared with boys, reported later onset of arousal, less frequency of arousal, less intense arousal, less distracting arousal, and were less likely to have experienced first arousal in response to visual cues. In the study by Gold and Gold (1991), men, relative to women, reported that their boyhood fantasies were more explicit and focused on the sexual acts themselves, more likely to have resulted from visual cues, more likely to have resulted in positive rather than negative affect, and that they were first experienced at an earlier age. Thus, sex differences in sexuality-related psychological responses appear to be present at least from preadolescence.

Method

Outcome measures were chosen to reflect long-term adjustment in a number of areas of concern to clinicians. These areas included: (i) self-acceptance; (ii) relations with parents, peers, and other adults; (iii) drug use; (iv) antisocial and criminal behavior; (v) suicidal ideation; (vi) social "problems" associated with sexual behavior (getting pregnant or having gotten someone pregnant, and getting an STD); and (vii) quality of sexual relationships, attitudes, and beliefs.

The UCLA Family Lifestyles Project (FLS) is a longitudinal investigation founded in 1973 to examine emergent family life-styles of that era. Fifty "conventional" and 154 "nonconventional" families, matched for ethnicity and socieconomic status (SES) according to Hollingshead's four-factor model (Hollingshead, 1975), were enrolled prior to the birth of the target child. All parents were of European American descent and were living in the State of California when recruited.

Conventional families were defined as those in a "married couple relationship" and were referred by a randomly selected sample of obstetricians from the San Francisco, San Diego, and Los Angeles areas. Nonconventional families were recruited through physician referral, birthing office records, alternative media announcements, and referral by already enrolled participants. Nonconventional family forms included intentional single mothers, couples living in communes or other group-living situations, and "social contract" (cohabiting) couples. During the most recent wave of data collection, target children were between the ages of 17 and 18 years.

For boys, exposure to primal scenes predicted reduced likelihood of having gotten an STD, or having gotten someone pregnant. The reverse was the case for girls, who were significantly more likely to have gotten an STD or to have become pregnant. This finding was independent of the extent of sexual behavior engaged in.

To determine extent of exposure to nudity and primal scenes, parents were asked two questions in a face-to-face interview at child's age 3: "Does mother (father) go nude in front of child?" and "Does mother (father) bathe or shower with the child?" The questions were followed by scales anchored by 1 (never) and 4 (regularly) or 1 (never) and 5 (daily). At child's age 6, parents were asked whether they (i) discouraged family nudity, (ii) felt OK about nudity within the family but not with others, or (iii) encouraged nudity within the family and with others.

Exposure to primal scenes was measured by two items. At child's age 3, parents were asked whether their child had ever seen them "have sex." They were offered a 4-point response format anchored by 1 (never) and 4 (regularly). At child's age 6, parents were again asked if their child had observed them having intercourse, and again offered a 4-point scale anchored by 1 (no) and 4 (regularly). Because of shifts in the identity of mothers' male partners for some of the families over the first 6 years, and the greater frequency of fathers working outside of the home and being unavailable for interview, missing data for fathers approach unacceptable levels. Therefore, only mothers' data were used for these analyses.

Results

The principal components analyses yielded five drug-use factors and four antisocial behavior factors. The drug-use factors are hence referred to as Hard Drugs (i) Sedatives, minor tranquilizers; (ii) Marijuana, hashish, psychedelic mushrooms, LSD, "Ecstasy"; (iii) PCP, major tranquilizers, other psychedelics, inhalants; (iv) Amyl nitrate, amphetamines, other narcotics; and (v) Heroin, barbiturates, cocaine, inhalants. The antisocial behavior variables are labeled antisocial behavior: theft, vandalism, felonies and fighting.

Frequencies for exposure to the main variables are as follows: For exposure to primal scenes, 32 percent of the children were exposed (boys, $n = 34$, girls, $n = 39$), whereas 68 percent of the children were not exposed. For exposure to parental nudity, 25 percent of children were not exposed to any parental nudity, 44 percent of children were exposed with moderate frequency, and 31 percent of children (boys, $n = 34$, girls, $n = 27$) were exposed frequently.

A number of trends were found that were significant. Exposure to parental nudity predicted lower likelihood of sexual activity in adolescence, but more positive sexual experiences among that group of participants who were sexually active. Exposure to parental nudity also predicted reduced instances of petty theft and shoplifting, but this was mediated by a sex of participant interaction indicating that this effect was attenuated or absent for women. Similarly, exposure to parental nudity was associated with reduced use of drugs such as marijuana, LSD, Ecstasy, and psychedelic mushrooms, but again, this effect was experienced primarily by men. Indeed, exposed women were very slightly more likely to have used these drugs.

At the level of trend, exposure to primal scenes was associated with higher levels of self-acceptance and improved relations with adults other than parents. There was also a trend for women exposed to primal scenes to have been less likely to use drugs such as PCP, major tranquilizers, inhalants, and psychedelics other than LSD or mushrooms.

Although a number of nonsignificant trends emerged, the only significant finding was that family sexual liberalism was associated with sexual liberalism at adolescence.

Discussion

This study, using a longitudinal design, is the first to examine long-term correlates of early childhood exposure to parental nudity and primal scenes. Consistent with the cross-sectional retrospective literature (and with our expectations), no harmful main effects of these experiences were found at ages 17–18. Indeed, trends in the data did not reach significance. Exposure to parental nudity was associated with positive, rather than negative, sexual experiences in adolescence, but with reduced sexual experience overall. Boys exposed to parental nudity were less likely to have engaged in theft in adolescence or to have used various psychedelic drugs and marijuana.

In the case of primal scenes, exposure was associated with improved relations with adults outside of the family and with higher levels of self-acceptance. Girls exposed to primal scenes were also less likely to have used drugs such as PCP, inhalants, or various psychedelics in adolescence. The one note of caution: males' exposure to primal scenes was associated with reduced risk of social "problems" associated with sexuality, while the opposite was the case for females. Women in our study who had been exposed to primal scenes reported increased instances of STD transmission and pregnancy. All findings were independent of the effects of SES, sex of participant, family stability, pathology, "pronaturalism," and beliefs and attitudes toward sexuality.

Taken as a whole then, effects are few, but generally beneficial in nature. Thus, results of this study add weight to the views of those who have opposed alarmist characterizations of childhood exposure both to nudity and incidental scenes of parental sexuality. Moreover, although the association of higher instance of sexually transmitted diseases and adolescent pregnancy among young women exposed to primal scenes might appear at first glance to represent harm unequivocally, more careful examination renders these findings somewhat ambiguous. In the case of increased instance of pregnancy among these women, for example, it should be noted that over half of those who reported having become pregnant (and almost half of the men who reported impregnating someone) rated their experience "good" rather than "bad." Although it is true that problems—sometimes serious problems—may attend such pregnancies in U.S. society, some data also suggest that these problems have been exaggerated (Stevens-Simon and White, 1991), and may often result more from low SES than from adolescent pregnancy itself (Trussell, 1988). Current treatment of adolescent pregnancy as intrinsically pathological may in part have generalized from an overall tendency to view adolescent sexual behaviors as problematic.

Even findings of increased instances of STD transmission among the women in our study need to be considered carefully. Symons (February 1995, personal communication) pointed out that increased instances of STDs and pregnancy among women exposed to primal scenes might be more parsimoniously understood as decreased use of condoms among the women. Regardless of problematic outcome, decreased use of condoms may be motivated by heightened desire (and capacity) for intimacy or higher levels of trust in partners—as well as by simple lack of sexual responsibility or self-destructive tendencies. In this respect it should be recalled that there was a (nonsignificant) trend toward higher levels of self-acceptance and improved relations with adults among these women.

Several outcome measures in the direction of beneficial correlates for boys were neutral or problematic correlates for girls. One interpretation would be that human males and females process sexuality-related events differently as the result of sexually dysmorphic psychological mechanisms that have evolved through natural and sexual selection (Buss, 1994). Moore (1995) has suggested the possibility that these mechanisms might begin to emerge reliably in childhood.

Other explanations of the gender interactions are also possible. For example, boys and girls are socialized differently throughout the world where sexuality is concerned, with girls being socialized more restrictively (Mead, 1967). Although these socialization procedures may also represent expressions of sexually dysmorphic psychological adaptation by natural and sexual selection, it could be argued that they instead represent temporally specific but worldwide sociocultural or socioeconomic forces related to patriarchal control of female sexuality. A third explanation of our results is more prosaic. These interactions by sex may be entirely artifactual statistical noise.

Additionally, while findings of beneficial outcomes are interesting, specific findings are not predicted by any theory that we know. In our view, then, the importance of the present investigation, apart from the suggestion of interactions by sex, lies not so much in positive findings as in the negative findings for harm—findings that converge on all of the available empirical data. Admittedly, any one set of negative results is not particularly informative. However, given virtually no evidence in this or any other empirical study that the behaviors examined in the current study are unambiguously harmful, the interesting question becomes: Why is it so widely believed in the United States and certain European nations that these practices are uniformly detrimental to the mental health of children? Such notions, certainly where exposure to parental nudity is concerned, are perhaps better conceptualized as myths. Whereas any of these behaviors of course may be experienced in an abusive context—and may also occasion harm under certain circumstances for certain individuals—their appearance per se does not appear to constitute cause for alarm.

Methodological limitations need to be addressed in interpreting results of this study. Most obviously, although the sample contains an interesting assortment of families that permitted the predictor variables to be studied in a number of contexts, these families undoubtedly differ in a number of potentially important ways from the "average" U.S. family. In addition to volunteer bias, the sample is made up entirely of European Americans residing in California at the time of enrollment, and "nonconventional" means exactly what it says—three-fourths of the sample were nonrepresentative of typical American life-style by definition. However, while not representative, the current sample was dedicated and attrition virtually nonexistent. This adds considerably to the meaningfulness of the analysis. Moreover, because the nonconventional families (whose members constituted approximately 75 percent of the total sample) were more likely to adhere to countercultural values supportive of free sexual expression, nudity within the family, and so forth, it is precisely in a data set such as this that one ought to expect to see elevated problems if these practices are in fact deleterious of themselves.

In any event, lack of reliability in the instruments used here would tend to reduce the probability of the type of findings that emerged. Lack of reliability should have produced null findings—not positive findings in a direction directly opposite that proposed by received wisdom. It is therefore difficult to imagine a methodological problem that could have erroneously painted such a consistent portrait of no harm.

Findings of the current study do not resolve the moral (or legal) issue of whether the behaviors we have examined represent "subtle sexual abuse." However, they do address the empirical question of whether these occurrences are harmful, at least within certain domains. Although evidence gathered for the present study is far from conclusive, at this point it is difficult to see the utility of referring to these events a priori as harmful, and even more difficult to see the utility of characterizing them globally as "abusive."

References

Abramson, P. R., and Pinkerton, S. (1995). *Sexual Nature, Sexual Culture*, University of Chicago Press, Chicago.

Berger, B. (1977). Child-rearing research in communes: The extension of adult sexual behavior to young children. In Oremland, E. K., and Oremland, J. D. (eds.), *The Sexual and Gender Development of Young Children: The Role of the Educator*, Ballinger, Cambridge, MA, pp. 159–164.

Buss, D. M. (1994). *The Evolution of Desire*, Basic Books, New York.

Buss, D. M. (1995). Evolutionary psychology: A new paradigm for psychological science. *Psychol. Inq.* 6: 1–30.

Caudhill, W., and Plath, D. W. (1966). Who sleeps by whom? Parent-child involvement in urban Japanese families. *Psychiatry* 29: 344–366.

Dahl, G. (1982). Notes on critical examinations of the primal scene concept. *J. Am. Psychiat. Assoc.* 30: 657–677.

DeCecco, J. P., and Shively, M. G. (1977). Children's development: Social sex-role and the hetero-homosexual orientation. In Oremland, E. K., and Oremland, J. D. (eds.), *The Sexual and Gender Development of Young Children: The Role of the Educator*, Ballinger, Cambridge, MA, pp. 89–90.

Esman, A. H. (1973). The primal scene: A review and a reconsideration. *Psychanal. Quart.* 28: 49–81.

Gold, S. R., and Gold, R. G. (1991). Gender differences in first sexual fantasies. *J. Sex Educ. Ther.* 17: 207–216.

Goodson, A. (1991). *Therapy, Nudity, and Joy*, Elysium Growth Press, Los Angeles.

Hartman, W. E., Fithian, M., and Johnson, D. (1991). *Nudist Society*, 2nd ed., Elysium Growth Press, Los Angeles.

Haynes-Seman, C., and Krugman, R. D. (1989). Sexualized attention: Normal interaction or precursor to sexual abuse? *Am. J Orthopsychiat.* 59: 238–245.

Hollingshead, A. (1975). *Four Factor Index of Social Position*, Yale University, New Haven, CT.

Hoyt, M. F. (1978). Primal scene experiences as recalled and reported by college students. *Psychiatry* 41: 57–71.

Hoyt, M. F. (1979). Primal-scene experiences: Quantitative assessment of an interview study. *Arch. Sex. Behav.* 8: 225–245.

Justice, B., and Justice, R. (1979). *The Broken Taboo*, Human Sciences, New York.

Knoth, R., Boyd, K., and Singer, B. (1988). Empirical tests of sexual selection theory: Predictions of sex differences in onset, intensity, and time course of sexual arousal. *J. Sex Res.* 24: 73–79.

Kritsberg, W. (1993). *The Invisible Wound: A New Approach to Healing Childhood Sexual Trauma*, Bantam, New York.

Krug, R. S. (1989). Adult male report of childhood sexual abuse by mothers: Case descriptions, motivations and long-term consequences. *Child Abuse Neg.* 13: 111–119.

Lewis, R. J., and Janda, L. H. (1988). The relationship between adult sexual adjustment and childhood experiences regarding exposure to nudity, sleeping in the parental bed, and parental attitudes toward sexuality. *Arch. Sex. Behav.* 17: 349–362.

Lozoff, B., Wolf, A. W., and Davis, N. S. (1984). Co-sleeping in urban families with young children in the United States. *Pediatrics* 74:171–182.

Martinson, F. M. (1977). Eroticism in childhood: A sociological perspective. In Oremland, E. K., and Oremland, J. D. (eds.), *The Sexual and Gender Development of Young Children: The Role of the Educator*, Ballinger, Cambridge, MA, pp. 73–82.

Mead, M. (1967). *Male and Female: A Study of the Sexes in a Changing World*, William Morrow, New York.

Moore, M. M. (1995). Courtship signaling and adolescents: "Girls just want to have fun"? *J. Sex Res.* 32: 319–328.

Morelli, G. A., Rogoff, B., Oppenheim, D., and Goldsmith, D. (1992). Culture variations in infant's sleeping arrangements: Questions of independence. *Dev. Psychol.* 28: 604–613.

Okami, P. (1995). Childhood exposure to parental nudity, parent-child co-sleeping, and "primal scenes": A review of clinical opinion and empirical evidence. *J. Sex Res.* 32: 51–64.

Okami, P., Olmstead, R., and Abramson, P. R. (1997). Sexual experiences in early childhood: 18-year data from the UCLA Family Life-styles Project. *J. Sex Res.* 34: 339–347.

Oleinick, M. S., Bahn, A. K., Eisenberg, L., and Lilienfield, A. M. (1966). Early socialization experiences. *Arch. Gen. Psychiat.* 15: 1966.

Rosenfeld, A. A., Smith, C. R., Wenegrat, M. A., Brewster, M. A., and Haavik, D. K. (1980). The primal scene: A study of prevalence. *Anti. J. Psychial.* 137: 1426–1428.

Smith, D. C., and Sparks, W. (1986). *The Naked Child: Growing Up Without Shame*, Elysium Growth Press, Los Angeles.

Sroufe, A. L., and Fleeson, J. (1986). Attachment and the construction of relationships. In Hartup, W. W., and Rubin, Z. (eds.), *Relationships and Development*, Erlbaum, Hillsdale, NJ, pp. 51–71.

Stevens-Simon, C., and White, M. (1991). Adolescent pregnancy. *Pediat. Ann.* 20: 322–331.

Story, M. D. (1979). Factors associated with more positive body self-concepts in preschool children. *J. Soc. Psychol.* 108: 49–56.

Trussell, J. (1988). Teenage pregnancy in the United States. *Fam. Plann. Perspect.* 20: 262–273.

Chapter 11

Negotiation of First Sexual Intercourse Among Latina Adolescent Mothers

Pamela I. Erickson

Pamela Erickson assumes a laborious task as she investigates cultural and social factors affecting the initiation of sexual intercourse among Latina adolescent mothers using the case study method. The data were drawn from life-history interviews with the young mothers and their sexual partners from 1994 to 1997.

The author's careful review of the research literature revealed a number of stereotyped gender behaviors influenced by Latino cultural norms. These patterns included the fact that, in some cases, the female adolescent wants a baby; she has a high incidence of older men or adolescents as sex partners; and her role models are peers, relatives, and/or a mother who experienced teenage pregnancy. However, Erickson suggests that changes in socio-economic realities, such as the emergence of an educated Latino middle class and exposure to more egalitarian gender norms in the United States, have resulted in greater variations in actual gender behavior among Latina adolescents and less stereotypical behavior.

As the case studies in Erickson's research unfold, patterns emerge: scripting of relationships; male pressure and female resistance; the absence of verbal consent; ignorance about sexuality; and male control along with female passivity. Readers are challenged to determine the role of cultural and societal factors in scenarios so deftly drawn by the data. How do these findings differ from those concerning other populations? Do these findings account for the fact that in 1995 the Latina adolescent birth rate surpassed that of African Americans for the first time? Is Erickson correct that Latino adolescent behavior is becoming less stereotypical? There is no lack of interesting questions for interested readers.

In the United States today, adolescent pregnancy and childbearing are perceived as serious health, social, and economic problems [1]. Despite a substantial research literature and numerous intervention programs, teenage childbearing rates have remained high for two decades [2]. The most recent statistics on adolescent birth rates indicate that those of Latina adolescents have now surpassed those of African Americans for the first time, and among Latina teens, birth rates are highest for those of Mexican descent [3]. This article explores the social and cultural context of romantic relationships in which Latina teen pregnancy occurs, using narratives from young mothers and their partners to illustrate experiences surrounding initiation of sexual intercourse and pregnancy.

The literature on teenage motherhood clearly demonstrates that adolescent childbearing is largely a socioeconomic class phenomenon intertwined with issues of race and ethnicity [2, 4]. Although it is commonly believed that teenage childbearing is disadvantageous for both mother and child [5], recent research suggests that adolescent childbearing may be an adaptive response to severe, generational, socioeconomic constraints experienced most acutely by adolescents of color [6–7].

Although political economy is an important factor in race and ethnic differences in adolescent childbearing, cultural expectations may also influence reproductive behavior [8]. In fact, Latina adolescents have distinct sexual behavior patterns. Compared to African-American and White (Non-Hispanic) adolescents, Latina adolescents have the lowest proportion of sexually active females, and they exhibit low use of family planning clinics, low use of contraceptive methods before becoming pregnant, and low use of abortion [9–11]. Latina adolescents may also be more likely to plan their pregnancies. Two surveys of primarily Mexican origin teen mothers in Los Angeles found that the proportion of young mothers who had planned to have a baby had increased from 34 percent in the 1986–87 survey to 58 percent in the 1992–94 survey [4]. In contrast, national data indicate that only 18 percent of pregnancies to adolescents of all races are planned [5]. In addition, greater acculturation has been associated with higher levels of sexual risk taking behavior and higher birth rates among Latina adolescents [9, 13–14].

Religious values are thought to buttress traditional gender role patterns through opposition to contraception and abortion [15]. In fact, however, Latinos are more similar to other Americans regarding both contraceptive use and attitudes about abortion [11, 15–16]. The use of abortion by Latinas actually exceeds that of Whites, although it may be used less often by Latina adolescents [11, 17].

Research and prevention efforts dealing with teenage pregnancy and childbearing have tended to assume three things: (1) that teenage motherhood is socially, economically, and often medically disadvantageous and should be prevented [1, 6]; (2) that all pregnancies should be consciously planned and young women should prevent unintended pregnancy through abstinence or contraception [5]; and (3) that young women have a choice about whether or not to engage in sex and they make decisions about sex and birth control after weighing the opportunity costs [18]. Yet, such a "rational decision-making" model of sex and reproduction seems to be a construct imposed by researchers, health practitioners, and other professionals dealing with adolescent pregnancy and childbearing issues. It is at odds with the emotional, highly intimate context in which sex is initiated by adolescents [19]. In the real world, sexual initiation is affected by a wide range of factors including emotions, sexual desire, coercion, and social, cultural, and moral norms [18–19].

In order to understand high rates of Latina adolescent childbearing it is important to understand how the social and cultural aspects of young Latinas' lives may put them at risk for early pregnancy. Latino culture places high value on family and motherhood, and childbearing occurs at younger ages than is normative in the broader American culture [20–21]. Latino cultural norms also tend to value premarital virginity and non-aggressive, modest, sexually ignorant, and sexually passive young women [21–23]. American cultural norms make young women the sexual gate-keepers in heterosexual relationships [19] and place high value on consciously chosen, responsible, planned motherhood [1, 5]. This non-traditional, essentially middle class, American gender role pattern may be one for which many Latina teens are not prepared.

The Current Study

Forty Latina teen mothers under age eighteen at the time they gave birth were recruited from a public hospital providing care to a low income, Latino population. The partners of the young mothers were also invited to participate subject to her permission. Fourteen male partners agreed to participate.[1]

Life histories of participants were collected during one to five informal interviews of one and two hours in length. Participants were simply asked to tell the story of their lives. Topics probed included neighborhood, school, and family, sex and romantic relationships, pregnancy and delivery, being a

parent, school and work, migration history, acculturation, health care, and future life plans and goals.

Narratives are presented for five cases which illustrate the range of experiences surrounding sexual debut for young mothers. The interviews suggest that for these young mothers, it was not really sex that was being negotiated, but the couple's entire relationship.[2] "Rational" decision making regarding sex, contraception, and STD prevention could only become the norm for these young couples after they had been having intercourse for some time.

Eva and Rudy[3]

At age sixteen, Eva moved out of her mother's house because they fought and she thought her mother drank too much, had too many boyfriends, and made her take care of her younger siblings all the time. Eva moved into a small apartment with her sister and another couple, but the situation was strained:

Eva: That's why I ended up living with Rudy.

Interviewer: When you were living with your sister, and you and Rudy were just *novios* (boyfriend/girlfriend)—you weren't really involved sexually yet. Did it happen after you moved in with Rudy?

Eva: After we moved to his house. He would like ask me, you know, if we could be together like. "No, no, no—I don't want it." Like, I didn't wanna go that far, you know: I was, like, scared. So he—well, he respected me. But we had tried for (having intercourse) sometimes, but it was like—oh! I wouldn't even know what to do. So, just forget it, you know. I was scared, so, I was like, no.

After six months of resistance, Eva gave in to Rudy's urging for sex and got pregnant in the first month.

Eva: The first time (we had sex), I was living with him, he just came outside, but I still got pregnant. (Sex) scared me at first because I was never introduced to my body or even a male's body. I didn't even know how my body worked, you know? To me, in my head it (premarital sex) was wrong.

Interviewer: Were you willing to *entregar* (give yourself up, surrender) yourself to him?

Eva: Yeah, because, see like, I really did love him a lot and I really did care for him, but it was just the fact that I was gonna lose my virginity. I mean, for a Hispanic girl, you know, that's like, God, that's a big thing! That's like something precious. And, you know, like, you just have to wait 'til you're married and stuff, you know? I did love him a lot, but I just didn't want to go that far. I didn't even know why. I just didn't want to do it . . . maybe because of what I had been taught. But I did. I didn't like being at home, and maybe it was a better way to stay away from home. So, being with him was better, and eventually I just gave up to it. But I was just looking for comfort, because I wasn't getting it at home.

Interviewer: Was it ever talked about, planned?

Eva: He would always ask me and I would say "No, no, no, no, no, no."

Eva and Rudy never talked about sex or contraception, but they had talked about a baby.

Eva: He had told me before that he wanted a baby, but I told him "I don't. I don't want a baby."

Eva was surprised that she got pregnant because they had only had sex that one time. By the time she realized she was pregnant she was about twelve to thirteen weeks and would not consider an abortion. After her daughter was born, Eva went back to high school and she is now in college. She and Rudy have a rocky relationship. They don't live together now, but he is very involved as a father and takes Sara frequently.

Rudy was born in Los Angeles and dropped out of school in ninth grade about the time his parents separated. He began working construction and met Eva when he was sixteen.

Rudy: . . . I used to mess around with a lot of girls. But not in, you know . . . to put it this way, I was a virgin. I let her think that I—I was a big time player with the girls. And, uh, she was my first one.

Interviewer: So, how did you decide to have sex?

Rudy: Well, to me it wasn't really hard, but you know, for Eva it was. 'cause . . . you know guys always they always leave them, you know. But the girl, like Eva, she was scared.

Interviewer: Was she scared about getting pregnant? Did you guys ever talk about that?

Rudy: She never did talk to me about that.

Interviewer: And were you trying to get her pregnant?

Rudy: Yeah, in a way, I was like . . . how does it feel to have a kid?

Interviewer: Were you in love with Eva?

Rudy: Well, see, I never loved someone, like really loved 'em (sic). You know? I don't know why. I'm just like that. I do like Eva and everything, but like, I miss her, but I don't like, love her, you know. Not yet. I don't know, we share a lot of things together, you know, but, I don't know how to love someone.

Julia and Juan

Juan met Julia in Mexico. He was born and raised in Los Angeles but was visiting his grandparents in Mexico. Julia's family lived in the same neighborhood and they were family friends of his grandparents. She was twelve years old when they first met, but told him she was fifteen. He was sixteen. For two years, he visited whenever he could. He was in love. He wrote her poems and called her on the phone.

Juan: I wasn't doing good (in school) 'cause all the time I was thinking about Julia—all the time . . . from one period to the next. I just couldn't stop. I couldn't help it. I tried not to think of her but I just couldn't stop.

Interviewer: You were really in love with her.

Juan: Yeah, but not—it was more, uh, spiritual, you know than just wanting to kiss her. No, it was true love. So I didn't want to have sex with her. I got tempted sometimes—when we were kissing so passionately—but I respected her. She was the first girl I respected.

Juan eventually found out that Julia had lied about her age and he agonized over how young she was. He wanted to wait until she was older before going out, to ask permission from her parents to date her, and then to have a long courtship. But when Julia was fourteen and Juan eighteen, her parents sent her to relatives in Los Angeles. She and Juan arranged to meet, and he took her to live with him at his mother's house.

Juan: I decided to steal her with her permission. She was having troubles with her brothers and with her parents. And everybody was trying to talk me out of it because I was too young, but I was really in love with her and didn't want her to go through any more pain. So, when she was here, I stole her. That's when I got on the bad side of her parents. And they really got upset with me and I understood, 'cause that made me feel like less of a man. So, I decided to go ahead and live with her. I didn't want to 'cause I wanted to get married first instead of taking her, because I knew that once she was there, where was she was gonna sleep? So, I just thought I might as well sleep with her, but I swear I wasn't thinking about the physical—the sexual part didn't hit me until a day before (she moved in).

Interviewer: So, did you and Julia talk about it (having sex)?

Juan: No, we just felt so free that it just happened. When you're in love, it's like a sense of freedom—like you could do anything. You feel real positive about things. I couldn't believe it that she was there with me. I mean one time she's in Mexico and the next she's in my room. She was so beautiful. And I was thinking, well, if I'm gonna marry her it might be OK. So, then, it just happened and it was like—we didn't—it wasn't even planned.

Julia was also in love with Juan.

Julia: He respected me a lot, and that day that I came (to live in his house)—I felt that I had to be with him.

Interviewer: Then, you didn't feel like he was pressuring you?

Julia: No, I knew what I was doing. He excites me, makes me happy. This is a love that is beautiful.

Interviewer: You intended to be his wife and have his children?

Julia: Yes.

Julia got pregnant about six months after they began having intercourse. They weren't using birth control because Julia had had an ovarian cyst in Mexico and she thought the doctor had told her she would never be able to have children. Juan and Julia wanted children someday, and they were hoping that Julia had been misdiagnosed, but they had not pursued medical follow-up in the United States. Thus, when she became pregnant, they were both surprised, but also very happy. They thought it was a little early and that they were a little young, but they were happy. Juan and Julia now have two children and they were married shortly after Julia's eighteenth birthday.

Sylvia

Sylvia, twenty years old at the time she was interviewed, was born in a small town in El Salvador. She came to the United States with her partner, Luís, when she was seventeen years old and three months pregnant with their daughter. Sylvia met and fell in love with Luís in El Salvador when she was fifteen. He was thirty. He had already moved to the United States, but had come back to visit relatives. Two years later when he returned to her village, she was still in love with him.

Luís began coming to her house and walking her to work. One day her stepfather caught them kissing, and her family tried to put an end to the relationship because he was so much older than she was. They threatened to call the police and have him put in jail, but Sylvia and Luís kept seeing each other secretly for about three months, and one day:

Sylvia: That's where it all started. He was going to take me to work, and from there we left. And the condemned man took me to a motel. And when I got there and he went in and I got to the door and I see the bed. Ay, I wanted to go but he grabbed me and wouldn't let me go. Well, maybe I wanted to, because then, we went together. I didn't know anything about condoms—nothing. And, I didn't protect myself. When I got pregnant he said: why didn't you take care of yourself (use contraception)?

In a later interview Sylvia continues with this theme:

Sylvia: Nobody educated me, nobody taught me (about sex). I think that's why I got pregnant so young. I'm not going to hide anything so that she (her daughter) can know. She has to know everything so she can choose what she wants to do. I never knew anything and because of that, I think, things happen.

Luís was surprised to find out that Sylvia was pregnant, and for awhile it was not clear what they would do. They finally decided that she would accompany him to the United States, but they have not married and Sylvia feels that their relationship is changing, or, perhaps that she thinks about things differently now.

Sylvia: When I gave in and got pregnant I was head over heels in love with him. Now I don't know. It could be due to the problems we had when we got here. He drank a lot. Maybe I lost a little of all that I felt for him. Now I love him and all, but not like we were before.

Luís would like another child, but Sylvia does not—not yet anyway. Until things get better financially and emotionally she is using the oral contraceptive pill, despite Luís not wanting her to contracept.

Erika

Erika is a U.S.-born Latina who grew up in the housing projects. She was thirteen when she met Junior, who was twenty at the time. She had her first baby at fourteen.

Erika: I met him on Halloween. I was just a Playboy Bunny (her Halloween costume), so I didn't look my age. I was wearing heels and makeup—all of that. In the beginning I didn't really care for him, to tell you the truth. He kept coming and coming, so I guess that is what made me like him because he kept on coming.

Erika and Junior dated for about seven months before they had sex for the first time. Erika did not plan to have sex with Junior, but she was clear that he did not force her into it. She said that she didn't want to do it, but at the same time she wanted to do it. They never talked about having sex or about using birth control. She got pregnant within the first month.

Interviewer: Were you trying to get pregnant, Erika?

Erika: In a way I was, but in a way I was like no, no. It was in between.

Interviewer: So, why did you want to get pregnant?

Erika: The truth, the truth because I didn't want to be older.

Interviewer: You didn't want to be a mother at an old age?

Erika: Uhuh. My friend, she got a baby too, she got pregnant at thirteen. I had her (first baby) at fourteen. But her sister got pregnant at fifteen, had her (child) at sixteen. Everybody I know had a man, you know? Everybody I know has kids. I only know two people that don't have kids from everyone I know.

Erika and Junior are still together and they now have two children.

Cori

Cori came to the United States from Mexico with her mother after her parents' divorce when she was a small child. When Cori was ten, her mother sent her to live with her father in Mexico because she had a new partner and was beginning another family. When Cori turned thirteen she began having problems with her stepmother and came back to East L.A., where she lived with her mother and stepfather until she was sixteen. They lived in a rough neighborhood with a lot of gang problems, but now Cori lives in an upscale beach community with her new partner. Cori thinks that the old neighborhood is part of the problem.

Cori: My old friends there, a lot of them want to get out. They don't want to live in the neighborhood and they try to get out and it's too hard. They end up like me getting pregnant, but then they just get on welfare and they just say: "Oh well, I get on welfare I won't have to work." They get all those girls pregnant and they just leave, and they don't think of their kids . . . when they need to give them money, to the girl, to take care of the kid, they are not there.

Cori met Carlos, her baby's father, through friends when she was fifteen. He was already eighteen and out of school, and she would ditch school

to be with him. They went out for about a year before they had sex for the first time.

Cori: I mean it (sex) just happened. (laughs) We didn't talk about sex. He did once and got—I slapped him really hard. (laughter) He told me because we were six months together and all his friends were having sex and he wanted a girlfriend and a girlfriend was somebody he could sleep with and be with, and you know. I didn't let him, and he tried grabbing my butt, and I punched him so hard, (laughs) and he didn't like that, and he got mad for a while but then we went back together again, and it happened after a year. Then, we kind of broke off for a while and went back together.

Interviewer: So then, you guys went back together . . .

Cori: . . . for like six more months and then we did (had sex).

Interviewer: And how did that happen? Were you ready for it? Did you want to?

Cori: I don't know. I didn't really want to. It just happened, because I left my house. My mom threw me out. I didn't have anywhere to go, and so I stayed (at his house). I felt like I was trapped, and I am not going to say that he forced me but I was trapped. . . . I don't know, we did it for the wrong reasons. I felt like I was so desperate, I had nothing else to live for. (I thought) "I don't care about anything else, you know? Forget it, it's just you (him, Carlos) now." It would get to a point that I really didn't care. Then I let him. I let him but I didn't feel like it. I don't know, afterwards I felt like oh! What did I do? I just, we did it twice, then after that I didn't want to. I thought I was too young for that. (Then) I went to my friend's, I didn't feel comfortable staying there (with Carlos), because he wanted me to sleep with him again, and I just didn't want to, so I left. And then I went to my other friend's house and I was just there with her. She has a baby and she is on welfare. She has been on welfare forever, since I know her. So then I said "I don't want to see myself like that—I don't," and I thought about it and I go "God! I could be pregnant." You know, it could happen. And I never, never let him touch me again. We did it twice or whatever, and he gave me something and got me pregnant. . . . I found out after, when I found out I was pregnant five months later, I had chlamydia. I was so mad. Afterwards, I found out that he was sleeping with my best friend. All my friends were sleeping with him. He was really cute.

Discussion

These case studies reveal the complexity of negotiating sexual behavior within a romantic relationship. Having sex was an act that, in the words of so many of these young people, "just happened." It was not negotiated verbally. The couple did not discuss or plan it. Rather, sexual involvement was negotiated physically through a gradual escalation in the level of intimate sexual contact allowed by the young woman during the times they were together. Verbal negotiation that occurred in the context of sexual passion consisted of little else but "please" and "no, not yet." One young man, Cori's boyfriend, who tried to discuss sexual involvement outside the context of hugging and kissing, was slapped for his efforts. That slap was a signal that conscious discussion about sexual involvement was not appropriate or appreciated.

In all cases the young man was the initiator of sexual involvement, and the young woman was the resistor and controller of passion. This is a familiar sexual "script" in contemporary American culture [19]. Most of the young women were able to resist having intercourse for a considerable length of time (several months to a year) before giving in to their partner's urging and, in many cases their own desire as well. This period of waiting was called respect. The respect the young men had for their girlfriends (pressuring for sex, but not too hard, and allowing her to make the decision about the timing of their first sexual intercourse) is interpreted by the young women as an indication of their partner's emotional involvement in the relationship. It is a sign of the young man's good intentions, a test period during which he proves that he cares for her, is not just after sex, and will stay with her in a committed relationship.

In some cases, as with Julia and Juan, sexual intercourse became a spontaneous symbol of commitment and love within the context of the development of their relationship. As the relationship evolved and they became emotionally closer, they naturally wanted to express this closeness physically. As they fell in love, sex became a natural part of the union of their two selves into one, the much sought after goal of passionate, romantic love [24]. For Cori and Eva, allowing intercourse to occur seemed to be a bid for greater commitment in the relationship, a strategy that ultimately failed for both of them. Erika and Sylvia both had much older partners, and intercourse took them by surprise, but was not unwelcome. Perhaps the powerful feelings inherent in passionate love in combination with cultural expectations about the importance of female virginity and naivete about sex preclude these young women from planning for sex, the circumstances under which it should occur (the timing of the event), and the prevention of pregnancy and STDs (use of contraception and condoms).

One of the more unfortunate precipitators of sexual debut for three of the cases presented here was conflict within the young women's home. Eva and Cori both felt pressure to leave their mothers' homes and said they had nowhere else to go. Julia, too, was having difficulties at home, and was sent to her aunt in the United States. All three of these young women eventually chose to live with their boyfriends. Julia clearly loved Juan and was ready to become his "wife." Eva and Cori both recognized that they were seeking a safe haven and comfort from their partners. Neither was ready to initiate intercourse. Eva thought it was morally wrong, and Cori thought she was too young. Both were also unsure of the depth of their own feelings for their partners—and their partner's feelings for them. Eva eventually came to love Rudy, but she was not in love with him when she moved in with him. She liked Rudy and was sexually attracted to him, but she needed a place to stay. Cori said she was not in love with Carlos. She gave in to sex because she needed a place to stay, because she thought he was cute, and because he was comforting.

An alternative reading of Cori's and Eva's stories, however, suggests that they only used the excuse of having nowhere else to go to justify the initiation of a sexual relationship with their boyfriends. Cori, it turns out, did have somewhere else to go, and Eva had a close school friend to whose family she probably could have turned had she wanted to do so. Instead, both arranged a scenario in which they could be blameless for engaging in sexual relations they felt were taboo.

Another striking chord in these narratives is the extent to which the young women were ignorant about the biology and physiology of human reproduction. Eva and Sylvia, in particular, thought this was a major reason for their unintended pregnancies—fear and ignorance of the mechanics of sex and contraception. For all except Julia, pregnancy was the consequence most feared by these young women. Although Erika wanted to get pregnant, she was somewhat ambivalent and considered abortion at the urging of her mother and Junior's mother, but all her friends had a man and kids, and she wanted to be like them. Junior was amenable to being a father and is still with her. Eva, Sylvia, and Cori had unintended pregnancies that changed their lives. Rudy wanted to see what being a father was like. He tried using withdrawal, but the method did not work well for him and Eva. Luís seemed to think pregnancy prevention was Sylvia's responsibility, but took on responsibility for her and their daughter. Carlos seemed to fit the pattern described by Cori in which young men take no responsibility for their sexual behavior at all. Cori contracted chlamydia and became pregnant. She was the only young mother who expressed any anger at her boyfriend's irresponsible behavior and at her own "stupidity." Interestingly, none of the young women talked about fear of STDs as a deterrent to having sex.

The role of older men dating teenage women and fathering children is just beginning to be addressed in the literature on adolescent pregnancy [25]. In the cases presented here, only Eva and Rudy were within two years in age. For the other four cases, age differences were three, four, six, and fifteen years. Certainly there can be knowledge and power differentials in such relationships, especially when the girl is a young teen (e.g., 12 to 15 years old) and the partner is an adult man. Sylvia's and Erika's families expressed concern about their dating much older men, and Juan also recognized it was problematic. In a later interview he said that he often felt more like Julia's father or her teacher than her husband and worried that perhaps he had stolen her girlhood. Despite their own and their families' concerns, they all persisted in their relationships.

Although none of these young women said they were forced into having sex, all, save Julia, did feel pressured by their partners. Cori came closest to describing a forced situation. She said she felt trapped, but it was a trap partly of her own making. The contradictions in some of these narratives both wanting and not wanting sex at the same time suggest the conflict in these young women's minds. For others, like Erika and Sylvia, sex was not unwelcome, but the timing was unexpected. Julia was the only one who seemed to embrace her sexual relationship with Juan, and her narrative stands in stark contrast to the other four, which depict conflicting desires, lack of preparation for sex, and uncertainty about their own or their partner's feelings.

Adult, middle-class health professionals working with adolescents tend to assume that anyone in a romantic relationship can be reasonably sure he or she might have sex and should be prepared to prevent unintended pregnancy and STDs. All of these respondents, however, indicated that their first intercourse experience together was neither expected nor planned. Moreover, almost all respondents, when asked how couples decide to have sex or use birth control, responded like Eva: "How do they decide? (long pause) They don't decide. They don't think about it." When adolescents say that they were not expecting or planning to have sex, even though they were involved in a romantic relationship that could reasonably be expected to include sexual involvement, we must take them at their word. As these cases indicate, both parties might have been thinking about sex, wanting to have sex, wondering when they would have sex, or trying to delay sex, but they were not consciously planning to have sex.

The implications of these findings for the prevention of pregnancy and STDs among young Latinas are not optimistic. The cultural scripting of gender roles in romantic relationships makes it almost certain that sex will be unplanned and unprotected. The young man pressures for sex, but allows his girlfriend to control the timing of the evolution of sexual intimacy within the relationship in order to prove his love and commitment. The young woman resists sex until she is sure of her partner's emotional commitment to her or wants to put it to the test, but she must remain unprepared for sex to be perceived as virtuous. Although this period of respect lasted six months to a year for these couples, abstinence eventually gave way to intercourse. These months were full of sexual uncertainty and emotional risk during which each person tested the other, and frank discussions about having sex, using birth control, or preventing STDs were culturally inappropriate and too emotionally risky for both parties. If either member of the couple violated these rules, he or she ran the risk of losing the partner.

Ironically, the initiation of sexual intercourse seemed to move the couple into another phase of their relationship in which they either broke up or developed mutual trust and affection that allowed for a more "rational" approach to sexual behavior and concern with its consequences. By this time, however, the young women were all pregnant and other decisions had to be made.

Cultural and social norms and values about appropriate sexual behavior, appropriate sexual partners, the importance of virginity, and contraception shape our experience of love and restrict what can be talked about at different stages of involvement in a romantic relationship. A script for romantic love that portrays spontaneous, unplanned, and unprotected sex after a protracted period of resistance by the female allows young women to retain their purity and relinquish their virginity at the same time. This script when enacted in the contemporary world of incurable STDs and the social and economic burdens of teenage motherhood places young women at enormous risk. Young couples will not behave as "rational decision-makers" in their sexual behavior until their society and community expect them to. Currently, as a society, we expect young people in love to behave "irrationally," to value spontaneous, unplanned (and therefore unprotected) sexual initiation. How, then, can we be surprised when they say, despite months of thinking about having sex, that they did not plan or expect to have sex. But, love can also accommodate prevention. Love, after all, is a valuing of the partner above the self. Surely, protection of the partner's health is part of love. We must teach our youth new scripts for falling in love, scripts that include this message.

References

1. R. A. Hatcher, J. Trussell, F. Stewart et al., *Contraceptive Technology*, Irvington Publishers, Inc., New York, 1994.
2. K. Luker, *Dubious Conceptions: The Politics of Teenage Pregnancy, and Childbearing*, Harvard University Press, Cambridge, MA, 1996.
3. T. J. Mathews, S. J. Ventura, S. C. Curtin, and J. A. Martin, Births of Hispanic Origin, 1989–95, *Monthly Vital Statistics Report*, 46: (6 Supplement), pp. 1–28, 1998.
4. P. I. Erickson, *Latina Adolescent Childbearing in East Los Angeles*, University of Texas Press, Austin, 1998.
5. S. S. Brown and L. Eisenberg, *The Best Intentions: Unintended Pregnancy and the Well-Being of Children and Families*, National Academy Press, Washington, D.C., 1995.
6. L. S. Zabin and S. C. Hayward, *Adolescent Sexual Behavior and Childbearing*, Sage Publications, Newbury Park, California, 1993.
7. L. M. Burton, Teenage Childbearing as an Alternative Life Course Strategy in Multigenerational Black Families, *Human Nature*, 1: 2, pp. 123–143, 1990.
8. J. B. Lancaster and B. A. Hamburg, *School-Age Pregnancy and Parenthood: Biosocial Dimensions*, Aldine, DeGruyter, New York, 1986.
9. C. S. Aneshensel, E. Fielder, and R. M. Becerra, Fertility and Fertility-Related Behavior among Mexican-American and Non-Hispanic White Female Adolescents, *Journal of Health and Social Behavior*, 30, pp. 56–76, March 1989.
10. R. M. Becerra and D. de Anda, Pregnancy and Motherhood among Mexican American Adolescents, *Health and Social Work*, 9: 2, pp. 106–123, 1984.
11. P. I. Erickson and C. P. Kaplan, Latinas and Abortion, in *The New Civil War: The Psychology, Culture and Politics of Abortion* (Chapter 6), L. J. Beckman and S. M. Harvey (eds.), American Psychological Association, Washington, D.C., pp. 133–155, 1998.
12. T. Reynoso, M. E. Felice, and P. Shragg, Does American Acculturation Affect Outcome of Mexican-American Teenage Pregnancy? *Journal of Adolescent Health*, 14: 4, pp. 257–261, 1993.
13. P. I. Erickson, Cultural Factors Affecting the Negotiation of First Sexual Intercourse among Latina Adolescent Parents, *International Quarterly of Community Health Education*, 18: 1, pp. 119–135, 1998–1999.
14. R. H. DuRant, R. Pendergast, and C. Seymore, Sexual Behavior among Hispanic Female Adolescents in the United States, *Pediatrics*, 85: 6, pp. 1051–1058, 1990.
15. H. Amaro, Women in the Mexican American Community: Religion, Culture, and Reproductive Attitudes and Experiences, *Journal of Community Psychology*, 16: 1, pp. 6–20, 1988.
16. H. Aviaro, Latina Attitudes towards Abortion, *Nuestro*, 5: 6, pp. 43–44, 1981.
17. L. M. Koonin, J. C. Smith, and M. Ramick, Abortion Surveillance—United States, 1991, *Morbidity and Mortality Weekly Report*, 44: SS-2, pp. 23–53, 1995.
18. J. Abma, A. Driscoll, and K. Moore, Young Women's Degree of Control over First Intercourse: An Exploratory Analysis, *Family Planning Perspectives*, 30: 1, pp. 12–18, 1998.
19. S. Thompson, *Going All the Way: Teenage Girls' Tales of Sex, Romance, and Pregnancy*, Hill and Wang, New York, 1995.
20. F. D. Bean and M. Tienda, *The Hispanic Population of the United States*, Russell Sage Foundation, New York, 1987.
21. B. R. Flores, *Chiquita's Cocoon: A "Cinderella Complex" for the Latina Woman*, Pepper Vine Press, Inc., Granite Bay, California, 1990.
22. N. Williams, *The Mexican-American Family: Tradition and Change*, General Hall, Inc., New York, 1990.
23. E. G. Pavich, A Chicana Perspective on Mexican Culture and Sexuality, *Journal of Social Work and Human Sexuality*, 4: 3, pp. 47–65, 1986.
24. E. S. Person, *Dreams of Love and Fateful Encounters: The Power of Romantic Passion*, Penguin Books, New York, 1988.
25. D. J. Landry and J. D. Forrest, How Old Are U.S. Fathers? *Family Planning Perspectives*, 27: 4, pp. 159–161, 1995.

Notes

1. About half of the young women had no partner at the time of recruitment or did not want us to contact him. Many men who were contacted declined due to time constraints of employment.
2. All of the participants were in consensual relationships, and 90 percent had had only one sexual partner in their lifetime. However, about one-third revealed a history of sexual abuse in the past.
3. Names and details that would identify respondents have been changed to protect confidentiality.

From Pamela I. Erickson, "Cultural Factors Affecting the Negotiation of First Sexual Intercourse Among Latina Adolescent Mothers." *International Quarterly of Community Health Education*, Vol. 18 (1), pp. 121–137. Copyright © 1998, Baywood Publishing Company, Inc. Reprinted by permission. ✦

Part III

Sexuality and the Life Cycle: Young Adulthood

The expanding definition of sexuality to encompass the entire lifespan is, perhaps, the most significant changing focus in human sexuality today. Sexuality researchers and clinicians who formerly worked to differentiate normative from nonnormative events first for children and, eventually, adolescents are now addressing developmental and transformational issues about sexuality in young adulthood and beyond. The chapters in Part III contribute to that process.

"A lot of kids are putting off sex, and not because they can't get a date. They've decided to wait, and they're proud of their chastity, not embarrassed by it. Suddenly, virgin geek is giving way to virgin chic" (Ingrassia 1994, 59). This 1994 *Newsweek* quote, used to introduce the topic of virginity on college campuses, could aptly be titled The Morals Revolution on Campuses. Oddly enough, that title belonged instead to a 1964 *Newsweek* story about virginity ("The Morals Revolution" 1964). The article claimed that men no longer expected to marry virgins, but that because sexual intercourse with anyone except "Mr. Right" was suspect, the question for young women should become, How many "Mr. Rights" make a wrong? Thirty years apart, these accounts by the popular media were merely reporting news of the day—one, a sexual revolution and the other, its counterpart, a sexual retrorevolution. Could it possibly be true, the more things change, the more they stay the same? After reading the Susan Sprecher and Pamela Regan selection, students can better discern the meaning of this conundrum.

Young adulthood poses specific challenges, one of which is intensifying personal individuation. According to Jung (1875–1961), a Swiss psychiatrist, individuation is a process of differentiation of self from others in the ongoing development of the personality (Hinsie and Campbell 1970, 390). Because our sexual self is an inseparable part of our persona, sex plays a considerable role in this real life drama. If, as claimed, emotions are the critical motivational forces promoting life-course individuation, it is prudent to explore the role of emotion in human sexual behavior. But, perhaps, we must first clarify the question, What is an emotion? Such questions have been the subject of debates by notables, ranging from Socrates to William James to present-day philosophers. In the search for answers, emotion has been perceived as being an inferior threat to reason and dismissed as merely an unintelligent feeling. Or conversely, emotion has been couched as true wisdom, the master of reason (Solomon 1993). But, even in the midst of such oppositional positions, most have agreed with two premises: virtually all emotion gets expressed in behavior and emotion has a cognitive dimension.

Of the many contextual factors included in the negotiation of sexual activity, both emotion and cognition are critical to decision making. Nelwyn Moore and Kenneth Davidson explore variables related to both rational decision making and its counterpoint, emotion; they also investigate the failure of college women to ask new partners about their sexual histories prior to sexual intercourse. Differentiating between health-promoting and health-defeating sexual behavior, this research provides valuable information for today's sexually active young adults, who are still in the process of achieving their own developmental task of individuation.

Human beings are designed to fall in love. That is the good news. The bad news from evolutionary psychology is that they are not designed to stay there. Further, there are many modern obstacles to monogamy. Life in large cities, with its anonymity, lends itself to extramarital relationships far more than does life in small-town America. Media messages, with their glossy images of playmates, offer alluring alternatives to monogamous devotion. But economic inequality may be the largest obstacle to lasting monogamy and a major player in extramarital sexual involvement. According to evolutionary psychologists, women seek the protection, resources, and genes of successful men, but men seek success to attract women, especially younger ones (Buss 1994).

Another modern obstacle to monogamous relationships is the changing roles of women and men. Social and occupational contacts with members of the opposite sex occur with increasing frequency among married persons, largely because of the burgeoning number of women working outside the home. In the world of work, women and men are often thrown into contact with attractive members of the opposite sex under conditions that exclude the spouse. As empathy is established in such relationships, sexual interest may surface. Thus, changing roles may explain why middle-aged women today are almost as likely as their husbands to have extramarital relationships. As Judith Treas and Deirdre Giesen approach the subject of infidelity from the vantage point of both marriage and cohabitation, they courageously study an issue about which more than 90 percent of Americans disapprove (Smith 1994). Readers of the article will be able to add their own opinions on this timely topic.

The Michael Wiederman replication of the earlier Darling and Davidson (1986) study about women pretending orgasm during sexual intercourse is a topic that apparently remains fascinating to college women who are sexually active, because more than one-half of them it seems, according to the study, do "pretend." But questions about this practice abound. Is this subterfuge because women fall prey to partners who ask, "Did you come?" Or, is it in response to the myths espoused in some women's magazines declaring that all able-bodied women should experience an orgasm 100 percent of the time? Seemingly, neither the earlier study a decade ago, using postcollege-age women, nor the present one, using college women, discovered answers to these difficult "why" questions. Although a major reason given by married women for pretending orgasm is "to get it over with," one would assume that this reason would not be as applicable to unmarried college women. Or would it? A perusal of the Wiederman study may prove this and other commonly held assumptions to be terminally flawed. Speculations aside, this selection should provoke a lively exchange among students.

References

Buss, D. M. (1994). *Evolution of Desire: Strategies of Human Mating.* New York: Basic Books.

Darling, C. A., and Davidson, J. K., Sr. (1986). "Enhancing Relationships: Understanding the Feminine Mystique of Pretending Orgasm." *Journal of Sex & Marital Therapy,* 12, 192–196.

Hinsie, L. E., and Campbell, R. J. (1970). "Individuation,." *Psychiatric Dictionary,* 4th Edition. New York: Oxford University Press.

Ingrassia, M. C. (1994, October 17). "Virgin Cool." *Newsweek,* pp. 59–62, 64, 69.

"The Morals Revolution on Campuses." (1964, April 6). *Newsweek,* p. 52.

Smith, T. W. (1994). "Attitudes Toward Sexual Permissiveness: Trends, Correlates, and Behavioral Connections." In A. S. Ross (Ed.), *Sexuality Across the Life Course* (pp. 63–97). Chicago: University of Chicago Press.

Solomon, R. C. (1993). "The Philosophy of Emotions." In M. Lewis and J. M. Haviland (Eds.), *Handbook of Emotions* (pp. 3–15). New York: Guilford. ✦

Chapter 12
College Virgins:
How Men and Women Perceive Their Sexual Status

Susan Sprecher
Pamela C. Regan

The sexual lives of college students have been the focus of research since 1938 when two female journalists, Dorothy Dunbar Bromley and Florence Haxton Britten, startled readers with a revealing report of sexual activity based on interviews with students at a number of colleges. But, through the years, very little research on college campuses has been concerned with those young adults who have chosen to remain virgins. In Erickson and Steffen's Kiss & Tell *(1999), which chronicles the history of sex surveys in the United States over a century filled with changing sexual mores, it is not surprising that only 10 of the 220 pages even mention the word "virginity." The body of knowledge about virginity that is found in the research literature concerns adolescents, and it generally explores the predictors of virginity status, not affective reactions. And still more rare are research findings about male virginity, a phrase more likely to be considered an oxymoron.*

This well-executed study of the reasons for virginity and the satisfaction with virgin status will provoke thoughtful responses. The more interesting questions may arise from the findings that emerged when differences in perceptions of virginity over time were examined. Why did more recent cohorts of virgins report more pride about their virginity status than those five years earlier? Does this represent changing mores? Is it really a sign of "virgin chic," as editorialized by Newsweek? *If so, does it challenge some time-worn assumptions? This article is an interesting commentary on campus life circa 2000 that shouldn't be missed.*

After the sexual revolution of the 1960s and the resulting freedom from sexual mores that promoted and glorified abstinence until marriage, it became somewhat socially gauche (and probably more difficult) for young adults to maintain their virginal status during college or the period immediately after high school (Rubin, 1990). Indeed, during the 1980s, a large majority of both males and females had made the transition to nonvirginity by the age of 19 (Miller & Moore, 1990). However, according to the popular media, we are in the midst of a sexual "retrorevolution" in which virginity is perceived as (and actually may be becoming) a more acceptable and popular choice among older adolescents and young adults; consequently, far from being embarrassed by their sexual status, some young adults who have remained virginal are proudly proclaiming their abstinence (Ingrassia, 1994). Interestingly, there have been few empirical attempts to examine systematically this anecdotal evidence about the feelings and reactions that adult virgins have about their sexual status.

Researchers have accumulated an extensive body of knowledge about the sexuality of adolescents, including the correlates of virginal/nonvirginal status and the factors that are associated with the loss of virginity (Gullotta, Adams, & Montemayor, 1993; Miller & Moore, 1990). We know much less about the virginity of adult men and women, perhaps because adult virgins still represent a relatively small proportion of the larger population (Billy, Tanfer, Grady, & Klepinger, 1993; Reinisch, Sanders, Hill, & Ziemba-Davis, 1992). Several researchers have included virginity as one variable among many in their studies of adult sexuality (Murstein & Mercy, 1994; Salts, Seismore, Lindholm, & Smith, 1994). Those few who have focused specifically upon adult virgins, like those who study adolescent virgins, have explored the correlates or predictors of virginity status (Schechterman & Hutchinson, 1991; Young, 1986). In addition, many have used samples composed solely of women (D'Augelli & Cross, 1975; Herold & Goodwin, 1981). Perhaps this is not surprising; after all, literary history is replete with the tales of sexually innocent young women who seek to preserve their premarital virginity and sexually knowledgeable men who seek to take it from them (Richardson, 1740/1971). Furthermore, modern literature and popular culture also have presented adult virginity as a female characteristic (e.g., the virgin protagonists on the primetime television shows *Beverly Hills 90210*, *Blossom*, and *L.A. Law* are women). However, although the majority of men (and women) are sexually active by the time they reach college age (Billy et al., 1993; Reinisch et al., 1992), adult virgins are found among both genders (e.g., Laumann, Gagnon, Michael, & Michaels, 1994).

107

Reasons for Virginity

By the time they are in college or engaged in a post-high school vocation, most young adults either have had opportunities for sexual intercourse or have considered whether they want the opportunity. Although the first intercourse experience itself is usually unplanned (e.g., Zelnik & Shah, 1983), the decision to make the transition from virgin to non-virgin is rarely spontaneous (DeLamater, 1989). Young adults weigh several factors while making this important decision about their sexual status, and some decide to postpone the transition (i.e., to remain a virgin). What are the reasons virginal men and women give for their virginity, and do they have the same reasons?

One major factor related to sexual behaviors (to have sex for the first time) is sexual standards or ideology (DeLamater & MacCorquodale, 1979). Considerable research conducted over the past few decades demonstrates that men hold more permissive attitudes toward casual (i.e., uncommitted) sexual activity than do women, whereas women are more likely than are men to view romantic love, emotional intimacy, and commitment as prerequisites for sexual activity (Sprecher, 1989). This gender difference has been explained from a number of theoretical perspectives. For example, evolutionary psychologists posit that men, whose reproductive success requires maximizing the number of genes passed on to the next generation, seek to engage in intercourse with many fertile partners, whereas women, whose reproductive success requires maximizing an offspring's chances of survival, confine their sexual activity to long-term relationships with partners who control many resources (Buss & Barnes, 1986). Social learning theorists suggest that men have received more reinforcement than have women for seeking sexual activity (Mischel, 1966), and script theorists point to societal norms that dictate that sexuality is tied more to the quality of the relationship for women than for men (Reiss, 1981). To the extent that women are more likely than men to associate sexual activity with such interpersonal phenomena as romantic love and emotional intimacy, women should place greater importance than men on lack of love and/or an appropriate relationship partner as reasons for remaining a virgin (i.e., abstaining from initial coitus).

Indeed, there is evidence to suggest that lack of a loving or committed relationship is a major reason why abstaining women choose not to have sex. In one of the few studies that focused on virgins and their decision-making processes, Herold and Goodwin (1981) asked Canadian college and high school women to indicate the most important reason why they had not engaged in sexual intercourse. A large number of the participants gave the reason that they had not yet met the "right" person. Also rated as important reasons by women were moral or religious beliefs, not being ready to have sexual intercourse, and fear of pregnancy. However, because Herold and Goodwin (1981) did not survey men, we do not know if virgin men have similar reasons.

A study conducted by Christopher and Cate (1985) suggests that young adult men may have different reasons than young adult women for remaining virginal. For part of a larger study (Christopher & Cate, 1984) these researchers asked college age, virgin men and women to indicate how important several factors would be in their decision to have sexual intercourse with an ideal partner for the first time. Women were more likely than men to rate relationship factors (e.g., love for partner) as a salient issue, which suggests that they would be more likely than men to abstain from sex in the absence of a loving relationship.

The first goal for this investigation, then, was to examine the reasons young adults have for maintaining their virginity status and to examine whether virgin men and women have the same reasons. In our investigation, we considered the reasons that were identified in the previous literature (moral or religious beliefs, fear of pregnancy, not being ready, not being in love enough, not having a willing partner). We also considered two other general categories of reasons that we believed might be relevant: fear of contracting AIDS and other sexually transmitted diseases (STDs) and perception of self-deficiency (i.e., the belief that one is not desirable, that one lacks desire for sex, or that one is too shy to initiate sex).

Affective Reactions to Virginity

Various emotions can be experienced as a consequence of engaging in sexual activity. DeLamater (1991) discussed four: sexual satisfaction/dissatisfaction, embarrassment, anxiety/fear, and frustration. Another negative emotion associated with sexual activity is guilt (Mosher & Cross, 1971). These emotions and others (e.g., pride), however, may also occur as a result of *not* having engaged in sexual activity.

Despite the recent media focus on the positive emotions ostensibly associated with virginity (Ingrassia, 1994), very few researchers have focused on how virgin men and women actually feel about their virginity. In an early study on adolescent sexuality, Sorensen (1973) concluded that the sexually inexperienced teenagers were satisfied with their status. He wrote: "They are, in the main, neither defensive nor ashamed of themselves, nor are they frustrated or preoccupied with the fact they do not have sex" (p. 154). Although Sorensen (1973) did not report whether there were gender differences in affective reactions, in a recent study of adolescent males and females, Langer, Zimmerman, and Katz (1995) found that male virgins were more likely than female virgins to report that they would feel better about themselves if they started having sex. In a study of college virgins, Young (1986) found more virgins of both genders were satisfied than frustrated, but a greater proportion of virgin men than of virgin women were frustrated. Furthermore, Walsh (1991) presented indirect evidence that men are more likely than women to experience a negative reaction to their virginity status. Virgin and nonvirgin women did not differ with respect to scores on a self-esteem scale; however, virgin men had significantly lower self-esteem scores than nonvirgin men. Although these studies suggest that gender differences in emotions associated with virginity in young adulthood exist, investigators have not studied how adult virgins react to their virginity status on a variety of both positive and negative emotions (including pride and embarrassment).

Thus, our second major goal was to examine the affective reactions virgins have in response to their virginity status and to examine gender differences in these affective reactions. We considered a number of emotional reactions—both positive (happiness and pride) and negative (anxiety, embarrassment, and guilt) and we hypothesized, based on previous research (Walsh, 1991; Young, 1986), that men would experience less positive and more negative affective reactions to their virginity than would women.

Associations Among Reasons, Affective Reactions, and Other Aspects of Virginity

The reasons young adults have for remaining virgins are likely to be related to their feelings about their virginity status. Young (1986) found that both male and female virgins who were satisfied with their sexual status reported greater religious commitment than did virgins who were frustrated by their sexual status. Perhaps reasons for remaining a virgin that reflect moral and religious beliefs are associated with positive affective reactions to virginity (e.g., pride, happiness), whereas reasons that reflect one's inability to initiate sexual intercourse with a partner or the partner's unwillingness to engage in sexual intercourse are associated with negative affective reactions to virginity (e.g., anxiety, embarrassment).

Furthermore, reasons for virginity and affective reactions to virginity may be related to the perceived likelihood of becoming a nonvirgin in the near future and the amount of support received from others for being a virgin. Virginity generally has been viewed as a discrete variable (i.e., one is either a virgin or not), but some researchers have further classified virgins by their perceived likelihood of becoming a nonvirgin before marriage. D'Augelli and her colleagues (1977) distinguished between "adamant virgins" and "potential nonvirgins." Adamant virgins have decided that they will not engage in premarital sexual intercourse, whereas potential nonvirgins are willing to consider premarital sex should they find themselves in the "right" situation with the "right" partner. These types of virgins are likely to have different reasons for remaining virgins. Herold and Goodwin (1981) classified their sample of high school and college women into adamant virgins and potential nonvirgins and asked them to select from an array of reasons the single most important reason why they had not engaged in intercourse. Half (50 percent) of the adamant virgins but only 2 percent of the potential nonvirgins endorsed the category encompassing moral and religious reasons (i.e., against religion, parental disapproval, premarital intercourse is wrong), whereas 54 percent of the potential nonvirgins but only 16 percent of the adamant virgins endorsed not having met the "right" person as the most important reason for abstaining from sexual intercourse.

The perceived likelihood of remaining a virgin before marriage may be associated with emotional reactions to virginity. Specifically, adamant virgins may have a more positive overall affective reaction to their virginity than do potential nonvirgins and in particular may feel prouder of their sexual status than do potential nonvirgins. Conversely, potential nonvirgins may feel more guilt, anxiety, and embarrassment than do adamant virgins.

Another factor that may push virgins toward having sexual intercourse is external—specifically, social pressure from others to become sexually active. Young adults who receive social pressure from others to become sexually active should be more likely than young adults who do not receive such pressure to perceive that they are likely to have sexual intercourse in the near future (i.e., to be potential nonvirgins). Furthermore, virgins who receive social pressure to remain a virgin should be less likely than virgins who do not receive this pressure to say that they are likely to begin having premarital sex.

Thus, our third goal was to examine the associations between reasons for virginity and affective reactions to virginity and to examine how both are related to other aspects of virginity, including the likelihood of becoming a nonvirgin and social pressure to become sexually active vs. to remain a virgin.

Changes Over Time in Virginity

As societal attitudes about sexuality change, so too should the experiences of young adults who are virginal when most of their cohort has had sexual intercourse. If, as suggested by the popular media, we are in the midst of a sexual "retrorevolution," then feelings and perceptions that adult virgins have about their sexual status should have changed over recent years. More specifically, fear of AIDS as a reason for being a virgin and positive reactions to virginity status have probably increased over time. Thus, our final goal was to explore the possibility that perceptions of virginity have changed.

In sum, scientists have collected very little data from adult virgins about their virginity. The purpose of this study was to examine reasons for virginity, affective reactions to virginity, and other perceptions of virginity with a sample of college age, virgin men and women obtained over a six-year period. We were particularly interested in how virgin men and women may differ.

THE CURRENT STUDY
Method

The participants in this study were selected from a nonprobability sample of undergraduate students enrolled at a Midwestern U.S. University who participated in a survey study of sexual attitudes and behaviors. To be classified as a virgin, the participant had to respond to two separate questions that he or she had not had sexual intercourse. There were not enough self-identified homosexual and bisexual virgins in the sample to examine the association between sexual orientation and reasons for and affective reactions to virginity. The final sample of 97 men and 192 women represented 11 percent and 13 percent, respectively, of the larger sample of men and women participants who were self-reported heterosexuals and had their gender identified.

The median age of the virgin participants was approximately 19.5. A majority (89 percent) identified themselves as White. On a question about religious preference, 44 percent identified themselves as Catholic, 19 percent were Protestants, 21 percent chose "other," 12 percent chose "none," and 4 percent described themselves as Jewish.

The virgin participants were presented with a list of 13 reasons "that people may have for not having premarital sexual intercourse." Participants responded to each item on a 1 = *not at all important* to 4 = *very important* response scale. An analysis conducted on the 13 items revealed 4 [major] factors. The first factor was labeled *Personal Beliefs* and included the following four items: "I believe that intercourse before marriage is wrong," "It is against my religious beliefs," "Fear of parental disapproval," and "I do not feel ready to have premarital intercourse." The second factor, labeled *Fear*, included three items: "I worry about contracting AIDS," "I worry about contracting another STD," and "Fear of pregnancy." *Inadequacy/Insecurity* was the third factor, which included four items: "I have been too shy or embarrassed to initiate sex with a partner," "I don't feel physically attractive or desirable," "I lack desire for sex," and "My current (or last) partner is (was) not willing." The final factor, labeled *Not Enough Love*, contained two items: "I have not been in a relationship long enough or been in love enough" and "I have not met a person I wanted to have intercourse with." Four scale scores were created based on the mean of the items loading on each particular factor, the higher the score, the more important the factor.

Participants were asked how *proud, guilty, anxious, embarrassed*, and *happy* they felt about their virginity status. We also created a summary measure, an index of *hedonic emotional tone*. A positive score on this index means that positive emotions were experienced to a greater intensity than were negative emotions; a negative score means that negative emotions were experienced to a greater intensity than were positive emotions.

Participants were also asked questions assessing the likelihood that they would remain a virgin and the social pressure they received to remain a virgin versus to become sexually active. *Likelihood of becoming a nonvirgin* was measured by the following three questions: "If you were in a close relationship with a partner who desired sexual intercourse and the opportunity were available, would you engage in premarital sexual intercourse?"; "How likely are you to engage in sexual intercourse before you get married?"; and "How likely are you to engage in sexual intercourse during the next year?" *Social pressure* was measured by the following two questions: "How much pressure have you received from others (e.g., dating partners, peers) to have sexual intercourse?" and "How much pressure have you received from others (e.g., parents, peers) to remain a virgin?"

Results

Reasons for Remaining a Virgin

Not all reasons for being a virgin were rated as equally important. For the total sample of virgins, the mean importance of the 4 factor scores derived from the 13 reasons were: Not Enough Love (M = 2.91), Fear (M = 2.86), Personal Beliefs (M = 2.21), and Inadequacy/Insecurity (M = 1.79). Women scored higher than men on Not Enough Love. Comparisons on the individual items indicated that women placed more importance than men on both items included in this factor (not been in a relationship long enough or been in love enough and not met the right person). Women also scored higher than men on the Personal Beliefs factor. In particular, virgin women, to a greater degree than virgin men, expressed fear of parental disapproval and stated that they were not ready. On the third factor, Fear, women also scored higher. However, women scored significantly higher than men on only one item included in this factor—fear of pregnancy. The only factor having a higher mean for men than for women was Inadequacy/Insecurity. Of the four items in this factor, men scored significantly higher than women on two: too shy or embarrassed to initiate sex and partner not willing.

Affective Reactions to Being a Virgin

In the total sample of virgins, participants reported being both proud and anxious about their virginity status. They also reported some happiness and embarrassment, but little guilt. The hedonic emotional tone index was positive, which indicates that positive emotions were experienced by the participants to a greater degree than were negative emotions.

As hypothesized, however, men and women differed in their emotional reactions to their virginity status. Women to a greater degree than men were proud and happy, and men to a greater degree than women were embarrassed and guilty. No significant gender difference was found on anxiety, although this emotion was experienced by men more than any other emotion (pride was the primary emotion women experienced). The hedonic emotional tone index was negative for men and positive for women; this difference was significant.

Reasons and Affective Reactions to Virginity

As hypothesized, personal beliefs (e.g., religious reasons) for virginity were strongly associated with positive affective reaction for both men and women. For men, interpersonal reasons (i.e., not enough love) were associated with a positive reaction. The fear factor was not associated with emotional reactions.

Men were more likely than women to believe that they would become a nonvirgin in the near future. There was a very strong correlation between the importance of personal beliefs as a reason for virginity and the perceived likelihood of becoming a nonvirgin. More specifically, the more important men and women rated personal beliefs (e.g., religious reasons) for their virginity, the more adamant they were about their virginity (the less likely they were to perceive that they would become a nonvirgin). In addition, for men only, higher scores on the Inadequacy/Insecurity factor were positively associated with the perceived likelihood of becoming a nonvirgin in the near future. Emotional reactions to virginity were also related to the perceived likelihood of becoming a nonvirgin. The men and women who believed it was likely that they would become a nonvirgin in the near future had the most negative and the least positive reaction to their virginity status.

Virgin men and women reported equal degrees of social pressure to begin to have sexual intercourse. However, virgin women reported more pressure to remain a virgin than did virgin men. Social pressure to become sexually active was negatively associated with women's hedonic emotional tone index; that is, social pressure to become sexually active was associated with a negative reaction to virginity. Conversely, social pressure to remain a virgin was associated with a positive reaction for women. For men, a strong association was found between social pressure to remain a virgin and their positive reaction as indicated by hedonic emotional tone; however, social pressure to become sexually active was unrelated to men's emotional reactions to virginity.

Changes in Virginity Over Time

Because our data were collected over a six-year period, we explored the possibility that there were changes over time in the reasons for and affective reactions to virginity. Over time both genders rated worry about contracting AIDS as increasingly important reasons for virginity. The importance rating of fear of pregnancy also became more important for women over time, as did the Inadequacy/Insecurity factor. The specific item that grew in importance for women was current partner is not willing. Some emotional reactions were also found to change significantly, in that over time men experienced greater pride and happiness. And, over time women reported feeling significantly greater pride and anxiety about their virginity.

Discussion

Reasons for Virginity

College virgins do not abstain from sexual intercourse because of lack of sexual desire. The least important reason for virginity for both men and women was "I lack desire for sex." This finding belies the stereotype of the "frigid" virgin and certainly can be used to argue against the common beliefs that sexual desire is an inherent aspect of the male but not the female experience (Regan & Berscheid, 1995) and that men have stronger and more frequent desires than do women (Richgels, 1992). Apparently, both men and women in our sample desired sex but abstained from it because they required an "appropriate" reason to become sexually active (e.g., the "right" person); sought to avoid some real, potentially negative consequences of sexual intercourse (e.g., unplanned pregnancy, disease); and were attempting to act in service of their personal beliefs. The reasons both men and women rated as most important had to do with not enough love or having not met the right partner. Overall, then, the relative ratings of the reasons were very similar for men and women.

Gender differences were found in the importance ratings given to many reasons. As expected, our virgin women participants were more concerned than their male counterparts with interpersonal reasons for virginity (i.e., not enough love or not having met the right person). These results are in accord with previous research that suggests that both sexually experienced and inexperienced women are more likely than men to associate sexual activity with love and/or committed relationships (Oliver & Hyde, 1993). Virgin women also placed greater importance than virgin men on such personal beliefs as not feeling ready to engage in sexual intercourse and on parental disapproval of premarital sex. The fact that during adolescence girls are more likely than boys to have discussed abstinence and other sexual topics with their parents (Leland & Barth, 1992) may explain why young adult women are more concerned with parental attitudes toward sexual activity (i.e., they may simply be more aware of their parents' views). Not surprisingly, the women in our sample were also more concerned than the men with the potential negative consequences of sexual intercourse (i.e., pregnancy).

However, men rated reasons having to do with inadequacy and insecurity as more important than did women. More specifically, men viewed their feelings of shyness or embarrassment about initiating sexual activity with a partner as a more important reason for their virginity than did women, and men were also more likely to point to their partners' unwillingness to engage in intercourse. A possible explanation for these gender differences is that the virgin men in our sample may have attempted to initiate sexual intercourse with a potential partner more often than did the virgin women; consequently, they may have experienced rejection more often than have women and may feel less inclined to (and more embarrassed about) making further initiation attempts. That is, this finding may stem from differential experiences of virgin men and virgin women. If virgin men and women perceive the male role in sexual interactions as primarily proactive and the female role as primarily reactive (Gagnon & Simon, 1973; Reiss, 1981), it makes sense that men would be more concerned than women with reasons associated with the initiation of sexual activity (e.g., partner's unwillingness, personal feelings of shyness).

Our results also indicate that the reasons young adult virgins maintain their sexual status have changed over time. Specifically, recent cohorts of virgins placed more importance than earlier cohorts on their fears of contracting AIDS and other STDs. Whether young adult virgins consciously decide not to have sex based upon this reason or simply provide it as an explanation for their current sexual status is not clear; however, sexually active individuals also have grown more aware of AIDS over time and appear to have altered their sexual behaviors as a consequence (e.g., are more likely to use condoms). Another reason that became more important over time, at least for women, was "My current (or last) partner is (was) not willing." Although heterosexual partners largely continue to adhere to the traditional script of male initiation of sexual activity (O'Sullivan & Byers, 1992), recent cohorts of women may be more comfortable with the role of sexual initiator and thus more likely to have experienced a partner's refusal to have intercourse. These changes found over a six-year period may indicate that the type of person who remains a virgin is changing and/or may indicate broader changes in societal attitudes about sexuality.

Affective Reactions to Virginity

Male and female virgins reported a variety of both positive and negative emotional responses to their sexual status; however, women's experiences were more positive than negative, whereas men's were more negative than positive. With respect to specific emotional reactions, women felt greater pride and happiness than did men, and men felt greater embarrassment and guilt than did women. These gender differences may be explained by cultural mandates regarding sexual intercourse that teach that sexual experience is an important aspect of masculinity. Virginity—defined here as not yet having engaged in sexual intercourse—therefore may represent a greater stigma for men than for women. Indeed, some people appear to believe that men are born sexually experienced; more than half the respondents in a survey conducted by Berger and Wenger (1973) argued that it made no sense to speak of "male virginity," and those who felt that such a concept did exist disagreed over the activities that constituted the loss of male virginity. It is not surprising, given these sociocultural expectations and beliefs, that virgin men demonstrate a negative response to their virginity. We might also then expect men to feel positively about the first occurrence of sexual intercourse; after all, it removes an undesired stigma. In fact, the feelings that men and women have about their virginity are to some extent the opposite of the reactions that men and women report to the loss of their virginity; that is, men tend to have a more positive emotional reaction to their first intercourse experience than do women (Darling, Davidson, & Passarello, 1992; Sprecher, Barbee, & Schwartz, 1995).

However, affective reactions to virginity, for both men and women, do appear to be changing over time. In particular, although virgin men continue to feel more negatively about their sexual status than do virgin women, more recent cohorts report greater pride and happiness than earlier cohorts. We also found that more recent cohorts of women reported more pride. These changes may reflect the fact that young adults—especially young men—have a greater number of publicly visible, virginal role models to emulate [for example, the group, Athletes for Abstinence includes a number of well-known male athletes (Newman, 1994)].

Associations Between Reasons and Affective Reactions

Men and women had a more positive overall reaction to their virginity if they viewed their sexual status as the result of their personal beliefs or values (i.e., against religious beliefs, believe that premarital sex is wrong, fear parental disapproval, not ready for intercourse). To the extent that virginity represents tangible evidence that one is living according to one's personal convictions, such positive feelings are understandable. Although we expected to find that men and women who choose to remain virgins because they have not found the right partner or been in love enough would feel less positive about their virginity status, no such association was found for women, and for men, such reasons were associated with a more positive overall affective response. Perhaps men who feel "good" about their virginity—and who are violating the stereotype of

the unhappy male virgin—are also those men who violate other stereotypes (who, for example, associate sex and love, which is not a stereotypically "male" response; Carroll et al., 1985). In addition, for men, but not women, reasons related to inadequacy/insecurity—a partner's unwillingness to have sex and the perception that one is unable to attract or initiate intercourse with a potential partner—were associated with a negative emotional reaction. To the extent that a man's virginity is not due to personal choice, but rather reflects an inability to overcome various individual (e.g., undesirability) and interpersonal (e.g., partner's refusal) barriers to sexual experience, it appears to engender negative affect.

Perceived Likelihood of Losing One's Virginity

Several researchers have suggested that virginity is not a discrete variable such that one is virginal or one is not virginal, but rather that there may be additional types of virgins. For example, D'Augelli and D'Augelli (1977) distinguished between "adamant virgins" (who believe that they will wait until marriage to have intercourse) and "potential nonvirgins" (who believe that they will have premarital sex under the "right" circumstances). We argue that it may be even more meaningful to conceptualize virginity along a continuum ranging from fully adamant about one's virginity to fully open to the possibility of losing one's virginity (becoming a nonvirgin).

Although the virgin women in our sample were more adamant than the virgin men about their sexual status, the more adamant that *both* genders were, the more importance they placed on personal beliefs for their virginity and the more positive their overall emotional reaction. Specifically, men and women who were more adamant about their virginity were more likely to experience pride and happiness and less likely to feel anxiety and guilt than were men and women who believed that they were likely to become sexually active in the near future. These results suggest that sexual decision making and affective reactions to virginity are inextricably interwoven. However, we do not know from these data whether individuals first make a sexual decision (i.e., to have sex) and then experience emotional reactions based on that decision or whether they have certain emotional reactions to their current situation (i.e., virginity) and then make a decision as a result of those reactions (e.g., a person realizes that he or she is unhappy about his or her sexual status, and this realization contributes to the decision to become a nonvirgin).

Social Pressure

This study represents an important preliminary step toward delineating the role that social pressure may play in informing the sexual attitudes and decisions of young adult virgins. First, we found several gender differences. Virgin men and women reported receiving equal amounts of pressure (presumably from dating partners and peers) to engage in sexual intercourse, but only women reported greater negative affect toward their virginity as the social pressure to have sex increased. Women also experienced greater pressure (presumably from parents) to abstain from intercourse than men, but both men and women felt more positive about their virginity as this type of social pressure increased.

In addition, the amount of social pressure respondents received to remain a virgin was unrelated to the amount of social pressure they received to lose their virginity, which suggests that young adult virgins may get conflicting messages from different network sectors (e.g., parents vs. friends). However, because we did not explicitly examine the different types of external pressure that virgins may experience (i.e., we asked our participants to indicate the amount of pressure they received from others in general rather than from specific subgroups of others), we do not know, for example, whether virgins received more pressure to have sex from their peers than from their parents, or whether gender differences exist such that virgin women received significantly more pressure to become sexually active from their (male) dating partners than virgin men received from their (female) dating partners. We also did not distinguish between overt pressure (e.g., a parent explicitly communicates his or her negative feelings about premarital sex to a child; a person verbally informs his or her dating partner that it is "time" to have sex) and indirect pressure (e.g., a virgin perceives that all of his or her friends are engaging in sex, regardless of their actual behavior) or how the type or quantity of pressure that a person receives from a particular element of his or her social network may change over time and/or with the interpersonal context.

Future Research Directions

We believe that it is important to include other subclassifications of virginity in research on adult virgins; for example, some virgins have engaged in "everything but" sexual intercourse (Rubin, 1990), whereas others have abstained from all intimate sexual activities. It is likely that sexually active but "technical" virgins will have different reasons for and emotional reactions to their sexual status than will virgins with very little sexual experience. A related issue worth examining is the phenomenon of "second virginity." This concept currently espoused by several social groups, refers to the notion that a sexually experienced man or woman can renew or reclaim virgin status by making the decision to discontinue further sexual activity until marriage (Ingrassia, 1994). Some researchers have in fact distinguished between "regretful nonvirgins" (those who had been sexually active but who planned to abstain from sex for a while) and other types of virgins (Schechterman & Hutchinson, 1991).

References

Berger, D. G., & Wenger, M. G. (1973). The ideology of virginity. *Journal of Marriage and the Family*, 35, 666–676.

Berscheid, E., Snyder, M., & Omoto, A. M. (1989). The relationship closeness inventory: Assessing the closeness of interpersonal relationships. *Journal of Personality and Social Psychology*, 57, 792–807.

Billy, J. O. G., Tanfer, K., Grady, W. R., & Klepinger, D. H. (1993). The sexual behavior of men in the United States. *Family Planning Perspectives*, 25, 52–60.

Brooks-Gunn, J., & Furstenberg, F F., Jr. (1989). Adolescent sexual behavior. *American Psychologist*, 44, 249–257.

Buss, D. M., & Barnes, M. (1986). Preferences in human mate selection. *Journal of Personality and Social Psychology*, 50, 559–570.

Carroll, J. L., Volk, K. D., & Hyde, J. S. (1985). Differences between males and females in motives for engaging in sexual intercourse. *Archives of Sexual Behavior*, 14, 131–139.

Christopher, F. S., & Cate, R. M. (1984). Factors involved in premarital sexual decision-making. *The Journal of Sex Research*, 20, 363–376.

Christopher, F. S., & Cate, R. M. (1985). Anticipated influences on sexual decision-making. *Family Relations*, 34, 265–270.

Christopher, F. S., & Roosa, M. W. (1991). Factors affecting sexual decisions in the premarital relationships of adolescents and young adults. In K. McKinney & S. Sprecher (Eds.), *Sexuality in Close Relationships* (pp. 111–133). Hillsdale, NJ: Lawrence Erlbaum.

Darling, C. A., Davidson, J. K, Sr., & Passarello, L. C. (1992). The mystique of first intercourse among college youth: The role of partners, contraceptive practices, and psychological reactions. *Journal of Youth and Adolescence*, 21, 97–117.

D'Augelli, J. F., & Cross, H. L. (1975). Relationship of sex guilt and moral reasoning to premarital sex in college women and in couples. *Journal of Consulting and Clinical Psychology*, 43, 40–47.

D'Augelli, J. F., & D'Augelli, A. R. (1977). Moral reasoning and premarital sexual behavior: Toward reasoning about relationships. *Journal of Social Issues*, 33, 44–66.

DeLamater, J. D. (1989). The social control of human sexuality. In K. McKinney & S. Sprecher (Eds.), *Human Sexuality: The Societal and Interpersonal Context* (pp. 30–62). Norwood, NJ: Ablex.

DeLamater, J. D. (1991). Emotions and sexuality. In K. McKinney & S. Sprecher (Eds.), *Sexuality in Close Relationships* (pp. 49–70). Norwood, NJ: Ablex.

DeLamater, J. D., & MacCorquodale, P. (1979). *Premarital Sexuality: Attitudes, Relationships, Behaviors*. Madison: University of Wisconsin Press.

Fielding, H. (1979). *The History of Tom Jones, a Foundling* (3rd ed.). New York: The New American Library. (Original work published 1749).

Fleming, A. T. (1995, February). Like a virgin, again. *Vogue*, pp. 68, 72.

Gagnon, J. H., & Simon, W. (1973). *Sexual Conduct: The Social Sources of Human Sexuality*. Chicago: Aldine.

Gullotta, T. P., Adams, G. R., & Montemayor, R. (Eds.). (1993). *Adolescent Sexuality*. Newbury Park, CA: Sage.

Herold, E. S., & Goodwin, M. S. (1981). Adamant virgins, potential nonvirgins and nonvirgins. *The Journal of Sex Research*, 17, 97–113.

Ingrassia, M. (1994, October 17). Virgin cool. *Newsweek*, pp. 59–62, 64, 69.

Langer, L. M., Zimmerman, R. S., & Katz, J. A. (1995). Virgins' expectations and nonvirgins' reports: How adolescents feel about themselves. *Journal of Adolescent Research*, 10, 291–306.

Laumann, E. O., Gagnon, J. H., Michael, R. T., & Michaels, S. (1994). *The Social Organization of Sexuality: Sexual Practices in the United States*. Chicago: University of Chicago Press.

Leite, R. M. C., Buoncompagno, E. M., Leite, A. C. C., Mergulhao, E. A., & Battistoni, M. M. M. (1994). Psychosexual characteristics of female university students in Brazil. *Adolescence*, 29, 439–460.

Leland, N. L., & Barth, R. P. (1992). Gender differences in knowledge, intentions, and behaviors concerning pregnancy and sexually transmitted disease prevention among adolescents. *Journal of Adolescent Health*, 13, 589–599.

Lewis, R., & Casto, R. (1978). Developmental transitions in male sexuality. *The Counseling Psychologist*, 4, 15–19.

Miller, B. C., & Moore, K. A. (1990). Adolescent sexual behavior, pregnancy, and parenting: Research through the 1980s. *Journal of Marriage and the Family*, 52, 1025–1044.

Mischel, W. (1966). A social-learning view of sex differences in behavior. In E. E. Maccoby (Ed.), *The Development of Sex Differences* (pp. 56–81). Stanford, CA: Stanford University Press.

Mosher, D. L., & Cross, J. J. (1971). Sex guilt and premarital sexual experience of college students. *Journal of Consulting and Clinical Psychology*, 36, 27–32.

Mosher, W. D., & Pratt, W. F. (1993). AIDS related behavior among women 15–44 years of age: United States, 1988 and 1990. *Advance Data from Vital and Health Statistics*, 239.

Murstein, B. I., & Mercy, T. (1994). Sex, drugs, relationships, contraception, and fears of disease on a college campus over 17 years. *Adolescence*, 29, 303–322.

Newman, J. (1994, June 19). Proud to be a virgin. *New York Times*, pp. 1, 6.

Oliver, M. B., & Hyde, J. S. (1993). Gender differences in sexuality: A meta-analysis. *Psychological Bulletin*, 114, 29–51.

O'Sullivan, L. F., & Byers, E. S. (1992). College students' incorporation of initiator and restrictor roles in sexual dating interactions. *The Journal of Sex Research*, 29, 435–446.

Peplau, L. A., Rubin, Z., & Hill, C. T. (1977). Sexual intimacy in dating relationships. *Journal of Social Issues*, 33(2), 86–109.

Peretti, P. O., Brown, S., & Richards, P. (1978). Female virgin and nonvirgin psychological orientations toward premarital virginity. *Acta Psychiatrica Belgica*, 78, 235–247.

Peretti, P. O., Brown, S., & Richards, R. (1979). Perceived value-orientations toward premarital virginity of female virgins and nonvirgins. *Acta Psychiatrica Belgica*, 79, 321–331.

Regan, P. C., & Berscheid, E. (1995). Gender differences in beliefs about the causes of male and female sexual desire. *Personal Relationships*, 2, 345–350.

Reinisch, J. M., Sanders, S. A., Hill, C. A., & Ziemba-Davis, M. (1992). High-risk sexual behavior among heterosexual undergraduates at a midwestern university. *Family Planning Perspectives*, 24, 116–121, 145.

Reiss, I. L. (1981). Some observations on ideology and sexuality in America. *Journal of Marriage and the Family*, 43, 271–283.

Richardson, S. (1971). *Pamela; or, Virtue Rewarded*. Boston: Houghton Mifflin. (Original work published 1740)

Richgels, P. B. (1992). Hypoactive sexual desire in heterosexual women: A feminist analysis. *Women and Therapy*, 12, 123–135.

Rubin, L. (1990). *Erotic Wars: What Happened to the Sexual Revolution?* New York: HarperCollins.

Salts, C. J., Seismore, M. D., Lindholm, B. W., & Smith, T. A. (1994). Attitudes toward marriage and premarital sexual activity of college freshmen. *Adolescence*, 29, 775–779.

Schechterman, A. L., & Hutchinson, R. L. (1991). Causal attributions, self-monitoring, and gender differences among four virginity status groups. *Adolescence*, 26, 659–678.

Smith, T. W. (1991). Adult sexual behavior in 1989: Number of partners, frequency of intercourse and risk of AIDS. *Family Planning Perspectives*, 23, 102–107.

Sonenstein, F. L., Pleck, J. H., & Ku, L. C. (1989). Sexual activity, condom use and AIDS awareness among adolescent males. *Family Planning Perspectives*, 21, 152–158.

Sorensen, R. C. (1973). *Adolescent Sexuality in Contemporary America*. New York: World.

Sprecher, S. (1989). Premarital sexual standards for different categories of individuals. *The Journal of Sex Research*, 26, 232–248.

Sprecher, S., Barbee, A., & Schwartz, P. (1995). "Was it good for you, too?": Gender differences in first sexual intercourse experiences. *The Journal of Sex Research*, 32, 3–15.

Sprecher, S., & Sedikides, C. (1993). Gender differences in perceptions of emotionality: The case of close, heterosexual relationships. *Sex Roles: A Journal of Research*, 28, 511–530.

Tiefer, L. (1995). *Sex Is Not a Natural Act and Other Essays*. Boulder, CO: Westview Press.

Tolman, D. L. (1991). Adolescent girls, women and sexuality: Discerning dilemmas of desire. *Women and Therapy*, 11, 55–69.

Walsh, A. (1991). Self-esteem and sexual behavior: Exploring gender differences. *Sex Roles*, 25, 441–450.

Young, M. (1986). Religiosity and satisfaction with virginity among college men and women. *Journal of College Student Personnel*, 27, 339–344.

Zelnik, M., & Shah, F. K. (1983). First intercourse among young Americans. *Family Planning Perspectives*, 15, 64–72.

Chapter 13

Communicating With New Sex Partners

College Women and Questions That Make a Difference

Nelwyn B. Moore
J. Kenneth Davidson, Sr.

When queried about their sexual script, most college students would probably reply, "What sexual script?" Yet, by adulthood, all persons have one. That there is a complex network of interacting variables within the individual that affects sexual behavior may seem to be a self-evident fact. But, when sexual decisions are close at hand, most individuals seldom consider the influence of family history, their personality make-up, or the culture in which they grew up, all variables that do indeed influence sexual behavior. Of course, the interaction effects of such factors must also be considered for persons who would wish to scientifically analyze their sexual lives, if any such persons exist! And, the fact that this process is dynamic, continuing to evolve throughout life in relationships with others, must also be factored in the equation for accurate appraisal.

Moore and Davidson focus on just one aspect of sexual scripting among young adults as they ask the question: Why do women fail to ask new sex partners about their sexual histories? This question should particularly resonate with women because lack of communication about sexual histories poses substantially greater risks for them than for men. This fact is based on widespread evidence that most college men have more lifetime sex partners than college women.

Although this study highlights primarily physiological factors, such as an unintended pregnancy or STDs in relation to lack of communication, can you suggest psychological risks that might also occur? If you are a sexually active, college female, you will find yourself in one of the three groups that differentiated the respondents. If so, what can you add from your own personal experience that might change the focus of future research on this topic? A heightened awareness of your own sexual script can enhance your role as director in the drama of your own developmental trajectory in life.

In today's society, numerous contextual factors surround the discussion and negotiation of sexual activity. Such sexual discourse often involves the representation of self and other in a creative game in which discussion of sexual pasts is avoided. This circumstance especially may be true for first sexual encounters. Added to this dilemma is the lack of an acceptable cultural language with which to negotiate disclosure of sexual histories (Pliskin, 1997). The fact that college women face gender-specific conflicts between the historically traditional and the more recent revolutionary understanding of their sexuality also is at issue. Society on the one hand condemns women who engage in casual sexual intercourse. At the same time, however, it advocates female sexual liberation (Dunn, 1998). And the very characteristics often associated with traditional gender roles, such as submissiveness, passivity, and nurturance, seemingly impair the woman's ability to effectively engage in rational decision making about involvement in sexual activity (Zellman & Goodchild 1983). Consequently, research suggests that women often are lacking in the training and socialization necessary to be effective communicators in sexual relationships (Murnen, Perot, & Bryne, 1989).

Despite the constant media barrage and the efforts of sexuality educators, many college women in the 1990s report being uninfluenced by information proclaiming the risks of contracting a sexually transmitted disease or initiating an unintentional pregnancy (Kusselling, Wenger, & Shapiro, 1995). Contrary to popular opinion, increased levels of awareness have not necessarily led to college women implementing behavioral changes in their sexual lives (Rubinson & De Rubertis, 1991). In one study, almost two thirds (62 percent) of college women indicated that awareness or concerns about AIDS had not affected their level of participation in sexual intercourse, and almost three fourths (72 percent) had not changed their level of involvement in oral-genital sex (Weinberg, Lottes, & Aveline, 1998). Even college women who claimed to have become more selective in their choice of sex partners were just as sexually active as those who had indicated no behavioral changes (Carroll, 1991). In fact, 19 percent of college women actually expressed the likelihood that they would eventually contract a sexually transmitted disease (STD) (Davidson & Moore, 1994).

REVIEW OF THE LITERATURE

First Sexual Intercourse

The age at first sexual intercourse for college women continued to decline during the 1990s, dropping to 16.5 years (Sprecher, Barbee, & Schwartz, 1995). Regardless of age, a person's first sexual intercourse experience often is viewed as a rite of passage to adulthood, potentially leading to affirmation of self-identity (Moore & Davidson, 1997). However, for many women, the first coital experience is disappointing both physically and emotionally (Darling, Davidson, & Passarello, 1992), perhaps in part, because only 50 percent of college women reported expecting first sexual intercourse to occur at that particular time (Sawyer & Smith, 1996). Additionally, the fact that college women are more likely to give implied consent rather than verbal consent for their first intercourse experience raises related questions (Moore & Davidson, 1997).

College women are more likely to experience feelings of anxiety, nervousness, embarrassment and guilt during their first sexual intercourse rather than excitement and pleasure (Guggino & Ponzetti, 1997). And only 38 percent of college women reported never feeling guilty about their first intercourse (Moore & Davidson, 1997). When asked to choose one word to describe their first sexual experience, only 24 percent of women chose a positive term, whereas 52 percent chose a negative term (Sawyer & Smith, 1996). Furthermore, the percentage of college women who indicated that they had experienced orgasm during first intercourse is only 7 percent (Sprecher, Barber, & Schwartz, 1995) to 8 percent (Sawyer & Smith, 1996).

In terms of safer sexual practices at first intercourse, the percentage of college women who were under the influence of alcohol ranges from 27 percent (Sprecher et al., 1995) to 31 percent (Moore & Davidson, 1997). In fact, 17 percent of the women reported being "drunk" (Sprecher et al., 1995). As for contraceptive usage during first intercourse, the ranges are from 55 percent (Moore & Davidson, 1997) to 74 percent (Sawyer & Smith, 1996), with the condom being the most frequently employed contraceptive method (Sprecher et al., 1995).

Sexual Risk-Taking

In general, incidence of risk-taking sexual behavior is elevated by several factors: decreased age at first sexual intercourse (Mauldon & Luker, 1996), low sexual self-esteem (Seal, Minichiello, & Omodei, 1997); 2 or more sex partners within the past year (Seidman, Mosher, & Aral, 1994); and consumption of alcoholic beverages prior to sexual intercourse (Leigh, Schafer, & Temple, 1995). Alcoholic beverages continue to play a substantial role in the sexual lives of college women. In one survey, 75 percent of college women indicated that they had gotten drunk within the past year. Of these respondents, 10 percent indicated that while drunk they had sexual intercourse with a stranger (Carroll & Carroll, 1995). College women who consumed greater quantities of alcohol and on a more frequent basis ranked high on sexual insecurity, and they perceived that consumption of alcohol could enhance the sexual experience (Mooney, 1995). In fact, 17 percent of college women reported deliberately drinking "more than normal" to make it easier to have sexual intercourse with someone (Anderson & Mathieu, 1996). Binge drinking, in particular, is a crucial factor in the equation. Among college women, 66 percent of binge drinkers, in contrast with only 33 percent of nonbinge drinkers, had had sexual intercourse while under the influence of alcohol since coming to college (Piombo & Piles, 1996). Although alcohol may enhance their sexual experiences, many college women also indicated that alcohol at some time had led to a negative effect on their sexual experience (Paulson, Eppler, Satterwaite, Wuensch, & Bass, 1998).

Although the overall percentage of college women who use a contraceptive is increasing (Sprecher et al., 1995), a related phenomenon is puzzling. Women who delay initiating sexual intercourse for the longest period of time are least likely to use contraception at first sexual intercourse. This finding is especially troubling, because it suggests that strategies that encourage postponement of the initiation of sexual intercourse may inadvertently discourage safer sex practices (Cooksey, Rindfuss, & Guilkey, 1996).

Even though two-thirds (66 percent) of college women today report "always" using contraception (Raj & Pollack, 1995), the percentage who "usually/always" have their sex partner use a condom ranges from 26 percent (Prince & Bernard, 1998) to 32 percent (Weinberg et al., 1998). This inconsistent condom use is in spite of the fact that the primary motivation for using a condom among unmarried women is disease prevention and not contraception (Anderson & Mathieu, 1996). Lower condom use occurs among college women with high perceptions of relative invulnerability (Thompson, Anderson, Freedman, & Swan, 1996), absence of negative emotions (i.e., worry and regret over nonusage) (Richard, de Vries, & Van der Plight, 1998), low perceptions of present risk (Basen-Engquist, 1992), and endorsement of the "relational ideal" (i.e., love and commitment as prerequisite for sexual intercourse) (Hynie, Lyndon, Côté, & Wiener, 1998). Thus, it should not be surprising that college women frequently perceived using a condom or the pill as an either/or choice, rather than perceiving both as necessary for maximum protection against STDs and unwanted pregnancy (Beckman, Harvey, & Tiersky, 1996). The perception of present risk is greatly diminished with the consumption of alcohol, especially among those who are binge drinkers. Of female college binge drinkers, 49 percent reported having unprotected/unsafe sexual intercourse since coming to college in comparison to only 25 percent of nonbinge drinkers (Piombo & Piles, 1996).

Finally, the prevalence of risk-taking sexual practices is related to perceived risk and self-efficacy rather than knowledge. High self-efficacy is associated with both the intention to discuss STD prevention (Hale & Trumbetta, 1996) and reported discussion of past sex partners with a current sex partner (Basen-Engquist, 1992). Yet the percentage of college women who indicated having asked their last sex partner about his sexual history before engaging in sexual intercourse ranges from 26 percent (Hawkins, Gray, & Hawkins, 1995) to 55 percent (Hale, Char, Nagy, & Stockton, 1993). The reasons that college women most frequently give for not discussing past sexual histories of their prospective sex partners relate to the vulnerability of their self-image (i.e., embarrassment and fear of rejection as a person and/or as a sex partner) (Cline, Johnson, & Freeman, 1992). Discussion of sexual history is of crucial importance, because the number of lifetime sex partners for college men ranges from 7.0 partners (Weinberg et al., 1998) to 8.0 partners (Reinisch, Hill, Sanders, & Ziemba-Davis, 1995). Since widespread evidence exists that most college men have more lifetime sex partners than college women, the lack of communication about sexual histories poses substantially greater risks for women than for men (Reinisch et al., 1995).

Sexual Satisfaction

In general, sexually active college women tend to report low levels of sexual satisfaction, especially those with inconsistent contraceptive usage and consumption of alcohol prior to sexual intercourse (Raj & Pollack, 1995). The importance of relationship factors as determinants of women's sexual functioning, including orgasmic consistency, are strongly supported (Rosen, Taylor, Leiblum, & Bachmann, 1993). But behavioral factors such as age at first intercourse, number of lifetime sex partners, and frequency of sexual intercourse are unrelated to experiencing orgasm during sexual intercourse (Raboch & Raboch, 1992).

Among college women, 78 percent rated coital orgasm as an important component of their sexual experience (Loos, Bridges, & Critelli, 1997). And the absence of orgasm at first sexual intercourse for college women also leads to a lower rating for subjective pleasure regarding the first sexual experience (Sprecher et al., 1995). Furthermore, 60 percent of college women reported feeling guilty if no orgasm was experienced during sexual intercourse. These women were also more likely to report being asked by their sex partner if they had experienced orgasm and less likely to indicate psychological sexual satisfaction (Davidson & Moore, 1994).

Why then do women fail to ask new sex partners about their sexual histories? Is this failure to act just one of a cluster of risk-taking behaviors? Are there family and personal background variables that differentiate women who do not ask from those who do? To answer these questions, this study investigated the correlation, if any, between the failure of college women to ask new sex partners about their sexual history prior to engaging in sexual intercourse and participation in other risk-taking sexual practices, as well as cognitive decision making and family and personal background variables.

METHODOLOGY

An anonymous questionnaire was administered to volunteer respondents in the schools of arts and sciences, business, and nursing at a midwestern, residential state university. This investigation was part of a larger research project designed to assess whether or not any significant changes in the sexual attitudes and behaviors of college students have occurred during the 1990s. Given the nature of the research question, the focus of this investigation was 438 women (77.7 percent) who reported having experienced sexual intercourse. Those women who gave no response to the question/variable "frequency/ask new sex partner/total number of previous sex partners prior to having sexual intercourse" (*N* = 28) were declared as missing values, providing a final sample of 410 sexually active women.

RESULTS

Overview

The initial data analyses revealed that of these college women, 32.7 percent (N = 134) reported "rarely", 19.5 percent (N = 80) reported "sometimes", and 47.8 percent (N = 196) reported "almost always" asking their new sex partner about his total number of previous sex partners. For ease of reporting the remaining data analyses, three respondent categories were subsequently established: AA group = almost always ask about previous sex partners; S group = sometimes ask about previous sex partners; and R group = rarely ask about previous sex partners. With regard to revealing their total number of sex partners, 44.0 percent of R group and 31.3 percent of S group women, in contrast to only 9.3 percent of AA group, reported "never" having discussed this matter with their new sex partner.

Of these women, 88.8 percent of R group, 92.5 percent of S group, and 88.7 percent of AA group women had received oral-genital stimulation. Further, 83.6 percent of R group, 90.0 percent of S group, and 87.2 percent of AA group had given oral-genital stimulation. S group women (65.0 percent) were more likely to have engaged in masturbation than either R group (45.5 percent) or AA group (45.9 percent) women. And 50.7 percent of R group, 53.8 percent of S group, and 60.7 percent of AA group women reported having experienced an orgasm while petting with an opposite-sex partner. However, S group (82.5 percent) and AA group women (72.4 percent) were more likely than R group (61.2 percent) women to indicate having ever experienced an orgasm during sexual intercourse.

Family and Personal Background

AA group women were more likely to have discussed sexually related topics with their mother figures than either R group or S group women. AA group women also were more likely than R group and S group women to believe that love should be a prerequisite for sexual intercourse and to desire to marry someone who had had sexual intercourse only with them. However, there were no significant differences between the groups for the following family background variables: feelings toward mother while growing up; mother figure uncommunicative; feelings toward father figure while growing up; father figure uncommunicative; and discussion of sexually related topics with father figure. There were no significant differences in religious denominations between groups; most women were either Mainline Protestant (46.7 percent) or Roman Catholic (43.0 percent). However, AA group women attended religious services more frequently than either R group or S group women.

First Sexual Intercourse

AA group women reported being in a committed love relationship with their sex partner at the time of their first sexual intercourse experience more often than either R group or S group women. AA group women also were older than R group and S group women at their first intercourse. However, there were no significant differences between groups for the age of first sex partner. Although not significant, the data suggest that, though voluntarily consenting, R group and S group women were more likely to have given implied rather than verbal consent for their first intercourse experience. Furthermore, R group and S group women, in comparison to AA group women, more frequently had been under the influence of alcohol or some other mind-altering substance at their first intercourse. Thus, as might be expected, AA group women more often employed a contraceptive at their initial sexual encounter than either R group or S group women.

There were no significant differences between groups with regard to first sexual intercourse either being physiologically or psychologically satisfying. Nor did any significant differences exist between groups with regard to feelings of guilt after having engaged in sexual intercourse.

Risk-Related Sexual Behaviors

The advent of AIDS resulted in the R group and S group women becoming less sexually active when compared to AA group women. AA group women were more likely than either R group or S group women to respond that AIDS had had "no effect" on their sexual activity. However, AA group women reported fewer sex partners in the past year and fewer lifetime sex partners than either R group or S group women.

There were no significant differences between groups for the following risk-related sexual behavior variables: experienced anal intercourse, ever diagnosed with STD, used condom during oral-genital sex, and used contraceptive during most recent sexual intercourse. But significant differences did exist with regard to other sexual risk-taking. AA group women were more likely to have planned their most recent sexual intercourse and to have discussed contraception prior to their most recent sexual intercourse than R group or S group women. In contrast, R group and S group women were more likely to have sexual intercourse without contraceptive use than AA group women. Furthermore, AA group women, when compared to R group and S group women, more often asked a new sex partner about his STD history. In addition, AA group women were less likely to believe that they would eventually contract an STD than the other women. Finally, a greater percentage of S group women than R group and AA group reported having ever been pregnant.

Role of Cognitive Decision Making

In exploring the role of cognitive factors in the decision-making process in the lives of AA group women, two variables were significant. These women were more likely than R group and S group women to set goals for themselves and to make sexual decisions based on their own thoughts rather than being influenced by others. However, no differences were found for the variable frequency/"feel optimistic about life."

Sexual Adjustment and Sexual Satisfaction

For all of these women, sexual guilt was not a distinguishing variable. There were no significant differences between groups for the following sexual guilt-related Likert-scale variables: feel guilty about masturbation, feel guilty about petting, feel guilty about current sexual intercourse, and feel guilty if no orgasm experienced during sexual intercourse. Furthermore there were no significant differences between groups with regard to level of comfort with sexuality and frequency of orgasm experienced during sexual intercourse. However, the sex partners of R group and S group women were more likely to ask them if they had experienced an orgasm during sexual intercourse when compared to the sex partners of AA group women. Furthermore, no significant differences between groups were found for the variable physiological sexual satisfaction in their sexual lives. However, AA group women, in contrast to R group and S group women, were more likely to report psychological sexual satisfaction in their sexual lives.

DISCUSSION

Given the nonrandomness of this sample, questions can be raised regarding the generalizability of the data, specifically the appropriateness of making inferences about college women in general. However, because these college women constituted 15 percent of the female students in each of the freshman, sophomore, junior, and senior classes and were from classes in various disciplines, this sample is thought to be a representative, albeit nonrandomly selected, group of American college women. Consequently, the investigators believe that this study can contribute to a better under-

standing of the communication practices of college women with their new sex partners.

Ideally, an anticipated first-time sex partner should share her or his previous sexual history, including number of lifetime sex partners, sexually transmitted disease history, and length of time since last partnered sexual activity. Although the content of such sexual discussions by these women was not determined in this investigation, the researchers propose that this is an important question for future research. Such a focus could help discern how young women actually make decisions pertaining to sexual intercourse, furnishing valuable information for professionals.

As the data unfold about young women who almost always ask new sex partners about their total number of sex partners, a clear portrait emerges of an apparently self-confident young woman whose sexual self-esteem is intact. This is consistent with the findings of Basen-Engquist (1992) that high self-efficacy is associated with intent to discuss past sex partners with a current sex partner. A gestalt of family and personal background factors offers a clue to the basis of healthy sexual communications in the young adult years. Perhaps the prototype for communicating freely with a new sex partner about sexual histories, hers and his, evolved from early discussions about sexuality that AA group women had with their mothers. Also, the frequent church attendance and valuing sexual intercourse within the context of love (i.e., no sexual intercourse without love, marrying a man who has had sexual intercourse only with them) are more likely rooted in family values than peer values.

Although self-efficacy was not directly measured in this study, one could reasonably extrapolate a high degree of such abilities in AA group women from the constellation of health-promoting sexual decisions involving their first sexual intercourse. For example, first intercourse frequently occurred in a committed love relationship and at a later age than for their peers, R group and S group women. They were more likely to have used a contraceptive and were less likely to have been under the influence of alcohol.

The role of alcohol in risk-taking sexual behavior implied by this research supports the findings of others that risk-taking is elevated by consumption of alcohol (Leigh et al., 1995). Given the findings of Mooney (1995), one would at least have to ask the question whether or not R and S group women who consumed greater quantities of alcohol and on a more frequent basis would rank high on sexual insecurity. Perhaps the risk takers in this study altered their perception of present risk with the consumption of alcohol as suggested by the Piombo and Piles (1996) study.

It is not surprising that in subsequent sexual intercourse experiences, AA group women exhibited healthier sexual behaviors than either R group or S group women, whose sexual behavior was characterized by risk-taking. Out of 11 statistically significant variables representing risk-related sexual behaviors, all but two variables were clearly health-promoting choices for AA group women. These women had fewer sexual intercourse partners in the past year and in their lifetime. Furthermore, they were less likely to have had sexual intercourse with a casual acquaintance or a person they had just met. Perhaps explicitly because of the foregoing health-promoting choices, they were least likely to believe that they would contract an STD in the future or to report that AIDS had had an effect on their current sexual activity. It is puzzling, however, that these low-risk women and the high-risk R group women were almost equally likely to have had a premarital pregnancy. Conceivably, this finding may be a function of the small n for this variable in general and for R group women in particular.

In assessing differences in the sexual behavior of these three groups of women, the key factor may lie in the cognitive dimension. AA group women were significantly more likely to base decisions on their own thoughts and goals that they had set for themselves. These cognitive variables may well be the chief ingredients in differentiating health-promoting and health-defeating sexual behavior among college women. Therefore, it is not surprising that AA group women were more likely than R and S group women to report psychological sexual satisfaction.

CONCLUSIONS

These findings do have at least two major implications for sex and family therapists. First, they lend further support to the crucial role that parent figures can play in the sexuality education of their children. Second, they demonstrate that the factors influencing young people to make healthy sexual decisions are far from simplistic. The health-promoting and health-defeating behaviors each appear to be constellations that, although observable, are by nature elusive in origin. If it is true that family/personal background factors and cognitive variables are singularly significant, practicing family professionals (such as sex educators, sex therapists, family therapists, and researchers) would be well-advised to focus less on the issue of imparting information about sexuality and more on strategies that support the development of high self-esteem and high self-efficacy in the developing person. Instruction and practice in decision-making skills and set-

ting short-range and long-range goals for self may be essential precursors to enacting sexual health-promoting behaviors. This perspective suggests that perhaps family professionals need to emphasize subjective as well as objective methods in their work. Furthermore, it suggests that researchers need to probe deeper than their quantitative data for qualitative answers.

References

Anderson, P. B., & Mathieu, D. A. (1996). College students' high-risk sexual behavior following alcohol consumption. *Journal of Sex & Marital Therapy, 22,* 259–264.

Basen-Engquist, K. (1992). Psychological predictors of "safer sex" behaviors in young adults. *AIDS Education and Prevention, 4,* 120–134.

Beckman, L. J., Harvey, S. M., & Tiersky, L. A. (1996). Attitudes about condom use among college students. *Journal of American College Health, 44,* 243–250.

Carroll, J. L., & Carroll, L. M. (1995). Alcohol use and risky sex among college students. *Psychological Reports, 76,* 723–726.

Carroll, L. M. (1991). Gender, knowledge about AIDS, reported behavioral change, and the sexuality of college students. *Journal of American College Health, 40,* 5–12.

Cline, R. J. W., Johnson, S. J., & Freeman, K. E. (1992). Talk among sexual partners about AIDS: Interpersonal communication for risk reduction or risk enhancement. *Health Communication, 4,* 39–56.

Cooksey, E. C., Rindfuss, R. B., & Guilkey, D. K. (1996). The initiation of adolescent sexual and contraceptive behavior during changing times. *Journal of Health and Social Behavior, 37,* 59–74.

Darling, C. A., Davidson, J. K., Sr., & Passarello, C. C. (1992). The mystique of first intercourse among college youth: The role of partners, contraceptive practices, and psychological reactions. *Journal of Youth and Adolescence, 21,* 97–117.

Davidson, J. K., Sr., & Moore, N. B. (1994). Guilt and lack of orgasm during sexual intercourse: Myth versus reality among college women. *Journal of Sex Education and Therapy, 20,* 153–174.

Dunn, J. L. (1998). Defining women: Notes toward an understanding of structure and agency in the negotiation of sex. *Journal of Contemporary Ethnology, 26,* 479–510.

Guggino, J. M., & Ponzetti, J. J., Jr. (1997). Gender differences in affective reactions to first coitus. *Journal of Adolescence, 20,* 189–200.

Hale, P. J., & Trumbetta, S. L. (1996). Women's self-efficacy and sexually transmitted disease preventative behaviors. *Research in Nursing and Health, 19,* 101–10.

Hale, R. W., Char, D. R., Nagy, K., & Stockert, N. (1993). Seventeen-year review of sexual and contraceptive behavior on a college campus. *American Journal of Obstretrics and Gynecology, 168,* 1833–1837.

Hawkins, M. J., Gray, C., & Hawkins, W. E. (1995). Gender differences of reported safer sex behaviors within a random sample of college students. *Psychological Reports, 77*, 963–968.

Hynie, M., Lydon, J. E., Côté, S., & Wiener, S. (1998). Relational sexual scripts and women's condom use: The importance of internalized norms. *Journal of Sex Research, 35*, 370–380.

Kusselling, F. S., Wenger, N. S., & Shapiro, M. F. (1995). Inconsistent contraceptive use among female college students: Implications for intervention. *Journal of American College Health, 43*, 191–195.

Leigh, B. C., Schafer, J., & Temple, M. T. (1995). Alcohol use and contraception at first sexual experiences. *Journal of Behavioral Medicine, 18*, 81–95.

Loos, V. E., Bridges, C. F., & Critelli, J. W. (1997). Weiner's attribution theory and female orgasmic consistency. *Journal of Sex Research, 23*, 348–361.

Mauldon, J., & Luker, K. (1996). The effects of contraceptive education on method use at first intercourse. *Family Planning Perspectives, 28*, 19–24, 41.

Mooney, D. K. (1995). The relationship between sexual insecurity, the alcohol expectation for enhanced sexual experience, and consumption patterns. *Addictive Behavior, 20*, 243–250.

Moore, N. B., & Davidson, J. K., Sr. (1997). Guilt about first intercourse: An antecedent of sexual dissatisfaction among college women. *Journal of Sex & Marital Therapy, 23*, 29–45.

Murnen, S. K., Perot, A., & Byrne, D. (1989). Coping with unwanted sexual activity: Normative responses, situational determinants, and individual differences. *Journal of Sexual Research, 26*, 85–106.

Paulson, R. L., Eppler, M. A., Satterwaite, T. N., Wuensch, K. L., & Bass, L. A. (1998). Alcohol consumption, strength of religious beliefs, and risky sexual behavior in college students. *Journal of American College Health, 46*, 227–232.

Piombo, M., & Piles, M. (1996). The relationship between drinking and their sexual behaviors. *Women's Health Issues, 6*, 221–228.

Pliskin, K. L. (1997). Verbal communication and sexual communication. *Medical Anthropology Quarterly, 11*, 89–109.

Prince, A., & Bernard, A. L. (1998). Alcohol use and safer sex behaviors of students at a commuter university. *Journal of Alcohol and Drug Education, 43*, 1–19.

Raboch, J., & Raboch, J. (1992). Infrequent orgasms in women. *Journal of Sex & Marital Therapy, 18*, 114–120.

Raj, A., & Pollack, R. H. (1995). Factors predicting high-risk sexual behavior in heterosexual college females. *Journal of Sex & Marital Therapy, 21*, 213–224.

Reinisch, J. M., Hill, C. A., Sanders, S. A., & Ziemba-Davis, M. (1995). High-risk sexual behavior at a midwestern university: A confirmatory survey. *Family Planning Perspectives, 27*, 79–82.

Richard, R., de Vries, N. K., & Van der Plight, J. (1998). Anticipated regret and precautionary behavior. *Journal of Applied Social Psychology, 28*, 1411–1428.

Rosen, R. C., Taylor, J. F., Leiblum, S. R., & Bachmann, G. A. (1993). Prevalence of sexual dysfunction in women: Results of a survey study of 329 women in a gynecological clinic. *Journal of Sex & Marital Therapy, 19*, 171–188.

Rubinson, L., & De Rubertis, L. (1991). Trends in sexual attitudes and behavior of a college population over a 15-year period. *Journal of Sex & Marital Therapy, 17*, 32–41.

Sawyer, R. G., & Smith, N. G. (1996). A survey of situational factors at first intercourse among college students. *American Journal of Health and Behavior, 20*, 208–217.

Seal, A., Minichiello, V., & Omodei, M. (1997). Young women's sexual risk-taking behavior: Re-visiting the influence of sexual self-efficacy and sexual self-esteem. *International Journal of Sexually Transmitted Diseases and AIDS, 8*, 159–165.

Seidman, S. N., Mosher, W. D., & Aral, S. O. (1994). Predictors of high-risk behavior in unmarried American women: Adolescent environment as a risk factor, *Journal of Adolescent Health, 15*, 126–132.

Sprecher, S., Barbee, A., & Schwartz, P. (1995). "Was it good for you, too?": Gender differences in first sexual intercourse experiences. *Journal of Sex Research, 32*, 3–15.

Thompson, S. C., Anderson, K., Freedman, D., & Swan, J. (1996). Illusions of safety in a risky world: A study of college students' condom use. *Journal of Applied Social Psychology, 26*, 189–210.

Weinberg, M. S., Lottes, I. L., & Aveline, D. (1998). AIDS risk reduction strategies among United States and Swedish heterosexual university students. *Archives of Sexual Behavior, 27*, 385–401.

Zellman, G. L., & Goodchilds, J. K. (1983). Becoming sexual in adolescence. In E. R. Allgeier & N. B. McCormick (Eds.), *Changing boundaries. Gender roles and sexual behavior* (pp. 49–63). Palo Alto, CA: Mayfield.

Chapter 14
Sexual Infidelity Among Married and Cohabiting Americans

Judith Treas
Deirdre Giesen

Tabloids herald extramarital sexual relationships of the famous and infamous. From Prince Charles to President Clinton, to the "woman or man on the street," no detail is too personal or too private to escape scrutiny. Sexual infidelity, it seems, captures the imagination of all America. Although the topic is a favorite pastime for the public, there is a dearth of empirical data about extramarital affairs. Treas and Giesen take a small step in correcting this imbalance.

If, as claimed by researchers, 90 percent of the general public believe that it is "always wrong" or "almost always wrong" to engage in extramarital sex, how do such beliefs translate into behavior? This is a fair but complex question in a society in which the percentage of women who have participated in extramarital affairs ranges from 15 percent to 29 percent and for men, 25 percent to 44 percent. Somehow the numbers confirming beliefs and behaviors don't compute.

Are psychological or sociological factors more influential in affecting the likelihood of extramarital affairs? And what is the role of permissive sexual values in infidelity? Reading the following article may help provide answers, but again, it may raise more questions than answers about this important topic.

Americans disapprove of sexual infidelity. More than 90 percent of the general public say it is "always" or "almost always" wrong for a married person to have sex with someone besides the marriage partner (Smith, 1994). About half the states in the U.S. retain laws against adultery that, although they are rarely enforced, would deny married persons who have extramarital sex the right to vote, serve alcohol, practice law, adopt children, or raise their own children (Constitutional barriers, 1992). American couples, whether married or cohabiting, agree that it is important to be monogamous (Greeley, 1991).

Couples' agreements about sexual exclusivity are a contractual condition of their unions. As with all contracts, bargains are sometimes broken. Although sexual fidelity is the dominant practice, recent surveys show that between 1.5 and 3.6 percent of married persons had a secondary sex partner in the past year (Choi, Catania, & Dolcini, 1994; Leigh, Temple, & Trocki, 1993). This article asks why some people are sexually exclusive while others have sex with someone besides their mate.

Previous Research

Research on sexual infidelity has focused on three domains—the personal values of the individual, the opportunities for extramarital sex, and the couple's relationship.

Permissive sexual values are associated with extramarital sex. Among Americans who believe extramarital relations are "not at all wrong," 76 percent report having had extramarital sex compared to only 10 percent of those who think extramarital sex is "always wrong" (Smith, 1994). Being male, African-American, and well educated are all associated with permissive sexual values (Smith, 1994). So is living in a big city. Extramarital permissiveness is linked to liberal political and religious ideologies (Smith, 1994). It is also related to gender egalitarianism and premarital permissiveness (Reiss, Anderson, & Sponaugle, 1980).

Opportunities, namely potential partners and circumstances assuring secrecy, facilitate extramarital sex. Some Americans admit they would have extramarital sex if their mate would not find out (Greeley, 1991). Couples who lead separate lives have more opportunities and are more likely to have secondary sex partners (Blumstein & Schwartz, 1983). Married people who perceive alternative partners to be available are more likely to have had extramarital sex (Maykovich, 1976). Of course, those predisposed to extramarital sex might be more likely to recognize opportunities that arise.

Dissatisfaction with the marital relationship itself is associated with extramarital sex (Brown, 1991; Vaughn, 1986). Those who engage in adultery are less likely to report happy marriages (Greeley, 1991). Infidelity has been linked to men's sexual dissatisfaction (Maykovich, 1976) and to women's perception of inequity in the marriage (Prins, Buunk, & Van Yperen, 1983). However, other studies fail to find a significant association for marital happiness

(Maykovich, 1976), marital adjustment (Johnson, 1970), seeing a mate as less affectionate (Edwards & Booth, 1976), or, for Whites, quality of marital sex (Choi et al., 1994). National surveys identify demographic risk factors for multiple sex partners. Education is positively related not only to permissive sexual values, but also to sexual infidelity (Leigh et al., 1993). Being African-American is associated with greater likelihood of multiple sexual relationships than being White (Smith, 1991). Men engage in more extramarital sex than women (Smith, 1991), perhaps because of male-female differences in reproductive strategies (Lancaster, 1994), the gendered nature of learned sexual scripts (Gagnon & Simon, 1973), or a double standard that judges men's sexual permissiveness less harshly than women's. The number of sex partners declines with age (Dolcini et al., 1993; Smith, 1991), which might reflect biological effects of aging (Edwards & Booth, 1994) or recent cohorts' more permissive sexual values (Smith, 1994). Compared to married couples, cohabitors are not as sexually exclusive (Forste & Tanfer, 1996)—consistent with their less conventional values (Clarkberg, Stolzenberg, & Waite, 1995), with the lower levels of commitment in cohabiting unions (Bumpass, Sweet, & Cherlin, 1991), and with differences in the sorts of partners chosen for cohabitation as opposed to marriage (Forste & Tanfer, 1996).

Conceptual Framework

Everyday accounts of extramarital sex often stress irrational causes like alcohol-impaired judgment or sexual addiction (Giddens, 1992). Although cultural scripts focus on romance and passion, people contemplating infidelity describe considered decisions. The self-conscious evaluation of extramarital options has been called "thinking" (Atwater, 1982) or "the debate" (Lawson, 1988). A wife reports making "a quick sort of negative and positive checklist" (Lawson, pp. 134–136). A husband confides, "(I)t's a question you have to ask yourself before. . . . 'Why am I doing this? What will I get out of it? How does this affect the status quo?'" (Lawson, p. 147).

Given social norms and strong dyadic expectations for sexual exclusivity, sexual infidelity demands calculated behavior. Theorizing about sex in terms of anticipated costs and gains yields useful insights, as Reiss and Miller (1979) suggested when hypothesizing a "reward-cost balance" for premarital permissiveness. A decision-making framework also serves to integrate piecemeal results of prior studies on extramarital sex.

Tastes and Values

A review of clinical and research studies identifies 31 reasons for extramarital relations; most, falling under the categories of sex, emotional intimacy, love, and ego bolstering, pertain to personal gratification (Glass & Wright, 1992). Some people's tastes and values increase the likelihood that they will engage in extramarital sex. People highly interested in sex might eschew sexual exclusivity because they anticipate greater pleasure from extramarital relations. On the other hand, nonpermissive values are known to be negatively associated with sexual infidelity, perhaps because people who hold these values anticipate discomfort reconciling dissonant beliefs and behavior (Lawson, 1988).

Hypothesis 1a: Greater interest in sex is associated with a greater likelihood of infidelity.

Hypothesis 1b: Nonpermissive sexual values are associated with a lower likelihood of infidelity.

Opportunities

People with fewer opportunities for undetected sex must go to greater lengths to have extramarital sex. Individual endowments and learned skills affect how many sexual opportunities come one's way. People with more sexual relationships in the past are more likely to have a secondary sex partner (Bozon, 1996). The sexually experienced might be more attractive; or they might have a "learned advantage" if they are more efficient than novices at recognizing sexual opportunities, recruiting sex partners, and managing sexual encounters.

H2a. Having had more sexual partners previously is associated with a greater likelihood of infidelity.

Social context also determines opportunities. As a place to socialize outside the company of a mate, the workplace offers access to potential partners (Lawson, 1988). Some work presents greater opportunities than other work. For instance, people whose jobs require overnight travel are more likely to have multiple sex partners (Wellings, Field, Johnson, & Wadsworth, 1994). Compared to small towns, big cities offer more opportunities for undetected sex—more potential partners, greater anonymity, and more permissive sexual values (Smith, 1994). In fact, big city residents do average more sex partners (Smith, 1991).

H2b. A job requiring personal contact with potential sex partners is associated with greater likelihood of infidelity.

H2c. Big city residence is associated with greater likelihood of infidelity.

Social networks composed of people who are apt to disapprove of adultery discourage extramarital relations, if only because one must go to greater lengths to keep sexual infidelity secret. Interestingly, married couples who became nonmonogamous "swingers" were insulated from social networks monitoring behavior and imposing costs on nonconformists: Swingers knew fewer neighbors, visited relatives less often, and joined fewer religious groups (Gilmartin, 1974).

H2d. When partners enjoy one another's kinship and friendship networks, the likelihood of infidelity is lower.

H2e. Controlling for sexual values, attending religious services more frequently is associated with lower likelihood of infidelity.

Primary Relationship

Because partners expect fidelity, potential costs to the primary relationship loom large in the face of infidelity. A mate who learns of a partner's infidelity might respond with emotionally draining recriminations, tit-for-tat infidelities, physical abuse, the withholding of couple services (e.g., sex, companionship, monetary support), and even divorce (Pittman, 1989).

Marital quality mediates costs. If a marriage is judged to be unrewarding, one has less to lose from extramarital sex. One can afford to be indifferent, both to costs to the marital relation and to sanctions a mate might offer. An extreme example is the "out-the-door" affair where one partner pursues an extramarital relationship to force a mate to end an unhappy marriage (Brown, 1991). Like subjective marital dissatisfaction, mates' social dissimilarity or heterogamy might prompt infidelity because social differences imply lower marital returns as a result of fewer stabilizing commonalities in the relationship (Lehrer & Chiswick, 1993).

H3a. Greater dissatisfaction with the union is associated with greater likelihood of infidelity.

H3b. Greater disparity in partners' social characteristics is associated with greater likelihood of infidelity.

People get locked into a union, however unfulfilling, by investments that they cannot recoup outside the relationship. Married people have more invested in their unions than do cohabitors. Besides a public commitment, the married are more likely to have children and to own a home jointly. They face higher exit costs should the relationship end. Because cohabitors risk less by an affair, it is not surprising that cohabitors are more likely to have secondary sex partners (Dolcini et al., 1993).

H3c. Cohabiting is associated with a greater likelihood of infidelity.

The likelihood of ever having been unfaithful increases with the duration of the union due to longer exposure to the risk of infidelity. At any given time, however, the likelihood of infidelity might vary with union duration. There are two competing arguments. If couples who have been together longer have made more stabilizing investments in their relationship, what they stand to lose will discourage infidelity. Yet, declines in coital frequency (Wellings et al., 1994) suggest that some marital benefits wane with time. If benefits jeopardized by infidelity decline over time, the likelihood of infidelity will increase at longer union durations.

H3d. (investment hypothesis) Longer union duration is associated with lower likelihood of infidelity at a given time.

H3e. (habituation hypothesis) Longer duration is associated with greater likelihood of infidelity at a given time.

Integrating prior findings on sexual infidelity, a decision-making framework generates hypotheses to be tested with superior survey data now available. We estimate a multivariate model of sexual infidelity incorporating personal tastes and values, the sexual opportunity structure, and features of the primary (i.e., marital or cohabiting) relationship. We control for demographic "risk factors" that might confound the associations among variables and consider whether factors informing sexual decision making can account for the effects of gender, race, age, and education.

THE CURRENT STUDY
Method

The 1992 National Health and Social Life Survey (NHSLS) is a national probability sample of 3,432 English-speaking Americans ages 18–59 who were interviewed about sexual attitudes and behavior (Laumann, Gagnon, Michael, & Michaels, 1994, pp. 42–73). In a face-to-face survey, interviewers asked about social background, health, fertility, sexual activities, attitudes, and fantasies. After answering demographic questions at the start of the interview, respondents filled out a short, self-administered questionnaire inquiring, among other things, whether they had ever had extramarital sex and whether they had had sex with someone besides their regular partner in the last 12 months. Interviewers then collected detailed marital, cohabitation, and sexual histories. Data quality is a concern with sensitive matters like extramarital sex. NHSLS self-reports of extramarital sex are consistent with those from the General Social Survey (Laumann et al., 1994).

On a self-administered questionnaire to be sealed in a "privacy" envelope, respondents marked whether they had ever had sex with someone other than their husband or wife while they were married. This self-recorded item was less vulnerable to social desirability bias than a person-to-person interview. Extramarital sex was reported by 15.5 percent of the 1,717 respondents in this category. Interviewer-collected data on the timing of sexual relationships showed 4.7 percent of the 2,010 respondents cohabiting and/or married in the past year had been unfaithful to their primary partner during this time.

Results

Expectations for Sexually Exclusive Unions

NHSLS respondents, whether married or cohabiting, held similarly high expectations for sexual exclusivity. Respondents who had had sex with a primary partner at least 10 times over the past year were asked about expectations for sexual fidelity. Nearly 99 percent of married persons expected their spouse to have sex only in marriage, and 99 percent assumed their partner expected sexual exclusivity of them. We found less than 1 percent of heterosexuals, married or cohabiting, reported that a partner had changed expectations for fidelity during the relationship.

Although cohabitors held less conventional gender and family values (Clarkberg et al., 1995), cohabiting heterosexuals were only slightly less likely (94 percent versus 99 percent) to expect sexual exclusivity than married persons who had never lived together. Once married, those who had once lived together held expectations that were not significantly different from the expectations of other married people. . . .

Cumulative Incidence of Extramarital Sex

If concerns about social acceptability deter people from admitting sexual infidelity, the self-administered questionnaire offered better data than the person-to-person interview. Tastes and values demonstrated the hypothesized relationships: Greater interest in sex was positively associated with the likelihood of infidelity, while nonpermissive sexual values were negatively associated. Thinking about sex daily instead of just a few times a week meant a 22 percent increase in the odds of ever having had extramarital sex.

The hypothesized link between infidelity and opportunities for undetected sex received mixed support. For once-married persons in central cities, compared to other communities the odds of extramarital sex were 39 percent higher. Partners' shared networks showed the predicted negative association: All things being equal, enjoying time spent with a mate's family lowered the odds of extramarital sex by 24 percent. Prior sexual experience, attendance at religious services, and workplace opportunities for extramarital sex were statistically insignificant.

As for the couple's relationship, no statistically significant association was found for any measures of social dissimilarity. However, living together before marriage raised the odds of marital infidelity by 39 percent even controlling for sexual values and frequency of attendance at religious services—variables that distinguish married couples who first cohabited from the more conventional married couples who did not.

Gender and race were statistically significant. All things considered, being male increased the odds of having engaged in extramarital sex by 79 percent. Being African-American [also] raised them by 106 percent even though education controlled for racial differences in socioeconomic status. Education showed a weak negative association. Both frankness and marital duration (i.e., exposure time) showed the expected positive relationships.

Cumulative Incidence for Married and Cohabiting Persons

Both cohabitors and married people expect sexual exclusivity. The gender's effect was markedly reduced when we added other variables hypothesized to affect sexual decision-making but [less] when sexual interest and nonpermissive values were considered. Analyses demonstrated that controlling for permissiveness eliminated most gender differences in infidelity: Because men's sexual values are more permissive, men faced fewer impediments to infidelity. By contrast, variables influencing decision-making did not much diminish the effect of being African-American.

Those with strong interest in sex—those apt to gain most from sexual encounters—were significantly more likely to have been unfaithful. Those facing stiffer personal costs—for example, those with nonpermissive values—were significantly less likely to engage in infidelity.

Early sexual experience and central city residence were positively associated with the likelihood of having ever been unfaithful. Sharing a mate's social network was negatively associated with infidelity. All things considered, befriending a partner's family was associated with a 26 percent decrease in the odds of sexual infidelity. Workplace sexual opportunities and religious service attendance were not statistically significant. Relationship measures of heterogamy were statistically insignificant, too. Cohabitation fell short of statistical significance at the .05 level.

Prevalence of Infidelity for Married and Cohabiting Persons

Sexual interest might prompt infidelity, but infidelity might stimulate interest in sex, leading to frequent erotic thoughts. Although permissive values no doubt encourage adultery, adulterers might rationalize their behavior by adopting permissive views. Results for short-term infidelity largely paralleled those from earlier analyses. Personal tastes and values were significantly associated with the likelihood of infidelity. With the exception of central city residence, so were measures of sexual opportunities. Even workplace opportunity, which was not statistically significant in earlier analyses, showed the hypothesized positive relationship for the previous 12 months. This suggests that characteristics of the job mattered, but the current job's social interactions did not adequately capture previous work conditions influencing past sexual behavior. Although previous cohabitation increased the odds of infidelity, other features of the relationship did not prove statistically significant. Union duration was not significant either, implying that the passage of time had no effect on the marital gains that would be jeopardized by sexual infidelity. Gender's effect—reduced when other factors were controlled—was not statistically significant for the previous 12 months. Race continued to be strongly significant, however.

Sexual opportunity measures—early sexual experience, workplace opportunity, central city residence—were all statistically significant. Heterogamy in education and age showed no hypothesized effects, but dissimilar religions raised the likelihood of sexual infidelity, suggesting that excluded variables like sexual values and religious service attendance accounted for the religious heterogamy effect. Gender and race were statistically significant. Youngest ages were associated with greater infidelity; all things being equal, the odds of infidelity were twice as high for those ages 18–30 as for those over 50.

Tastes and values were statistically significant. When "cosmopolitan" values were incorporated, the effect of central city residence ceased to be statistically significant. Other measures of sexual opportunity—whether clearly prior or less remote in time—showed the predicted associations. The odds of a recent infidelity were more than twice as high for cohabitors than for married persons. Although

cohabitation increased the likelihood significantly, we did not find the predicted association between partners' social dissimilarity and sexual infidelity. Subjective dissatisfaction, however, *was* positively and significantly associated with the likelihood of infidelity in the preceding 12 months. Most people reported high satisfaction with both the emotional and physical aspects of their union.

Subjective perception of the relationship was more closely associated with infidelity than objective heterogamy measures, which—although stable and causally prior to infidelity—did not demonstrate uniform effects on sexual behavior. Whether subjective dissatisfaction prompted infidelity or vice versa, any effect might be relatively short-term, especially if unhappy partners either reconciled or separated after an infidelity. If subjective evaluations of the match were not very stable, this might explain why prior studies did not always find current marital evaluations to be significantly associated with cumulative incidence of infidelity over the course of a union.

Discussion

Although previous research has reported personal values, sexual opportunities, and the marital relationship as determinants of extramarital sex, these studies have been largely piecemeal and based on small samples of limited generalizability. To the best of our knowledge, our research is the first to include measures of all three sets of determinants in multivariate analyses based on a large, representative sample of the U.S. population. The analyses show that values, opportunities, and the marital relationship are associated with sexual infidelity, even when other factors and demographic risk variables are controlled.

As we predicted, people who were more interested in sex were more likely to have multiple partners. As we hypothesized, people with nonpermissive values were less likely to engage in sexual infidelity. Considering sexual opportunities, we found evidence that prior sexual experiences were positively associated with infidelity. The behavioral constraints posed by overlap of mates' social networks reduced the likelihood of infidelity. In the short run, so did involvement in a religious community: Those who often attended religious services were less likely to have had multiple sex partners in the previous year, even when sexual values associated with religiosity were controlled. Sexual opportunities of the workplace also increased the likelihood of infidelity during the last 12 months. At least in the short run, however, any effect of city residence was substantially reduced when "cosmopolitan" sexual values and tastes were controlled.

The nature of the primary relationship proved important. We found cohabitors more likely than married people to engage in infidelity, even when we controlled for permissiveness of personal values regarding extramarital sex. This finding suggests that cohabitors' lower investments in their unions, not their less conventional values, accounted for their greater risk of infidelity. Cohabitors who went on to marry were no less likely to demand sexual exclusivity than people who married without having lived together. Neither the habituation nor the investment hypothesis about the effects of union duration was empirically supported.

As for measures of marital quality, partners' social dissimilarity was statistically insignificant, but subjective dissatisfaction with a union was associated with greater likelihood of recent infidelity. Prior studies yielded inconsistent results on whether poor relationships led to extramarital sex. Current relationship quality might not demonstrate an association with cumulative incidence—that is, having ever been unfaithful: Relationship problems were apt to be short-term if couples either reconciled or divorced soon after an infidelity.

Although epidemiological research consistently reports men to be at higher risk of infidelity than women, studies have not usually included indicators of sexual values and tastes. When we controlled for interest in sex and permissiveness of sexual values, we found that the main effects of gender were markedly reduced or even eliminated. Consistent with prior research, we found that being African-American was positively associated with multiple sex partners, even when educational attainment (an indicator of socioeconomic status) and other variables were controlled. The persistence of this effect points to the need for further research to clarify the role of race. Because we found the sexual opportunity structure to be important in understanding sexual behavior, racial differences in the sex ratio might influence the likelihood of having multiple partners.

We argue for thinking about sexual infidelity as the product of rational decision-making. Assuming sexual behavior is subject to rational calculation, we derived a series of testable hypotheses. NHSLS measures did not permit us to examine intrapsychic, cognitive processes or to compare directly preferences for alternative courses of behavior. To the extent that preferences are revealed in behavior, however, we can evaluate our approach by asking whether empirical results are consistent with predictions. Indeed, they are largely consistent even given different operationalizations of sexual infidelity.

Previous research reported that sexual infidelity is associated with values, opportunities for secret sex, the quality of the primary relationship, and sociodemographic risk factors. Integrating these piecemeal findings into a unified model revealed some well-documented relationships to be spurious. Our multivariate model also clarified the mechanisms by which variables might influence infidelity. For example, differences in tastes and values largely accounted for the effects of city residence and male gender. Controlling for sexual values, however, did not eliminate the significant association between infidelity and cohabitation, a result that pointed to commitment mechanisms as likely influences on sexual behavior. Nor could sexual values account for the negative association of church-going and recent infidelity. The multivariate analysis suggested that religiosity constrained sexual behavior not only through internalized moral beliefs, but also via supportive social networks. The integrated model pointed to one clear result: Being subject to preferences, constraints, and opportunities, sexual behavior is social behavior.

References

Atwater, L. (1982). *The Extramarital Connection: Sex, Intimacy, and Identity.* New York: Irvington.

Blumstein, P., & Schwartz, P. (1983). *American Couples.* New York: Morrow.

Bozon, M. (1996). Reaching adult sexuality: First intercourse and its implications. In M. Bozon & H. Letridon (Eds.), *Sexuality and the Social Sciences* (pp. 143–175). Aldershot, England: Dartmouth.

Brown, E. M. (1991). *Patterns of Infidelity and Their Treatment.* New York: Brunner-Mazel.

Bumpass, L. L., Sweet, J. A., & Cherlin, A. (1991). The role of cohabitation in declining rates of marriage. *Journal of Marriage and the Family, 53,* 913–927.

Choi, K.-H., Catania, J. A., & Dolcini, M. M. (1994). Extramarital sex and HIV risk behavior among American adults: Results from the National AIDS Behavioral Survey. *American Journal of Public Health, 84,* 2003–2007.

Clarkberg, M., Stolzenberg, R. M., & Waite, L. J. (1995). Attitudes, values, and entrance into cohabitational versus marital unions. *Social Forces, 51,* 609–633.

Constitutional barriers to civil and criminal restrictions on pre- and extramarital sex. (1993). *Harvard Law Review, 104,* 1660–1680.

Dolcini, M. M., Catania, J. A., Coates, T. J., Stall, R., Hudes, E. S., Gagnon, J. H., & Pollack, L. M. (1993). Demographic characteristics of heterosexuals with multiple partners: The National AIDS Behavior Surveys. *Family Planning Perspectives, 25,* 208–214.

Edwards, J. N., & Booth, A. (1976). Sexual behavior in and out of marriage: An assessment of correlates. *Journal of Marriage and the Family, 38,* 73–83.

Edwards, J. N., & Booth, A. (1994). Sexuality, marriage, and well-being: The middle years. In A. S. Rossi (Ed.), *Sexuality Across the Life Course* (pp. 233–299). Chicago: University of Chicago Press.

Forste, R., & Tanfer, K. (1996). Sexual exclusivity among dating, cohabiting, and married women. *Journal of Marriage and the Family, 58,* 33–47.

Gagnon, J., & Simon, W. (1973). *Sexual Conduct: The Social Sources of Human Sexuality.* Chicago: Aldine.

Giddens, A. (1992). *The Transformation of Intimacy: Sexuality, Love and Eroticism in Modern Societies*. Cambridge, England: Polity Press.

Gilmartin, B. G. (1974). Sexual deviance and social networks: A study of social, family, and marital interaction patterns among co-marital sex participants. In J. R. Smith & L. G. Smith (Eds.), *Beyond Monogamy* (pp. 291–323). Baltimore, MD: Johns Hopkins University Press.

Glass, S. P., & Wright, T L. (1992). Justifications for extramarital relationships: The association between attitudes, behaviors and gender. *The Journal of Sex Research, 29,* 361–387.

Greeley, A. M. (1991). *Faithful Attraction*. New York: A Tom Doherty Associates Book.

Johnson, R. E. (1970). Some correlates of extramarital coitus. *Journal of Marriage and the Family, 32,* 449–456.

Lancaster, J. (1994). Human sexuality, life histories, and evolutionary ecology. In A. S. Rossi (Ed.), *Sexuality Across the Life Course* (pp. 39–62). Chicago: University of Chicago Press.

Laumann, E. O., Gagnon, J. H., Michael, R. T. & Michaels, S. (1994). *The Social Organization of Sexuality*. Chicago: University of Chicago Press.

Lawson, A. (1988). *Adultery: An Analysis of Love and Betrayal*. New York: Basic Books.

Lehrer, E. L., & Chiswick, C. U. (1993). Religion as a determinant of marital instability. *Demography, 30,* 385–404.

Leigh, B. C., Temple, M. T., & Trocki, K. F. (1993). The sexual behavior of U.S. adults: Results from a national survey. *American Journal of Public Health, 83,* 1400–1408.

Maykovich, M. K. (1976). Attitudes versus behavior in extramarital sexual relations. *Journal of Marriage and the Family, 38,* 693–699.

Pittman, F. (1989). *Private Lives: Infidelity and the Betrayal of Intimacy*. New York: W. W. Norton.

Prins, K. S., Buunk, B. P., & Van Yperen, N. W. (1983). Equity, normative disapproval, and extramarital relations. *Journal of Social and Personal Relationships, 10,* 39–53.

Reiss, I. L., Anderson, R. E., & Sponaugle, G. C. (1980). A multivariate model of the determinants of extramarital sexual permissiveness. *Journal of Marriage and the Family, 42,* 395–411.

Reiss, I. L., & Miller, B. C. (1979). Heterosexual permissiveness: A theoretical analysis. In W. R. Burr, R. Hill, F. I. Nye, & I. L. Reiss (Eds.), *Contemporary Theories About the Family* (Vol. 1, pp. 57–100). New York: Free Press.

Siegel, M. J. (1992). For better or worse: Adultery, crime and the Constitution. *Journal of Family Law, 30,* 45–95.

Smith, T. W. (1991). Adult sexual behavior in 1989: Numbers of partners, frequency of intercourse and risk of AIDS. *Family Planning Perspectives, 23,* 102–107.

Smith, T. W. (1994). Attitudes toward sexual permissiveness: Trends, correlates, and behavioral connections. In A. S. Rossi (Ed.), *Sexuality Across the Life Course* (pp. 63–97). Chicago: University of Chicago Press.

Vaughn, D. (1986). *Uncoupling*. Oxford, England: Oxford University Press.

Wellings, K., Field, J., Johnson, A., & Wadsworth, J. (1994). *Sexual Behavior in Britain*. London: Penguin Books.

Chapter 15
Pretending Orgasm During Sexual Intercourse

Michael W. Wiederman

During the past two decades, the traditional view
that women are less sexual than men has largely disappeared, and the sexual needs of women have been
increasingly recognized and accepted. Therefore,
today a woman who perceives herself as sexually un-
responsive may become embarrassed or experience
other stressful emotions, such as guilt.

Although the vast majority of men usually experience orgasm with every episode of sexual intercourse,
this research suggests that this is not true for many
women. The reported percentage of women who always or almost always experience orgasm during sexual intercourse is about one-half. But, because most
men consider a woman's orgasm as symbolic of their
prowess as lovers, many women feel pressured to
have an orgasm during sexual intercourse. Thus, it is
known that a majority of women at least occasionally
pretend to experience an orgasm. This not-to-be-
missed selection will furnish an interesting perspective on a topic assumed to be of considerable interest,
if one believes the hype in popular women's magazines.

To the extent that women are expected to be sexually responsive to their partners, women may experience some degree of pressure to experience an orgasm during sexual intercourse. In response to such
pressure, some women may pretend, or "fake," an
orgasm during coitus. Indeed, popular films (e.g.,
When Harry Met Sally) and television programs
(e.g., *Seinfeld*) have tackled the issue of women pretending orgasms during sexual intercourse. In contrast, it is surprising how little empirical research
has been conducted on the phenomenon.

In the only study focused on the topic, Darling
and Davidson[1] explored the prevalence and correlates of pretending orgasm in a large sample of professional nurses. In their sample, 58 percent of the
women reported ever having pretended orgasm
during sexual intercourse. In comparing "pretenders" to "nonpretenders," Darling and Davidson
found that the pretenders were more likely to have
masturbated and explored a variety of techniques
for achieving orgasm (e.g., use of vibrators, erotic
literature, fantasy). Also, relative to the nonpretenders, pretenders were slightly older, had started
having sexual intercourse at a younger age, and had
greater numbers of lifetime intercourse partners.

The results from Darling and Davidson's survey
are interesting. However, many questions remain.
Pretending orgasm appears to be related to greater
sexual experience, but why? Is pretending orgasm
related to more liberal sexual attitudes? To sexual
esteem? If pretending orgasm is related to increased numbers of sexual partners, unrelated to
sexually permissive attitudes, and related to decreased sexual esteem, pretending orgasm may be
one way some women attempt to compensate for
feeling less than adequate as a sexual partner. Such
women may have had more partners not because of
permissive attitudes or high sexual esteem but,
rather, in an attempt to find male acceptance.

Similarly, is pretending orgasm related to physical attractiveness or, at least, self-perception of attractiveness? Women's physical attractiveness is
more highly related to their sexual desirability than
is men's physical attractiveness.[2] Correspondingly,
women with negative body image appear to have
less sexual experience.[3] It would stand to reason
that women who were less attractive, or believed
themselves to be, might attempt to compensate
through being more sexually responsive, even to the
point of pretending orgasm during coitus.

Is pretending orgasm related to more general
self-monitoring propensities? Self-monitoring refers to the degree to which the individual tends to
regulate self-presentation for the sake of desired
public appearance.[4] Highly self-monitoring persons are said to exhibit greater responsiveness to
social and interpersonal cues of situationally appropriate performance, whereas the expressive behavior of less self-monitoring persons is said to
more closely reflect enduring and momentary inner
states, including the person's attitudes, traits, and
feelings.[5] Self-monitoring has been shown to be
positively related to sexual experience,[6] and it
would stand to reason that highly self-monitoring
people would be more likely to pretend orgasm.
That is, women who typically monitor their own expressive behavior in social situations might be expected to be more likely to "act" when in a sexual situation with a partner.

The objective of the current study was to investigate potential relationships between having pre-

tended orgasm and sexual experience, sexual attitudes and sexual esteem, actual and self-perceived physical attractiveness, and self-monitoring. I decided to attempt to replicate Darling and Davidson's findings[1] regarding greater number of sex partners among women who pretended orgasm because they did not trim statistical outliers before conducting their analyses. That is, in their study, the range in number of lifetime intercourse partners appeared larger for the pretenders (range: 1–75) than for the nonpretenders (range: 1–35). So, the apparent difference between the mean number of sex partners in each group may have been due to a few statistical outliers among the pretenders.[7] Also, in their study, pretenders were older and had started having sexual intercourse at a younger age than nonpretenders. The apparent group differences in lifetime number of sex partners could have been due to the pretenders simply having been sexually active longer. I also chose a younger sample than that employed by Darling and Davidson[1] so as to explore the phenomenon during courtship. The mean age of the women in their sample was approximately 30 years, the mean age at which these women first experienced sexual intercourse was approximately 20 years, and a large proportion of the women were (or had been) married.

THE CURRENT STUDY
Method

Sample

Initial research participants were 232 women recruited from introductory psychology classes at a midsize Midwestern state university who received research credit toward partial completion of their psychology course. To ensure a rather homogeneous sample with regard to age, women ages 29 and older were excluded from further analysis. However, 24.4 percent of these women reported not having had sexual intercourse. Therefore, the final sample consisted of 161 young women who reported having experienced coitus, and nearly all (94.4 percent) of the women were between the ages of 18 and 22 years. The large majority of these participants (88.8 percent) were white, 8.7 percent were black, and the remaining 2.5 percent were Latino.

Measures

Respondents were asked whether they had ever experienced "sexual intercourse with a male (penis in vagina)," the age at which they had first experienced sexual intercourse, and the number of different males with whom they had ever experienced sexual intercourse. Additionally, respondents were asked whether they had ever experienced oral stimulation of their genitals by a male, and if so, with how many different males. Lastly, respondents were asked whether they had ever orally stimulated a male's genitals, and if so, with how many different males. Respondents also were asked to indicate "true" or "false" in response to the statement, "I have, at one time or another, pretended to have an orgasm during sexual intercourse."

Sexual Attitudes

Respondents completed the brief form of the Sexual Opinion Survey (SOS)[8] as a measure of their affective orientation toward erotic stimuli. Specifically, respondents indicated their degree of agreement or disagreement with each of five statements using a seven-point scale (ranging from 1, "Strongly agree," to 7, "Strongly disagree").

Sexual esteem, or the tendency to evaluate oneself positively as a sexual partner, was measured with the short form[9] of the sexual esteem scale from Snell and Papini's Sexuality Scale.[10] Respondents indicated their degree of agreement or disagreement with each of the five statements using a five-point scale (ranging from 1, "Strongly disagree," to 5, "Strongly agree"). Respondents were asked to rate the overall attractiveness of their face and their body separately, using a seven-point scale for each rating (ranging from 1, "Well below average," to 4, "Average," and 7, "Well above average"). As a measure of actual facial attractiveness (as opposed to self-reported facial attractiveness), research participants were unobtrusively and independently rated by a male and female research assistant using a seven-point scale (ranging from 1, "Not attractive," to 4, "Average attractiveness," and 7, "Very attractive"). Participants completed the 18-item revised Self-Monitoring Scale[8] by indicating whether each of the items was "true" or "false." Higher scores indicate a greater tendency to engage in self-monitoring of expressive behavior. Briggs and Cheek[11] demonstrated that the Self-Monitoring Scale is composed of two distinct factors, one having to do with "other-directedness" (five items) and one having to do with "public performing" (eight items).

Results

Of the 161 women, 55.9 percent reported having pretended orgasm during sexual intercourse. Relative to nonpretenders, women who reported having pretended orgasm during coitus were slightly older, had more liberal sexual attitudes, had higher sexual esteem, had started having coitus at a younger age, and perceived themselves to be more facially attractive. Surprisingly, there were no group differences in experimenter-rated facial attractiveness, self-perceived body attractiveness, or self-monitoring. Still, pretenders reported greater numbers of sexual intercourse and oral sex partners relative to nonpretenders.

Both age and age at first coitus were significant predictors. And, [number of] fellatio partners and age at first intercourse were marginally significant. Age was not a significant predictor nor was self-rated facial attractiveness. However, SOS scores and sexual esteem scores were significant predictors, even after controlling for age and self-rated facial attractiveness.

Discussion

In the current sample of young adult women who had experienced sexual intercourse, more than one-half reported having pretended orgasm during coitus. The rate of 55 percent reporting having pretended orgasm was very similar to the 58 percent rate in Darling and Davidson's sample,[1] even though those authors surveyed women who were 10 years older on average than were the women in the current sample. In attempting to understand the nature of this phenomenon, it is important to note the variables that were expected to be related but were not. For example, I expected women who were more highly self-monitoring of their expressive behavior in social situations to be more likely to have pretended orgasm. However, pretenders and nonpretenders did not differ in their self-monitoring scores.

Pretenders and nonpretenders also did not differ in self-rated body attractiveness or in experimenter-rated facial attractiveness. However, pretenders rated their own facial attractiveness higher than the self-ratings of nonpretenders, [but] this relationship disappeared after controlling for other variables on which pretenders and nonpretenders differed.

As with Darling and Davidson,[1] pretenders in the current study reported having greater numbers of lifetime intercourse as well as cunnilingus partners relative to nonpretenders. However, this difference apparently was due to the pretenders' being older and having had sexual intercourse at a younger age. In other words, pretenders and nonpretenders did not differ in their mean number of intercourse and cunnilingus partners per unit of time during their sexual careers after statistically controlling for current age and age at first sexual intercourse.

With regard to fellatio partners, however, pretenders had marginally more lifetime partners than nonpretenders, even after controlling for current age and age at first intercourse. This finding suggests that young women who pretend orgasm may be more focused on their partners' satisfaction, or more invested in appeasing their sexual partners, than young women who do not pretend orgasm during sexual intercourse. This speculation fits with Darling and Davidson's finding[1] that, to an open-ended question regarding personal feelings about faking orgasm, the most frequent response was "feel guilty, but it is important that I satisfy my partner" (p. 192).

The only unique predictor of having pretended orgasm during coitus was sexual esteem scores. Young women who reported having pretended orgasm had higher sexual esteem scores than women who denied ever having pretended orgasm. The items that constitute the sexual esteem scale refer generically to rating oneself "high" as a sex partner or being "confident" as a sex partner. The results of the current study raise interesting questions regarding the nature of sexual esteem for young women. It may be that, for women, being a "good" sexual partner is defined as being responsive to one's partner. If that is the case, women who can "put on an act" during sexual intercourse apparently view themselves as "good" sexual partners. Another possibility is that women who are confident as sex partners are simply more comfortable pretending orgasm should the situation, in their judgment, call for it.

A third explanation for the unique relationship between women's sexual esteem and having pretended orgasm has to do with orgasm consistency. Darling and Davidson[1] found that pretenders in their study had experienced orgasm in response to a greater number of different forms of stimulation than had nonpretenders. Also, pretenders were more likely than nonpretenders to experience guilt if they did not experience an orgasm during sexual intercourse. It may be that pretenders in the current study experience higher sexual esteem because they generally are more sexually responsive (have orgasms more consistently) than nonpretenders. If this were the case, pretenders might be holding themselves to a higher standard of sexual performance and engaging in pretended orgasm to compensate for perceived deficits in sexual responsiveness. Unfortunately, in the current study, respondents did not report on orgasm consistency or self-expectations regarding sexual responsiveness.

The results of the current study, coupled with those of Darling and Davidson,[1] indicate that pretending orgasm during sexual intercourse is a fairly widespread phenomenon among women and is related to their self-view as a sexual partner. Further investigation is needed to elucidate how pretending orgasm is related to women's attributions and sexual interactions with partners. For example, how is pretending orgasm related to sexual communication, sexual satisfaction, and expectations within the dyad? How do women communicate a pretend orgasm, and what effect, if any, does pretending have on women's sexual partners? Do their partners perceive or suspect a faked orgasm? What cues do partners use to make such a judgment? Do women who pretend orgasm to please a partner differ from those who pretend in order to enhance their own sexual appeal or to end an unsatisfying sexual interaction? All these questions await further research.

References

1. Darling CA, Davidson JK: Enhancing relationships: Understanding the feminine mystique of pretending orgasm. *J Sex Marital Ther 12*: 182–196, 1986.
2. Gangestad SW: Sexual selection and physical attractiveness: Implications for mating dynamics. *Hum Nature 4*: 205–235, 1993.
3. Faith MS, Schare ML: The role of body image in sexually avoidant behavior. *Arch Sexual Behavior 22*: 345–356, 1993.
4. Snyder M: *Public appearance/private realities: The psychology of self-monitoring*. New York, Freeman, 1987.
5. Snyder M, Gangestad S: On the nature of self-monitoring: Matters of assessment, matters of validity. *J Pers Soc Psychol 51*: 125–139, 1986.
6. Snyder M, Simpson JA, Gangestad S: Personality and sexual relations. *J Pers Soc Psychol 51*: 181–190, 1986.
7. Tabachnick BG, Fidell LS: *Using multivariate statistics* (3rd ed). New York, HarperCollins, 1996.
8. Fisher WA, Byrne D, White LA, Kelly K: Erotophobia-erotophilia as a dimension of personality. *J Sex Res 25*: 123–151, 1988.
9. Wiederman MW, Allgeier ER: The measurement of sexual esteem: Investigation of Snell and Papini's (1989) Sexuality Scale. *J Res Pers 27*: 88–102, 1993.
10. Snell WE, Papini DR: The sexuality scale: An instrument to measure sexual-esteem, sexual-depression, and sexual-preoccupation. *J Sex Res 26*: 256–263, 1989.
11. Briggs SR, Cheek JM: On the nature of self-monitoring: Problems with assessment, problems with validity. *J Pers Soc Psychol 54*: 663–678, 1988.

Part IV

Sexuality and the Life Cycle: Middle and Later Adulthood

The woman of 60, flying to her winter home in Florida, conveyed a somewhat convoluted saga to her seatmate. Her latest boyfriend, a 70-year-old businessman, had recently acquired a mark of distinction from his peers when sued by a young female employee for sexual harassment. Although neither the woman nor the jury faulted her boyfriend, it troubled her mother, age 85, whose 91-year-old fifth husband had read about it in a professional business journal he had received in his office (Clendinen 2000). Such copy may seem to set the stage for an off-Broadway play, but this actually occurred, epitomizing "third-stage adulthood"—the fastest growing demographic category in America.

A recent Harris poll found that almost one-half of persons ages 65 to 69 consider themselves as middle-aged, as do one-third of those in their 70s. Elliot Jacques, a psychologist who began to write about midlife crisis when he was age 38, now at age 83 has proposed the name "third-stage adulthood" for ages 62 to 85. According to Jacques, the first stage is from ages 18 to 40 and the second stage, ages 40 to 62. It was not until the second half of the twentieth century that changing demographics, resulting from the "graying of America," spawned the fertile field of geriatrics to care for America's fastest growing population, the elderly. In this process, a face was finally placed on sexuality throughout a lengthening life span.

Sex therapists and sexuality educators with a life-span perspective have responded to the need to expand their services to encompass new markets. Sexuality researchers have also expanded their parameters beyond the issues of the early adolescent and the young adult years, as reflected in the selections in this unit that showcase sexuality in the middle and later years. Regardless of the market or issues, a firm understanding of life-span sexuality development can contribute to personal happiness or professional success. This knowledge is especially important for today's aspiring sexuality professionals, who will work with myriad populations in search of individual and family stability.

Helping couples decode the language of their sexuality in "Passionate Marriage," David Schnarch addresses what he calls the vortex of the emotional struggle in marriage, in which to grow up, each must hold on to self in the context of the other. This seasoned therapist is a founder of the Sexual Crucible Approach, which conceptually integrates individual sexual and marital therapies. The article is included here not just for those few who would be sex therapists. It is included for all because it illustrates that sexual-marital therapy is an excellent context for gratifying personal growth and relationship development. This selection is a timely feature about the middle adult years, one of the foci of this unit. When marriages end through divorce at this juncture in life, they usually do so because of having been "neglected to death." As such malaise is addressed, nearly always, sexuality is raised as an issue. Those whose interest is piqued by the article are referred to Schnarch's (1991) breakthrough book, *Constructing the Sexual Crucible: An Integration of Sexual and Marital Therapy*. In presenting the reality of our struggles with sex, he engages in highly explicit discussion of what goes on in bed. The time spent reading this selection will yield rich dividends.

Pavlov wrote to the academic youth of Soviet Russia in 1935 just before his death, "Do not become the archivists of facts. Try to penetrate to the secret of their occurrence . . ." (Elias 1979, 73). More than three-quarters of a century later, sexuality researchers must still resist the tendency to become "archivists of facts" in their efforts to correctly assess changes in sexual attitudes and behaviors. Jenna Mahay, Edward Laumann, and Stuart Michaels seem to have mastered this feat in their chapter, "Race, Gender, and Class in Sexual Scripts." Although many scholars have documented group differences in sexual behaviors and attitudes, this research team "penetrates the secret of their occurrence" by examining the broader sexual scripts in which specific acts are embedded and by determining how race/ethnicity, gender, and class intersect to shape those scripts.

The fact that the respondents were primarily middle-aged, rather than those from younger respondents in the convenience samples generally surveyed in sexuality research, underscores the significance of this study for Part IV. Also, many of the earlier sexuality studies on racial/ethnic and class differences failed because they lacked data from representative samples collected at the same time; and they covered only a narrow range of sexual behaviors. The use of the rich descriptive resources of the National Health and Social Life Survey allowed these researchers to overcome such limitations.

Beginning with the premise that changes in sexual attitudes and behaviors can only be understood in relation to other elements in the fabric of our social structure, the authors explore what they labeled as master status variables: age, religion, marital status, and family composition. Readers will be intrigued with the differences in sexual attitudes and behavior that did surface between race/ethnicity, gender, and class when these master statuses were controlled. Certainly, this compelling chapter will not be quickly read, but the lack of technical research jargon does make it student friendly.

The review of aging and sexuality by Sheryl Kingsberg is a useful addition to this unit on later adulthood. Although the article's primary emphasis concerns the psychological and physiological impact of aging on sexual function in women and their partners, it contains a wealth of information on related sociological and physiological factors. For example, the author pays particular attention to the impact of sexuality on the baby-boomer generation and its different approaches to sexuality at midlife than those dictated by cultural stereotypes. Even though this offering overviews the major sexual problems attributable to the aging process, its most valuable contribution may be the excellent development of the idea that sexual intimacy later in life is very much a reality that may assume many different faces. Kingsberg's assertion that new, exciting sexual relationships are as likely to occur in midlife as in young adulthood may be a novel idea to many young readers who have a difficult time perceiving older adults, such as parent figures, as sexual beings.

Nobel laureate Gary Becker suggested that the physical extension of life may be the greatest single achievement of the twentieth century, and this reality could prove to be the greatest single influence on the current century. That is the good news. The bad news is that redefinitions of life do not come easily. Even with all of the excitement about the map of the human genomes, the work of recrafting the language of longevity is just beginning (Clendinen 2000). Lore Wright's research is a small but significant step in this direction, adding to the sparse data about the effects of Alzheimer's disease on affection and sexuality among married couples. Contrasting normal aging with pathological deviations and framing aging itself within a human development perspective, this study draws some surprising conclusions. Although more data are certainly needed due to the very small sample, the work's value is enhanced by its longitudinal design. This effort expands our thinking about an important personal and social issue.

References

Clendinen, D. (2000, July 14). "Third-Stage Adulthood Is Fast-Growing Demographics." *New York Times*, p. 15A.

Elias, V. D. (1979). "Interpreting Data on Sexual Conduct and Social Change." In V. L. Bullough (ed.), *The Frontiers of Science* (pp. 71–76). Buffalo, NY: Prometheus.

Schnarch, D. (1991). *Constructing the Sexual Crucible: An Integration of Sexual and Marital Therapy.* New York: Norton. ✦

Chapter 16
Passionate Marriage

David M. Schnarch

Individuals for whom orgasm is the ultimate in sexual functioning may find David Schnarch's article simply boring. His counter-belief that sexual potential extends far beyond the physical point of release is skillfully woven into the case of Betty and Donald, an actual married couple with real-life issues. Challenging the common foci of many sex therapists, i.e., sexual technique, reversal of sexual symptoms, or the pursuit of intimacy for intimacy's sake, Schnarch proposes another theory. From his perspective, it is within what he calls the "sexual crucible" that unresolved individual and relationship problems surface to reveal themselves in common dysfunctional sexual styles.

One does not have to be an aspiring sex therapist to be enlightened and liberated by this important work. Of the many insights to be gained, two points are especially helpful for young persons just embarking on their personal odysseys. The first is the distinction between a person's genital prime, the peak years of physical reproductive maturity, and one's sexual prime, the human capacity for adult eroticism and emotional connection. The potential for sex to be even better in the sexual prime that occurs with age than in the genital prime of youth has to be an intriguing concept for all mortals because aging is seldom an option. The second point, concerning the author's thesis that mutual completion of the sexual response cycle is not the same thing as intimacy, is well-supported. Although this assertion may be assumed to be self-evident, the number of failed marriages among Americans perhaps belies this assumption. This is a definitely not-to-be-missed offering.

Betty, a designer in a high-powered advertising firm, and Donald, a college professor bucking for tenure, had been married for 15 years. They spent the first 10 minutes in my office invoking the standard litany of our times as an explanation for their lousy sex life—they were both just too busy. Not that this focus precluded blaming each other for their difficulties. "Betty gets home from work so late that we barely see each other anymore, let alone have sex," said Donald resentfully. "We're collaborators in child raising and mortgage paying, but we're hardly lovers anymore. I've taken over a lot of the household chores, but she often doesn't get home until 9 p.m.—and most nights, she says she's just 'too tired' for sex." Betty sighed in exasperation. "Sometimes I think Donald wants me to leap from the front door to the bedroom and take care of him," she said. "But I'm being swallowed up by a sea of obligations—my boss, the kids, the house, the dog, Donald, everybody wants a big chunk of me. Right now, I feel there's nothing left of me for *me*, let alone for *him*. He just doesn't get it that I need more time for myself before I'm interested in sex." I asked them to be specific about how the stress from their very demanding lives revealed itself in bed—exactly what happened, and in what order, when they had sex. Several moments of awkward silence and a number of false starts ensued before another, much more intimate, level of their marital landscape revealed itself.

Betty looked hard at Donald, then at me. "The fact of the matter is, he doesn't even know how to kiss me!" she said grimly.

"How would you know? It's been so long since you *let* me kiss you!" hissed Donald.

When I asked them to describe their foreplay, Betty looked embarrassed and Donald sounded frustrated. "During sex, she turns her face to the side and I end up kissing her cheek. She won't kiss me on the mouth. I think she just wants to get sex over with as fast as possible. Not that we have much sex." Betty shook her head in distaste. "He always just rams his tongue halfway down my throat—I feel like I can't breathe. Besides, why would I want to kiss him, when I can't even talk to him! We don't communicate at all."

Over the years, I've worked with many couples who complain bitterly that the other kisses—or touches, fondles, caresses, strokes—the "wrong" way. I used to take these complaints at face value, trying to help the couple solve their problems through various forms of marital bargaining and forbearance—listen empathetically, give a little to get a little, do something for me and I'll do something for you—teach them the finer points of sexual technique and send them home with detailed prescriptions (which they usually didn't follow) until I realized that their sexual dissatisfactions did not stem from ignorance, ineptitude or a "failure to communicate." On the contrary, "communicating" is exactly what Donald and Betty were already doing very well, only neither much liked the "message" the other was sending. The way this couple kissed each other, indeed their "vocabulary" of foreplay, constituted a very rich and purposeful dialogue, replete with symbolic meanings. Through this finely nuanced, but unmistakable language, both partners expressed their feelings about themselves and each other and negotiated what the entire sexual encounter would be like—the degree and quality of eroticism, connection and intimacy, or their virtual absence.

Donald and Betty had tried marital therapy before, but their therapist had taken the usual approach of dealing with each complaint individually—job demands, parenting responsibilities, housework division and sexual difficulties—as if they were all separate but equal situational problems. Typically, the clinician had tried to help Donald and Betty resolve their difficulties through a skill-building course on compromise, setting priorities, time management and "mirroring" each other for mutual validation, acceptance and, of course, better communication. The net result of all this work was that they felt even worse than before, even more incompetent, inadequate and neurotic, when sex didn't improve.

Knowing that Betty and Donald were most certainly communicating something via their gridlocked sexual styles, I asked them, "Even if you are not talking, what do you think you might actually be 'saying' to each other when you kiss?" After a minute, Donald said resentfully, "She's telling me I'm inadequate, that I'm not a good lover, I can't make her happy and she doesn't want me anyway." Betty defensively countered, "He's saying he wants me to do everything exactly his way and if I don't just cave in, he'll go ahead and do what he likes, whether I like it or not!" I asked her why she was willing to have intercourse at all if she didn't even want to kiss him. "Because he is such a sullen pain in the ass if I don't have sex," Betty replied without hesitation. "Besides, I like having orgasms."

Donald and Betty perfectly illustrated the almost universal, but widely unrecognized, reality that sex does not merely constitute a "part" of a relationship, but literally and metaphorically embodies the depth and quality of the couple's entire emotional connection. We think of foreplay as a way couples establish connection, but more often it's a means of establishing disconnection. Betty was a living rebuttal of the common gender stereotype that all women always want more foreplay; she cut it short so they could get sex done with as quickly as possible—and Donald understood. Donald returned the compliment by "telling" Betty he knew she didn't like him much, but he was going to get something out of her anyway—with or without her presence, so to speak.

Clearly, foreplay for this couple was not simply a mechanical technique for arousal, amenable to the engineering, skill-building approach still dictated by popular sex manuals. Nor were they likely to improve sex just by being more "open" with each other, "asking for what they wanted"—another popular remedy in self-help guides and among marital therapists—as if they weren't already "telling" each other what each did and did not want, and what each was or was not willing to give. Instead of trying to spackle over these normal and typical "dysfunctional" sexual patterns with a heavy coat of how-to lessons, I have learned that it makes much more sense to help the couple analyze their behavior, to look for the meaning of what they were already doing before they focused on changing the mechanics.

Rather than "work on their relationship" as if it were some sort of hobby or home-building project, Betty and Donald, like every other couple I have seen, needed to understand that what they did in bed was a remarkably salient and authentic expression of themselves and their feeling for each other. The nuances of their kissing style may have seemed trivial compared to the screaming fights they had about money or long days of injured silence, but in fact was an open window into their deepest human experience—who they were as people, what they really felt about each other, how much intimacy they were willing to risk with each other and how much growing up they still had to do.

As in any elaborate and nuanced language, the small details of sex carry a wealth of meaning, so while Donald and Betty were surprised that I focused on a "little thing" like kissing, rather than the main event—frequency of intercourse, for example—they were startled to find how truly revealing it was, about their personal histories as well as their marriage. I told Betty I thought she had probably come from an intrusive and dominating family that never dealt openly or successfully with anxiety and conflict. "So now, you have a hard time using your mouth to tell Donald not to be so overbearing, rather than turning it away to keep him from getting inside it. You've become very good at taking evasive action to avoid being overwhelmed," I said. "You're right about my family," Betty said softly, "we kids didn't have any privacy or freedom in my family, and we were never allowed to complain openly about anything—just do what we were told, and keep our mouths shut."

On the other hand, I said, I imagined Donald had never felt worthwhile in his family's eyes. He had spent a lot of time trying to please his parents without knowing what he was supposed to do, but he got so little response that he never learned how to read other people's cues—he just forged blindly ahead, trying to force his way into people's good graces and prove himself without waiting to see how he was coming across. "Come back here and give me a chance to prove myself!" his behavior screamed. "Are you so used to being out of contact with the people you love that you can successfully ignore how out of sync you are with them?" I asked. To Donald's credit, he didn't dodge the question, though he seemed dazed by the speed with which we'd zoomed in on such a core issue.

Nevertheless, Donald and Betty discovered that their discomfort in describing, in exact detail, what was done by whom, when, how and where, was outweighed by their fascination at what they were finding out about themselves—far more than was remotely possible from a seminar on sex skills. Betty, for example, had suggested that once kissing had stopped and intercourse had started, her sexual life was just fine—after all, she had orgasms and she "liked" them. But when I asked her to describe her experience of rear-entry intercourse—a common practice with this couple—she did not make it sound like a richly sensual, erotic or even particularly pleasant encounter. During the act, she positioned herself on elbows and knees, her torso held tense and rigidly parallel to the mattress while she protectively braced her body for a painful battering. Instead of moving into each thrust from Donald, she kept moving away from him, as if trying to escape. He, on the other hand, clasped her hips and kept trying to pull her to him, but never got a feeling of solid physical or emotional connection.

In spite of the fact that both were able to reach orgasm—widely considered the only significant measurement of successful sex—Betty and Donald's minute-by-minute description of what they did made it obvious that a lot more was happening than a technically proficient sex act. I told Betty I was glad she had told me these details, which all suggested that she thought it was pretty hopeless trying to work out conflicts with people she loved. "I suspect you've gotten used to swallowing your disappointment and sadness without telling anybody, and just getting along by yourself as best you can," I said. "It sounds very lonely." At that point, much to Donald's shock, Betty burst into tears. I said to Donald that he still seemed resigned to chase after people he loved to get them to love and accept him. "I guess you just don't believe they could possibly love you without being pressured into it. In fact, I think both of you use sex to confirm the negative beliefs you already have about yourselves."

For several seconds Donald looked at his lap, while Betty quietly cried in the next chair. "I suppose we must be pretty screwed up, huh?" Betty snuffled. "Nope," I said. "Much of what's going on between you is not only understandable, it's predictable, normal and even healthy—although it doesn't look or feel that way right now." They were describing the inevitable struggle involved in seeking individual growth and self-development within the context of marriage.

Betty said she used to enjoy sex until she became overinvolved with her job, but I suggested that the case was more likely the reverse—that the demands of her job gave her a needed emotional distance from Donald. Her conscious desire to "escape" from Donald stemmed from emotional fusion with him—she found herself invaded by his worries, his anxieties, his insecurities and his needs as if she had contracted a virus from him. "You may feel that you don't have enough inside you to satisfy his needs and still remain a separate, whole person yourself," I said. "Your work is a way of keeping some 'self' *for* yourself, to prevent being absorbed by him. That's the same reason you turn your head away when he tries to kiss you."

I suggested that Donald's problem was a complementary version of the same thing: in order to forestall the conviction that he had no worthwhile self at all, he felt he had to pressure Betty, or anybody he loved, to demonstrate they loved him—over and over. Donald, of course, did not see that he was as important to Betty as she was to him, but their mutual need for each other was really a function of two fragile and insecure selves shoring each other up.

Like most of us, neither Betty nor Donald was very mature when they married; neither had really learned the grown-up ability to soothe their own emotional anxieties or find their own internal equilibrium during the inevitable conflicts and contretemps of marriage. And, like most couples after a few years of marriage, they made up for their own insecurities by demanding that the other provide constant, unconditional acceptance, empathy, reciprocity and validation to help them each sustain a desired self-image. "I'm okay if, but only if, you think I'm okay," they said, in effect, to each other, and worked doubly hard both to please and be pleased, hide and adapt, shuffle and dance, smile and agree. The more time passes, the more frightened either partner is of letting the other know who he or she *really* is.

This joint back-patting compact works for a while to keep each partner feeling secure, but eventually the game becomes too exhausting to play. Gradually, partners become less inclined to please each other, more resentful of the cost of continually selling themselves out for ersatz peace and tranquillity, less willing to put out or give in. The ensuing "symptoms"—low sexual desire, sexual boredom, control battles, heavy silences—often take on the coloring of a deathly struggle for selfhood, fought on the implicit assumption that there is only room for one whole self in the marriage. "It's going to be my way or no way, my self or no self!" partners say in effect, in bed and out—leading to a kind of classic standoff.

Far from being signs of a deeply "pathological" marital breakdown, however, as Donald and Betty were convinced, this stalemate is a normal and inevitable process of growth built into every marriage, as well as a golden opportunity. Like grains of sand inexorably funneling toward the "narrows" of an hourglass, marriage predictably forces couples into a vortex of emotional struggle, where each dares to hold onto himself or herself in the context of each other, in order to grow up. At the narrowest, most constricting part of the funnel—where alienation, stagnation, infidelity, separation and divorce typically occur—couples can begin not only to find their individual selves, but in the process acquire a far greater capacity for love, passion and intimacy with each other than they ever thought possible.

At this excruciating point in a marriage, every couple has four options: each partner can try to control the other (Donald's initial ploy, which did not succeed), accommodate even more (Betty had done so to the limits of her tolerance), withdraw physically or emotionally (Betty's job helped her to do this) or learn to soothe his or her own anxiety and not get hijacked by the anxiety of the other. In other words, they could work on growing up, using their marriage as a kind of differentiation fitness center par excellence.

Differentiation is a lifelong process by which we become more uniquely ourselves by maintaining ourselves in relationship with those we love. It allows us to have our cake and eat it too, to experience fully our biologically based drives for both emotional connection and individual self-direction. The more differentiated we are—the stronger our sense of self-definition and the better we can hold ourselves together during conflicts with our partners—the more intimacy we can tolerate with someone we love without fear of losing our sense of who we are as separate beings. This uniquely human balancing act is summed up in the striking paradox of our species, that we are famously willing both to die for others, and to die rather than be controlled by others.

Of all the many schools of hard experience life has to offer, perhaps none but marriage is so perfectly calibrated to help us differentiate—if we can steel ourselves to take advantage of its rigorous lessons, and not be prematurely defeated by what feels at first like abject failure. Furthermore, a couple's sexual struggle—what I call the sexual crucible—is the most powerful route both to individual maturity and the capacity for intimate relationship, because it evokes people's deepest vulnerabilities and fears, and also taps into their potential for profound love, passion, even spiritual transcendence.

In the typically constricted sexuality of the mid-marriage blues, Betty and Donald's sexual repertoire consisted of "leftovers"—whatever was left over after eliminating every practice that made one or the other nervous or uncomfortable. The less differentiated a couple, the less they can tolerate the anxiety of possibly "offending" one another, the more anxiety they experience during sex and the more inhibited, rigid and inflexible their sexual style becomes: people have sex only up to the limits of their sexual and emotional development. Unsurprisingly, Donald and Betty's sexual routine had become as predictable, repetitious, unadventurous and boring as a weekly hamburger at McDonald's. This is why the standard advice to improve sex by negotiating and compromising is doomed to failure—most normally anxious couples have already long since negotiated and compromised themselves out of any excitement, variety or sexual passion, anyway.

And yet, it would have been pointless and counterproductive to march Donald and Betty through a variety of new sexual techniques. Using sex as a vehicle for personal and relational growth is not the same as just doing something new that raises anxieties. Rather, it depends on maintaining a high level of personal connection with someone known and loved during sex—allowing ourselves to really see and be seen by our partners, feel and be felt, know and be known by them. Most couples have spent years trying not to truly reveal themselves to each other in order to maintain the illusion of complete togetherness, thus effectively smothering any true emotional connection, with predictably disastrous effects on sex.

Donald and Betty were so obsessed with sexual behavior, so caught up in their anxieties about who was doing or failing to do what to whom in bed, that they were not really emotionally or even physically aware of each other when they touched. Like people "air kissing" on social occasions, they were going through the motions while keeping a kind of emotional *cordon sanitaire* between them. Their sex was more like the parallel play of young children than an adult interaction—except that they each watched the other's "play" with resentment and hurt feelings. Betty complained that Donald touched her too roughly—"He's crude and selfish!" she said, "and just uses me to please himself." Her complaint undercut Donald's sense of self, and he defensively accused her of being a demanding bitch, never satisfied and fundamentally unpleasable—thereby undermining her sense of self.

In order to help them each find a self and each other, I had to redirect their gaze away from their obsession with mutually disappointing sexual behavior, and encourage them to "follow the connection"—rediscover or establish some vital physical and emotional link as a first building block to greater intimacy. To consciously "follow the connection," however, requires the full presence and consent of both partners, each purposely slowing down and giving full attention to the other, feeling and experiencing the other's reality.

The next session, Donald reported that he now understood why Betty felt he was too "rough"; he said the experience made him realize that he usually touched her with about as much care and sensitivity as if he was scouring a frying pan! But slowing down to really become conscious of what he was doing made him experience a sudden jolt of emotional connection with Betty. This awareness was an unnerving sensation for someone who had spent his life performing for other people (including his wife) rather than actually being *with* them.

Betty, too, was shaken by the jarring reality of their connection. She hadn't liked being touched roughly, but the concentration and attention in Donald's hands as he really felt and got to know her body was deeply disturbing; she found herself suddenly and unexpectedly sobbing with grief and deprivation for the warmth and love she'd missed as a child, and that she had both craved and feared in her marriage. Later that night, they had the best sex they had experienced in a very long time.

Buoyed by this first success, more hopeful about their future together, they both wanted to know how they could enhance this new and still tentative sense of connection. I suggested they try something called "hugging till relaxed," a powerful method for increasing intimacy that harnesses the language and dynamics of sex without requiring either nudity or sexual contact. Hugging, one of the most ordinary, least threatening gestures of affection and closeness, is also one of the most telling. When they hugged, Betty complained that Donald always leaned on her—making her stagger backward—while Donald accused Betty of pulling away from him, letting go "too soon," and leaving him "hugging air."

I suggested that Betty and Donald each stand firmly on their own two feet, loosely put their arms around each other, focus on their own individual experience and concentrate on quieting themselves down while in the embrace—neither clutching nor pulling away from or leaning on each other. Once both partners can learn to soothe themselves and maintain their individual equilibrium, shifting their own positions when necessary for comfort, they get a brief, physical experience of intimate connection without fusion, a sense of stability and security without overdependency.

While practicing hugging until relaxed with Donald, Betty found that as she learned to quiet her own anxiety, she could allow herself to be held longer by Donald without feeling claustrophobic. Just relax-ing in the hug also made her realize that she normally carried chronic anxiety like a kind of body armor. As Betty calmed down and began to melt peacefully into the hug, not pulling away from fear that Donald would, literally, invade her space, he noticed his own impulse to break it off before she wanted to. When they each could settle down in the hug, they discovered that together they eventually would enter a space of great peace and tranquillity, deeply connected and in touch with each other but secure in their self.

Soon, they could experience some of the same kind of deep peace during sex, which not only eliminated much of the anxiety, resentment and disappointment they had felt before, but vastly increased the eroticism of the encounter. Now that they knew what they were looking for, they could tell when it was absent. Later, in my office, while Betty gently stroked his arm, Donald teared up as he told me about the new sense of quiet but electric connection he felt with her. "I just had no idea what we were missing; she seemed so precious to me that it almost hurt to touch her," he said, his voice thick with emotion.

This leap in personal development didn't simply occur through behavioral desensitization. Sometimes, Betty and Donald got more anxious as their unresolved issues surfaced in their physical embrace. At times, when Betty dared to shift to a more comfortable position, Donald felt she was squirming to avoid him. It was my job to help them see how this reflected the same emotional dynamics present in other aspects of their marriage. Betty was attempting to "hold onto herself" while remaining close to someone she loved, and likewise, Donald was refusing to chase after a loved one to get himself accepted. Insight alone didn't help much; a lot of self-soothing was required. Ultimately, they stopped taking each other's experience and reaction as a reflection on themselves and recognized that two separate realities existed even during their most profound physical union.

Building on their new stockpiles of courage earned in these experiments with each other, I suggested that Donald and Betty consider eyes-open sex, the thought of which leaves many couples aghast. Indeed, Donald's first response to the suggestion was that if he and Betty tried opening their eyes during sex, they wouldn't need birth control because the very thought made him so anxious he could feel his testicles retreating up into his windpipe! But eyes-open sex is a powerful way of revealing the chasm between sensation-focused sex and real intimacy. Most couples close their eyes in order to better tune out their partners so that they can concentrate on their physical feelings; it is a shocking revelation that to reach orgasm—supposedly the most intimate human act—most people cannot tolerate too much intimacy with their partners, so they block the emotional connection and concentrate on body parts.

Eyes-open sex is not simply a matter of two pairs of eyeballs staring at each other, but a way to intensify the mutual awareness and connection begun during foreplay; to really "see" and "be seen" is an extension of feeling and being felt when touching one another. But if allowing oneself to be known by touch is threatening, actually being seen can be positively terrifying. Bravely pursuing eyes-open sex in spite of these misgivings helps couples not only learn to tolerate more intimacy, it increases differentiation—it requires a degree of inner calm and independent selfhood to let somebody see what's inside your head without freaking out.

But the experience was also exhilarating. As Donald and Betty progressed from shy, little, peekaboo glimpses into each other's faces to long, warm gazes and soft smiles, each found their encounters more deeply moving. Betty slowly realized that whereas before she had wanted to escape from Donald, now she yearned to see all of him, and for him to see all of her. "I felt so vulnerable, as if he could see all my inadequacies, but the way he looked at me and smiled made all that unimportant." Donald gradually relinquished the self-image of a needy loser; he no longer needed to pursue Betty for reassurance and found, to his delight, that she wanted him—a breathtaking experience. "Her eyes are so big and deep, I feel I could dive into them," he said in wonder.

Both began to experience an increasing sense of self-acceptance and personal security. "We're having better sex now than we've ever had in our lives," Betty reported, "And I thought we were getting to be too old and far too married for exciting sex." Donald agreed. Betty and Donald, like society at large, were confusing genital prime—the peak years of physical reproductive maturity—with sexual prime—the specifically human capacity for adult eroticism and emotional connection. "Are you better in bed or worse now than you were as an adolescent?" I asked them. "Most people definitely get better as they get older, at least potentially. No 17-year-old boy is sufficiently mature to be capable of profound intimacy—he's too preoccupied with proving his manhood; and a young woman is too worried about being 'used' or too hung up about romance and reputation to really experience her own eroticism. Most 50-year-olds, on the other hand, have a much better developed sense of who they are, and more inner resources to bring to sex. You could say that cellulite and sexual potential are highly correlated."

As far as issues of gender equality are concerned, both men and women become more similar as they age and approach their sexual potential. Men are not as frightened of letting their partners take the lead in making love to them, and they develop far greater capacity and appreciation for emotional connection and tenderness than they had as young men. Women, on the other hand, become more comfortable with their own sexuality, more likely to enjoy sex for its own sake and less inclined to apologize for their eroticism or hide behind the ingenue's mask of modesty. As they age, women feel less obligated to protect their mate's sexual self-esteem at the cost of their own sexual pleasure.

Once a couple's sexual potential has been tapped, partners are no longer afraid to let their fantasies run free with each other. Donald, for example, let Betty know that he dreamed of her tying him up and "ravishing" him sexually—so one day, she bought four long, silk scarves and that night, wearing three-inch high heels and a little black lace, she trussed him to the bed and gave him what he asked for, astounding him and surprising herself with her own dramatic flair. Betty had always secretly cherished a fantasy of being a dangerous, sexually powerful femme fatale, but Donald's clingy neediness had dampened her enthusiasm for trying out the dream—also she had been afraid it would make him even more demanding. But now, knowing he was capable of being himself regardless of what she did or did not do, Betty felt much more comfortable expressing her own sense of erotic play.

The Sexual Crucible Approach encourages people to make use of the opportunity offered by marriage to become more married and better married, by becoming more grown-up and better at staking out their own selfhood. But the lessons learned by Betty and Donald, or any couple, extend far beyond sex. The same emotional development that makes for more mature and passionate sexuality also helps couples negotiate the other potential shoals of marriage—money issues, childrearing questions, career decisions—because differentiation is not confined to sex. In every trouble spot, each partner has the same four options: dominate, submit, withdraw or differentiate. Differentiation does not guarantee that spouses can always have things their own individual way and an unfailingly harmonious marriage besides. Marriage is full of hard, unpleasant choices, including the choice between safety, security and sexual boredom, on the one hand, and challenge, anxiety and sexual passion, on the other.

But spouses who have learned to stand on their own two feet within marriage are not as likely to force their own choices on the other or give in or give up entirely just to keep their anxiety in check and shore up their own frail sense of self. Learning to soothe ourselves in the middle of a fight with a spouse over, say, the choice of schools for our child or a decision to move, not only helps keep the discussion more rational, but makes us more capable of mutuality, of hearing our partner, of putting his or her agenda on a par with our own. The fight stops being, for example, a struggle between your personal needs and your spouse's personal needs, often regarded by each as my "good idea" and her/his "selfishness," but which is really often my fragile, undeveloped self versus his/her equally fragile, undeveloped self. Instead, we can begin to see that the struggle is inside each of us individually, between wanting what we want for ourselves personally, and wanting for our beloved partner what he or she wants for himself or herself. Becoming more differentiated is possibly the most loving thing you can do in your lifetime—for those you love as well as yourself. Someone once said that if you're going to "give yourself" to your partner like a bouquet of flowers, you should at least first arrange the gift!

There is no way this process can be foreshortened into a technical quick-fix, no matter how infatuated our culture is with speed, efficiency and cost containment. Courage, commitment, a willingness to forgo obvious "solutions," tolerating the anxiety of living without a clear, prewritten script, as well as the patience to take the time to grow up are all necessary conditions, not only for a good marriage, but for a good life. At the same time, reducing all marital problems to the fallout from our miserable childhoods or to gender differences not only badly underestimates our own ability to develop far beyond the limitations of our circumstances, but misjudges the inherent power of emotionally committed relationships to bring us (drag us, actually, often kicking and screaming) more deeply and fully into our own being. Marriage is a magnificent system, not only for humanizing us, maturing us and teaching us how to love, but also perhaps for bringing us closer to what is divine in our natures.

From David M. Schnarch, "Passionate Marriage." *Family Therapy Networker*, (September/October): 42, 44–49. Copyright © 1997, *The Psychotherapy Networker*. Reprinted by permission. ✦

Chapter 17

Race, Gender, and Class in Sexual Scripts

Jenna Mahay
Edward O. Laumann
Stuart Michaels

What do your race/ethnicity, gender, and class have to do with your sexuality? How do your cultural scenarios differ from those of your best friends? Or, just how unique is your interpersonal script, which translates abstract sexual scenarios into strategies appropriate to particular situations? Certainly your intrapsychic script, your sexual dialogue with self that elicits and sustains sexual arousal, is unlike that of any other. Or is it? You as a sexuality student, and perhaps even your erudite professors will be interested in discovering answers to these rather personal questions in this chapter.

Using the rich descriptive resources of the National Health and Social Life Survey (NHSLS), Mahay, Laumann, and Michaels weave the variables of race/ethnicity, gender, and class into a piece that avoids the limitations of previous studies. The use of master status variables, that is, age, religious affiliation, marital status, and family composition, in analyzing each category was a massive undertaking, but one that spelled success for the authors, who broke new ground on old premises. As you read this chapter, challenge yourself to make two lists: one with findings that surprise you and one with reaffirmations of your long-held attitudes about race/ethnicity, gender, and class as related to sexuality. Regardless of which list is longer, the contents of both are guaranteed to challenge you with new unanswered questions and offer a fertile field for class discussion.

While sexuality is popularly described in highly individualistic terms, this chapter examines the ways in which sexual norms, practices, and prefer-ences are shaped by race, gender, and class. Many scholars have already documented group differ-ences in specific sexual behaviors, such as age at first sex, use of condoms, and number of partners. This chapter examines the broader sexual scripts in which these specific acts are embedded and how race, gender, and class intersect to shape those scripts.

A middle-aged, working-class African American man explains what he sees as racial differences in sexual scripts:

> When it comes to woman and man relationships, white people have a tendency to be too damn in-tellectual. Now that is not one of the true prereq-uisites of making love. It's the emotion, the pas-sion. You don't have time to ask a woman what kind of degree she has. You see what I'm saying? (quoted in Duneier 1992, 44)

A white woman describes how gender shapes the way she approaches sex with her partner:

> It is sort of an issue that I don't initiate sex. I would always wait for him. And finally he said, "Look, I'm not going to initiate sex all the time," and I would give him the argument: "Oh, men say they want women to initiate sex, but really when it happens they're, like, 'I have a headache to-night, honey.'" So in my mind there was a reason not to initiate it because it threatened him. (quoted in Blumstein and Schwartz 1983, 212)

An African American woman discusses how class plays a part in who she believes is a suitable partner:

> It is difficult to find a person that one is truly compatible with, and that's especially true for a highly educated woman whose expectations of-ten differ from those of most women and are not always consistent with the eligible pool [similar status] of men, who seem to have some prefer-ence for "traditional" women. (quoted in Staples 1981, 83)

Race, gender, and class, however, do not operate in-dependently in forming sexual scripts; they "inter-sect" (cf. Connell 1995; Nagel 1999). In the third quote presented above, for example, ideas of who is a suitable partner and of the difficulties the woman has in finding one have to do not only with class but with race and gender as well. Unfortunately, until recently, there has been an absence of data allowing simultaneous comparisons by race/ethnicity, gen-der, and class on the broad range of sexual atti-tudes, practices, and preferences that make up sex-ual scripts. This chapter uses the rich descriptive resources of the National Health and Social Life Survey (NHSLS) to overcome this limitation. We first develop a theoretical perspective on the sys-tematic variations in the sexual scripts adopted by persons with particular status attributes. We then analyze the similarities and differences in the sexual scripts of racial/ethnic groups and the gender and class variations within those groups.

Theorizing Variations in Sexual Scripts

Sexual scripts operate at three levels: the cultural, the interpersonal, and the intrapsychic (Simon and Gagnon 1987b). *Cultural scenarios* are the societal norms and narratives that provide guidelines for sexual conduct, thereby broadly indicating appropriate partners and sex acts, where and when to perform those acts, and even what emotions and feelings are appropriate. Thus, actors engaged in sexual interactions create *interpersonal scripts* that translate abstract cultural scenarios into scripts appropriate to particular situations. Interpersonal scripts, then, are the strategies for carrying out an individual's own sexual wishes with regard to the actual or anticipated responses of another person. While interpersonal scripts can be seen as "sexual dialogues" with others, *intrapsychic scripts* are sexual dialogues with the self. The intrapsychic script is a person's sexual fantasies, the sequence of acts, postures, objects, and gestures that elicit and sustain sexual arousal (Simon and Gagnon 1987b). Intrapsychic scripts should be seen, not merely as expressions of an individual's biologically generated appetites or drives, but rather as inextricably linked to what that person has learned to mean or understand as *being sexual*.

In the United States, cultural scenarios frequently stipulate that people of races or ethnicities different from one's own are inappropriate for sexual partnerships. In addition, because sex partners are generally chosen from a circumscribed group of people who are met through mutual friends, at work, or in neighborhood activities, the high level of racial segregation in these areas of social life also results in choosing others from the same racial/ethnic group. Indeed, as was reported in *The Social Organization of Sexuality (SOS)*, 93 percent of those who were married in the last ten years chose marriage partners of the same race or ethnicity. Even among those who had had a very short-term sexual relationship, 91 percent chose partners of the same race or ethnicity. In short, SOS (p. 255) reported that racial homophily was higher than all the other types of homophily, including age, education, and religious affiliation.

Because sexual partnering is so highly segregated racially, we would expect different sexual scripts to develop within these segregated subpopulations with their distinctive age, class, religious, and marital compositions. Sexual scripting creates and stages a drama wherein the roles take on meaning in relation to the enactment of related roles and the specific cast of actors (Simon and Gagnon 1987a). Thus, we would expect different dramas and roles to be staged when distinctive and segregated casts of actors perform them. Because sexual scripts are *socially* produced, individuals must call on shared meanings and expectations to produce them. Thus, we would expect an independent effect of race/ethnicity after controlling for age, religion, class, and marital status.

In addition to race, gender centrally organizes sexual scripting. Most sexual scripts involve gendered roles, where certain sexual practices take on meaning as either masculine or feminine in relation to the enactment of particular roles by the "appropriate" sex. Cultural scenarios, interpersonal scripts, and intrapsychic scripts all involve assumptions about gender differences in sexuality. For example, at the level of the cultural scenario, the social norm may be that boys are expected to have sex before marriage but that girls are not. At the level of the interpersonal script, it may be that men are generally more aggressive in initiating sexual encounters and that women are more passive sexually. At the intrapsychic level, men and women may find different sexual practices appealing or have different kinds of sexual fantasies. As sexual scripts vary between racial/ethnic groups, so will the gender roles and expectations regarding men's and women's sexual behavior.

Finally, many have speculated on the relation between race and class in sexual behavior, but the data limitations of previous studies have precluded an evaluation of their relative importance. This chapter examines the effects of race and class separately, to test whether racial/ethnic differences in sexual behavior can, in fact, be explained by class alone, after taking into account gender, marital status, age, religion, and family composition.

Other Studies of Race, Gender, and Class in Sexual Behavior

Racial/Ethnic Differences in Sexual Behavior

Social scientists have long studied race and ethnicity in American society and its effect on attitudes and social life (cf. Jaynes and Williams 1989), but only limited attention has been paid to sexual practices. While some ethnographic studies of particular racial/ethnic communities have included information on their sexual attitudes and practices, this qualitative information does not readily lend itself to comparisons across groups. Quantitative studies, on the other hand, have made such comparisons but have been restricted only to adolescent sexual practices or a very limited range of adult sexual practices. One more comprehensive analysis (Weinberg and Williams 1988) identified interesting differences across racial and class groupings but was based on different samples drawn at different times and different geographic locations. What has been lacking are data from representative samples of the major racial/ethnic groups collected at the same time and covering a wide range of sexual behaviors.

It is clear from the literature that the sexual practices and attitudes of different racial/ethnic groups must be analyzed in relation to each other because sexual relations within racial/ethnic groups are often affected and defined by the race relations between groups (Spelman 1988, 106). For example, in his ethnography of middle-aged working-class African American men in Chicago, Duneier (1992) found his informants to be very aware of the stereotype of themselves as sexual exploiters, an image they self-consciously tried to live down. But Bowser (1994) claims that the hypersexuality attributed to African Americans by whites has been incorporated into the self-identity of younger African Americans, motivating them to become experienced as soon as possible and to prove to themselves and their partners that they are sexually superior. In addition, the influence of race relations on specific sexual practices is shown by Sterk-Elifson's (1994) finding that many African Americans considered birth control, masturbation, and anal and oral sex evils that white people invented.

Only a very limited range of sexual experiences has been studied in existing quantitative work on racial/ethnic differences in sexual practices, however. Many studies focus on age at first intercourse, condom use, and teenage pregnancy and thus are concerned mainly with adolescent sexuality (see, e.g., Udry and Billy 1987; Duncan and Hoffman 1991; Furstenberg et al. 1987; Lauritsen 1994; Brewster 1994). There have been several national surveys of the sexual behavior of adolescents, such as John Kantner and Melvin Zelnik's 1971 and 1976 National Surveys of Young Women and the 1979 National Survey of Young Men and Women. Sonenstein has more recently conducted the 1988 and 1990 National Surveys of Adolescent Males.

While numerous studies have been conducted on specific sexual practices (e.g., sexual debut and condom use), we know much less about the prevalence and meanings given to such sexual practices as masturbation, oral sex, anal sex, and same-gender sexual activity. The General Social Survey (GSS) included only a limited number of questions about sexual behavior in its national surveys, and the 1990 National AIDS Behavioral Surveys asked detailed questions about vaginal and anal intercourse only

of respondents who reported an HIV risk factor. Moreover, sexual behavior cannot be understood apart from the attitudes that give insight into the meaning of various sexual activities. The NHSLS provides a much more comprehensive and detailed picture of people's sexual activities, preferences, and attitudes than has previously been available.

Gender Differences in Sexual Practices

Most sexual practices are highly gendered, meaning that certain sexual practices, such as engaging in a high frequency of sex and having multiple sex partners, are identified as masculine, others, such as waiting until marriage to have sex, as feminine. Many studies of sexual behavior, however, study only one gender (see, e.g., Sterk-Elifson 1994; Gilmore, DeLamater, and Wagstaff 1996; Brewster 1994). This makes it very difficult to compare the experiences and sexual roles of men and women in relation to each other within and across racial and ethnic groups.

Several studies of gender differences in sexuality have been conducted within specific racial/ethnic and class groups. Anderson (1990) found that adolescent African American men and women living in the ghetto have sharply contrasting orientations toward sexuality. Anderson describes the "game" of men and the "dream" of women. Men see women as objects of a sexual game to be won as trophies for their own personal aggrandizement; sex is used as an important means of enhancing their social status among their male peers. Women dream of having a boyfriend, a fiancé, or a husband and the fairy-tale prospect of living happily ever after with one's children in a nice house in a good neighborhood: the dream of a middle-class lifestyle and the nuclear family. The reality of inner-city African American men's poor employment prospects means that this dream is not likely to be realized (Anderson 1993).

Gender roles also have an important but different effect on sexual behavior among Latinos (see, e.g., Marín 1996). Women cannot be sexual if they want to be considered "good," resulting in the feelings of discomfort about sex commonly reported by Latino women. At the same time, men are expected to be passionate and to have a constant sexual desire that, once ignited, is beyond their control. For a Latino man, sexual conquest is a proof of masculinity. Because men generally have more status and power than women in Latino culture, women are at a disadvantage in dealing with coercion by men. The norms requiring virginity for women and encouraging men to seduce women create an ongoing tension between the sexes. In Mexican culture, men are allowed to have multiple sex partners, while women are required to be faithful. When a young woman does engage in premarital intercourse, her sexuality is more accepted if it is seen as "bounded." For example, she was in love with her boyfriend and gave in to his sexual demands in a moment of passion (Horowitz 1983). Among mainly middle-class whites, Blumstein and Schwartz (1983) found that gender also affects what a person desires in a relationship and how he or she behaves in one. Men are expected to be more aggressive sexually and are thought to be more lustful than women, while women are supposed to be more passive.

While the literature has clearly documented significant gender differences in sexual scripts within racial/ethnic groups, studies typically treat only a single racial or ethnic group and fail directly to compare gender differences *across* racial and ethnic groups. Some authors have speculated that gender differences in sexual practices are smaller for African Americans than for whites. Bowser (1994) argues that African American gender differences in sexual practices are smaller because it is more acceptable for African American women to engage in casual sex. African American men assume that African American women are, like the men themselves, having sex before marriage and having multiple sex partners. Sterk-Elifson (1994) found that many young African American women felt pressured to have sex because they feared that their partners would leave them if they did not.

Weinberg and Williams (1988) found male-female differences in sexual practices were substantially larger among African Americans than among whites. Compared to African American women, African American men have first intercourse at a much younger age, have a higher frequency of premarital sexual activity, and have more sex partners. They suggest that this is because African American men are in a social milieu that is sexually permissive and in which sexual opportunities are relatively available, while white men are more constrained by their cultural environment. These conclusions were based on data collected only through 1970 and may not accurately represent women and men who came of age after the sexual revolution.

The Effect of Education on Sexual Practices

Studying racial/ethnic differences in sexual scripts is difficult because race and ethnicity are themselves highly correlated with educational attainment. Findings regarding the relative effect of education versus race on sexual practices have been contradictory. Numerous studies have shown that class has an effect on age at first intercourse (Kinsey, Pomeroy, and Martin 1948; Hollingshead 1949; Sterk-Elifson 1994). In an early sociological community study, Hollingshead (1949) found that

class was a major factor in shaping white adolescents' sexual practices. Adolescents in the lower classes tended to begin having sexual intercourse at an earlier age than those in the working or middle classes. Most lower-class couples did not use contraception, and there was a high rate of pregnancy before marriage. In more recent analysis comparing two different studies, Weinberg and Williams (1980) found that class, as measured by education level, is important among males in predicting the onset of sexual activity and the incidence and frequency of such sexual behaviors as masturbation and oral sex during adolescence. For females, class was negatively related to early sexual activity and positively related to good feelings about first sexual experiences.

The increasing polarization of the African American population by socioeconomic class (Wilson 1978) suggests that class may have an even greater effect on African Americans' sexual behavior. Hogan and Kitagawa (1985) examined the linkages between social status, family structures, and neighborhood characteristics as they affected fertility patterns among adolescent African American women in 1979. They found that social class was a significant factor, inversely related to teenage pregnancy.

Anderson (1993) also argues that black ghetto sexual behaviors and values are a result of the "economic noose" in the ghetto—the structural conditions that allow girls to conclude that they have no future to derail by having a baby and boys to conclude that they will be unable to become economically self-reliant and support a family. The same strains are not experienced by middle-class blacks. In addition, middle-class youths have a much higher level of practical education about birth control and sexuality in general.

Other studies have shown that sexual relationships are still sharply organized around racial and ethnic categories. *SOS* found a higher degree of race than class homophily (as measured by education) in sexual partnerships. Weinberg and Williams (1988) concluded that cultural differences between races override differences in social class, finding that the effects of race were still prominent even after class was taken into account. Regardless of class status, African Americans were more likely to engage in premarital sex earlier and more frequently than whites. African American men had a greater number of partners, and African Americans in general were more liberal and accepting of sex, pursued it more, and reported fewer problems with it. They found no support for Kinsey's hypothesis that these differences are explained by social class. Weinberg and Williams (1988) argued that their finding that social class is not a complete explanatory factor for racial differences in sexual behavior is due to a distinct subculture created by African Americans as a result of their specific historical and social circumstances, which have given particular meaning to sexuality for them. In addition, the continuing segregation of blacks and whites regardless of social class has sustained these cultural patterns.

Measuring Class

Furstenberg et al. (1987) conclude that African Americans have sex earlier than whites because of racial differences in attitudes and norms regarding sexual behavior and that this is particularly true for African Americans in highly segregated schools. They found that African Americans are more likely to expect parenthood before or at the same time as marriage and that they are more likely to report having peers who are sexually active. These studies lead one to expect that race will have a larger effect on sexual scripts than class, given that distinctive sexual scripts will develop in racially segregated populations.

One difficulty in comparing the effects of race/ethnicity and class is that, while *race* and *ethnicity* are reasonably well-defined, socially sanctioned categories, *class* is less easily defined and measured. Previous studies of sexuality that have focused simply on age at first sex, number of partners, and condom use have defined *class* as the potential for upward mobility and thus have used complex composite measures that take into account parents' education, occupation, family income, and labor force experience (cf. Hogan and Kitagawa 1985). However, the concept of class most pertinent to our analysis of broader sexual scripts is that of groups of individuals who share a "style of life," social positions that are characterized by value orientations, attitudes, behavior, and conventions. Thus, each dimension of lifestyle, including the sexual, expresses a similar logic. Education has often been thought to be a better measure of this conception of class than occupation or income since cultural capital has a greater influence on one's values and beliefs than does economic capital (Mayer 1997; DiMaggio 1994). Thus, although it is not a perfect measure, we use respondent's education as a simple measure of class and the potential for upward mobility and a factor that largely defines the pool of potential sex partners. We have broken education into three categories: no high school degree, high school degree, and more than high school degree (which includes vocational degree, some college, college degree, and advanced degrees). We grouped those with vocational degrees and some college with those who had a college or an advanced degree because, in general,

they are more similar to the latter than to the high school graduates.

Racial/Ethnic Categories

There are definitional issues related to ethnicity that also require careful consideration. First, race and ethnicity are not mutually exclusive. Some respondents, primarily Hispanics, do not consider themselves white or black, selecting the category *other* on the question about race, and, when queried, specify their race as Hispanic. For this reason, in following what is the standard practice in reporting census data, we start by dividing the population into Hispanic and non-Hispanic, then break the latter into racial categories: white, black, Asian/Pacific Islander, or Native American. However, the Hispanic group does not form a single homogeneous entity in terms of either race or national origin. It is therefore problematic to treat Hispanics as a single category when comparing them to blacks and whites. One solution is to break them into smaller, more homogeneous groupings. Since Mexican Americans constitute the majority of Hispanics in the United States, we analyze them as a separate group. Unfortunately, no other Hispanic subgroups in our sample are large enough to analyze separately.

Second, the fact that Hispanics are very heterogeneous reminds us that whites also have many ethnic origins. According to the GSS (1988-94), no more than 20 percent of whites in the United States under sixty years of age came from any one country of origin. The most common white family origin is Germany (18 percent), followed by England (12 percent) and Ireland (11 percent). Smaller percentages report family origins in Italy (5 percent), Scotland (3 percent), and Poland (3 percent). Reflecting this diversity in countries of origin is the religious heterogeneity among whites. Whites reporting a religious affiliation in the NHSLS were evenly divided among Catholics, Mainline Protestants, and Fundamentalist Protestants.

Understanding Racial/Ethnic Differences

Whites

The whites have, on the average, more school years completed when compared to the other three racial and ethnic groups. Only about 11 percent of the whites in our sample did not finish a high school degree, while over 60 percent had at least some college or vocational training. They were also somewhat older. About 40 percent of the whites were between forty and fifty-nine years of age. Whites were very heterogeneous in terms of religious affiliation, almost evenly divided among Catholicism, Mainline Protestantism, and evangelical and fundamentalist Protestantism, with about 12 percent reporting no religious affiliation. About 55 percent of the men and 59 percent of the women were married at the time of the survey. The white profile is generally older, married, and college educated, but religion is mixed.

African Americans

Compared to the whites in our sample, African Americans had a lower level of educational achievement. About 22 percent of the African Americans had not finished high school, twice the percentage of whites, and only about 40 percent had at least some college or vocational school. African Americans had an age composition similar to that of whites, with about 36 percent between forty and fifty-nine years of age. A much lower percentage of African Americans than whites were currently married. Only 39 percent of the men and 36 percent of the women were married at the time of the interview. The vast majority, 64 percent of the men and 75 percent of the women, were affiliated with more conservative Protestant denominations, such as the Baptist and Pentecostal Churches. The African American profile is thus typified by older, moderately educated, and unmarried conservative Protestants.

Mexican Americans

Of our four racial and ethnic groups, Mexican Americans had the lowest level of educational attainment. Almost 38 percent had not completed high school. Mexican Americans in our sample also tended to be much younger than representatives of the other groups. Almost 80 percent of the Mexican American women were between eighteen and forty, and 45 percent were between eighteen and twenty-nine. Almost 70 percent of Mexican American men were between eighteen and forty years of age, and 49 percent were between eighteen and twenty-nine. Despite their younger ages, however, the proportion married was similar to the proportion of whites married, with 50 percent of the men and 57 percent of the women married at the time of the interview. The vast majority of Mexican Americans in our sample were Catholic, 75 percent of the men and 67 percent of the women. Mexican Americans were concentrated in the Southwest. The Mexican American profile is one of young, less-educated, strongly Catholic married couples.

Data and Methods

To study cultural scenarios, we analyze the responses to the NHSLS questions regarding sexual attitudes. These questions ask respondents whether they think that certain sexual practices are wrong, and the answers to these questions thus form a picture of the social guidelines and norms surrounding sexual behavior. Second, we examine interpersonal scripts by analyzing the responses to the NHSLS questions regarding the sexual practices in which the respondents have engaged, both in their lifetime and in their last sexual event. Third, to study intrapsychic scripts or individual fantasies and desires, we analyze the responses to the NHSLS questions regarding which sexual practices the respondent finds appealing.

Definition of Variables

Master Statuses

Age is divided into four cohorts: eighteen to twenty-nine, thirty to thirty-nine, forty to forty-nine, and fifty to fifty-nine. The oldest cohort reached adolescence well before the sexual revolution; the youngest cohort came of age after the AIDS epidemic began (1981).

There are four categories of religious affiliation: no religious affiliation, Mainline Protestant, Evangelical Protestant, and Catholic. Mainline Protestant mainly includes such Protestant denominations as the Episcopalians, Lutherans, Presbyterians, and Methodists. Evangelical Protestant includes the Baptists and Pentecostals and other fundamentalist sectarian churches.

Respondent's marital status was treated differently for different dependent variables. When the dependent variable pertained to sexual activities performed over the lifetime, such as whether the respondent had ever experienced fellatio, marital status distinguished between the ever married and the never married. When the dependent variable referred to sexual activities in the past twelve months, marital status distinguished the currently married from the not currently married.

Family composition was determined from the question, "Were you living with both your own mother and father when you were 14?" (if no: "With whom were you living around that time?") Three categories were identified: (1) lived with both biological parents; (2) lived with a parent and a stepparent; and (3) lived with a single parent.

Measures of Cultural Scenarios

Aspects of sexual cultural scenarios were measured by the respondents' attitudes toward certain sexual practices. These attitudes concern the age at which the respondent believes sex is appropriate, the appropriate relationship to one's sex partner, the feelings one is supposed to have for one's sex partner, the sexual acts deemed appropriate in a sexual encounter, and the appropriate gender of a sex partner. *SOS* reported a cluster analysis of nine attitudes that identified three broad normative orientations toward sexuality: traditional, relational, and recreational.

Strongly disapproving attitudes toward premarital sex and teenage sex as well as agreement with the statement that religious beliefs shape the respondent's sexual behavior are used to indicate support for the traditional cultural scenario that regards reproduction as the sole purpose of sex, which should take place only within marriage. This orientation is rooted in religious convictions, with the Roman Catholic and more conservative Protestant churches being strong advocates of these ideas. Respondents were asked, "If a man and a woman have sex relations before marriage, do you think it is always wrong, almost always wrong, wrong only sometimes, or not wrong at all?" and, "What if they are in their teens, say 14–16 years old?" Those who answered always wrong or almost always wrong to these questions were coded as having a traditional cultural scenario. In addition, respondents were asked to respond to the statement, "My religious beliefs have shaped and guided my sexual behavior." Those who responded strongly agree or agree were coded as having a traditional cultural scenario (*SOS*).

Relational orientation toward sexuality was identified by agreement with the statement, "I would not have sex with someone unless I was in love with them." Those who answered strongly agree or agree were coded as holding a cultural scenario in which sex should take place in an intimate, loving relationship (thus, a relational cultural scenario allows for premarital sex, but only within a loving relationship).

A recreational cultural scenario is one in which attitudes toward sexual practices do not relate directly either to procreation or to the intimacy of the relationship. This was measured by asking respondents whether they agreed with the statement, "Any kind of sexual activity between adults is okay as long as both persons freely agree to it." Again, those who answered strongly agree or agree were coded as holding a recreational attitude toward sexuality. This item was used because it was thought to measure a modern, pleasure-centered view of sex, where sex is considered a good in itself as long as it does not hurt anyone.

Finally, respondents' attitudes toward homosexuality are often quite distinct from any of their attitudes toward other sexual matters, and we thus analyze this issue separately. We distinguished between those who regarded homosexual activity as always or almost always wrong and those who said that it was wrong only sometimes or not wrong at all.

Measures of Interpersonal Scripts

We examined the respondent's actual sexual practices, including both adolescent and adult sexual experiences. Interpersonal scripts can be divided, like cultural scenarios, into three categories: traditional, relational, and recreational.

Two central aspects of interpersonal scripts are the age at the time of first sexual intercourse and the relationship to one's first sex partner. Respondents were asked, "How old were you the *first* time you had vaginal intercourse with a (. . . male/female)?". It was specified that the interviewer was asking only about the first intercourse after puberty, not about childhood sexual experiences before puberty. We coded those who had sex before age sixteen as having an early initiation into sexual activity and thus have a less traditional interpersonal script. Respondents were then asked, "What was your relationship to this person [i.e.,. the person with whom respondent had first vaginal intercourse]?". Those who were married to their first sex partner at the time they had their first sex can be seen as being traditional on this measure. Those who reported that they were in love with their first sex partner (but not necessarily married) were considered to be more relational in their sexual practices than people who reported that they were not in love with their first sex partner. People who reported their first sex as being with someone with whom they were not in love were considered more recreational in their sexual practices.

Another aspect of interpersonal scripts concerns the reasons people report for having decided to have sex for the first time. First, we asked whether this first sexual intercourse was "something you wanted to happen at the time? . . . something you went along with, but did not want to happen? . . . [or] something that you were forced to do against your will?". For those whose first sex was wanted, the interviewer continued: "What was the main reason you decided to go along with having sexual intercourse this first time?". The answers fell mainly into four categories: affection for partner, curious/ready for sex, physical pleasure, and wedding night. Those who reported their first sex because it was their wedding night were considered more traditional in their interpersonal scripts. Having first sex because of affection for one's partner indicated a relational script, while having it because of curiosity/readiness or for physical pleasure indicated a more recreational script. We also asked respondents how many sex partners they had had in the past twelve months. Those who reported having three or more partners in the last year were considered more recreational in their sexual practices.

Finally, we asked about the sexual acts occurring in sexual encounters. To determine whether respondents had ever had fellatio or cunnilingus, they were asked, "Have you ever performed oral sex on a [opposite sex: man/woman]?" and, "Has a [opposite sex: man/woman] ever performed oral sex on you?" Regarding heterosexual anal sex, we asked, "Have you ever had anal sex with a [opposite sex: man/woman]?". The sexual acts in which people engage are not readily associated with particular normative orientations, but they do seem to indicate conventional interpersonal scripts (never having experienced oral or anal sex) as opposed to elaborated interpersonal scripts (ever having experienced oral or anal sex).

Measures of Intrapsychic Scripts

The respondent's own sexual preferences will serve as measures of his or her intrapsychic scripts. Respondents were asked whether they found certain sex acts, such as vaginal intercourse, watching their partner undress, a partner performing oral sex on them, or performing oral sex on a partner, very appealing, somewhat appealing, not appealing, or not at all appealing. We simply dichotomized the responses into the categories appealing and not appealing. Those who found only vaginal intercourse appealing, a substantial majority of the NHSLS respondents, will be treated as being more conventional in their Intrapsychic scripts, while those who find any other sexual act appealing will be regarded as having more elaborated intrapsychic scripts.

Analyses and Results

Race, Gender, and Class in Sexual Cultural Scenarios

Overall, the majority of both men and women in all the racial/ethnic groups considered do not believe that premarital sex is wrong but do believe that teenage sex (between the ages of fourteen and sixteen years) is wrong. The majority also agree that any sexual activity between two consenting adults is OK. Finally, the majority believe that homosexual activity is wrong. Even after controlling for the other master statuses, the attitudes of Mexican Americans and African American women are more traditional where sex is concerned, while whites are less traditional, and African American men are the least traditional of all.

More specifically, Mexican Americans are more than twice as likely as whites to regard premarital sex as wrong when we control for the other master statuses. Mexican American women are also three times more likely than white women to believe that teenage sex is wrong, and Mexican American men are more than twice as likely as white men to believe that religion shapes their sexual behavior. Thus, Mexican Americans are more likely than whites to embrace traditional sexual attitudes. Mexican American women are also over three times more likely than white women to report that homosexual activity is wrong.

In comparison to Mexican Americans, who hold mostly traditional attitudes, whites are more secular and less traditional. For example, whites are less likely than Mexican Americans to report that religion shapes their sexual behavior. Whites are also less likely than Mexican Americans to regard premarital sex as wrong. In addition, whites, and particularly white women, are much more liberal in their attitudes toward homosexual activity. While the vast majority of whites believe that teenage sex is wrong, white women are less likely than Mexican American women to believe this, particularly after taking into account the other master statuses.

The attitudes of African Americans are similar to those of whites on several issues, such as premarital sex and teenage sex. However, gender differences between African American men and women are so large that it is difficult to analyze them together. The attitudes of African American women are more traditional than those of whites in some respects, while those of African American men are not. For example, after controlling for other master-status characteristics, African American women are almost twice as likely as white women to say that their religion shapes their sexual behavior. They are also slightly more likely than white women to regard premarital sex as wrong, although this result is reduced to nonsignificance when other master statuses are taken into account. Although the attitudes of African American men are also very similar to those of white men where sex is concerned, African American men are significantly less likely than men of other racial/ethnic groups to say that they would have sex only if they were in love. African American men, in short, hold less relational attitudes than men and women of other racial/ethnic groups.

While the racial/ethnic differences are significant, gender plays the central role in shaping sexual attitudes. In fact, attitudes toward teenage sex, one's relationship to one's sex partner, and religious beliefs guiding sexual behavior differ more by gender than by race or ethnicity. More women than men in all racial/ethnic groups regard premarital and teenage sex as wrong and assert that their religious beliefs shape their sexual behavior and that they would not have sex unless they were in love. This may reflect the sexual double standard that places more restrictions on women's sexuality than on men's. The gender gap appears largest among African Americans. While 77 percent of African American women say that they would have sex only if they were in love, only 43 percent of African American men agree. And, while 69 percent of African American women say that their religious beliefs shape their sexual behavior, only 50 percent of African American men say this. The gender gap in attitudes toward premarital sex and teenage sex is also large for Mexican Americans. However, there are no significant gender differences in attitudes toward recreational sexual activity and homosexuality, with the exception of white men's and women's attitudes toward homosexuality.

What are the effects of class and other master-status variables on sexual attitudes? Education, age, religion, marital status, and family composition during adolescence do not diminish racial/ethnic differences in the attitudes toward premarital sex, teenage sex, religious influence on sexual behavior, and having sex only if in love. The one exception is that African American women do not differ from whites in regarding premarital sex as wrong once the other master statuses are taken into account.

In most cases, when we control for these other social factors, racial/ethnic differences are even stronger. For example, only after controlling for these other master statuses are Mexican American men more than twice as likely as white men to regard premarital sex as wrong and to say that their religious beliefs shape their sexual behavior. Differences for Mexican American and other Hispanic women (compared to white women) in the influence of religion on sexual behavior also approach significance once these other social factors are taken into account. Education, for example, has an effect on women's attitudes toward teenage sex; women with a college education are more likely to regard teenage sex as wrong. For men, education has an effect on men's reporting that their religious beliefs shape their sexual behavior. In the end, however, these attitudes are still largely organized around racial/ethnic lines, with variations according to age and religion.

Other sexual attitudes, however, appear to be more a function of class than of race/ethnicity. Attitudes about recreational sexual and homosexual activity are strongly affected by education. Controlling for education does diminish racial/ethnic differences in attitudes toward homosexual activity and other sexual practices between adults. Those with at least some college are significantly less likely to believe that homosexual activity is wrong. After controlling for education, age, religion, marital status, and family composition, there are no significant racial/ethnic differences among men in attitudes toward homosexuality. The difference in attitudes toward homosexuality between African American women and white women is diminished, although the difference between Mexican American women and white women is only slightly reduced, suggesting perhaps that there is a particular proscription against homosexuality in Mexican American culture.

Education also has a significant effect on whether the respondent believes that any sexual activity between two consenting adults is OK. Among both men and women, those with at least some college are about half as likely as those who did not finish high school to believe that any sexual activity between two consenting adults is OK. Controlling for these other variables, the difference between Mexican American women and white women is reduced to nonsignificance, but the difference between African American women and white women remains.

In conclusion, education has the strongest effect on attitudes toward recreational sexual practices and homosexuality, at times causing racial/ethnic differences to disappear. This suggests that these attitudes are more related to class and other social characteristics, such as age and religious affiliation, than racial/ethnic group affiliation. However, for other sexual attitudes, racial/ethnic differences largely remain, or become even stronger, after controlling for education and these other social characteristics. Thus, attitudes toward premarital and teenage sex, religious influence on sexual behavior, and having sex only if in love vary more by race and ethnicity than by class.

Race, Class, and Gender in Interpersonal Scripts

Now that we have a picture of the role of race, gender, and class in sexual cultural scenarios, how do these relate to interpersonal scripts or actual sexual practices? Recall that interpersonal scripts refer to the ways in which cultural scenarios are used and adapted to fit specific situations, representing the actor's response to the external world. We first briefly summarize the racial/ethnic similarities and differences in sexual practices and then examine the effects of class and other master statuses on these sexual practices.

Just as in the case of cultural scenarios, racial/ethnic groups share basic interpersonal scripts. For example, the majority of men and women in all racial/ethnic groups have had premarital sex. The majority of men and women also report that their first sex was something they wanted to do at the time. In terms of current sexual practices, the majority of people had fewer than three sex partners in the past year and had sex once a week or more in the past twelve months.

Despite these basic similarities among racial/ethnic groups, it is clear that significant differences also exist among the racial/ethnic groups in almost all aspects of interpersonal scripts examined here. For example, even after controlling for other master statuses, whites have sex later in adolescence but engage in more elaborated sexual practices, including oral and anal sex, as adults. Mexican Americans' adolescent sexual behavior is similar to that of whites, but the former are much less likely to engage in oral sex as adults. African Americans have had sex earlier, and have a much higher rate of premarital sex, but are still very conventional in terms of adult sexual practices, being much less likely to engage in oral and anal sex.

When we compare actual sexual practices to the cultural scenarios of the racial/ethnic groups, we find that these two levels of sexual scripts do not always coincide. For example, while Mexican Americans have more traditional attitudes than whites toward premarital sex and teenage sex, their sexual practices are little different from those of whites. And, while African American women hold more traditional sexual attitudes than white women, their actual sexual practices are less traditional. While African American men hold attitudes similar to those of men in other racial/ethnic groups regarding premarital sex and teenage sex, they are much less traditional and relational in practice. These disjunctures between the cultural scenario and the interpersonal script suggest that the situational contexts of sexual encounters for racial/ethnic groups are different, leading to differences in the ways in which those cultural scenarios are used.

Adolescent Interpersonal Scripts

Whites are slightly more conventional than other racial/ethnic groups in terms of their early sexual experiences. While the vast majority of whites have had premarital sex, most did not have sex until after they were sixteen. About three-fourths of white women were in love with their first sex partner and reported wanting their first sex at the time. There is a significant gender difference, however, in that only 42 percent of white men reported being in love with their first sex partner. In addition, most white men report wanting their first sex out of curiosity/

readiness, while most white women report wanting their first sex because of affection for their partner.

Despite the fact that Mexican Americans have more traditional attitudes than whites, there is no significant difference between the two groups in the proportion who have had teenage sex or premarital sex. Over 90 percent of the men and about 80 percent of Mexican American women had premarital sex, and about 30 percent of the men and 20 percent of the women had sex before they were sixteen. Mexican American women are twice as likely as white women, however, to report being in love with their first sex partner, after controlling for the other master statuses. The higher percentage of Mexican American women who report being in love with their first sex partner is consistent with the feminine ideal in the Mexican American community that makes premarital sex more acceptable for a woman if it is done out of love for her boyfriend (Horowitz 1983). Despite the fact that a higher proportion of Mexican American women report being in love with their first sex partner, almost 30 percent of Mexican American women also report that their first sex was something they went along with but did not want. This, too, may reflect the Mexican American feminine ideal that requires submission to the sexual demands of a boyfriend, particularly when in love.

Although the attitudes of African Americans toward premarital sex and teenage sex are not significantly different from those of whites, African Americans do have higher rates of premarital and teenage sex and are less likely than whites to be in love with their first sex partner, even after controlling for the other master statuses. Almost 98 percent of African American men and 93 percent of African American women had premarital sex. African Americans also had a higher rate of teenage sex, with 51 percent of African American men and 24 percent of African American women having sex before they were sixteen. African American women are also the least likely to report that their first sex was wanted at the time even after controlling for other master statuses.

Differences in interpersonal scripts among racial/ethnic groups, despite similarities in cultural scenarios, may be the result of the different situational contexts in which the cultural scenario is used. For example, barriers to their economic success may help explain why African American men have sex before they are sixteen more often than do men in other racial/ethnic groups (despite shared attitudes about teenage sex). In a situation where economic opportunities are blocked, sex during early adolescence is likely to have meaning beyond the sexual, affirming identity as a socially competent, high-status person (Simon and Gagnon

1987b). As noted before, twice as many African American men as white men have no high school degree, an indicator of limited later socioeconomic success. However, even after controlling for education, African American men are still three times more likely than white men to have had sex before they were sixteen. In short, blocked opportunities, as measured by education at least, cannot account for all the effects of race on early sexual intercourse.

While having sex early may be a way for African American adolescent males to affirm their status, the literature does not offer the same explanation with regard to African American women. For some African American women, early sex may instead be something that they go along with because they have no future to derail (Anderson 1993). First, African American women are significantly more likely than white women to report that their first sex was something that they went along with but did not want to happen. This may be a result of the very different cultural scenarios with which African American men and women approach the sexual encounter. Education, (a measure of future opportunities) has a very strong effect on age at first sex for women at both the high school and the college level. For women, then, the racial/ethnic differences in the percentage having sex before age sixteen disappear when we control for education and the other master statuses.

Gender differences in the percentage actually having sex before age sixteen reflect the differences in attitudes toward teenage sex that are part of the cultural scenarios. A significantly lower percentage of women than men had premarital and teenage sex in most racial/ethnic groups. Women are also more likely than men to be in love with their first sex partner and to have sex because of affection for their partner. In all racial/ethnic groups, however, women are significantly less likely than men to report that their first sex was wanted.

Adult Interpersonal Scripts

We now turn to an examination of sexual practices occurring in the past twelve months. Compared to other racial/ethnic groups, whites have lower numbers of sex partners but much greater elaboration in sexual practices. The vast majority of whites (90 percent of the men and 96 percent of the women) have fewer than three sex partners in the past twelve months, and most whites have sex once a week or more. About three-fourths of whites have engaged in oral sex, with 30 percent of the men and 21 percent of the women having experienced fellatio in the last event and similar percentages having experienced cunnilingus.

Mexican Americans' number of partners in the last twelve months is very similar to that of whites. There is also no significant difference in the frequency of partnered sex. However, Mexican Americans are more conventional with regard to other sexual practices, being less than half as likely as whites to engage in oral sex, even after controlling for the other master statuses.

African American men and women are more likely than those in other racial/ethnic groups to have three or more partners in the last twelve months, although, for women, this difference disappears after controlling for other master statuses. Despite the fact that a higher proportion of African American men have three or more sex partners in the past twelve months, there is no significant racial/ethnic difference in the frequency of partnered sex. In terms of other sexual practices, African Americans are more conventional than whites, with African American women being less likely than white women to have ever performed fellatio and African American men and women both being less likely than whites ever to have experienced cunnilingus. African American women are also significantly less likely than white women to have had anal sex, although there is no racial difference among men.

Race, Class, and Gender in Intrapsychic Scripts

Let us now turn to racial/ethnic similarities and differences in individuals' sexual desires and fantasies, key elements of the intrapsychic sexual script. We find that the intrapsychic scripts of racial/ethnic groups generally coincide with their interpersonal scripts. For example, as with their interpersonal scripts, whites had more elaborated intrapsychic scripts than African Americans and Mexican Americans when one counted the number of sexual techniques, such as oral or anal sex and manual stimulation, that respondents found very appealing. White men had the highest mean number of *very appealing* responses, 2.60. African American men had a significantly lower mean number of *very appealing* responses, 2.47, and Hispanic men had an even lower mean number, 2.38. Women in all the racial/ethnic groups had lower mean numbers of *very appealing* responses than men, but they also differed significantly between racial and ethnic groups. White women reported a mean of 1.68 techniques to be very appealing, which was close to Hispanic women's mean of 1.65. African American women, however, found a mean of only 1.48 techniques very appealing. In general, African Americans and Hispanics find fewer sexual techniques very appealing.

Vaginal intercourse enjoys almost universal appeal and constitutes a part of the vast majority of people's intrapsychic scripts in all the racial/ethnic groups. However, there are some racial/ethnic variations among women in the appeal of vaginal intercourse. Other Hispanic women are significantly less likely than women of the other racial/ethnic groups analyzed here to find vaginal intercourse very or somewhat appealing. However, there were no racial or gender differences in whether vaginal intercourse occurred in the last event. When we look at the percentage of people who both find vaginal intercourse appealing and actually had vaginal intercourse in the last event, we find that African American and Mexican American women who find vaginal intercourse appealing are more likely than white women or other Hispanic women to have had vaginal intercourse in the last event.

While vaginal intercourse is almost universally appealing, the appeal of oral sex varies greatly by race and ethnicity. While the vast majority of white men (82 percent) find fellatio appealing, a substantially lower proportion of African American men (55 percent) find it appealing. Mexican American and the other Hispanic men find fellatio appealing more often than African American men do but still less often than white men do. Similarly, while 55 percent of white women find fellatio appealing, only 25 percent of African American women do. It is apparent that there are also significant gender differences in the percentage finding fellatio appealing in all racial/ethnic groups. For example, among African Americans, more than twice as many men as women find fellatio appealing.

The appeal of cunnilingus also varied widely among racial/ethnic groups. A much higher percentage of white men (77 percent) than African American men (42 percent) reported that they found cunnilingus appealing. Likewise, a higher percentage of white women (65 percent) than African American women (40 percent) found cunnilingus appealing. Again, Mexican Americans and the other Hispanics are between African Americans and whites in the percentage finding cunnilingus appealing. However, unlike for fellatio, there is no significant gender difference in the proportion finding cunnilingus appealing, except among whites. There is also a significant difference between white men and white women in the percentage who both find cunnilingus appealing and reported that it occurred in the last sexual event: a higher percentage of white men than white women who find cunnilingus appealing reported that it occurred in the last event.

When we control for education and other master statuses, racial/ethnic differences in the proportion finding oral sex appealing remain. While education does have a significant effect on preferences for cunnilingus and fellatio, as it does for the actual practice of these acts, the racial/ethnic differences are not diminished.

Thus, while vaginal intercourse is part of the intrapsychic scripts of all four racial/ethnic groups, whites include fellatio and cunnilingus to a larger degree in their intrapsychic scripts, while Mexican Americans and other Hispanics include these sexual practices to a lesser extent. African Americans are the least likely to include fellatio and cunnilingus in their intrapsychic scripts.

Summary: Racial/Ethnic Similarities and Differences in Sexual Scripts

First, we found that racial and ethnic groups share many aspects of their sexual scripts. The majority of people in all racial/ethnic groups, for example, believe that teenage sex and same-gender sex are wrong and report that they would not have sex unless they were in love. In terms of sexual practices, most people have had premarital sex but waited until they were at least sixteen to have sexual intercourse, have fewer than three sex partners in the last twelve months, and have sex once a week or more. In intrapsychic scripts, vaginal intercourse is found to be almost universally appealing, but only smaller pluralities find most other sexual practices appealing.

However, even after controlling for other master-status variables, there are still significant racial/ethnic variations in these aspects of sexual scripts and even larger differences in the practices of other sexual activities, such as oral sex. Because race and ethnicity are highly correlated with other master statuses, different sexual scripts develop within these sexually segregated racial/ethnic groups. These sexual scripts become the norm for those in racial/ethnic groups and are used even by members of those groups who differ on other master statuses. Thus, we get an independent effect for racial and ethnic group affiliation after controlling for the other master statuses. Below, we summarize the predominant sexual scripts for whites, African Americans, and Mexican Americans.

Secular Cultural Scenario, Relational-Elaborated Interpersonal Scripts

Regarding interpersonal scripts, whites can best be described as relational-elaborated. While the overwhelming majority of whites had premarital sex and thus cannot be considered traditional in that respect, they are more likely than African Americans to say that they were in love with their first sex partner, indicating a more relational orientation. Whites are also much more likely than the other racial/ethnic groups to engage in elaborated sexual behavior, such as oral and anal sex. One hypothesis is that the more elaborated and less procreation-oriented sexual script of whites is due to a weakening of religious influence on sexual attitudes and practices. A lower proportion of whites than of the other racial/ethnic groups assert that their religious beliefs shape and guide their sexual behavior in every age cohort younger than fifty to fifty-nine, even after the other master statuses are taken into account. Evidence that religion is linked to less elaborated sexual practices is found in the fact that respondents who agree that their religious beliefs shape and guide their sexual behavior are less than half as likely to have ever engaged in fellatio or cunnilingus.

Gendered Cultural Scenario, Recreational-Conventional Interpersonal Scripts

Characterizing the cultural scenarios of African Americans as a whole is difficult because men and women embrace such different sexual scripts. African American women hold more traditional and relational attitudes toward premarital sex, homosexuality, teenage sex, the influence of religion on sexual behavior, and having sex only if in love than African American men. They are much less likely to describe their first sexual experience as wanted at the time than women in any other group.

Regarding interpersonal scripts, African Americans are typically recreational-conventional in orientation. They are more likely than the other groups to report that they were not in love with their first sex partner, that they had their first sex because of curiosity/readiness or physical pleasure, and that they had three or more partners in the past year. At the same time, they are much more conventional than whites in what they do in sexual encounters, being much less likely to engage in oral or anal sex.

One explanation for the more conventional features of African Americans' sexual scripts is the legacy of fundamentalist and evangelical Protestantism. About 64 percent of African American men and 75 percent of African American women are affiliated with conservative Protestant churches, and similar proportions were raised in such churches. This is over twice, and sometimes more than three times, the rate of affiliation for any of the other racial/ethnic groups. African Americans, particularly women, are especially likely to say that their religious beliefs shape and guide their sexual behavior. Support for the hypothesis that conventional sexual practices are the result of conservative religious af-

filiation is found in the fact that whites affiliated with fundamentalist and evangelical Protestant churches are also much less likely to have had experience with oral or anal sex. More research is surely needed to clarify how recreational scripts came to dominate the orientations of African American men.

Traditional Cultural Scenario, Relational-Conventional Interpersonal Scripts

Mexican Americans' cultural scenarios are traditional in orientation with respect to attitudes toward premarital sex, homosexuality, religious influences on sexual behavior (for men), and attitudes toward teenage sex (for women).

Regarding interpersonal scripts, Mexican Americans are relational-conventional. They cannot be considered traditional because the vast majority have engaged in premarital sex. They are, however, relational in their interpersonal scripts because Mexican American women are twice as likely as white women to report that they were in love with their first sex partner, after controlling for the other master statuses. Mexican Americans are also less likely than African Americans to have had three or more partners in the last year. In terms of specific sex acts, Mexican Americans are more conventional than whites in that they are less likely to engage in fellatio or cunnilingus.

Mexican Americans' traditionalism in sexual scripts may be rooted in their Catholicism, which emphasizes procreational sexual practices within the context of marriage. Three-fourths of Mexican American men and two-thirds of Mexican American women are Catholic. Over 50 percent of Mexican American men and over 60 percent of Mexican American women report that their religious beliefs shape and guide their sexual behavior.

Although Mexican American women overwhelmingly reported being in love with their first sex partner, a fairly high percentage (30 percent) also reported that their first sex was something they went along with but did not want.

Elaboration of Sexual Script by Class, Age, Religious Affiliation, and Marital Status

Master statuses other than race and ethnicity also exert significant effects on sexual attitudes, preferences, and practices. The younger age cohorts are less traditional in their attitudes and more likely to have sex earlier, to have more sex partners, to have sex more frequently, and to engage in oral sex. The college educated are also significantly more likely to engage in cunnilingus and fellatio, to find those practices appealing, and to express more liberal views toward homosexuality. Those who are conservative Protestants are less likely to engage in or find oral sex appealing and more likely to regard teenage sex, premarital sex, and homosexual activity as wrong. Married people, compared to the never married, are more likely to regard premarital sex and teenage sex as wrong. They report fewer sex partners but have partnered sex more frequently.

Conclusion

While racial/ethnic groups share basic similarities in their sexual scripts, important differences remain even after one takes the effects of education, religion, age, and marital status into account. We hypothesize that the racial/ethnic segregation of sexual partnering results in sexual scripts that are particularized to each group. When a specific sexual script becomes the norm in a group, it may be used by other members of the group regardless of their other master statuses. Because the script is *socially* produced, individuals must call on shared meanings and expectations in order to enact them. Further research must be conducted if we are to understand how actual networks and social contexts of sexual partnering facilitate the development and transmission of sexual scripts.

The sexual scripts approach also revealed the complex patterns in which specific sexual practices are embedded. For example, while African Americans may be less traditional in their age at and the context of first intercourse, they are actually more traditional in their actual sexual practices in adulthood. We also found contradictions between the cultural scenarios and the interpersonal scripts of some groups. These disjunctures highlight the different contexts in which these generally shared cultural narratives are applied in actual situations. Along these lines, some have argued that the racial/ethnic differences in sexual behavior are really an effect of class locations. But we found that, although education does have a significant effect on many sexual behaviors, race/ethnicity retains an independent effect.

Finally, we found that, for many aspects of sexual scripts, gender differences are more substantial than racial/ethnic differences. And, where the gender differences in cultural scenarios were the greatest, so were the number of women who reported that their first sex was something that they went along with but did not want. Gender is thus an integral part of sexual scripts, with profound consequences for men's and women's sexual experiences.

References

Anderson, E. 1990. *Streetwise: Race, class, and change in an urban community*. Chicago: University of Chicago Press.

Anderson, E. 1993. Sex codes and family life among poor inner-city youths. In *The ghetto underclass: Social science perspectives*, ed. W. J. Wilson. Newbury Park, Calif.: Sage.

Blumstein, P., and P. Schwartz. 1983. *American couples: Money, work, sex*. New York: Morrow.

Bowser, B. 1994. African-American male sexuality through the early life course. In *Sexuality across the life course*, ed. A Rossi. Chicago: University of Chicago Press.

Brewster, K. L. 1994. Race differences in sexual activity among adolescent women: The role of neighborhood characteristics. *American Sociological Review* 59 (June): 408–24.

Connell, R. W. 1995. *Masculinities: Knowledge, power, and social change*. Berkley and Los Angeles: University of California Press.

DiMaggio, P. 1994. Social stratification, life-style, and social cognition. In *Social stratification: Class, race, and gender in sociological perspective*, ed. D. B. Grusky. Boulder, Colo.: Westview.

Duncan, G. J., and S. D. Hoffman. 1991. Teenage underclass behavior and subsequent poverty: Have the rules changed? In *The urban underclass*, ed. C. Jencks and P. Peterson. Washington, D.C.: Brookings.

Duneier, M. 1992. *Slim's table: Race, respectability, and masculinity*. Chicago: University of Chicago Press.

Furstenberg, F., P. Morgan, K. Moore, and J. Peterson. 1987. Race differences in the timeing of adolescent intercourse. *American Sociological Review* 52:511–18.

Gilmore, S., J. DeLamater, and D. Wagstaff. 1996. Sexual decision making by inner city black adolescent males: A focus group study. *Journal of Sex Research* 33, no. 4:363–71.

Hogan, D., and E. Kitagawa. 1985. The impact of social status, family structure, and neighborhood on the fertility of black adolescents. *American Journal of Sociology* 90, no. 4:825–55.

Hollingshead, A. B. 1949. *Elmtown's youth: The impact of social classes on adolescents*. New Brunswick, N.J.: Rutgers University Press.

Horowitz, M. J. 1983. *Honor and the American dream: Culture and identity in a Chicano community*. New Brunswick, N. J.: Rutgers University Press.

Jaynes, G. D., and Robert M. Williams, ed. 1989. *A common destiny: Blacks and American society*. Washington, D.C.: National Academy Press.

Kinsey, A. C., W. B. Pomeroy, and C. E. Martin. 1948. *Sexual behavior in the human male*. Philadelphia: W. B. Saunders.

Laumann, E. O., J. H. Gagnon, R. T. Michael, and S. Michaels. 1994. *The social organizations of sexuality: Sexual practices in the United States*. Chicago: University of Chicago Press.

Lauritsen, J. L. 1994. Explaining race and gender differences in adolescent sexual behavior. *Social Forces* 72, no. 3:859–84.

Marin, B. V. 1996. Cultural issues in HIV prevention for Latinos: Should we try to change gender roles? In *Understanding and preventing HIV risk behavior: Safer sex and drug use*, ed. S. Oskamp and S. C. Thompson. Thousand Oaks, Calif.: Sage.

Mayer, S. 1997. *What money can't buy: Family income and children's life chances*. Cambridge, Mass.: Harvard University Press.

Nagel, J. 1999. Ethnosexual frontiers: Constructing and crossing racial, ethnic, nationalist, and sexual boundaries. Paper presented at the annual meeting of the American Sociological Association, 9 August.

Simon, W., and J. H. Gagnon. 1987a. Sexual scripts: Permanence and change. *Archives of Sexual Behavior* 52:97–120.

Simon, W., and J. H. Gagnon. 1987b. A sexual scripts approach. In *Theories of human sexuality*, ed. W. T. O'Donohue. New York: Plenum.

Sonenstein, F. L., J. H. Pleck, and L. C. Ku. 1989. Sexual activity, condom use, and AIDS awareness among adolescent males. *Family Planning Perspectives* 21:152–158.

Staples, R. 1981. *The world of black singles: Changing patterns of male/female relations*. Westport, Conn.: Greenwood.

Sterk-Elifson, C. 1994. Sexuality among African-American women. In *Sexuality across the life course*, ed. A. S. Rossi. Chicago: University of Chicago Press.

Udry, J. R., and J. Billy. 1987. Initiation of coitus in early adolescence. *American Sociological Review* 52:841–55.

Weinberg, M., and C. Williams. 1980. Sexual embourgeoisement? Social class and sexual activity, 1938–1970. *American Sociological Review* 45:33–48.

Weinberg, M., and C. Williams. 1988. Black sexuality: A test of two theories. *Journal of Sex Research* 25, no. 2:197–218.

Wilson, W. J. 1978. *The declining significance of race*. Chicago: University of Chicago Press.

Zelnik, M., and J. F. Kantner. 1980. Sexual activity, contraceptive use, and pregnancy among metropolitan-area teenagers, 1971–1979. *Family Planning Perspectives* 12:230–37.

Chapter 18
The Impact of Aging on Sexual Function in Women and Their Partners

Sheryl A. Kingsberg

What does the self-perception theory, or the over-justification hypothesis, or the cognitive dissonance theory have to do with aging and sexuality? Read Kingsberg's offering to find the answer linking this unusual company of players. In this chapter about the impact of aging on sexual functioning in women and their partners, the author deftly relates all three of these psychosocial theories to the understanding of desire and the female response cycle.

In her lucid coverage of hypoactive sexual desire disorder, the most prevalent female sexual dysfunction, Kingsberg distinguishes among the three related, but separate, components of desire: drive; beliefs and values; and motivation. As you read this section of the chapter, ask yourself which, if any, of the three concepts applies singularly to aging sexuality? As you can quickly conclude from your answer to this question, there is danger in oversubscribing age as a problem in and of itself when it comes to sexuality.

Among the uninformed myths concerning the "nonsexual senior," perhaps the most popular is that sexual activity is not prevalent among the elderly. In reality, sexual needs do not change abruptly with age; in fact, the potential for sexual expression continues until death. Although sexual vigor is not necessarily age-related, age does appear to have its effects on both women and men as physiological changes occur in the later years. As a result, touching, caressing, and masturbation are all forms of sexual activity that may be increasingly enjoyed by later-age seniors in addition to sexual intercourse.

Unfortunately, the lack of informed opinion about aging and sexuality is not limited to the public. Despite the explosion of knowledge about sexuality, most physicians receive little, if any, sexuality educa-tion in medical school, especially that which pertains to the elderly. Similarly, nursing home staffs are only moderately knowledgeable about sexuality in older persons and are often, as a result, highly restrictive and judgmental in their attitudes and rules about elderly sexuality. What are the sources of such repression of sexual fulfillment for the elderly? Certainly lack of knowledge is a factor. But, the negative reaction of health professionals may also be a manifestation of their own fears of aging or, simply, nonacceptance of their own sexuality. Which would you guess?

Introduction

The psychological and physiological impact of aging on sexuality in women is a particularly timely topic for a number of reasons. The first reason I have labeled the "Viagratization" of America. Whether or not Viagra (and now the other PDE5 inhibitors) ultimately lives up to its promise to be the sexual salvation for aging men and their increasingly unreliable penises (Feldman, Goldstein, Hatzichristou, Krane, & McKinlay, 1994), its arrival into our culture has renewed attention to the topic of sexuality in older people. Since Viagra came to market in March 1998, sex in aging Americans has been the cover story of virtually every magazine and newspaper. Second, and almost as obvious a reason, is the fact that the baby boomers have arrived at middle age, a trend popularly termed "the graying of America." In the next two decades, almost 40 million women will experience menopause. Women can now expect to live an average of 82 years, which means that women will now live one-third of their lives postmenopausally. Third, the baby boomer generation has never been known for passively accepting models for living handed down from prior generations. It is already evident that the women of this generation are negotiating midlife and menopause in different ways from their mothers and grandmothers. Cultural stereotypes of the middle-aged woman as gray-haired, frail, and asexual have given way to images of strong, active, and sexual women. Examples include Sigourney Weaver, age 51, who after 20 years in her role as Lt. Ripley from the *Alien* movie series is stronger and more independent than ever, and Tina Turner, who, at 62, arguably has the sexiest legs and the most energy of the entire entertainment industry. Fourth, and most central to the topic, interest and research on postmenopausal sexuality has finally begun receiving the kind of attention that has resulted in a more refined conceptualization of women's sexual lives and improvements in treating sexual problems.

Age of Relationship Versus Age of Partners

Sexual activity for women often occurs within the context of a relationship. However, the age and developmental stage of life of a woman provide no reliable predictors of where she may be in a relationship. Menopausal women and partners may be involved in a new passionate relationship, a long-standing intimate relationship, a long-standing nonintimate/distant relationship or no relationship at all. Therefore, physicians must be careful not to make assumptions about the type of relationship in which their menopausal patients are involved. Women may benefit from a reminder to hold realistic expectations about sexuality in long-standing relationships (that are not related to aging) as well as to hold realistic expectations that *are* about age limitations.

Schnarch (1997) reminds us to appreciate the advantages of longer relationships and more mature partners. He argues that most of us are best able to achieve our "sexual potential" in midlife. His distinction between "genital prime" and "sexual prime" suggests that sexual peak has more to do with who one is as a person than with the speed at which one's body works. True sexual intimacy is only achievable by individuals who are mature, independent, and have good self-esteem and who trust and respect their partners; in short, those who have the capacity for *emotional* intimacy. Maturity and independence are more likely to be attained by men and women who are also chronologically mature. Similarly, lasting or long-term relationships are fairly exclusive to "older" couples because these terms require by definition that a relationship exists for many years. Recall, however, that older age does not effectively predict that someone is in a long-term relationship just as older age is not a guarantee that someone actually has achieved independence and emotional maturity. Older age can be considered a necessary but not sufficient component to maturity.

Although a long-term relationship allows for true sexual intimacy, there are also some compelling sexual advantages that are only experienced within the context of a new relationship. The excitement of new love (or even lust), the mystery, the challenge, and the discovery are often the ingredients that make sex during this stage of a relationship incredibly passionate and exciting. There is much less risk of emotional dependence early on because, typically at this early stage of a relationship, each partner's identity is still independent of the other (though possibly not fully developed or healthy). But don't confuse new with young. These new exciting relationships are as likely to occur in midlife as in young adulthood.

The Impact of Aging on Sexuality

The impact of aging on sexuality can be understood only by putting it in a greater context of all adult sexuality. The fact is that sexual dysfunction is highly prevalent in both men and women. The National Health and Social Life Survey (NHSLS; Laumann, Paik, & Rosen, 1999) surveyed 1,410 men and 1,749 women between the ages of 18 and 59 years and reported that 31 percent of men and 43 percent of women had experienced a sexual dysfunction. However, the NHSLS also noted that the prevalence of sexual dysfunction in women, unlike that in men, tends to decline with age. This corresponds with the results of the Massachusetts Male Aging Study (Feldman et al., 1994), which reported that by age 40, 40 percent of the men surveyed experienced mild-to-severe erectile dysfunction and this increased to 67 percent by age 70. In contrast, the 1998 NCOA (The National Council on the Aging) survey of 1,300 "older" (over age 60) Americans helped to provide a slightly different perspective on sexuality in this population (NCOA, 1998). Their results indicate that sexual activity plays an important role in relationships among these "older" men and women. Forty-eight percent reported that they were sexually active (sex at least once per month). Of these respondents, 79 percent of men and 66 percent of women said that sex was an important component of their relationship with their partner. Seventy-four percent of the sexually active men and 70 percent of the sexually active women reported being as satisfied or even more satisfied with their sexual lives than they were in their 40s. It is fair to state that when older people are sexually abstinent, it is likely because they have no available partner or because of health problems.

Age-Related Factors That Impact Sexual Functioning

Female sexual satisfaction does not appear to decline appreciably with age (Avis, Stellato, Crawford, Johannes, & Longscope, 2000; Laumann et al., 1999). However, the physical changes that may occur as a result of the menopausal transition have the potential to interfere with sexual functioning. Declining estrogen levels that occur during perimenopause often result in vaginal dryness and atrophy due to diminished blood flow to the vagina. The vagina is a cylindrical organ, 7–15 cm in length. With sexual arousal, lubrication occurs as a result of secretions from the uterine glands and transudate from the subepithelial vasculature. The blood and nerve supplies to the vagina are similar to those of the penile shaft. Arterial blood flow branches off the uterine, pudendal, and ovarian arteries. The changes in the epithelial lining of the vagina occur relatively rapidly as estrogen levels decline. Subsequent vascular, muscular, and connective tissue changes occur over time. Decreased vascularization starves the surrounding tissues of nutrients and makes it more difficult for engorgement and lubrication. The vagina also loses its elasticity.

Estrogen replacement therapy, unless medically contraindicated, will often prevent genital atrophy and preserves the epithelial integrity of urogenital tissues (Freedman, 2000). Topical estrogen cream or a vaginal estradiol ring may also help prevent genital atrophy and vaginal dryness (Berman & Goldstein, 2001).

The clitoris is composed of the clitoral gland and two corporal bodies that extend for perhaps 9–10 cm behind the head of the clitoris and along the undersurface of the vagina. These corporal bodies are made of erectile tissue covered with a unilaminar tunica, rather than the trilayer tunica found in the penis. Clitoral changes from aging include shrinkage, a decrease in perfusion, diminished engorgement during the desire and arousal phases, and a decline in the neurophysiological response, including slowed nerve impulses and a decrease in touch perception, vibratory sensation, and reaction time. Decreased muscle tension may increase the time it takes for arousal to lead to orgasm, diminish the peak of orgasm, and cause a more rapid resolution. Additionally, the uterus typically contracts with orgasm, and with advancing age, those contractions may become painful. However, although all this sounds pretty ominous for older women, the actual perception of sexual satisfaction does not necessarily change.

Androgens and Postmenopausal Sexuality

The role of androgens and androgen replacement for postmenopausal women is currently receiving tremendous attention and has incurred lively debate. The fact that androgens have a role in female sexual drive has been known for 60 years (Greenblatt, 1942). However, the current controversy revolves around whether there is a clinical syndrome of "androgen deficiency."

Women achieve peak androgen production in their mid-20s. Beginning in their early 30s, they gradually lose testosterone (Davis, 2001). By the time most women reach their 60s, their testosterone levels are half of what they were before age 40.

In contrast to the gradual decline in testosterone of naturally menopausal women, there is a sudden decline in testosterone following bilateral oophorectomy because the ovaries produce 40 percent of circulating testosterone. Testosterone, together with its metabolite dihydrotestosterone, is the most potent endogenous androgen in both men and women. Testosterone is bound to albumin and sex hormone-binding globulin (SHBG). During the time of the perimenopausal transition, as estrogen levels are declining, women also experience a decrease in SHBG, which binds both estrogen and testosterone and, in fact, tends to bind testosterone more than it does estrogen. Some perimenopausal women will notice an increase in sexual desire and activity, perhaps because the declining levels of SHBG frees up more testosterone. In contrast, some premenopausal women who use oral contraceptives may increase their SHBG levels and lower their free testosterone levels and may notice a decrease in sexual desire.

In response to the controversy over whether androgen deficiency exists in women, a panel of experts reviewed the existing literature in this area. This panel proposed that there is a clinical syndrome that they have labeled "Female Androgen Insufficiency" (FAI). FAI is defined as a pattern of clinical symptoms in the presence of decreased bioavailable testosterone and normal estrogen status. The clinical symptoms include impaired sexual function, mood alterations, and diminished energy and well-being (Bachman et al., 2002).

The panel used the term *insufficiency* and not *deficiency* because we do not yet know enough about normal levels of androgens in women to be able to state what is considered a deficiency. There is not yet a clear range below which a deficiency can be diagnosed. Most commercially available methods are inaccurate or unreliable. Equilibrium dialysis is the current gold standard but it is not readily available in most laboratory settings. In addition to difficulty with determining normal values, there is considerable variability among women who show low levels of free testosterone. Not all women experience the symptoms, even when they may have declining levels of free testosterone. There are also some long-term side effects, some potentially irreversible. These include virilization (e.g., hirsutism, clitoral enlargement, deepened voice), acne, and liver damage (Berman & Goldstein, 2001).

Another problem with the concept of female androgen insufficiency is that healthcare providers may overuse this simple medical diagnosis. Unfortunately (or fortunately), this is not the case with regard to any female sexual dysfunction, and this is particularly true with regard to aging women and decreased sexual desire. Female sexuality and hypoactive desire disorder are very complicated and cannot be summed up by a simple biologic theory. In fact, even when androgen insufficiency may be involved, there are a number of other psychosocial factors that are at least as important, if not more important, in understanding the problem and treating it.

Aging and Sexual Desire

Hypoactive sexual desire disorder is the most prevalent female sexual dysfunction for all women (Laumann et al., 1999). It is also the sexual dysfunction that has often been linked to menopause because of the declining levels of testosterone that occur during this time. However, recent large-scale studies do not support this long-held belief. Instead it is age much more than menopausal status that is related to decreased sexual drive. In fact, one of the most significant and universal changes that occur with age is a decline in the drive component of sexual desire. The false assumption that menopause automatically results in loss of sexual drive has often resulted in haphazard and inappropriate treatments. Unfortunately, many healthcare providers and women themselves do not accurately understand the complexity of desire.

Desire refers to one's interest in being sexual and is determined by the interaction of three related but separate components: (1) drive; (2) beliefs/values; and (3) motivation (Levine, 1992). Drive is the biologic component of desire. It is the result of neuroendocrine mechanisms and is experienced as spontaneous, endogenous sexual interest. Drive is typically manifested by sexual thoughts, feelings, fantasies or dreams, increased erotic attraction to others in proximity, seeking out sexual activity (alone or with a partner), and genital tingling or increased genital sensitivity. This is the component that is impacted by declining testosterone levels. The second component of desire reflects an individual's expectations, beliefs, and values about sexual activity. The more positive the person's beliefs and values are about sexuality, the greater the person's desire to behave sexually. The third component of desire is the psychological and interpersonal motivation. Motivation is driven by emotional or interpersonal factors and is characterized by the willingness of a person to behave sexually with a given partner. This component tends to have the greatest impact overall on desire and is the most complex and elusive.

This distinction between drive and desire is absolutely essential for any physician assessing or treating sexual problems because treatment is vastly different on the basis of which component or components of desire have declined. For example, a woman might have a very strong sexual drive but if she is not motivated to be sexual, say if she is angry with her partner, dealing with a stressful work problem or suffering from depression, she will not act on the drive. In fact, it is virtually wiped out.

On the other hand, if a woman has lost some of her drive but remains motivated to be close to and intimate with her partner, then despite having little physical cues or interest, she still enjoys the sexual experience. This differentiation of drive from desire is particularly important to the understanding of female sexuality and points out some of the gender differences in prevalence of particular sexual problems. It also underscores the relative gender differences in the sexual response cycle itself and is very consistent with Basson's model of a nonlinear female response cycle (Basson, 2000). For many women, particularly postmenopausal women, drive fades and is no longer the initial step (or never was) in the response cycle. Instead, desire follows arousal and many women begin to respond from a point of sexual neutrality. Arousal may come from a conscious decision or from a stimulus or as a result of seduction or suggestion from a partner (receptivity). Healthcare providers must understand this to normalize this reality for women who have come to believe that because the initial drive has gone they have a sexual dysfunction (which then can lead to a self-fulfilling prophecy).

Psychosocial Factors Impacting Sexuality

In addition to understanding desire and the female response cycle in order to fully understand the complexity of female sexuality, it is helpful to observe it from a completely different context than medicine has done so far—social psychology theory. The first social psychology concept that is relevant to female sexuality and desire is called *self-perception theory*. Self-perception theory proposes that people make attributions about their own attitudes, feelings, and behaviors by relying on their observations of external behaviors and the circumstances in which those behaviors occur (Bem, 1965). Consider, for example, a 55-year-old woman who has been married for 20 years. Throughout her marriage, she has had drive to be sexual about once per week but her husband has had the drive to be sexual three times per week. This has resulted in the husband always being the initiator. On the basis of this, the wife observes her own behavior and sees that she only engages in sex when asked. Even though she was often receptive to the initiation and enjoyed the encounters, her self-perception is that she has little desire and is not a sexual person because she hardly ever thinks of it on her own and never initiates.

Another example is the self-perceptions that occur as a result of the disadvantage of long-term relationships. In this case, both partners observe that they are no longer passionate with each other. When they were first lovers, it was exciting and the challenge, mystery, danger, and novelty kept the passion alive. But as with every long-term relationship, passion ebbs as comfort, security, and partnership step in. But many couples do not understand this natural occurrence and perceive it as a flaw in their own relationship. Therefore, they observe their own decline in passion and interpret this as meaning they no longer desire their partner.

The second social psychology concept is called the *overjustification hypothesis*. This predicts that when an external reward is given to a person for performing an intrinsically rewarding activity, the person's intrinsic interest will decrease (Lepper, Greene, & Nisbett, 1973). In this case, if this 55-year-old woman responds to her husband's sexual initiation and the result is that she experiences a reward, such as relief from guilt (a form of negative reinforcement), relief from a whiney crabby husband, or lots of gratitude and more chores done the next day, the actual enjoyment of the sexual encounter may decline for her. Why? Because she now interprets her enjoyment as being primarily from the reward instead of the actual activity. We can also explain this in the opposite direction using the concept of *insufficient justification*. This concept is based on the classic *cognitive dissonance theory*, which states that an inconsistency between two cognitions or between a cognition and a behavior will create such discomfort in a person that they will alter one of the cognitions or behaviors to restore consistency and reduce this distress (Festinger, 1957). If this same woman responds to her husband's advances but does not perceive any external reward for this, that is, no relief of guilt, no reduction in whining, no gratitude and so forth, the need for cognitive balance or consistency between her observed behaviors and thoughts would lead her to attribute her behavior to intrinsic enjoyment of sex.

One of the classic cognitive dissonance studies illustrates this wonderfully (Festinger & Carlsmith, 1959). In this study, participants participated in a dull experiment and were then paid either $1 or $20 to tell potential participants that the experiment had actually been interesting and fun. When the original participants were subsequently asked to evaluate the dull experiment, the group that was paid $1 had changed their attitude toward the experiment and described it as actually being enjoyable. The investigators concluded that the $20 group had sufficient justification for lying and thus did not feel any dissonance and had no need to alter their cognitions and continued to consider the task as dull. The dollar group felt insufficient justification for lying and therefore felt dissonance, which they reduced by changing their attitude and deciding that the experiment was actually fun. The importance of recognizing how women interpret their own behaviors cannot be overstated. Many women, because of self-perception theory and overjustification, perceive sex as a chore or an obligation rather than an enjoyable experience and consider themselves sexually inadequate. In addition, many couples in long-term relationships misinterpret the natural decrease in excitement and passion as being a symptom of a failed marriage. Therefore, even if healthcare providers improve drive and overall desire but do not address and then alter these long-held misattributions with patients, treatment will be undermined.

Healthcare providers must also be sensitive to a patient's culture to gain an accurate assessment of her sexual functioning. A woman's sexual self-perception is influenced by her race, gender, ethnicity, educational background, socioeconomic status, sexual orientation, financial resources, and religion. For example, in many Asian societies, women are expected to be obedient, yielding, timid, respectful, and unselfish (American Medical Association, 2001). Obviously, this culturally determined behavior pattern could greatly impact the sexual lives of women who follow it. Culture also influences women's perceptions of menopause and its impact on health, self-image, and sexuality. Pharmacia Corporation recently surveyed 1,200 women to see how ethnicity impacted these perceptions of menopause. They found that African American women were the most optimistic, Caucasian women were the most anxious, Asian women were more muted about symptoms, and Hispanic women were the most stoic (Pharmacia Corporation, 2001).

Age-Related Factors: The Impact of Partner Sexual Dysfunction

In keeping with this model of looking at context to understand female sexuality, one of the most significant psychosocial or contextual variables that affect women is the impact of their partner having a sexual dysfunction. Many older heterosexual couples cease being sexual because the male partner's interest declines, usually because of his experiencing erectile dysfunction. Erectile dysfunction is a major source of poor body image and resulting low desire for men. Many postmenopausal women are abstinent because of their male partner's erectile difficulties or his decline in drive.

The Massachusetts Male Aging Study (Feldman et al., 1994) indicates that by middle age, the majority of men will experience some erectile dysfunction. Men who had mild dysfunction in their 40s tended to progress to moderate or complete dysfunction as they age. In midlife, men begin to experience changes in hormone levels, blood flow, libido, sensitivity, and ejaculation. Those changes may compromise their ability to achieve and maintain erections as well as the quality of the erections. Arousal takes longer to achieve and the plateau phase is prolonged, delaying ejaculation. In addition, ejaculation may be slow or absent. Overall, with age, blood flow to all organs decreases (Feldman et al., 1994; Schiavi, 1999).

Although Viagra has helped many men overcome erectile dysfunction, a problem to recognize is that it may now cause a shift in a couple's sexual equilibrium. As women first adjusted to the sexual equilibrium of abstinence due to their partner's dysfunction, now they must once again accommodate to another change in equilibrium. This creates a challenge. Not only do older people require a longer adjustment period to make the necessary accompanying cognitive shift, but older women definitely need time for their bodies to readjust to a partnered sexual life. However, give a man a reliable erection, and he typically wants to immediately use it (that is, unless there are other psychogenic factors contributing to avoidance and low desire other than an unreliable penis). Unfortunately, if he and his female partner have not had intercourse for a long time, her aging vagina has likely narrowed and atrophied and will not immediately accommodate a penis without risking pain and/or injury. This may lead to a secondary female sexual dysfunction of dyspareunia or vaginismus. For heterosexual postmenopausal women who have been sexually abstinent for a long time, they must begin by slowly stretching and "exercising" their vaginas. They need to start by penetration with a finger or dilator and gradually stretch the vagina to accommodate a penis. They cannot return to sexual functioning instantaneously, if sexual functioning for them has always meant intercourse.

Age-Related Factors: Health Changes

Not only does the aging body experience problems with sexual functioning, but also the likelihood of developing other health problems increases in older age with a subsequent impact on relationships and sexuality. Sexual problems may be primarily due to physical limitations, lack of energy, side effects of medications, or poor self-image as a "sick person." From minor problems such as decreased energy or strength to major problems such as cardiovascular disease, arthritis, cancer, diabetes, and other serious illnesses, the physical decline of the aging body must be faced and accommodated to maintain a satisfying sexual life. The equilibrium of the emotional component of a relationship also changes when one or both partners in a couple become ill or develop chronic health problems. One partner may end up as the nurse or fulltime caregiver to the other. Even excluding the physical problems, the imbalance of these roles in this case would likely result in sexual problems with one or both partners losing desire.

Translating Theory Into Practice

Although aging may contribute to changes in the sexual dynamics of a relationship, a number of treatment modalities are available, both psychological and medical. An extensive review of these treatments, which include counseling and medical interventions, is beyond the scope of this paper. In fact, such detail works against the main point; healthcare providers do not need to be trained as sex therapists to effectively address many of the sexual problems of their peri- and postmenopausal patients. Instead, physicians can provide help simply by minimally expanding what they are already trained to do: first, assess and evaluate. Second, treat and/or refer. Simply initiating a discussion of sexual concerns is often the most valuable component to treatment for women and their partners. By asking about sexuality, the healthcare provider informs the patient that it is appropriate to discuss sexual problems in that setting and validates an older woman's self-perception as a sexual being. It is hard to provide an effective intervention, regardless of the type of treatment, if there is no mention of a problem.

Healthcare providers can be extremely helpful in giving permission to women to expand or change their sexual repertoire or by providing basic sex education. For example, many couples are ignorant of the fact that despite erectile dysfunction, men are still able to experience desire, arousal, and orgasm. Despite our sexually enlightened culture, many older couples still hold onto fairly restrictive and conservative views of what is "appropriate" and "normal." Therefore, treatment would be defined as helping older women and couples to redefine what normal sexual activity entails. For example, the suggestion that some heterosexual couples may no longer want to rely on intercourse as their main sexual event can provide an optimistic perspective for couples having difficulty due to genital atrophy or erectile dysfunction. It may be difficult, though very satisfying, for older couples to move away from the standard missionary position and intercourse and toward different positions and ways of stimulation (e.g., increased use of oral sex, manual stimulation, sexual aids, and sensual nongenital activities like bathing together, massage, or erotic movies/literature; Leiblum, 1991). Change does not have to be extreme for couples to notice significant improvement in sexual fulfillment. It may imply something as simple (but often not considered) as suggesting that couples make love in the morning when older people have more energy rather than late in the evening when there is a greater likelihood of fatigue. Furthermore, it is important to remind older couples to learn to communicate better both in and out of bedroom. As their sexual repertoire requires some adjustment or change, a couple needs to effectively communicate in order to smoothly accomplish this. In addition, communication itself can be seductive, enticing, and sexual. Effective communication in everyday life is also important for the quality of the overall relationship, which is also critical to couples' sexual lives. Finally, healthcare providers must be culturally competent.

References

American Medical Association. (2001). *Talking to patients about sex: Training program for Physicians*. /chicago: Author.

Avis, N. E., Stellato, R., Crawford, S., Johannes, C., & Longscope, C. (2000). Is there an association between menopause status and sexual functioning? *Menopause, 7*, 297–309.

Bachman, G., Bancroft, J., Braunstein, G., Burger, H., Davis, S., Dennerstein, L., et al. (2002). Female androgen insufficiency: The Princeton consensus statement on definition, classification, and assessment. *Fertility and Sterility, 77*, 660–665.

Basson, R. (2000). The female sexual response. A different model. *Journal of Sex and Marital Therapy, 26*, 51–65.

Bern, D. (1965). An experimental analysis of self-persuasion. *Journal of Experimental Social Psychology, 1*, 199–218.

Berman, J. R., & Goldstein, I. (2001). Female sexual dysfunction. *Urologic Clinics of North America, 28*, 405–416.

Davis, S. R. (2001). Testosterone treatment: Psychological and physical effects in postmenopausal women. *Menopausal Medicine, 9(2)*, 1–6.

Feldman, H. A., Goldstein, I., Hatzichristou, D. G., Krane, R. J., & McKinlay, J. B. (1994). Impotence and its medical and psychosocial correlates: Results of the Massachusetts Male Aging Study. *Journal of Urology, 151*, 54–61.

Festinger, L. (1957). *A theory of cognitive disonnance*. Stanford, CA: Stanford University Press.

Festinger, L., & Carlsmith, J. (1959). Cognitive consequences of forced compliance. *Journal of Abnormal and Social Psychology, 58*, 203–210.

Freedman, M. (2000). Sexuality in post-menopausal women. *Menopausal Medicine, 8*, 1–4.

Greenblatt, R. B. (1942). Hormone factors in libido. *Journal of Clinical Endocrinology and Metabolism, 3*, 305.

Laumann, E. O., Paik, A., & Rosen, R. C. (1999). Sexual dysfunction in the United States. *Journal of the American Medical Association, 281*, 537–544.

Leiblum, S. R. (1991, October). *The midlife and beyond*. Paper presented at the 24th Annual Postgraduate Course of the Psychology Professional Interest Group of the American Fertility Society on Sexual Dysfunction: Patient Concerns and Practical Strategies, Orlando, FL.

Lepper, M., Greene, D., & Nisbett, R. (1973). Undermining children's interests with extrinsic rewards: A test of the "overjustification hypothesis." *Journal of Personality and Social Psychology, 28*, 129–137.

Levine, S. B. (1992). *Sexual life*. New York: Plenum.

Pharmacia Corporation. (2001, November 15). *New research on menopause and sexuality finds women are not seeking medial help for chronic symptoms affecting intimate relationship* (Press release). Peapack, NJ: Author.

Schiavi, R. C. (1999). *Aging and male sexuality*. Cambridge, UK: Cambridge University Press.

Schnarch, D. (1997). *Passionate marriage*. New York: Henry Holt.

The National Council on Aging (1998, September). *Healthy sexuality and vital aging*. Washington, DC: Author.

Chapter 19
Affection and Sexuality in the Presence of Alzheimer's Disease

Lore K. Wright

Variations in sexual capacity and performance among the elderly are greater than among persons in the young or middle years. Add to this already imbalanced equation the disease of Alzheimer's and the scale of sexual satisfaction is bound to tip. Or is it?

The interesting findings in the Wright study will raise questions in the minds of the readers of previous articles in this anthology. For example, because men tend to underreport the frequency of sexual contact and women to overreport it, why was this issue not raised in interpreting the findings in this study? Also, could the reported increase in sexual desire for some be the result of Alzheimer's disease or could it perhaps be related to medication? L-Dopa reportedly does enhance sexual desire in Parkinson's disease patients. In spite of limited sample size, this research makes a significant contribution to a pressing problem about which we have very limited empirical data.

Affection and sexual intimacy in adult relationships are physical expressions of affirmation and caring between two people. It is generally accepted that in community residing older adults, expression of affection increases with age (1,2), interest in sexuality remains high (3), but frequency of sexual intercourse declines (3). These findings are mostly based on cross-sections data; they were challenged to some extent by George and Weiler (4), who found that over a period of six years, sexual activity remained stable for three adult cohorts (ages 46–55, 56–65, and 66–71).

Various physical ailments are known to adversely impact a couple's intimate relationship, and conditions such as cardiovascular disease, cancer, arthritis, diabetes, as well as the adverse effects on sexuality from medications, surgery, and radiation treatment have been researched extensively (5). However, the presence of cognitive impairment and its impact on affection and sexuality have been the focus of only a few investigations. Yet it is cognitive ability, perhaps more so than physical health, which sustains the quality of affectional expressions between partners, and cognitive ability is necessary to perform sexual activities in a manner which shows awareness of the partner's feelings and needs (6).

Progressive loss of cognitive ability is the cardinal feature of Alzheimer's disease (AD), an illness that affects over four million Americans, typically after age 65. The illness is characterized by initial forgetfulness which progresses to loss of independent social functioning, followed by loss of physical abilities to a stage of total dependence on a caregiver (7). This decline typically occurs over the course of eight to 12 years.

Duffy (6) provided rich data on how Alzheimer's disease affects intimate relationships. Of husband and wife caregivers, close to 80 percent perceived a change in their emotional relationship to the AD spouse, characterizing the relationship in non-sexual terms as the illness progressed; a similar percentage experienced a change in sexual intimacy with a gradual decline in interest most commonly reported (9). Hypersexual interest displayed by a few male afflicted spouses caused wife caregivers to have feelings ranging from mild irritation to strong aversion; male caregivers, however, did not report such sentiments to an afflicted wife's increased receptiveness to sexual overtures (6). Wright (8) reported similar findings for sexual activities of AD couples, but, based on cross-sectional data, found that expression of affection was not significantly different for AD couples and healthy couples. Davies, Zeiss, and Tinklenberg (9) distinguished between sexual problems within the marital relationship and inappropriate sexual behavior in social situations. Their research showed that 53 percent of men reported erectile failure since the onset of AD symptoms, but inappropriate sexual behavior such as exposing or masturbation in public was rare (10). Taken together, these findings provide important insights into a sensitive topic, but fail to provide a long-range perspective of affection and sexuality which contrasts normal aging and illness.

THE CURRENT STUDY

The purpose of this study was to investigate longitudinal trends of marital intimacy in the presence of a dementing illness, AD, versus healthy aging. The study sought answers to the following questions: (1) Are affectional interactions different for AD couples compared to healthy couples, and do affectional interactions change over time? (2) Is sexual intimacy different for AD couples compared to healthy couples, and does it change over time? (3) Are affection and sexual expression related to the afflicted spouse's longitudinal outcome variables?

Method

The sample consisted of two groups of community-residing couples, an "AD group" and a comparison group or "well group" recruited from 10 agencies in two southeastern states. The AD group comprised 30 couples each: an AD afflicted spouse and the other spouse functioned as the primary caregiver. There were 24 male and 6 female afflicted spouses; all were in the early to middle phases of the illness. The comparison group comprised 17 couples without cognitive impairment in either spouse, but several spouses had common medical problems such as arthritis, hypertension, and heart disease. The two groups were similar in age, years of education, and monthly income. However, mean length of marriage was 38 years for the AD group and 45 years for the comparison group. The difference was due to greater numbers of second and third marriages in the AD group.

Affection was measured with the Dyadic Adjustment Rating Scale (11). In addition to the original item, "kissing the spouse," five new items were added; these were "touching the spouse lovingly," "caressing the spouse," "holding hands," "putting an arm around the spouse," and "sleeping in the same bed." Sexual intimacy data were based on two measures, frequency of and agreement over sexual intimacy. Frequency of current sexual intimacy per month was ascertained through direct questioning. Agreement over sexual expression was assessed with the Dyadic Adjustment Rating Scale (10) which questioned the degree to which spouses agreed over sexual relations.

Retrospective (time 1) data were conceptualized as the time prior to onset of memory problems in the AD spouse, and for the comparison group as the time prior to a spouse's retirement. These data were obtained from caregivers and well spouses. Concurrent (time 2) data were conceptualized as "now," i.e., thinking about the past few weeks. These data were obtained from all spouses including the afflicted, but spouses were interviewed in separate rooms. Follow-up (time 3) data were obtained from caregivers and well spouses two years after the home interview, with a response rate of 98 percent.

First, congruence between answers from each husband-wife dyad was tested. This showed that answers given by husbands-wives from both groups were very similar for frequency of affection. Answers for frequency and agreement over sexual relations were also nearly identical for husbands-wives of the well group. Answers from AD group couples differed significantly, with afflicted spouses reporting higher agreement than caregivers. In addition, approximately one-fourth of AD afflicted spouses reported more frequent sexual contacts per month than the respective caregiver spouse. Because answers from afflicted spouses were considered less reliable, comparisons between the AD and well groups were made as follows: Only caregiver spouses' answers were used to represent the AD group; to represent the comparison group, answers from only one spouse per well couple were used.

Results

Affection

Perception of past affection (time 1) was very similar for both groups of couples for the AD group and for the well group. At the time of the home interview (time 2), affectional expression had declined significantly for the AD group, but differences between the AD and well group remained insignificant. Two years later (time 3), outcomes for afflicted spouses had to be considered. Only 43 percent of couples in the AD group still lived at home together, 27 percent of the afflicted spouses were in a nursing home, and 30 percent were deceased. Among well couples, only one spouse had died, and no spouse had been placed into a nursing home. Information on time 3 affection was obtained from all intact well couples and from AD caregivers who either continued to be in-home caregivers or had placed the spouse into a nursing home.

Past (time 1) affection was similar for continued in-home caregivers, nursing home placement caregivers, and well spouses, but was lower for caregivers whose spouses had died by time 3. At the time of the home interview (time 2), affection was rated markedly lower by those caregivers who subsequently became widowed and also by caregivers who subsequently placed the spouse into a nursing home. However, those who would continue in-home caregiving and the well spouses remained at similar levels of affection as observed for time 1. Another interesting effect can be noted for time 3 in that the nursing home placement caregivers increased significantly in their rating of affection, while well spouses and in-home caregivers remained fairly stable.

Sexual Intimacy

Only 27 percent of AD couples were sexually active at time 2 (about 5 years after the onset of AD) in contrast to 82 percent of well couples. Mean sexual contacts per month were 8.0 for AD couples and 3.8 for well couples. Range of sexual contacts was 1 to 14 (or more) times per month for AD couples and < 1 to 10 times per month for well couples.

Demand for frequent sexual contacts by AD spouses was reported by 14 percent of caregivers when the entire group was counted, but this translated to 50 percent when only the still sexually active couples were considered. Caregivers' reaction to hypersexuality ranged from acceptance to strong aversion. Of the intact AD couples, only 19 percent were reported to be still sexually active. Mean number of sexual contacts at time 3 was 3.75 per month for the AD group. Among intact well couples, 62.5 percent were still sexually active. Their mean number of sexual contacts per month was 5.2. The difference between the two groups was not significant.

An intriguing question is whether sexual activity at time 2 is related to outcomes of afflicted spouses at time 3, i.e., still at home, nursing home, or deceased. Of the 73 percent AD couples who had not been sexually active at time 2, only 32 percent still lived together at time 3, and nursing home placement and death had resulted at similar frequencies. However, of the 27 percent AD couples who were sexually active at time 2, 75 percent were still living together at home two years later (time 3).

For AD couples, about five years into the illness (time 2), sexual activity was significantly related to the caregivers' better physical health and lower depressed moods but not to the afflicted spouses' mental status. There were no significant relationships between these variables and AD couples' sexual activity two years later (time 3). For well couples, sexual activity at time 2 was significantly related to better physical health and being younger. At time 3, only better physical health was related to sexual activity.

In addition to frequency of sexual intimacy, agreement over sexual relations was evaluated longitudinally. There was no significant difference between the groups' past perception of agreement. By time 2, the home interview, caregivers rated agreement over sexual issues lower than well spouses but this difference was not statistically significant. Taking outcomes for afflicted spouses into consideration, agreement for the still at home and the nursing home placement groups bounced back from a lower level at time 2 to similar levels as those reported by well spouses at time 3.

Discussion

This study began by asking whether, compared to normal aging, affection and sexual intimacy are different and change over time when a spouse has AD. The data support that yes, the illness leads to differences between the two groups of couples, and there is change over time.

The fact that ratings of past affection and past agreement over sexual relations were very similar for the two groups lends support to the validity of the findings, despite the limitations inherent in generalizing from a small sample size. Most likely these couples were not different in their affectionate and sexual relationships when all were well, but it was illness, i.e., AD, which brought about significant changes: affection declined significantly, fewer AD than well couples were sexually active (27 percent versus 82 percent), and frequency of sex per month was significantly higher for the AD group (Mean of 8.0 versus 3.8). Poor physical health and depression in caregivers was related to less frequent sexual contacts. This supports findings from other studies documenting that physical and emotional health of both partners influence the sexual relationship (4).

Approximately five years after the onset of AD, demands for frequent sexual contacts occurred by a small percentage of AD afflicted spouses, and their behavior was distressing to caregiver spouses. However, two years later, which amounts to seven years since the onset of AD, this higher frequency of sexual relations had declined for all but one couple. Agreement over sexual relations was rated lowest by caregiver spouses at time 2, but was again similar to that reported by the well group at time 3, when for the AD group the problem had abated for all but one couple.

When examining the pattern for well group couples, affection shows stability over time. The stable pattern of affection could be attributed to the relatively short time frame examined (seven years in total) and to the measure of affection used in this study. Behavioral indicators such as kissing, caressing, and putting an arm around the spouse do not necessarily capture the emotional bond between spouses. Feelings of trust, being comfortable with each other, and helping each other are other indicators of affection which may increase with age, and which could be assessed in future studies.

The percent of well couples who remained sexually active did decline over time (from 82 percent to 62.5 percent). This is consistent with most other studies (3,5), and is further supported by the negative correlation between age and frequency of sex per month found in this study for time 2 and also by the positive correlation with physical health and frequency of sexual intimacy at time 2 and time 3.

But in addition to an overall decline, some stability over time was found which is consistent with findings by George and Weiler (4). In this study, several well couples with high sexual activity at time 2 remained high, i.e., actually reported an increase at time 3.

Intriguing are the findings for affection and sexual relations when outcomes of still being together at home, the afflicted spouse having been placed into a nursing home, or the afflicted spouse having died are taken into consideration. Normal aging is clearly different compared to the life of couples with AD. Despite the fact that well group couples had a variety of physical illnesses such as heart disease, arthritis, and hypertension, only one spouse had died over a two-year period, and no spouse had been institutionalized. Yet in the AD group, 30 percent of afflicted spouses had died, and 27 percent were in a nursing home. From a human developmental perspective, this loss demonstrates what Riegel (12) termed pathological deviations from normal development or the "catastrophic" impact of disease for over half of the couples. AD robbed 30 percent of couples of any further interactions and, one would anticipate, severely limited interactions for another 27 percent of couples due to the nursing home placement of the afflicted spouse.

It should be remembered that at the time of home interview (time 2), neither caregivers nor the researcher knew what the outcomes would be at time 3, and the reports of affection given at time 2 can be considered genuine reflections of spousal interactions at that time. Affection was rated significantly lower by those caregivers who subsequently became widowed and by those who subsequently placed the spouse into a nursing home. So the question arises whether caregivers had "given up" on the ill spouses, and whether this lack of interaction between spouses contributed to the afflicted spouses' death or their institutionalization.

It is, therefore, surprising to see that frequency of affection increased dramatically at time 3 for the nursing home placement group. Possibly, the stress of in-home caregiving had been alleviated, and positive feelings for the ill spouse could re-emerge. King et al. (13) have reported that spouses visit the nursing home almost daily and want to be involved in the care of their mate. The increase in affection after nursing home placement noted in this study may reflect this. Caregivers may indeed be re-experiencing positive feelings toward their mate, intertwined perhaps with some feelings of guilt for earlier inattention. Another interesting observation is that a much higher percentage of afflicted spouses who were sexually active at time 2 had remained at home by time 3. But the numbers on which these percentages are based are too small to speculate on their meaning.

Findings from this longitudinal study have several implications. The middle phase of AD seems to be the most problematic for sexual intimacy. Health professionals need to ask about the sensitive issue of sexual relations when interacting with caregivers and afflicted spouses. The use of prescription tranquilizers is debatable, but caregivers can be supported in their need to limit sexual relations. Distraction techniques and environmental manipulation (e.g., separate bedrooms) can be taught.

A professional who observes affectional gestures by a caregiver can provide positive reinforcement by commenting that such expressions are likely to contribute to the afflicted spouses' comfort. But professionals should not use findings from this study as a "threat" by telling caregivers that absence of affection may contribute to nursing home placement or early death.

Nursing home staff need to be especially sensitive to the needs of spouses who have relinquished the caregiver role. Visiting the afflicted spouse, kissing, hugging, and caressing are expressions of the bond between two people, no matter how difficult the years prior to nursing home placement may have been. When memory has been lost, expressions of affection are all that is left to form a bridge to the past. Connecting to that past in a positive way may be important for the caregiver's continued and future development.

References

1. Reedy M.N., Birren J.E., Schaie K.W.: Age and sex differences in satisfying love relationships across the adult life span. In *Readings in Adult Development and Aging*, K. Schaie, J. Geiwitz (eds). Boston, Little, Brown and Company, 1982, pp. 158–160.
2. Wright L.K.: *Alzheimer's Disease and Marriage*. Newbury Park, Sage, 1993.
3. Brecher E.M.: *Love, Sex, and Aging*. Boston, Little, Brown and Company, 1984.
4. George L.K., Weiler S.J.: Sexuality in middle and late life. *Arch Gen Psychiatry*, 38: 919–923, 1981.
5. Wright L.K.: Sexual dysfunction in the elderly. Forthcoming in Meridean L. Mass (ed.), *Nursing Diagnoses and Interventions for the Elderly* (second edition). Newbury Park, Sage.
6. Duffy L.M.: Sexual behavior and marital intimacy in Alzheimer's couples: A family theory perspective. *Sexuality & Disability*, 13(3): 239–254, 1995.
7. Reisberg B.: Dementia: A systematic approach to identifying reversible causes. *Geriatrics*, 41(4): 30–46, 1986.
8. Wright L.K.: The impact of Alzheimer's disease on the marital relationship. *Gerontologist*, 31(2): 224–237, 1991.

9. Davies H.D., Zeiss A., and Tinklenberg J.R.: 'Til death do us part: Intimacy and sexuality in the marriages of Alzheimer's patients. *Journal of Psychosocial Nursing*, 30(11): 5–10, 1992.

10. Zeiss A.M., Davies H.D., Wood M., Tinklenberg J.R.: The incidence and correlates of erectile problems in patients with Alzheimer's disease. *Archives of Sexual Behavior*, 19(4): 325–331, 1990.

11. Spanier G.B. and Thompson L.: A confirmatory analysis of the Dyad Adjustment Scale. *Journal Marriage and the Family*, 38: 731–741, 1982.

12. Riegal, K.F.: Foundation of dialectal psychology. New York, Academic Press, 1979.

13. King S., Collins C., Given B., and Vredevoogd J.: Institutionalization of an elderly family member: Reactions of spouse and nonspouse caregivers. *Archives of Psychiatric Nursing*, 5(6): 323–330, 1991.

Part V

Sexual Desire and Gender

"Sex Drugs for Women?" Four years ago, *Harper's Bazaar* posed this question in a lead article that focused attention on University of Chicago survey data which revealed sexual dysfunction to be a bigger problem for women than for men (Fishman 2000). At that time, the writer suggested it was possible that within two years women would have their own tested version of Viagra. But, not so fast, warned Irwin Goldstein, a physician at Boston University School of Medicine. A leader in the science of female response, it was Goldstein who, ironically, had authored a 1998 paper showing that Viagra—an angina drug that had the unwanted side effect of producing erections—was a safe and effective treatment for male erectile dysfunction. According to Goldstein, results for women are 20 years behind those of men mainly because female sexual dysfunction is underresearched and a poorly understood area of medicine (Fishman 2000). Apparently, he is correct. In the four years since the Fishman article's publication, men now have two additional choices of "sex drugs" (*Levitra* and *Cialis*), but the score for women is still zero to nothing!

In Part V, the subjects of sexual desire and gender are addressed from several perspectives. But, before students encounter various approaches to understanding these issues so vital to their sexual health, a challenge might be in order. They could be encouraged to search the offerings for any clues that might help explain a female-male imbalance such as that evidenced in the drug research.

Although American society has always had a great fascination with sexuality, this has long been a conversational taboo, especially in mixed-sex groups. However, the flurry of media attention around the Clinton-Lewinsky scandal during the Clinton Presidency bestowed a certain legitimacy upon this controversial topic. In fact, sex became the subject of dinner-table conversation for many American families faced with answering questions from their young children about the news of the day. The debacle even sent sexologists and sex therapists scrambling to justify or denigrate newly suggested definitions of "sexual relations" that would exclude oral sex. One of the inescapable questions after reading the Lewis Lapham chapter, which explores sex, Americans, scandal, and morality, is How much have things really changed since the early twentieth century? If Will and Ariel Durant accurately assessed the garden of tabloid delight of their own day in the opening quote for this selection, the answer is Not much.

To state that sexual desire is a popular pastime among young adults today may be a classic understatement, without any dissenters. But add the subject of gender to the mix of sexual desire and the screen immediately scrolls down to the category of "debate." Pepper Schwartz and Virginia Rutter manage a fascinating, readable combination of the two often disparate topics, addressing many of the fallacies and facts along the way. Their promise is alluring: Who we're attracted to and what we find sexually satisfying is not just a matter of the genital equipment we're born with. This chapter explains why.

Beginning with the thesis that gender is the most significant dimension of sexuality, the authors take issue with the assumptions that sexuality is naturally gendered, being rooted in biology, and that women and men are different sexually. They aptly review three competing explanations of differences in sexual desire between women and men to substantiate their claims: the biological; the sociobiological and evolutionary psychological; and the social constructionist view. But Schwartz and Rutter expand what could be just a well-done review of the

171

three opposing perspectives about gender differences in sexual desire when they propose the use of an "integrative" view. Defining *integrationist* as "one who will raise questions about biology when social context is emphasized as cause and will raise questions about social contexts when biological causes are emphasized," they encourage students to reason for themselves (Schwartz and Rutter 1998, 36). This is a lengthy reading, but one that is guaranteed to pique the interest of even the most reluctant of readers.

"How refreshing it is to find a book that sees through 30 years of blather about sexual politics and calls a gene, a gene; a reproductive strategy, a reproductive strategy; a survival mechanism, a survival mechanism" (Angier 2000, *Frontspiece*). Erica Jong's observation in the *New York Observer* was but one of numerous accolades praising Natalie Angier's book, *Woman: An Intimate Geography*, a *New York Times* bestseller that has been translated into nineteen (19) languages. Pulitzer-Prize winning author Angier, science writer for the *New York Times*, challenges widely accepted Darwinian-based gender stereotypes in her latest book. She shows how cultural biases have influenced research in evolutionary psychology, leading to what she describes as dubious conclusions about female nature. In the chapter "Venus in Furs: Estrogen and Desire," Angier admits that we do not understand how estrogen works on the brain to elicit desire. But, in her words, "there are enough indirect strands of evidence to knit a serviceable thinking cap with which to mull over estrogen's meaning" (Angier 2000, 214). Not only will students resonate to the message Angier sends, they will also appreciate the language with which she offers an optimistic, fresh vision of womanhood. Some may even be motivated to read more on this topic than required.

Barry McCarthy takes an interesting oppositional stance on the role of intimacy in facilitating sexual desire and functioning. Asserting that increasing intimacy is not the answer for couples, he embarks on a road less traveled in therapy circles. Using John Gottman's (1994) four marital styles derived from empirical research to frame his thesis, McCarthy postulates that a mutually comfortable and agreeable level of intimacy is the key to sexual desire. Most therapists would agree with him about the importance of achieving intimacy early in the marriage. In fact, in the first two years of marriage, one of the most important couple-tasks is to work out the relationship rules in the areas of intimacy as well as in the area of power (Lewis, Beavers, Gossett, and Phillips 1976). It is interesting that as the sexual strengths and vulnerabilities of each of Gottman's marital styles are explored by McCarthy, nowhere does the concept of power in relationship to healthy sexual functioning receive more than a passing glance. In contrast, therapist Keith Miller (1997) gives power top rating in his book, *Compelled to Control: Recovering Intimacy in Broken Relationships*. Miller, who portrays sex as the outward sign of intimacy, views power, or the compulsion to control, as the number one enemy of intimacy. Students may find this intimacy-power debate central to their own questions concerning sexual desire.

When levels of sexual satisfaction and sexual drive in women with spinal cord (SCI) injuries, were examined by Kimberly Black, Marsha Sipski, and Susanne Strauss, an important step was made for SCI women. Especially so because this study was the first to compare the sexual functioning of SCI women with those who are able-bodied. However, along with good news, there were some bad-news elements related to the study. The fact that all of the subjects were members of the National Spinal Cord Injury Association, with a membership of only 346 women, can raise questions concerning the representativeness of the sample. Although such women are assumed to be much more educated about the effect of spinal cord injury on sexuality, it is problematic that the procedure for selecting the comparison group was not random. In spite of these methodological issues, the study does furnish a rare glimpse into a neglected area of sexuality, and thus it makes a valuable contribution to the research.

References

Angier, N. (2000). *Woman: An Intimate Geography*. New York: Anchor Books.

Fishman, S. (2000, March). "Sex Drugs for Women?" *Harper's Bazaar*, pp. 388–392.

Gottman, J. (1994). *Why Marriages Succeed or Fail*. New York: Simon & Schuster.

Lewis, J. M., Beavers, W. R., Gossett, J. T., and Phillips, W. A. (1976). *No Single Thread: Psychological Health in Family Systems*. New York: Brunner/Mazel.

Miller, J. K. (1997). *Compelled to Control: Recovering Intimacy in Broken Relationships*. Deerfield Beach, FL: Health Communications.

Schwartz, P., and Rutter, V. (1998). *The Gender of Sexuality*. Thousand Oaks, CA: Pine Forge. ✦

Chapter 20

In the Garden of Tabloid Delight

Notes on Sex, Americans, Scandal, and Morality

Lewis H. Lapham

Master of metaphor, Lapham attains the very essence of "tabloid delight" with musings from his notes on sex, Americans, scandal, and morality—an irony that is hopefully not lost on the reader. Although the litany of sexual scandals in the summer of 1997 fostered both pious "op-ed page sermonettes" and "ribald commentary" in the media, most Americans barely acknowledged the blip on their screens of conscience. The flash of media attention did, however, legitimize talking about sexuality in a society that has always had a great fascination with sex but a conversational taboo against it.

The fact that a commercial presentation of sexuality as a commodity allows consumers to select from a smorgasbord of options seems to offer the best in the world of choice and exchange. Nevertheless, Lapham believes the resulting contradictions lead to confusion about what is moral and what is virtue, existential questions for which there are no societally-sanctioned answers. The author raises issues that are germane not only for a mooringless society, but also for individuals who operate without the strength of a moral order, risking their chance for love or meaning in life. Citing the failure of the nation's moral guidebook to adapt to political, economic, social, and technological changes of the last century, Lapham urges a reassessment of both our sexual behavior and the rules by which we play.

> Caught in the relaxing interval between one moral code and the next, an unmoored generation surrenders itself to luxury, corruption, and a restless disorder of family and morals.
>
> —*Will and Ariel Durant*

The news media in May of 1997 bloomed with so exuberant a profusion of sexual scandal that by the first week of summer it was hard to tell the difference between the front-page political reporting and the classified advertising placed by men seeking women and women seeking men. Every day for thirty days some sort of new or rare flowering appeared in the garden of tabloid delight, prompting the headline writers to dance joyously around the maypoles of 72-point type, singing their songs of spring with lyrics supplied by a grand jury or the police. Some of the stories were better than others, and although not all of them resulted in invitations to talk to Oprah, even a brief summary of the leading attractions fairly describes the gifts of the season's abundance.

May 2—Eddie Murphy, noted comedian and screen actor, found by sheriff's deputies, at 4:45 a.m. on Santa Monica Boulevard in West Hollywood, in the company of a transvestite prostitute.

May 10—Congressman Joseph P. Kennedy declines to explain how it came to pass that his younger brother Michael, thirty-nine, embarked upon a love affair with the fourteen-year-old girl employed as the baby-sitter to his infant son.

May 22—Frank Gifford, a famous television sportscaster, reported to have been photographed in a New York hotel room, parading around on a bed with a woman not his wife.

May 22—Lieutenant Kelly Flinn, "the perfect picture girl" of the United States Air Force and the first woman to command a B-52 bomber, drummed out of the service for committing adultery with a civilian soccer coach.

May 27—The Supreme Court directs the President of the United States to answer questions about the administration of his penis, all nine justices concurring in the opinion that the discussion cannot be postponed for reasons of state.

May 30—Staff Sergeant Vernell Robinson Jr. expelled from the United States Army and sentenced to six months in prison for forcing sodomy on five female recruits.

June 1—Robert S. Bennett, the Washington lawyer defending President Clinton against the charges brought by Paula Corbin Jones (attempted sodomy, violation of civil rights), informs two television networks that he intends to entertain the court with tales of the plaintiff's lurid past.

June 2—Major General John E. Longhouser announces his retirement from the Army and resigns his command of the Aberdeen Proving Ground (the scene of the crimes committed by Sergeant Robinson) because an anonymous tipster telephoned headquarters to report that five years ago, while briefly separated from his wife, the general had formed a liaison with a female civilian.

June 3—Concerned Women for America characterizes Lawyer Bennett's legal tactics as those "normally used by a rapist's attorney" and reminds him that two years ago President Clinton signed a law excusing sexually abused women from questions about their prior conduct.

June 4 (late morning)—Lawyer Bennett disavows his proposed line of questioning. "I'm not a fool. It's my intention to take the high ground. . . . Her sex life is of no particular concern to me."

June 4 (early afternoon)—Secretary of Defense William S. Cohen recommends the appointment of Air Force General Joseph Ralston as the next Chairman of the Joint Chiefs of Staff, despite the General's confession that fourteen years ago (while separated from his wife) he carried on a love affair with a woman in the CIA. Secretary Cohen says that the time has come "to draw a line" against "the frenzy" of allegations spreading panic among military officers in all grades and ranks: "We need to come back to a rule of reason instead of a rule of thumb."

June 6—The major news media, allied with indignant voices in both Houses of Congress, overrule Secretary Cohen's call for reason. If bomber pilot Flinn must wear the scarlet letter, how then does fighter pilot Ralston escape the same marking?

June 7—Congressman Kennedy informs 2,000 cheering delegates to the Democratic State Convention in Salem, Massachusetts, that he is "so very sorry, so very, very sorry" for any damage that his brother might have done to the baby-sitter or the baby-sitter's family.

June 9—General Ralston withdraws his name from consideration as Chairman of the Joint Chiefs of Staff.

The news offered so many occasions for pious or ribald commentary that any chance of agreement about what any of it meant was lost in a vast din of clucking and sniggering. The upscale newspapers published prim, op-ed-page sermonettes (about the country misplacing the hope chest filled with old family values); down-market talk-radio hosts told prurient jokes (about Paula's mouth, or Marv's toupee, or Bill's mole); the television anchorpersons were merely happy to be told that a lot of important people (many of them grown-ups and some of them celebrities) had been seen loitering (well past their bedtimes) on Love Street.

Although a few of the country's more high-minded commentators attempted professions of shock and alarm, the sentiments didn't draw much of a crowd. Most Americans know by now that the country's moral guidebooks (government-inspected, church-approved) fail to account for the political, economic, social, and technological changes that over the last 100 years have reconfigured not only the relation between the sexes but also the Christian definitions of right and wrong. The old guidebooks were written for nineteenth-century travelers apt to fall afoul of Satan in a San Francisco

bordello, and either they require extensive revision or we need to adjust our present behavior. For the time being, the words don't match the deeds, and the ensuing confusion inflates the currencies of scandal. But because not enough people can agree to common terms of discourse, whether to begin with A for Abortion or with C for Clone, whether to proceed with reference to the *Bible* or to the *Kinsey Report*, we avoid the arguments by classifying human sexuality as a consumer product—a commodity, like cereal or furniture polish, packaged under as many brands and in as many forms (powdered or freeze-dried) as can be crowded onto the shelves in the supermarkets of desire. The commercial presentations allow us to have it both ways from the end and all ways from the middle—to meet the demand for hard-line feminist theory and the *Victoria's Secret* catalogue, for Robert Bork's sermons and Tony Kushner's plays, for breast or penile implants and software programs blocking out displays of nudity on the Internet, for as many different kinds of marriage (homosexual, heterosexual, open, closed, Christian, pagan, alternative, frankly perverse) as can meet with the approval of a landlord. The contradictions show up in every quarter of the society—posted on billboards and flashing on neon signs, available twenty-four hours a day on both the Playboy and the Disney channels, in the fashion photographs selling Donna Karan's dresses and Giorgio Armani's suits, in David Letterman's jokes and Senator Strom Thurmond's speeches, in the mirrors behind a hotel bar or on the walls of a health club, in the leaflets and lectures distributed (sometimes with condoms) to grammar school students, in newspaper ads hawking big-city prostitutes with the same adjectives that greengrocers assign to the grapefruit and the plums.

As might be expected of people engulfed in a haze of quasi-pornographic images, the subsequent confusion raises questions to which nobody has any good answers but which in the meantime provide the topics for the best-selling books of ethical self-help. What is moral, and where is virtue? Who is a man and who is a woman, and how do I know the difference? Is marriage forever, or is it another one of those institutions (like the churches and the schools) wrecked on the reefs of progress? Do the doors of the future open only to people who observe the rules and watch their diets, or must we, as true Americans and therefore rebellious at birth, knock down the walls of social convention? Suppose for a moment that we wish to obey the rules: What do they mean and where are they written?

During the daylight hours such questions take the form of political disputes—about a woman's due or a man's debt, about the reasons why a gay and lesbian alliance is marching in Beverly Hills, about the academic poetess who didn't receive tenure, or the diaspora of Real American Men (hard-drinking and unshaven) tracking the spoor of William Faulkner's bear in a Mississippi forest. Like CNN or Batman, the questions never sleep, and late at night they turn inward and existential—am I inside the television set with Marv and Paula and Kathie Lee, or am I out here in the middle of nowhere with the wrong nail polish and last season's beer? Is the search for the perfect orgasm like the search for the perfect apartment—always lost and never found? If I highlight my hair and redistribute the weight of my stomach, will I live happily ever after in the land of Calvin Klein?

Maybe the questions need never be answered, but when and if we get around to doing so, we at least should admit that the events of the last fifty years can't be ignored or reversed. It's no good demanding (as do quite a few of our prophets on the Christian and neoconservative right) that the changes be sent back for credit to Bloomingdale's or L. L. Bean, or that somehow it still might be possible to bring back the summer of 1947. Most of the changes probably have been for the better rather than the worse. It's true that freedom doesn't come without its costs, but how many people willingly would return to a society that insisted upon the rigid suppressions of human sexuality dictated by a frightened aunt or a village scold? In 1947 a Hollywood movie couldn't be released to the public without the prior consent of the Hayes office, a bureau of censors loyal to the rules of decorum in effect at a New England school for girls. Husbands and wives couldn't be seen occupying the same bed, and children were brought into the world by storks. Under the threat of boycott by the Catholic Archdiocese of New York, Leo Durocher, the manager of the Brooklyn Dodgers, was suspended from the team during the 1947 season because he was conducting a love affair with Laraine Day, an actress to whom he was not married. The booksellers in Boston banned the sale of novels found guilty of sentences that described either the hero or heroine in states of wanton undress. Young men at college in 1947 hadn't been introduced to television, much less to Robert Mapplethorpe or Helmut Newton; genetics was a subject that had to do mostly with mice, a woman's place was in the home, and sex was something that happened in France.

Looking back on the transformations that have occurred within the span of my own lifetime, I remember that during the decade of the 1960s, in the early stages of what later became known as the sexual revolution, the photographs in Hugh Hefner's *Playboy* magazine opened a window in what I suddenly saw as a prison wall made of sermons in Protestant stone. I lose track of chronological sequence,

but the rules seemed to change every year with the new fall clothes—first the forwardness of young women relieved of their inhibitions by the birth control pill, then the grievances (some of them surprising, most of them just) revealed in the commotion of the feminist movement, eventually the enlarged and public assertions of the gay and lesbian points of view, lastly the news that women no longer require men to perform the functions of husband and father. These days a woman of almost any age can choose to bear and raise a child under circumstances matched to her own history and understanding of the world—with a husband, with a man not her husband, from a zygote supplied by a sperm bank, by a fertilized egg borrowed from her daughter or mother, by adoption with a gay man, by adoption with a lesbian companion, by adoption with herself as the sole parent.

Nor have the changes been confined to what Pat Robertson likes to imagine as the red-light districts of Los Angeles and New York, as if the appetite for sexual fantasy presupposed a jaded, metropolitan taste. When the news of adultery usurped the headlines in late May, the *New York Times* dispatched a reporter to search the country for pockets of Christian rebuke. Generals were falling like ninepins into the gutters of lust, and the editors assumed that west of the Hudson somebody cared. The reporter, Carey Goldberg, returned with the news that not many did. A woman in Greenville, South Carolina, speaking on behalf of a clear majority, observed that although adultery wasn't legal in her state, "In this day and time, it's going on everywhere, and I mean everywhere." Were the authorities to enforce the law, she said, "everybody'd be in jail."

Among the guests who entertain Ricki Lake's afternoon television audiences with tales of their cross-dressing and cosmetic surgery, most of the people onstage come from places like Des Moines, Iowa, or Grand Rapids, Michigan. To meet the demand of the nation's video stores (most of them located in suburban shopping malls) the pornographic film industry last year provided 7,852 new releases (as opposed to the 471 supplied by Hollywood), and under the tolerant auspices of the World Wide Web, any child of nine sitting at a computer in Medford, Oregon, or Opa-Locka, Florida, can explore the landscape of sexual deviance first mapped by the Marquis de Sade.

About the perils of the voyage to paradise, the old moral guidebooks were not wrong. What at first glance looks like a ticket to the islands of bliss often proves more nearly to resemble a reserved seat in one of the eight dress circles of Dante's *Inferno*. I think of the numbers of people I've known over the last twenty or thirty years who sacrificed themselves on the altars of the imaginary self—marooned in a desolate marriage, so paralyzed by so many sexual options that nothing ever came of their talent and ambition, dead of AIDS at the age of thirty-one. The glittering invitations to everlasting orgy that decorate the drugstores and the movie screens are meant to be understood not as representations of reality but as symbols and allegories. Any customer so foolish as to mistake the commercial intent has failed to read properly the instructions on the label. One is supposed to look, not touch; to abandon oneself to one's desire not in a cocktail lounge but in a nearby mall.

The credit-card statements don't show the arithmetic of human suffering and unhappiness. It might well be true that if South Carolina enforced the laws against adultery, everybody would be in jail, but it is also true that sexual promiscuity and infidelity cause more misery (for the featured players as well as for the children in the supporting cast) than ever gets explained in the program notes. Over the years I've listened to a good many stories of bewilderment and loss, but none sadder than the one that appeared in the New York tabloids on June 9 about the eighteen-year-old girl, a student at the Lacey Township School in Ocean County, New Jersey, to whom a son was born at her graduation prom. During a break in the music, she left the ballroom, gave birth to the baby in a bathroom stall, wrapped it in paper towels, discarded it in a wastebasket, washed her hands, smoothed her evening dress, and returned for the next dance. From the perspective of the consumer market, the girl's actions make perfect sense. Sex is merchandising, and the product of desire, like Kleenex, is disposable. In the garden of tabloid delight, there is always a clean towel and another song.[1]

Like the high-speed computers that collate restaurant checks with telephone bills and drugstore receipts, the market can't tell the difference between adultery and a program of aerobic exercise; it doesn't know or care who said what to whom or whether the whip was meant to be used on a horse from Kentucky or a gentleman from Toledo.

Human beings who tailor themselves to the measures of the market float like numbers across the surface of the computer screen. Without the strength and frame of a moral order—some code or rule or custom that provides them with a way and a place to stand against the flood of their own incoherent desire—they too often lose the chance for love or meaning in their lives, unable or unwilling to locate the character of their own minds or build the shelters of their own happiness.

The loss of identity is good for business. The conditions of weightlessness not only set up the demand for ballast—heavier gold jewelry, more golf clubs, bigger cigars—but also encourage the free exchange of sexual identities, which, like the liquidity of cash, preserves the illusion of infinite options and holds out the ceaselessly renewable prospect of buying into a better deal. The pilgrims in search of a more attractive or plausible face can try on the 1,001 masks to which Freud gave the name of polymorphous perverse and to which the trendier fashion designers now affix the labels of androgynous chic. The structures of gender present themselves as so much troublesome baggage impeding the migration into F. Scott Fitzgerald's "orgiastic future." Let human sexuality be understood as a substance as pliable as modeling clay, and maybe it becomes an asset, easily worked into the shape of a stock-market deal, a music video, a celebrity crime.

Transferred to what was once known as the public square, the descent into narcissism makes of politics a trivial pursuit. A society adjusted to the specifications of the tabloid press draws no invidious distinctions between the foreign and domestic policies of the President's penis and the threat of nuclear annihilation. Both stories guarantee record sales at the newsstands. On the day after the Supreme Court certified Paula's complaint about Bill (which also happened to be the day on which Boris Yeltsin announced at the NATO conference in Paris that Russia no longer would target its missiles on New York and Washington) the newspapers assigned the bigger headlines to the targeting error that either did or did not take place six years ago in an upstairs room of the Excelsior Hotel in Little Rock, Arkansas.

The distribution of news value should have come as no surprise. The voters last November saw in Clinton's narcissism a reflection of their own self-preoccupations, and although well aware of his appetites for hard women and soft money, they were happy to send him to Washington as a representative of their collective moral confusion—a man no better than the other men that one was likely to meet at a sales conference or in a topless bar, always smiling and polite but in it for the money, in his own way as much of a hustler as Paula, as lost as most everybody else in the maze of amorphous sexuality. One day he appears in his masculine character (speaking sternly to the Serbs or the Albanians, making the strong, decisive, executive movements expected of a successful American businessman); the next day he shows up smiling like a debutante, pouring sentiment and sympathy into the teacups of the White House press corps, bravely holding back the tears that he otherwise would shed for a flood victim, a welfare mother, or a sick dog. Who but the old fools at the Pentagon could expect such a man to keep his penis in his pants or his fingers out of the Boston cream pie? The poor fellow is always so desperately needy, so insatiably eager for approval and affection, that it's a wonder he hasn't yet sold the Lincoln Memorial to a Korean amusement park.

A President so obviously unable or unwilling to tell the difference between right and wrong (much less, God forbid, to stand on or for anything other than the platform of his own need) clearly cannot ask anybody to grow up. He presents a role model not unlike that of Peter Pan (albeit an increasingly stout Peter Pan) and so excuses the rest of the class from the tedium of moral homework. With such a President, why bother to aspire to an adult code of ethics? We need not seek our own best selves, and in the meantime we inoculate ourselves against the viruses of age and idealism, which, as the advertising agencies well know depress sales and sour the feasts of consumption.

Sex in the United States is no laughing matter, and although the commercial synthetics tend to leech the life out of the enterprise—the chance of meaning and the hope of intimacy as well as humor and eroticism—I take it for granted that the promises of eternal youth and everlasting orgy will continue to be more widely available and more innovatively sold. I'm glad that I'm not twenty years old, my name, address, and DNA stored in a data bank available to any mail-order operation. I expect that it probably would take me another twenty years to solve the riddle of my own identity, which is, of course, the point. If I knew who I was, why would I keep buying new brands of aftershave lotion, and how then would I add to the sum of the gross domestic product?

Given the sophistication of our current marketing techniques and the boundless resource of human curiosity and desire, the media undoubtedly will continue to post their scarlet letters and deliver their bouquets of scandal. The demand for gaudier sensations, for more telephone sex and brighter lip gloss, presumably will foster competing markets in small-time puritanism. Absent a unified field of moral law that commands a sufficiently large number of people to obedience and belief, with what else do we fill in the blanks except a lot of little rules—rules about how to address persons of differing colors or sexual orientation, about when to wear fur and when not to eat grapes, about what to read or where to smoke?

Although I can imagine books of rules as extensive as encyclopedias, I can't imagine them quieting the rage of the market. If I can lust after the girls on 300 pornographic cable channels, why can't I order one from a shopping network? If the editors of the *Globe* can pay an airline stewardess $75,000 to pose with Frank Gifford for the video camera in the Regency Hotel, what will they bid for the sight of a fireman in bed with Barbara Walters?

For the time being, and not yet having discovered a system of moral value that corresponds to the workings of big-time, postindustrial capitalism, where else can we live except in the garden of tabloid delight with Marv and Bill and Paula and Batman? Unless we wish to say that what is moral is what an insurance company will pay for (which, in our present circumstances, comes fairly close to the truth), what other arrangement meets the presumption—accepted as revered truth on both the liberal and conservative sides of the bed—that ethics and politics constitute increasingly marginal subsections of economics? If the lights must never go out and the music must always play, how do we even begin to talk about the discovery or construction of such a thing as a new moral order? Who has time for so slow a conversation? Who could hear what was being said?

Note

1. Babies dropped into garbage cans sometimes survive, but the one who died at the prom reminded me of another newspaper story I had read several weeks earlier about the Lacey Township School. The administrators apparently were worried about rumors of sexual malfeasance on the part of faculty or staff, and so they had ordered all adult personnel to approach the students with extreme caution. No touching, no hugs, no possibly suspicious pats on the shoulder, and when face to face with a student at a distance of less than three feet, the teachers and custodians were to raise both arms above their heads in a gesture of surrender. Both incidents (the one brutal, the other absurd) exemplify the character of what Will and Ariel Durant described as an "unmoored generation" drifting between one moral order and the next.

Chapter 21
Sexual Desire and Gender

Pepper Schwartz
Virginia E. Rutter

Fisher, Buss, and Schwartz are all names instantly recognized by colleagues in their respective disciplines of anthropology, psychology, and sociology. What do these different professionals have in common? All have written about the subject of sexual desire. Helen Fisher and David Buss are but two of the names of researchers you will encounter in the following chapter as Schwartz and Rutter carefully review the current knowledge about the intriguing subject of sexual desire and gender.

In anthropologist Helen Fisher's (2004) new book, Why We Love: The Nature and Chemistry of Romantic Love, *she postulates that romantic love is a primary motivation system in the brain, a fundamental human mating drive. She accepts neuroscientist Don Pfaff's definition of a drive as a "neural state that energizes and directs behavior to acquire a particular biological need to survive or reproduce" (Fisher 2004, 74). In her research, Fisher and colleagues worked with a team of scientists who scanned the brains of people who had just fallen "madly in love." The scans revealed that specific areas of the brains of "in love" subjects actually "light up" with increased blood flow. The research team concluded that romantic passion is hardwired into our brains by millions of years of evolution; it is not an emotion, but a drive as powerful as hunger, even if less predictable.*

Buss's work, reported in The Evolution of Human Desire: Strategies of Human Mating *(1994), was based on the most massive study of human mating ever undertaken. It encompassed more than 10,000 people of all ages from thirty-seven (37) world-wide cultures. According to Buss, to understand the elusive subject of sexual desire, we must look into our evolutionary past. Presenting a unique theory of human mating behavior, he details what women want, what men want, and then explains why their desires differ radically.*

After reading this chapter from Schwartz and Rutter's book, The Gender of Sexuality, *you will be better able to claim your own territory in the land of sexual dissention. Ask yourself if you fit most neatly into the biological camp, the evolutionary psychological one, or the social-constructionist one. Or perhaps with Schwartz and Rutter, you will embrace the position of an integrationist, questioning biology when social contexts are emphasized as cause and questioning social contexts when biological causes are emphasized. Whatever your answers when you have finished reading this next offering, your opinion will be better informed than before.*

The gender of the person you desire is a serious matter seemingly fundamental to the whole business of romance. And it isn't simply a matter of whether someone is male or female; how well the person fulfills a lover's expectations of masculinity or femininity is of great consequence, as two examples from the movies illustrate.

In the movie *The Truth About Cats & Dogs* (1996), Brian falls in love with Abby over the phone, and she with him. They find each other warm, clever, charming, and intriguing. But she, thinking herself too plain, asks her beautiful friend Noelle to impersonate her when the man and woman are scheduled to meet. Although the man becomes very confused about which woman he really desires, in the end the telephone lovers are united. The match depended on social matters far more than physical matters.

In the British drama *The Crying Game* (1994), Fergus, an Irish Republican Army underling, meets and falls in love with the lover (Dil) of Jody, a British soldier whom Fergus befriended prior to being ordered to execute him. The movie was about passionate love, war, betrayal, and, in the end, loyalty and commitment. Fergus seeks out Jody's girlfriend in London out of guilt and curiosity. But Fergus's guilt over Jody's death turns into love, and the pair become romantically and sexually involved. In the end, although Fergus is jailed for terrorist activities, Fergus and Dil have solidified their bond and are committed and, it seems, in love. The story of sexual conquest and love is familiar, but this particular story grabbed imaginations because of a single, crucial detail. Jody's girlfriend Dil, Fergus discovers, turns out to be (physically) a man. Although Fergus is horrified when he discovers his lover is biologically different from what he had expected, in the end their relationship survives.

These movies raise an interesting point about sexual desire. Although sex is experienced as one of the most basic and biological of activities, in human beings it is profoundly affected by things other than the body's urges. Who we're attracted to and what we find sexually satisfying is not just a matter of the genital equipment we're born with. This chapter explains why.

Before we delve into the whys and wherefores of sex, we need to come to an understanding about what sex is. This is not as easy a task as it may seem, because sex has a number of dimensions.

On one level, sex can be regarded as having both a biological and a social context. The biological refers to how people use their genital equipment to reproduce. In addition, as simple as it seems, bodies make the experience of sexual pleasure available—whether the pleasure involves other bodies or just one's own body and mind. It should be obvious, however, that people engage in sex even when they do not intend to reproduce. They have sex for fun, as a way to communicate their feelings to each other, as a way to satisfy their ego, and for any number of other reasons relating to the way they see themselves and interact with others.

Another dimension of sex involves both what we do and how we think about it. *Sexual behavior* refers to the sexual acts that people engage in. These acts involve not only petting and intercourse but also seduction and courtship. Sexual behavior also involves the things people do alone for pleasure and stimulation and the things they do with other people. *Sexual desire*, on the other hand, is the motivation to engage in sexual acts. It relates to what turns people on. A person's *sexuality* consists of both behavior and desire.

The most significant dimension of sexuality is *gender*. Gender relates both to the biological and social contexts of sexual behavior and desire. People tend to believe they know whether someone is a man or a woman not because we do a physical examination and determine that the person is biologically male or biologically female. Instead, we notice whether a person is masculine or feminine. Gender is a social characteristic of individuals in our society that is only sometimes consistent with biological sex. Thus, animals, like people, tend to be identified as male and female in accordance with the reproductive function, but only people are described by their gender, as a man or a woman.

When we say something is *gendered* we mean that social processes have determined what is appropriately masculine and feminine and that gender has thereby become integral to the definition of the phenomenon. For example, marriage is a gendered institution: The definition of marriage involves a masculine part (husband) and a feminine part (wife). Gendered phenomena, like marriage, tend to appear "naturally" so. But, as recent debates about same-sex marriage underscore, the role of gender in marriage is the product of social processes and beliefs about men, women, and marriage. In examining how gender influences sexuality, moreover, you will see that gender rarely operates alone: Class, culture, race, and individual differences also combine to influence sexuality. This chapter explores and takes issue with the assumptions that sexuality is naturally gendered and rooted in biology, that men and women are different sexually, and that this difference is consistent and universal across societies.

Sexuality is a complex bit of business. The study of sexuality presents methodological challenges. Sexual thoughts and behavior are typically private. Researchers must rely on what people say they want and do sexually, and these reports, as much as the desire and behavior itself, are influenced by what people believe they are supposed to feel and say. We will piece together this puzzle of acts, thoughts, and feelings with insights provided by survey research, physiological studies, ethnography, history, philosophy, and even art, cinema, and literature.

Desire: Attraction and Arousal

The most salient fact about sex is that nearly everybody is interested in it. Most people like to have sex, and they talk about it, hear about it, and think about it. But some people are obsessed with sex and willing to have sex with anyone or anything. Others are aroused only by particular conditions and hold exacting criteria. For example, some people will have sex only if they are positive that they are in love, that their partner loves them, and that the act is sanctified by marriage. Others view sex as not much different from eating a sandwich. They neither love nor hate the sandwich; they are merely hungry, and they want something to satisfy that hunger. What we are talking about here are differences in desire. As you have undoubtedly noticed, people differ in what they find attractive, and they are also physically aroused by different things.

Many people assume that differences in sexual desire have a lot to do with whether a person is female or male. In large representative surveys about sexual behavior, the men as a group inevitably report more frequent sex, with more partners, and in more diverse ways than the women as a group do. We will review that evidence. First, we should consider the approaches we might use to interpret it. Many observers argue that when it comes to sex, men and women have fundamentally different biological wiring. Others use the evidence to argue that culture has produced marked sexual differences among men and women. We believe, however, that it is hard to tease apart biological differences and social differences. As soon as a baby enters the world, it receives messages about gender and sexuality. In the United States, for example, disposable diapers come adorned in pink for girls and blue for boys. In case people aren't sure whether to treat the baby as masculine or feminine in its first years of life, the diaper signals them. The assumption is that girl babies really are different from boy babies and the difference ought to be displayed. This different treatment continues throughout life, and therefore a sex difference at birth becomes amplified into gender difference as people mature.

Gendered experiences have a great deal of influence on sexual desire. As a boy enters adolescence, he hears jokes about boys' uncontainable desire. Girls are told the same thing and told that their job is to resist. These gender messages have power not only over attitudes and behavior (such as whether a person grows up to prefer sex with a lover rather than a stranger) but also over physical and biological experience. For example, a girl may be discouraged from vigorous competitive activity, which will subsequently influence how she develops physically, how she feels about her body, and even how she relates to the adrenaline rush associated with physical competition. Hypothetically, a person who is accustomed to adrenaline responses experiences sexual attraction differently from one who is not.

What follows are three "competing" explanations of differences in sexual desire between men and women: a biological explanation, socio-biological and evolutionary psychological explanations, and an explanation that acknowledges the social construction of sexuality. We call these competing approaches because each tends to be presented as a complete explanation in itself, to the exclusion of other explanations. Our goal, however, is to provide a clearer picture of how "nature" and "nurture" are intertwined in the production of sexualities.

The Biology of Desire: Nature's Explanation

Biology is admittedly a critical factor in sexuality. Few human beings fall in love with fish or sexualize trees. Humans are designed to respond to other humans. And human activity is, to some extent, organized by the physical equipment humans are born with. Imagine if people had fins instead of arms or laid eggs instead of fertilizing them during intercourse. Romance would look quite different.

Although biology seems to be a constant (i.e., a component of sex that is fixed and unchanging), the social world tends to mold biology as much as biology shapes humans' sexuality. Each society has its own rules for sex. Therefore, how people experience their biology varies widely. In some societies, women act intensely aroused and active during sex; in others, they have no concept of orgasm. In fact, women in some settings, when told about orgasm,

do not even believe it exists, as anthropologists discovered in some parts of Nepal. Clearly, culture—not biology—is at work, because we know that orgasm is physically possible, barring damage to or destruction of the sex organs. Even ejaculation is culturally dictated. In some countries, it is considered healthy to ejaculate early and often; in others, men are told to conserve semen and ejaculate as rarely as possible. The biological capacity may not be so different, but the way bodies behave during sex varies according to social beliefs.

Sometimes the dictates of culture are so rigid and powerful that the so-called laws of nature can be overridden. Infertility treatment provides an example: For couples who cannot produce children "naturally," a several billion dollar industry has provided technology that can, in a small proportion of cases, overcome this biological problem (Rutter 1996). Recently, in California, a child was born to a 63-year-old woman who had been implanted with fertilized eggs. The cultural emphasis on reproduction and parenthood, in this case, overrode the biological incapacity to produce children. Nevertheless, some researchers have focused on the biological foundations of sexual desire. They have examined the endocrine system and hormones, brain structure, and genetics. Others have observed the mechanisms of arousal. What all biological research on sex has in common is the proposition that many so-called sexual choices are not choices at all but are dictated by the body.

The Influence of Hormones

Biological explanations of sexual desire concentrate on the role of hormones. *Testosterone*, sometimes called the male sex hormone, appears to be the most important hormone for sexual function. Numerous research studies identify testosterone as an enabler for male sexual arousal (Bancroft 1978; Masters, Johnson, and Kolodny 1995). But we cannot predict a man's sexual tastes, desires, or behavior by measuring his testosterone. Although a low level of testosterone in men is sometimes associated with lower sexual desire, this is not predictably the case. Furthermore, testosterone level does not always influence sexual performance. Indeed, testosterone is being experimented with as a male contraceptive (Wu et al. 1996), thus demonstrating that desire and the biological goal of reproduction need not be linked to sexual desire.

Testosterone has also been implicated in nonsexual behaviors, such as aggression. Furthermore, male aggression sometimes crosses into male sexuality, generating sexual violence. But recent research on testosterone and aggression in men has turned the testosterone-aggression connection on its head: Low levels of testosterone have been associated with aggression, and higher levels have been associated with calmness, happiness, and friendliness (Angier 1995).

Testosterone is also found in women, although at levels as little as one-fifth those of men. This discrepancy in levels of testosterone has incorrectly been used as evidence for "natural" gender differences in sex drives. However, women's testosterone receptors are simply more sensitive than men's to smaller amounts of testosterone (Kolodny, Masters, and Johnson 1979).

Estrogen, which is associated with the menstrual cycle, is known as the female hormone. Like testosterone, however, estrogen is found in both women and men. Furthermore, estrogen may be the more influential hormone in human aggression. Researchers are currently investigating the association between adolescents' moodiness and their levels of estrogen (Angier 1995). Of course, many social factors—such as changes in parental behavior toward their teenagers—help explain moodiness among adolescents (Rutter 1995).

Some biological evidence indicates that a woman's sexual desire may be linked to the impact of hormones as levels change during her reproductive cycle. (No evidence shows men's sexual desire to be cyclical.) Some scientists believe that women's sexual arousal is linked to the fertile portion of their cycle (Stanislaw and Rice 1988). They believe that sexual interest in women is best explained as the product of thousands of years of natural selection. Natural selection would favor for survival those women who are sexually aroused during ovulation (the time women are most likely to become pregnant). These women would be reproductively successful and therefore pass on to their children the propensity for arousal during ovulation. Neat though this theory is, it doesn't fit all the data. Other research (Bancroft et al. 1983) finds no evidence of increased sexual interest among women who are ovulating. Instead, the evidence suggests that women's sexual interest actually tends to peak well before ovulation. Still other evidence finds no variation in sexual desire or sexual activity in connection to the menstrual cycle (Meuwissen and Over 1992).

Testosterone and estrogen are not clearly linked to either men's desire or women's. Research shows a complicated relationship between hormones and sexuality. Hormonal fluctuations may not be the central cause of sexual behavior or any social acts; instead, social circumstances may be the cause of hormonal fluctuation.

The Mechanisms of Arousal

Biological explanations of gender differences in sexuality owe a great deal to the work of William Masters and Virginia Johnson, who studied the human sexual arousal system. Unlike other researchers, who had relied on self-reports, these pioneers actually hooked up their participants to machines that could provide information on physiological responses to sexual stimuli. They based their findings on laboratory observation of over 10,000 sexual episodes experienced by 382 women and 312 men (Masters and Johnson 1966). The research team photographed the inside of women's vaginas during arousal and observed circulatory and nipple response, and they observed the rise and fall of men's penises.

Notice that Masters and Johnson focused on bodies rather than the social and relationship contexts in which sex occurs. From the start, the research was limited to information about the mechanisms of sexuality. It's not hard to imagine that the responses of men and women hooked to machines and under observation might well be different from a loving couple's first (or 91st) sexual episode. In addition, the participants were far from "typical" or randomly selected. To the contrary, they were sexual extroverts such as prostitutes, who, as far as we can tell, were not really representative of the population.

Nevertheless, with this information Masters and Johnson created the new field of sex therapy, which sought to understand and modify the mechanisms of human sexual response or, as the case might be, nonresponse. The sexual therapies they developed were based on what they inferred from their data to be differences between male and female patterns of arousal.

One of Masters and Johnson's most important observations was a sexual difference between men and women in the timing of the excitement cycle. The key difference is that male sexual physiology has a quicker trigger. Comparing men's and women's sexual responses is like comparing sprinters (men) to long-distance runners (women). Men are excited sooner, have an orgasm sooner, relatively quickly lose their erection, and require a "refractory" period before sexual excitation and erection can begin again. This refractory period among young or exceptional men could be very brief. But for the majority of men, 20 minutes, an hour, or even a day might be necessary.

The female cycle is, in general, a slower and more sustained proposition. The increase of blood to the genital area that accompanies arousal takes longer and remains longer after orgasm. This slower buildup may in part account for the longer time it typically takes women to be ready for sexual intercourse. Additionally, the longer time women take to reach and stay in the plateau phase theoretically makes orgasm less automatic than it is for men. However, the fact that blood leaves the genital area slowly after orgasm means that many women require little or no refractory period if restimulated. Consequently, Masters and Johnson described women as potentially "multi-orgasmic." In other words, some women can have more than one orgasm in fairly short succession.

These physiological findings were the basis for a theory about female and male mating styles. Masters and Johnson considered men's more quickly triggered mechanisms to be at odds with the slower mechanisms of women. On the other hand, the ability of women to have more than one orgasm suggested that women might be the superior sexual athletes under certain conditions. Masters and Johnson's followers work within a model that addresses sexual problems by matching male and female sexual strategies more closely than they believe nature has done. In fact, it might be argued that Masters and Johnson's general approach to sexual counseling was to teach men to understand and cope with the slower female sexual response and to modify their own sexual response so that they do not reach orgasm before their partner is fully aroused.

Sociobiology and Evolutionary Psychology

The past few decades of research on sexuality have produced a new school of human behavior—*sociobiology* and a related discipline, *evolutionary psychology*—that explains most gender differences as strategies of sexual reproduction. According to evolutionary psychologist David Buss (1995), "Evolutionary psychologists predict that the sexes will differ in precisely those domains in which women and men have faced different sorts of adaptive problems" (p. 164). By "those domains," Buss refers to reproduction, which is the only human function that depends on a biological difference between men and women.

The key assumption of sociobiological/evolutionary theory is that humans have an innate, genetically triggered impulse to pass on their genetic material through successful reproduction: This impulse is called *reproductive fitness*. The human species, like other species that sociobiologists study, achieves immortality by having children who live to the age of reproductive maturity and produce children themselves. Sociobiologists and evolutionary psychologists seek to demonstrate that almost all male and female behavior, and especially sexuality, is influenced by this one simple but powerful proposition.

Sociobiologists start at the species level. Species are divided into r and K reproductive categories. Those with r strategies obtain immortality by mass production of eggs and sperm. The r species is best illustrated by fish. The female manufactures thousands of eggs, the male squirts millions of sperm over them, and that is the extent of parenting. According to this theory, the male and female fish need not pair up to nurture their offspring. Although thousands of fertilized fish eggs are consumed by predators, only a small proportion of the massive quantity of fertilized eggs must survive for the species to continue. In the r species, parents need not stay together for the sake of the kids.

In contrast, humans are a K-strategy species, which has a greater investment in each fertilized egg. Human females and most female mammals have very few eggs, especially compared to fish. Moreover, offspring take a long time to mature in the mother's womb and are quite helpless after they are born, with no independent survival ability. Human babies need years of supervision before they are independent. Thus, if a woman wants to pass on her genes (or at least the half her child will inherit from her), she must take good care of her dependent child. The baby is a scarce resource. Even if a woman is pregnant from sexual maturation until menopause, the number of children she can produce is quite limited. This limitation was particularly true thousands of years ago. Before medical advances of the nineteenth and twentieth centuries, women were highly unlikely to live to the age of menopause. Complications from childbirth commonly caused women to die in their 20s or 30s. Where the food supply was scarce, women were less likely to be successful at conceiving, further reducing the possibility of generating offspring.

Sociobiologists and evolutionary psychologists say that men inseminate, women incubate. The human female's reproductive constraints (usually one child at a time, only so many children over a life cycle, and a helpless infant for a long period of time) shape most of women's sexual and emotional approaches to men and mating. According to their theory, women have good reason to be more selective than men about potential mates. They want to find a man who will stick around and continue to provide resources and protection to this child at least until the child has a good chance of survival. Furthermore, because a woman needs to create an incentive for a man to remain with her, females have developed more sophisticated sexual and emotional skills specifically geared toward creating male loyalty and commitment to their mutual off-spring.

Sociobiologists and evolutionary psychologists say that differences in reproductive capacity and strategy also shape sexual desire. Buss asserts that reproductive strategies form most of the categories of desire: Older men generally pick younger women because they are more fertile; younger women seek older men who have more status, power, and resources (a cultural practice known as *hypergamy*) because such men can provide for their children. Furthermore, health and reproductive capacity make youth generally sexier, and even certain shapes of women's bodies (such as an "ideal" hip-to-waist ratio epitomized by an hourglass figure, which correlate with ability to readily reproduce), are widely preferred (Buss 1994)—despite varying standards of beauty across cultures. Likewise, men who have demonstrated their fertility by producing children are more sought after than men who have not (Buss 1994).

According to evolutionary psychologists, men's tastes for recreational sex, unambivalent lust, and a variety of partners are consistent with maximizing their production of children. Men's sexual interest is also more easily aroused because sex involves fewer costs to them than to women, and the ability for rapid ejaculation has a reproductive payoff. On the other hand, women's taste for relationship-based intimacy and greater investment in each sexual act is congruent with women's reproductive strategies.

In a field that tends to emphasize male's "natural" influence over reproductive strategies, evolutionary anthropologist Helen Fisher (1992) offers a feminist twist. Her study of hundreds of societies shows that divorce, or its informal equivalent, occurs most typically in the third or fourth year of a marriage and then peaks about every four years after that. Fisher hypothesizes that some of the breakups have to do with a woman's attempt to obtain the best genes and best survival chances for her offspring. In both agrarian and hunter-gatherer societies, Fisher explains, women breast-feed their child for three or four years—a practice that is economical and sometimes helps to prevent further pregnancy. At the end of this period, the woman is ready and able to have another child. She reenters the mating marketplace and assesses her options to see if she can improve on her previous mate. If she can get a better guy, she will leave the previous partner and team up with a new one. In Fisher's vision, unlike the traditional sociobiological view, different male and female reproductive strategies do not necessarily imply female sexual passivity and preference for lifelong monogamy.

Sociobiologists and evolutionary psychologists tell a fascinating story of how male and female reproductive differences might shape sexuality. To accept sociobiological arguments, one must accept the premise that most animal and human behavior is driven by the instinct to reproduce and improve the gene pool. Furthermore, a flaw of sociobiology as a theory is that it does not provide a unique account of sexual behavior with the potential to be tested empirically. Furthermore, other social science explanations for the same phenomena are supported by more immediate, close-range evidence.

The Social Origins of Desire

Your own experience should indicate that biology and genetics alone do not shape human sexuality. From the moment you entered the world, cues from the environment were telling you which desires and behaviors were "normal" and which were not. The result is that people who grow up in different circumstances tend to have different sexualities. Who has not had their sexual behavior influenced by their parents' or guardians' explicit or implicit rules? You may break the rules or follow them, but you can't forget them. On a societal level, in Sweden, for example, premarital sex is accepted, and people are expected to be sexually knowledgeable and experienced. Swedes are likely to associate sex with pleasure in this *"sex positive"* society. In Ireland, however, Catholics are supposed to heed the Church's strict prohibitions against sex outside of marriage, birth control, and the expression of lust. In Ireland the experience of sexuality is different from the experience of sexuality in Sweden because the rules are different. Certainly, biology in Sweden is no different from biology in Ireland, nor is the physical capacity to experience pleasure different. But in Ireland, nonmarital sex is clandestine and shameful. Perhaps the taboo adds excitement to the experience. In Sweden, nonmarital sex is acceptable. In the absence of social constraint, it may even feel a bit mundane. These culturally specific sexual rules and experiences arise from different *norms*, the well-known, unwritten rules of society.

Another sign that social influences play a bigger role in shaping sexuality than does biology is the changing notions historically of male and female differences in desire. Throughout history, varied explanations of male and female desire have been popular. At times, woman was portrayed as the stormy temptress and man the reluctant participant, as in the *Bible* story of Adam and Eve. At other times, women were seen as pure in thought and deed while men were voracious sexual beasts, as the Victorians would have it.

These shifting ideas about gender are the social "clothing" for sexuality. The concept of gender typically relies on a dichotomy of male versus female sexual categories, just as the tradition of women wearing dresses and men wearing pants has in the past made the shape of men and women appear quite different. Consider high heels, an on-again off-again Western fashion. Shoes have no innate sexual function, but high heels have often been understood to be "sexy" for women, even though (or perhaps because) they render women less physically agile. So feminine are high heels understood to be that a man in high heels, in some sort of visual comedy gag, guarantees a laugh from the audience. Alternatively, high heels are a required emblem of femininity for cross-dressing men. Such distinctions are an important tool of society; they provide guidance to human beings about how to be a "culturally correct" male or female.

The Social Construction of Sexuality

Social constructionists believe that cues from the environment shape human beings from the moment they enter the world. The sexual customs, values, and expectations of a culture, passed on to the young through teaching and by example, exert a powerful influence. When Fletcher Christian sailed into Tahiti in Charles Nordhoff's 1932 account, *Mutiny on the Bounty*, he and his nineteenth-century English crew were surprised at how sexually available, playful, guilt-free, and amorous the Tahitian women were. Free from the Judeo-Christian precepts and customs that inhibited English society, the women of Tahiti regarded their sexuality joyfully and without shame. The Englishmen were delighted and refused to leave the island. The women back in England had been socialized within their Victorian culture to be modest, scared of sex, protective of their reputation, and threatened by physical pleasure. The source of the difference was not physiological differences between Tahitian and English women; it was sexual *socialization* within their differing families and cultures.

If we look back at the Victorian, nineteenth-century England that Nordhoff refers to, we can identify *social structures* that influenced the norms of women's and men's sexuality. A burgeoning, new, urban middle class created separate spheres in the division of family labor. Instead of sharing home and farm or small business, the tasks of adults in families became specialized: Men went out to earn money, women stayed home to raise children and take care of the home. Although this division of labor was not the norm in all classes and ethnicities in England at the time, the image of middle-class femininity and masculinity became pervasive. The new

division of labor increased women's economic dependence on men, which further curbed women's sexual license but not men's. When gender organizes one aspect of life—such as men's and women's positions in the economy—it also organizes other aspects of life, including sex.

In a heterogeneous and individualistic culture like North America, sexual socialization is complex. A society creates an "ideal" sexuality, but different families and subcultures have their own values. For example, even though contemporary society at large may now accept premarital sexuality, a given family may lay down the law: Sex before marriage is against the family's religion and an offense against God's teaching. A teenager who grows up in such a household may suppress feelings of sexual arousal or channel them into outlets that are more acceptable to the family. Or the teenager may react against her or his background, reject parental and community opinion, and search for what she or he perceives to be a more "authentic" self. Variables like birth order or observations of a sibling's social and sexual expression can also influence a person's development.

As important as family and social background are, so are individual differences in response to that background. In the abstract, people raised to celebrate their sexuality must surely have a different approach to enjoying their bodies than those who are taught that their bodies are a venal part of human nature. Yet whether or not a person is raised to be at ease with physicality does not always help predict adult sexual behavior. Sexual sybarites and libertines may have grown up in sexually repressive environments, as did pop culture icon and Catholic-raised Madonna. Sometimes individuals whose families promoted sex education and free personal expression are content with minimal sexual expression.

Even with the nearly infinite variety of sexuality that individual experience produces, social circumstances shape sexual patterns. For example, research shows that people who have had more premarital sexual intercourse are likely to have more extramarital intercourse, or sex with someone other than their spouse (Blumstein and Schwartz 1983). Perhaps early experience creates a desire for sexual variety and makes it harder for a person to be monogamous. On the other hand, higher levels of sexual desire may generate both the premarital and extramarital propensities. Or perhaps nonmonogamous, sexually active individuals are "rule breakers" and resist not only the traditional rules of sex but also other social norms they encounter. Sexual history is useful for predicting sexual future, but it does not provide a complete explanation.

To make explanations more useful, sociologists refer to societal-level explanations as the *macro* view and to individual-level explanations as the *micro* view. At the macrolevel, the questions pertain to the patterns among different groups. For example, we may note in our culture that some women wear skirts and all men do not. Why do women and men, generally speaking, differ in this way? *Social conflict theory*, which examines the way that groups gain and maintain power over resources and other groups, is often used to address macrolevel questions. One might ask: Whose interest does this custom serve, and how did it evolve? What does it constrain or encourage? If the custom changes, what social forces have promoted the change?

Symbolic interactionism supplements this macrolevel view by looking at the microlevel: How does a particular custom gain its meaning through social interaction? For example, what is really happening when a man opens a door for a woman? *Symbolic interactionism* proposes that social rules are learned and reinforced through everyday interaction in both small acts, such as a man's paying for a woman's dinner, and larger enactments of male and female roles, such as weddings, manners, movies, and television. Through such everyday social interaction, norms are confirmed or resisted. When an adult tells a little girl "good girls don't do this," or when boys make fun of her for wanting to be on the football team, or when she sees women joining a military school getting hazed and harassed, she is learning her society's rules of behavior.

When it comes to sexuality, all these social and behavioral theories hold that biological impulses are subservient to the influence of social systems. Consider high heels again. As anyone who has done so knows, wearing high heels has physical consequences, such as flexed calves while wearing them and aching feet at the end of an evening. But nothing in the physiology of women makes wearing high-heeled shoes necessary, and the propensity to wear high heels is not programmed into women's DNA. A sociobiologist might note that any additional ways a society can invent for women to be sexy accelerate reproductive success. A symbolic interactionist would counter that most rules of sexuality go way beyond what's needed for reproductive success. Society orchestrates male and female sexuality so that its values are served. A social conflict theorist would go a step further and note that the enactment of gendered fashion norms serves the political agenda of groups in power (in this case men) at the macrolevel.

An astounding example of gender-based social control of sexuality was the practice of binding the feet of upper-class women in China starting around the tenth century. Each foot was bound so tightly that the last two toes shriveled and fell off. What was left was so deformed that the woman could barely walk and had to be carried. The function was to allow upper-class men to control the mobility of their women. Bound feet, which were thus associated with status and wealth, became erotically charged. Unbound feet were seen as repugnant. By the eighteenth and nineteenth centuries, even poor women participated in this practice. This practice was so associated with sexual acceptability and marriageability that it was difficult to disrupt, even when nineteenth century missionaries from the West labeled the practice barbaric and unsafe. Only later, in the twentieth century, did foot binding become illegal (Greenhalgh 1977).

Social Control of Sexuality

So powerful are norms as they are transmitted through both social structures and everyday life that it is impossible to imagine the absence of norms that control sexuality. In fact, most images of "liberated" sexuality involve breaking a social norm—say, having sex in public rather than in private. The social norm is always the reference point. Because people are influenced from birth by the social and physical contexts of sexuality, their desires are shaped by those norms. For the past two centuries in North America, people have sought "true love" through personal choice in dating and mating (D'Emilio and Freedman 1988). Although this form of sexual liberation has generated a small increase in the number of mixed pairs—interracial, interethnic, interfaith pairs—the rule of *homogamy*, or marrying within one's class, religion, and ethnicity, still constitutes one of the robust social facts of romantic life. Freedom to choose the person one loves turns out not to be as free as one might suppose.

Despite the norm of true love currently accepted in our culture, personal choice and indiscriminate sexuality have often been construed across cultures and across history as socially disruptive. Disruptions to the social order include liaisons between poor and rich; between people of different races, ethnicities, or faiths; and between members of the same sex. Traditional norms of marriage and sexuality have maintained social order by keeping people in familiar and "appropriate" categories. Offenders have been punished by ostracism, curtailed civil rights, or in some societies, death. Conformists are rewarded with social approval and material advantages. Although it hardly seems possible today, mixed-race marriage was against the law in the United States until 1967. Committed same-sex couples continue to be denied legal marriages, income tax breaks, and health insurance benefits; heterosexual couples take these social benefits for granted.

Some social theorists observe that societies control sexuality through construction of a dichotomized or gendered (male-female) sexuality (Foucault 1978). Society's rules about pleasure seeking and procreating are enforced by norms about appropriate male and female behavior. For example, saying that masculinity is enhanced by sexual experimentation while femininity is demeaned by it gives men sexual privilege (and pleasure) and denies it to women.

Societies control sexuality in part because they have a pragmatic investment in it. Eighteenth-century economic theorist T. R. Malthus ([1798] 1929) highlighted the relationship between reproductive practices and economics in *The Principle of Population*. According to Malthus, excessive fertility would result in the exhaustion of food and other resources. His recommendation to curb the birth rate represents an intervention into the sexual behavior of individuals for the well-being of society. A more recent example is the one-child policy in modern China. Alarmed by the predictions of famine and other disastrous consequences of rapid population growth, Mao Tse-tung and subsequent Chinese leaders instituted a program of enforced fertility control, which included monitoring women's menstrual cycles, requiring involuntary abortions, and delaying the legal age for marriage. To this state, sexual behavior isn't really an intimate, private act at all; it is a social and even economically significant activity. Such policies influence society at large, but they influence private experience as well. In China, raising the legal age for marriage resulted in a shift toward tolerance regarding premarital sex, a practice that became more common.

Society's interest in controlling sexuality is expressed in the debates regarding sex education. Debates about sex education in grade school and high school illustrate the importance to society of both the control of desire and its social construction. The debates raise the question, does formal learning about sex increase or deter early sexual experimentation? The point is, opponents and proponents of sex education all want to know how to control sexuality in young people. Those who favor sex education hold that children benefit from early, comprehensive information about sex, in the belief that people learn about sexuality from birth and are sexual at least from the time of puberty. Providing young people with an appropriate vocabulary and accurate information both discourages early sexual activity and encourages safe sexual practices for those teenagers who, according to the evidence, will not be deterred from sexual activity (Sexuality Information and Education Council of the United States [SIECUS] 1995). On the other hand, opponents of sex education are intensely committed to the belief that information about sex changes teenagers' reactions and values and leads to early, and what they believe are inappropriate, sexual behaviors (Whitehead 1994). Conservative groups hold that sex education, if it occurs at all, should emphasize abstinence as opposed to practical information.

These conflicting points of view about sex education are both concerned with managing adolescent sexual desire. Conservatives fear that education creates desire; liberals feel that information merely enables better decision making. So who is correct? In various studies, a majority of both conservative and liberal sex education programs have demonstrated little effect on behavior.

[But] the passionate debate about sex education is played out with high emotions. Political ideology, parental fears, and the election strategies of politicians all influence this mode of social control. In the final analysis, however, teaching about sex clearly does not have an intense impact on the pupil. In terms of trends within groups, however, it appears that sex education tends to delay sexual activity and makes teenage sex safer when it happens.

To summarize, social constructionists believe that a society influences sexual behavior through its norms. Some norms are explicit, such as laws against adult sexual activity with minors. Others are implicit, such as norms of fidelity and parental responsibility. In a stable, homogeneous society, it is relatively easy to understand such rules. But in a changing, complex society like the United States, the rules may be in flux or indistinct. Perhaps this ambiguity is what makes some issues of sexuality so controversial today.

An Integrative Perspective on Gender and Sexuality

Social constructionist explanations of contemporary sexual patterns are typically pitted against the biology of desire and the evolutionary understanding of biological adaptations. Some social constructionists believe there is no inflexible biological reality; everything we regard as either female or male sexuality is culturally imposed. In contrast, *essentialists*—those who take a biological, sociobiological, or evolutionary point of view—believe people's sexual desires and orientations are innate and hard-wired and that social impact is minimal. Gender differences follow from reproductive differences. Men inseminate, women incubate. People are born with sexual drives, attractions, and natures that simply play themselves out at the appropriate developmental age. Even if social constraints conspire to make men and women more similar to each other, people's essential nature is the same: Man is the hunter, warrior, and trailblazer, and woman is the gatherer, nurturer, and reproducer. In short, essentialists think the innate differences between women and men are the cause of gendered sexuality; social constructionists think the differences between men and women are the result of gendering sexuality through social processes.

Using either the social constructionist or essentialist approach to the exclusion of the other constrains understanding of sexuality. We believe the evidence shows that gender differences are more plausibly an outcome of social processes than the other way around. But a social constructionist view is most powerful when it takes the essentialist view into account. We describe this view of gender differences in sexual desire as *integrative*. Although people tend to think of sex as primarily a biological function—tab B goes into slot A—biology is only one part of the context of desire. Such sociological factors as family relationships and social structure also influence sex. A complex mix of anatomy, hormones, and the brain provides the basic outline for the range of acts and desires possible, but biology is neither where sexuality begins nor where it ends. Social and biological contexts link to define human sexual possibilities.

The integrative approach follows from a great deal that sexuality researchers have observed. A very personal matter that seems to be utterly physical—penile erection, or more specifically a man's inability to get an erection. How might an erection be socially constructed? It is more or less understood in the United States that a penis should be hard and ready when a man's sexual opportunity is available. And it is more or less understood that the failure to get or maintain an erection in a sexual situation has two meanings: The guy isn't "man enough," or the other person isn't attractive enough. But there are many other explanations, not the least of which has been poetically explained by Shakespeare (and scientifically documented):

> Lechery, sir, [alcohol] provokes and unprovokes: it provokes the desire, but it takes away the performance. Therefore much drink may be said to be an equivocator with lechery: it makes him, and it mars him; it sets him on, and it takes him off; it persuades him, and disheartens him; makes him stand to, and not stand to; in conclusion, equivocates him in a sleep, and, giving him the lie, leaves him. (*Macbeth*, Act 11, Scene iii)

The Shakespearean speech refers to the way in which alcohol can undermine robust sexual desire by leaving the penis flaccid. The performance is not the intimate interaction of bodies in pursuit of pleasure; it is strictly focused on the penis, which ought to "stand to." The speech emphasizes the humiliation—the "mar"—for a man who fails to sustain an erection. Though the speech refers to the toll that alcohol takes on the circulatory system that assists penises in becoming erect, the discussion is about the social experience of a man failed by his penis.

Even in the absence of drinking, penises are not nearly so reliable as the mythology of masculinity and attraction would maintain. Erections appear to come and go with odd timing. For example, erections rise and fall on babies and young boys; men often wake up with erections. None of these instances has to do with machismo or sexual desire. Erections are not always evidence of romantic interest, though our culture tends to interpret them as such. But their absence or presence, which is a physical phenomenon, takes on great meaning thanks to Western culture's prevailing beliefs and norms.

Even biological research has supported the integrative perspective. A quarter century ago, one team of scientists found that homosexual men had lower testosterone levels than a matched group of heterosexual men (Kreuz, Rose, and Jennings 1972). The traditional interpretation at the time of the study was that homosexual men were less "masculine" than the comparison group and that their lower testosterone levels explained why they were gay. But a group of active military men were also measured and found to be low in testosterone. The researchers were loath to believe that an unusual number of military men were gay or that military men were below average hormonally, so they found an alternative explanation for low testosterone. The researchers speculated that stress, anxiety, and similar negative emotions had temporarily lowered hormone levels in both soldiers and homosexuals. The stressful social context—as either a gay man living in a straight world or as a military man being bossed around constantly—had shaped a biological response, the researchers concluded. Hormones were the cart, not the horse. Biology influences desire, but social context influences biology and gives meaning to bodily sensation.

What do these examples from research illustrate? Sexual desire—in fact, all sexuality—is influenced by the cultural, personal, and situational. But these examples also tell us that people can't escape the biological context of sex and sexuality—nor can they rely on it. Such an *integrative approach*—the intimate relationship between social context and biological experience—is central to understanding sexuality.

What are the implications of using an integrative approach to sexuality? First, an integrationist will raise questions about biology when social context is emphasized as cause, and will raise questions about social context when biological causes are emphasized. The point is, everything sexual and physical occurs and achieves meaning in a social context.

Sexual Identity and Orientation

Nowhere does the essentialist versus social constructionist argument grow more vehement than in the debate over *sexual identity* and *sexual orientation*. These terms are used to mean a variety of things. We use these terms to refer to how people tend to classify themselves sexually—either as *gay, lesbian, bisexual,* or *straight*. Sexual behavior and sexual desire may or may not be consistent with sexual identity. That is, people may identify themselves as heterosexual, but desire people of the same sex—or vice versa.

It is hard to argue with the observation that human desire is, after all, organized. Humans do not generally desire cows or horses. More to the point, humans are usually quite specific about which sex is desirable to them and even whether the object of their desire is short or tall, dark or light, hairy or sleek.

In the United States, people tend to be identified as either *homosexual* or *heterosexual*. Other cultures (and prior eras in the United States) have not distinguished between these two sexual orientations. However, our culture embraces the perspective that, whether gay or straight, one has an essential, inborn desire, and it cannot change. Many people seem convinced that homosexuality is an essence rather than a sexual act. For essentialists, it is crucial to establish the primacy of one kind of desire or another and to build a world around that identity. People tend to assume that the object of desire is a matter of the gender of the object. That is, they think even homosexual men desire someone who is feminine and that homosexual women desire someone who is masculine. In other words, even among gay men and lesbians, it is assumed that they will desire opposite-gendered people, even if they are of the same sex.

Historians have chronicled in Western culture the evolution of homosexuality from a behavior into an identity (e.g., D'Emilio and Freedman 1988). In the past, people might engage in same-gender sexuality, but only in the twentieth century has it become a well-defined (and diverse) lifestyle and self-definition. Nevertheless, other evidence shows that homosexual identity has existed for a long time. The distinguished historian John Boswell (1994) believes that homosexuals as a group and homosexuality as an identity have existed from the very earliest of recorded history. He used evidence of early Christian same-sex "marriage" to support his thesis. Social scientist Fred Whitman (1983) has looked at homosexuality across cultures and declared that the evidence of a social type, including men who use certain effeminate gestures and have diverse sexual tastes, goes far beyond any one culture. Geneticist Dean Hamer provides evidence that sexual attraction may be genetically programmed, suggesting that it has persisted over time and been passed down through generations.

On the other side of the debate is the idea that sexuality has always been invented and that sexual orientations are socially created. A gay man's or lesbian's sexual orientation has been created by a social context. Although this creation takes place in a society that prefers dichotomous, polarized categories, the social constructionist vision of sexuality at least poses the possibility that sexuality could involve a continuum of behavior that is matched by a continuum of fantasy, ability to love, and sense of self.

The jury is still out on the scientific origins of heterosexuality and homosexuality. One series of studies on the brain (LeVay 1993) identified some differences in the makeup of the brains of heterosexual and homosexual men. This research has been criticized because the brain samples for the homosexual population were taken from men who had died from AIDS, which may have systematically altered the brain structure of the men. Nevertheless, some researchers believe that sexual orientation is wired into the brain, perhaps even dictating the intensity and specificity of sexual tastes.

Genetics researcher Michael Bailey and colleagues looked at identical twins (who have identical genetic material) reared apart. The studies found a likelihood much greater than chance that if one male twin is homosexual, the other will also be homosexual (Bailey et al. 1993). Because the twins in the study did not share the same environment, this finding suggests that the twins' common genes made them similar in their sexual orientation. On the other hand, other recent genetic and twin studies have highlighted the fact that having a certain *genotype* (DNA coded for a particular characteristic, such as heart disease) does not always produce the corresponding *phenotype* (the physical expression of that characteristic, such as actually suffering from heart disease). Researchers speculate that environment and individual history influence the expression or suppression of genetic types (Wright 1995).

These are just a few of the studies that, in some people's opinions, support the idea that homosexuality is not a choice but a naturally occurring phenomenon in a predetermined proportion of births. By extension, they believe, much human sexual desire and behavior must be biologically determined. Of course, social constructionists would disagree. But if biology does not determine whether one is heterosexual or homosexual, is sexual orientation a choice? Not exactly. The notion that sexuality is a preference supposes a person goes to a sexuality bazaar and picks out what to be today. That is not the case either. Physical and social structures and individual biography join together to produce sexual desire and behavior in an individual that may vary over time. Because of powerful social norms regarding sexuality, people are more likely to sustain a single sexual orientation throughout adulthood. The overwhelming evidence supports the idea that biology is a player in the game of sexual orientation but is not the only player or even captain of the team.

The Continuum of Desire

Variation among people has been examined more than changes in sexual orientation within an individual. Alfred Kinsey (see Kinsey, Pomeroy, and Martin 1948), in his pioneering studies on human sexualities in the late 1940s and 1950s, introduced the Kinsey Heterosexual-Homosexual Rating Scale. A person was coded using a zero for "completely heterosexual," a six for "completely homosexual," or a number in between to represent a more ambiguous orientation. Kinsey measured his participants' reports of interest in or attraction to and explicit past experiences with both same-sex and other-sex people and figured out where his participants fit on the continuum. However, his measurements were more of an art than a science. One cannot weigh or calibrate sexuality so finely. But Kinsey did examine actual behavior, fantasy, intensity of feeling, and other important elements that contribute to a person's sexuality.

Although such a rating scale may be an imperfect way of providing individuals with some sort of sex score, Kinsey made the point that a dichotomous vision of sexual orientation is even more inadequate and inaccurate. The Kinsey scale still defines the polarities of sexuality as heterosexuality and homosexuality, and in that sense it is essentialist. However, it provides alternatives beyond "yes," "no," or "in denial."

Kinsey opened the door to thinking in terms of the diversity of sexualities. People may use dichotomous terms in everyday life, but the idea that many people have the capacity to relate sexually to both males and females (at a single point in their life or intermittently over a lifetime) is part of the legacy of Kinsey's sex research.

By using a sexual continuum that blurs the edges of heterosexuality and homosexuality, Kinsey advanced the idea of bisexuality. The mere existence of *bisexuality* (the common term for some history of attraction to or sex with both men and women) is troubling for essentialists, who see sexuality as fixed and linked to procreation. However, biologists can show that bisexuality exists in the animal kingdom. Evolutionary psychologists and anthropologists hypothesize that bisexuality could be useful for a group's bonding and thus have survival value (Fisher 1992). The explanation is that adults who are like aunts and uncles to children—and who are intimate with parents—provide additional support for maintaining a family. But committed essentialists do not usually buy the idea that "true" bisexuality exists. Instead, they code men and women as "true" heterosexuals or homosexuals who have some modest taste in the other direction.

Given the evidence, it is possible to believe that the biological context tends to encourage an individual to acquire one sexual orientation or another but also to believe that society exerts greater influence than biology over behavior. Kinsey's data, as well as controversial data from a small gay and lesbian subsample from the National Health and Social Life Survey (NHSLS; Laumann, Michael, and Gagnon 1994), indicate that many more people report homosexual desire and behavior than those who claim homosexuality or bisexuality as their main sexual orientation or sexual identity. Essentialists might say people who admit to homosexual behavior but deny being homosexuals are kidding themselves. Social constructionists say people are always kidding themselves; in other words, people acquire the desires and behaviors that are available and appealing. These choices will be based on personal history as well as social norms and will emerge in idiosyncratic and diverse ways across the continuum of sexuality. They will also be based on the costs and benefits in a given social system. How many people might code their fantasies differently if it were prestigious to be bisexual? Surely people's impulse to code themselves dichotomously is in part influenced by the social and emotional costs of doing otherwise.

An interesting issue that puzzles essentialists is how different male homosexuality seems to be from female homosexuality. More men than women identify as homosexual, but more women claim homosexual desire and/or behavior than men in those categories. In Lever's (1994) *Advocate Survey*, as well, more men than women identify themselves as homosexual. Indeed, much of the sexual attraction and behavior between women is not labeled as sexual. Women hug and kiss each other with impunity, and not necessarily with specific sexual intent. They can have extended sex play in their youth, or even in adulthood, without being instantly labeled as homosexual, as men who engaged in similar behavior would be. Women are also more likely to report that a same-sex sexual episode had less to do with sexual attraction than with love.

Historically, the waters are even murkier. As Lillian Faderman illustrates in *Surpassing the Love of Men* (1981), eighteenth- and nineteenth-century women were allowed such license to love each other that they could declare truly passionate feelings for one another without labels and identities being bandied about. For example, Faderman (1981) quotes Rousseau's eighteenth-century novel *La Nouvelle Héloïse*, in which Julie writes to Clair: "The most important thing of my life has been to love you. From the very beginning my heart has been absorbed in yours" (p. 77). If these women expressed these sentiments today, observers would assume them to be homosexual. Are these the words simply of passionate friends? Essentialists would say these were lesbian lovers who did not have social permission to know who they really were. Historians and sociologists are divided as to whether these women experienced their love as sexual or romantic in the contemporary understanding of those feelings. It is difficult to label people's emotions for them after the fact and from a different historical and psychological vantage point. Just as beliefs and biases influence the way social science is conducted in the present, so such biases influence the views and interpretations of the past. We need to remember that sexual orientation, along with desire and other manifestations of sexuality, is socially constructed and culturally specific.

Gender as the Basis for Sexual Identity

Sexual orientation, as nearly everyone in Western culture has come to understand the phrase, signifies the identity one has based on the gender of the sexual partners one tends to pair with—either at a particular time or over a lifetime. In our culture, gender is the focus of sexual identity. Thus, the whole notion of sexual identity requires strict distinctions between male and female. The fact that the gender of sexual partners is of great social interest highlights yet again how gender organizes the definitions of sexuality.

Few can resist gendered distinctions. But a challenge comes from *transsexuals*, men and women who believe they were born in the wrong body. Although anatomically they are one sex, transsexuals experience themselves as the other sex, much the way we described Dil, in *The Crying Game* at the beginning of the chapter, who felt like a woman but was built like a man. Sometimes transsexuals "cor-

rect" their bodies with surgery or hormone treatments. And their sexual orientations are diverse. Some male-to-female transsexuals pair with men, some with women. The same is true for female-to-male transsexuals. One male-to-female person, speaking at a sexuality conference in the 1970s, declared, "Personally, I feel it is sexist to love on the basis of gender. You love the person, whatever their sex might be!"

Conclusion

There are, it seems, two arguments that help explain the way the genders express sexual desire. On the one hand are the images and statistics showing that men and women have distinct (albeit shifting) patterns of sexual expression, regardless of sexual orientation. On the other hand, the wide range of sexualities among men or among women also calls for an explanation. A continuum of passion, of desire, of sexual acts and feelings is a useful way to reconcile these phenomena. Furthermore, it helps to recognize that sexual phenomena are socially scripted but also highly individualized. Although sexual desire tends to be described in orderly and quantifiable terms, sexual desire is a chaotic playing field on which we, as sociologists, attempt to place some order to understand it better.

Biology or, more simply stated, bodies are the site for passionate experience, even if that experience is in the brain, in the absence of actual sensations in the skin or other sexual organs. In this sense, biology is a prominent context for sexuality. However, interpersonal, biographical, social, and political contexts influence sexuality and interact with biology in surprising ways. Thus, the continuum of sexuality we propose becomes even more diverse.

Diversity and change in behavior are at the center of social science. Sexuality is one of the most diverse, pervasive, and enigmatic of human experiences. Therefore, far from naming a single sexuality or a dichotomous sexuality, we may more accurately say that there are as many sexualities as there are people. Yet detecting patterns within the diversity can advance an understanding of gender, sex, and society and show how differences and similarities among groups of men and women came into being and are sustained through social practices. The categorical language of sexuality is difficult to avoid.

References

Angier, N. 1995. "Does Testosterone Equal Aggression? Maybe Not." *New York Times*, June 20, p. A1.

Bailey, J. M., R. C. Pillard, M. C. Neale, and Y. Agyei. 1993. "Heritable Factors Influence Sexual Orientation in Women." *Archives of General Psychiatry* 50:217–23.

Bancroft, J. 1978. "The Relationship between Hormones and Sexual Behavior in Humans." Pp. 493–519 in *Biological Determinants of Sexual Behavior*, edited by J. B. Hutchinson. New York: Wiley.

Bancroft, J., D. Sanders, D. Davidson, and P. Warner. 1983. "Mood, Sexuality, Hormones, and the Menstrual Cycle: III. Sexuality and the Role of Androgens." *Psychosomatic Medicine* 45:508–24.

Boswell, J. 1994. *Same-Sex Unions in Pre-Modern Europe*. New York: Villard.

Buss, D. 1994. *The Evolution of Desire: Strategies of Human Mating*. New York: Basic Books.

Buss, D. 1995. "Psychological Sex Differences: Origins through Sexual Selection. *American Psychologist* 50:164–68.

D'Emilio, J. D. and E. Freedman. 1988. *Intimate Matters: A History of Sexuality in America*. New York: Harper & Row.

Faderman, L. 1981. *Surpassing the Love of Men: Romantic Friendship and Love between Women from the Renaissance to the Present*. New York: William Morrow.

Fisher, H. (2004). *Why we love: The nature and chemistry of romantic love*. New York: Henry Holt.

Fisher, H. E. 1992. *Anatomy of Love: The Natural History of Monogamy, Adultery, and Divorce*. New York: Norton.

Foucalt, M. 1978. *A History of Sexuality: An Introduction. A History of Sexuality: An Introduction*. New York: Pantheon.

Greenhalgh, S. 1977. "Hobbled Feet, Hobbled Lives: Women in Old China." *Frontiers* 2:7–21.

Kinsey, A. C., W. B. Pomeroy, and C. E. Martin. 1948. *Sexual Behavior in the Human Male*. Philadelphia: W. B. Saunders.

Kolodny, R. C., W. H. Masters, and V. E. Johnson. 1979. *Textbook of Sexual Medicine*. Boston: Little, Brown.

Kreuz. L. E., R. M. Rose, and J. R. Jennings. 1972. "Suppression of Plasma Testosterone Levels and Psychological Stress: A Longitudinal Study of Young Men in Officer Candidate School." *Archives of General Psychiatry* 26:479–82.

Laumann, E. O., R. T. Michael, and J. H. Gagnon. 1994. *The Social Organization of Sexuality: Sexual Practices in the United States*. Chicago: University of Chicago Press.

LeVay, S. 1993. *The Sexual Brain*. Cambridge: MIT Press.

Lever, J. 1994. "The 1994 Advocate Survey of Sexuality and Relationships: The Men." *The Advocate: The National Gay and Lesbian News Magazine*, August 22, pp. 22–30.

Malthus, T. R. [1798] 1929. *An Essay on the Principle of Population as It Affects the Future Improvement of Society*. New York and London: MacMillan.

Masters, W. H. and V. E. Johnson. 1966. *Human Sexual Response*. Boston: Little, Brown.

Masters, W. H., V. E. Johnson, and R. C. Kolodny. 1995. *Human Sexuality*. 5th ed. New York: Harper Collins College.

Meuwissen, I. and R. Over. 1992. "Sexual Arousal across Phases of the Human Menstrual Cycle." Archives of Sexual Behavior 2:101–19.

Nordhoff, C. and J. N. Hall. 1932. *Mutiny on the Bounty*. Boston: Little, Brown.

Rutter, V. 1995. "Adolescence: Whose Hell Is It?" *Psychology Today*, January/February, pp. 54–66.

Rutter, V. 1996. "Who Stole Fertility?" *Psychology Today*, March/April, pp. 44–70.

Sexuality Information and Education Council of the United States. 1995. A Report on Adolescent Sexuality. New York: SIECUS.

Stanislaw, H. and F. J. Rice. 1988. "The Correlation between Sexual Desire and Menstrual Cycle Changes." *Archives of Sexual Behavior* 17:499–508.

Whitehead, B. D. 1994. "The Failure of Sex Education." *Atlantic Monthly*, October, pp. 55–80.

Whiteman, F. 1983. "Culturally Invariable Properties of Male Homosexualities: Tentative Conclusions from Cross-Cultural Research." *Archives of Sexual Behavior* 12:207–26.

Wright, L. 1995. "A Reporter at Large: Double Mystery. *New Yorker* 8/7:44–50.

Wu, F. C., T. M. Farley, A. Peregondon, and G. M. Waites. 1996. "Effects of Testosterone Enanthate in Normal Men: Experience from a Multicenter Contraceptive Efficacy Study." *Fertility and Sterility* 65:626–36.

Chapter 22
Venus in Furs: Estrogen and Desire

Natalie Angier

The biology of scorpions, disputes over the Human Genome Project, the ubiquitousness of philandering in the animal kingdom, and estrogen and desire: How could this wide array of scientific topics possibly be related? As you read this chapter from Natalie Angier's book, Woman: An Intimate Geography, *you can sense why this science writer for the* New York Times *won a Pulitzer Prize in the category of "Beat Reporting" for a series of articles on such topics. And, you will understand why Angier's book has been so highly lauded. According to the* Washington Post, *"ultimately this grand tour of the female body provides a new vision of the role of women in the history of our species" (Angier 2000, ii). Gloria Steinem quipped, "Think you know it all? Think again. [It] is nothing less than liberation biology. . . . Anyone living in or near a female body should read this book" (Angier 2000, ii).*

But, before you read this tell-tale chapter about estrogen and sexual desire, ask yourself, what do I currently know about the relationship of estrogen to sexual behavior? To check this out, label the following statements as myths or facts:

There is a positive correlation between a woman's ovulatory cycle and

- *Frequency of sexual intercourse*
- *Frequency of orgasm*
- *Frequency of sexual fantasy*
- *Frequency of masturbation*
- *Physical arousability (genitals swell and lubricate)*
- *Sexual hunger*
- *A rise in hemlines*

You will find the answers to these less than academic-sounding questions in the pages of this chapter, along with a wealth of other scientific information couched in readable language. Whether you are of the female or male sex, some surprises may be in store for you as you mine this fertile field of sexuality information about estrogen and desire. And, without

a doubt, this reading has the potential to invoke still other questions that might lead to a lively class debate among inquiring minds.

A female rat can't mate if she is not in estrus. I don't mean that she doesn't want to mate, or that she won't find a partner if she's not in heat and sending forth the appropriate spectrum of olfactory and auditory enticements. I mean that she is physically incapable of copulating. Unless she is in estrus, her ovaries do not secrete estrogen and progesterone, and without hormonal stimulation, the rat can't assume the mating position known as *lordosis*, in which she arches her back and flicks aside her tail. The lordosis posture changes the angle and aperture of the vagina, making it accessible to the male rat's penis once he has mounted her from behind. There is no rat's version of the *Kama Sutra*. An ovariectomized female won't assume lordosis, and hence she can't mate—unless, that is, she is given hormone shots to compensate for the loss of the natural ablutions of the ovarian follicle.

For the rats, as well as for many other female animals, mechanics and motivation are intertwined. Only when she is in heat is the female driven to seek a mate, and only when she is in heat can her body oblige her. Estrogen controls her sexual appetite and sexual physics alike.

A female primate can copulate whenever she pleases, whether she is ovulating or not. There is no connection between the mechanics of her reproductive tract and the status of her hormones. Estrogen does not control the nerves and muscles that would impel her to hoist her rear end in the air, angle her genitals just so, and whip her tail out of the way, if she has one. A female does not have to be capable of becoming pregnant in order to partake of sex. She can have sex every day, and if she's a bonobo, she will have sex more than once a day, or once an hour. A female primate has been unshackled from the tyranny of hormones. In an almost literal sense, the *key* to her door has been taken away from her ovaries and placed in her hands.

Yet she still cycles. Her blood bears estrogen from place to place, including to the portions of the brain where desire and emotion and libido dwell, in the limbic system, the hypothalamus, the amygdala. The female primate has been freed from the rigidity of hormonal control. Now she can take the sex steroid and apply it subtly, to integrate, modulate, and interpret a wealth of sensory and psychological cues. For rats, hormones are thumpish, unmistakable, the world in black and white; for primates, they act like a box of crayons, the sixty-four pack, with a color for every occasion and at least three names for every color. Do you want it in pink, blush, or fuchsia?

"In primates, all the effects of hormones on sexual behavior have become focused on psychological mechanisms, not physical ones," Kim Wallen, of Emory University, says to me. "The decoupling of physical from psychological allows primates to use sex in different contexts, for economic reasons or political reasons. Or emotional reasons, or to keep from getting bored." As Wallen speaks, we watch a group of five rhesus monkeys at the Yerkes Primate Research Center chase two other rhesus monkeys around and around in their enclosure, all seven swearing back and forth at each other in rhesusese, as you can tell because the more they scream, the faster everybody runs. In a primate, Wallen continues, hormone pulses may not make the female bow down in lordosis, but they clearly influence her sexual motivation. He points at the group of rhesus monkeys. The seven samurai are still screaming and running. Several other monkeys look on with rapt anxiety, like bettors at a racetrack. One large, scruffy male ignores everything and picks his teeth. None is doing anything remotely sexual. Rhesus monkeys are Calvinists, Wallen says, prudish and autocratic in matters of sex. When a female rhesus is alone with a familiar male and no other monkeys are there to spy on her, she will mate with the male regardless of where she is in her breeding cycle. But a female under the constraints of the social group does not have the luxury of freewheeling carnality. If she sidles up to a male and begins engaging in a bit of heavy petting, other group members strive to intervene, raucously and snappishly. A female rhesus doesn't often bother defying convention. What does she look like, a bonobo?

Hormones change everything. They tint her judgment and sweep her from Kansas to Oz. When she is ovulating and her estrogen levels soar, her craving overcomes her political instincts and she will mate madly and profligately, all the while out snarling those who would dare to interfere.

We know that there's a macaque darting about in the genomic background and that we feel like monkeys and can act like them too. The moment a young girl enters adolescence, she begins dwelling on sex, consciously, unconsciously, in her dreams, alone in the bath—however or wherever it happens, it happens. Her desire is aroused. The changes of puberty are largely hormonal changes. The shifting of the chemical setting stirs desire. Intellectually, we accept the idea that sexuality is a hormonally inflected experience, but we still resent the connection. If hormones count, we worry that they count too much and that therefore we have no free will, and so we deny that they count, all the while knowing that they count, because we see it in our teenage children and we remember, please goddess, our teenage greed.

Rather than denying the obvious, we should try to appreciate the ways in which estrogen and other hormones affect behavior. Granted, our knowledge of neurobiology is primitive. We don't understand how estrogen or any other substance works on the brain to elicit desire, or feed a fantasy, or muffle an impulse. But there are enough indirect strands of evidence to knit a serviceable thinking cap with which to mull over estrogen's meaning.

If you don't reproduce during a particular cycle, it won't kill you. Humans are long-lived creatures who operate on the implicit assumption that they will have many opportunities to breed and can afford to override the whims and impulses of Eros for months, years, decades, and, oops, a lifetime if conditions of the moment are not quite optimal. Animals in whom reproductive drives are as relentless as thirst are short-lived species who may have only one or two breeding seasons in which to leave their Mendelian badge on the world. A corollary of longevity is a rich emotional life and a complex sexuality. We mistakenly equate emotionality with the primitive and rationality with the advanced, but in fact the more intelligent the animal, the deeper its passions. The greater the intelligence, the greater the demand on the emotions to expand their capacity and multiply their zippers and compartments.

We impugn emotions, but we are lucky to be so thick with them. They give us something to think about and decode. We are brilliant because of them, not in spite of them. Hormones are part of the suitcase, and they are part of the contents. They relay information about themselves, and they carry information about others. They do not make us do anything, but they may make the doing of something easier or more pleasurable when all else conspires in favor of it.

Estrogen, puckish estrogen, works through many intermediaries in the brain, many neuropeptides and neurotransmitters. It works through nerve growth factor, and it works through serotonin, a neuropeptide best known for its role in depression. It works through natural opiates and it works through oxytocin. It may be thought of as a conjoiner or a facilitator, or as leavening, like yeast or baking soda. Estrogen has no particular emotion in mind, yet it permits emoting. For years researchers have sought to link estrogen levels to women's sexual behavior. The assumption is logical. Estrogen concentrations rise steadily as the egg follicle grows each month; peaking with the moment of ovulation, when the egg is released into the fallopian tube. If the egg has a need, a desire to be fertilized, in theory it could make the need known to the brain through estrogen, and estrogen would then stimulate a neuropeptide to encourage a particular behavior—to wit, seeking a sexual partner like a thirsty pedestrian seeks a water fountain.

The difficulties of correlating estrogen to human sexual behavior are considerable. What sort of behavior are you looking at? What are the relevant data points? Frequency of intercourse? Frequency of orgasm? Frequency of masturbation or sexual fantasy? The sudden urge to buy *Cosmopolitan*? Here is what we know. There is no association between rate of intercourse and where a woman is in her ovulatory cycle. Women do not have sex more often during ovulation than they do at any other time of the month, unless they're consciously on the fertility quest. But the completion of a behavior tells you little about the subliminal provocations of that behavior. If you plot the incidence of intercourse among couples, you'll see an amazing statistical high point, and it's called the weekend—not because people necessarily feel sexy each Sunday, but because people have sex when it's convenient, when they're not exhausted by work, and when they have the whole day to toy with. A hormone may lead you to water, but it can't make you drink.

There is also no correlation between estrogen levels and physical arousability—the tendency of the genitals to swell and lubricate in response to an overt sexual stimulus, such as a lovemaking scene in a movie. Women have been shown to be fairly invariate in their display of physiological arousal, regardless of their cycle. But physiological arousal says little about meaningful sexual motivation or hunger, for some women will lubricate during rape, and Ellen Laan, of the University of Amsterdam, has shown that women's genitals congest robustly when they watch pornography that the women later describe as stupid, trite, and distinctly unerotic.

We get a somewhat better kinship between hormones and sexuality when we look at desire rather than at genital performance. Some studies have taken female initiation of sex as the marker of desire. The results have varied considerably, depending on the type of birth control used, but they list in the predicted direction. Women on oral contraceptives, which interfere with normal hormonal oscillations, are no more likely to come on to their partners at the middle of the cycle than they are at other times. When the birth control method is reliable but nonhormonal—a vasectomized husband, for example—women show a tendency to be the initiators of sex at the peak of ovulation more than they are during other times of the month, suggesting that the estrogen high is beckoning to them. Add in the complicating factor of a less trustworthy barrier, such as a diaphragm or condom, and the likelihood of midpeak propositioning subsides. No great enigma there: if you don't want to get pregnant, you might

not be eager to fool around when you think you're at your most fertile. In a study of lesbian couples, who have no fear of pregnancy, don't use birth control, and are free of supposedly confounding factors of male expectations and manipulations, psychologists found that women were about 25 percent more likely to initiate sex and had twice as many orgasms during the midpoint of their cycle than at other times of the month.

The strongest correlations between hormones and sexuality are seen when pure, disembodied desire is the object of scrutiny. In one large study, five hundred women were asked to take their basal temperatures every day for several months and to mark down the day of the month when they first noticed the stirrings of sexual desire. The pooled results show an extraordinary concordance between the onset of sexual hunger and the time that basal temperature readings suggest the women were at or nearing ovulation. Women may even express desire through unconscious body language. In a study of young women who spent a lot of time dancing in nightclubs, the scientists found that as the women approached the day of ovulation, their outfits became progressively skimpier, more flaunting of flesh: the hemlines rose with estrogen levels as if with a bull market. (Of course, it doesn't hurt that midcycle is also the best time to wear your tightest and most revealing clothing, as that is when you are free of premenstrual water retention and blemishes and any fear of leaking menstrual blood.)

A number of researchers lately have suggested that it is testosterone, not estrogen, that is the "true" hormone of libido, in men and women alike. They point out that the ovaries generate testosterone as well as estrogen and that androgen levels spike at midcycle just as estrogen levels do. How can we neglect testosterone when men have so much of it and men love sex so madly, don't they? Many textbooks on human sexuality declare flatly that testosterone is the source of all lust, and some women have added testosterone to their hormone replacement regimens in an effort to shore up their ebbing libido. But if testosterone is relevant to female lust, evidence suggests that it is as a handmaiden to estrogen rather than as Eros descended. As it happens, some proteins in the blood will cling to both testosterone and estrogen and in so clinging prevent the hormones from penetrating the barrier between blood and brain. Estrogen accelerates the production of these binding proteins, but the proteins have a slight preference for testosterone. Hence, as the levels of sex hormones and binding proteins climb with the menstrual cycle, the binding proteins seek out testosterone prejudicially, defusing it in the blood below before it can accomplish much of psychodynamic interest above. The testosterone proves useful indirectly, though: by occupying the binding proteins, it frees estrogen to reach the brain unimpeded. This power of distraction could explain why testosterone therapy works for some women with low libidos: it keeps the blood proteins busy and lets estrogen breaststroke straight to the brain.

But to view estrogen as the hormone of libido is to overstate it and underrate it. If estrogen is the messenger of the egg, we should expect the brain to pay attention, but not in any simple, linear fashion. Just as the mechanics of our genitals have been released from the hormonal chokehold, so have our motives and behaviors. We would not appreciate a hormonal signal that is a blind nymphomaniac, an egg groupie, telling us we're horny and must fornicate. We do not want to indulge an egg just because it is there. We live in the world, and we have constraints and desires of our own. What we might like, though, is a pair of well-appointed glasses, to read the fine print better. Estrogen's basic behavioral strategy is to hone the senses. It pinches us and says, Pay attention. A number of studies have suggested that a woman's vision and sense of smell are heightened at ovulation. So too do the senses shine at other times of high estrogenicity, such as right before menstruation, when your progesterone levels have dropped way down and left estrogen to act unopposed. During pregnancy, you can smell a dirty cat box from two flights away, and you can see dim stars and the pores on every face you meet. It must be emphasized that we don't need estrogen to pay attention or to smell a thing, but there it is, coursing from blood to brain and lending the brain a mild buzz, just as it does the bones and heart and breast and little gray basket.

If estrogen is to help at all, it should help us best when our minds must be wonderfully concentrated. Ovulation is a time of danger and of possibility. Estrogen is like hunting magic, the hallucinogenic drug that Amazonian Indians extract from the skin of the poison-dart frog to lend them the sensorial strength of heroes. The more we are of the world, the greater are our chances of meeting others who suit us, but the more incumbent it is on us to notice and assess those around us. If there is such a thing as feminine intuition, it may lie in the occasional gift of a really sweet estrogen high, the great emulsifier, bringing together disparate observations. But estrogen is also at the behest of history and current affairs: If you are in a sour, reclusive mood to begin with, the hump of estrogen at ovulation, or its unopposed premenstrual energy, may make you feel more rather than less reclusive. Estrogen is a promoter, not an initiator. We can understand this by considering how estrogen contributes to breast cancer. The hormone is not, strictly speaking, a carcinogen. It does not crack or destabilize the genetic material of breast cells, in the way radioactivity or toxins such as benzene can. Yet if an abnormal cell exists, estrogen may stoke and stimulate it, abetting its growth until a minor aberration that might otherwise regress or be cleaned up by the immune system survives and expands to malignant dimensions.

The strength of estrogen lies in its being context-dependent. It does not make us do anything, but it may make us notice certain things we might otherwise neglect. Estrogen may enhance sensory perception, giving us a slight and fluctuating advantage overlaid on the background of the self. If we are good, we may have our moments of being very, very good, and if we are mediocre, well, we can blame it on our hormones. They are there to be used.

As a lubricant for learning, estrogen is of greatest benefit in young women, who are sorting themselves out and gathering cues and experiences. Young women may reap advantages from intuition for lack of anything better to draw on as they assess the motives and character of another. But we can become too enamored of our intuitive prowess, our insight into others, and believe too unshakably in the correctness of our snap judgments. The older we get, the softer the peaks and valleys of our estrogen cycles are, and the less we need them. Experience, after all, is a trustworthier friend than intuition. How many times do you have to encounter a man who reminds you of your cold, aloof, angry, hypercritical, and infinitely alluring father before you can recognize the phenotype in your sleep and know enough to keep your eyes and nose and hormones far, far away?

Each of us is a privately held chemistry lab, and we can play with ourselves if we want. You may find your ovarian cycle too boring to dwell on or you may try to explore its offerings, and you may be disappointed or you may not. It took me many years to realize that my orgasms were very strong at midcycle. I always knew that they were good right before menstruation, but I thought that had to do with mechanics, the congesting of the pelvis with premenstrual fluid, and I didn't attend to the other side of the equation, because I didn't believe in it. When I started to investigate the link between rising estradiol and the quality of climax, I found a wonderful connection. The midway orgasms are deep and resounding, accentuated, maybe by estrogen, maybe by decoy testosterone, maybe by autohypnosis. I could be experiencing a placebo aphrodisiac. It doesn't matter. As a chemist, I'm an amateur, and I can't do a controlled experiment with myself. Nevertheless, on matters that count I'm a quick study, and I've learned to find my way home to ecstasy whatever the moon, month, menses, may be doing.

We each of us have but one chemistry set and brain to explore, and the effects of estrogen will vary from head to head. Yet if there is a principle to be drawn from the general recognition that hormones can stimulate and emulsify the brain and sensitize it to experience and input, it is this: puberty counts. Under the influence of steroid hormones, the brain in early adolescence is a brain expanding, a Japanese flower dropped in water. It is also vulnerable to the deposition of dreck and pain, which can take a lifetime to dump back out again. The plasticity of the pubertal mind is grievously underestimated. We've obsessed over the brain of early childhood and the brain of the fetus, and though those brains matter deeply to the development of all-round intelligence, character, and skill, the adolescent brain counts in another way. As the brain stumbles toward maturity, and as it is buffeted by the output of the adrenal glands at age ten and of the gonads a year or two later, it seeks to define itself sexually and socially. The brain of a prepubertal girl is primed to absorb the definitions of womanness, of what counts and what doesn't, of what power is and how she can get it or how she will never get it. We've all heard about the crisis of self-confidence that supposedly strikes girls as they leave childhood and climb the Bunker Hill of junior high, but what has been less recognized is the correspondence between this period of frailty, this tendency for the personality to mutate beyond recognition, and the hormonal squall in the head. The pubertal brain is so aware of the world that it throbs, it aches, it wants to find the paths to calm it down and make sense of the world. It is an exposed brain, as tender as a molted crab, and it can be seared deeply. Who can forget adolescence? And who has ever recovered from it?

At the same time that hormones challenge the pubertal brain, they change the body. A girl's high estrogen content helps in the deposition of body fat on the breasts, hips, thighs, and buttocks, subcutaneously, everywhere. Because of estrogen and auxiliary hormones, women have more body fat than men. The body of the average woman is 27 percent fat, that of the average man 1.5 percent fat. The leanest elite female athletes may get their body fat down to 11 or 12 percent, but that is nearly double the percentage of body fat found on the elite male athlete, who is as spare as a pronghorn antelope. We can look at the deposition of body fat that comes with womanhood and say it's natural for girls to fatten up when they mature, but what natural means is subject to cultural definition, and our culture still hasn't figured out how to handle fat. On the one hand, we're getting fatter by the year, we westerners generally and North Americans particularly, and why should we expect otherwise? We are stapled to our desks; food is never far from our hands and mouths, and that food tends to be starchy and fatty and overrich; and we get exercise only if we exert willpower, not because sustained body movement is an integrated feature of work, social life, or travel. On the other hand, we are intolerant of fatness, we are repulsed by it, and we see it as a sign of weak character and sloth. Contradictory messages assail us from all sides: we must work all the time, the world is a competitive place, and technology requires that our work be sedentary, cerebral, but we must not get too fat, because fat is unhealthy and looks self-indulgent. So we must exercise and control our bodies, because our natural lives won't do it for us.

Girls, poor girls, are in the thick of our intolerance and vacillation. Girls put on body fat as they pass into adulthood. They put on fat more easily than boys do, thank you very much, Lady Estradiol. And then they are subject to the creed of total control, the idea that we can subdue and discipline our bodies if we work very very hard at it. The message of self-control is amplified by the pubescent brain, which is flailing about for the tools to control and soothe itself and to find what works, how to gather personal and sexual power. Dieting becomes a proxy for power, not simply because girls are exposed through the media to a smothering assemblage of slender, beautiful models, but because adolescent girls today are laying down a bit of fat in an era when fat is creeping up everywhere and is everywhere despised. How is a girl to know that her first blush of fatness will ever stop, when we're tearing our hair out over how the national fat index keeps on rising and we must wrestle it to the ground right now?

There are other, obvious reasons that a girl's brain might decide that a fixation on appearance is the swiftest route to power. There are too many of these Beauty 'n' You, Beast magazines around, far more than when I was a prepubescent girl circa 1970. (There were too many of them back then.) Supermarkets now offer no-candy checkout aisles for parents who don't want their children screaming for Mars bars as they wait in line. Where are the no-women's-magazine aisles? Where are the aisles to escape from the fascism of the Face? Any sane and observant girl is bound to conclude that her looks matter and that she can control her face as she controls her body, through makeup and the proper skin care regimen and parsing her facial features and staying on guard and paying attention and thinking about it, really thinking about it. No wonder a girl loses confidence. If she is smart, she knows that it is foolish to obsess over her appearance. It is depressing and disappointing; for this she learned to read, speak passable Spanish, and do calculus? But if she is smart, she has observed the ubiquitous Face and knows of its staggering power and wants that power. A girl wants to learn the possible powers. By all indications, a controlled body and a beautiful face practically guarantee a powerful womanhood.

I'm not saying anything new here, but I argue that people should see adolescence as an opportunity, a fresh coat of paint on the clapboards of the brain. Girls learn from women: fake women, amalgamated women, real women. The Face is inescapable, but it can be raspberried, sabotaged, emotionally exfoliated. Repetition helps. Reassuring a girl that she is great and strong and gorgeous helps. The exhilarating, indoctrinating rah-rah spirit of the new girl-power movement helps. Girls helping each other helps, because girls take cues from other girls as well as from women. Ritual helps, and antiritual helps. We can denude totemic objects and reinfuse them with arbitrary mania. Girls can use lipstick to draw scarification patterns on each other's backs or faces, or a line of supernumerary nipples from armpit to pelvis. Build a hammock with brassieres and fill it with doughnuts and Diet Coke. Combine the covers of women's magazines with cutout parts from nature magazines to make human-animal chimerical masks: Ellephant MacPherson, Naomi Camel. Glue rubber insects and Monopoly hotels onto the top of a bathroom scale. Girls can imagine futures for each other, with outrageous careers and a string of extraordinary lovers, because it is easier to be generous to another than to yourself, but imagining greatness for a friend makes it thinkable for yourself. Sports help. Karate helps. Sticking by your girlfriends helps. Writing atonal songs with meaningless lyrics helps more than you might think. Learn to play the drums. The world needs more girl drummers. The world needs your wild, pounding, dreaming heart.

Chapter 23
Marital Style and Its Effects on Sexual Desire and Functioning

Barry W. McCarthy

In the Woody Allen movie Annie Hall, *an interesting scenario evolves in two scenes set in a marriage therapist's office. In the first scene, the therapist is inquiring of the wife, "How frequently do you two have sex?" to which she replies, "All the time, maybe twice a week." In the second scene, when the same question is posed to the husband, he answers, "Hardly ever, maybe twice a week." After reading the following article based on Gottman's four marital styles, put on a therapist's hat and classify the Woody Allen characters. Are they a complementary couple or a conflict-minimizing couple? If engaging in the stereotypical struggle in which the woman argues for closeness and affection and the man for intercourse frequency, it would probably be a conflict-minimizing marriage. If they are a couple who play very traditional roles in sex, then the complementary style is a better guess.*

McCarthy argues that when sex in marriage is good, it is a 15 percent to 20 percent factor in a positive marital bond. And, when sex is problematic, it is a 50 percent to 75 percent negative factor, draining the marriage of intimacy. This article is guaranteed to intrigue with its sweeping, and at times perhaps controversial statements about the importance of sexuality in marriage.

Research in the marriage therapy field has yielded extremely impressive results in the last decade. This is in contrast to the stagnation in the sex therapy field, especially in terms of outcome research. The lay public work of Gottman (1994), and Markman, Stanley, and Blumberg (1994) are particularly impressive. Interestingly, these authors give very little attention to the sexual dimensions of marriage,

which is consistent with trends in marital research and therapy. Other therapists (Schnarch, 1991; Kaplan, 1995; and LoPiccolo, 1992) have explored the integration of marital and sexual therapy. This [chapter] explores the relationship between marital styles and sexual functioning, with a special focus on desire issues.

Rather than only one viable marital style, empirical research has identified at least four potentially viable marital styles (Gottman, 1993). By order of frequency they are:

1. Complementary couples—The most common marital style, involves respect for each spouse's contribution, each person has power in certain domains, moderate amounts of intimacy.

2. Conflict-minimizing couples—This is the most stable marital style, marriage is organized along culturally dictated gender roles, avoidance of strong emotional expression, especially anger, limited intimacy, and emphasis on child, family and religious values.

3. Best-friend couples—This style is characterized by highest degree of intimacy and sharing, equitably assigning roles and responsibilities, and a strong commitment to a vital marriage. This marital style runs the risk of disappointment and alienation if expectations are not met, resulting in inhibited sexual desire and marital dissolution.

4. Emotionally-expressive couples—This is the most volatile and unstable marital style, but the most engaging, erotic, and fun. Intimacy is like an accordion, sometimes very close, other times quite distant. Emotion is strongly felt and expressed—joy, anger, and eroticism.

Of course, there are not "pure" styles. A prime couple task during the first two years of marriage is to adopt a comfortable, functional marital style (McCarthy, 1998). A chief issue is to find a mutually comfortable level of intimacy.

How important is sexuality in marriage? McCarthy and McCarthy (1998) postulate that when sex is good, it is a positive, integral factor in the marital bond, but not dominant (15–20 percent). The functions of marital sex are a shared pleasure, a means to deepen and reinforce intimacy, and a tension reducer to deal with the stresses of life and marriage. Sexuality energizes the marital bond and reinforces feelings of specialness. Dysfunctional sex or a nonsexual relationship plays an inordinately powerful role, 50–75 percent, draining the marriage of intimacy and good feelings. Paradoxically, problematic sex plays a more powerful negative role than vital sex plays a positive role in marriage.

Sexual functioning is divided into four components—desire, arousal, orgasm, and satisfaction. The original focus of sex therapy was arousal and orgasm. It is now understood that desire and satisfaction are the core dimensions in marital sexuality. Inhibited sexual desire or discrepancies in sexual desire are the major problems which bring couples to sex therapy. Problems involving sexual desire affect approximately one-third of couples and over 50 percent of those in sex therapy (Rosen and Leiblum, 1995). Key concepts for desire are sexual anticipation and feeling deserving of sexual pleasure. Having a variety of ways to connect—emotionally, affectionally, sensually, and erotically—is valuable. Developing individual and couple bridges for sexual desire is crucial for maintaining vital marital sexuality (McCarthy, 1995). Even more than a specific dysfunction, a non-sexual relationship is a major drain on the marital bond. If you define a non-sexual marriage as being sexual less than ten times a year, one in five married couples have a non-sexual relationship (Michael, Gagnon, Laumann, and Kolata, 1994).

Sexual Strengths and Vulnerabilities of Each Marital Style

What degree of intimacy facilitates sexual desire and functioning? Contrary to cultural and media myths, increasing intimacy is not the answer for couples. The therapeutic focus is finding a mutually comfortable and agreeable level of intimacy, one which facilitates sexual desire (Lobitz and Lobitz, 1996).

Complementary Couples

Complementary (also called validating or supportive) couples have moderate degrees of intimacy, maintaining a balance between autonomy and coupleness. They reinforce each other's competency, validate the spouse's worth, experience an intimate connection and value the marital bond. This promotes sexual desire and functioning. However, complementary couples can fall into the trap of routine, mechanical sex. Sex becomes a low priority, occurring late at night after all the important things in life like putting the children to sleep, paying bills, walking the dog, and watching Jay Leno are completed. Sex might be functional, but it is low quality. The couple wistfully looks back on the romantic love/passionate sex of the premarital years. Couple sexuality cannot rest on its laurels—couple time and valuing intimate sexuality are crucial. The core intervention for complementary couples is to either make sexual initiation a shared domain or one

spouse claims it as his/her domain. Ideally, each spouse would be comfortable initiating, each spouse could say no or preferably offer an alternative, there would be individual and couple bridges to sexual desire, and both spouses would value affection, pleasuring and eroticism.

In complementary marriages, one spouse, traditionally the male, makes sexuality his domain. Sexuality being one spouse's domain prevents sex from being treated with benign neglect or avoided. It's unusual for complementary marriages to degenerate into a non-sexual relationship. The danger is the male overemphasizes intercourse at the expense of intimacy, affection, and pleasuring so the woman's anticipation and satisfaction is lowered. The other danger, especially with the aging of the person and the marriage, is the male's performance/intercourse orientation subverts sexuality. Males over forty are vulnerable to the cycle of anticipatory anxiety, tense and dysfunctional sex, and avoidance. The sexual relationship becomes a source of embarrassment and withers. Revitalizing sexual desire is a couple task. The key is establishing a broad based, flexible, intimate, interactive couple style (McCarthy, 1997). That's easier to do if the woman has her own sexual voice. When both people value intimacy, pleasuring, and eroticism, the couple are inoculated against sexual dysfunction.

Conflict-Minimizing Couples

Conflict-minimizing (also called conflict avoiding or traditional) marriages are the most stable marital style. The rules of the marriage are easily understood and implemented. These marriages are organized around traditional male-female roles. The emphasis is stability, family, and religion. Strong emotional expression is discouraged, including sexual expression. Sexual conflicts are minimized and dealt with by avoidance of both the conflict and sex.

Typically, it's the husband who initiates sex and establishes the sexual style. The sexual scenario emphasizes intercourse, with foreplay to get the woman ready for intercourse. The expectation is her orgasmic pattern should mimic his, a single orgasm during intercourse. Sex is his domain, not hers. Intimacy and expression of feelings is her domain. What is unacceptable are intense feelings, especially anger. Demands and threats are unacceptable. These couples value security over intimacy and family over coupleness.

The danger in this marital style is sex settles into a predictable, mechanical routine. Sexuality is undervalued, becoming marginal and mechanical. The double standard sexual scenario makes them vulnerable to sexual dysfunction and inhibited desire as the male ages and no longer has easy, automatic functioning. When couples stop having sex, whether at 40 or 60, it is the man's unilateral nonverbal decision. He is too frustrated or embarrassed by sexual problems, and decides sex isn't worth the effort. The couple has not been intimate friends, so it is hard to make the transition to intimate, interactive sex.

Best-Friend Couples

The marital style that most values intimacy is the best-friend (also called close or intimate) couple. This is the cultural ideal of marriage—the more intimacy the better. These couples are characterized by high degrees of acceptance, intimacy, satisfaction, and security. Sex is a positive, integral, vital element. Sexuality energizes the marital bond and makes it special. They have a strong bond of respect, trust, and intimacy. These couples value touching both inside and outside the bedroom and enjoy pleasuring and eroticism. They develop a sexual style that is flexible and responsive to the feelings and preferences of both partners.

What are the potential pitfalls of the best-friend marital style? Unfortunately, for most couples this is not a viable model. Best-friend couples have a high divorce rate, based on unmet expectations, anger, and alienation. Marriage cannot live up to the "love means never having to say you're sorry" promise. These couples lack conflict resolution skills and are bitter over thwarted expectations and hopes. They sacrifice autonomy and individuality for the sake of coupleness. The trap for best-friend couples is sacrificing autonomy and then being resentful and blaming.

The biggest sexual trap is inhibited desire. Intimacy and couple time are prime bridges to sexual desire, but too much intimacy stifles erotic feelings. The couple needs to have a mutually comfortable level of intimacy which promotes connection and sexual desire.

Best-friend couples are not assertive in dealing with sexual dysfunction or dissatisfaction. When there's a sexual problem, love is not enough. It is beneficial and necessary to develop sexual comfort and skill, especially making sexual requests. Positive feelings and closeness are helpful, but not enough to overcome dysfunctions such as early ejaculation or vaginismus. When one person develops a secondary dysfunction, erection or female non-orgasmic response, the spouse alternates between blaming self and blaming the partner. The therapeutic stance is to institute a one-two combination of taking personal responsibility for change and working as an intimate team. Best-friend couples often become stuck in a cycle of avoidance, not wanting to push the spouse, waiting for the spouse to initiate. Avoidance further drains the intimate bond.

Emotionally-Expressive Couples

Emotionally-expressive (also called volatile or explosive) couples have the highest intensity of feelings, both loving and angry. Intimacy is like an accordion—sometimes very close, other times alienated. When these marriages work they are exciting and vibrant. Sexually they are passionate and fun. Unfortunately, this is the most unstable marital style, most likely to result in divorce. Emotionally-expressive couples often have physical abuse incidents. A particularly unhealthy pattern is to use sex to make up after an abusive incident. Physical or emotional fights serve as foreplay for sex, a poisonous pattern.

Emotionally-expressive couples who thrive maintain awareness of personal boundaries. They express conflict, anger, and disappointment, but do not cross the line into personal put-downs, contempt, and loss of respect. These couples value intimacy and vibrancy while not being afraid of conflict or anger. Sex is likely to be spontaneous, playful, adventuresome, and energizing.

If one or both spouses develop a sexual dysfunction it is hard to adopt a stepwise, cognitive-behavioral sexual exercise approach. If the dysfunction is not quickly resolved, they easily become demoralized, bitter, and can't tolerate the sexual hiatus. Problematic sex results in affairs and marital dissolution.

Couple Style and Sexuality

Couples with incompatible needs are likely to have a "fatally flawed" marriage. The wife who wants an emotionally-expressive marriage while the husband wants a conflict-minimizing style are vulnerable. On the other hand, a wife who prefers a complementary couple style while the husband prefers a best-friend marriage are likely to negotiate a mutually satisfying degree of connection and intimacy.

The two sexual issues most important to resolve are the amount of intimacy and the importance of sexuality. Intimacy includes sexuality but is much more than sexuality (Schaefer and Olson, 1981). One spouse desiring high levels of intimacy while the other wants a high level of autonomy with the major connection being sex are likely to develop inhibited sexual desire. The traditional pattern is the woman wants more intimacy, affection, and sensuality. The man withdraws emotionally and sees intercourse as the best way to reconnect. They engage in the stereotypic Ann Landers struggle with the woman arguing for closeness and affection while the man argues for intercourse frequency. For vital sexual functioning, the couple needs to break from rigid sex roles (this is hardest for conflict-minimizing couples). Each spouse would value intimacy, affection, pleasuring, eroticism, and intercourse. Each would be comfortable initiating, saying no, and offering an alternative sensual or erotic scenario.

Each marital style has strengths and vulnerabilities. The marital style least influenced by sexual issues is the conflict-minimizing couple. Sexual expectations are low and sex is not highly valued. What is most disruptive is an extra-marital affair, especially the wife's. Marital rules are very important for conflict-minimizing couples. They are more likely to emphasize rebuilding trust than rebuilding sexual vitality. Another vulnerability is an infertility problem. Having children is normal, so infertility is unexpected and unacceptable. The medical assessment procedures and intercourse on a rigorous schedule has a high probability of causing erectile dysfunction and/or inhibited sexual desire for one or both spouses.

Inhibited sexual desire and a non-sexual marriage are the death knell for best-friend marriages, and even more so for emotionally-expressive couples. Bad sex is better than no sex, especially when the lack of intercourse generalizes to avoidance of affection and sensuality. The best-friend couple feels betrayed and personally rejected. Lack of physical connection—whether affectionate, sensual, or sexual—is a major drain on the marital bond. The closeness and sharing which typifies the best-friend marriage is devastated by a non-sexual relationship.

The issues are different for an emotionally-expressive couple. Sexuality has been one of their joys and energizers. Rather than feeling support and gradually regaining sexual confidence, the couple explode in a torrent of accusations, anger, and tears. There is a great deal of heat and drama, too much for a traditional sex therapy program to contain. Interestingly, emotionally-expressive couples find it easier to recover from an affair than other couples. The best-friend marriage finds it very difficult to recover from an extra-marital affair, especially a comparison affair. Even more than sex are feelings of personal betrayal. These couples spend so much time and energy on trust and intimacy issues that they find it difficult to revitalize sexual desire and view the spouse as an erotic partner.

Complementary couples find sexuality the easiest fit with their marital style. The woman's domain is affection and intimacy while the man's domain is sexual initiation and intercourse. Both people value their contribution, including flexibility in roles. The man values intimacy and does initiate affectionate touching. The woman values eroticism and orgasm, and initiates sexual encounters. Sexuality is broad based and flexible, reinforcing desire and functioning.

A vibrant sexual relationship is most important for emotionally-expressive couples and least important for conflict-minimizing couples. Without a vital sexual life, emotionally-expressive couples question the value of the marriage. More than any other couple style, sexuality plays a dominant role for emotionally-expressive couples. Happiness and excitement can be expressed in a multitude of ways, but when not expressed sexually this void is starkly apparent. Conflict-minimizing couples deny the impact of sexual problems; this is especially true of the traditional wife. Even if the sex is unfulfilling she makes herself available. Unless the sexual problem interferes with fertility, the traditional wife does not complain about unfulfilled sexual needs. With the birth of children and the aging of the marriage, the importance of sex is further downplayed.

Complementary couples and best-friend marriages find it easiest to accept the guideline of sexuality being 15–20 percent. A satisfying sexual relationship energizes and makes special the marital bond. Couples adopt a broad-based, flexible approach to affectionate, sensual, erotic, and intercourse expression. Having a variety of ways and levels to emotionally and physically connect promotes intimacy. Having his, her, and our bridges to sexual desire ensures a vital sexual relationship. Sexuality can fulfill a multitude of functions and be expressed in a multitude of ways. Touching can be initiated by the woman or man, and occur inside or outside the bedroom. Touching is worthwhile whether or not it culminates in intercourse. These couples respond to the intimacy, nondemand pleasuring, eroticism prescription for maintaining satisfying marital sexuality.

Complementary couples are less emotionally vulnerable and less likely to overreact to a sexual problem than best-friend couples. Best-friend couples have a greater struggle with issues of autonomy and personal boundaries. If one spouse develops a sexual dysfunction, the partner feels responsible or guilty. Complementary couples emphasize individuation and maintain a sexual relationship. For example, if he develops an erection problem she is empathic and supportive, but doesn't blame herself or reduce her sexual interest. This is helpful since her desire and responsivity is a positive resource for marital sex. This facilitates regaining sexual comfort and confidence. The most powerful aphrodisiac is an involved, aroused partner. The wife in the best-friend couple overreacts and is demoralized by erectile dysfunction. Her desire and arousal are lessened. Both become passive spectators on the state of his penis. Self-consciousness, tentativeness, and second-guessing interfere with erotic flow. Each person is responsible for his/her desire, arousal, and orgasm. From this base, they work as an intimate team to revitalize sexual desire and functioning.

Closing Thoughts

This [work] is a heuristic attempt to integrate findings from marital theory and therapy with concepts of sexual desire, function and dysfunction. The couple's marital style—complementary, conflict-minimizing, best-friend, emotionally-expressive—has important implications for sexuality. A crucial concept is when sexuality functions well, it's a positive, integral component in the marriage, contributing 15–20 percent. The functions of sexuality are a shared pleasure, a means to deepen and reinforce intimacy, and a tension reducer to lessen the stresses of life and marriage. Sexuality energizes and makes special the marital bond. However, when sexuality is dysfunctional or non-existent it plays an inordinately powerful role, 50–75 percent, robbing the marriage of intimacy and vitality. Especially for best-friend and emotionally-expressive couples, sexual problems destroy marital viability.

Each marital style entails sexual strengths and vulnerabilities. This is reflected both in the degree of intimacy and the importance of sex in the relationship. There is a need for empirical and clinical exploration of the reciprocal effects of marital style with sexual desire and functioning.

References

Gottman, J. (1993). The roles of conflict engagement, escalation, and avoidance in marital interaction: A longitudinal view of five types of couples. *Journal of Consulting and Clinical Psychology, 61,* 6–15.

Gottman, J. (1994). *Why Marriages Succeed or Fail.* New York: Simon and Schuster.

Kaplan, H. (1995). *The Sexual Desire Disorders.* New York: Brunner/Mazel.

Lobitz, W. & Lobitz, G. (1996). Resolving the sexual intimacy paradox: A developmental model for the treatment of sexual desire disorders. *Journal of Sex and Marital Therapy, 22,* 71–84.

LoPiccolo, J. (1992). Postmodern sex therapy for erectile failure. In R. Rosen & S. Leiblum (Eds.). *Erectile Disorders: Assessment and Treatment* (pp. 171–197). New York: Guilford.

Markman, H., Stanley, S., & Blumberg, S. (1994). *Fighting for Your Marriage.* San Francisco: Jossey Bass.

McCarthy, B. (1995). Bridges to sexual desire. *Journal of Sex Education and Therapy, 21,* 132–141.

McCarthy, B. (1997). Strategies and techniques for revitalizing a non-sexual marriage. *Journal of Sex and Marital Therapy, 23,* 231–240.

McCarthy, B. (1998). Sex in the first two years of marriage. *Journal of Family Psychology.*

McCarthy, B. & McCarthy, E. (1998). *Couple Sexual Awareness, 9(4),* 4–11. New York: Carroll and Graf.

Michael, R., Gagnon, J., Laumann, F., & Kolata, G. (1994). *Sex in America.* Boston: Little, Brown.

Rosen, R. & Leiblum, S. (Eds.) (1995). Hypoactive sexual desire. *Psychiatric Clinics of North America, 18,* 107–121.

Schaefer, M. & Olson, D. (1981). Assessing intimacy. *Journal of Marital and Family Therapy, 7,* 47–60.

Schnarch, D. (1991). *Constructing the Sexual Crucible.* New York: Norton.

From Barry W. McCarthy, "Marital Style and Its Effects on Sexual Desire and Functioning." *Journal of Family Psychotherapy, 10(3),* 1–12. Copyright © 1999, The Haworth Press, Inc. Reprinted by permission. ✦

Chapter 24

Sexual Satisfaction and Sexual Drive in Spinal Cord Injured Women

Kimberly Black

Marca L. Sipski

Susanne S. Strauss

The recognition that Christopher Reeves has brought to issues surrounding spinal cord (SC) injury is noteworthy. His willingness to openly share his recovery process has raised public awareness and sensitivity about the need for SC injury research. Not much awareness exists, however, concerning the effects of spinal cord injury on a person's sexual functioning. This is especially true for SC injured women. The little research that has been conducted on this population focuses mainly on pregnancy and childbirth issues. After reading this selection, students should be better able to formulate questions for continued research on the psychological aspects of sexuality and sexual functioning after SC injuries. Perhaps at least one reader will be challenged to undertake such an ambitious project as a future professional.

Introduction

Women with spinal cord injuries (SCI) have been underrepresented in research that examined sexual functioning of individuals with SCI. Most of the previous research available on women with spinal cord injuries and sexual functioning focused primarily on pregnancy and childbirth.[1-2] Recently, studies have begun to measure and compare sexual functioning in women pre-SCI to that of post-SCI.[3-4] However, this method is subject to the limitations of retrospective studies and does not take into account the percentage of subjects with sexual dysfunction that occurs in the able-bodied (AB) population. No studies comparing the sexuality and sexual functioning of SCI women with that of AB women were identified.

Women with SCI continue to engage in sexual activities. White et al.[5] studied the sexual activities of 40 SCI women and reported that 80 percent of the women had had a sexual relationship (emotional, physical, or both) since the time of injury, and 65 percent had had a physical relationship within the previous year. Having had a physical relationship since injury was significantly related to age at onset and years since injury. Women who had been involved in a physical relationship since injury were younger at the onset of injury and had been injured for a longer time than those who had not had such a relationship.

Sexual intercourse is one activity many SCI women continue to engage in. White et al.[5] reported that 72 percent of women had had sexual intercourse since their injury and 58 percent had had intercourse within the previous 12 months. Having had intercourse since their injury was correlated with age at onset; women who had had intercourse since injury were younger at the onset of injury. Sipski and Alexander[6] noted that although intercourse had been the favored activity pre-injury, kissing, hugging, and touching were the favored activities post-injury. After injury, 76 percent of the women engaged in both kissing and hugging, 68 percent in penis-vagina intercourse, 68 percent in touching, 56 percent in oral sex, 40 percent in manual stimulation, 24 percent in vibratory stimulation, and 12 percent in anal intercourse.

Although sexual activity continues post-injury, the frequency of sexual activity decreases. Sipski and Alexander[6] assessed sexual functioning pre- and post-injury in 25 SCI women, 64 percent of the women had engaged in a sexual activity at least one time per week pre-injury and only 48 percent had engaged in a sexual activity at least one time per week post-injury.

Charlifue et al.[4] surveyed 231 SCI women and found that prior to injury, 76 percent of the women reported having had sexual contact at least once a week; after injury, only 52 percent reported having had sexual contact at least once a week (with 34 percent having sexual contact less than once per month). Factors interfering with sexual activity included spasticity, lack of spontaneity, motion limitations, catheter interference, inadequate vaginal lubrication, and autonomic hyperreflexia. Zwerner,[7] reporting on the frequency of sexual activity in SCI females, found that just under half had a decrease in frequency post-injury, approximately 37 percent had no change, and 15 percent had an increase. Women with very high (daily) or very low (less than once a month) pre-injury sexual activity had less change in frequency than women with moderate (two to three times a week) sexual activity pre-injury. Age and marital status were thought to have influenced the frequency of sexual activity in these women.

Level of sexual satisfaction has also been found to decrease following SCI. In Sipski and Alexander's study,[6] 72 percent of the women felt sexually satisfied or very satisfied prior to injury, whereas only 48 percent of the women felt satisfied post-injury. Charlifue et al.[4] also noted that 69 percent of the women in their study expressed satisfaction with their post-injury sexual experiences.

Whereas the earlier studies began to examine the impact of SCI on sexuality, none of them compared the SCI population with the general population. However, Sipski et al.[8] conducted a laboratory-based assessment of the characteristics and physiological sexual responses during orgasm in 25 SCI women and compared their responses with those of 9 AB women. AB women reported greater levels of sexual satisfaction than did SCI women; however, SCI women had a more integrated gender role definition. Further, subjects who achieved orgasm had a higher sex drive and were significantly more educated about sexual functioning.

The Current Study

In the present study comparing SCI subjects with an AB comparison group, the DSFI was used to measure differences in sexuality and sexual functioning in 10 areas: information, experience, drive, attitude, psychological symptoms, affect, gender role definition, fantasy, body image, and sexual satisfaction.

Methods

Subjects included 84 women with SCI and 37 able-bodied (AB) women. Ages ranged from 18 to 61 years with a median age of 37 for SCI women and 32 for AB women. Most of the women were single and never married (40.5 percent of SCI and 41.7 percent of AB); however, the next largest group reported being currently married (27.0 percent and 35.7 percent, respectively). Number of children ranged from 0 to 5, with the majority of women having 0 children (75.7 percent and 57.1 percent). Education ranged from completing some high school to earning a graduate degree. The two largest categories of SCI women were those describing their highest level of education as four years of college (24.7 percent) or a graduate degree (23.5 percent). The two largest categories of AB women were those reporting some college (18.8 percent) or a graduate degree (18.8 percent). Annual incomes ranged from less

than $10,000 to more than $40,000, with means of $27,000 for SCI women and $25,000 for AB women.

The largest group of SCI women reported injury in the thoracic region (38.6 percent) and the next largest group reported injury in the cervical region (32.5 percent). Of those who responded, 52 percent reported complete lesions and 48 percent reported incomplete lesions.

Subjects were recruited from a national list produced by the National Spinal Cord Injury Association (NSCIA). Return-addressed, stamped postcards requesting voluntary participation were mailed [and] one hundred twenty-six women returned the postcards, for a response rate of 36 percent. Two questionnaires were mailed to the respondents: one for each SCI woman and one for the SCI woman to give to an able-bodied friend. Eighty-four questionnaires were returned by SCI women and 37 were returned by AB women.

We used the DSFI,[9] a multidimensional test designed to measure current level of sexual functioning. It consists of 10 subsets: *Information* measures the subject's general knowledge regarding sexual functioning. *Experience* measures the variety of sexual behaviors that the subject has experienced. *Drive* assesses the person's level of interest in sex as determined by the frequency of various sexual activities. *Attitude* measures attitudes toward sexual activities and relationships. *Psychological symptoms* measure distress arising from psychological symptoms. *Affect* measures the subject's mood status. *Gender role definition* measures the balance between the subject's masculine and feminine characteristics. *Fantasy* assesses the number of different sexual fantasies acknowledged by the subject. *Body image* assesses the subject's satisfaction with her own body. *Sexual satisfaction* measures the degree to which the subject is gratified by her sexual life.

Results

Scores on drive, sexual satisfaction, psychological symptoms, and affect all differed at a significant level between SCI and AB women. SCI women scored significantly lower than AB women on the drive subscale and significantly lower on the sexual satisfaction subscale. Thus, SCI women engaged in sexual activities less frequently and experienced lower levels of sexual satisfaction in their current relationships than did AB women. SCI women scored significantly higher on the psychological symptoms subscale than did AB women and significantly lower on the affect subscale. SCI women experienced higher levels of psychological distress and higher negative affect than did AB women.

Age was found to be significantly related to sexual satisfaction among both SCI and AB women, but in opposite directions. The older the SCI women, the lower the score on the sexual satisfaction subscale. In contrast, the older the able-bodied women, the higher the score on the sexual satisfaction subscale. Women who were older at the time of injury indicated less sexual satisfaction in their current relationships by scoring significantly lower on the sexual satisfaction subscale. These women expressed more liberal attitudes about sexuality, had a more integrated gender role definition, and had more fantasies than did women whose injuries were of shorter duration. However, no significant associations were found with level of injury or severity of lesion.

Among SCI women, significant findings were also reported for income and education. The higher the income, the higher the score on the drive subscale. Educated SCI women experienced lower levels of psychological distress, felt more positive affect, and established a more integrated gender role definition. Lower levels of sexual satisfaction were [not found] among SCI women who were married.

Discussion

Married SCI women were no less sexually satisfied than AB women. Partner availability may influence levels of sexual satisfaction. Unmarried SCI women may have had more difficulty finding partners and thus achieving high levels of sexual satisfaction. Married SCI women may have found more security in their relationships, may have been more willing to experiment with different techniques, and may have found alternate ways of achieving sexual satisfaction. Similarly, Nosek et al.[10] found that women with disabilities who lived with a significant other reported greater sexual satisfaction and had a higher level of sexual activity.

Interpretation of the data poses certain challenges. In this study, responses were self-reported. Only perceptions of behavior were assessed, as opposed to actual behavior. Sexual functioning, sexual experiences, and sexual satisfaction are subject to response bias and subject uncertainty. There was also a relatively low response rate from both SCI and AB women. It is unclear whether women who were more adjusted and who felt more comfortable in answering questions on sexuality were more likely to respond.

In the present study, the procedure for selecting the comparison group was not random. The size of the comparison group in the present study [also] was less substantial than the SCI group, weakening the power of the analyses. Further, many of the women in the present sample were highly educated, single, and childless; therefore, the findings of this study may be most appropriately generalized to similar groups of women. However, Nosek et al.[10] also found that women with disabilities were more likely to be single and were much less likely to bear children than AB women. Similarly, the women in their study were well educated; 54 percent of women with disabilities and 42 percent of able-bodied women had college degrees.

The results of the present study indicate a need to continue addressing both the psychological and physiological aspects of female sexual functioning in SCI. Laboratory assessment can clarify the physiological aspects of sexual functioning. In the laboratory-based assessment of Sipski et al.,[8] 52 percent of SCI women were able to stimulate to orgasm. The ability to achieve orgasm in SCI women was not related to the degree or type of injury; no significant differences were found between any of the subject groups for heart rate and systolic and diastolic blood pressure during orgasm and no characteristics were identified that would have allowed prediction of which SCI women would be able to achieve orgasm. However, the ability to have an orgasm was related to the level of sexual knowledge and level of desire.

Further research is needed to identify possible predictors of orgasmic ability and the relationship of the predictors to sex drive and sexual satisfaction. Examination of the influence of both psychological and physiological factors on female sexual functioning is important in order to reach a more accurate diagnosis and identify treatment interventions that maximize sexual satisfaction in women with SCI.

References

1. Comarr A. Observations on menstruation and pregnancy among female spinal cord injury patients. *Paraplegia* 1996; 3: 263–272.
2. Ohry A, Peleg D, Goldman J, David A, Rozin R. Sexual function, pregnancy and delivery in spinal cord injured women. *Gyn Obstet Invest* 1978; 9: 281–291.
3. Kettl P, Zarefoss S, Jacoby K, et al. Female sexuality after spinal cord injury. *Sexual Disabil* 1991; 9: 287–295.
4. Charlifue SW, Gerhart KA, Mentor RR, Whiteneck GG, Manley MS. Sexual issues of women with spinal cord injuries. *Paraplegia* 1992; 30: 192–199.
5. White M, Rintala D, Hart KA, Fuhrer MJ. Sexual activities, concerns and interests of women with spinal cord injury living in the community. *Amer J Phys Med Rehabil* 1993; 72: 372–378.
6. Sipski ML, Alexander CJ. Sexual activities, response and satisfaction in women pre- and post-spinal cord injury. *Arch Phys Med Rehabil* 1993; 74: 1025–1029.

7. Zwerner J. Yes, we have trouble but nobody's listening: Sexual issues of women with spinal cord injury. *Sexual Disabil* 1982; 5: 158–171.

8. Sipski ML, Alexander CJ, Rosen RC. Orgasm in women with spinal cord injuries: A laboratory-based assessment. *Arch Phys Med Rehabil* 1995; 76: 1097–1102.

9. Derogatis L. Derogatis sexual functioning inventory. Baltimore; *Clinical Psychometrics,* 1975.

10. Nosek MA, Rintala DH, Young ME, et al. Sexual functioning among women with physical disabilities. *Arch Phys Med Rehabil* 1996; 77: 107–115.

Part VI

Sexually Transmitted Diseases and Abortion

The vast majority of adults have engaged in sexual behavior that could potentially result in conception or sexually transmitted diseases, or both. We know this fact because only 2.8 percent of adults report never having had sex with a partner, and of those who have, 97 percent have had vaginal intercourse (Laumann et al. 1994). But, when connecting the dots in the game of "sex and consequences," a number of outcomes are possible, some of which are by choice and others by chance. Those variables subject to choice are fertility, sexual practices, and fertility control. Disconnecting these dots at any point can separate the act of safer sex from the consequence of chance. In the chapter about abortion in Part VI, the subject of abortion by choice is raised.

First known to Americans as RU-486, the French abortion pill was hailed by leading contraceptive researchers as the only real discovery in birth control since the pill. At the same time, it was denounced by the Pope as the "Pill of Cain, the monster that cynically kills its brothers." With such confusing messages, readers could go down the science versus religion path in this controversy. But as the facts of Mifepristone and home Misoprostol unfold in the chapter by Fielding, Edmunds, and Schaff, a number of other related variables surface.

Most troubling to both factions in the abortion conflict is the issue of viability, an ever-present moral dilemma of gigantic proportions. Because viability is almost solely defined by evolving medical technology, it is a constantly moving target. And, for the majority of Americans, the concept of timing does make a difference in their opinion about abortion. For example, given the ability of a fetus at six months to survive outside of the womb, many per-

sons are rethinking their positions on late-term abortions.

Marie Bass, a pro-choice political consultant in Washington who worked for years to help bring RU-486 to this country, has questioned the stance of the pro-choice leaders who believe they have to stand their ground against all restrictions on choice, calling the issue a "slippery slope" (Talbot 1999); Bass is not sure she would go that far. Margaret Talbot reported in her feature coverage of abortion in a *New York Times Magazine* article that to her knowledge, no country in the world does not heavily regulate second- and third-trimester abortions. For example, in France, abortion is legal only until 12 weeks. But it is not socially stigmatized before then, and because it is state-financed, it is easily accessible (Talbot 1999). Does, then, the fact that medical abortions can be accomplished so much earlier in pregnancy than most surgical abortions make them the more desirable of the two options? Talbot warned against placing too much hope for social change on any one technological innovation. But, she suggested that "if Americans do care as much as they say they do about making abortion happen earlier, then medical abortion is the best means yet for enacting that shift" (Talbot 1999, 48).

Fielding and colleagues provide an excellent chapter to promote a lively class debate, a part of which would focus on the question of the physiological and psychological effects of abortion. At the present time, considerably more is known about the subsequent physiological health of women who have had abortions than about the psychological effects. In fact, few, if any, longitudinal studies report data about long-term effects. This chapter, which skillfully uses case studies to report both the physiological and psychological effects of abortion, is a critical addition to the literature.

The sexual behavior patterns of individuals affect not only their chances for involvement in an unplanned pregnancy, but also their chances for contracting sexually transmitted diseases (STDs). The Centers for Disease Control (CDC) estimates that 15.3 million Americans become infected with STDs each year, two-thirds of whom are under age 25 (Kelly 2004). The CDC estimates that in the United States, 900,000 persons have the HIV infection, and it reports that 40,000 new cases are diagnosed each year (Centers for Disease Control 2003).

Searching for the operative word in the chapter concerning risk, identity, and love in the age of AIDS, students will discover that the word is community. From Judith Levine's controversial book, *Harmful to Minors: The Perils of Protecting Children From Sex*, this exposé about sexuality education and HIV prevention programs among youth clearly features the concept of *community as process*. However, this emotionally charged phrase represents more than the usual meanings ascribed to the word *community*: "consensus, socialization, and solidarity." Levine's concept of community is more analogous to "community-feeling", or *gemeinschaft* a word Alfred Adler (1924) used to describe a sense of relationship between the individual and the community. Adler contended that out of community-feelings ". . . are developed tenderness, love of neighbor, friendship and love, and the desire for power unfolding itself in a veiled manner and seeking secretly to push its way along the path of group consciousness" (Hinsie and Campbell 1970, 139). Therapists have long emphasized the value of such a sense of community by including socio-environmental and interpersonal influences in their treatment protocols. Theoretically, at least, patients who identify with a social group will modify their social attitudes and behavior because of a growing awareness of their roles in relationships with others (Wilmer 1958).

Reading about Levine's field work in the Minneapolis and St. Paul, Minnesota area to study the issue of AIDS, students will encounter what is described as "an imperiled, yet flourishing community of gay, lesbian, bisexual, and homeless youth [who] are the recipients of some extraordinary adult care and attention" (Levine 2000, 202). Could such success be expressly because of community-feeling? Perhaps. It will be hard for students to read this chapter without putting a face on their own sense of community. They will at least find this broad sense of community in the two principles that Levine believes to be essential in successful programs that target prevention of AIDS: (1) to recognize the urgency of the problem and the pressing needs of the people targeted and (2) to respect social norms, identities, values, and desires of clients as expressed in the relationships between individuals and within communities. Readers of this offering may learn the simple lessons of meeting people where they are and of respecting their choices—both valuable lessons for community programs and for life.

Although the likelihood of contracting any STD is affected by behavioral risk factors, knowledge about STDs is not always associated with a reduction in risk-taking behavior. Large numbers of informed college students continue to report nonuse of condoms, sexual intercourse with persons just met, and sexual intercourse while under the influence of alcohol (Hingson et al. 2003). Research indicates that sexual activity that is anonymous, casual, with multiple partners, and/or with high-risk partners substantially increases the likelihood of contracting an STD, but that condom use greatly reduces this likelihood. Why then do so many sexually-active persons fail to use condoms? Perhaps because consistent condom use is a complex issue, affected by psychological, interpersonal, and cultural factors.

More than 15 million Americans become infected with sexually transmitted diseases annually. Of these, the human papilloma virus (HPV), evidenced in genital warts, represents one-third of the cases. An estimated 20 million persons in the United States today have HPV (Dailard 2003). Such numbers place our nation near the top of the HPV charts in the developed countries of the world. Like the genital herpes virus, HPV is a "gift" that keeps on giving, and as a result, over 5.5 million new cases of genital warts require treatment annually (Hyde and DeLamater 2003). Not only can subsequent partners be affected, but HPV can also be transmitted to a baby during vaginal delivery if the warts are on the cervix or in the vagina.

To break the chains of transmission, education is vital. The chapter by Robert D. Burk and colleagues, derived from their presentation at the International Human Papillomavirus (HPV) Conference in Amsterdam, Holland, contributes to this end with its rigorous design and execution by a team of medical researchers. Testing the hypothesis that sexual behavior and partner characteristics are the major risk factors for HPV in young women, this reasearch team reveals data valuable for young persons in today's uncertain world. The chapter may sound a like a cacophonous note of educational facts for those who prefer to rely on their feelings. But, at least the facts will have been heard; silence is unacceptable.

References

Adler, A. (1924). *The Practice and Theory of Individual Psychology*. (P. Radin, Trans). London: Humanities Press.

Centers for Disease Control. (2003). *HIV/AIDS Surveillance Report, 2002*. Atlanta, GA: Centers for Disease Control and Prevention.

Dailard, C. (2003). "HPV in the United States and Developing Nations: A Problem of Public Health or Politics?" *The Guttmacher Report*, 6(3), 1–5.

Hingson, R., Heeren, T., Winter, M. R., and Wechsler, H. (2003). "Early Age at First Drunkenness as a Factor in College Students' Unplanned and Unprotected Sex Attributable to Drinking." *Pediatrics*, 111, 34–41.

Hinsie, L. E., and Campbell, R. E. (1970). "Community. In L. E. Hinsie and R. E. Campbell, *Psychiatric Dictionary* (4th Edition). New York: Oxford University Press.

Hyde, J. S., and DeLamater, J. D. (2003). *Understanding Human Sexuality* (8th Edition). Boston: McGraw-Hill.

Kelly, G. F. (2004). *Sexuality Today: The Human Perspective* (7th Edition). New York: McGraw-Hill.

Laumann, E. O., Gagnon, J. H., Michael, R. T., and Michaels, S. (1994). *The Social Organization of Sexuality: Sexual Practices in the United States*. Chicago: University of Chicago Press.

Levine, J. (2002). *Harmful to Minors: The Perils of Protecting Minors from Sex*. Minneapolis: University of Minnesota Press.

Talbot, M. (1999, July 11). "The Little White Bombshell." *New York Times Magazine*, pp. 38–43, 48, 61–63.

Wilmer, H. A. (1958). "Toward a Definition of Community." *Journal of Psychiatry*, 114, 824–833. ✦

Chapter 25

Having an Abortion Using Mifepristone and Home Misoprostol

A Qualitative Analysis of Women's Experiences

Stephen L. Fielding

Emme Edmunds

Eric A. Schaff

Abortion. A weighty word that engendered one of the most contentious debates of the past century and survived to become a singular political focus in the first presidential election of the twenty-first century. One and one-third million abortions are performed every year in the United States, making it the most common surgical procedure for women. Guaranteed to spark yet another dimension of debate is a new method of abortion with enormous political consequences for both the pro-choice advocates and the right-to-life advocates: RU-486, or the French abortion pill, a method of medication-induced abortion that offers an alternative to the traditional westernized method of surgical abortion. We are told that women choose medical over surgical abortion for several reasons: it is more natural, more private, and less painful. Many may choose the medical method because of the timing factor: the option to have the abortion before seven weeks gestation, thought by most practitioners to be too early for a surgical abortion. In a feature article in the New York Times Magazine, titled "The Little White Bombshell," Margaret Talbot questioned whether this new method is the shape of abortion to come (Talbot 1999). That depends.

At the time of its occurrence, an abortion may raise many concerns in a woman's mind. She may worry about disapproval by her family or friends, her partner's reaction, or not being able to have another child or to become a mother. A woman may also feel anger toward her sex partner for not using an effective contraceptive or toward her parents for providing inadequate information about contraception. Intense feelings may range from guilt to relief, from being sad about aborting the fetus to being happy not to be pregnant.

The in-depth before and after interviews in the following research furnish insight into a woman's perceptions during the medical abortion process. In this qualitative study, one of the first of its kind, at least some clues, if not answers, have been provided to address what some consider to be a conundrum, a problem admitting no satisfactory answer.

Before reading this chapter, consider some common perceptions and emotions about medical abortions reported by respondents in this study: control, emotional distress, anxiety, uncertainty over efficacy, guilt, concern about long-term health effects, comfort, ambivalence, and fear. Which of these perceptions do you believe to be most common? When do you think each of these perceptions was of most concern to participants, before or after the procedure? Make a note of your answers. After discovering the correct answers in the research, look at your answers and ask yourself, on what basis were they predicated? Values? Fact? Prejudice? If you compared your judgments with those of your classmates, would they differ significantly? Do you believe your answers would have been different if the abortion procedure in question were surgical rather than medical? These are important questions to be entertained by the nation's brightest young people, many of whom could be tomorrow's researchers and all of whom will be recipients of scientific findings. After all, eventually, there may be no such thing as a conundrum.

You may find that reading the interviews of the young women in this chapter is a somewhat sobering experience. But this qualitative analysis of women's first-hand experiences with a medication-induced abortion by uniquely qualified practitioners, professors of family medicine, Fielding and Schaff and Planned-Parenthood nurse-midwife Edmunds, will expand your thinking critically. You will be better informed about abortion in general and the differences between surgical and medical abortions in particular. And, you can congratulate yourself, having read an offering that makes a valuable contribution to the literature.

Women base their decision to have an abortion on their current life setting, even though having an abortion may conflict with their moral or religious beliefs. Researchers who conducted in-depth interviews with women with unwanted pregnancies

210

found that the decision whether to have a surgical abortion or carry a pregnancy to term was based more on practical and personal considerations than on political and ethical arguments about abortion.[1] A study of Puerto Rican women who had decided to have an abortion revealed that women integrated their decisions with other parts of their lives and considered how their lives and relationships might change if they did not have an abortion.[2] These women sought to maintain their current identities, preserve their emotional and physical health, cope with the threat of abandonment by their partners after giving birth and, for women whose partner wanted them to have a baby, resist male control. A study of American women reported that upon deciding to have an abortion, women expressed feelings of developing a new self, coming to terms with their bodies and using contraception, and adjusting to shifting personal relationships.[3]

Several studies have examined women's preferences for medical versus surgical abortion. One article reviewed 12 published studies in which respondents were offered a choice of techniques and found that 60-70 percent of patients chose the medical procedure.[4] The most common reasons women gave for selecting medical abortion were that the procedure offered greater privacy and autonomy, was less invasive and was more natural than surgery. A study that demonstrated the psychological safety of medical abortion also found that younger women in this study were more likely to select a surgical procedure than older women. Overall, the reasons most women listed as "very important" when deciding to have a medical abortion were the timing (the option to have the abortion before seven weeks' gestation, which is thought by most practitioners to be too early for a surgical abortion), privacy and fear of surgery.[5] An additional study found that women chose mifepristone with home misoprostol to avoid surgery, because of the perceived naturalness of the procedure and for its privacy.[6]

Only one qualitative study exists on women's views about mifepristone followed by misoprostol versus vacuum aspiration. The researchers conducted eight focus groups at family planning clinics in three major cities, comprising 73 women who were not pregnant and had not had an abortion within the previous two years. They found that women lacked information about the drugs, how they worked, the pain and expulsion process and the role of providers. The women also said that the social, personal and cultural aspects of their lives would play a role in their decision. The researchers also found that emotional problems related to the procedure would be more likely among women with little or no social support, women who were younger and less-educated (and more dependent on others), and women who were not Protestant.[7]

A secondary analysis of responses to an open-ended questionnaire among participants in a national clinical trial of mifepristone revealed that women had six clear concerns when considering an abortion procedure: side effects, privacy, avoiding surgery, control, the naturalness of the procedure and personal conflict. Nearly all women, regardless of age or educational level, experienced a strong sense of relief when the medical abortion procedure was over.[8] We develop these findings here to provide a more detailed understanding of how patients view induced abortion using mifepristone.

METHODS

Since 1996, Abortion Rights Mobilization (ARM) of New York City has funded several clinical trials of mifepristone through the University of Rochester, New York, at abortion clinics and private practices around the country. At the time we conducted our research, 3,143 women at 16 sites had participated in these national trials.

With some variations by trial, women are given 200 mg of mifepristone upon their first visit with a provider. After 1-2 days, women take 800 mcg of misoprostol at home, which women are randomly assigned to take orally or vaginally. At women's discretion, they are to return to the clinic 3-8 days after their first visit. Providers alert women to expect cramping and bleeding, and advise them about how to effectively manage these symptoms. Women also receive guidance about seeking medical care if pain and bleeding become excessive. At intake, women provide information about their demographic characteristics. They later respond to a questionnaire regarding their feelings about the medical abortion procedure, including whether they find the pain acceptable and whether they would recommend home use of misoprostol.

For our study, we recruited 43 women from a clinic affiliated with the Reproductive Health Program at the University of Rochester. We enrolled 22 women who previously had had an uncomplicated surgical abortion and 21 who had never had an abortion so that we could determine whether previous experience with a surgical abortion influenced women's perceptions of medical abortion. We excluded women if they previously had had a medical abortion, because we wanted to avoid having their experiences influence their current responses.

All of the women in our study completed a brief questionnaire prior to receiving counseling and taking mifepristone. They completed the same questionnaire at their follow-up visit to the clinic 4-8 days after taking misoprostol, before seeing the provider. The questionnaire had two open-ended questions: "What feelings or concerns are you experiencing?" and "What does having this procedure mean to you?"

We conducted in-depth interviews with 30 women either by phone or in person 1-6 weeks following their abortion, asking the same two questions from the questionnaire. We probed with additional questions unique to each interview, as needed. The interviews were recorded on cassettes and transcribed. One researcher listened to each recording and reread the interviews during the coding process. The same researcher identified important themes that emerged from the first questionnaire, the follow-up questionnaire and in-depth interviews.

We analyzed the predominant themes in women's experiences at each of the three points in time—the first visit, the follow-up visit and the in-depth interview—rather than tracking each woman's responses. Therefore, and because this study is more descriptive than causal, we present our results in the chronological order of the medical abortion procedure according to these themes.

RESULTS

Sample Characteristics

Despite a few differences, the women in our study are generally representative of those in the overall ARM trials. A larger proportion of women in our study were white (77 percent vs. 66 percent) and single (75 percent vs. 66 percent). The proportion of women finding that the level of pain associated with the procedure was acceptable was smaller in our sample than in the larger ARM sample (63 percent vs. 72 percent). The same was true for women's opinions about whether home use of misoprostol was acceptable (82 percent vs. 88 percent). However, there were no differences in their mean years of education (14) or age (26), or in the proportion agreeing that the overall mifepristone procedure was acceptable (93 percent vs. 91 percent). We found no substantive differences between the accounts of women who had had prior surgical abortions and those of women who had never had an abortion. The employment status of women in our sample is similar to that of women nationally in that most of them worked full-time.[9]

The First Visit

When women arrive at an abortion clinic, they have completed much of the difficult process of deciding to have an abortion. Though some women in our study had little difficulty making this decision, for most it was difficult. When we asked women about the feelings and concerns they were experiencing, they referred to guilt; ambivalence; anxiety and uncertainty over efficacy; cramping and pain; and wanting to avoid surgery. The following are typical remarks:

> I am torn. I feel guilty but at the same time would feel relief.
>
> *—33-year-old mother of three*

> My feelings are sad but strong that this is what I need to do. I do, however, also feel angry at myself because I am pregnant, just due to the fact of not being able to carry this pregnancy out.
>
> *—25-year-old mother of three*

The influence of psychological and sociological factors—the politicization of abortion, questions about the morality of abortion and the expectations placed on women—were at least partially displaced by a more pragmatic focus at the first visit. Women asked questions such as "Will it work?" "Will it hurt?" "Will there be any long-lasting effects?" Five women expressed concerns about how the drugs would work. One typical response from a 19-year-old childless woman was, "I am feeling nervous, scared. And I am concerned about my health and how I am going to feel afterwards."

Remarks of nine women indicated that pain was a concern. For example:

> I just want something that is not going to hurt when having an abortion.
>
> *—26-year-old mother of three*

> I am most concerned about the pain of [a medical] abortion, and about any problems it will cause between me and my partner, as he wants children more than I do.
>
> *—31-year-old childless woman*

Sixteen women said they wanted to avoid a surgical procedure. A typical statement was that of a 19-year-old childless woman who said that medical abortion sounded "a little bit more relieving [mentally] than the surgical procedure."

One woman's statement, less typical of women who expressed this concern, was much stronger:

> To avoid having a machine inserted into my uterus, I would have gone to France, if necessary.
>
> *—31-year-old childless woman*

These women's desire to avoid surgery involved wanting to maintain control, to avoid pain and physical trauma, to reduce vulnerability to judgmental clinic staff and to minimize guilt.

When we asked women what the procedure meant to them, the overarching theme—expressed by 24 women—was directly related to control. This theme had two dimensions, one related to the medical abortion procedure, the other to the impact of abortion in general in their lives. For example, one woman was delighted to have the option of medical abortion:

> This procedure means to me that a woman's decision about her body can finally happen, that a woman finally has more options that were not available before.
>
> —*22-year-old childless woman*

She went on to say that taking mifepristone was both mentally and physically easier on her because its result was more like having a period than an abortion.

Younger women without children primarily expressed a need to maintain control over their future:

> I also have dreams and goals in my future that I can't accomplish if I had a baby.
>
> —*20-year-old childless woman*

The comments of another woman make it clear that abortion often is a difficult decision because women have to weigh their own interests against what is expected of them, as society still views motherhood as women's central role:

> I've made a mistake by being pregnant at the wrong time in my life. Hopefully, this will give me the opportunity to continue with my studies and pursue my career. I do want to have children in the future.
>
> —*27-year-old woman without children*

Because this woman did not participate in the in-depth interview, we do not know what she meant by a "mistake." Her declaration that she intends to have children in the future may indicate a genuine desire or an attempt to demonstrate that she is not rejecting motherhood.

By contrast, older women with children focused more on maintaining control in terms of their current families. One woman talked about "not having to worry about the responsibility of bringing another child into my life right now." She explained:

> I wish things could have been different. I do feel terrible, but financially and economically, I can't have three kids.
>
> —*29-year-old mother of two*

She said that her life was comfortable and she was afraid that if she had another child, she would have to go on welfare. Another woman, who could not afford day care, was concerned that a fourth child would jeopardize her job. She said that having an abortion means:

> I can go on with my life, not have to worry about another mouth to feed. I have no support from the father of this child. He [already] has one child with me, and I do not get support [for] her.
>
> —*33-year-old single mother of three*

The Follow-Up Visit

Women's responses at their follow-up visit 4-8 days after taking mifepristone revealed greater psychological comfort than their replies to the initial questionnaire. Nine women expressed relief. One woman who had had positive feelings on the first day also had felt uncertain about the outcome. At her follow-up visit, she reported:

> Now that the experience is over, I feel relieved. The scariest part of the whole thing was not really knowing what to expect from my body. Everything went smoothly. I did experience a lot of pain for about five hours, but that was it.
>
> —*23-year-old childless woman*

Other women felt both relief and guilt at their follow-up visit, or intimated that they might feel sad later on:

> I am relieved that it is over with. The cramping was the worst part of it. I don't really feel sad. I guess it hasn't really hit me yet. I know in my heart that this was the best thing for me to do.
>
> —*19-year-old childless woman*

Still, eight women were eager to receive medical confirmation that everything was fine:

> I'm relieved that this procedure, assuming it worked, was so relatively uncomplicated and painless. My only concern is that it will not have been successful.
>
> —*31-year-old childless woman*

This statement illustrates the influence that medical providers have, as some women do not recognize or believe that their symptoms are real and think that they are no longer pregnant until a clinician has rendered a diagnosis. Even though a woman may have experienced cramping and bleeding, she cannot know for certain that her abortion is complete until a provider performs either a sonogram or a hormonal pregnancy test.

Five women were concerned about whether there would be any long-term health effects. A 29-year-old woman with one child was concerned about "any side effects that can happen to a pregnancy I plan some time down the road." She expressed this concern again during her in-depth interview, even though she said that the clinic staff had answered all of her questions about long-term effects clearly. Similarly, an 18-year-old woman without children said, "I'm wondering, since it is a study drug, if there will be some kind of side effect that no one could know until I'm 60 years old or something."

Control over their lives remained a major theme of women's responses to the question of what having this procedure meant to them. Nine women spoke about control. A 38-year-old mother said that if the procedure is effective, "it will have allowed me to continue to focus on my two children, ages six and nine." Other women were less concrete in their response, like the 23-year-old mother of two who asserted that having the procedure means "I have a chance to do whatever it takes to make sure I don't have to go through this again . . . I will be more careful."

But still others were more pragmatic:

It means I didn't miss much work and I didn't have to explain to anyone what I was doing or why I was gone.

—31-year-old mother of one

In-Depth Interview

The interviews provide much better insight into women's experiences, not only because they were more personal and took place at a time convenient to the women, but also because they took place 1-6 weeks after their abortion, giving women time to return to their daily lives and reflect on how their abortion influenced their lives. Two women—a 33-year-old mother and a 19-year-old childless woman—who had expressed guilt in their questionnaire responses now expressed positive feelings about their decision. Three other women expressed concerns similar to those of a college senior who was preparing for a career in theater:

I really don't know if it has to do with the actual abortion pills that I took, but the most feelings and concerns I'm having right now are of getting pregnant again.

—22-year-old childless woman

Long-term health effects continued to concern eight women. This remark is illustrative:

Well my concern now, at this point, is I'm wondering if, since it's a test, if there is going to be any long-term effects that they had no way of knowing about.

—18-year-old childless woman

Two women wondered about the baby they would have had. One of them, lowering her voice and obviously feeling a loss, said:

Well, sometimes you wonder what this life would've been—who he or she [would have been], what kind of person, what they would have looked like.

—41-year-old childless woman

Some women were concerned about the morality of their decision, including one divorced woman who felt very irresponsible and had been concerned about her decision since the day she took the mifepristone:

There's always, always going to be just a struggle, I think, with the whole moral issue. And that will always be there, I'm sure, for the rest of my life. And I'll just have to, you know, work on that myself.

—38-year-old mother of two

Another woman said that she had not wanted to get pregnant and felt that she had not taken adequate precautions. She had not told her family about the abortion and had had to lie about her doctor visits and feeling sick:

I don't regret having to do it. I mean there are times when I get upset and I think, you know, I killed a baby, but at the same time it wasn't really a child. And I think people should be allowed to have an abortion if they so choose without someone directing negative feelings about it.

—22-year-old childless woman

The themes that were most prominent in the questionnaires—the importance of continuing school, devoting resources to current families and avoiding surgery—were also common in the in-depth interviews. Women referred to these issues 27 times. Given their limited time and financial and emotional resources, women saw limiting the number of children they had as an important way to preserve their family's quality of life. One woman summed up this view as follows:

The day I found out that I was pregnant it was like everything came to me. . . . I had plans to go to school. . . . I don't have health insurance. My husband don't have either. . . . I'm giving everything I can to my daughter.

—28-year-old mother of one

Having an Abortion at Home

Through our interviews, we investigated whether women felt comfortable taking misoprostol at home. Eighteen women said that being at home was a comfortable experience, even though they had cramping and nausea. (Despite this, compared with the ARM sample, somewhat smaller proportions of women in this sample agreed that pain and the home use of misoprostol were acceptable.) For example, one woman was home alone and prepared for her at-home abortion by stocking up on food and magazines to make the process easier while she watched television. By contrast, another woman recounted a less-private experience:

> I was in my own home. I wasn't in a hospital bed or anything. . . . I was with my family. . . . My ex was there with me. My mom was there. My sister was, but she just thought I was just sick. And my dad was at work. . . . I had friends calling.
>
> —*22-year-old childless woman*

Even among women who said they experienced a significant amount of pain, having their abortion at home was manageable, as the following cases illustrate:

> I mean, it was painful, but that's to be expected. . . . I don't think it was really a terrible, terrible experience. You know what I mean. I didn't die or [have] anything major happen. . . . I was expecting like my worst period, and this was just like phenomenal . . . for three hours . . . I took two more pain killers, and I went back to bed.
>
> —*28-year-old childless woman*

Avoiding Surgery

Women's reports of a relatively comfortable experience of medical abortion stood in strong contrast to reports of 10 women who previously had had a surgical procedure or had heard accounts of friends' surgical procedures. The theme of wanting to avoid surgery surfaced many times throughout the questionnaire responses and interviews. Presumably, these experiences would have created an additional incentive for these women to try something other than a surgical abortion. Many women said something similar to the following statement:

> I was so thankful that there was an alternative to having a surgical abortion. And that was . . . my biggest concern.
>
> —*23-year-old childless woman*

Women reported several reasons for this attitude, including fear of pain and of the procedure's invasiveness and the feeling that surgical abortion patients are moved along a production line or are judged by clinic staff. One woman told us what her best friend had told her about her abortion when the latter was 27 years old:

> She was told that she should know better at this point . . . [than] to get pregnant and that, as she put it, they insert the scraper or vacuum tube or something inside of you, and it's like having your soul scraped. And she said that the doctor was just kind of moralistic and cold.
>
> —*31-year-old childless woman*

Similarly, a 22-year-old childless woman recalled that when a friend's sister had an abortion at age 16, "she said it was excruciating."

Images like these are passed on not only through families and friends, but also through schools. Two women described how abortion was presented to them in class. One said:

> I can still see images in my head from sophomore year [in health class], when they showed us the video on abortion. And they showed them sucking the baby out and all that stuff, and . . . it was just an awful, horrible video of . . . badly performed abortions, surgically done.
>
> —*18-year-old childless woman*

A few women who had had a surgical abortion gave accounts of the impersonality of abortion clinics:

> They kind of herded you in like cattle, and there were like five or six women sitting in the same room. And then one by one you got called in and you could hear the screaming in the other room. It was like the fear of the unknown; it was just horrible. I mean, I know it's not that bad anymore for surgical procedures, but that was my thought [when I was deciding what to do].
>
> —*29-year-old mother of two*

DISCUSSION

This study confirms past findings that some women choose medical abortion for its naturalness, for the privacy it affords and to avoid the perceived pain and trauma of surgery. There is evidence that women's experience of pain associated with medical abortion is partially related to their reproductive history. One clinical trial showed that women who had had one or more live births were 2.7 times more likely to find the pain associated with a medical abortion acceptable than women who had not given birth.[10] For most women, emotional distress was most intense at the first visit, decreased by the time of their follow-up visit and remained low at their in-depth interview.

Throughout the interviews, personal control was the most common theme that emerged from women's responses. Contrary to abortion opponents' criticism that women who have abortions are selfish for denying their motherhood role, most of the women in our sample either planned to have or already had one or more children. Control is perhaps most acute for poorer women. The reality is that public policy subjects poor women to a double bind. On one hand, they are criticized for being on welfare, which has become more difficult to qualify for and is limited to five years. On the other hand, young women from poor backgrounds who have children are more likely to remain trapped in poverty than those who do not have children.[11] This is illustrated by the women who said that having an abortion would allow them to fulfill their goals. If a woman's education is curtailed because she carried an unwanted pregnancy, she could risk not only her future, but the future of her children, who would be less likely to be prepared emotionally, occupationally and financially to contribute to society.

Many women also are in a precarious position as the result of the feminization of poverty over the last 30 years, illustrated by two women who cited financial reasons for not being able to have another child. Census data clearly show that the proportion of women who are the sole heads of households is rising[12] and that women are poorer than men.[13] Women's median income in 1998 constant dollars was only 54 percent of men's median income.[14] Being the sole head of a household is a heavy burden for women, as many do not receive child support from their former partners.

The appeal of medical abortion for women who want to maintain personal control has several implications for clinicians and counselors. Providers need to account for the amount of time needed for counseling women about medical abortion, which generally takes more time than counseling about surgical abortion because women need to know how to take misoprostol and what to expect thereafter. In addition, eliciting from women whether they are concerned about control may be a way for clinicians to identify women who are appropriate candidates for medical abortion. Our experience indicates that with adequate information, women often select the abortion procedure most appropriate for them. Furthermore, we have learned that women who indicate that they want more control are more likely to follow through with the regimen, thus increasing the odds of a positive outcome.

Our findings are in concert with those of a study that found that only 5 percent of women experience strong guilt about having an abortion.[15] However, this is not to say that psychological and sociological factors do not play a role in making this decision difficult. For example, the 22-year-old woman who said she sometimes thought about how she had "killed a baby" said others should not direct negative feelings toward women who have an abortion. Her statement and use of the term "baby" illustrate that some women perceive that society disapproves of their decision to have an abortion. Women's use of the term "baby" was often related to feelings of guilt or conflict, possibly because the notion that life begins at the moment of conception has been emphasized by several religious denominations and strongly proclaimed by anti-abortion groups.

But in spite of some women's expressions of guilt, at their first visit to the clinic, their concerns were related less to their moral or religious beliefs than to the practical considerations of pain, side effects and efficacy. Although there have been no scientific studies of the long-term effects of mifepristone abortion, no patients over the last 13 years have reported long-term effects.

It occurred to us only after we had reviewed the interviews in detail that women's concerns about side effects may be similar to those experienced by patients undergoing other medical or surgical procedures. Thus, while some anxiety is related to the moral and political issues surrounding abortion, these may be less influential than previously thought.

Women's negative comments about surgical abortion facilities and providers may reflect the realities of current abortion practice or the influence of anti-abortion media campaigns that portray abortion providers negatively. Although these accounts could be based on women's experiences with insensitive staff, they could also reflect the reality of crowded facilities, given the shortage of clinics and providers around the country. Many clinics can perform abortions only on days when a physician, possibly one who must travel from out of town, is present.

Although we cannot generalize our findings to all women who have medical abortions, we conclude that clinicians could ease the intense feelings of many patients at their first visit by explaining that some of their feelings may be related to the uncertainties that any medical procedure poses. Clinicians should also reemphasize at the follow-up visit that there are no long-term health effects related to abortion.

Introduction Reference

Talbot, M. (1999, July 11). "The Little White Bombshell." *New York Times Magazine*, pp. 38–43, 48, 61–63.

References

1. Maloy K and Patterson MJ, *Birth or Abortion? Private Struggles in a Political World*, New York: Plenum Press, 1992.
2. Peterman JP, *Telling Their Stories: Puerto Rican Women and Abortion*, Boulder, CO: Westview Press, 1996, pp. 13–25.

3. Kushner E, *Experiencing Abortion: A Weaving of Women's Words,* New York: Haworth Park Press, 1997.

4. Winikoff B, Acceptability of medical abortion in early pregnancy, *Family Planning Perspectives,* 1995, 27(4): 142–148.

5. Henshaw R et al., Psychological responses following medical abortion (using mifepristone and gemeprost) and surgical vacuum aspiration: A patient-centered, partially randomized prospective study, *Acta Obstetricia et Gynecologica Scandinavica,* 1994, 73(10): 812–818.

6. Elul B et al., In-depth interviews with medical abortion clients: thoughts on the method and home administration of misoprostol, *Journal of the American Medical Women's Association,* 2000, 55(Suppl. 3): 169–172.

7. Castle MA et al., Listening and learning from women about mifepristone: Implications for counseling and health education, *Women's Health Issues,* 1995, 5(3): 130–138.

8. Fielding SL and Fuller LL, *The influence of race and educational level on women's perceptions in a clinical trial of mifepristone (RU-486),* Rochester, NY: University of Rochester, 2001.

9. Stevens LK, Register CA and Sessions DN, The abortion decision: A qualitative approach, *Social Indicators Research,* 1992, 27(4): 327–344.

10. Schaff EA et al., Vaginal misoprostol administered 1, 2, or 3 days after mifepristone for early abortion: a randomized trial, *Journal of the American Medical Association,* 2000, 284(15): 1948–1953.

11. Barber JS, Axinn WG and Thornton A, Unwanted childbearing, health, and mother-child relationships, *Journal of Health and Social Behavior,* 1999, 40(3): 231–257.

12. U.S. Bureau of the Census, *Historical Poverty Tables, 2000,* http://www.census.gov/hhes/poverty/histpov/hstpov4.html, Table 4.

13. U.S. Bureau of the Census, *HH-1 Households by Type: 1940 to Present, 2001,* http://www.census.gov/population/socdemo/hh-fam/tabHH-1.txt.

14. U.S. Bureau of the Census, *Statistical Abstract of the United States: 2000,* Washington, DC: U.S. Government Printing Office, 2000, Table. 751.

15. Fielding SL and Fuller LL,, 2001, op. cit. (see reference 8).

Chapter 26
Community
Risk, Identity, and Love in the Age of AIDS

Judith Levine

The type of "love" in the age of AIDS highlighted in this offering may surprise you. In her controversial book, Harmful to Minors: The Perils of Protecting Children from Sex, *Judith Levine provides prescriptions for how adults might do better in guiding children toward "loving well," meaning safely, pleasurably, and with respect for others and themselves. But, the love featured in this chapter is about* agape *love, a Greek word meaning "selfless love."*

Levine is a journalist of national renown whose lively writing about sex, gender, and families has spanned two decades. She is well-qualified to report on the success of the sexuality education and HIV prevention programs she investigated in the Minneapolis and St. Paul areas. Do not expect academic "program evaluations," however, from this hands-on "beat-reporter." She uses interviews with young people and their parents, stories drawn from today's headlines, as well as visits to classrooms and clinics to inform her writing. And, in the process she will inform your opinion. Chronicling the lives of the gay, lesbian, bisexual, and homeless youth in the Twin Cities, she poignantly portrays a community of caring adults who embody the essence of agape love in their programs and practice.

Levine's chapter promises to challenge your critical thinking. On the one hand, it may raise anxieties, on the other, it may provoke questions about conflicting views. In either case, you will be among friends—that large group of people who admit that they do not yet have all the answers about sex or about agape love.

"But what about AIDS?" The question arises immediately, almost every time I hazard the opinion that sex is not harmful to minors. Often it is not a question at all but a kind of preemptive statement: as long as there is AIDS, there cannot be adolescent sex. In 1981, when only gay men and their friends knew about the incipient epidemic, "chastity education" was a laughingstock. But as soon as HIV hit the cover of *Newsweek*, not far behind was the remarkable popular consensus that no-sex was the best thing to teach and the best thing for teens to practice. Just when mass public education about transmission, condoms, and nonpenetrative forms of sex was most crucial, AIDS became the rationale for not talking about sex. "The right wing's demand to 'teach' abstinence created the next generation's paradox," wrote Cindy Patton in her searing *Fatal Advice: How Safe-Sex Education Went Wrong.* "[E]quating 'no sex' and safe sex suggests that no sex is safe."[1]

That paradox did not yield mass abstention. Sex continued more or less unabated, but instead of safely, many youths did it ignorant of the difference between those acts that abetted HIV transmission, those that were relatively safer, and those that virtually precluded transmission. And exactly as the militant AIDS activist group ACT UP warned, silence has equaled death. By the mid-1990s, a young person was being infected with HIV every hour of every day.[2] And while AIDS deaths dropped in the general U.S. population,[3] the disease became the leading cause of mortality for people ages twenty-five to forty-four, many of whom had likely contracted the virus in their teens.[4]

If abstinence is not the key, what is? Public-health experts have long observed that the populations hit hardest by AIDS overlap in predictable ways with those otherwise afflicted by poor health, education, or housing—and a poor standing in America's social hierarchies. Infection rates have fallen dramatically among adult men who have sex with men, especially white, middle-class, out gay men.[5] Nevertheless, it was estimated in the 1990s that 20 to 30 percent of gay youths would be infected by their thirtieth birthday.[6] Of all HIV-infected American youths in 1998, 63 percent were black.[7] And a survey of young, gay men of color conducted in six major cities by the National Centers for Disease Control from 1998 to 2000 revealed an even more astonishing figure: almost a third of gay black men in their twenties are HIV positive.[8]

People in extremis, as usual, are at more extreme risk. Runaway teens show infection rates as high as 10 percent.[9] Half of New York City's people with HIV in the 1990s were intravenous drug users,[10] many of whom were young and marginally housed or employed.

These patterns are even more baldly visible globally. For instance, as the disease has ravaged Africa and steadily crept over South Asia, the United Nations reports that the near-total sexual, social, and economic abjection of women in those regions is translating into catastrophic rates of HIV infection and AIDS deaths among them.[11] The 1997 International AIDS Conference had predicted such dire developments. "Social norms and structural factors" exert a major impact on the spread and containment of the epidemic, the conferees concluded, advising policymakers to start paying more attention to such factors.[12]

Risk, in other words, is like sex itself: it is made up of acts that are given meaning and relative gravity by social context. Without basic changes in the most encompassing of those contexts (those "structural factors" such as economic, racial, and gender inequality), the AIDS plague will not end. Stagnant social structures are the reason the relatively wealthy, middle-class, urban, gay white male populations of the United States were able to stem the spread of the disease relatively quickly in the 1980s and why today many seropositive men in those communities are living longer, healthier lives with the help of expensive drugs and medical care. It's also why the same thing has not happened among poor people of color, women, and drug addicts in America and Eastern Europe. In Africa, countries already decimated by war and famine now watch their populations stagger while international lawyers adjudicate their "rights" to buy cheaper generic versions of exorbitantly expensive AIDS drugs patented in the global North.

The good news is that social norms even within these stubborn structures can change—if people feel it's in their interest to change and if what they're changing to isn't vastly more onerous than what they are used to doing. The failure of abstinence education may prove less about the intransigence of young people's mores (these can turn on an advertiser-flipped coin) than about the plain fact that sex is more appealing than abstinence. Abstaining promises a definite negative (you don't have sex, and you don't get pregnant or sick) in place of a positive linked only to a possible negative (you do have sex, and you may not get pregnant or sick).

The norm of safe sex has taken hold most firmly where it has represented not a wholesale reversal of already established norms but rather a variation on those norms. Some early gay AIDS activists such as Larry Kramer and Michelangelo Signorelli have since repented of their earlier sexual libertarianism and indicted the "promiscuity" of gay men for their own demise. But other activist-intellectuals such as Douglas Crimp and Jeffrey Weeks argue far more persuasively that the inventive public sexual culture that defined the liberationist gay community also provided the motherlode of techniques from which safe sex was mined and the sexual frankness and intimate networks that got the word out. Similarly, AIDS-prevention workers in distressed communities have adopted the strategy of "harm reduction":

they don't try to make drug addicts stop using before getting help, for instance (though they offer treatment when possible). Instead, they promote needle sterilization and clean-needle exchange programs so that intravenous users won't share dirty needles, one of the main transmitters of HIV.

Successful AIDS prevention, then, must be based on at least two principles: It must recognize the urgency of the problem of HIV and the exigencies, both personal and structural, of the people it is targeting. And it must respect their social norms: their identities, values, and desires, expressed in the relationships between individuals and within communities.

To witness sexuality education and HIV prevention where these principles are taken intelligently, creatively, and passionately to heart, I traveled in the spring of 1998 to Minneapolis and St. Paul, Minnesota, where the imperiled yet flourishing communities of gay, lesbian, bisexual, and homeless youths are the recipients of some extraordinary adult care and attention.[13]

As communities go, the Twin Cities are hardly the worst place to be young, gay, homeless, or at risk of dropping out, having a baby, getting HIV, or otherwise losing your way. A slow-moving, leafy metropolis of manageable size, with a history of progressive politics and philanthropy, a well-funded network of social service agencies, a university that has done groundbreaking work on sexuality and AIDS, and a cottage industry of "recovery" facilities, the Twin Cities are also blessed with a committed cadre of gay and lesbian public-health and youth workers. These people are determined to make growing up gay happier and safer for this generation than it was for theirs.

Not everything is perfect in the Twin Cities, of course. There aren't enough beds for homeless kids, for instance. As elsewhere, some of the neediest clients slip through the cracks: by definition runaways and street kids are fliers by night. The majority of youth and AIDS professionals in the Twin Cities are male, white, educated, healthy, and handsome, whereas many of their clients meet few of the above descriptions. State policymakers don't always appear to be on the same page as the workers on the ground. For instance, during the snack break of a student-taught HIV-prevention class run by a drop-in agency for homeless youth called Project Offstreets, the young staffer told me her program was about to lose its funding. Why? Because youth AIDS cases were diminishing in the Twin Cities. "Well duh-uh," commented the frustrated worker. "Maybe prevention is working."

If AIDS prevention is working, why is it? How are the strategies developed over twenty years by progressive grassroots gay and lesbian organizers and public-health educators being applied? What lessons can we take from the Twin Cities about sex and safe-sex education as part of young people's lives?

Meet People Where They Are: Identity and Exigency

Out-of-the-closet gay youths have one thing going for them. Whereas abstinence-only sex education gives straight kids the message that sex is not a seminal part of adolescence, when a kid announces his identity in sexual terms, the people around him have no choice but to deal with him as a sexual person. That's both a blessing and a curse.

Coming out can give a kid a secure affiliation, a way to fit into the scheme of things. But the evil twin of affiliation is conformity, and the rigidly homophobic monoculture of the average high school hallway dictates that "queers" be punished—that they be reminded continually that they don't fit anywhere in the scheme. Some states, with Minnesota in the lead, have instituted legal antiharassment policies and student-faculty gay-straight alliances throughout the public schools. Nevertheless, facing ostracism and violence, gay students drop out at high rates.

Family life can be awful for a homosexual child, too. Youth who come out meet with parental grief, confusion, denial, or rage so hot that, for everyone involved, the prospect of the child eating from dumpsters and sleeping under bridges may be preferable to coexisting under the same roof. "My brother says to my mom, 'You have a faggot-ass son,'" said Stephen Graham, a twenty-year-old African American gay activist, recalling his early teens. He was speaking at a sexuality-education conference for teachers run by the young denizens of District 202, Minneapolis's drop-in center run "by and for gay, lesbian, bi, and transgendered youth." "My mom just said to me, 'I can't agree with it. I can't love you.'" Stephen's pastor also branded him a sinner and banished him from the church. The boy ended up in state institutions, in squats, and crashing at friends' places throughout much of his adolescence.

Family hostility, in fact, is a leading cause of homelessness among gay youth. Of 150 youngsters surveyed in 1997 at District 202, 40 percent said they had been homeless at some time.[14] In cities nationwide, 25 to 40 percent of homeless youth identify themselves as gay or lesbian.[15] And what they do when they leave home isn't always the safest things. "Parents' abandonment or overt rejection of homosexual adolescents is partially responsible for the dramatic rise of teen male prostitution in the United States," wrote adolescent public-health doctors Martha Sturdevant and Gary Remafedi in a review of the special health needs of homosexual youth.[16] If you're fourteen and can't get a worker's permit or even a driver's license, sex is one of the few services you've got to offer on the labor market. "This may be the most politically unsavvy thing I can say," averred Paul Thoemke, Offstreets' gay lesbian bisexual transsexual (GLBT) case manager. "But I sometimes think the greatest risk for these kids is their families."

It is hardly surprising that among gay and lesbian youth drug and alcohol use is high,[17] and while getting high does not cause people to take risks, people tend to do a number of dangerous and self-destructive things at the same time.[18] Despair plus disinhibition can equal death, as the disproportionate number of gay and lesbian kids in the suicide statistics suggests.[19]

A gay identity can present other, less obvious troubles in growing up and shaping a self. A straight kid's straightness does not box his identity in; he is straight, yes, but mostly he's seen as African American or Filipino or Jewish, a jock or a gangsta or a nerd. But a gay kid is defined by what he is not: he is not straight. That makes it hard even for a securely gay or lesbian teen to express his or her individuality. "Coming out gives kids the freedom to express and explore their sexuality," said Ed Kegle, a youth worker at District 202. "But it's also limiting, because that's the only way other people see you, as 'that little fag' or 'that little dyke.'" A sixteen-year-old lesbian activist summed up the dilemma: "I love being queer," she told me, running a hand through her cherry-red crew cut. "But sometimes I just wanna be Jenny, not Queer Jenny."

Many kids may feel that a gay identity describes them no more accurately than the names they inherited from the communities that expelled them. In one study of seventh- to twelfth-graders in Minneapolis, more than 10 percent said they were unsure of their sexual orientation.[20] "I meet a lot more kids who say they're bi, or just 'sexual,' not homo or hetero," said Rob Yaeger, the high-wattage risk-reduction educator for the community-based Minnesota AIDS Project and member of the Safer Sex Sluts. Courie Parker, a District 202 youth who identifies herself as bisexual, described her orientation this way: "There are the consonants and the vowels—a, e, i, o, u, and sometimes y. That's me: *sometimes y.*'"

The dangers of coming out and teens' disinclination to join one sexual "team" or another can flummox those who are trying to deliver culturally specific or community-based safe-sex education to them. This is especially true when the adults, like those in Minneapolis, come from strongly gay-identified politics, social circles, and even career paths.

One way everyone seems to have dealt with this fluidity of identity is to classify it as an "identity," too. In the lengthening train of labels attached to "queer" youth, GLBTQ, the Q stands not for "queer" but for "questioning." In a sense, it's a description that could fit almost every teenager.

Of course, sexuality is not the only way that people identify themselves. Even if their parents may sometimes regard them as foundlings, queer youngsters are not born in some independent offshore Queer Nation and imported to Boston's Italian American South Side or Utah's Mormon Salt Lake City. Nor do all kids reject their religious or ethnic communities of origin, even when some people in those communities reject them. The best safe-sex education takes into account the complex interplay of identities and loyalties in any given person or group.

In the African American community of north Minneapolis, a group of young women and men calling themselves the Check Yo'self Crew got started producing one poster with the slogans "Check yo'self before you wreck yo'self," "Educate your mind, protect your body," and "No parachute, no jump" emblazoned over a photo of a bunch of hip-looking black kids. After their poster won an award, they got grants to put up six billboards of the same image and message, and then they hunkered down in the neighborhood, channeling gangs' energy into HIV peer education and establishing a free condom source on every block. A similar project was later undertaken in a Latino community in town.

Some of the smartest and most moving culturally specific HIV/AIDS youth work in the Twin Cities is masterminded by the Minnesota American Indian Task Force. Its Director is Sharon Day, a forty-six-year-old Ojibwa Indian, out lesbian, mother of two, and custodial grandmother of one. "We need to understand what has allowed us native people to survive since time began," Day told me in a voice as soft and tough as chamois. Her theater work began with that and related questions. "If the birth rate is an indication of the frequency of the sex act," she reasoned, Native Americans' high birth rate "shows we haven't gotten so depressed that we've lost that ability to be sexual. Why is that?" Western psychological models don't explain it. Even if parents are alcoholic or otherwise "dysfunctional," Native American children like herself have survived intact by gleaning intimacy and security from the extended family and the wider community. In directing the task force's youth theater troupe, which travels to community centers, schools, and reservations statewide, doing AIDS-awareness plays, Day said, "We are trying to recapture those traditions and expressions that have kept our people emotionally and sexually healthy."

My Grandmother's Love, written by Day in collaboration with the young actors, is one part family soap opera, one part Native American vision quest, one part safe-sex agit-prop political propaganda skit. It opens with four boys beating one large drum and chanting the traditional men's songs in their high children's voices. Then it moves to short reminiscences about grandmothers, whose photos are projected onto a large screen. "She's a good cook, her hair is all black, no gray," one boy says. "She's a basic grandma." The main story concerns a gay college boy (played by an androgynous fourteen-year-old girl) who returns home to tell his family he is HIV positive. "You little faggot!" the father explodes, pounding his fist on the kitchen table. Scared and depressed, the young man withdraws. But he is sustained, and finally restored, by his grandmother's unconditional love and a dream-vision of running to safety. In the final scene, the group chants his vision—"I have been to the brink, to the rim of the canyon. I've looked over the edge. It's not so scary to me anymore"—and asks the audience to pray for the ill. Family, spirituality, community, said Day: "This is what has enabled native people to survive, gay or straight."

By the same token, Day knows that as much as sex education must focus on specific cultural beliefs and practices, it must also be catholic enough to accommodate young people who fall victim to those same beliefs and practices. Stephen Graham, the gay boy rejected by his pastor, for instance, was lucky to find another African American church whose dogma and liturgy resembled his old congregation's, with the major difference that this one embraced him, sexuality and all. Other gay youth have felt driven more radically from their faith communities by antagonism toward homosexuality, so they've had to find other sources to satisfy their spiritual needs. In the 1997 District 202 survey, almost every respondent filled in the blank under religious affiliation. But the largest single group called themselves Pagan.

Don't Box People In: The "Risk-Group" Fallacy

Identities are multiple. Their facets sometimes harmonize; at other times they are dissonant. In AIDS prevention, the challenge is to find people where they affiliate and speak to their sense of belonging for the purpose of instilling and reinforcing safe-sex values and habits. But the construction of categories can also be perilous. Indeed, the error (some say the fatal error) of AIDS prevention over the past two decades has been its strategy of labeling groups of people, not as potentially powerful allies in fighting the disease, but as collections of mutually antagonistic virus-carrying harm-spreaders, or "risk groups."

The first decade of public-health AIDS education told us there were two kinds of people in the world of AIDS. The "high-risk groups" included gay men, Haitian immigrants, and intravenous drug users and their sex partners and babies. These people used to be called AIDS victims but were actually thought of as AIDS victimizers. In the "low- or no-risk groups" were suburban teens, heterosexuals, white Yuppies—as Patton put it, the people who qualified as bona fide "citizens." Prevention for the "low-risk" folks meant avoiding the poisonous populations, first, by steering clear of people who looked suspicious and, second, by practicing "partner selection": interrogating potential partners for their possible inclusion or interaction with "high-risk" persons and rejecting those who might be "unsafe" lovers.[21] Teens did not have to perform this discretionary process. They were instructed to say no to everyone.

The concept of the risk group helped neither presumptive group. The people supposedly inside it were either stigmatized (and neglected by policymakers) for their allegedly self-destructive lifestyles or ignored. Some of those relegated to this status used it as a powerful political motivator—ACT UP emerged from gay men's rage at being excluded as legitimate recipients of health care resources. For others, however, being branded "at risk" only induced fatalism. The idea that one is likely to die simply by virtue of being a certain kind of person does not concentrate the mind wonderfully on life-saving strategies. And for already hurt people, this new denigration only compounded hopelessness. "Individuals who have been at high risk," like kids who have been abused, lived on the streets, or turned tricks, "are likely to see themselves as at risk of getting HIV," said Gary Remafedi, Director of the University of Minnesota's Youth & AIDS Project. "Or they'll say, 'I'm gay. It's inevitable I'm gonna die. So what?'" According to Jeffrey Escoffier, a New York public educator, sociologist, and AIDS activist, research shows that gay men who learn that all gay-associated sex, including fellatio, is equally fatal come to believe they are doomed, so they engage in more of the riskiest behaviors. In one San Francisco survey of seventeen- to nineteen-year-old men who have sex with men, 28 percent had recently had unprotected anal sex, the behavior carrying the highest risk for HIV transmission;[22] in a six-city study of young gay men of color, almost half had done so in the preceding six months.[23]

For people both "inside" and "outside," however, the risk-group theory had a profound flaw: *there is no such thing as a discrete social-sexual population.* No group is an island; all risk is shared, potentially, with a limitless universe of partners. While in America most people travel in social ruts, apart from other races and classes, not even the most insular, cautious people always stay in those ruts. Drug users don't congregate only in crack houses; they also frequent trendy nightclubs. And a man who has unprotected sex with a seropositive teenage hustler in a downtown city park may have sex the next day with a guy he knows from a neighborhood bar, and that guy will have sex with his middle-class suburban wife the next.

One way to circumvent the hazards of the risk-group assumption, while being realistic about the fact that it's been drummed into everybody's head, is to use it to get people's attention, then redirect their thinking. Rather than choosing or rejecting certain people or "kinds" of people, specific *behaviors* can be rejected. As a pamphlet displayed with a couple dozen others on District 202's wall put it: "Being young and gay does NOT have to mean being at risk for HIV & AIDS. . . . But being unsafe does."

Taking a kernel of wisdom from the "risk-group" concept—that individuals within certain social or sexual groups may more commonly engage in behaviors that can transmit HIV—and tempering it with the understanding of the fluidity of communities and individual diversity within them, AIDS-prevention professionals have lately conceived the notion of "target populations." These comprise not people who are "by nature" risk-prone but those who live in situations of high risk, say, in a neighborhood or social circle a large number of whose members are seropositive. Most important, educators identify these populations by sexual behavior: not by how they dress, where they drink, or what they call themselves, but by what acts they do. MSM, for example, is HIV/AIDS shorthand for "men who have sex with men, a category that takes in both the Puerto Rican husband and father who lives in upper Manhattan but occasionally goes to a bar in the Bronx and has sex with a man and the teenage Anglo who dies his hair green and marches in the Castro Street Gay Pride parade in a goatee and tutu."

In Minneapolis, I watched numerous AIDS-ed workers in various settings, from off-the-cuff conversations in a scruffy city park to the makeshift stage in a Native American cultural center, from a peer-run class in a high school for returning dropouts to sex-and AIDS-ed sessions at District 202. In all of these, instructors started with the acts they believed their students might engage in, making these broadest determinations by the group's sexual or age identity or perhaps its religious or ethnic affiliation. But they assumed nothing about the specifics of any individual's predilections. A lesbian group at District 202 discussed the use of a square of latex called a dental dam that can be laid over a partner's vagina before performing cunnilingus. At the Center's conference for teachers, a quick safe-sex rap by the twenty-year-old peer educator Toyin Adebanjo reminded the audience not to forget such youth-specific contaminated-blood risks as body piercing and tattooing. At the same time, the woman addressing the young lesbians talked about contraceptive and safe-sex precautions for penile-vaginal intercourse. And a youth worker addressing fifteen-year-olds did not neglect information on the HIV transmission risks of breast feeding.

Gary Remafedi, who educates young gay men, described the balance of the main message, identity, and personal taste this way: "One message is, 'Always use condoms while you're fucking.' But that assumes that every gay man fucks. So the other message is, 'Fucking is not a fundamental part of being a gay man. Not everyone likes it. And everyone can enjoy safe sex behavior that is not intercourse.'"

Respect People's Choices as Rational

A fair number of the youngsters who find their way to Offstreets, District 202, or Remafedi's program at the university either regularly or occasionally turn to prostitution to get by. In the risk-benefit calculus of life on the street, sex is both a plus and a minus.[24] "Survival sex"—sex in trade for a bed, a shower, or a pair of shoes—may also offer some personal rewards, such as adult companionship and affirmation. And like other adult-minor sex, it is not always an interaction of utter abjection on the young person's side. "A lot of the youth don't see survival sex as prostitution," said Ludfi Noor, the easy-going Director of Offstreets' HIV education. Added Gonne (pronounced "Honnah") Asser, a young outreach worker, "This youth was talking the other day, saying, 'I was going to clubs and getting lucky. Older people wanted to have sex with me.'" Of the here-to-day-gone-tomorrow relationships between youngsters and adults, she added, "It can be a relationship that lasts a week, but to the kid, it's still a relationship."

Of course, prostitution without even that rudimentary relationship poses its own risks. Working girls (and boys) have long adopted their own health and safety practices, notably condom use. Among homeless youth, it appears that when the trick is a stranger, condom use is also the rule.[25] No educator should underestimate a young person's ability to

make informed decisions about sex. To make informed decisions, though, people need information, and some AIDS experts argue that what they need is the kind of detailed information about risk that is available throughout most of Europe but that U.S. Health Departments are reluctant to give out. Rather than listing acts as either safe or unsafe, period, so-called relative-risk data disseminated in Paris or Berlin tell you that such-and-such behavior has led to HIV transmission in a particular number of known cases in this or that country, or that findings about this other behavior are still inconclusive. Armed with such data, people can make choices about their sex lives in the same way they craft the rest of their lives: by weighing desires and rewards against dangers and unwanted consequences.

That said, there are a lot of reasons not to put on a rubber if you're a young person selling or bartering sex. Sex without a condom demands a higher price than sex with one, so taking a higher risk per trick in order to turn fewer tricks overall may feel like a reasonable business decision. (Other considerations go into the equation, too: receiving fellatio, a fairly common act of male prostitution, is of extremely low risk to the receptor. For a young woman in heterosexual sex, the opposite is true: as the giver of oral sex and the receiver of vaginal intercourse, she takes practically all the risk of HIV and other STD transmission.)[26]

A homeless kid turning a trick may not protect himself or herself for some subtler and sadder reasons as well. Such youngsters typically have been the victims of inordinate violence; "more than half have been physically abused, more than one-third sexually abused, more than one-third beaten by an intimate partner during the last year," said a report of Minneapolis's gay, lesbian, bisexual, and transgender homeless youth conducted by the Wilder Research Center in 1996.[27] About once a week, said Paul Thoemke, a girl comes into Offstreets and says she's been raped. For people who have been treated with routine cruelty, particularly by their "loved" ones, self-care can be a foreign concept. "A lot of women and girls don't see sex as a source of pleasure or their bodies as something they have control over," noted Beth Zemsky, a lesbian AIDS educator who works on gay and lesbian student issues at the University of Minnesota. Ine Vanwesenbeeck, in a study of sexual power and powerlessness among Dutch prostitutes and other young women, found that those who capitulated to johns' demands that they forgo a condom were more often younger, drug users, and immigrants and "had experienced more victimization, both in childhood and in adult life, both on and off the job." Once they'd become known as "risk takers," they were "most often visited by recalcitrant condom users."[28]

AIDS prevention for the street kids of the Twin Cities, then, means more than pressing a bundle of condoms into a hustler's tight jeans pocket. "So many of the youth I work with have been treated in such a disrespectful way, they can't respect themselves," said Youth & AIDS Project caseworker Jerry Terrell. "A third of the people I see are suicidal, a fifth are actively using chemicals, and then for the homeless youth, there's no tomorrow; everything is today. The main thing is helping them to imagine that there is a future and beginning to get a toehold in whatever that might be. HIV is at the end of a long line of other issues."

Those issues are both emotional and material. When the Wilder researchers queried homeless youth on what would really make a difference in their lives, their sights usually focused somewhere between hand and mouth. Several suggested access to a free washing machine. "I can wear dirty clothes, pants, shirts, and stuff," said one girl. "As long as I can have clean underwear, I'm okay." Under such circumstances, safe sex can be a rather abstract and distant notion. "Safety means finding a bed tonight," explained Amber Hollibaugh, former Head of the Lesbian AIDS Project at GMHC in New York. "Putting on a condom is not exactly the Number One priority."[29]

Still, risk taking should not be considered a symptom of pathology, as it so often is among teachers, adolescent psychologists, and public-health professionals. Instead, said Jeffrey Escoffier: "People are also doing a rational assessment of their environments. They tally the odds." On the street, kids know their lives are by definition unsafe, that they can't eliminate all risk. So the task is to figure out the route of greatest reward—financial, practical, emotional—with the least endangerment along the way. It is the job of prevention workers to understand that calculus, too, and help young people incrementally refigure the emotional and material factors so that they can make more self-protective decisions in their sexual behavior and stick to them. In "sex education" with his young hustlers, Jerry Terrell told me, "most of what I do is not about sexuality."

Rethink All Assumptions: Pleasure, Love, and Trust

Street kids are not another species. Even for them, sex is not all work, exploitation, or pain. "Sex is nice, it's intimate, it's fun, it doesn't cost anything," Project Offstreets' Thoemke said, in answer to my question about the role of pleasure in his clients' lives. "These kids, not having close relationships with their families, or if they were abused, sex was a really awful thing. To find sex as a pleasure, that's so great." He grumbled at the relentless Lutheran-ness of the bureaucrats who check up on his agency. "They come in, and they're appalled that we have condoms available at our front door or the kids are watching cartoons or smoking cigarettes." Homeless kids carry all the responsibilities of adult independence, he reasoned. Why not get a few of the perquisites? He paused. "But sex is the easiest thing in the world. It's love that's hard to find."

The personality structures and circumstances of disenfranchised youths vex the already difficult search for love. On one hand, as abused or rejected children, they are desperate to love, to plunge into trusting. On the other, as abused or rejected children-turned-street rats, they are trained in mistrust, and touchy, sometimes paranoid. They want stability and monogamy, yet they are also hot to try out their sexuality, sometimes with many partners (these last two contradictory desires are often split by gender, with girls and women rushing to the altar, so to speak, and boys and men reveling in sexual novelty, variety, and quantity). On balance, though, homeless boys and girls want what everyone wants, Thoemke insists: love *and* sex, plus a measure of security—"a permanent partner and not to worry about how the bills will get paid."

Love? A permanent partner? Regular bill paying? These wishes would bring sunshine to the hearts of the bureaucrats at Offstreets' door or to the abstinence-until-marriage campaigners, who claim that a committed relationship is the best and only prophylactic against AIDS. But the fact is, love is no fortress against sexual risk. One of the biggest paradoxes of HIV prevention is that love—not just careless love, but also love that is desperately coveted and conscientiously nurtured—may compound the dangers of sex. Contrary to the propaganda that advertises the perils of the backroom or the bathhouse, *people, both gay and straight, are more likely to have unsafe sex inside a committed, loving relationship than in casual encounters.*[30] Trust, conceived in the way we currently conceive it, can be "a risky practice."[31]

"One of the most striking and consistent findings of behavioral research on gay men is that high-risk sex is more frequently reported with someone described as a 'regular partner or lover,'" wrote the British medical sociologist Graham Hart. In a study of 677 men, Hart and his colleagues found that "unprotected intercourse . . . was a way of expressing the love and commitment to a shared life that the men felt."[32] Sarah Phillips's survey of heterosexual adolescents' condom use came to similar conclusions: "[B]oth young men and women who claimed to be in love with their partners were significantly more likely to agree to sexual intercourse without a condom than were those who reported that they were not in love."[33] The certainty that the other person is perfectly monogamous is viewed, by people of all classes, as an automatic right conferred in loving that person. "Once I'm married, that's it," declared Keisha, a seventeen year-old Minneapolis peer educator, ramming a firm fist into her hip and raising an instructing finger to face height. "If he brings me home AIDS, then I have a right to kill him." If the implicit agreement of Keisha's marriage is that her husband knows he'll be "killed" if he admits to having been unfaithful—and therefore feels he can't tell her—then he may end up killing her too, only more slowly.

Although many definitions of trust cross gender lines, those that do not tend to put women at a disadvantage. "There was a strong shared understanding that 'steady' relationships are based on trust," wrote the psychologist Carla Willig, paraphrasing the conclusions of some researchers who interviewed inner-city young women. ""At the same time [the women] identified a tendency to define a relationship as 'steady' in order to justify sex. Since discontinuation of condom use can signify increasing commitment to a relationship, condom use within 'steady' relationships is difficult to maintain." Among a group of Canadian college students, "for women [the implicit compact between committed lovers] meant trusting that one's partner would disclose relevant information, and for men it meant trusting that one's partner had nothing to disclose. As a result, women found it very difficult to request condom use from partners whom they knew well, but ironically, 'they were most able to protect themselves from all three dangers—pregnancy, disease, and emotional hurt—in casual encounters.'"[34] The prejudice that respectable girls are nonsexual (except with the current partner), moreover, makes safe sex additionally difficult for young women. Planned HIV prevention can give a girl a bad reputation, sex educator Rob Yaeger said. "Girls say, 'If I pull out a condom, he'll think I'm a slut.'" Because women are far more likely to contract HIV from a male partner than vice versa, and young women's vaginal linings are more fragile than mature women's and therefore additionally infection-prone, these gendered assumptions endanger young women disproportionately.

For many people, simply bringing up the subject of protection is so threatening to trust that trust requires absolute censorship. Some of the people Willig interviewed went so far as to say that requiring long-term couples to start talking about or, worse, using condoms would mean an irreparable rent in the social fabric. "I mean there's got to be some sort of element of trust somewhere," said a young man named John, "unless life as we know it ain't gonna happen."[35]

True love is monogamous, trust depends on monogamy and monogamy on trust, and trust is the cornerstone of love: unfortunately, from the point of view of the sexually transmitted virus, this formulation is heavy with potential dangers. First, although statistics vary widely depending on the surveyor, the way the questions are asked, and the sexuality of the subjects, at least a significant number of married and committed couples stray at least once, at least a third of teens do,[36] and even youths who are monogamous are only serially so.[37] Meanwhile, fewer than 60 percent of sexually active adolescent boys who use only condoms say they use them every time.[38]

Yet many of these people predicate their relationship on unerring fidelity. That sets up an untenable dilemma: the confession of a lapse fatally threatens the relationship, but keeping a secret fatally threatens both the person and his or her beloved. Carla Willig's informant John accepted that maintaining a societal and personal contract of trusting silence might mean the sacrifice of a few "innocent victims" whose partners committed crimes of omission.[39] Is the symbolic and moral risk of abandoning loving trust "as we know it" really greater than the risk of rampaging HIV infection? Federally funded abstinence-only education says yes, by teaching, contrary to evidence, that the only safe sex is within a "traditional" committed (read unquestionably monogamous) heterosexual marriage.

Fortunately, some independent AIDS educators are going wholeheartedly in the other direction. "I tell them, *love is not the answer,*" said Rob Yaeger. "Love will not protect you. The virus doesn't care if you're in love, if you're married. It doesn't care what your favorite song is." And it doesn't care what your favorite song says love is, either. Given the urgent historical circumstances, a policy of confession and forgiveness when a partner strays from intended monogamy might be *more* loving than censorship enforced by the expectation of rage and rejection. But such ways of relating require less dependency, less jealousy, less unwavering confidence in the other person's ability and willingness to take care of you, and at the same time, more personal maturity, flexibility, independence, and self-esteem, and more altruism from both partners.

Aside from altruism, these emotions are different from the ones we are used to associating with love. Nevertheless, it is these qualities and values, not the blind faith of "true" love and, the hound dog's acuity for "risky" partners, that we need to be nurturing in kids.

Cultivate the Best Values: Create Brave New Communities

Plenty of the teens who flow through the agencies where I hung out in Minneapolis and St. Paul are notoriously tough cases. It's hard to get them back to the clinic for a follow-up visit, much less to a GED class or job-training program. District 202 youth volunteer Courie Parker, who has been homeless herself, explained why homeless kids drift further and further from "normalizing," adult-overseen institutions such as school and work. "You can't plug in an alarm clock under a bridge," she said simply.

But exclusion from the mainstream can also engender tight affiliation, and as history has shown for blacks, women, gays, and the disabled, collective survival is the first step toward the creation of a resistant community identity. Homeless youth form scruffy mutual-aid societies, tight little tribes that scavenge food or locate shelter for each other, often moving about with a brace of equally disenfranchised dogs. To the Offstreets kids, group cohesiveness is everything, said Thoemke. "They always want to say 'we.' If we could harness that good energy, we'd have a powerful community."

During the early years of gay liberation, despised communities harnessed the energy of the hatred directed at them and transformed it into pride—for instance, appropriating as flags of distinction the derogatory terms *dyke, faggot,* and *queer.* When the AIDS epidemic hit them, gay men and women turned that energy toward aggressive political confrontation that, for all its outward rage, was fueled by love, both fraternal and erotic. "The AIDS crisis, in all its frightening impact, bearing the burden of fear of disease and death in the wake of pleasure and desire, seems to many to embody the downside of the transformation of sexuality in recent years, a warning of the dangers of things 'going too far,'" wrote the British social critic Jeffrey Weeks. "Yet in many of the responses to it we can see something else: a quickening of humanity, the engagement of solidarity, and the broadening of the meanings of love, love in the face of death."[40]

Self-love and self-esteem are necessary to practicing safe sex. But this history speaks of love that goes beyond the self and even beyond the beloved. This is *communal* love, a kind of modern agape, based in shared pride of identity and collective self-defense and practiced within circles of personal friendship and desire. *Love and loyalty, the same feelings that can discourage safe sex, can also motivate it.* People care about their communities even when their communities are hostile to them, and they put on a condom with that caring in mind. "When people are asked why they practice safe sex," said Jeffrey Escoffier, "one of the main reasons they give is altruism." He cited a study of gay Latino men, done by the Rafael Diaz Center for AIDS Prevention Studies in San Francisco. "The most common response was, 'There are people who count on me.'" Escoffier noted that the people who depend on those men were not necessarily part of any gay community but rather family members, friends, and neighbors in their Latino communities of origin. What this study and others uncovered, he said, was "a high level of integration even into a community that they feel ambivalent about. A lot of [HIV] prevention aims at self-interest," he concluded. "That's a mistake."

America has made many grievous mistakes in trying to protect its children from the dangers of sex. Underlying these errors is fear. Some is "good" fear, that they will be sickened or traumatized, will lose their direction, their ambition, their sense of self. But much is fear of eros, to which we attribute anarchic, obliterating power—the power to destroy individuals and civilization itself.

Yet eros is not a wild animal prowling outside the civilizing meanings we assign it, beyond the moralities with which we govern it. We create eros for ourselves and for our children; it is we who teach our young the meanings and moralities of sex. In the age of AIDS, we must invent new iterations of the best old values, creating new expressions of love, trust, loyalty, and mutual protection. Inspired and sheltered by the values of caring, young people can discover their sexual power without dominating or diminishing others; they can find romance without surrendering self-protection. They can arrive at the divine oblivion of sex consciously, with responsibility, forethought, and consent.

While laboring to vanquish AIDS and the conditions that abet it, we must remember what we were taught by the gay and lesbian heroes of one of modern sexuality's most terrible epochs. The infinite gifts of the erotic can empower people and unite communities. The embrace of pleasure can be the greatest defense against peril.

References

1. Cindy Patton, *Fatal Advice: How Safe-Sex Education Went Wrong.* (Durham, NC: Duke University Press, 1996), 34.
2. Bill Alexander, "Adolescent HIV Rates Soar; Government Piddles," *Youth Today* (March/April 1997): 29.
3. Lawrence K. Altman, "AIDS Deaths Drop 48% in New York," *New York Times,* February 3, 1998, A1.
4. Philip J. Hilts, "AIDS Deaths Continue to Rise in 25–44 Age Group, U.S. Says," *New York Times,* January 16, 1996, A22.

5. Centers for Disease Control, Atlanta, Ga., March 1996.

6. Interview with Gary Remafedi, Director of the University of Minnesota/Minneapolis Youth & AIDS Project, 1998.

7. "Rate of AIDS Has Slowed," *New York Times,* April 25, 1998, A9.

8. Lawrence K. Altman, "Study in 6 Cities Finds HIV in 30% of Young Black Gays," *New York Times,* February 6, 2001.

9. Cherrie B. Boyer and Susan M. Kegeles, "AIDS Risk and Prevention among Adolescents," *Social Science Medicine* 33, no. 1 (1991): 11–23.

10. New York City Health Department, phone interview, April 1999.

11. Barbara Crossette, "In India and Africa, Women's Low Status Worsens Their Risk of AIDS," *New York Times,* February 26, 2001 [sic].

12. B. R. Simon Rossner, "New Directions in HIV Prevention," *SIECUS Report 26* (December 1997/January 1998): 6.

13. The following remarks from people in the Twin Cities came from interviews that I conducted during my visit there in 1998.

14. *District 202 Youth Survey* (Minneapolis, 1997).

15. *District 202 Youth Survey.*

16. Marsha S. Sturdevant and Gary Remafedi, "Special Health Needs of Homosexual Youth," in *Adolescent Medicine: State of the Art Reviews* (Philadelphia: Hanley and Belfus, 1992), 364.

17. R. Stall and J. Wiley, "A Comparison of Alcohol and Drug Use Patterns of Homosexual and Heterosexual Men: The San Francisco Men's Health Study," *Drug and Alcohol Dependence* 22 (1988): 63–73.

18. Marina McNamara, "Adolescent Behavior II. Socio-Psychological Factors," *Advocates for Youth Fact Sheet,* Washington, D.C., September 1997 [sic].

19. Alan Bell and Martin Weinberg, *Homosexualities* (New York: Simon and Schuster, 1978).

20. Gary Remadefi, Michael Resnick, Robert Blum, and Linda Harris, "Demography of Sexual Orientation in Adolescents," *Pediatrics* 89, no. 4 (April 1992).

21. Patton, *Fatal Advice.*

22. U.S. Conference of Mayors, "Safer Sex Relapse: A Contemporary Challenge, *AIDS Information Exchange* 11, no. 4 (1994): 1–8.

23. Altman, "Study in 6 Cities."

24. D. Boyer, "Male Prostitution and Homosexual Identity," *Journal of Homosexuality* 9 (1984): 105.

25. S. L. Bailey et al., "Substance Use and Risky Sexual Behavior Among Homeless and Runaway Youth," *Journal of Adolescent Health* 23 (December 1998): 378–388.

26. Amy Bracken, "STDs Discriminate," *Youth Today* (March 2001): 7–8.

27. *Minnesota's Youth Without Homes* (St. Paul: Wilder Research Center, 1997), 5.

28. Ine Vanwesenbeeck, "The Context of Women's Power(lessness) in Heterosexual Interactions," in *New Sexual Agendas,* ed. Lynne Segal (New York: New York University Press, 1997), 173.

29. Author interview, New York, 1999.

30. E. Matinka-Tyndale, "Sexual Scripts and AIDS Prevention: Variations in Adherence to Safer Sex Guidelines in Heterosexual Adolescents," *Journal of Sex Research* 28 (1991): 45–66.

31. Carla Willig, "Trust as a Risky Practice," in *New Sexual Agendas,* ed. Segal, 125–135.

32. Graham Hart, " 'Yes, but Does It Work?' Impediments to Rigorous Evaluations of Gay Men's Health Promotion," in *New Sexual Agendas,* ed. Segal, 119.

33. Sarah R. Phillips, "Turning Research into Policy: A Survey on Adolescent Condom Use," *SIECUS Report* (October/November 1995): 10.

34. Willig, "Trust as a Risky Practice," 126.

35. Willig, "Trust as a Risky Practice," 130.

36. Pepper Schwartz and Philip Blumstein, *American Couples: Money, Work, Sex* (New York: Pocket Books, 1983).

37. Susan L. Rosenthal et al., "Heterosexual Romantic Relationships and Sexual Behaviors of Young Adolescent Girls," *Journal of Adolescent Health* 21 (1997): 238–243.

38. Freya L. Sonenstein and Joseph H. Pleck et al., "Change in Sexual Behavior and Contraception among Adolescent Males: 1998 and 1995," *Urban Institue Report,* Washington, D.C., 1996 [sic].

39. Willig, "Trust as a Risky Practice," 130.

40. Jeffrey Weeks, *Invented Moralities: Sexual Values in an Age of Uncertainty* (New York: Columbia University Press, 1995), 42.

Chapter 27

Predominant Risk Factors for Genital Papillomavirus Infection

Robert D. Burk

Gloria Y. F. Ho

Leah Beardsley

Michele Lempa

Michael Peters

Robert Bierman

Human papillomavirus (HPV), believed to be the most common STD in the United States, has been identified as the major cause of cervical cancer, and to have a strong association with cancer of the vulva, vagina, anus, and/or penis. Commonly called genital warts, the virus primarily affects persons ages 15 to 40. These highly contagious warts are transmitted through direct bodily contact during vaginal, oral, or anal intercourse as well as through nongenital contact. The problem is magnified because many infected male sex partners have no visible signs of these warts, which may be only inside the urethra. Additionally, a partner may be a carrier of the virus, which has not as yet produced warts. Therefore, the most common form of transmission is by a person who is asymptomatic. Adding to the bad news, no accurate screening test is currently available for this STD.

Because of these somewhat sobering facts, the Burk et al. epidemiological study that examines certain sexual behavior and partner characteristics as risk factors for HPV is an important link in the chain of sexuality education needed by young persons today. The article may prove to be of special value for those who are already sexually active, especially those with multiple sex partners. The somewhat inconsistent findings of prior studies underscore the need for this carefully designed and well-executed piece of re-search, which, in spite of its acknowledged limitations, is an important addition to this anthology.

Cervical cancer is the second most common cancer in women worldwide and accounted for ~5000 deaths in the United States in 1994 [1]. Epidemiologic studies have identified human papillomavirus (HPV) as the major cause of cervical cancer and cervical dysplasia [2–4]. Infection of the female genital tract with HPV is now recognized as one of the most, if not the most, common sexually transmitted diseases (STDs) [5–7]. However, studies that have examined the role of sexual behavior as a risk factor for HPV infection have yielded inconsistent results. Potential explanations accounting for this discrepancy include limitations in population size, differences in sampling strategies, and varying sensitivity, specificity, and accuracy of HPV detection methods [8–10]. In addition, little is known about how the behavior of the male partner is related to the risk of female genital HPV infection.

THE CURRENT STUDY

This study sought to test the hypothesis that sexual behavior and partner characteristics are the major risk factors for HPV infection in young women. A cohort of predominantly young college women was recruited through advertisement in order to assemble a group with heterogeneous sexual behavior.

Subjects and Methods

Between September 1992 and March 1994, women students from a state university were invited to participate in a longitudinal study designed to investigate the natural history of HPV infection. Women were eligible if they fulfilled the following criteria: first or second year in college and/or planning to stay in the area for at least 2.5 years; not currently pregnant and without plans to become pregnant in the next 3 years; and never had a cervical biopsy or invasive treatment for cervical lesions.

The ethnic distribution of the participants was representative of the ethnic distribution of the total female undergraduate population (i.e., 70 percent white, 9 percent Asian, 11 percent black, 8 percent Hispanic, and 2 percent other). Characteristics of the eligible nonparticipants (*n* = 308) and participants (*n* = 598) who completed the telephone screening were compared. Compared with nonparticipants, participants were slightly older and had more lifetime male sex partners. Hence, this study sample could overestimate the HPV prevalence in the general female college population.

At the baseline visit, each subject completed a self-administered questionnaire that obtained information on demographic background, sexual history, characteristics of sex partners, smoking history, recreational drug and alcohol use, oral contraceptive usage, and pertinent medical history.

Detailed sexual behavior of the subjects in the 6-month period before the baseline visit was assessed. Two types of sex partners were distinguished in the questionnaire: regular partners were sex partners with whom subjects had ongoing sexual contact for > 1 month, whereas casual partners were defined as partners with whom subjects had sex for < 1 month, including "one-night stand" relationships. For each regular partner, subjects provided information on the partner's demographic and lifestyle characteristics, as well as the frequency of having different types of sex, such as vaginal, oral, and anal sex, with that particular partner.

A pelvic examination was done at the baseline visit [and] a Pap smear was obtained. Thus, 604 subjects were included in this analysis.

Results

Characteristics of Study Population

Mean age of the 604 study subjects was 20.0 years; 83 percent were recruited through advertisements in the mail, on bulletin boards, or in the campus newspaper and 17 percent through word of mouth. The majority of subjects were in the first (50.7 percent) or second (30.6 percent) year of college. The study population was predominantly white (57.1 percent), with 13.1 percent Hispanic, 12.1 percent black, 9.6 percent Asian, and 8.1 percent other ethnicities. Median annual family income was $40,000–$49,999. Most of the subjects were sexually experienced; of the 12.6 percent who denied having had vaginal intercourse, 5.1 percent had had oral and/or anal sex. Among the 87.4 percent who had vaginal intercourse, the median age of first coitus was 16, and the median number of lifetime male sex partners was 3. STDs were rare.

Characteristics of Subjects That Were Risk Factors for HPV Infection

HPV DNA was detected in 27.8 percent of 604 subjects. The subjects' demographic and behavioral characteristics were examined for their associations with HPV positivity. Prevalent HPV infection was strongly associated with the subject's demographic characteristics—age, ethnicity, and year in college; sexual behavior—experience with vaginal sex, number of lifetime male partners for vaginal sex, frequency of douching after sexual intercourse, concern of having been exposed to an STD, and sexual activities in the last 6 months as indicated by the number of male partners for vaginal sex, number of regular sex partners, and having had casual sex; and other lifestyle and behavior characteristics, including frequency of attending religious service and number of smokers in the household. Variables not significantly associated with HPV infection included annual family income, frequency of giving or receiving oral sex in the last 6 months, and having had anal intercourse in the last 6 months.

Black and Hispanic subjects were more likely to be HPV-positive than the other subjects, who were predominantly white. HPV positivity increased proportionately with lifetime as well as more recent (6 months) numbers of male sex partners. None of the lifestyle or behavioral risk factors identified were significant, except the numbers of smokers in the household. Subjects who lived with people who smoked were more likely to have HPV infection than those who did not.

Characteristics of Subjects' Male Sex Partners That Were Risk Factors for HPV Infection in Subjects

The following regular male partner's characteristics [were] independently associated with an increased risk of genital HPV infection in women: age 20 years, black or Hispanic ethnicity, currently not attending college, and increased number of lifetime female sex partners. Subjects who had sex with their regular partner under the influence of alcohol or drugs and those who had a sexual relationship with their partner for 12 months also had an increased risk of HPV.

The subject's age (21–23 years), ethnicity (black and Hispanic), number of smokers in subject's household, lifetime number of male sex partners, duration of the sexual relationship, whether subject's partner was currently in school, and lifetime number of partners of the subject's regular male partner were significant risk factors for HPV infection in the subject.

Discussion

HPV infection was detected in 27.8 percent of a population-based group of young women participating in a study advertised throughout a college campus. Increasing numbers of sex partners for either the female subject or her regular male partner were the predominant risk factors for HPV infection, providing compelling evidence for the sexual transmission of HPV infection mediated through sexual promiscuity.

Association between sexual behavior and female HPV infection in previous studies has not been reported consistently in the literature [10, 12]. For example, Rohan et al. [15] did not identify number of sex partners as a risk factor for genital HPV in a student health clinic population. The lack of association could be attributed, in part, to differences in sample collection [13–14], virus detection methods lacking adequate sensitivity and specificity [9], or population characteristics.

An important feature of this study was the establishment of the cohort through advertisement. This attracted a diverse spectrum of the female college population with greater heterogeneity in sexual behaviors than women attending the health service for gynecologic exams. This latter point is relevant since demonstration of sexual behavior as the quintessential risk factor for HPV is analytically a comparison between groups in a cohort. The importance of how a population has been recruited becomes relevant when interpreting risk factors for HPV infection. Populations that tend to be more homogeneous in their or their partners' level of sexual promiscuity will diminish findings on the relationship between sexual behavior and HPV.

Three studies have reported significant association with lifetime number of sex partners and HPV infection in young women [6, 11–12]. The Berkeley study [6, 11] reported 33 percent of 467 subjects with cervical HPV infection and 46 percent with HPV detected in the vulvar or cervical swab specimen. The New Mexico study [12] reported that 44.3 percent of 357 women attending the University Student Health Center for routine gynecologic care were HPV-positive on cervical swabs. In both studies, HPV positivity was independently correlated with increasing numbers of sex partners. Consistent with the higher prevalence of HPV detected in these latter two studies, two differences in the populations should be noted. In the current study, a population-based cohort was obtained by advertisement, in contrast to the Berkeley and New Mexico studies, which both recruited women coming in for gynecologic care. The mean age of the women in both studies was 23 years, 3 years older than the current population.

A population-based Swedish study [16] detected cervical HPV infection in 20 percent of 581 women who were 19–25 years old. Lifetime number of male sex partners was the only independent risk factor for cervical HPV infection and showed a linear trend, similar to the current report. Moreover, in the Swedish study, 4 percent of 55 non-sexually active women were HPV-positive compared to 33 percent of women with 5 lifetime sex partners.

Taken together, the three previous studies [11–12, 16] and the current report all show a significant association with lifetime number of sex partners and HPV infection in young women.

The relationship between lifetime partners and prevalent HPV infection is not as dramatic in older populations of women, in whom recent numbers of sex partners is more strongly associated with HPV [10]. This may reflect differences in the sexual experience of college-aged women, whose lifetime number of sex partners reflects sexual encounters in the recent time period. In contrast, for women 30 years of age, the period of time encompassing numbers of lifetime sex partners may span decades, thus accentuating differences between recent and lifetime number of partners. Moreover, the differences in risk for prevalent HPV infection in distinct age groups of women from lifetime versus recent partners may reflect the transient nature of most cervical HPV infections [10, 18]. Discrepant with the predominant sexual transmission of HPV, however, is the detection of HPV in virginal or non-sexually active women, albeit at a much lower prevalence.

The information on sexual behavior of the women in the current study indicates that cervical HPV infection is associated with vaginal intercourse and not oral or anal sex. Only lifetime and recent number of male vaginal sex partners remained significant, suggesting exposure to different men as the predominant risk, in contrast to frequency of sex. Alternatively, these other risk factors may just be correlated with number of partners. Surprisingly, subjects who claimed to use condoms all of the time still had a relatively high rate of HPV infection (25 percent). Thus, this study did not provide compelling evidence that condoms offer adequate protection from transmission of HPV infection. In addition, subjects who believed they had been exposed to an STD had a higher prevalence of HPV than those not anticipating such a risk.

Only age, ethnicity, and number of smokers in the household were independently associated with HPV. Similar age trends have been seen in other studies of college-aged women [11, 19]. These trends probably reflect the sexual behavior patterns of college-aged women who enter college relatively sexually quiescent and become more sexually active as they expand their social networks in their upper years of college. In support of this notion, the prevalence of HPV went from 25 percent in the first 2 years of college to 46 percent in the later years. Different ethnic groups display varying prevalences of HPV in college populations [11–12]. Similar to our findings, the Berkeley study identified being black as an independent risk factor for HPV infection [11]. Hispanic women were at increased risk in our study but not in the New Mexico study [12]. Reasons for ethnic differences as risk factors for prevalent HPV infection may include genetic predisposition for acquisition or persistence of HPV infection. Alternatively, different levels of endemic HPV may exist in given groups, thus yielding a higher risk of exposure to a group member. This later mechanism has been proposed as an important variable in the high rate of cervical cancer in Latin America [20]. Similarly, the unexpected independent risk factor of a woman living in a household with smokers might be construed as placing the subject at risk through association with friends who engage in risky sexual behaviors [21].

This is the first report to investigate the behaviors of the regular male sex partners of women as risk factors for HPV infection in the women. The significant factors among male partners imparting risk to the subjects included older age, black and Hispanic ethnicity, educational status, increasing number of sex partners, a short-term relationship, frequent sex while intoxicated, rarely using seat belts, and less attendance at religious service. Taken together, these risk factors paint the picture of male partners of HPV-infected women as being more sexually promiscuous, as indicated by lifetime number of partners, duration of relationship, and frequency of sex. In addition, male partners of infected women exhibit characteristics of risk-taking behaviors, as evidenced by lack of seat belt use and substance abuse. These observations strengthen the importance of the "male factor" in HPV infection in women and are consistent with the recent observation of HPV type-specific concordance in sex partners [22]. The lifetime numbers of both female and male partners were independently associated with HPV in subjects, as was ethnicity, college status of partner, duration of sexual relationship, and number of smokers in household.

Certain limitations apply to this study. The cohort of women studied is relatively young and early in their sexual behavior patterns and thus is not likely representative of older women. The information on male partners was obtained from the subjects and may be biased by each subject's own sexual behaviors and assumptions concerning her partner. In addition, differences in geographic or ethnic variation of endemic HPV could be significant variables influencing risk factors for HPV infection.

In summary, our data suggest three main areas of risk for college-aged women to have an HPV infection. The first and most significant is sexual exposure through multiple male sex partners. The second is their partners' level of promiscuity as evidenced by his lifetime number of partners. Last, the probability of a woman having HPV infection was related to the prevalence of HPV in her social/sexual contact pool. Characteristics of contact groups appear to be associated with ethnicity, college status, having short-term relationships, and living with persons who smoke.

References

1. Boring C, Squires TS, Tong T, Montgomery S. Cancer statistics, 1994. *CA Cancer J Clin* 1994; 44: 7–26.
2. Schiffman MH. Epidemiology of cervical human papillomavirus infections. *Curr Top Microbiol Immunol* 1994; 186: 55–81.
3. Koutsky LA, Holmes KK, Critchlow CW, et al. A cohort study of the risk of cervical intraepithelial neoplasia grade 2 or 3 in relation to papillomavirus infection. *N Engl J Med* 1992; 327: 1272–1278.
4. Munoz N, Bosch FX, De Sanjose S, et al. The causal link between human papillomavirus and invasive cervical cancer: a population-based case-control study in Colombia and Spain. *Int J Cancer* 1992; 52: 743–749.
5. Kiviat NB, Koutsky LA, Paavonen JA, et al. Prevalence of genital papillomavirus infection among women attending a college student health clinic or a sexually transmitted disease clinic. *J Infect Dis* 1989; 159: 293–302.
6. Bauer HM, YiTing MS, Greer CE, et al. Genital human papillomavirus infection in female university students as determined by a PCR-based method. *JAMA* 1991; 265: 472–477.
7. Jamison JH, Kaplan DW, Hamman R, Eagar R, Beach R, Douglas JM Jr. Spectrum of genital human papillomavirus infection in a female adolescent population. *Sex Transm Dis* 1995; 22: 236–243.
8. Schiffman MH, Schatzkin A. Test reliability is critically important to molecular epidemiology: an example from studies of human papillomavirus infection and cervical neoplasia. *Cancer Res* 1994; 54(suppl 7): 1944s–1947s.
9. Franco EL. Measurement errors in epidemiological studies of human papillomavirus and cervical cancer. *IARC Sci Publ* 1992; 119: 181–197.
10. Hildesheim A, Gravitt P, Schiffman MH, et al. Determinants of genital human papillomavirus infection in low-income women in Washington, DC. *Sex Transm Dis* 1993; 20: 279–285.
11. Ley C, Bauer HM, Reingold A, et al. Determinants of genital human papillomavirus infection in young women. *J Natl Cancer Inst* 1991; 83: 997–1003.
12. Wheeler CM, Parmenter CA, Hunt WC, et al. Determinants of genital human papillomavirus infection among cytologically normal women attending the University of New Mexico Student Health Center. *Sex Transm Dis* 1993; 20: 286–289.
13. Vermund SH, Schiffman MH, Goldberg GL, Ritter DB, Weltman A, Burk RD. Molecular diagnosis of genital human papillomavirus infection: comparison of the methods used to collect exfoliated cervical cells. *Am J Obstet Gynecol* 1989; 160: 304–308.

14. Goldberg GL, Vermund SH, Schiffman MH, Ritter DB, Spitzer C, Burk RD. Comparison of cytobrush and cervicovaginal lavage sampling methods for the detection of genital human papillomavirus. *Am J Obstet Gynecol* 1989; 161: 1669–1672.

15. Rohan T, Mann V, McLaughlin J, et al. PCR-detected genital papillomavirus infection: prevalence and association with risk factors for cervical cancer. *Int J Cancer* 1991; 49: 856–60.

16. Karlsson R, Jonsson M, Edlund K, et al. Lifetime number of partners as the only independent risk factor for human papillomavirus infection: a population-based study. *Sex Transm Dis* 1995; 22: 119–127.

17. Rosenfeld WD, Rose E, Vemund SH, Schreiber K, Burk RD. Follow-up evaluation of human papillomavirus infection in adolescents. *J Pediatr* 1992; 121: 307–311.

18. Hildesheim A, Schiffman MH, Gravitt PE, et al. Persistence of type-specific human papillomavirus infection among cytologically normal women. *J Infect Dis* 1994; 169: 235–240.

19. Melkert PW, Hopman E, van den Brule AJ, et al. Prevalence of HPV in cytomorphologically normal cervical smears, as determined by the polymerase chain reaction, is age-dependent. *Int J Cancer* 1993; 53: 919–923.

20. Bosch FX, Munoz N, de Sanjose S, et al. Importance of human papillomavirus endemicity in the incidence of cervical cancer: an extension of the hypothesis on sexual behavior. *Cancer Epidemiol Biomarkers Prev* 1994; 3: 375–379.

21. Millstein SG, Moscicki AB. Sexually transmitted disease in female adolescents: effects of psychosocial factors and high risk behaviors. *J Adolesc Health* 1995; 17: 83–90.

22. Baken LA, Koutsky LA, Kuypers J, et al. Genital human papillomavirus infection among male and female sex partners: prevalence and type-specific concordance. *J Infect Dis* 1995; 171: 429–432.

Part VII

Sexual Orientation

The word *homosexuality* was coined in 1869 when Hungarian Karoly Benkert first used the term; but it was British sexologist Havelock Ellis who introduced its English usage in the 1880s (Weeks 1981). Thereafter, the medical model of homosexuality as a form of mental disease was prevalent until the mid-1950s, when University of California psychologist Evelyn Hooker's pioneer study of matched samples of heterosexuals and homosexuals found that there were no significant differences in psychological functioning between the groups. However, it was not until 20 years later in 1974, after a number of other studies found similar results, that the American Psychiatric Association removed "self-accepting homosexuality" from its list of mental disorders (Troiden 1988).

The two basic perspectives of homosexuality in both popular and scientific thought are essentialism and social constructionism (Stein 1992). The popular, widespread view of essentialism relates homosexuality to biological or psychological factors. Ascribing a genetic causal model, this perspective is embraced by many scholars and researchers as well. Conversely, social constructionists question the universality of such categories as homosexuality and heterosexuality, proposing instead that concepts of sexual orientation and practices have changed over time and that they vary across societies. Persons who subscribe to either of these positions can be pro-gay or anti-gay in their beliefs. Although social constructionism was mainly developed by pro-gay intellectuals who denied the innateness of homosexuality, in a twist of fate, some of their arguments of denial have been embraced by the right-wing anti-gays who use this position to support the view that homosexuality is a choice, and therefore, a sin (Laumann, et al. 1994).

A difference in perspectives concerning the origin of homosexuality is at the heart of many issues. The Parents and Friends of Lesbians and Gays (PFLAG) support organization is firmly behind any research that implicates biology as the source of homosexuality, possibly because it assuages any guilt for responsibility that they might feel. Conversely, many lesbians and gays have a growing skepticism about the search for the cause(s) of homosexuality, believing such a search implies that homosexuality is deviant and, therefore, needs to be cured. Hooker stated: "Why do we want to know the cause? If we understood . . . and accept it as a given, then we come closer to the kinds of attitudes that will make it possible for homosexuals to live a decent life in society." (Gelman, et al. 1992, 53)

One wonders if tolerance and acceptance of gays and lesbians would increase if we, without any reservations, could conclude that homosexuality is genetically linked. Or, if we discovered a homosexual gene, would pregnant women obtain an abortion if the fetus were gay or lesbian? Would these women echo the sentiments of the mother of an adult gay man, who in a *Newsweek* feature said, "Had I known that I was to have a gay child, I would probably not want to have a gay child" (Gelman et al. 1992, 50). Hard questions without easy answers are on the horizon for twenty-first century pilgrims. The articles on sexual orientation in Part VII enable readers to assess just how far society has progressed in its attitudes about homosexuality and, perhaps, the distance they themselves have traveled in their own journey.

Richard Pillard and Michael Bailey's technical, well-written review of the behavioral genetics research on sexual orientation includes studies of twins, the hypothalamus, and evolutionary trends. To determine if homosexuality runs in families, the authors examine sibling, twin, and adoption concordance rates that are compatible with the hypothesis that genes account for at least one-half of any variable in sexual orientation. Supporting the essentialist perspective of the authors, research findings are presented about gender atypicality as a forerunner of adult homosexuality, an unresolved topic that has been in the research literature for over a century. In raising the issue of a reproductive disadvantage of a homosexual orientation, this psychiatrist and psychologist team of Pillard and Bailey offers an evolutionary slant different from the William Byne selection that follows.

After considering the heritable component of sexual orientation, a number of important questions surface. For example, why do lesbians and gays have fewer children than heterosexuals? Why are women more often bisexual than men? Is the fact that gay men tend to be born later into the family a significant factor to be explored in studying sexual orientation? Why are more gays found in urban than in rural areas? Is it because of more tolerance or anonymity there, or are other factors operating? And, finally, does homosexuality run in families? This selection is guaranteed to raise more questions than answers about an important and timely topic.

Byne is well-qualified to counter the argument that human sexual orientation has a heritable component. As a neuroanatomist and psychiatrist at Mt. Sinai School of Medicine, he studies correlations between brain structure and behavior in health and disease. He does not deny that all mental phenomena have a biological substructure, but he questions the precise contribution that certain biological factors may have in the development of sexual orientation. Although somewhat technical, the selection clearly and succinctly reviews several widely acclaimed studies suggesting a biological basis for sexual orientation and draws surprising conclusions. Addressing what he believes to be incomplete or misleading findings, Byne makes a cogent case for controlled, carefully designed longitudinal studies. To properly debate the issue of the origin(s) of homosexuality, students will need the insights gained from this article as well as the previous one by Pillard and Bailey.

In our society, four to eight million lesbian and gay families are rearing three to fourteen million children, figures that are admittedly estimates (Lowry 1999). More precise numbers are difficult to discern for various reasons—some obvious, others obscure. Obviously, many homosexual parents choose to remain anonymous because of discrimination, which can lead to loss of employment, loss of child custody, ostracism, or anti-gay and lesbian violence. Others may be ambivalent about their ho-

mosexuality, making it impossible for researchers to accurately assess the number of lesbian and gay parents. For example, when Michael Huffington, the 1998 California Republican senatorial candidate, announced that he was gay, did his heterosexual family suddenly become a gay family? And, how might we best categorize families of bisexuals or transsexual/transgendered persons? Readers who wish to expand their knowledge beyond Susan Golombok and Fiona Tasker's experimentally designed British study on these topics are referred to a recent article by therapists Ariel and McPherson (2000), who address a number of such issues in their work with lesbian and gay parents and their children.

Of the hot topics pertaining to homosexual parenting, psychological stability is perhaps the most debated. Do lesbian or gay parents differ from heterosexual parents in their ability to nurture their children? Some people apparently believe so. A Florida court in 1996 removed a child from her biological mother, who was a lesbian, and awarded custody to the child's father, who had been convicted of murdering his first wife. Moreover, the mother mysteriously died when the case was being appealed (*Ward v. Ward* 1996). Golombok and Tasker also contrast biological and psychological theories as they address the subject of parental influence on the sexual orientation of children. An excellent, easy-to-follow review of various explanations of the causes of sexual orientation precedes the research in this British study.

A number of years ago, psychotherapist Rollo May (1969), in his classic work, *Love and Will*, decried the *Playboy* mentality in our society that took the fig leaf from the genitals and placed it on the face, resulting in much bed-hopping but little intimacy. Ritch Savin-Williams' litany of poignant quotes by lesbian/gay youth emphasizes the role of society in institutionalizing such a reality among homosexual youth. But for heterosexual and homosexual youth, the underlying causes of sex without intimacy appear to differ. That is, the sexual promiscuity of heterosexuals addressed by May had at least partial roots in society's changing sexual mores. Conversely, the plight of lesbian/gay youth in establishing intimacy seems more related to the failure of sexual mores to change at all.

The inherent problems for lesbians and gays in accomplishing the developmental tasks of youth that are dramatically and knowledgeably magnified by Savin-Williams may be novel ideas for the vast majority of readers, who themselves are heterosexuals. Probably few adults recognize the significant role that dating has played, or can play, in their lives by helping them to achieve their own developmental tasks. For example, dating not only affords recreation and a venue for selecting a life partner, but through interaction with others, persons are also socialized for various life roles, become more independent, and are better able to meet their status and ego needs (Adams 1986). This offering will not only raise consciousness about the negativism that lesbian, gay, and bisexual youth are prone to experience in romantic relationships with same-sex partners, but it will also move readers along their own path of decision making about the role that society needs to play in this real-life drama.

Gays and lesbians represent a small minority of the population in the United States. Of this number, approximately 600,000 same-sex couples were counted in the 2000 Census. Where do they live? Like all couples, they live in all states. But, if the District of Columbia were a state, it would lead the nation with 1.5 percent of its households formed by same-sex couples. Vermont and California have .8 percent each, with Massachusetts and Washington State close behind with .7 percent (Lane 2004).

James Madison warned that majority rule unchecked can become majority tyranny. It can be argued that the system of representative government, separation of powers, checks and balances, and the Bill of Rights was designed to protect the unpopular minority from the tyranny of the majority (Madison 1987). Some would suggest that at the beginning of the twenty-first century the issue of same-sex marriage is such a work in progress. Others would vehemently disagree.

Personal beliefs about marriage are usually related to a person's religious belief, based on denominational interpretations of the *Bible*. But, the U.S. Constitution states that no religion shall be established through law or government policy, a provision that, over the years, has been interpreted by courts to mean that there must be a separation of church and state. Despite this doctrine, clergy are permitted to act as state officials in performing marriage ceremonies. However, they cannot grant divorces; a marriage can be dissolved only by a state court decree. Because marriage is not mentioned in the Constitution as an area of federal jurisdiction, legislating laws related to marriage has been left to the individual states, a reality evidenced in the wide variety of divorce laws existing in the United States.

The 2003 U.S. Supreme Court decision, ruling that state sodomy laws are unconstitutional, ushered into America a sea change if not a tsunami. Many fear that the court will use this equal protection clause in the Constitution to also declare the laws banning same-sex marriage to be unconstitutional. Many fear they will not. "The War Over Gay Marriage," a "must read" feature included here as an ending to Part VII, is only the beginning of a lengthy process of change facing every American today!

References

Adams, B. N. (1986). *The Family: A Sociological Interpretation*, Fourth Edition. San Diego: Harcourt Brace Jovanovich.

Ariel, J., and McPherson, D. W. (2000). "Therapy With Lesbian and Gay Parents and Their Children." *Journal of Marital and Family Therapy*, 26, 421–432.

Gelman, D., Foote, D., Barrett, D., and Talbot, M. (1992, February 24). "Born or Bred?" *Newsweek*, pp. 46–50, 52–53.

Lane, C. (2004, February 5). "Massachusetts Court Backs Gay Marriage; 'Civil Unions' Rejected; Same Sex Couples to Have Equal Status for First Time." *Washington Post*, p. A01.

Laumann, E. O., Gagnon, J. H., Michael, R. T., and Michaels, S. (1994). *The Social Organization of Sexuality: Sexual Practices in the United States*. Chicago: University of Chicago Press.

Lowry, J. (1999, March 7). "Gay Adoption Backlash Growing." *San Francisco Examiner*, p. A20.

Madison, J. (1987). *Federalist 10, The Federalist Papers*. New York: Penguin Classics.

May, R. (1969). *Love and Will*. New York: Norton.

Stein, E. (Ed.). (1992). *Forms of Desire: Sexual Orientation and the Social Constructionist Controversy*. New York: Routledge.

Troiden, R. R. (1988). *Gay and Lesbian Identity: A Sociological Analysis*. Dix Hills, NY: General Hall.

Ward v. Ward, No. 95-4184, 1996 *Fla. App. LEXIS 9130* (Fla. Dis. Ct. App. Aug. 30, 1996).

Weeks, J. (1981). "Discourse, Desire, and Deviance: Some Problems in a History of Homosexuality." In K. Plummer (Ed.), *The Making of the Modern Homosexual* (pp. 76–111). London: Hutchinson. ✦

Chapter 28
Human Sexual Orientation Has a Heritable Component

Richard C. Pillard

J. Michael Bailey

Homosexuality, as a topic, was discussed previously in this book when Reiss and Reiss gave an excellent accounting of the homosexual revolution in 1969 that began at Stonewich Inn, a gay bar in Greenwich Village, and of the subsequent birth of the Gay Liberation Front. Another beginning article in Part I by Bullough detailed the history of Kinsey's work on the topic of homosexuality from a different vantage point. Now, in this overview of behavioral genetics research on homosexual and heterosexual orientation, Pillard, a psychiatrist, and Bailey, a psychologist, team up to explore the heritability component of human sexual orientation. Against a backdrop of data about female and male sexual orientation, they impose recent research findings suggesting that sexual orientation is, at least in part, genetically based. Whether confirming or confounding for the reader, their research is an important contribution to understanding this still debatable topic.

A powerful generalization about human sexual desire is that members of the two sexes are attracted to each other but attracted by different qualities. Traditionally, men seek youth and beauty in a woman (although the standard of beauty may vary with time and place), whereas women seek in a man good health, high status, and evidence of willingness to provide for children (Symons 1979). These generalizations are intuitively compatible with evolutionary theory. The healthy, the young (women), and the rich (men) are more likely to produce viable offspring and raise them to maturity than the sick, the old, and the poor. (One example of fecundity en-hanced by wealth and status: the late King Sombhuza of Swaziland was reported to have over 600 children.)

For a given individual the selection of a mate may be an inexact marker of sexual attraction because in many societies the individual has limited mate choice and sometimes no choice at all. Community expectations and the social and political ambitions of the family often override individual desires. Also, atypical sexual desires result in censure and therefore may be effectively concealed. Nevertheless, heterosexual attraction, broadly speaking, must be the paradigmatic adaptation. Men and women attracted to one another sufficiently to copulate, pair bond, and raise children to self-sufficiency are a precondition for hominid evolution (Symons 1979).

The development and mechanisms of human sexual attraction have only recently become objects of study. Visual animals that we are, visual cues are doubtless important triggers of sexual response. Olfactory cues may also play a role in sexual attraction, although the nature of the cues and their relative strength remain in controversy (Kohl 1995). (It is interesting to note that blind persons report that they can be sexually attracted by a particular tone of voice.) Whatever cues attract men and women to each other, it is hard to escape the conclusion that they are more or less wired in, the product of an evolutionary history parallel to that of sexual reproduction itself.

Homosexuality, the sexual desire for a person of the same sex, is an interesting challenge to an evolutionary account of sexual attraction, one reason that psychosocial theories have been dominant. Homosexuality is not the only trait that poses the problem of the apparent selection of a reproductively disadvantageous trait. Schizophrenia is ubiquitous in humankind, too frequent to be the result of occasional mutations, and it is genetically influenced and results in decreased fecundity. What can one make of traits that seem so evidently to defeat the biological imperative of optimizing reproductive success?

Here, we present some background data about male and female sexual orientation and follow with some recent research that in our opinion suggests that sexual orientation has a genetic component. Finally, we comment on some possible explanations for the paradox presented by the persistence of a trait that appears inimical to reproductive success.

Phenotype

Sexual orientation refers to an individual's erotic desire for a member of his or her own sex (homosexuality), the opposite sex (heterosexuality), or both sexes (bisexuality). Recognition of one's orientation generally comes during adolescence, although some individuals are aware of sex-specific attractions in childhood. A homosexual orientation may be concealed for practical reasons, but by adulthood it is almost always a conscious and more or less permanent personality trait. Psychological constructs such as "unconscious" or "latent" homosexuality have use for some clinicians but have dropped out of the research literature.

The ascertainment of an individual's sexual orientation for research purposes is generally done by a questionnaire or a sexual history interview, ideally conducted by a clinician with experience in sex history interviewing. Alfred Kinsey and his colleagues pioneered sex history interviewing with volunteer subjects, and a detailed account of the technique and content of the interviews upon which their survey research was based has been published (Kinsey et al. 1948). The information collected in a sexual history interview may include data about sexual feelings and behavior during the life epochs: childhood, adolescence, adulthood, and old age. Other information is obtained as the research protocol dictates, for example, the timing of developmental milestones (puberty, first sexual experience, marriage, menopause, etc.), the presence of sexual dysfunctions, safer sex practices, and sexual traumas.

As with any psychometric assessment, it is important to ensure the validity and reliability of the measures, and considerable work has been done on this issue (Bogaert 1996; Catania et al. 1995). Some researchers use physiological measures, such as penile plethysmography (Miner et al. 1995) or a vaginal probe, to evaluate sexual responsiveness to stimuli, usually presented by slides or videos. In this way responses to different erotic situations can be compared. These techniques, besides being somewhat invasive, require expensive instrumentation and their validity has not been fully established. Questionnaire and interview responses can be valid and reliable indicators of sexual behavior; as one example, respondents' accounts of their sexual activity can predict the occurrence of sexually transmitted diseases. The studies cited make use of interviews and questionnaires to ascertain the sexual orientation of research subjects. Despite sources of error, such as volunteer bias, pressure to give socially desirable responses, differences in interviewer technique and questionnaire items, these data give as clear and consistent a picture of the frequency and direction of sexual feeling and behavior as can be obtained from interview data on almost any other topic of interest to behavioral science.

Frequency of Homosexual Orientation

Some commentators in the early sexology literature believed that homosexuality was increasing because of the corrupting influences of city life (von Krafft-Ebing 1901). What they probably observed was the urbanization of nineteenth-century Europe bringing to the cities gays and lesbians who recognized that the opportunities for discreet liaisons were maximized there. More recently, Laumann et al. (1994) found that the percentage of gay men in large U.S. cities is much higher than that in rural areas. Some of this differential is the result of the migration of gays from country to city, but Laumann also found that gay men were disproportionately born in urban areas. This could result from environmental exposure, a reporting artifact (urban gays might be more candid about their orientation), or a genetic effect such that people with "gay genes" are more likely to be city dwellers.

Surveys of sexual orientation began with the Kinsey reports of 1948 and 1953 (Kinsey et al. 1948, 1953). With respect to sexual orientation, the Kinsey team estimated the *relative* amounts of heterosexual and homosexual behavior, placing each subject on a 7-point scale from 0 (completely heterosexual) to 6 (completely homosexual) with intermediate points to describe mixtures of the two. Kinsey's data led to the much-cited estimate that 1 in 10 men are "more or less exclusively homosexual." Kinsey's colleague, Gebhard (1972), recognized the overrepresentation of subsamples with unusually high rates of homosexuality. By adjusting the sample weightings, Gebhard concluded that only 3–4 percent of men and 1–2 percent of women in the United States are exclusively homosexual or virtually so.

The Kinsey group also found that the frequency of more or less exclusive homosexuality was about the same in older subjects as in younger subjects. More recent surveys, although on a smaller scale, give estimates close to those from the Kinsey survey (as adjusted by Gebhard) a half-century ago (Seidman and Rieder 1994; Laumann et al. 1994). Thus, despite differences in definition, methodology, and time frame, these surveys taken together suggest that the frequency of gay and lesbian behavior in the United States has remained stable over several generations in spite of the revolutionary changes in the social status of homosexuality. Although comparable data from other countries would be useful, few are available. Some recent surveys report a frequency of homosexual behavior in the 1–2 percent range (Sell et al. 1995).

Bisexuality occupies a controversial place in the literature (Fox 1996). Kinsey suggested that bisexuality was both common and normal. His graphic presentations using a cumulative frequency distribution make it difficult for the reader to recognize that he found more respondents toward the extreme homosexual end of the spectrum (5 and 6 on the Kinsey scale) than in the intermediate range. Diamond (1993) concluded from his own survey that "exclusive or predominantly exclusive homosexual activities are more common than bisexual activities" (p. 291). In our experience this bimodality is more evident among men, whereas bisexuality is relatively more common in women.

Bisexuality is also more frequently endorsed among the young. Adult subjects are usually unequivocally able to say which sex they prefer in a partner, that is, which sex most strongly engages their fantasies and desires. On the other hand, people engage in sexual relations with the nonpreferred sex for any number of reasons, and therefore frequency counts of behavior alone, particularly if sampled over a stretch of time, often result in a pattern that appears more bisexual than would be the case if desire alone prompted behavior. By the time they reach their mid-twenties, most men and most women give a clear and unambiguous answer when asked, Would you rather have sex with a woman or a man?

Gender Atypicality

Gay men and to a lesser extent lesbian women are often labeled as gender atypical. The term "gender atypical" is chosen to avoid prejudging whether the behaviors at issue are typically those of the other sex or simply not typical of the assigned sex. For men atypicality is evidenced in childhood by association with girl playmates, preference for girls' toys and games, and avoidance of boyish rough-and-tumble play. In adulthood gay men often have preference for female-typical activities and vocations. Lesbian women recollect tomboy behavior in childhood and preference for boys' games and companionship. As adults, lesbians tend to adopt male-typical social and vocational roles more often than do heterosexual women.

Gender atypicality as a forerunner of adult homosexuality has been noted in the sexology literature for more than 100 years (Ulrichs 1994). It is a robust phenomenon confirmed in both prospective and retrospective studies (Bailey, Miller et al. 1993; Bailey and Zucker 1995; Bailey, Nothnagel et al. 1995; Green 1987; Phillips and Over 1995). Whitam found that gender atypicality is a culturally invariable childhood trait for gay men (Whitam 1983) and women (Whitam and Mathy 1991) in such diverse cultures as Brazil, Peru, Guatemala, and the Philippines.

Of course there are many possible kinds of gender atypicality and many ways that a child or adult can feel and behave atypically. Nevertheless, comparing the gender behavior of gays and heterosexuals makes clear that this trait is not simply a matter of feeling lonely, isolated, different, or depressed. The feelings and behaviors are often strikingly and specifically those of the other sex (Pillard 1991).

Gender typical and atypical behaviors emerge in children at similar ages, around 2 to 4 years. Observers of gender-atypical children at play are struck by the pervasive and tenacious nature of this trait. Moreover, some gender-atypical children even look different. Zucker and his colleagues gave photographs of prepubertal gender-typical and gender-atypical boys (Zucker et al. 1993) and girls (Fridell et al. 1996) to raters blind to the child's behavior status. Raters described gender-atypical boys as "cuter," "prettier," and "more attractive" than the gender-typical boys and described the converse for the atypical girls. Apparently, in addition to their behavior, something in the physiognomy of these children marks them already in childhood as gender atypical. What we know about the natural history of this trait suggests that a larger than expected percentage will become gay and lesbian adults. A theory of the development of sexual orientation must take account of the robust and frequently replicated data on the coincidence of atypical behavior in early childhood followed by same-sex attraction in adolescence and adulthood [for an alternative view, see Bem (1996)].

With the onset of adolescence same-sex or opposite-sex attractions become prominent in the gay or lesbian adult-to-be, but some measure of gender atypicality usually remains. Standard personality tests often include so-called masculinity-femininity (M-F) scales purporting to reflect the degree to which an individual matches the "maleness" or "femaleness" typical of his or her sex. Most such items are transparent: "I think I would like the work of a nurse" or "I like to read *Popular Mechanics* magazine" obviously will have different endorsement rates for the two sexes. What is surprising is how large the differences are, how consistent they are across cultures, and how little they have changed over time despite the profound changes in available gender appropriate activities and role models (Gough et al. 1968). The endorsement of female-typical pursuits and interests by gay men found by Terman and Miles (1936) on their M-F scale can be replicated today, again despite profound changes in the roles and social status of women and of gays.

Are gays and lesbians also atypical in other domains in which the sexes differ, such as patterns of cognitive abilities, brain lateralization, or incidence of physical and mental illness? These questions have not been well studied, and results are uneven (Bogaert and Blanchard 1996; Hall and Kimura 1995; Reite et al. 1995). Furthermore, there are at least some traits on which gender atypicality seems to be minimal or absent; for example, gay men tend not to show a female-typical interest in child care (Stringer and Grygier 1976).

The research just cited naturally led investigators seeking neuroanatomical correlates of sexual orientation to look at the hypothalamus, because it subserves reproductive functions, and at nuclei within the hypothalamus known to be gender dimorphic. Two recent articles reported differences between gay and heterosexual men in the size of hypothalamic nuclei. LeVay (1991) found that gay men have a smaller anterior hypothalamic nucleus, which is also smaller in women than in men. However, Swaab and Hoffman (1990) found that gay men have a larger suprachiasmatic nucleus, although it is *not* gender dimorphic. It thus appears that homosexual attraction and gender atypicality are more complex than simply a skewed mix of typically masculine and feminine qualities.

Birth Order

Blanchard and Bogaert (1996) have recently reported that gay men tend to be born later in the sibship, and this trend is accounted for by the presence of older brothers but not older sisters. A psychosocial explanation for this observation certainly seems plausible. Perhaps having an older brother stimulates homosexual attraction, perhaps the family's reaction to a younger brother is such as to bend him in a homosexual direction. There are also purely biological possibilities; for example, placental cells invade the uterine endometrium, and it is now known that protein fragments from these cells may remain in the maternal system for many years. Their effect (if any) is unknown, but their existence raises the possibility of an influence on later gestations (Blanchard and Bogaert 1996).

Familial Aggregation of Male and Female Sexual Orientation

Characteristics of interest to the behavioral geneticist generally run in families; familial aggregation suggests but does not prove a genetic contribution to the trait. Sexologists a half-century ago observed that sexual orientation may be familial (Hirschfeld 1936), but systematic research on the issue is relatively recent. Pillard and Weinrich (1986) used newspaper and radio advertisements to recruit subjects for studies of "personality, sexual behavior, and mental abilities." Some ads were placed in papers with a mostly gay readership to enrich the participation of the minority orientation and were written to be candid yet to conceal the specific hypotheses of the study. Volunteers were interviewed and given psychological tests; then permission was requested to recruit their sibs. A large number of sibs were enrolled and (to avoid bias) interviewed.

Pillard and Weinrich's (1986) primary finding was that nonheterosexual males (2–6 on the Kinsey scale) had an excess of nonheterosexual brothers (22 percent), whereas heterosexual males (0 or 1 on the Kinsey scale) had only 4 percent nonheterosexual brothers, close to the population average. We use the term "nonheterosexual" to highlight another finding: The few males who were bisexual (2–4 on the Kinsey scale) had as many gay brothers as did males who were exclusively gay. Individuals who had "more than occasional" gay contacts, even if most of their contacts were heterosexual, shared the tendency toward familial aggregation as strongly as did the exclusive homosexuals. An additional finding was that probands [brothers] were able to accurately report their sibs' orientation so long as they made the assessment with a high degree of confidence.

To summarize, we note that nonheterosexual males have from 2 to 5 times as many nonheterosexual brothers as do heterosexual males. The heterosexual males, in turn, have rates of nonheterosexuality among their brothers that are about equal to the population frequency, based on other large survey studies. Nonheterosexual women also appear to have more nonheterosexual sisters than do heterosexual women, although the familiality estimates for women vary more widely.

There is a trend for nonheterosexual men to have more nonheterosexual sisters [however, this was not found by Pillard and Weinrich (1986)], whereas nonheterosexual women tend to have more nonheterosexual brothers. However, the estimates varied considerably, leaving open the important issue of cofamiliality of male and female homosexuality.

Family trees with the systematically ascertained sexual orientation of parents, children, and other relatives of gay and lesbian probands are rarely published. Pillard et al. (1982) noted that, when males reported other gay or lesbian relatives, they usually came from the maternal side of the family, an observation also made by Hamer et al. (1993). This pattern suggests that some male homosexuality may be X-chromosome linked, an issue more fully discussed by Pattatucci (1998).

Female and Male Twins and Adoptees

The traditional method used by behavioral geneticists to disentangle genetic and environmental components of trait variance is the comparison of concordance between monozygotic (MZ) twins, dizygotic (DZ) twins, and adopted siblings (i.e., biologically unrelated individuals) reared together. If the influence of genes is paramount, MZ twins will be frequently concordant, whereas DZ twins will have the same concordance as nontwin siblings (in the absence of a congenital factor). Adopted siblings, sharing the family's environment but not their genes, will share the trait no more often than an average sample of the population.

Several twin studies of sexual orientation have been conducted recently. Bailey and Pillard (1991) and Bailey, Pillard et al. (1993) recruited two kinds of gay males: those with twins and those with adopted brothers or sisters. Males were interviewed concerning the sexual orientation of their co-twin or adopted sib, who was contacted where possible. Males were generally accurate in assessing their sibling's sexual orientation. In the male sample 56 MZ twins were ascertained, 52 percent of whom were concordant for a nonheterosexual orientation, 54 DZ twins were ascertained, 22 percent of whom were concordant [the same as for nontwin brothers according to Pillard and Weinrich (1986)], and 57 adopted male sibs were ascertained, 11 percent of whom were concordant with the gay male sib.

The female study yielded concordance rates of 48 percent for MZ twins, 16 percent for DZ twins, and 6 percent for adopted sisters. Heritability estimates for women were likewise substantial. However, more recent data obtained by Bailey et al. (1996) on twins from an Australian twin registry showed little difference in concordance rates between female MZ and DZ twins and thus gave essentially zero heritability for females. This result may be due to the different manner in which the twins were recruited.

Neither age of first recognition of gay or lesbian feelings, extreme Kinsey scale score, nor extent of childhood gender atypicality related to genetic liability for a homosexual orientation. However, both male and female *concordant* MZ twin pairs were also highly similar in their gender atypicality scores, suggesting a genetic basis for this trait. Whitam et al. (1993) reported somewhat higher concordance rates for both MZ and DZ twins. They also reported three sets of triplets. One set consisted of an MZ male pair, concordant for homosexuality, and a heterosexual sister. A second set of three sisters consisted of an MZ pair, both lesbian, and a DZ

heterosexual sister. The third set consisted of three MZ brothers, all gay.

The few available examples of MZ twins *raised apart* (Eckert et al. 1986; Whitam et al. 1993) show a degree of concordance, at least for males, similar to the cited observations of MZ twins raised together. Concordance in several male MZ pairs reared apart extended to an interesting variety of personality traits as well.

The conclusion that sexual orientation has a heritable component depends on a set of assumptions, which we now examine. The primary assumption is that volunteer bias does not distort the outcome. Probands [subjects] for the twin studies were obtained through advertisements in gay-oriented publications. It may be that persons who read these publications and who volunteer for a study are systematically different from the larger population of gay twins or siblings. This possibility can be tested by comparing volunteer data with those from a captive sample, such as from a clinic, or with subjects randomly drawn from a census tract or phone book.

There may also be a systematic concordant-dependent bias; that is, twins or sibs who share a trait may be more (or less) likely to volunteer than those who are discordant. The cited heritability analyses examined the effects of concordance-dependent bias and found that heritability estimates remained substantial over a wide range of assumptions about that kind of bias. Moreover, we found that the concordance rate of DZ twins was similar to the rate of nontwin siblings in other studies of men (Pillard and Weinrich 1986) and women (Bailey and Benishay 1993). We doubt that concordance estimates from the sibling studies were seriously biased because the hypothesis of those studies was concealed from subjects.

The possibility of *asymmetric* concordance-dependent bias could more seriously affect the heritability estimates. This could happen if, for example, concordant MZ twins were relatively more likely to volunteer than concordant DZ twins or adopted siblings. This possibility cannot be completely ruled out; however, the degree of volunteer asymmetry would have to be large to result in a true zero difference in concordance rates between MZ and DZ pairs.

Heritability calculations assume that MZ twins, DZ twins, and adopted siblings share environments that are not systematically different—in this case, not different on variables salient to sexual orientation. At first thought, it must seem that MZ twins are so alike that their family and friends could not help but treat them almost as one individual. Perhaps so, but studies suggest that a violation of the equal-environments assumption does not seem to have much effect. Twins whose parents make a deliberate effort to differentiate them (different clothing, names, schools, etc.) turn out to be as similar on a variety of personality traits as twins treated alike. Furthermore, MZ twins mistakenly thought by their family to be DZ twins are as similar as if they were correctly labeled (Plomin et al. 1990). However, it may be that we simply do not know the relevant environmental precursors of sexual orientation and so cannot judge the extent to which siblings share them.

Twin concordance estimates are affected by the way twins are selected. Hundreds of pairs may have to be screened to obtain a stable estimate of concordance for an infrequent trait. It is much easier just to advertise for twin probands [subjects] expressing the trait of interest. This proband-wise concordance will always produce an overestimate of true concordance simply because there are more concordant individuals eligible to respond. Proband-wise concordance is the probability that a homosexual twin will have a homosexual co-twin.

For clarity of exposition the discussion to this point has tacitly assumed a simple causal model for sexual orientation, an assumption that is almost certainly incorrect. It seems likely, for example, that the orientation of women and men may be differently determined. As already noted, women and men experience sexual attraction in different ways; women are more often bisexual than men, there seems to be less familiality between than within the sexes, and the X-chromosome linkage site reported for men has not been replicated for women (Hu et al. 1995). Extrapolating from what is known about the genetics of other traits, one can see that there may be dozens or even hundreds of alleles [a series of two or more different genes that occupy the same location on a specific chromosome] relevant to sexual orientation. Some alleles may be quite rare, and some may interact with the environment in complex and unexpected ways. The physical and functional identification of genes for sexual orientation is still a distant goal.

Evolutionary Significance

Many human traits are thought to have a genetic component because they run in families and because twin and adoptee concordance rates are compatible with the known principles of genetic transmission. Such traits include the shyness-extroversion axis, certain cognitive abilities, aggressiveness, manic-depressive illness, Tourette's syndrome, specific language disorders, self-esteem, some mental disorders, and some social attitudes (Plomin et al. 1994). A few of these traits (e.g., spatial ability) are thought to have animal analogs.

However, for none of the named traits has a specific gene (or genes) been found. The pathway from gene to behavior is unknown. Environmental sources of variance, substantial in our studies, may include the biological environment, for example, prenatal hormone exposure, the psychosocial environment, or some combination of the two. The interplay between genetic predisposition and environmental releasers or suppressers of a trait is presumably complicated, and at present, nothing is known with respect to sexual orientation.

The special problems posed by the evolution of traits that reduce fecundity have interested biologists since Darwin. If an individual possesses a gene that reduces his or her reproductive ability even slightly, that trait will be negatively selected, although it may reappear in other kindreds by means of a new mutation. But, as noted 25 years ago by Moran (1972), the frequency of homosexual orientation is too great by orders of magnitude to make plausible that it is replenished by random mutations.

The selective disadvantage of homosexuality must be very large in modern society. Bell et al. (1981) found that homosexuals have only one-fifth as many children as heterosexuals. Lesbians and gay men without children are a common feature of the urban milieu and give rise to the further paradox that social tolerance toward gays is the very condition that should promote the negative selection of "gay genes" (Hamer and Copeland 1994). In societies remote from Western influence, lesbians and gay men may more often marry and have children, but some probably adopt nonreproductive roles as celibates, priests, and so forth. In these societies the reproductive loss would be diminished but still present. If a genetic predisposition for a homosexual orientation exists, what advantage could it confer to pay the cost of lost reproduction to the individual?

Three sorts of answers are usually given to this question. One proposes a reproductive advantage to the heterozygote. Fisher (1922) pointed out that for a condition that is reproductively deleterious in the homozygote, there must be a selective advantage for the heterozygote. This issue has been developed by Weinrich and others (Weinrich 1987; MacIntyre and Estep 1993). The hypothetical advantage to the heterozygote need not have anything to do with sexual attraction. It could involve genes with other attributes: conferring resistance to an endemic disease, promoting a larger sibship or coding for personality traits or patterns of cognitive abilities that, for example, help their possessor to hunt the leopard or harvest the yams. It seems likely that the selecting environment "sees" other associated traits, and sexual desire or behaviors carried along as an exaptation.

A second possibility to account for the persistence of "gay genes" is that they prompt their possessor to undertake acts of altruism toward kin such that kin survival more than offsets the reproductive loss (in genetic terms) to the altruist. (Altruism is defined as an act that benefits another at a cost to the altruist.) Examples of kin altruism are reported for animal species and clearly are evolved behaviors (Packer et al. 1991). There is some evidence, both anecdotal and systematic, that gay persons behave more altruistically (Salais and Fischer 1995), but whether this is the behavior that maintains the genotype is of course anyone's guess.

A third possibility for persistence comes from the finding of a putative linkage site on the X chromosome (Hu et al. 1995). A gene conferring reproductive advantage to females (e.g., by making them more beautiful, more desirable as mates) could persist, although it is detrimental to males. Women have two X chromosomes, whereas men have only one, so a fairly small genetic advantage to a female could offset the cost to the male. We reiterate that the three mechanisms are simply speculations, arguments on the general question of the persistence of a phenotype that reduces fecundity. There is no evidence that any one of these mechanisms operates to maintain "gay genes" in a balanced polymorphism in human populations.

A limitation of the family and twin studies is that they can give no clue about where the "gay genes" are or what they do. Specific gene finding techniques are needed to address this issue. Should such genes be found, one question that begs for an answer is the transcultural nature of homosexuality. Herdt (1994) and others have described "third gender" members in various societies—shamans, priests, berdaches, celibates, etc. Some of these individuals are described as having cross-gender attributes and homosexual behaviors possibly analogous to gay and lesbian behavior in Western societies. One hypothesis is that there is a "gay genotype" of ancient origin, now widely dispersed in human societies, the phenotypic expression of which takes the many forms of third genderness described by social scientists.

Research on the presumed selective advantage of a gay genotype will be difficult to implement, first, because the environment that selected it, presumably over generations of prehistoric time, may be different from the one in which it now exists. Second, the selective advantage need be very small, only a percentage point or two, to balance the lost fertility of the individual gay or bisexual family member. These small effects are often buried in noise. Despite these formidable challenges to re-search on the genetics of sexual orientation, we believe that this topic has much to contribute to a more complete understanding of human nature.

References

Bailey, J.M., and D. Benishay. 1993. Familial aggregation of female sexual orientation. *Am. J. Psychiatr.* 150: 272–277.

Bailey, J.M., and R.C. Pillard. 1991. A genetic study of male sexual orientation. *Arch. Gen. Psychiatr.* 48: 1089–1096.

Bailey, J.M., and K.J. Zucker. 1995. Childhood sex-typed behavior and sexual orientation: A conceptual analysis and quantitative review. *Devel. Psychol.* 31: 43–55.

Bailey, J.M., M.P. Dunne, and N.G. Martin. 1996. Distribution correlates and determinants of sexual orientation in a national twin sample. Unpublished.

Bailey, J.M., J. Miller, and L. Willerman. 1993. Maternally rated childhood gender nonconformity in homosexuals and heterosexuals. *Arch. Sex. Behav.* 22: 461–469.

Bailey, J.M., J. Nothnagel, and M. Wolfe. 1995. Retrospectively measured individual differences in childhood sex-typed behavior among gay men: Correspondence between self and maternal reports. *Arch. Sex. Behav.* 24: 613–622.

Bailey, J.M., R.C. Pillard, M.C. Neale et al. 1993. Heritable factors influence sexual orientation in women. *Arch. Gen. Psychiatr.* 50: 217–223.

Bell, A.P., M.S. Weinberg, and S.K. Hammersmith. 1981. *Sexual Preference: Its Development in Men and Women.* Bloomington, IN: Indiana University Press.

Bem, D.J. 1996. Exotic becomes erotic: A developmental theory of sexual orientation. *Psychol. Rev.* 103: 320–335.

Blanchard, R., and A.F. Bogaert. 1996. Homosexuality in men and number of older brothers. *Am. J. Psychiatr.* 153: 27–31.

Bogaert, A.F. 1996. Volunteer bias in human sexuality research: Evidence for both sexuality and personality differences in males. *Arch. Sex. Behav.* 25: 125–140.

Bogaert, A.F., and R. Blanchard. 1996. Handedness in homosexual and heterosexual men in the Kinsey interview data. *Arch. Sex. Behav.* 25: 373–378.

Catania, J.A., D. Binson, A. van der Straten et al. 1995. Methodological research on sexual behavior in the AIDS era. In *Annual Review of Sex Research: An Integrative and Interdisciplinary Review*, R.C. Rosen, ed. Mount Vernon, IA: Society for the Scientific Study of Sexuality, 77–125.

Diamond, M. 1993. Homosexuality and bisexuality in different populations. *Arch. Sex. Behav.* 32: 291–310.

Eckert, E.D., T.J. Bouchard, J. Bohlen et al. 1986. Homosexuality in monozygotic twins reared apart. *Br. J. Psychiatr.* 148: 421–425.

Fisher, R. A. 1922. On the dominance ratio. *Proc. R. Soc. Edinburgh* 42: 321–341.

Fox, R.C. 1996. Bisexuality: An examination of theory and research. In *Textbook of Homosexuality and Men-*

tal Health, R.P. Cabaj and T.S. Stein, eds. Washington, DC: American Psychiatric Press, 147–172.

Fridell, S.R., K.J. Zucker, S.J. Bradley et al. 1996. Physical attractiveness of girls with gender identity disorder. *Arch. Sex. Behav.* 25: 17–31.

Gebhard, P. 1972. Incidence of overt homosexuality in the United States and Western Europe. *In National Institute of Mental Health Task Force on Homosexuality: Final Report and Background Papers*, J. Livingood, ed. DHEW Publication (HMS) 72-9116. Washington, DC: US Department of Health, Education, and Welfare, 22–29.

Gough, H.G., K. Chun, and Y.E. Chung. 1968. Validation of the CPI femininity scale in Korea. *Psychol. Rep.* 22: 155–160.

Green, R. 1987. *The "Sissy Boy Syndrome" and the Development of Homosexuality*. New Haven, CT: Yale University Press.

Hall, J.A.Y., and D. Kimura. 1995. Sexual orientation and performance on sexually dimorphic motor tasks. *Arch. Sex. Behav.* 24: 395–407.

Hamer, D., S. Hu, V.L. Magnuson et al. 1993. A linkage between DNA markers on the X chromosome and male sexual orientation. *Science* 261: 321–327.

Hamer, D., and P. Copeland. 1994. *The Science of Desire: The Search for the Gay Gene and the Biology of Behavior*. New York: Simon and Schuster.

Herdt, G., ed. 1994. *Third Sex, Third Gender: Beyond Sexual Dimorphism in Culture and History*. New York: Zone Books.

Hirschfeld, M. 1936. Homosexuality. In *Encyclopaedia Sexualis: A Comprehensive Encyclopedia/Dictionary of the Sexual Sciences*, V. Robinson, ed. New York: Dingwall-Rock, 321–334.

Hu, S., A. Pattatucci, C. Patterson et al. 1995. Linkage between sexual orientation and chromosome Xq28 in males but not in females. *Natur. Genet.* 11: 248–256.

Kinsey, A.C., W.B. Pomeroy, and C.E. Martin. 1948. *Sexual Behavior in the Human Male*. Philadelphia, PA: W.B. Saunders.

Kinsey, A.C., W.B. Pomeroy, C.E. Martin et al. 1953. *Sexual Behavior in the Human Female*. Philadelphia, PA: W.B. Saunders.

Kohl, J.V. 1995. *The Scent of Eros: Mysteries of Odor in Human Sexuality*. New York: Continuum Publishing.

Laumann, E., J. Gagnon, R. Michael et al. 1994. *The Social Organization of Sexuality: Sexual Practices in the United States*. Chicago, IL: University of Chicago Press.

LeVay, S. 1991. A difference in hypothalamic structure between heterosexual and homosexual men. *Science.* 255: 1034–1037.

MacIntyre, F., and K.W. Estep. 1993. Sperm competition and the persistence of genes for male homosexuality. *Biosystems* 31: 223–233.

Miner, M.H., M.A. West, and D.M. Day. 1995. Sexual preference for child and aggressive stimuli: Comparison of rapists and child molesters using auditory and visual stimuli. *Behav. Res. Ther.* 33: 545–551.

Moran, P.A.P. 1972. Familial effects in schizophrenia and homosexuality. *Aust. N.Z.J. Psychiatr.* 6: 116–119.

Packer, C., D.A. Gilbert, and A.E. Pusey. 1991. A molecular genetic analysis of kinship and cooperation in African lions. *Nature* 351: 562–564.

Pattatucci, A.M.L. 1998. Molecular investigations into complex behavior: Lessons from sexual orientation studies. *Hum. Biol.* 70(2): 367–386.

Phillips, G., and R. Over. 1995. Differences between heterosexual, bisexual, and lesbian women in recalled childhood experiences. *Arch. Sex. Behav.* 24: 1–20.

Pillard, R.C. 1991. Masculinity and femininity in homosexuality: "Inversion" revisited. In *Homosexuality: Research Implications for Public Policy*, J. Gonsiorek and J.D. Weinrich, eds. Newbury Park, CA: Sage Publications, 32–43.

Pillard, R.C., and J.D. Weinrich. 1986. Evidence of familial nature of male homosexuality. *Arch. Gen. Psychiatr.* 43: 808–812.

Pillard, R.C., J.I. Poumadere, and R.A. Carretta. 1982. A family study of sexual orientation. *Arch. Sex. Behav.* 11: 511–520.

Plomin, R., J.C. DeFries, and G.E. McClearn. 1990. *Behavioral Genetics: A Primer*. New York: W.H. Freeman.

Plomin, R., M.J. Owen, and P. McGuffin. 1994. The genetic basis of complex human behaviors. *Science* 264: 1733–1739.

Reite, M., J. Sheeder, D. Richardson et al. 1995. Cerebral laterality in homosexual males: Preliminary communication using magnetoencephalography. *Arch. Sex. Behav.* 24: 585–593.

Rogers, S., and C. Turner. 1991. Male-male sexual contact in the USA: Findings from five sample surveys, 1970–1990. *J. Sex Res.* 28: 491–519.

Salais, D., and R.B. Fischer. 1995. Sexual preference and altruism. *J. Homosex.* 28: 185–196.

Seidman, S.N., and R.O. Rieder. 1994. A review of sexual behavior in the United States. *Am. J. Psychiatr.* 151: 330–341.

Sell, R.L., J.A. Wells, and D. Wypij. 1995. The prevalence of homosexual behavior and attraction in the United States, the United Kingdom, and France: Results of national population-based samples. *Arch. Sex. Behav.* 24: 235–248.

Stringer, P., and T. Grygier. 1976. Male homosexuality, psychiatric patient status, and psychological masculinity and femininity. *Arch. Sex. Behav.* 5: 15–27.

Swaab, D.F., and M.A. Hoffman. 1990. An enlarged suprachiasmatic nucleus in homosexual men. *Brain Res.* 537: 141–148.

Symons, D. 1979. *The Evolution of Human Sexuality*. New York: Oxford University Press.

Terman, L.A., and C. Miles. 1936. *Sex and Personality: Studies in Masculinity and Femininity*. New York: McGraw-Hill.

Ulrichs, K.H. 1994. *The Riddle of "Man-Manly" Love: The Pioneering Work on Male Homosexuality*, M.A. Lombardi-Nash, trans. Buffalo, NY: Prometheus Books.

von Krafft-Ebing, R. 1901. *Psychopathia Sexualis*, 3d ed., translation of 10th German ed. Chicago, IL: W.T. Keener.

Weinrich, J.D. 1987. *Sexual Landscapes*. New York: Scribner's.

Whitam, F.L. 1983. Culturally invariable properties of male homosexuality: Tentative conclusions from cross-cultural research. *Arch. Sex. Behav.* 22: 207–226.

Whitam, F.L., and R.M. Mathy. 1991. Childhood cross-gender behavior of homosexual females in Brazil, Peru, the Philippines, and the United States. *Arch. Sex. Behav.* 20: 151–170.

Whitam, F.L., M. Diamond, and J. Martin. 1993. Homosexual orientation in twins: A report of 61 pairs and three triplet sets. *Arch. Sex. Behav.* 22: 187–206.

Zucker, K., J. Wild, S. Bradley et al. 1993. Physical attractiveness of boys with gender identity disorder. *Arch. Sex. Behav.* 22: 23–36.

Chapter 29
Why We Cannot Conclude Sexual Orientation Is a Biological Phenomenon

William M. Byne

After reading the previous article, claiming that human sexual orientation has a heritable component, readers will be challenged to broaden their conclusions by the Byne selection, which presents counterarguments to a number of scientific studies. For example, are the often quoted LeVay research findings focused more clearly by evidence that the medication used to treat AIDS causes change in the size of the hypothalamus gland? And what conclusions can be drawn from the information that the hormone profiles of gays and lesbians are reportedly indistinguishable from those of heterosexuals? These and other intriguing facts raise issues without answers. But the author, a medical researcher of brain structures and behavior, asks far more penetrating questions. Does biology simply provide a slate of neural circuitry upon which sexual orientation is inscribed by experience? Or do biological factors influence sexual orientation only indirectly by affecting personality variables that influence the environment in social relationships which in turn shape sexual orientation? Students, like more learned scholars, will be unable to answer the questions decisively after finishing this offering, but they will be farther along the path of scientific thought about this matter.

I would like to challenge [the following statement]: "Sexual orientation is primarily a biological phenomenon," from three different perspectives. First, we have to ask whether sexual orientation is a unitary phenomenon that can be accounted for by a single explanation. If, as seems more likely, there are multiple pathways to the same endpoint of relative sexual attraction to men or to women, then biology might play a greater or lesser role for different individuals depending on the idiosyncrasies of their individual developmental pathways. [To say that]: "Sexual orientation is primarily a biological phenomenon," fails to anticipate the need for analysis at such a level of complexity.

Second, what do we mean when we assert that sexual orientation is "primarily biological"? All psychological phenomena are primarily biological in the sense that they cannot exist in the absence of the biological activity of a living brain. "Primarily biological" must mean something else—perhaps, that biological factors are more important than psychosocial or experiential factors. But the processes integral to experience, namely perception, internalization, association, and assimilation, are themselves inextricably enmeshed with biology. How, then, can biological and experiential factors be teased apart, and what are the units of measurement that would allow them to be individually quantified and weighed against one another in order to determine which is more important? I believe that it would be more productive to explore the pathways through which biological and experiential factors might interact, than to argue about the primacy of one set of factors over the other.

The final perspective from which I wish to challenge the debate statement is to address the weakness of the biological database itself. Much of the commonly offered biological evidence has yet to be replicated or has to be discounted because it has failed replication (Byne, 1995, 1996; Byne & Parsons, 1993; Fausto-Sterling, 1992). Even the replicable data are often uninterpretable because of confounded experimental designs (Byne, 1995; Fausto-Sterling, 1992). Beyond these difficulties the research to date has produced purely correlational data. Correlations, no matter how robust, cannot demonstrate that sexual orientation is primarily biological in the absence of adequately controlled longitudinal studies that delineate the intermediate causal mechanisms (Byne, 1996)

Much of the research is premised on assumptions of questionable validity. Most biological research that addresses sexual orientation seeks to demonstrate that the brains of homosexuals are in some ways like those of the other sex (Byne & Parsons, 1993). The rationale behind this research is as follows: First, sexual orientation is assumed to be a unitary brain function that is sexually dimorphic. By sexually dimorphic, I mean that it takes two forms and differs between heterosexual men and heterosexual women. Researchers then seek to define two archetypes for the human brain: One of these they suggest would be shared by gay men and heterosexual women and would drive sexual attraction to men, while the other would be shared by heterosexual men and lesbians and would drive sexual attraction to women. Even a cursory review of human sexuality in historical and cross-cultural perspective suggests that these assumptions are culture bound and inadequate (Boswell, 1980; Ford & Beach, 1951).

Without questioning the validity of these assumptions, some researchers propose that the differentiation of these two archetypes is accomplished prenatally in response to sex differences in exposure to particular hormones (Allen & Gorski, 1992; Gladue et al., 1984; LeVay, 1991). This prenatal hormonal hypothesis draws upon animal research showing that a sexually receptive female mating posture called lordosis can be elicited from male rodents that were deprived of androgens during a critical period of brain development. Conversely, females that were experimentally treated with androgens during that same period fail to show lordosis in adulthood, but will show increased levels of male-typical mounting behavior (Goy & McEwen, 1980).

There are major problems in extrapolating from these findings to sexual orientation in humans. First, in the paradigm of the neuroendocrine laboratory, the male rat that shows lordosis [bending backward] when mounted by another male is considered the homosexual. But it is important to note that lordosis is little more than a reflex, and that the male that displays lordosis when mounted by another male will also display the posture if its back is stroked by a researcher. We cannot infer much about the sexual motivation of the male that exhibits this posture. Ironically, however, the animal that does display sexual motivation—the male that mounts another male—escapes scientific scrutiny and labeling as does the female that displays lordosis when mounted by another female. Some researchers have begun to acknowledge the problem of equating behaviors in rodents with sexual orientation, and have begun to employ a variety of strategies to actually assess partner preference in animals (Paredes & Baum, 1995).

But even these studies may have no relevance to human sexual orientation. This is because in order for the genetic male to behave as a female, with respect to either partner preference or lordosis behavior, he must be exposed to extreme hormonal abnormalities that are unlikely to occur outside the neuroendocrine laboratory. Not only must he be castrated as a neonate, depriving him of androgens, but in order to activate the display of female-typical behaviors and preferences, he must also be injected with estrogens in adulthood (Paredes & Baum, 1995).

It is difficult to see how this situation has any bearing on human sexual orientation when healthy gay men and lesbians have hormonal profiles that are indistinguishable from those of their heterosexual counterparts. Nor do the vast majority of homosexuals exhibit physical stigmata indicative of sexually atypical prenatal hormone levels (Meyer-Bahlburg, 1984).

However, if it proves to be replicable, Simon LeVay's report (1991) concerning the third interstitial nucleus of the anterior hypothalamus could be considered as evidence that some homosexual men experienced low androgen levels prenatally. Specifically, LeVay reported that the third nucleus is smaller in women and gay men than in presumed heterosexual men. The third nucleus in humans closely resembles a structure which, in rats, is much larger in males than in females. In rats, the size of this structure which is known as the sexually dimorphic nucleus of the preoptic area is primarily determined by perinatal hormones (Gorski et al., 1978).

LeVay's report that the size of the third nucleus varies with sexual orientation has been faulted for a number of technical reasons, such as small sample size, inadequate assessment of sexual orientation, and the reliance on the brains of gay subjects with AIDS. The small sample size really isn't a problem. In fact, statistical power analysis suggests that differences as large as those he reported could be detected with even smaller sample sizes. Also, by adding to uncontrolled variance, poor sexual histories would decrease rather than increase the probability of detecting statistically significant differences.

Unfortunately, there has been little discussion of the hormonal abnormalities associated with AIDS and the possible impact of such abnormalities on LeVay's findings. HIV-related hormonal abnormalities need to be taken into account because in some species the size of sexually dimorphic hypothalamic nuclei varies with the amount of testosterone in the adult animal's bloodstream (Commins & Yahr, 1984). Whether or not the nucleus is present is related to prenatal hormonal status. However, if an adult male is castrated, the size of his nucleus will decrease by half. This shrinkage can be prevented by the administration of testosterone, suggesting that testosterone is necessary to maintain the size of the nucleus in the mature animal (Commins & Yahr, 1984).

These findings are potentially highly relevant to LeVay's report because the testes fail in HIV infection and testosterone levels decline. Furthermore, some drugs used commonly to treat the opportunistic infections of AIDS also decrease testosterone levels and the side effects of other medications may elevate estrogen levels (Croxson et al., 1989). Thus, it is entirely possible that the effects on the size of the third nucleus that LeVay attributed to sexual orientation were actually due to some hormonal abnormality resulting from AIDS or its treatment. His inclusion of a few heterosexual men who died with AIDS did not adequately control for this possibility.

In interpreting his study, LeVay (1991) has suggested that the third interstitial nucleus is involved in the "generation of male-typical sexual behavior." But this suggestion is made on the basis of an imprecise reading of the literature. While he is technically correct when he writes that lesions in the region of the rat's sexually dimorphic nucleus disrupt male sexual behavior, the effective lesion site lies above, not within, that nucleus (Arendash & Gorski, 1983). Furthermore, Gary Arendash and Roger Gorski at UCLA have shown that the sexually dimorphic nucleus can be destroyed on both sides of the brain without any effect on mounting behavior (Arendash & Gorski, 1983).

LeVay and Hamer (1994) conclude that similarly placed lesions in male rhesus monkeys cause them to become "completely sexually indifferent to females." But what the paper they cite actually shows is quite different. While dorsally placed medial preoptic lesions did decrease mounting, they by no means eliminated it (Slimp et al., 1978). Moreover, the males in this study pressed a lever for access to females more frequently following the lesions than before. So contrary to LeVay's interpretation, one cannot conclude that the lesioned males were sexually indifferent to females.

In another highly publicized neuroanatomical study, Laura Allen and Roger Gorski reported that the anterior commissure is larger in women and homosexual men than in presumed heterosexual men (Allen & Gorski, 1992). The major problem for this study is that the only other group to study the anterior commissure for sexual dimorphism found a sex difference but in the opposite direction (Demeter et al., 1988).

To summarize so far, then, the neuroendocrinological and neuroanatomical evidence does not allow one to resolve that sexual orientation is primarily biological, and as I will now show, the same can be said about the genetic evidence.

Until only two years ago, the evidence that heritable factors influence sexual orientation consisted only of reports that homosexuality tends to run in families and that identical twins are more likely to share the same sexual orientation than are fraternal twins (Byne & Parsons, 1993). Such studies are not helpful in distinguishing between biological and environmental influences because related individuals share environmental variables as well as genes. Adoption studies are necessary to avoid this confound.

One of the recent heritability studies did include an adoption component, and this suggested a significant environmental contribution to the development of sexual orientation (Bailey & Pillard, 1991). This study included not only identical and fraternal twins, but also the unrelated adopted brothers of the gay probands [subjects]. If there were no environmental effect on sexual orientation, then the rate of homosexuality among the adopted brothers should be equal to the base rate of homosexuality in the population, which recent studies place at somewhere between 2 and 5 percent (Hamer et al., 1993). The fact that the observed concordance rate was 11 percent—that is 2 to 5 times higher than expected—suggests a major environmental contribution—especially when we consider that the rate of homosexuality in the non-twin biological brothers was only 9 percent in the study of Bailey and Pillard (1991), and 13.5 percent in a study by Dean Hamer et al. (1993). If the concordance rate for homosexuality among non-twin brothers is the same whether or not the brothers are biologically related, the concordance cannot be explained genetically.

Of all the recent biological studies, the genetic linkage study by Dean Hamer's group (Hamer et al., 1993) is the most complex conceptually, and the most likely to be misinterpreted, especially by those unfamiliar with the rationale of linkage studies. While this study did suggest that homosexuality may be linked to the X-chromosome in at least one cohort of men, the study did not uncover any particular genetic sequence associated with homosexuality as is commonly believed.

The verdict is still out as to whether or not Hamer's study can be independently replicated. Recent work done by George Ebers's group in London, Ontario, raises doubt. This group is convinced that sexual orientation is genetically determined and is currently screening approximately 10 markers a day distributed across the human genome. While they are confident that they will eventually establish a genetic linkage for homosexuality, they are equally confident that it will not be to the X-chromosome. To date, their family studies based on over 200 gay probands have failed to show any evidence of X linkage (Ebers, personal communication).

In closing, we are a long way from understanding the factors that contribute to sexual orientation. Even if the size of certain brain structures does turn out to be correlated with sexual orientation, current understanding of the brain is inadequate to explain how such quantitative differences could produce qualitative differences in a psychological phenomenon as complex as sexual orientation. Similarly, confirmation of genetic linkage would make clear neither precisely what is inherited nor how the heritable factor influences sexual orientation. For instance, would the heritable factor influence the organization of hypothetical neural circuits that mediate sexual orientation? Or would it act more indirectly, perhaps influencing temperamental variants that in turn influence how one interacts with the environment in constructing the social relationships and experiences from which sexual orientation emerges (Byne, 1996)? The existing biological data are equally compatible with both scenarios, and certainly do not allow us to resolve that sexual orientation is primarily biological.

As research into the biology of sexual orientation proceeds, we should ask why we as a society are so emotionally invested in its outcome. Will it—or should it—make any difference in the way we perceive ourselves and others or in the way we live our lives and allow others to live theirs? Perhaps the answers to the most salient questions in this debate reside not in the biology of human brains, but within the cultures those brains have created.

References

Allen, L. S., & Gorski, R. A. (1992). Sexual orientation and the size of the anterior commissure in the human brain. *Proceedings of the National Academy of Sciences, USA, 89*, 7199–7202.

Arendash, G. W., & Gorski, R. A. (1983). Effects of discrete lesions of the sexually dimorphic nucleus of the preoptic area or other medial preoptic regions on the sexual behavior of male rats. *Brain Research Bulletin, 10*, 147–154.

Bailey, J. M., & Pillard, R. C. (1991). A genetic study of male sexual orientation. *Archives of General Psychiatry, 48*, 1089–1096.

Boswell, J. (1980). *Social tolerance, Christianity, and homosexuality*. Chicago, IL: University of Chicago Press.

Byne, W. (1995). Science and belief: Psychobiological research on sexual orientation. *Journal of Homosexuality 28*, 303–344.

Byne, W. (1996). Biology and homosexuality: Implications of neuroendocrinological and neuroanatomical studies. In R. P. Cabaj & T. S. Stein (Eds.) *Textbook of homosexuality and mental health* (pp. 129–146). Washington, DC: American Psychiatric.

Byne, W., & Parsons, B. (1993). Sexual orientation: The biological theories reappraised. *Archives of General Psychiatry, 50*, 228–239.

Commins, D., & Yahr, P. (1984). Adult testosterone levels influence the morphology of a sexually dimorphic area in the Mongolian gerbil brain. *Journal of Comparative Neurology, 224*, 132–140.

Croxson, T. S., Chapman, W. E., Miller, L. K., Levit, C. D., Senie, R., & Zumoff, B. (1989). Changes in the hypothalamic-pituitary-gonadal axis in human immunodeficiency virus-infected men. *Journal of Clinical Endocrinology and Metabolism, 89*, 317–321.

Demeter, S., Ringo, J. L., & Doty, R. W. (1988). Morphometric analysis of the human corpus callosum and anterior commissure. *Human Neurobiol, 6*, 219–226.

Fausto-Sterling, A. (1992). *Myths of gender: Biological theories about women and men*. New York: Basic Books.

Ford, C. S., & Beach, F. A. (1951). *Patterns of sexual behavior*. New York: Harper and Bros.

Gladue, B. A., Green, R., & Hellman, R. E. (1984). Neuroendocrine response to estrogen and sexual orientation. *Science, 225*, 1496–1499.

Gorski, R. A., Gordon, J. H., Shryne, J. E., & Southam, A. M. (1978). Evidence for a morphological sex difference in the medical preoptic area of the rat brain. *Brain Research, 148*, 333–346.

Goy, R. W., & McEwen, B. S. (1980). *Sexual differentiation of the brain*. Cambridge, MA: MIT Press.

Hamer, D. H., Hu, S., Magnuson, V. L., Hu, N., & Pattatucci, A. M. L. (1993). A linkage between DNA markers on the X chromosome and male sexual orientation. *Science, 261*, 321–327.

LeVay, S. (1991). A difference in hypothalamic structure between heterosexual and homosexual men. *Science, 253*, 1034–1037.

LeVay, S., & Hamer, D. (1994). Evidence for a biological influence in male homosexuality. *Scientific American, 270*, 44–49.

Meyer-Bahlburg, H. F. L. (1984). Psychoendocrine research on sexual orientation: Current status and future options. *Progress in Brain Research, 71*, 375–397.

Paredes, R. G., & Baum, M. J. (1995). Altered sexual partner preference in male ferrets given excitotoxic lesions of the preoptic area/anterior hypothalamus. *Journal of Neuroscience, 15*, 6619–6630.

Slimp, J. C., Hart, B. L., & Goy, R. W. (1978). Heterosexual, autosexual, and social behavior of adult male rhesus monkeys with medial preoptic anterior hypothalamic lesions. *Brain Res, 142*, 105–122.

Chapter 30
Do Parents Influence the Sexual Orientation of Their Children?

Susan E. Golombok

Fiona L. Tasker

A subject of major interest to many students is whether having a homosexual parent will predispose a person to a lesbian or gay identity. Golombok and Tasker investigate family environment as a causative factor in sexual orientation, identifying several factors that may influence whether children grow up to be heterosexual or homosexual. With one exception, they go a step beyond other investigations of adult daughters of lesbian mothers, which have focused on children rather than on adults and have failed to address sexual orientation.

In addition, use of a comparison group of heterosexual parents definitely differentiates this research design from other such studies. But most important is its prospective nature, an approach that allows data about the sexual orientation of young adults reared by lesbian mothers to be examined. Thus, we receive a rare glimpse into the process through which childhood family characteristics and experiences may influence sexual orientation during the transition to adult life. Readers are cautioned, however, to interpret the data with care because respondent attrition in the follow-up stage of the study substantially reduced the sample size. This ambitious piece of research, which challenges readers with far from staid conclusions or "pat" answers, may inspire or incite, yet it definitely will inform.

Opinion varies among biological and psychological theorists regarding the extent to which it is possible for parents to influence the sexual orientation of their children. From a purely biological perspective, parents should make little difference. In contrast, psychoanalytic theorists believe that relationships with parents in childhood are central to the development of sexual orientation in adult life. Research on adults raised in lesbian families provides an opportunity to test theoretical assumptions about the role of parents in their children's sexual orientation; if parents are influential in whether their children grow up to be heterosexual, lesbian, or gay, then it might be expected that lesbian parents would be more likely than heterosexual parents to have lesbian daughters and gay sons. With the exception of Gottman's (1990) investigation of adult daughters of lesbian mothers in which actual sexual behavior was not reported, research on lesbian families has focused on children rather than adults, and sexual orientation has not been assessed (Golombok, Spencer, & Rutter, 1983; Green, Mandel, Hotvedt, Gray, & Smith, 1986; Patterson, 1992).

From the existing literature, it seems that no single factor determines whether a person will identify as heterosexual or homosexual. The current view is that there are a variety of influences, from the prenatal period onward, which may shape development in one direction or the other. Studies of gay men with twin brothers (Bailey & Pillard, 1991) and lesbian women with twin sisters (Bailey, Pillard, Neale, & Agyei, 1993) have found that a significantly greater proportion of monozygotic than dizygotic co-twins were gay or lesbian. The greater concordance between identical than nonidentical twin pairs indicates a genetic link to homosexuality, although this does not mean that a homosexual (or heterosexual) orientation is dependent on a specific genetic pattern. The identification of a genetic marker for male homosexuality has recently been reported by Hamer, Hu, Magnuson, Hu, and Pattatucci (1993). Of 40 pairs of brothers, both of whom were homosexual, 33 pairs were found to have a marker in a small region of the X chromosome, suggesting that there may be a specific gene, yet to be located, which is linked to male homosexuality. However, the presence of this gene, if it exists, would not necessarily determine a homosexual orientation, and not all homosexual men would necessarily possess the gene (the marker was not found in 7 pairs of brothers). Instead, it may be one of many factors that influence development along a homosexual rather than a heterosexual course.

Gonadal hormone levels may constitute another such factor. Although no consistent differences in gonadal hormone levels between heterosexual and homosexual adults have been identified (Meyer-Bahlburg, 1984), there is evidence to suggest that the prenatal hormonal environment may play some part in the development of sexual orientation. Studies of women with congenital adrenal hyperplasia (CAH), a genetically transmitted disorder in which malfunctioning adrenal glands produce high levels of androgens from the prenatal period onward, have found that these women were more likely to consider themselves to be bisexual or lesbian than were women who do not have the disorder, suggesting that raised levels of androgens prenatally may be associated with a lesbian sexual orientation (Dittman, Kappes, & Kappes, 1992; Money, Schwartz, & Lewis, 1984). In addition, a significantly greater proportion of women exposed in utero to the synthetic estrogen diethylstilbestrol (DES), an androgen derivative, reported bisexual or lesbian responsiveness compared with both unexposed women from the same clinic and their unexposed sisters (Ehrhardt et al., 1985). It is important to note, however, that most of the women with CAH, and most of the women prenatally exposed to DES, were heterosexual despite their atypical endocrine history.

On the basis of this research, together with animal research which has demonstrated that gonadal hormones influence the development of sex-typed behavior and sex differences in brain morphology (Goy & McEwen, 1980), it has been proposed that prenatal gonadal hormones may act on the human brain to facilitate development as heterosexual or homosexual (Hines & Green, 1990; Money, 1988). However, the mechanisms involved in the link between prenatal gonadal hormones, sex differences in brain morphology, and sexual orientation have not been established (Byne & Parsons, 1993). Although an anatomical difference in the hypothalamus of homosexual and heterosexual men has recently been identified (LeVay, 1991), the reason for this difference, and how it may influence sexual orientation, remains unknown.

A number of investigations point to a relationship between nonconventional gender role behavior in childhood and adult homosexuality. In retrospective studies, differences in childhood gender role behavior have been found between homosexual and heterosexual men (Bell, Weinberg, & Hammersmith, 1981; Whitam, 1977) and between lesbian and heterosexual women (Bell et al., 1981; Whitam & Mathy, 1991), with homosexual men and lesbian women consistently reporting greater involvement in cross-gender activities. Prospective studies of boys with gender identity disorder (American Psychiatric Association, 1994)—children who express a strong desire to be the other sex and characteristically engage in cross-gender behavior including a marked preference for friends of the other sex—have shown that more than two thirds of the children develop a bisexual or homosexual orientation in adulthood (Green, 1987). Nevertheless, the identification of a link between cross-gender behavior in childhood and homosexuality in adulthood does not mean that all or even most adults who identify as homosexual were nonconventional in their gender role behavior as children. A substantial proportion of gay and lesbian adults who participated in the retrospective studies reported no or few cross-gender behaviors in childhood, and the prospective studies examined gay men who had been referred in childhood to a clinic because of marked cross-gender behavior and thus were not representative of the general population of adult homosexual men. Investigations of parental influences on childhood gender nonconformity have failed to identify a clear and consistent association between the two, either for boys (Roberts, Green, Williams, & Goodman, 1987) or for girls (Green, Williams, & Goodman, 1982). However, to the extent that sexual orientation results from complex interactions between the individual and the social environment, studies that have demonstrated a link between boyhood cross-gender behavior and adult homosexuality suggest that feminine boys, and possibly masculine girls, in lesbian families may be more likely than their counterparts in heterosexual families to develop a sexual orientation toward partners of the same sex.

From the perspective of classical social learning theory, the two processes that are important for children's gender development are differential reinforcement and the modeling of same-sex individuals, particularly same-sex parents (Bandura, 1977; Lytton & Romney, 1991; Mischel, 1966). Although social learning theorists have focused on the development of gender role behavior rather than on sexual orientation, insofar as sexual orientation results from social learning, the processes of reinforcement and modeling would also apply. From this viewpoint, it could be expected that different patterns of reinforcement may be operating in lesbian than in heterosexual families, such that young people in lesbian families would be less likely to be discouraged from embarking upon lesbian or gay relationships. With respect to modeling, contemporary social learning theorists now believe that it is the modeling of gender stereotypes, rather than same-sex parents, that promotes gender development (Bandura, 1986; Perry & Bussey, 1979). Thus, girls would no longer be expected to adopt a lesbian identity simply by observing and imitating their lesbian mother. But by virtue of their nontraditional family, the sons and daughters of lesbian mothers may hold less rigid stereotypes about what constitutes acceptable male and female sexual behavior than their peers in heterosexual families, and they may be more open to involvement in lesbian or gay relationships themselves. Thus, from a social learning theory perspective, children's sexual orientation may be influenced by attitudes toward sexuality in the family in which they are raised.

In examining the cognitive mechanisms involved in gender development, cognitive developmental theorists, like social learning theorists, have focused on the acquisition of sex-typed behavior rather than on sexual orientation (Kohlberg, 1966; Martin, 1993). Cognitive developmental explanations of gender development emphasize that children actively construct for themselves, from the gendered world around them, what it means to be male or female, and they adopt behaviors and characteristics that they perceive as being consistent with their own sex. Again, gender stereotypes, rather than parents, are viewed as being the primary source of gender-related information. To the extent that cognitive processes are contributing to the adoption of a heterosexual or homosexual orientation, it would seem that young people seek out information that is in line with their emerging sexual orientation, and they come to value and identify with those characteristics that are consistent with their view of themselves as heterosexual, lesbian, or gay. Cognitive developmental theorists would place less emphasis on the role of parental attitudes than on prevailing attitudes in the wider social environment. Thus, the social context of the family, within a wider community that is either accepting or rejecting of homosexuality, would be considered to facilitate or inhibit respectively young people's exploration of relationships with partners of the same sex as themselves.

Social constructionist theories start from the premise that sexual feelings are not essential qualities that the individual is born with or that are socialized by childhood experiences (Kitzinger, 1987; Simon & Gagnon, 1987). What these approaches have in common is an emphasis on the individual's active role, guided by his or her culture, in structuring reality and creating sexual meanings for particular acts. Sexual identity is considered to be constructed throughout the life course; the individual first becomes aware of cultural scenarios for sexual encounters and then develops internal fantasies associated with sexual arousal and interpersonal scripts for orchestrating specific sexual acts (Gagnon, 1990). Identification with significant others is believed to be important for enabling an individual either to neutralize a homosexual potential or to construct a homosexual identity. For example, heterosexual parents may respond negatively to what they perceive as children's same-gender sexual activity (Gagnon, 1977). Plummer (1975) suggested that awareness of others who identify as homosexual validates feelings of same-gender attraction that might otherwise go unnoticed or be denied. From a social constructionist perspective, therefore, children raised in lesbian families would be expected to be more likely than children in heterosexual families to adopt a lesbian or gay identity themselves as a result of their exposure to lesbian lifestyles, and often to gay lifestyles as well.

Although psychoanalytically oriented theorists hold the view that homosexuality arises from disturbed relationships with parents (Freud, 1920/1955, 1933; Socarides, 1978), empirical studies of the influence of parent-child relationships on the development of a gay or lesbian identity have produced inconclusive results. In a study of psychoanalysts' reports of the family relationships of their male homosexual patients, the fathers of gay men were described as hostile or distant and the mothers as close—binding, intimate, and dominant (Bieber et al., 1962). With a nonpatient sample, Evans (1969) also showed a similar pattern of a close mother and a detached father. However, Bene (1965) found no evidence that homosexual men who were not in therapy were more likely to have been overprotected by, overindulged by, or strongly attached to their mother than heterosexual men, and in a well-controlled large-scale study by Siegelman (1974), no differences were identified in parental background between homosexual and heterosexual men who were low on neuroticism. Studies of the parents of lesbian women have similarly failed to produce consistent findings, although some investigations have reported mothers of lesbian women to be dominant and fathers to be inferior or weak (Bell et al., 1981; Newcombe, 1985).

Although existing research has failed to produce empirical evidence to demonstrate that parents' behavior influences the development of their children's sexual orientation, all of the studies to date have investigated heterosexual families. In addition, these studies have focused on the quality of parent-child relationships rather than on other aspects of the family environment. By investigating the sexual partner preferences of young adults who have grown up in a lesbian family, we hoped to examine the impact on sexual orientation of being raised by a lesbian mother, and thus to address the question of what influence, if any, parents may have in their children's development as heterosexual, lesbian, or gay. As data in this study were first collected from the families when the children were school age, this prospective investigation not only provides data on the sexual orientation of young adults raised by lesbian mothers, but it also allows an examination of the processes through which childhood family characteristics and experiences may influence the development of sexual orientation during the transition to adult life.

THE CURRENT STUDY
Method

Sample

Twenty-seven lesbian mothers and their 39 children and a control group of 27 heterosexual single mothers and their 39 children first participated in the study when the average age of the children was 9.5 years (Golombok et al., 1983). The two types of family were alike in that the children were being raised by women in the absence of a father in the household, but they differed with respect to the sexual orientation of the mother. The criteria for inclusion were that the lesbian mothers regarded themselves as predominantly or wholly lesbian in their sexual orientation and that their current or most recent sexual relationship was with a woman. The single-parent group was defined in terms of mothers whose most recent sexual relationship had been heterosexual but who did not have a male partner living with them at the time of the original study. The two groups were matched for the age and social class of the mothers, and all of the children had been conceived within a heterosexual relationship.

In 1992–1993, the children, who were 23.5 years old on average, were seen again. For ethical reasons, it was necessary to locate the mothers in the first instance to request permission to recontact their children. Fifty-one of the 54 mothers who participated in the original study were traced. The follow-up sample comprised 25 young adults raised in lesbian families (8 men and 17 women) and 21 young adults raised in heterosexual families (12 men and 9 women).

An examination of the demographic characteristics of the young people who participated at follow-up showed no statistically significant differences between those from lesbian and those from heterosexual single-parent homes with respect to age, gender, ethnicity, and educational qualifications. There were seven pairs of siblings in the lesbian group and five pairs of siblings in the heterosexual group. By the time of the follow-up study, all but one of the original group of heterosexual single mothers were reported by their children to have had at least one heterosexual relationship, and in most cases (18 out of 20), the new male partner had cohabited with the mother while the children were living at home. Likewise, all but one of the children in lesbian families reported that their mother had had at least one lesbian relationship, and in 22 out of 24 cases, their mother's female partner had resided with them. Thus, the large majority of children in both groups had lived in a stepfamily during their adolescent years.

Measures

Data on the young adults' sexual orientation were gathered in the follow-up study by using a semistructured interview with a standardized coding scheme that had been developed specifically for the present investigation (Tasker & Golombok, in press). Each man and woman was interviewed either at home or at the university by a female interviewer (Fiona Tasker). The psychosexual history section of the interview commenced with questions on experience of prepubertal sexual play with same-gender and opposite-gender children and about interest in other children's bodies and physical development during puberty. The men and women were then asked to recall their first crush and subsequent crushes from the beginning of puberty through to their first sexual relationship in order to establish the extent of same-gender and opposite-gender attraction. To further assess the presence or absence of same gender attraction, we asked the participants whether they had ever thought that they might be physically attracted to a friend of the same gender, and whether they had ever had sexual fantasies about someone of the same gender. A chronological sexual relationship history was then given by each interviewee detailing their age when the relationship began, the gender of their partner, the level of sexual contact, and the duration of the relationship. In addition, information was obtained regarding their current sexual identity as heterosexual, bisexual, lesbian, or gay.

Five variables relating to sexual orientation were derived from the interview material: (a) The presence of *same-gender attraction* was established from data on sexual object choice in crushes, fantasies, and sexual relationships from puberty onward. (b) *Consideration of lesbian or gay relationships* was rated according to whether participants had ever previously thought that they might experience same-gender attraction or relationships, or whether they thought it possible that they might do so in the future. (c) *Same-gender sexual relationships* ranged from a single encounter involving only kissing to cohabitation lasting over 1 year. (d) For the variable *sexual identity*, men and women were categorized according to whether they identified as bisexual, lesbian, or gay and expressed a commitment to a bisexual, lesbian, or gay identity in the future. (e) A composite rating of *same-gender sexual interest* was made for each participant.

Family Characteristics

Using an adaptation of a standardized interview previously designed to assess family functioning (Quinton, Rutter, & Rowlands, 1976), we obtained data on characteristics of the lesbian family environment that may be hypothesized to influence the development of children's sexual orientation from the lesbian mothers in the initial study when the children were school age. The variables derived from the initial study were the following: (a) number of years the child had been raised in a heterosexual home, (b) the mother's warmth to the child, (c) the child's contact with his or her father, (d) the child's gender role behavior, (e) quality of the child's peer relationships, (f) quality of the mother's relationship with her current female partner, (g) the mother's relationship history, (h) the mother's openness in showing physical affection, (i) the mother's contentment with her sexual identity, (j) the mother's political involvement, (k) the mother's preference for the child's sexual orientation, and (l) the mother's attitude toward men. Comparable data from the initial study are not available for the young people raised in heterosexual families as it would not have been meaningful to ask the heterosexual mothers questions about lesbian relationships when they had not experienced any (e.g., about physical affection shown toward their female partner in front of the child).

Results

Sexual Orientation: Comparison Between Young Adults Raised in Lesbian and Heterosexual Families

There was no significant difference between adults raised in lesbian families and their peers from single-mother heterosexual households in the proportion who reported sexual attraction to someone of the same gender.

Distinct from the experience of same-gender attraction is consideration of having a lesbian or gay relationship. Significantly more of the young adults from lesbian family backgrounds stated that they had previously considered, or thought it a future possibility, that they might experience same-gender attraction or have a same-gender sexual relationship or both. Fourteen children of lesbian mothers reported this to be the case compared with 3 children of heterosexual mothers. Daughters of lesbian mothers were significantly more likely to consider that they might experience same-gender attraction or have a lesbian relationship than daughters of heterosexual mothers. There was no significant difference between sons from the two family types for this variable.

With respect to actual involvement in same-gender sexual relationships, there was a significant difference between groups such that young adults raised by lesbian mothers were more likely to have had a sexual relationship with someone of the same gender than young adults raised by heterosexual mothers. None of the children from heterosexual families had experienced a lesbian or gay relationship. In contrast, 6 children from lesbian families had become involved in one or more sexual relationships with a partner of the same gender. It was also found that all of the men and women from lesbian (as well as from heterosexual) backgrounds had experienced at least one opposite-gender sexual relationship.

In terms of sexual identity, the large majority of young adults with lesbian mothers identified as heterosexual. Only 2 young women from lesbian families identified as lesbian compared with none from heterosexual families. This group difference did not reach statistical significance.

Childhood Family Characteristics and Adult Sexual Orientation

To examine prospectively the processes that may result in the children of lesbian mothers being more likely to engage in same-gender relationships than those raised by heterosexual mothers, we correlated variables from the initial study relating to family characteristics with the overall rating of same-gender sexual interest for the group of young adults raised by lesbian mothers. Young adults whose mothers had reported greater openness in showing physical affection to their female partner when their children were school age and young adults whose mothers had reported a greater number of lesbian relationships when their children were school age were more likely to report same-gender sexual interest. No significant associations were found between same-gender sexual interest in adulthood and the number of years the child had been raised in a heterosexual household, the mother's warmth to the child, the child's contact with the father, the child's gender role behavior, the quality of the child's peer relationships, the quality of the mother's relationship with her female partner, the mother's contentment with her sexual identity, the mother's political involvement, or the mother's attitude toward men. Similarly, data obtained from the heterosexual mothers in the initial study on the mother's warmth to the child, the child's contact with the father, the child's gender role behavior, and the quality of the child's peer relationships showed no significant association between these variables and the overall rating of the young adults' same-gender sexual interest.

Discussion

The sample studied in the present investigation is unique in that it constitutes the first group of young people raised in lesbian families to be followed from childhood to adulthood. As information about childhood family environment was collected before the participants began to engage in sexual relationships, the findings relating to the characteristics of the lesbian and heterosexual families in which these young people grew up are not confounded by knowledge of their sexual orientation in adult life.

Although no significant difference was found between the proportions of young adults from lesbian and heterosexual families who reported feelings of attraction toward someone of the same gender, those who had grown up in a lesbian family were more likely to consider the possibility of having lesbian or gay relationships, and to actually do so. However, the commonly held assumption that children brought up by lesbian mothers will themselves grow up to be lesbian or gay is not supported by the findings of the study; the majority of children who grew up in lesbian families identified as heterosexual in adulthood, and there was no statistically significant difference between young adults from lesbian and heterosexual family backgrounds with respect to sexual orientation.

It is important to remember that this research was conducted with volunteer samples of lesbian and heterosexual families, thus the generalizability of the findings is reduced. It is not possible to recruit a representative sample of lesbian mothers given that many do not publicly declare their sexual identity. However, both the lesbian and heterosexual groups reflected a diversity of families nationwide, from different socioeconomic backgrounds, and with different political or apolitical perspectives. Although our interviewees may have been reluctant to admit to same-gender sexual preferences, if underreporting took place, it seems reasonable to assume that this would have been more prevalent among men and women from heterosexual homes, as young adults from lesbian families appeared to be more comfortable in discussing lesbian and gay issues in general. Because of limitations of sample size, data have been presented for more than one child per family, which could have inflated significance. However, the 2 daughters who identified as lesbian were from different families, and of the 6 young adults from lesbian families who reported a same-gender relationship, only 2 belonged to the same family, suggesting that the findings cannot be explained in this way. To definitively address the questions raised in this article, one would require a large-scale epidemiological study following children of lesbian and heterosexual parents from childhood to adulthood with respect to their family characteristics and sexual identity development.

The greater proportion of young adults from lesbian families than from heterosexual families who reported consideration of, and involvement in, same-gender sexual relationships suggests an association between childhood family environment and these aspects of sexual development. Moreover, the association found in lesbian families between the degree of openness and acceptance of lesbian and gay relationships and young adults' same-gender sexual interest indicates that family attitudes toward sexual orientation, that is, as accepting or rejecting of gay and lesbian lifestyles, constitute one of the many influences that may shape development in either a heterosexual or a homosexual direction. It seems that growing up in an accepting atmosphere enables individuals who are attracted to same-sex partners to pursue these relationships. This may facilitate the development of a lesbian or gay sexual orientation for some individuals. But, interestingly, the opportunity to explore same-sex relationships may, for others, confirm their heterosexual identity. In the present sample, 4 of the 6 young adults who had experienced same-gender sexual relationships identified as heterosexual in early adulthood. Although the findings suggest that daughters of lesbian mothers are more open to same-sex relationships than are sons, in the initial investigation, there was a higher ratio of sons to daughters in the lesbian group and a higher ratio of daughters to sons in the heterosexual group, which remained at the follow-up. Thus a higher proportion of women than men who reported consideration of, and involvement in, same-sex relationships may reflect this sampling bias.

It is important to point out that the mothers and children who participated in the research were genetically related to each other, and thus it is not possible to disentangle the influence of genetic and social aspects of the parent-child relationship, that is, the influence of parental genetic material as opposed to parental behavior. It cannot be ruled out that the outcomes for these young people would have been the same had they been raised by parents who were genetically unrelated to them (e.g., adoptive parents). However, the results suggest that the group difference in same-gender sexual interest is a consequence of the children's experiences with lesbian and heterosexual mothers while growing up, particularly in view of the finding that the childhood family environments of young adults from lesbian families who reported same-gender sexual interest were characterized by an openness and acceptance of a lesbian lifestyle. It should be noted that the young adults raised in lesbian households were no more likely than those from heterosexual households to experience mental health problems, and both groups obtained scores on standardized measures of emotional well-being that did not differ significantly from those of general population samples (Tasker & Golombok, in press).

Although not inconsistent with biological theories that propose that sexual orientation results from interactions between prenatal factors and postnatal experience (Money, 1988), the findings of this investigation are also compatible with social-cognitive and social constructionist explanations of the psychological mechanisms involved in gender development. What these latter theories have in common is the view that sexual orientation is influenced, to some extent at least, by social norms. From this perspective, if children grow up in an atmosphere of positive attitudes toward homosexuality, they would be expected to be more open to involvement in gay or lesbian relationships themselves. Different aspects of sexual orientation may be influenced to a greater or lesser degree by experiential factors such that sexual experimentation with same-gender partners may be more dependent on a conducive family environment than the development of a lesbian or gay identity. It is worth noting that none of the sons or daughters of lesbian mothers in the present investigation showed marked childhood cross-gender behavior of the type associated with a later lesbian or gay identity. In addition, no difference in childhood role behavior was found between young adults who reported same-gender sexual interest and those who did not.

Whereas there is no evidence from the present investigation to suggest that parents have a determining influence on the sexual orientation of their children, the findings do indicate that by creating a climate of acceptance or rejection of homosexuality within the family, parents may have some impact on their children's sexual experimentation as heterosexual, lesbian, or gay.

Growing attention has been paid in recent years to the social context of families and to the processes through which social environments affect family relationships. It is important to remember that the young adults in this study were born at a time when there was less social acceptance of lesbian women and gay men. As Gagnon (1990) pointed out, young people are now better informed about lesbian and gay lifestyles and know about lesbian and gay possibilities at an earlier age. How the changing social climate may influence exploration of same-gender relationships remains open to speculation. It is conceivable, however, that children born at the present time to heterosexual parents who are accepting of lesbian and gay relationships will be just as open to same-sex exploration in adulthood as their counterparts from lesbian families are today.

References

American Psychiatric Association. (1994). *Diagnostic and statistical manual of mental disorders* (4th ed.). Washington, DC: Author.

Bailey, J. M., & Pillard, R. C. (1991). A genetic study of male sexual orientation. *Archives of General Psychiatry, 48*, 1089–1096.

Bailey, J. M., Pillard, R. C., Neale, M. C., & Agyei, Y. (1993). Heritable factors influence sexual orientation in women. *Archives of General Psychiatry, 50*, 217–223.

Bandura, A. (1977). *Social learning theory.* Englewood Cliffs, NJ: Prentice Hall.

Bandura, A. (1986). *Social foundations of thought and action: A social cognitive theory.* Englewood Cliffs, NJ: Prentice Hall.

Bell, A. P., Weinberg, M. S., & Hammersmith, S. K. (1981). *Sexual preference: Its development in men and women.* Bloomington: Indiana University Press.

Bene, E. (1965). On the genesis of male homosexuality: An attempt at clarifying the role of the parents. *British Journal of Psychiatry, 111*, 803–813.

Bieber, I., Dain, H., Dince, P., Drellick, M., Grand, H., Gondlack, R., Kremer, R., Rifkin, A., Wilber, C., & Bieber, T. (1962). *Homosexuality: A psychoanalytic study.* New York: Basic Books.

Byne, W., & Parsons, B. (1993). Human sexual orientation: The biologic theories reappraised. *Archives of General Psychiatry, 50*, 228–239.

Dittman, R. W., Kappes, M. E., & Kappes, M. H. (1992). Sexual behavior in adolescent and adult females with congenital adrenal hyperplasia. *Psychoneuroendocrinology, 17*, 1–18.

Ehrhardt, A. A., Meyer-Bahlburg, H. F. L., Rosen, L., Feldman, L., Verdiano, N., Zimmerman, I., & McEwen, B. (1985). Sexual orientation after prenatal exposure to exogenous estrogen. *Archives of Sexual Behavior, 14*, 57–77.

Evans, R. (1969). Childhood parental relationships of homosexual men. *Journal of Consulting and Clinical Psychology, 33*, 129–135.

Freud, S. (1933). *Psychology of women: New introductory lectures on psychoanalysis.* London: Hogarth Press.

Freud, S. (1955). Beyond the pleasure principle. In J. Strachey (Ed.), *The standard edition of the complete works of Sigmund Freud* (Vol. 18, pp. 3–68). London: Hogarth Press. (Original work published 1920.)

Gagnon, J. H. (1977). *Human sexuality.* Glenview, IL: Scott Foresman.

Gagnon, J. H. (1990). Gender preference in erotic relations: The Kinsey scale and sexual scripts. In. D. P. McWhirter, S. A. Sanders, & J. M. Reinisch (Eds.), *Homosexuality/heterosexuality: Concepts of sexual orientation* (pp. 177–207). Oxford, England: Oxford University Press.

Golombok, S., Spencer, A., & Rutter, M. (1983). Children in lesbian and single-parent households: Psychosexual and psychiatric appraisal. *Journal of Child Psychological Psychiatry, 24*, 551–572.

Gottman, J. S. (1990). Children of gay and lesbian parents. In F. W. Bozett & M. B. Sussman (Eds.), *Homo-*

sexuality and family relations (pp. 177–196). New York: Harrington Park.

Goy, R. W., & McEwen, B. S. (1980). *Sexual differentiation in the brain*. Cambridge, MA: MIT Press.

Green, R. (1987). *The "sissy boy syndrome" and the development of homosexuality*. New Haven, CT: Yale University Press.

Green, R., Mandel, J., Hotvedt, M., Gray, J., & Smith, L. (1986). Lesbian mothers and their children: A comparison with solo parent heterosexual mothers and their children. *Archives of Sexual Behavior, 15,* 167–184.

Green, R., Williams, K., & Goodman, M. (1982). Ninety-nine "tomboys" and "non-tomboys": Behavioral contrasts and demographic similarities. *Archives of Sexual Behavior, 11,* 247–266.

Hamer, D., Hu, S., Magnuson, V., Hu, N., & Pattatucci, A. (1993). A linkage between DNA markers on the X-chromosome and male sexual orientation. *Science, 261,* 321–327.

Hines, M., & Green, R. (1990). Human hormonal and neural correlates of sex-typed behaviors. *Review of Psychiatry, 10,* 536–555.

Kitzinger, C. (1987). *The social construction of lesbianism*. London: Sage.

Kohlberg, L. (1966). A cognitive-developmental analysis of children's sex-role concepts and attitudes. In E. E. Maccoby (Ed.), *The development of sex differences* (pp. 82–173). Stanford, CA: Stanford University Press.

LeVay, S. (1991). A difference in hypothalamic structure between heterosexual and homosexual men. *Science, 253,* 1034–1037.

Lytton, H., & Romney, D. M. (1991). Parents' differential socialization of boys and girls: A meta-analysis. *Psychological Bulletin, 109,* 267–296.

Martin, C. L. (1993). New directions for assessing children's gender knowledge. *Developmental Review, 13,* 184–204.

Meyer-Bahlburg, H. F. L. (1984). Psychoendocrine research on sexual orientation: Current status and future options. *Progress in Brain Research, 61,* 375–398.

Mischel, W. (1966). A social learning view of sex differences in behavior. In E. E. Maccoby (Ed.), *The development of sex differences* (pp. 56–81). Stanford, CA: Stanford University Press.

Money, J. (1988). *Gay, straight or in-between: The sexology of erotic orientation*. New York: Oxford University Press.

Money, J., Schwartz, M., & Lewis, V. (1984). Adult heterosexual status and fetal hormonal masculinization and demasculinization: 46, XX congenital virilizing adrenal hyperplasia and 46, XY androgen-insensitivity syndrome compared. *Psychoneuroendocrinology, 9,* 405–414.

Newcombe, M. (1985). The role of perceived relative parent personality in the development of heterosexuals, homosexuals, and transvestites. *Archives of Sexual Behavior, 14,* 147–164.

Patterson, C. (1992). Children of lesbian and gay parents. *Child Development, 63,* 1025–1042.

Perry, D. G., & Bussey, K. (1979). The social learning theory of sex difference: Imitation is alive and well. *Journal of Personality and Social Psychology, 37,* 1699–1712.

Plummer, K. (1975). *Sexual stigma: An interactionist account*. London: Routledge & Kegan Paul.

Quinton, D., Rutter, M., & Rowlands, O. (1976). An evaluation of an interview assessment of marriage. *Psychological Medicine, 6,* 577–586.

Roberts, C. W., Green, R., Williams, K., & Goodman, M. (1987). Boyhood gender identity development: A statistical contract of two family groups. *Developmental Psychology, 23,* 544–557.

Siegelman, M. (1974). Parental background of male homosexuals and heterosexuals. *Archives of Sexual Behavior, 6,* 89–96.

Simon, W., & Gagnon, J. H. (1987). A sexual scripts approach. In J. H. Geer & W. T. O'Donahue (Eds.), *Theories of human sexuality* (pp. 363–383). London: Plenum Press.

Socarides, C. W. (1978). *Homosexuality*. New York: Jason Aronson.

Tasker, F., & Golombok, S. (in press). *Growing up in a lesbian family*. New York: Guilford Press.

Whitam, F. (1977). Childhood indicators of male homosexuality. *Archives of Sexual Behavior, 6,* 89–96.

Whitam, F., & Mathy, R. (1991). Childhood cross-gender behavior of homosexual females in Brazil, Peru, the Philippines and the United States. *Archives of Sexual Behavior, 20,* 151–170.

From Susan E. Golombok, and Fiona L. Tasker, "Do Parents Influence the Sexual Orientation of Their Children? Findings From a Longitudinal Study of Lesbian Families." *Developmental Psychology, 32,* 3–11. Copyright © 1996, American Psychological Association. Adapted by permission. ◆

Chapter 31

Dating and Romantic Relationships Among Gay, Lesbian, and Bisexual Youths

Ritch C. Savin-Williams

The Savin-Williams article will be a revelation to many heterosexual students who think of homosexuality in terms of sexual behavior. The brief, poignant quotes add a clear description of the unhappiness experienced by gay/lesbian youth who feel deprived of romantic/love relationships so naturally formed by their heterosexual friends. Although the author stops short of labeling such homosexual youth as developmentally delayed, this assumption could possibly be made from the stories presented that detail the separation of a youth's homoerotic passion from socially sanctioned heterosexual dating. Students with a background in adolescent development will be most likely to understand the possible effects of these nuances in the gay/lesbian youths' growing up experiences. The fact that the termination of a close homosexual relationship for one college man was more stressful than revealing his sexual orientation to his parents portrays in bold relief the significance of a partnered relationship.

One of the limitations of the article is the failure to differentiate the circumstances for bisexual youth from those of homosexual youth. Nevertheless, the article is guaranteed to provoke a lively class discussion for students who feel safe enough to venture into largely uncharted territory.

The Importance of Dating and Romance

According to Scarf (1987), the developmental significance of an intimate relationship is to help us "contact archaic, dimly perceived and yet powerfully meaningful aspects of our inner selves" (p. 79). We desire closeness within the context of a trusting, intimate relationship. Attachment theory posits that humans are prewired for loving and developing strongly felt emotional attachments (Bowlby, 1973). When established, we experience safety, security, and nurturance. Early attachments, including those in infancy, are thought to circumscribe an internal blueprint that profoundly affects future relationships, such as the establishment of intimate friendships and romances in adolescence and adulthood (Hazan & Shaver, 1987).

Developmentally, dating is a means by which romantic relationships are practiced, pursued, and established. It serves a number of important functions, such as entertainment, recreation, and socialization, that assist participants in developing appropriate means of interacting. It also enhances peer group status and facilitates the selection of a mate (Skipper & Nass, 1966). Adolescents who are most confident in their dating abilities begin dating during early adolescence, date frequently, are satisfied with their dating, and are most likely to become involved in a "committed" dating relationship (Herold, 1979).

The establishment of romantic relationships is important for youths regardless of sexual orientation. Isay (1989) noted that falling in love was a critical factor in helping his gay clients feel comfortable with their gay identity and that "the self-affirming value of a mutual relationship over time cannot be overemphasized" (p. 50). Browning (1987) regarded lesbian love relationships as an opportunity to enhance:

> . . . the development of the individual's adult identity by validating her personhood, reinforcing that she deserves to receive and give love. A relationship can also be a source of tremendous emotional support as the woman explores her goals, values, and relationship to the world. (p. 51)

Because dating experience increases the likelihood that an intimate romantic relationship will evolve, the absence of this opportunity may have long-term repercussions. Malyon (1981) noted some of the reverberations:

> Their most charged sexual desires are usually seen as perverted, and their deepest feelings of psychological attachment are regarded as unac-

ceptable. This social disapproval interferes with the preintimacy involvement that fosters the evolution of maturity and self-respect in the domain of object relations. (p. 326)

Culture's Devaluation of Same-Sex Relationships

Relatively speaking, our culture is far more willing to turn a blind eye to sexual than to romantic relationships among same-sex adolescent partners. Same-sex activity may appear "temporary," an experiment, a phase, or a perverted source of fun. But falling in love with someone of the same gender and maintaining a sustained emotional involvement with that person implies an irreversible deviancy at worst and a bad decision at best. In our homes, schools, religious institutions, and media, we teach that intense relationships after early adolescence among members of the same sex "should" raise the concern of good parents, good friends, and good teachers. One result is that youths of all sexual orientations may become frightened of developing close friendships with same-sex peers. They fear that these friendships will be viewed as sexually intimate.

It is hardly surprising that a sexual-minority adolescent can easily become "the loneliest person . . . in the typical high school of today" (Norton, 1976: 376):

> For the homosexual-identified student, high school is often a lonely place where, from every vantage point, there are couples: couples holding hands as they enter school; couples dissolving into an endless wet kiss between school bells; couples exchanging rings with ephemeral vows of devotion and love. (Sears, 1991: 326–327)

The separation of a youth's homoerotic passion from the socially sanctioned act of heterosexual dating can generate self-doubt, anger, and resentment, and can ultimately retard or distort the development of interpersonal intimacy during the adolescent years. Thus, many youths never consider same-sex dating to be a reasonable option, except in their fantasies. Scientific and clinical writings that ignore same-sex romance and dating among youth contribute to this conspiracy of silence. Sexual-minority youth struggle with issues of identity and intimacy because important impediments rooted in our cultural values and attitudes deter them from dating those they love and instead mandate that they date those they cannot love.

Empirical Studies of Same-Sex Romantic Relationships Among Youth

Until the last several years same-sex relationships among sexual-minority youths were seldom recognized in the empirical, scientific literature. With the recent visibility of gay, bisexual, and lesbian youths in the culture at large, social and behavioral scientists are beginning to conduct research focusing on various developmental processes of such youths, including their sexuality and intimacy.

Bisexual, lesbian, and gay youths, whether in Detroit, Minneapolis, Pennsylvania, New York, or the Netherlands, report that they desire to have long-lasting, committed same-sex romantic relationships in their future (D'Augelli, 1991; Sanders, 1980; Savin-Williams, 1990). According to Silverstein (1981), establishing a romantic relationship with a same-sex partner helps one to feel "chosen," to resolve issues of sexual identity, and to feel more complete. Indeed, those who are in a long-term love relationship generally have high levels of self-esteem and self-acceptance.[1]

Although there are few published studies of teens that focus primarily on their same-sex dating or romantic relationships, there are suggestive data that debunk the myth in our culture that gays, lesbians, and bisexuals neither want nor maintain steady, loving same-sex relationships. In two studies of gay and bisexual male youths, same-sex relationships are regarded as highly desirable. Among 29 Minnesota youths, 10 had a steady male partner at the time of the interview, 11 had been in a same-sex relationship, and, most tellingly, all but 2 hoped for a steady male partner in their future (Remafedi, 1987). For these youths, many of whom were living independently with friends or on the street, being in a long-term relationship was considered to be an ideal state. With a college-age sample of 61 males, D'Augelli (1991) reported similar results. One half of his sample was "partnered," and their most troubling mental health concern was termination of a close relationship, ranking just ahead of telling parents about their homosexuality.

The difficulty, however, is to maintain a visible same-sex romance in high school. Sears (1991) interviewed 36 Southern late adolescent and young adult lesbians, gays, and bisexuals. He discovered that although nearly everyone had heterosexually dated in high school, very few dated a member of the same sex during that time. Because of concerns about secrecy and the lack of social support, most same-sex romances involved little emotional commitment and were of short duration. None were overt.

Research with over 300 gay, bisexual, and lesbian youths between the ages of 14 and 23 years (Savin-

Williams, 1990) supports the finding that sexual-minority youths have romantic relationships during adolescence and young adulthood. Almost 90 percent of the females and two thirds of the males reported that they have had a romantic relationship. Of the total number of romances listed, 60 percent were with same-sex partners. The male youths were slightly more likely than lesbian and bisexual female youths to begin their romantic career with a same-sex, rather than an opposite-sex partner.

In the same study, the lesbians and bisexual females who had a high proportion of same-sex romances were most likely to be "out" to others. However, their self-esteem level was essentially the same as those who had a high percentage of heterosexual relationships. If she began same-sex dating early, during adolescence, then a lesbian or bisexual female also tended to be in a current relationship and to experience long-lasting romances. Gay and bisexual male youths who had a large percentage of adolescent romantic relationships with boys had high self-esteem. They were more likely to be publicly "out" to friends and family if they had had a large number of romances. Boys who initiated same-sex romances at an early age were more likely to report that they have had long-term and multiple same-sex relationships.

The findings from these studies are admittedly sparse and do not provide the depth and insight that are needed to help us better understand the experience of being in a same-sex romantic relationship. They do illustrate that youths have same-sex romances while in high school. Where there is desire, some youths will find a way. Sexually active same-sex friendships may evolve into romantic relationships (Savin-Williams, 1995), and those most publicly out are most likely to have had adolescent same-sex romances. Certainly, most lesbian, gay, and bisexual youths value the importance of a same-sex, lifelong, committed relationship in their adult years.

Perhaps the primary issue is not the absence of same-sex romances during adolescence, but the hidden nature of the romances. They are seldom recognized and rarely supported or celebrated. The research data offer little information regarding the psychological impact of not being involved in a same-sex romantic relationship or of having to hide such a relationship when it exists. For this, one must turn to stories of the personal struggles of adolescents.

Personal Struggles

Youths who have same-sex romances during their adolescence face a severe struggle to have these relationships acknowledged and supported. Gibson (1989) noted the troubling contradictions:

> The first romantic involvements of lesbian and gay male youth are a source of great joy to them in affirming their sexual identity, providing them with support, and assuring them that they too can experience love. However, society places extreme hardships on these relationships that make them difficult to establish and maintain. (p. 130)

A significant number of youths, perhaps those feeling most insecure regarding their sexual identity, may fantasize about being sexually intimate with a same-sex partner but have little hope that it could in fact become a reality. One youth, Lawrence, reported this feeling in his coming-out story:

> While growing up, love was something I watched other people experience and enjoy. . . . The countless men I secretly loved and fantasized about were only in private, empty dreams in which love was never returned. I seemed to be the only person in the world with no need for love and companionship. . . . Throughout high school and college I had no way to meet people of the same sex and sexual orientation. These were more years of isolation and secrecy. I saw what other guys my age did, listened to what they said and how they felt. I was expected to be part of a world with which I had nothing in common. (Curtis, 1988:109–110)

A young lesbian, Diane, recalled that "love of women was never a possibility that I even realized could be. You loved your mother and your aunts, and you had girlfriends for a while. Someday, though, you would always meet a man" (Stanley & Wolfe, 1980:47). Girls dated boys and not other girls. Because she did not want to date boys, she did not date.

Another youth knew he had homoerotic attractions, but he never fathomed that they could be expressed to the boy that he most admired, his high school soccer teammate. It took alcohol and the right situation:

> I knew I was checking out the guys in the shower after soccer practice. I thought of myself as hetero who had the urge for males. I fought it, said it was a phase. And then it happened.

> Derek was my best friend. After soccer practice the fall of our junior year we celebrated both making the "A" team by getting really drunk. We were just fooling around and suddenly our pants were off. I was so scared I stayed out of school for three days but we kept being friends and nothing was said until a year later when I came out to everyone and he came up to me with these tears and asked if he made me homosexual. (Savin-Williams, 1995)

It is never easy for youths to directly confront the mores of peers whose values and attitudes are routinely supported by the culture. Nearly all youths know implicitly the rules of socially appropriate behavior and the consequences of nonconformity. This single, most influential barrier to same-sex dating, the threat posed by peers, can have severe repercussions. The penalty for crossing the line of "normalcy" can result in emotional and physical pain.

Peer Harassment as a Barrier to Dating

Price (1982) concluded, "Adolescents can be very cruel to others who are different, who do not conform to the expectations of the peer group" (p. 472). Very little has changed in the last decade. For example, 17-year-old actor Ryan Phillippe worried about the consequences on his family and friends if he played a gay teen on ABC's soap opera *One Life to Live* (Gable, 1992:3D). David Ruffin, 19, of Ferndale, Michigan, explained why he boycotted his high school senior prom: "The kids could tell I was different from them, and I think I was different because I was gay. And when you're dealing with young people, different means not cool" (Bruni, 1992: 10A).

Unlike heterosexual dating, little social advantage, such as peer popularity or acceptance, is gained by holding hands and kissing a same-sex peer in school hallways, shopping malls, or synagogues. Lies are spun to protect secrets and to avoid peer harassment. One lesbian youth, Kim, felt that she had to be an actress around her friends. She lied to friends by creating "Andrew" when she was dating "Andrea" over the weekend (Bruni, 1992).

To avoid harassment, sexual minority adolescents may monitor their interpersonal interactions. They may wonder, "Am I standing too close?" or "Do I appear too happy to see him(her)?" (Anderson, 1987). Hetrick and Martin (1987) found that youths are often apprehensive to show "friendship for a friend of the same sex for fear of being misunderstood or giving away their secretly held sexual orientation" (p. 31). If erotic desires become aroused and threaten expression, youths may seek to terminate same-sex friendships rather than risk revealing their secret. For many adolescents, especially bisexual youths, relationships with the other sex may be easier to develop. The appeal of such relationships is that the youths will be viewed by peers as heterosexual, thus peer acceptance will be enhanced and the threat of harassment and rejection will be reduced. The result is that some sexual-minority youths feel inherently "fake" and they therefore retreat from becoming intimate with others. Although they may meet the implicit and explicit demands of their culture, it is at a cost—their sense of authenticity.

Faking It: Heterosexual Sex and Dating

Retrospective data from gay, bisexual, and lesbian adults reveal the extent to which heterosexual dating and sex are commonplace during the adolescent and young adult years (Bell & Weinberg, 1978; Schafer, 1976; Troiden & Goode, 1980). These might be one-night stands, brief romances, or long-term relationships. Across various studies, nearly two-thirds of gay men and three-quarters of lesbians report having had heterosexual sex in their past. Motivations include fun, curiosity, denial of homoerotic feelings, and pressure to conform to society's insistence on heterosexual norms and behaviors. Even though heterosexual sex often results in a low level of sexual gratification, it is deemed a necessary sacrifice to meet the expectations of peers and, by extension, receive their approval. Only later, as adults, when they have the opportunity to compare these heterosexual relationships with same-sex ones do they fully realize that which they had missed during their younger years.

Several studies with lesbian, bisexual, and gay adolescents document the extent to which they are sexually involved with opposite-sex partners. Few gay and bisexual [male] youth had *extensive* sexual contact with females, even among those who began heterosexual sex at an early age. Sex with one or two girls was usually considered "quite enough." Not infrequently these girls were best friends who expressed a romantic or sexual interest in the gay boys. The male youths liked the girls, but they preferred friendships rather than sexual relations. One youth expressed this dilemma:

> She was a year older and we had been friends for a long time before beginning dating. It was a date with the full thing: dinner, theater, alcohol, making out, sex. At her house and I think we both came during intercourse. I was disappointed because it was such hard work—not physically I mean but emotionally. Later on in my masturbation my fantasies were never of her. We did it once more in high school and then once more when we were in college. I labeled it love but not sexual love. I really wanted them to occur together. It all ended when I labeled myself gay. (Savin-Williams, 1995)

An even greater percentage of lesbian and bisexual female adolescents engaged in heterosexual sexual experiences—2 of every 3 (Herdt & Boxer, 1993), 3 of every 4 (Sears, 1991), and 8 of 10 (Savin-Williams, 1990). Heterosexual activity began as early as second grade and as late as senior year in high school. Few of these girls, however, had extensive sex with boys—usually with two or three boys within the context of dating. Eighteen-year-old Kimba noted that she went through a heterosexual stage:

> . . . trying to figure out what was so great about guys sexually. I still don't understand. I guess that, for straights, it is like it is for me when I am with a woman. . . . I experimented in whatever ways I thought would make a difference, but it was no go. My closest friends are guys; there is caring and closeness between us. (Heron, 1983:82)

Georgina also tried to follow a heterosexual script:

> In sixth and seventh grades you start wearing makeup, you start getting your hair cut, you start liking boys—you start thinking about letting them "French kiss" you. I did all those major things. But, I still didn't feel very satisfied with myself. I remember I never really wanted to be intimate with any guy. I always wanted to be their best friend. (Sears, 1991:327)

One young lesbian, Lisa, found herself "having sex with boys to prove I wasn't gay. Maybe I was even trying to prove it to myself! I didn't enjoy having sex with boys" (Heron, 1983:76). These three lesbian youths forfeited a sense of authenticity, intimacy, and love because they were taught that emotional intimacy can only be achieved with members of the other sex.

The reasons sexual-minority adolescents gave as to why they engaged in heterosexual sex were similar to those reported in retrospective studies by adults. The youths needed to test whether their heterosexual attractions were as strong as their homoerotic ones—thus attempting to disconfirm their homosexuality—and to mask their homosexuality so as to win peer- and self-acceptance and to avoid peer rejection. Many youths believed that they could not really know whether they were lesbian, gay, bisexual, or heterosexual without first experiencing heterosexual sex. For many, however, heterosexual activities consisted of sex without feelings that they tried to enjoy without much success (Herdt & Boxer, 1993). Heterosexual sex felt unnatural because it lacked the desired emotional intensity. One young gay youth reported:

> We'd been dating for three months. I was 15 and she, a year or so older. We had petted previously and so she planned this event. We attempted intercourse in her barn, but I was too nervous. I didn't feel good afterwards because it was not successful. We did it every week for a month or so. It was fun but it wasn't a big deal. But then I did not have a great lust or drive. This was just

normal I guess. It gave me something to do to tell the other guys who were always bragging. (Savin-Williams, 1995)

Similarly, Kimberly always had a steady heterosexual relationship: "It was like I was just going through the motions. It was expected of me, so I did it. I'd kiss him or embrace him but it was like I was just there. He was probably enjoying it, but I wasn't" (Sears, 1991:327).

Jacob, an African American adolescent, dated the prettiest girls in his school in order to maintain his image: "It was more like President Reagan entertaining heads of state. It's expected of you when you're in a certain position" (Sears, 1991: 126–127). Another Southern male youth, Grant, used "group dates" to reinforce his heterosexual image. Rumors that he was gay were squelched because his jock friends came to his defense: "He's not a fag. He has a girlfriend" (Sears, 1991: 328).

These and other personal stories of youths vividly recount the use of heterosexual sex and dating as a cover for an emerging same-sex or bisexual identity. Dating provides opportunities to temporarily "pass" as straight until the meaning of homoerotic feelings are resolved or youths find a safe haven to be lesbian or gay. Heterosexual sex and dating may be less pleasurable than same-sex encounters, but many sexual-minority youths feel that the former are the only safe, acceptable options.

Impediments and Consequences

The difficulties inherent in dating same-sex partners during adolescence are monumental. First is the fundamental difficulty of finding a suitable partner. The vast majority of lesbian, bisexual, and gay youths are closeted, not out to themselves, let alone to others. A second barrier is the consequences of same-sex dating, such as verbal and physical harassment from peers. A third impediment is the lack of public recognition or "celebration" of those who are romantically involved with a member of the same gender. Thus, same-sex dating remains hidden and mysterious, something that is either ridiculed, condemned, or ignored.

The consequences of an exclusively heterosexually oriented atmosphere in the peer social world can be severe and enduring. An adolescent may feel isolated and socially excluded from the world of peers. Sex with others of the same gender may be associated exclusively with anonymous, guilt-ridden encounters, handicapping the ability to develop healthy intimate relationships in adulthood. Denied the opportunity for romantic involvement with someone of the same sex, a youth may suffer impaired self-esteem that reinforces the belief that one is unworthy of love, affection, and intimacy. One youth, Rick, even doubted his ability to love:

> When I started my senior year, I was still unclear about my sexuality. I had dated women with increasing frequency, but never felt love for any of them. I discovered that I could perform sexually with a woman, but heterosexual experiences were not satisfying emotionally. I felt neither love nor emotional oneness with women. Indeed, I had concluded that I was incapable of human love. (Heron, 1983:95–96)

If youths are to take advantage of opportunities to explore their erotic sexuality, it is sometimes, at least for males, confined to clandestine sexual encounters, void of romance, affection, and intimacy but replete with misgivings, anonymity, and guilt.

> Ted was 21 and me, 16. It was New Year's Eve and it was a swimming pool party at my rich friend's house. Not sure why Ted was there but he really came on to me, even putting his arm around me in front of everyone. I wasn't ready for that but I liked it. New Year's Day, every time Ted looked at me I looked away because I thought it was obvious that we had had sex. It did clarify things for me. It didn't feel like I was cheating on [my girlfriend] Beth because the sex felt so different, so right. (Savin-Williams, 1995)

A gay youth may have genital contact with another boy without ever kissing him because to do so would be too meaningful. Remafedi (1990) found this escape from intimacy to be very damaging: "Without appropriate opportunities for peer dating and socialization, gay youth frequently eschew intimacy altogether and resort to transient and anonymous sexual encounters with adults" (p. 1173). One consequence is the increased risk for contracting sexually transmitted diseases, including HIV. This is particularly risky for youths who turn to prostitution to meet their intimacy needs (Coleman, 1989).

When youths eventually match their erotic and intimacy needs, they may be surprised with the results. This was Jacob's experience (Sears, 1991) when he fell in love with Warren, an African American senior who also sang in the choir. Sex quickly evolved into "an emotional thing." Jacob explained: "He got to the point of telling me he loved me. That was the first time anybody ever said any thing like that. It was kind of hard to believe that even after sex there are really feelings" (p. 127).

Equally common, however, especially among closeted youths, is that lesbian, bisexual, and gay teens may experience a poverty of intimacy in their lives and considerable social and emotional isolation. One youth, Grant, enjoyed occasional sex with a star football player, but he was devastated by the subsequent exclusion the athlete meted out to him:

"We would see each other and barely speak but after school we'd see each other a lot. He had his image that he had to keep up and, since it was rumored that I was gay, he didn't want to get a close identity with me" (Sears, 1991: 330).

Largely because of negative peer prohibitions and the lack of social support and recognition, same-sex romances that are initiated have difficulty flourishing. Irwin met Benji in the eighth grade and was immediately attracted to him (Sears, 1991). They shared interests in music and academics and enjoyed long conversations, playing music, and riding in the countryside. Eventually, their attractions for each other were expressed and a romantic, sexual relationship began. Although Irwin was in love with Benji, their relationship soon ended because it was no match for the social pressures and personal goals that conflicted with Irwin being in a same-sex relationship.

Georgina's relationship with Kay began dramatically with intense feelings that were at times ambivalent for both of them. At one point she overheard Kay praying, "Dear Lord, forgive me for the way I am" (Sears, 1991: 333). Georgina's parents demanded that she end her "friendship" with Kay. Georgina told classmates they were just "good friends" and began dating boys as a cover. Despite her love for Kay, the relationship ended when Georgina's boyfriend told her that no one liked her because she hung around "that dyke, Kay." In retropect, Georgina wished: "If everybody would have accepted everybody, I would have stayed with Kay" (p. 334).

Given this situation, lesbian, bisexual, and gay youths in same-sex relationships may place unreasonable and ultimately destructive demands on each other. For example, they may expect that the relationship will resolve all fears of loneliness and isolation and validate all aspects of their personal identity (Browning, 1987).

A Success Story

A vivid account of how a same-sex romantic relationship can empower a youth is depicted in the seminal autobiography of Aaron Fricke (1981), *Reflections of a Rock Lobster*. He fell in love with a classmate, Paul:

> With Paul's help, I started to challenge all the prejudice I had encountered during 16 1/2 years of life. Sure, it was scary to think that half my classmates might hate me if they knew my secret, but from Paul's example I knew it was possible to one day be strong and face them without apprehension. (Fricke, 1981: 44)

Through Paul, Aaron became more resilient and self-confident:

> His strengths were my strengths. . . . I realized that my feelings for him were unlike anything I had felt before. The sense of camaraderie was familiar from other friendships; the deep spiritual love I felt for Paul was new. So was the openness, the sense of communication with another. (Fricke, 1981: 45)

Life gained significance. He wrote poems. He planned a future. He learned to express both kindness and strength. Aaron was in love, with another boy. But no guidelines or models existed on how best to express these feelings:

> Heterosexuals learn early in life what behavior is expected of them. They get practice in their early teens having crushes, talking to their friends about their feelings, going on first dates and to chaperoned parties, and figuring out their feelings. Paul and I hadn't gotten all that practice; our relationship was formed without much of a model to base it on. It was the first time either of us had been in love like this and we spent much of our time just figuring out what that meant for us. (Fricke, 1981: 46)

Eventually, after a court case that received national attention, Aaron won the right to take Paul to the senior prom as his date. This victory was relatively minor compared to the self-respect, authenticity, and pride in being gay that their relationship won for each of them.

Final Reflections

As a clinical and developmental psychologist, I find it disheartening to observe our culture ignoring and condemning sexual-minority youth. One consequence is that myths and stereotypes are perpetuated that interfere with or prevent youths from developing intimate same-sex relationships with those to whom they are erotically and emotionally attracted. Separating passion from affection, engaging in sex with strangers in impersonal and sometimes unsafe places, and finding alienation rather than intimacy in those relationships are not conducive to psychological health. In one study the most common reason given for initial suicide attempts by lesbians and gay men was relationship problems (Bell & Weinberg, 1978).

A youth's limited ability to meet other bisexual, lesbian, and gay adolescents compounds a sense of isolation and alienation. Crushes may develop on "unknowing friends, teachers, and peers. These are often cases of unrequited love with the youth never revealing their true feelings" (Gibson, 1989: 131).

Sexual-minority youths need the validation of those around them as they attempt to develop a personal integrity and to discover those similar to themselves. How long can gay, bisexual, and lesbian adolescents maintain their charades before they encounter difficulty separating the pretensions from the realities? Many "use" heterosexual dating to blind themselves and others. By so doing they attempt to disconfirm to themselves the growing encroachment of their homoerotic attractions while escaping derogatory name calling and gaining peer status and prestige. The incidence of heterosexual sex and relationships in the adolescence of gay men and lesbians attests to these desires.

Future generations of adolescents will no doubt find it easier to establish same-sex relationships. This is due in part to the dramatic increase in the visibility that adult same-sex relationships have received during the last few years. Domestic partnership ordinances in several cities and counties, victories for spousal equivalency rights in businesses, court cases addressing adoption by lesbian couples and challenges to marriage laws by several male couples, the dramatic story of the life partnership of Karen Thompson and Sharon Kowalski, and the "marriage" of former Mr. Universe Bob Paris to male Supermodel Rod Jackson raise public awareness of same-sex romantic relationships. Even Ann Landers (1992) is spreading the word. In a column, an 18-year-old gay teen from Santa Barbara requested that girls quit hitting on him because, as he explained, "I have a very special friend who is a student at the local university . . . and [we] are very happy with each other" (Landers, 1992: 2B).

A decade after Aaron Fricke fought for and won the right to take his boyfriend to the prom, a dozen lesbian, gay, and bisexual youths in the Detroit–Ann Arbor area arranged to have their own prom. Most felt excluded from the traditional high school prom, which they considered "a final, bitter postscript to painful years of feeling left out" (Bruni, 1992: 10A). Seventeen-year-old Brenda said, "I want to feel rich for one moment. I want to feel all glamorous, just for one night" (Bruni, 1992: 10A). Going to the "Fantasy" prom was a celebration that created a sense of pride, a connection with other sexual-minority teens, and a chance to dance—"two girls together, unguarded and unashamed, in the middle of a room filled with teenagers just like them" (Bruni, 1992: 10A). One year later, I attended this prom with my life partner and the number of youths in attendance had increased sixfold.

We need to listen to youths such as Aaron, Diane, and Georgina, to hear their concerns, insights, and solutions. Most of all, we need to end the invisibility of same-sex romantic relationships. It is easily within our power to enhance the well-being of millions of youths, including "Billy Joe," a character in a famous Bobbie Gentry song. If Billy Joe had seen an option to a heterosexual life style, he might have considered an alternative to ending his life by jumping off the Tallahatchie Bridge.

Note

1. The causal pathway, however, is unclear (Savin-Williams, 1990). That is, being in a same-sex romance may build positive self-regard, but it may also be true that those with high self-esteem are more likely to form love relationships and to stay in them.

References

Anderson, D. (1987). Family and peer relations of gay adolescents. In S. C. Geinstein (Ed.), *Adolescent psychiatry: Developmental and clinical studies: Vol. 14* (pp. 162–178). Chicago: The University of Chicago Press.

Bell, A. P., & Weinberg, M. S. (1978). *Homosexualities: A study of diversity among men and women*. New York: Simon & Schuster.

Bowlby, J. (1973). *Attachment and loss: Vol. 2. Separation*. New York: Basic Books.

Browning, C. (1987). Therapeutic issues and intervention strategies with young adult lesbian clients: A developmental approach. *Journal of Homosexuality, 14,* 45–52.

Bruni, F. (1992, May 22). A prom night of their own to dance, laugh, reminisce. *Detroit Free Press,* pp. 1A, 10A.

Coleman, E. (1989). The development of male prostitution activity among gay and bisexual adolescents. *Journal of Homosexuality, 17,* 131–149.

Curtis, W. (Ed.). (1988). *Revelations: A collection of gay male coming out stories*. Boston: Alyson.

D'Augelli, A. R. (1991). Gay men in college: Identity processes and adaptations. *Journal of College Student Development, 32,* 140–146.

Fricke, A. (1981). *Reflections of a rock lobster: A story about growing up gay*. Boston: Alyson.

Gable, D. (1992, June 2). "Life" story looks at roots of homophobia. *USA Today,* p. 3D.

Gibson, P. (1989). Gay male and lesbian youth suicide. In M. R. Feinleib (Ed.), *Report of the secretary's task force on youth suicide, Vol. 3: Prevention and interventions in youth suicide (3-110-3-142)*. Rockville, MD: U.S. Department of Health and Human Services.

Hazan, C., & Shaver, P. (1987). Romantic love conceptualized as an attachment process. *Journal of Personality and Social Psychology, 52,* 511–524.

Herdt, G., & Boxer, A. (1993). *Children of horizons: How gay and lesbian teens are leading a new way out of the closet*. Boston: Beacon.

Herold, E. S. (1979). Variables influencing the dating adjustment of university students. *Journal of Youth and Adolescence, 8,* 73–79.

Heron, A. (Ed.). (1983). *One teenager in ten*. Boston: Alyson.

Hetrick, E. S., & Martin, A. D. (1987). Developmental issues and their resolution for gay and lesbian adolescents. *Journal of Homosexuality, 14,* 25–44.

Isay, R. A. (1989). *Being homosexual: Gay men and their development*. New York: Avon.

Landers, A. (1992, May 26). Gay teen tired of advances from sexually aggressive girls. *Detroit Free Press,* p. 2B.

Malyon, A. K. (1981). The homosexual adolescent: Developmental issues and social bias. *Child Welfare, 60,* 321–330.

Norton, J. L. (1976). The homosexual and counseling. *Personnel and Guidance Journal, 54,* 374–377.

Price, J. H. (1982). High school students' attitudes toward homosexuality. *Journal of School Health, 52,* 469–474.

Remafedi, G. (1987). Male homosexuality: The adolescent's perspective. *Pediatrics, 79,* 326–330.

Remafedi, G. (1990). Fundamental issues in the care of homosexual youth. *Adolescent Medicine, 74,* 1169–1179.

Sanders, G. (1980). Homosexualities in the Netherlands. *Alternative Lifestyles, 3,* 278–311.

Savin-Williams, R. C. (1990). *Gay and lesbian youth: Expressions of identity*. New York: Hemisphere.

Savin-Williams, R. C. (1994). Dating those you can't love and loving those you can't date. In R. Montemayor, G. R. Adams, & T. P. Gullotta (Eds.), *Personal relationships during adolescence: Vol 6. Advances in adolescent development* (pp. 196–215). Newbury Park, CA: Sage.

Savin-Williams, R. C. (1995). *Sex and sexual identity among gay and bisexual males*. Manuscript in preparation, Cornell University, Ithaca, NY.

Scarf, M. (1987). *Intimate partners: Patterns in love and marriage*. New York: Random House.

Schafer, S. (1976). Sexual and social problems of lesbians. *Journal of Sex Research, 12,* 50–69.

Sears, J. T. (1991). *Growing up gay in the South: Race, gender, and journeys of the spirit*. New York: Harrington Park Press.

Silverstein, C. (1981). *Man to man: Gay couples in America*. New York: William Morrow.

Skipper, J. K., Jr., & Nass, G. (1966). Dating behavior: A framework for analysis and an illustration. *Journal of Marriage and the Family, 27,* 412–420.

Stanley, J. P., & Wolfe, S. J. (Eds.). (1980). *The coming out stories*. New York: Persephone.

Troiden, R. R., & Goode, E. (1980). Variables related to the acquisition of a gay identity. *Journal of Homosexuality, 5,* 383–392.

Chapter 32
The War Over Gay Marriage

Evan W. Thomas

A *plethora of polls seems to be the order of the day in the cultural war over gay marriage. The* Newsweek *article that you are about to read quickly followed the U.S. Supreme Court's June 2003 decision declaring anti-sodomy laws unconstitutional. Since that time, the issue of same-sex marriages has been a constantly moving target for state and national pollsters and pundits, armed with their wares. The results of national polls have varied considerably, with the acceptance of gay-lesbian marriage ranging from 34 percent (Sedlye and Elder 2003) to 50 percent (Grossman 2003). However, up to 63 percent of registered voters have supported the idea that gays and lesbians should receive the same civil rights afforded to married persons (The Gallup Organization 2003). Further, 33 percent would also approve granting civil marriage licenses to gay and lesbian couples if religious institutions did not have to recognize or perform the marriages (Morin and Cooperman 2003).*

For readers whose minds insist upon order, here is a time line of recent events surrounding same-sex marriages:

> *June 2003. The U.S. Supreme Court declared anti-sodomy laws to be unconstitutional, based on the constitutional rights of privacy and due process (Lawrence et al. v. Texas 2003). This decision legitimized the right to engage in oral-genital sex or anal intercourse, or both, with persons of the same or opposite sex, married or unmarried.*

> *November 2003. Using the equal protection and due process provisions of the state constitution, the Supreme Judicial Court of Massachusetts ruled that same-sex couples were legally entitled to marry in Massachusetts. The court gave the legislature 180 days to change state law to comply with this decision (Burge 2003). However, on behalf of the state, attorneys presented new arguments that same-sex marriages should not be permitted, asking the Massachusetts Supreme Judicial Court to reconsider its decision.*

> *January 2004. The Supreme Judicial Court of Massachusetts cleared the path to marriage for gay*

> *and lesbian couples in their state when it ruled that government attorneys had failed to identify adequate constitutional reasons to deny the partners' right to marry (Lane 2004). This ruling set into motion new legal battlegrounds, with advocates on both sides of the issue. Governor Mitt Romney denounced the decision and declared that he would work for a constitutional amendment to overturn the ruling. However, the earliest that such an amendment could come before the voters in a referendum is in 2006 (Lane 2004).*

> *February 2004. The Massachusetts Court's ruling set the tone for the 2004 Presidential debates. President Bush announced that he endorsed the concept of an amendment to the U.S. Constitution that would restrict marriage to two persons of the opposite sex, but leave open the possibility for states to allow civil unions (Feldmann 2004). Democratic nominee John Kerry declared his support for civil unions, but at the same time, he stated his belief that the decision for a state constitutional amendment about same sex marriages should be left up to the individual states (Phillips 2004).*

> *March 2004. At this time, thirty-eight (38) states have in place a Defense of Marriage Act, that bans same-sex marriage (Feldman 2004). Meanwhile, Oregon and New Jersey have joined California, New York, New Mexico, and Washington State in issuing marriage licenses to same-sex couples on the grounds that refusing to do so is unconstitutional in their states. However, such actions are believed to be illegal by many legal experts (Bayles 2004).*

If by now you, the reader, are confused by the facts as they have unfolded, take a number! It may be tomorrow or it may well be years from now when the ball is in your court that such political issues are finally settled. Welcome to the world of politics at the beginning of the twenty-first century.

I
t was a homey scene. Standing in their warm kitchen on a winter's day in 2001, Julie and Hillary Goodridge, a couple for 16 years, played the old Beatles song "All You Need Is Love" for their young daughter, Annie. Hillary asked Annie if she knew any people who loved each other. The little girl rattled off the names of her mothers' married friends, heterosexuals all. "What about Mommy and Ma?," asked Hillary. "Well," the child replied, "if you loved each other you'd get married."

"That did it. My heart just dropped," said Hillary. The gay couple headed far the Massachusetts Department of Public Health to get a marriage license. Julie was optimistic, Hillary less so. "I thought we'd be led away in handcuffs," Hillary recalled. Blood tests and $30 in hand, they anxiously asked for an application. "No, you're not allowed to," responded the woman behind the counter. "I'll need two grooms first." Hillary and Julie asked to speak to the department's director. The woman politely told them, "No, you can't get married, and there's nothing you can do about it."

Actually, there was. With the help of the Gay & Lesbian Advocates & Defenders (GLAD), Hillary and Julie sued for the right to be legally wed. Any day now, the Massachusetts Supreme Judicial Court is expected to decide their case. No court in America has ever recognized gay marital vows. But last week Hillary and Julie—and every gay person who wants to be married or adopt a child or hold a job or receive a government benefit or simply enjoy the right to be respected—received a tremendous boost from the highest court in the land.

The outcome of *Lawrence et al. v. Texas*, handed down on the final day of the Supreme Court's 2002–2003 term, was not unexpected. In a Houston apartment five years ago, Tyron Garner and John Geddes Lawrence had been arrested by police for performing a homosexual act and fined $200. By a 6–3 vote, the high court struck down the Texas anti-sodomy law. In some ways, the Supreme Court was just catching up to public opinion. In 1986, in *Bowers v. Hardwick*, a decision that lived in infamy among gays in America, the court had upheld a Georgia anti-sodomy law. At the time, 25 states had such laws. Some 17 years later, only four states banned sodomy between homosexuals (an additional nine states had laws, on the books but rarely enforced, barring sodomy between any sexual partners).

What stunned court watchers—and what promises to change forever the status of homosexuals in America—was the far reach of the court's reasoning. Gays "are entitled to respect for their private lives," said Justice Anthony Kennedy, reading from his majority opinion from the high court's mahogany bench. His voice was quiet and he seemed a little nervous, but his words rang with lasting meaning. Under the due-process clause of the 14th Amendment of the Constitution, Kennedy ruled, gays were entitled to a right of privacy. "The state cannot demean their existence or control their destiny by making their private sexual conduct a crime," said Kennedy. In the crowded courtroom, some of the gay activists and lawyers silently but visibly wept as they listened.

Justice Kennedy's ruling in the Lawrence case "may be one of the two most important opinions of the last 100 years," says David Garrow, legal scholar at Emory University and Pulitzer Prize-winning biographer of Martin Luther King Jr. "It's the most libertarian majority opinion ever issued by the Supreme Court. It's arguably bigger than *Roe v. Wade*,"

said Garrow, referring to the 1973 Supreme Court decision giving women a right to abortion. At least in symbolic terms, Garrow put the decision on a par with *Brown v. Board of Education*, the landmark 1954 ruling declaring that separate was not equal in the nation's public schools.

But it may be years before the ripple effects of *Lawrence* are felt. Just as schools were still segregated in parts of the South a decade after the *Brown* decision, it is likely that attempts to give gays true legal equality with heterosexuals will encounter fierce resistance from people and institutions that still regard homosexuality as morally deviant. The battle—over gay marriage, gay adoption, gays in the military and gays in the workplace—will be fought out court to court, state to state for years to come. Nonetheless, there is no question that the Lawrence case represents a sea change, not just in the Supreme Court, a normally cautious institution, but also in society as a whole.

In 1986, when the court had ruled in the *Bowers* case, Justice Byron White curtly dismissed the argument that the Constitution protected the right of homosexuals to have sex in their own homes. Writing for the majority of justices, White had called such an assertion "facetious." But social norms have been transformed over the past two decades. How mainstream is the idea of "gay rights"? Of the six justices who voted to strike down laws against homosexual sodomy, four were appointed by Republican presidents. (Kennedy, David Souter and John Paul Stevens all subscribed to a right of privacy for gays; Justice Sandra Day O'Connor stuck to the narrower ground that it was unfair to punish gays but not heterosexuals for sodomy.) Polls showed that the justices have public opinion behind them: some six out of 10 Americans believe that homosexual sex between consenting adults should be legal.

One veteran gay activist could sense the change in the attitudes of the justices. Kevin Cathcart, Executive Director of the Lambda Legal Defense and Education Fund, has been part of a small but determined circle of lawyers plotting gay-rights strategy since 1984. In the past, he had to deal with what he called the "ick factor"—the revulsion some heterosexuals feel about homosexual acts. "The Kennedy opinion not only does not have an ick factor," says Cathcart, "but is almost an apology for the ick factor 17 years ago."

One justice was still full of disgust. In a biting, sarcastic voice, Justice Antonin Scalia read his dissent from the bench. He denounced his colleagues for "taking sides in the culture war." He accused the court's majority of having "largely signed on to the so-called homosexual agenda." Most Americans, Scalia warned, "do not want persons who openly engage in homosexual conduct as partners in their business, as scoutmasters for their children, as teachers in their children's schools, or as boarders in their homes." Scalia predicted that the court's decision would cause "a massive disruption of the current social order" by calling into question the government's right to legislate morality. While noting the majority's statement that the case did not involve gay marriage, Scalia scoffed, "Do not believe it."

Scalia's fulmination was impressive, but (as even he might privately concede) it was also an overstatement of the legal and political reality, at least for the immediate future. While gays can now claim some constitutional protection—their new right to privacy under the Lawrence decision—the federal government and the states can override those rights if they have a good enough reason, a "legitimate state interest." Thus, national security could trump privacy in the military and preserve the Pentagon's "don't ask, don't tell" policy on gays. Or the state's interest in preserving "traditional institutions"—like marriage between different-sex couples—might overcome a homosexual's right to not be "demeaned," as Justice Kennedy put it. After *Lawrence*, gays can no longer be branded as criminals. But that does not mean they will enjoy all the rights of "straight" citizens. The current Supreme Court has shown, albeit erratically, a federalist streak: it will not lightly trample "states' rights"—that is, second-guess the power of states to make up their own rules, especially if popular opinion is running strong.

Inevitably, politics will play a role. "People of faith are not going to lie down and allow their faith to be trampled because a politically correct court has run amok," promised the Rev. Lou Sheldon, President of the Traditional Values Coalition. He offered a hint of the battles that lie ahead when a vacancy opens up on the high court. "In this court, you do not have friends of the Judeo-Christian standard. We know who our friends are. And we know who needs to be replaced," said Sheldon. Sandy Rios, President of the Concerned Women for America, predicted moral Armageddon. "We're opening up a complete Pandora's box," she said. Some conservatives, including Justice Scalia, warned that the court's decision would undermine laws barring bigamy, incest and prostitution. Maybe. But states will still be able to ban sexual practices that are obviously hurtful or exploitative of women or minors. Nonetheless, the fear of legalized wantonness will quickly become a campaign issue. Last week the White House—which decided not to file a brief in the case—was taking cover; White House spokesman Ari Fleischer defensively mumbled that gay rights were a matter for the states to decide. Bush's

political handlers were fearful of alienating either gay voters or the legion of Christian conservatives who provided Bush with his electoral base in 2000. "Bush officials apparently think homosexual activists make better leaders than the conservative activists who delivered millions of votes," taunted Bob Knight, Director of the conservative Culture and Family Institute. The fight over gay rights could easily become a "wedge issue" in the 2004 presidential campaign, though Democrats, too, will be wary of getting ahead of public opinion. For the most part, gay rights will be fought out at the local and state level. The struggle will be protracted and there may be a real backlash. An overview of the main battlegrounds:

Gay Marriage

Although gay couples routinely have commitment ceremonies and the *New York Times* wedding pages now run photos of gay and lesbian pairings, no state in the country recognizes or grants gay marriages. (Churches are badly split, with some denominations honoring same-sex unions and others vehemently opposing them.) Vermont comes the closest of any state with "civil unions" that bestow many of the same rights and responsibilities as marriage, but give it a different name—for purely political reasons. A few other states, most notably Massachusetts and California, seem to be edging toward the recognition of gay marriage, either by legislation or judicial fiat. But the stronger movement, at least for now, appears to be in the other direction. Some 37 states—and the federal government—have adopted "Defense of Marriage Acts," which define marriage as applying only to a man and a woman, and—significantly—bar recognition of same-sex marriage from other states.

These laws will inevitably be challenged in the courts under the *Lawrence* decision. On June 11, a court in Ontario, Canada, ruled that same-sex marriages are legal (they are also legal in the Netherlands and Belgium). [The] last weekend [of June 2003] in Toronto, during the city's Gay Pride celebration, the city's marriage office stayed open for extended hours. A dozen of the first 200 customers were Americans who had driven across the border. Legal experts are divided over whether a gay couple with a Canadian marriage license will be recognized back in the States, but they are sure that sooner or later the issue of gay marriage will wind up in the Supreme Court, though probably not for several years.

By then the court may be, as the saying goes, following the election returns. Gary Bauer, the President of American Values and a former presidential candidate, warned that if the Republicans do not take a stand against gay marriage in the 2004 election, then GOP "family values" activists might just sit home rather than work for the party. On the other hand, Bush may pick up votes from libertarians and Republican moderates (the "soccer moms") if he is seen as being compassionate or tolerant of different sexual orientations.

Adoption and Custody

Most states now permit single gays to adopt children. Resistance to gay adoption has waned as studies show that children raised by gays look a lot like those raised by straights—and are no more or less likely to be gay. Still, only 11 states permit same-sex couples to adopt children. The rest of the states are a patchwork of conflicting rules. Florida, swayed by Anita Bryant's 1977 "Save the Children" campaign, is the most restrictive, banning adoption by any gay or lesbian individuals. That law, based largely on moral disapproval, seems vulnerable after *Lawrence*.

The most immediate impact of *Lawrence* will be on custody battles. One Virginia judge, for instance, asked a lesbian to detail her homosexual acts in court testimony and then told her she would lose her child because her behavior was immoral. That sort of reasoning will likely no longer pass constitutional muster.

Gays in the Workplace, Schools and the Military

Big employers have already gotten the message. In 1992 only one of the Fortune 500 companies offered benefits to gay partners. Today the number is 197; including 27 of the top 50. Unfounded worries about getting tagged with massive AIDS bills have been replaced by top companies' desire to compete for gay workers.

Schools and the military will be slower going. Teachers fear harassment or retribution if they support student efforts to form "gay-straight alliances" (even so, there are some 1,700 pro-tolerance clubs in 50 states). The Pentagon will argue that "unit cohesion" will suffer if gays are openly tolerated in the military. Part of the underlying legal basis for the armed services' restrictive "don't ask, don't tell" policy, a federal anti-sodomy law, is likely to be struck down. Still, the courts are very reluctant to interfere with the military.

Despite the challenges ahead, the alliance of gay lawyers who have been working for two decades to overturn discriminatory laws can feel the ground shifting beneath their feet. Susan Sommer, the Supervising Attorney at the Lambda Legal Defense and Education Fund, noted: "But now I feel like when I walk in the courtroom I've got a powerful symbol on our side, the ringing words of Justice Kennedy that *Bowers v. Hardwick* had demeaned gay people."

Lambda is trying to soften up public opinion with town-hall meetings designed to show that gay families are good for the community. "The town halls we're doing tell people, 'Hey, we're just like anyone else-a middle-class, hometown suburban couple that's been called boring'," says Cindy Meneghin, 45, who with her partner, Maureen Kilian, also 45, and their two children, Joshua, 10, and Sarah, 8, are suing to be recognized as a legal family in New Jersey. "You can't look at our beautiful, charming kids and not notice that we're a family, and the myths start tumbling down. What we've found is that people get to know us as people with families and kids, that I coach soccer and take pictures, and Maureen is the best dessert maker in town, and, oh yes, Maureen and Cindy are a gay couple."

At their home in the liberal Boston enclave of Jamaica Plain, Julie and Hillary Goodridge (who adopted the common last name from Hillary's grandmother because it sounded "positive") have found acceptance—except for the time a bunch of high-school kids urinated on their car and yelled "Dyke!" Last week Julie sat down with their daughter, Annie, to explain the *Lawrence* decision. "I had to do it without talking about sodomy," said Julie. "I mean, she's only 7 and three quarters!" "The Supreme Court made an important decision yesterday," Julie told Annie. "They said it was OK for lesbians and gays to love each other." "That's good," said Annie. But she still wants her parents to be married.

Introduction References

Burge, M. H. (2003, November 19). "Gays Have Right to Marry, SJC Says in Historic Ruling Legislature Given 180 Days to Change Law." *Boston Globe*, p. A1.

Feldmann, L. (2004, February 26). "Bush Backs a Marriage Amendment; Announcing Support for a Constitutional Ban on Gay Marriage; Bush Appeals to Conservative Ban." *Christian Science Monitor*, p. 1.

Grossman, C. L. (2003, October 7). "Public Opinion Divided on Gay Marriage." *USA Today*, p. A21.

Lane, C. (2004, February 5). "Massachusetts Court Backs Gay Marriage; 'Civil Unions' Rejected; Same-Sex Couples to Have Equal Status for First Time." *Washington Post*, p. A01.

Lawrence et al. v. Texas, 539 U.S. 102, (2003).

Morin, R., and Cooperman, A. (2003, August 14). "Poll Finds 60; Oppose Recognition by Churches, Especially Their Own Same-Sex Unions Unblessed." *Pittsburgh Post-Gazette*, p. A13.

Phillips, F. (2004, February 27). "Romney Calls Kerry's Stance on Gay Marriage Confusing." *Boston Globe*, p. B1.

Sedlye, K. Q., and Elder, J. (2003, December, 21). "Strong Support Is Found for Ban on Gay Marriage." *New York Times*, p. A1.

The Gallop Organization (2003, May 15). "Six Out of 10 Americans Say Homosexual Relationships Should Be Recognized as Legal." Princeton, NJ: Author.

Part VIII

Sexual Victimization and Compulsion

As illustrated by the topics in Part VIII, sexual victimization and compulsion can run the gamut, ranging from child sexual abuse to cybersex. The one variable inherent in all victimization is power and its misuse. Even though all sexual relationships include an element of power, when this power is shared, partners are empowered and relationships strengthened. But, coercive sexuality is characterized by a clash of personal power (Carroll and Wolpe 1996). Whether evidenced in child sexual abuse, sexual aggression, sexual harassment, or cybersex, an unequal power structure inevitably results in harm.

All adults in our society are called upon to play a role in stemming the tide of sexual victimization. When underage children or adolescents are victims of sexual abuse, laws mandate that any person with knowledge of the incident must play the role of reporter. Once the abuse becomes known and verified by the authorities, professionals become involved. The role of medical and mental health professionals is assessment and, eventually, the role of the therapist is to address healing (Faller 1995). Legal roles may also play a part in the sexual victimization picture as evidenced by various state laws and institutional policies pertaining to sexual aggression and sexual harassment in occupational, educational, medical, and therapeutic settings. But the laws and roles involved in the protection against sexual victimization are not always clear-cut or embraced by everyone. As readers will see, some people question whether or not the government should have any role at all when the setting is in the bedroom.

A number of models of sexual abuse have been advanced, but a comprehensive theory of sexual aggression has yet to be proposed. Such a theoretical vacuum exists in spite of the fact that almost one-half of Americans are affected by this serious social problem as either victims or perpetrators (Laumann, et al. 1994). Viewing sexual aggression only as a societal problem ignores the horrendous personal emotional pain experienced by millions. But, neither is it a purely personal problem. Sexual aggression should be considered a broad mix of both social processes and interpersonal relationships.

Any theoretical model for child sexual abuse must take into account possible immediate causes of sexual abuse, such as the psychology of the abuser and interpersonal relationships as well as possible contextual factors such as social variables and values that make children more or less likely to be victimized (Glaser and Frosh 1988). Sexual victimization of the young arises from two sources: outside factors, including child and adolescent sex rings, pornography, adolescent runaways, and juvenile prostitution, and inside factors, including incest, a family affair. The David Finkelhor, Gerald Hotaling, I. A. Lewis, and Christine Smith (1990) research based on a national survey of adult women and men is considered a classic study in this field.

Nice women don't say "yes," and real men don't say "no." For more than a decade, Charlene Muehlenhard (1988) has maintained a research interest in the controversial topic of sexual scripting. The concept of stereotypes has also involved a number of other researchers studying gender and cultural differences in communication about sexual intercourse. Readers intrigued by the Charlene Muehlenhard and Carie Rodgers' selection are referred to the Sprecher, Hatfield, Cortese, Potapova, and Levitskaya (1994) research, which added yet another dimension to this issue when they investigated the reverse of token resistance, saying "yes" when meaning "no."

If in fact token resistance, as defined by the authors, is a "scripted refusal," it is prudent to ask more about the phenomenon of sexual scripts. Accordingly, many women are reluctant to acknowledge their desire for sexual intercourse, lacking psychological permission to do so because of social norms dictating that "nice girls" should avoid engaging in sexual intercourse before marriage. But what is the basis of such sexual scripts? To answer that question, we must begin at the beginning when, in the first years of life, children discover their genitals and parents begin the long process of imparting their sexual attitudes and behaviors to their offspring. Other family members, and eventually peers, soon join this parade of values. Whether these and successive sexual experiences in the culture in which children are reared relay positive or negative sexual messages, by adulthood, a person has fairly well-established sexual attitudes and ways of interacting sexually. This personal model is called a sexual script. The Muehlenhard and Rodgers selection leads students into yet uncharted waters in search of answers to ongoing communication dilemmas that occur when sexual scripts collide.

In previous chapters, students have read about gender differences related to sexuality on a number of dimensions: desire, infidelity, sexual dysfunction, and drug research to name only a few. The research by Cindy Struckman-Johnson, David Struckman-Johnson, and Peter Anderson investigates gender differences in a subject long considered to be uniquely a feminine experience: sexual coercion. Based on the assumption that language is power, the chapter challenges students to clarify the term "sexual coercion" and its various uses. Struckman-Johnson and colleagues define sexual coercion for their purposes as the act of using pressure, alcohol or drugs, or force to have sexual contact with someone against her or his will. The fact that the sample studied in this research consists of university women and men makes the research believable, if not a *déjà vu* experience, for students.

But, upon finishing this selection, students may find themselves with more questions than answers and in considerable disagreement with their classmates. What constitutes verbal pressure? What constitutes force? Does sexual coercion include threats of physical force as well as physical force? And, just how intoxicated does the person have to be? Does the alcohol or drug need to be given by the perpetrator? What if both persons are intoxicated? Clearly, most readers will be interested in what this research offers to clarify such cloudy issues. And, those who are motivated to expand their thinking beyond these obvious questions will find at least some other recent research on the topic.

One of the more interesting new studies investigates the subject of gender and coercive sexual behavior within the framework of "social rules." Researchers posed two questions: (1) Are there social rules regarding sexual behavior that indicate when sex may be desired, expected, or obligatory? (2) Do some rules legitimize a man's initiation of sex with a woman, regardless of the woman's desires or intentions (Anderson, Taylor-Simpson, and Herrmann 2004)? Using the "Rules About Sex" questionnaire, which was developed to study these questions, gender differences were discovered in the use of rules that would indicate when sex may be desired. Girls and women endorsed fewer rules than did boys and men, and university students endorsed fewer rules than did middle school children. An association between boys' and men's self-reported sexually coercive behavior and beliefs about who should initiate sex was also found. Students who explore relationships between these findings and those in the Struckman-Johnson et al. study will exercise their critical thinking skills and, perhaps, even those of their professor.

Gordon Hall, Amy Windover, and Gloria Maramba's exploration of numerous types of sexual aggression provides a well-developed review of empirical research in the general population, even though the article's focus is on Asian Americans. This study raises many questions. Is the low rate of sexual aggression among Asian Americans because this group is less likely than others to experience developmental, motivational, and situational risk factors? In the Asian culture, does the emphasis on self-control of sexual and aggressive behavior serve as a protective factor? In this population, what are the relative roles of internal and external factors? These and other such queries can be more factually answered after reading Hall and colleagues' offering.

Handwritten love letters carried by Pony Express, telephone conversations between lovers on different continents, and online chats in cyberspace. What are the differences? Years of technological advances in communication (Occhetti 2003). The September–October 2002 issue of the *Family Therapy Magazine* was devoted to the subject "relationships in cyberspace." It featured several articles illustrating that human communication in its many forms is vital to the fabric of all societies. The Jennifer Schneider chapter, highlighting cybersex addiction and its effects on the family, is an important new feature in Part VIII on sexual victimization. The survey, which was completed by women and men who had experienced serious adverse consequences of their partner's cybersex involvement, offers a wealth of information on a relatively new and controversial subject.

One of the more significant facts revealed by the survey was that almost one-third of the respondents indicated that the cybersex activities of their spouse were a continuation of preexisting compulsive sexual behaviors. This finding raises interesting questions about cause and effect: Does Internet use cause or is it the result of an addiction? Also, what is normal Internet usage? And, what about terminology? Is such behavior an addiction or is it sexual compulsivity?

Eli Coleman (1992), Director of the Human Sexuality Program at the University of Minnesota Medical School, has argued that sexual activity, if inadequately controlled, is an *obsessive-compulsive disorder* (OCD). Thus, he believes that the syndrome should be called sexual compulsivity rather than sexual addiction. Coleman points to the fact that, unlike OCD, the syndrome of sexual addiction has never been included in the standard diagnostic classification system used in the United States—*The Diagnostic and Statistical Manual of Mental Disorders* (American Psychiatric Association 1994). Gold (2001) has stated, "The lack of a clear, widely agreed upon definition of sexual addiction itself has created considerable confusion about the concept and its practical application" (p. 347). Not surprisingly, the Internet itself has spawned a proliferation of websites with personal and professional opinions about this puzzle. Students surfing the Internet will discover new terms emerging, such as Pathological Internet Use (PID) and Internet Addiction Disorder (IAD) (Occhetti 2003). Most authorities, however, believe the jury is still out on the subject of what inadequately controlled sexual behavior on the Internet should be called. There appears to be an ever widening circle of choices: IAD, PID, OCD, or CA (cybersex addiction).

Although answers about causal relationships between online behavior and its effects are lacking, research does confirm that online usage is a problem when it interferes with a person's normal life and relationships (Kraut et al. 1998). All of which begs the question: "If a rose by any other name is a rose," is a problem by any other name a problem? The scenarios in this offering will, without question, infuse a dose of reality into the minds of students, most of whom have spent an entire lifetime in a cyberspace world. We can all hope that, as a jury, they will reach reasoned opinions on this subject.

The Nova Sweet and Richard Tewksbury study provides a glimpse into the personal and background characteristics of sex workers in the stripping industry. But, this work does not simply focus on factors usually studied in the genre, such as who strippers are and how they perform their jobs. Instead, by collecting firsthand accounts of early background experiences of women who work in this much maligned industry, the authors invite readers to a holistic perspective about the subject. Surprising concepts, such as ordinal position, the ugly duckling syndrome, and exhibitionism, are brought to life in this qualitative analysis of experiential factors revealed in words of young women who have chosen stripping as a career.

This chapter will challenge readers to review their knowledge about contemporary feminist theorists and ways in which they analyze circumstances shaping women's lives and the social and political understanding of what it means to be a woman. Astute readers who consider the subjects of sex workers, sexual deviance, and sexual victimization may search for feminist language, looking for words such as *subordination, marginalization,* or *commodization*. But, these words will not be found. Nor will the authors talk about the "saleability" of female sexuality that contributes to women's devaluation and objectification (Davis 2001). Searching beneath the words for meaning, however, readers will recognize the practical application of many of these concepts.

This selection about stripping does not address theory, but its content is not atheoretical. Students who are knowledgeable about feminist theories will probably be better able to form generalizations of their own and ask questions that could lead to a spirited class discussion. Even though this work is not an analytical discussion of all of the variables that will surface in the readers' minds, it is a rare glimpse into the reality of Act I in "The Life Scenes Behind the Act of Stripping."

References

American Psychiatric Association. (1994). *Diagnostic and Statistical Manual of Mental Disorders,* Fourth Edition. Washington, DC: Author.

Anderson, V. N., Taylor-Simpson, D., and Hermann, D. J. (2004). "Gender, Age, and Rape-Supportive Rules." *Sex Roles,* 50, 77–90.

Carroll, J. L., and Wolpe, P. R. (1996). *Sexuality and Gender in Society.* New York: HarperCollins.

Coleman, E. (1992). "Is Your Patient Suffering From Compulsive Sexual Behavior?" *Psychiatric Annuals,* 22, 320–325.

Davis, N. (2001). "Theories of Sexual Deviance, Feminist." In N. Davis and G. Geis (Vol. Eds.), *Encyclopedia of Criminal and Deviant Behavior,* Vol 3. Sexual deviance (pp. 409–414). Philadelphia, PA: Taylor and Francis.

Faller, K. C. (1995). "Assessment and Treatment in Child Sexual Abuse." In G. A. Rekers (Ed.), *Handbook of Child and Adolescent Sexual Problems* (pp. 209–231). New York: Lexington.

Finkelhor, D., Hotaling, G., Lewis, I. A., and Smith, C. (1990). "Sexual Abuse in a National Survey of adult Men and Women: Prevalence, Characteristics, and Rick Factors." *Child Abuse and Neglect,* 14, 14–28.

Glaser, D., and Frosh, S. (1988). *Child and Sexual Abuse.* Chicago: Dorsey.

Gold, S. N. (2001). "Sexual Addiction." In N. Davis and G. Geis (Vols. Eds.), *Encyclopedia of Clinical and Deviant Behavior,* Vol. 3. Sexual deviance (pp. 347–350). Philadelphia, PA: Taylor and Francis.

Kraut, P., Patterson, M., Lundamark, V., Kiesler, S., Mukophadhyay, T., and Scherlis, W. (1998). "Internet Paradox: A Social Technology That Reduces Social Involvement and Psychological Well-being? *American Psychologist,* 53, 1017–1031.

Laumann, E. O., Gagnon, J. H., Michael, R. T., and Michaels, S. (1994). *The Social Organization of Sexuality: Sexual Practices in the United States.* Chicago: University of Chicago Press.

Muehlenhard, C. L. (1988). " 'Nice Women' Don't Say Yes and 'Real Men' Don't Say No: How Miscommunication and the Double Standard Can Cause Sexual Problems." *Women and Therapy,* 7, 95–108.

Occhetti, D. R. (2003, September-October). "E-Communication: Pros and Cons." *Family Therapy Magazine,* pp. 28–31.

Sprecher, S., Hatfield, E., Cortese, A., Potapova, E., and Levitskaya, A. (1994). "Token Resistance to Sexual Intercourse: College Students' Dating Experiences in Three Countries." *Journal of Sex Research,* 31, 125–132. ✦

Chapter 33
Sexual Abuse in a National Survey of Adult Men and Women

David Finkelhor

Gerald Hotaling

I. A. Lewis

Christine Smith

The Finkelhor et al. widely cited research, based on a national probability sample, is regarded by many professionals as the "gold standard" concerning the prevalence of child sexual abuse in the United States. Although the data, collected in 1985, are fifteen years old, they have assumed a life of their own, analogous in a lesser way to the Kinsey work. Those familiar with the Laumann et al. findings concerning persons who under the age of 18 were sexually abused will note a significantly larger percentage reported in this earlier study of a decade ago. Many questions could be raised by such differences. Are fewer reported cases of child sexual abuse in the later study a function of the research design or data collection techniques? Or is it safe to assume that actually there is less child sexual abuse today than formerly? Although the answers to those questions do not appear in this selection, the carefully reported findings on this important topic do furnish information with which students can form a hypothesis concerning such issues. The strong predictors of child sexual abuse found in this study may not be as surprising for students of family studies or child development as for those less familiar with the myriad effects of an unhappy family life. Nevertheless, this selection will challenge the thinking of all students about a compelling topic so important to the well-being of society.

Much of the important scientific knowledge about the nature, prevalence, and impact of child sexual abuse has come from community surveys of adults, reporting on their histories of abuse (Finkelhor, 1984; Russell, 1986). The revelations of these studies have suggested that even larger studies and ones using nationally representative samples could provide additional, valuable answers to questions about prevalence and risk factors. This paper reports on a large, national survey on the subject of sexual abuse and presents its findings concerning prevalence and risk factors.

THE CURRENT STUDY
Methodology

The survey was conducted in late July 1985. The *Los Angeles Times* Poll, a highly respected and experienced survey research organization, interviewed a sample of 2,626 American men and women 18 years of age or older, over the phone. The sampling frame was all residential telephones in the U.S., including the states of Alaska and Hawaii. The sample of 1,145 men and 1,481 women were questioned for approximately a half hour on topics related to sexual abuse—their attitude toward the problem, their own experiences, and their opinions about what should be done. The sample conformed in all respects to census demographics for the United States as a whole and to demographics for other similar telephone surveys. The refusal rate was 24 percent.

A history of sexual abuse was elicited through responses to four questions:

1. When you were a child (age 18 or under), can you remember having any experience you would now consider sexual abuse—like someone trying or succeeding in having any kind of sexual intercourse with you, or anything like that?

2. When you were a child, can you remember any kind of experience that you would now consider sexual abuse involving someone touching you, or grabbing you, or kissing you, or rubbing up against your body either in a public place or private—or anything like that?

3. When you were a child, can you remember any kind of experience that you would now consider sexual abuse involving someone taking nude photographs of you, or someone exhibiting parts of their body to you, or someone performing some sex act in your presence—or anything like that?

4. When you were a child, can you remember any kind of experience that you would now consider sexual abuse involving oral sex or sodomy—or anything like that?

These screening questions are more comprehensive than some that have been used in earlier surveys, but they also have some problems, in part because they allow for a partially undefined interpretation of sexual abuse. Experiences some researchers might define as abuse could be left out because the respondent did not consider them as abuse. Other experiences of a minor nature that many researchers would exclude could have been counted because of a respondent's broad interpretation of the phrase "anything like that." Unfortunately, no subsequent questions were asked about the sexual acts that could have been used to exclude experiences that did not meet researchers' criteria.

On the other hand, these screening questions are an improvement over surveys which asked only a single broad question about a history of abuse. Comparison among studies has shown that respondents disclose more experiences when they are given multiple opportunities to disclose and a variety of cues about the kinds of events researchers are interested in as opposed to a single screening question (Peters, Wyatt, & Finkelhor, 1986).

Findings

Prevalence and Characteristics

The responses to the four screening questions are shown in Table 33.1. If we count as a victim anyone who answered yes to any one of the four questions, a history of sexual abuse was disclosed by 27 percent of the women and 16 percent of the men. More information on the nature of these experiences appears in Tables 33.2 and 33.3. The median age of abuse was 9.9 for boys and 9.6 for girls, with the victimization of 22 percent of the boys and 23 percent of the girls occurring before age 8. Boys were more likely to be abused by strangers, whereas girls were more likely to be abused by family members. Of the girl victims, 6 percent were abused by a father or stepfather. Half the offenders were seen by the victims to be authority figures. Both men and women reported that most of their abuse was perpetrated by men: 83 percent of the offenders against boys and 98 percent of the offenders against girls. Most of the offenders were 10 or more years older than their victims, but boys were more likely to be abused by younger offenders, most of whom were older adolescents. Very little of the abuse was by peers. Of the male victims, 62 percent and 49 percent of the female victims said they had experienced

Table 33.1
Types of Sexual Abuse

Type of Abuse	Men* %	Women* %
Sexual intercourse	9.5	14.6
Touch, Grab, Kiss	4.5	19.6
Exhibition, Nude Photos, Performing		
Photos	—	0.1
Exhibition	1.0	3.2
Performing	0.3	0.3
Other	0.3	0.1
Oral Sex, Sodomy	0.4	0.1

* Men (n = 1145); Women (n = 1481).

Table 33.2
Age of Sexual Abuse Victim

Age of Victim	Men* %	Women* %
Age at Time of Abuse		
0–6	12	14
7	10	9
8	12	11
9	6	7
10	11	15
11	7	8
12	11	14
13	11	8
14	8	4
15	3	2
16–18	6	6
Don't know	3	2
Median	**9.9**	**9.6**

* Men (n = 1145); Women (n = 1481).

Table 33.3
Characteristics of Sexual Abuse Perpetrators

Characteristics of Perpetrators	Men* %	Women* %
Gender of Perpetrator		
Male	83	98
Female	17	1
Age Difference		
3 years or less	3	4
4 to 10 years	34	19
10 years or more	61	72
Don't know	2	5
Relationship to Perpetrator		
Stranger	40	21
Known	31	33
Friend	13	8
Cousin	5	5
Uncle/Aunt	5	14
Sibling	1	2
Grandparent	0	2
Stepparent	0	3
Natural/parent	0	3
Other	5	9
Authority figure	49	49

* Men (*n* = 1145); Women (*n* = 1481).

actual or attempted intercourse. Force was used in only 15 percent of the incidents to boys and 19 percent of the incidents to girls. A majority of the experiences were one-time events, and there was no significant gender difference in the percentage of experiences lasting more than a year. However, boys were somewhat more likely never to have disclosed the experience to anyone.

Overall, the description of abuse experiences from this national survey conforms to findings from other surveys (see Finkelhor, 1987; Russell, 1986) with two main exceptions. There was an unusually large amount of actual or attempted intercourse (49 percent of girls in this survey compared to only 20 percent in Russell's survey) and an unusually small amount of coercion (only 19 percent of the incidents to girls in this survey compared to 41 percent in Russell). Both of these differences are probably due to quirks of particular survey questions. The question on coercion introduced a bias; it asked, "Did this person use any kind of force when this happened; for example, did this person strike you or use a weapon or threaten to harm you in any way or to restrain you by physical strength." Because force is illustrated in this question with exam-

ples of very serious force, victims who were bullied, intimidated or felt that the act was against their wishes may have been reluctant to say yes. Half or more of victims in other surveys (Finkelhor, 1979) report force or coercion. We are inclined to discount the findings from this survey on intercourse and force.

Risk Factors

Men and women were more likely to have been victimized if they reported that their family life had been unhappy, if their predominant family situation had been one without one of their natural parents, or if they were currently living in the Pacific region. Men, in addition, were at higher risk if their family came from English or Scandinavian ancestry. Women were at higher risk if they received an inadequate sex education. Older women were also at lower risk compared to younger women. Aside from these factors, other possible background characteristics such as race, parents' education, and having few friends were not related to victimization.

Unhappy Family Life

Growing up in an unhappy family appeared to be the most powerful risk factor for abuse. Both men and women who described their families this way were more than twice as likely to be abused. It is easy to understand why a child from an unhappy family might be vulnerable to the manipulations of an abuser who was offering affection or companionship to trick a child.

However, it is also possible that the causal relationship might be reversed. Some victims may have been describing their family life as an unhappy one because they were abused there or because they could never confide their secret there. To test for this, we repeated the analysis twice: first, for victims of extra-familial abuse only; and second, only for victims who had disclosed their abuse to a family member (girls only—there were too few boys who had disclosed).

An unhappy family life was still a strong predictor of abuse. This suggests that unhappy family life is a true risk factor and not simply a distorted perception that a victim develops as a result of having been abused. Moreover, an unhappy family life may contribute to the risk for abuse outside as well as inside the family for two reasons (Finkelhor & Baron, 1986): first, children in such families probably receive poorer supervision when out of the home; and, such children, who may have particularly strong needs for positive attention and affection, may be more vulnerable to the ploys of nonfamily perpetrators who offer attention and affection as a lure.

Living Without a Natural Parent

Separation from a natural parent for a major portion of one's childhood was a risk factor in this study as in a number of other studies (Bagley & Ramsay, 1986; Finkelhor, 1979; Russell, 1986). Interestingly, girls showed markedly higher risk under all family circumstances except that of living with two natural parents and particularly when living alone with father or with two non-natural parents. Moreover, this higher risk held for all types of sexual abuse, not just the intrafamily type. Boys, in contrast, were primarily at risk only in two family constellations: when they lived with their mothers alone or with two non-natural parents. It would seem that almost any long-term disruption of the natural parent situation is risky for girls but not so for boys. Moreover, the transition from a single mother alone to a single mother with stepfather increases the risk for girls but not for boys.

Region

This first national survey of sexual abuse showed a markedly higher rate of abuse for Pacific states (California, Oregon, Washington, Alaska, and Hawaii). The rate in California for women was particularly high (42 percent). Several explanations are possible. First, Westerners may have been more candid about disclosing sexual abuse. California is one of the places where the social movement originated that first drew attention to the problem of sexual abuse. It is the state with the most advanced system of prevention and treatment (as evidenced by recent legislation mandating sexual abuse prevention for all school children). Moreover, Californians at the time of the survey had been barraged by news coverage of the notorious McMartin preschool abuse case. People there may be much more knowledgeable and comfortable about the subject and thus more prepared to disclose histories.

A second plausible explanation: There may be more abuse going on in the West. The West is and has been the frontier, perhaps attracting deviance. There is more sexual assault and other violence reported to the police in the West, a disproportion not necessarily explained by readiness to report (Baron & Straus, 1984). The West is also reputed to have a different ethic in regard to sex which may affect the prevalence of sexual abuse. The only problem here is that one study (Wyatt & Peters, 1986) looking into this hypothesis failed to find more abuse among those Californians raised in California than those raised elsewhere.

A third explanation may be that the West may tend to attract a disproportionate number of adult victims. Many people who suffered sexual abuse in childhood would justifiably feel alienated from their family and community and seek to settle elsewhere, away from the bad memories. Where have people in this country traditionally gone when they wanted to get away from a past? The West. So it is not clear whether being from the West puts someone at greater risk. But the issue needs further research.

Ethnicity

Men who reported English or Scandinavian heritage were at higher risk for abuse. The explanation for this is not clear. Associations between ethnicity and abuse have been found in a previous study (Finkelhor, 1979), but not these particular ethnicities.

Age

This national survey shows significantly lower rates of abuse for women over 60 and significantly higher rates for women 40 to 49, with a similar nonsignificant trend apparent for the men. This is additional fuel for the debate over the existence of historical trends or cohort effects. Also, Russell (1986) in a survey almost 10 years earlier did find lower rates among the oldest cohort of women and higher rates for a cohort then in their 30s.

One of the issues in the cohort debate concerns whether differences are real or reflect greater willingness among some age groups either to remember or report candidly on their experiences. Lower rates among older respondents could stem from memory loss about events that happened a long time earlier or greater embarrassment due to the values of an earlier historical era. However, Russell (1986) found the cohort effects for only some types of victimization, suggesting that the rate differences were real.

Addressing the element of embarrassment, the *Los Angeles Times* survey itself asked a question about the level of comfort in discussing the subject of sexual abuse. Respondents were asked early in the survey how much difficulty they had discussing the subject of sexual abuse. Only 23 percent claimed some, little, or great difficulty. The rest said hardly any at all. Surprisingly it was the youngest, not the oldest cohort, that had the highest level of discomfort. Moreover, it was only among the women of this youngest cohort that reporting an experience bore any relationship to level of discomfort. Women of this age who said they had had difficulty discussing sexual abuse revealed about one-third fewer experiences of abuse. Among the older groups of both men and women, there were no significant differences in rates between those with difficulty discussing sexual abuse and those without. This suggests that embarrassment is not a factor in the lower rates of the oldest group, although it is still possible that memory loss could be.

The *Los Angeles Times* survey does argue against the idea that there has been a precipitous rise in the amount of abuse in the very recent past, for example, in the wake of the "sexual revolution" of the 1960s. That is, the rates for the youngest cohorts (those growing up in the 1960s and 70s) are not higher than their immediate predecessors. The particularly higher risk in the age 40 to 49 cohort may be associated with women who had childhoods interrupted by World War II. It was a time when many fathers were gone from their families and returned after long absence. Separation from a natural father has been shown to be a risk factor both in this study and a number of other studies (Parker & Parker, 1986; Russell, 1986). In the current study, the cohorts do not vary significantly in the types of families (single parent, stepfather, etc.) reported by women. But the survey asked only about predominant family type during all of childhood, not about periods of significant absences.

Inadequate Sex Education

Women who described the sex education they received as inadequate were at higher risk for abuse. Adequate sex education may well protect children because it gives specific sexual abuse prevention information, like the kind advocated by prevention education programs (Finkelhor, 1986). Or it may be that inadequately educated children have unfulfilled curiosity about sex, a vulnerability which potential perpetrators can more easily manipulate. However, it is also possible that the causal order is reversed here. A child who has been abused could readily conclude that she had not received adequate sex education to help her avoid becoming a victim.

Conclusion

This first national prevalence study of sexual abuse does not itself break much new ground in its findings about the prevalence, nature, or risk factors for sexual abuse, but it does confirm much of what other more local studies have determined. A history of sexual abuse can be found in the backgrounds of an important fraction of men and women in the general population. Most of these experiences are at the hands of a person known to the child. Many of the victims never disclosed about the experiences to anyone, and children at risk were of-

ten ones from troubled families whose parents left home, were sick, or died. Having these findings confirmed on a national level adds weight to what we already know. Some problems with methodology however, particularly the imprecision of the screening questions, do caution against relying on findings from this study alone in absence of supporting evidence from other research. Replications with other large samples are needed. Perhaps the two most interesting new findings seem to be the disproportion of disclosures from victims in California and those born in 1936–1945.

References

Badgley, R., Allard, H., McCormick, N., Proudfoot, P., Fortin, D., Ogilvie, D., Rae-Grant, Q., Celinas, P., Pepin, L., & Sutherland, S. Committee on Sexual Offenses Against Children and Youth. (1984). *Sexual offenses against children* (Vol. 1). Ottawa: Canadian Government Publishing Centre.

Bagley, C., & Ramsey, R. (1986). Sexual abuse in childhood: Psychosocial outcomes and implications for social work practice. *Journal of Social Work and Human Sexuality, 4,* 33–47.

Baron, L., & Straus, M. (1984). Sexual stratification, pornography, and rape in the United States. In N. Malamuth and E. Donnerstein (Eds.), *Pornography and sexual aggression.* Orlando FL: Academic Press.

Finkelhor, D. (1979). *Sexually victimized children.* New York: Free Press.

Finkelhor, D. (1984). *Child sexual abuse: New theory and research.* New York: Free Press.

Finkelhor, D. (1986). *Sourcebook on child sexual abuse.* Newbury Park CA: Sage.

Finkelhor, D. (1987). The sexual abuse of children: Current research reviewed. *Psychiatric Annals: The Journal of Continuing Psychiatric Education, 17,* 233–241.

Finkelhor, D., & Baron, L. (1986). High-risk children. In D. Finkelhor and Associates (Eds.), *Sourcebook on child sexual abuse.* Newbury Park CA: Sage.

Parker, H., & Parker, S. (1986). Father-daughter sexual abuse: An emerging perspective. *American Journal of Orthopsychiatry, 56,* 531–549.

Peters, S., Wyatt, G., & Finkelhor, D. (1986). Prevalence. In D. Finkelhor and Associates (Eds.), *Sourcebook on child sexual abuse.* Newbury Park CA: Sage.

Russell, D. (1986). *The secret trauma: Incest in the lives of girls and women.* New York: Basic Books.

Wyatt, G. & Peters, S. (1986). Issues in the definition of child sexual abuse in prevalence research. *Child Abuse & Neglect 10,* 231–240.

Chapter 34
Token Resistance to Sex
New Perspectives on an Old Stereotype

Charlene L. Muehlenhard
Carie S. Rodgers

This intriguing, easy-to-follow study contains candid respondent narratives guaranteed to evoke thoughtful reader reactions. The fact that Muehlenhard, a feminist psychologist, is a noted authority on the issue of token resistance (i.e., "does no mean yes" or "do nice girls say no") can quickly be confirmed with a perusal of the article's bibliography. Although sexuality researchers typically only use survey responses in their data collection, this contribution is unique in its use of first person case studies.

Sexually active students will probably ask themselves several questions after reading this selection. Have I ever said "no" when I really wanted to have sexual intercourse and intended to do so? What role, if any, has the "swept away" phenomenon played in my sexual intercourse experience? Has male domination been a factor in instances when, as a female, I said "no" and meant "no," but sexual intercourse followed? What are the implications of implied consent versus verbal consent to have sexual intercourse? Being clear about one's own sexual intercourse experience or one's intentions for eventually engaging in sexual intercourse will add a dimension of reason that can take the "mis" out of miscommunication for women and men. A not-to-be-missed article.

The traditional sexual script dictates that women "are not supposed to indicate directly their sexual interest or engage freely in sexuality," and that men are supposed to "take the initiative even when a woman indicates verbally that she is unwilling to have sex (presumably because of the male belief that a woman's initial resistance is only token)"

(Check & Malamuth, 1983, p. 344). This script incorporates the idea of "token resistance," which can be defined as refusing or resisting sexual activity while intending to engage in that activity. The traditional sexual script perpetuates the belief that women's refusals of sexual advances are often insincere and need not be taken seriously.

Popular culture has a long history of perpetuating the idea that women say "no" when they mean yes. This idea appeared in Louisa May Alcott's *Little Women* (1868–1869/1968) and in Jane Austen's (1813/1931) *Pride and Prejudice*. Many popular movies and television programs, as well as pornography, have incorporated the theme of token resistance (Cowan, Lee, Levy, & Snyder, 1988; Warshaw, 1994). There is both anecdotal and laboratory evidence that some men do not believe women's refusals. Anecdotally, women have reported cases of attempted and completed rape in which the male perpetrator seemed to believe that their resistance was insincere (Warshaw, 1994). In one laboratory study, men read a scenario in which a modestly dressed woman said "no" to her date's sexual advances three times and tried to move away (Muehlenhard, Linton, Felts, & Andrews, 1985). When the men were asked to rate how much the woman wanted to have sexual intercourse, their mean rating was 4.5 on a scale of 1 to 9. Further evidence came from the men's ratings of how justified the woman's date was in having sexual intercourse with her under these circumstances (rape-justifiability ratings) and how likely they themselves would be to behave similarly (self-likelihood ratings). Men's initial rape-justifiability and self-likelihood ratings decreased significantly when they were instructed to assume that the woman really meant no when she said "no," suggesting that the men had not initially believed her refusals. In another study, men watched a videotaped depiction of a woman and man on a date. Even when the woman told the man that she did not want to do "anything more than kiss," many men indicated that it was likely that she wanted to engage in petting and sexual intercourse (Muehlenhard, Andrews, & Beal, 1996). When asked directly, men have estimated that between 31 and 45 percent (B. A. Hunter & Shotland, 1994) of women have engaged in token resistance to sex.

Previous research has shown that some women do, in fact, report having experienced the following situation, which has commonly been used as an operational definition of token resistance to sexual intercourse:

> You were with a guy who wanted to engage in sexual intercourse and you wanted to also, but for some reason you indicated that you didn't want to, although you had every intention to and

were willing to engage in sexual intercourse. In other words, you indicated "no" and you meant "yes." (Muehlenhard & Hollabaugh, 1988, p. 874)

The percentages of U.S. and Japanese college women in various studies who reported engaging in token resistance to sexual intercourse, as described previously, have been surprisingly consistent, ranging between 37 and 40 percent (Muehlenhard & Mc-Coy, 1991; Shotland & Hunter, 1995; Sprecher, Hatfield, Cortese, Potapova, & Levitskaya, 1994). The highest prevalence—59 percent—was found by Sprecher et al. (1994) in a sample of Russian women using a questionnaire translated into Russian; this higher prevalence might reflect cultural differences or might have involved subtle but important changes in the meaning of the question when it was translated. Taken together, these results suggest that a substantial minority of women have—at least once—indicated no to sex when they meant yes.

Shotland and Hunter (1995) challenged this conclusion. They suggested that many of the women in these studies had really meant no when they indicated no; later, however, the women may have agreed to participate in sexual intercourse without ever actually saying "yes." Due to memory consolidation, some of these women may have recalled indicating no while meaning yes. Some research findings support this conclusion. For example, in one study, some of the women reported engaging in token resistance out of fear of pregnancy or sexually transmitted diseases (STDs) (Muehlenhard & Hollabaugh, 1988). Shotland and Hunter (1995) pointed out that these concerns are not addressed by engaging in token resistance; having refused prior to sexual intercourse does nothing to protect women from pregnancy or STDs. These fears are reasons for indicating no and meaning no, however. In another study, women who reported having engaged in token resistance reported feeling significantly more negative about the incident when it resulted in sexual intercourse than when it did not (Muehlenhard & McCoy, 1991). This seems inconsistent with the definition of token resistance used on the questionnaire: "He wanted to engage in sexual intercourse and *you wanted to also*" (p. 451, italics added). Shotland and Hunter (1995) found that, in situations in which women reported engaging in token resistance, most (83 percent) reported having more than one sexual intention during the situation, saying "no" and meaning either no or maybe prior to saying "no" and meaning yes.

Perhaps Shotland and Hunter's (1995) memory consolidation hypothesis is correct. Alternatively, it may be that the research participants did not realize

that situations such as indicating no but changing their minds or indicating "no" and meaning no even though in some ways they wanted to engage in sex did not fit the definition of token resistance. We conducted the present study to investigate these issues.

The stereotype is that women—and only women—engage in token resistance. If men engage in this behavior, token resistance can no longer be viewed as a gender-specific behavior in which women are stereotyped as manipulative teases. In fact, some researchers have found that significantly more men than women reported having engaged in token resistance to sexual intercourse (Sprecher et al., 1994). Others, however, have reported no gender differences in this behavior (B. A. Hunter & Shotland, 1994). Thus, we also investigated whether men engage in token resistance. Most studies of token resistance, with one exception (O'Sullivan & Allgeier, 1994), have investigated token resistance to heterosexual intercourse. In the present study, we gave respondents the opportunity to report token resistance to any type of sexual activity, rather than limiting their reports to sexual intercourse. Instead of describing a situation and asking respondents merely to indicate whether they had or had not experienced such a situation, we asked them to describe what took place in their own words. By allowing respondents to relay their own accounts, we hoped to learn whether they meant "yes" when they indicated "no," or whether they changed their intentions as the situation progressed, or whether they never meant "yes" at all. They could also report situations involving homosexual as well as heterosexual behavior.

Method

Respondents were 65 female and 64 male introductory psychology students at the University of Kansas. Their mean age was 18.9 for the women and 19.4 for the men. Most (90.7 percent), of the participants were White/European/European American.

Respondents were asked about their experiences in three situations. The first situation (Situation A) was as follows:

You were with a guy [for women's questionnaires]/girl [for men's questionnaires] you had never had sexual intercourse with before. He/she wanted to engage in sexual intercourse, and you wanted to also, but for some reason you indicated that you didn't want to, although you had every intention to and were willing to engage in sexual intercourse. In other words, you indicated "no" and you meant "yes."

The second situation (Situation B) was identical except that it began, "You were with a guy/girl you had previously had sexual intercourse with." The third situation (Situation C) was gender neutral and included any sexual activity with a new or previous partner. It read,

> You were with someone who wanted to engage in some type of sexual activity (such as kissing, or caressing, or oral sex, etc.) with you, and you wanted to also, but for some reason you indicated that you didn't want to, although you had every intention to and were willing to engage in sexual activity. In other words, you indicated "no" and you meant "yes."

Respondents were asked to indicate how many times they had been involved in each situation. If they had been involved in all three situations, they were asked to pick two to describe. If they had been in only one situation, they were asked to describe that situation and then make up a fictitious situation and describe it. If they had never been in any of the situations, they were asked to make up two situations and describe both. They checked blanks indicating whether each situation was real or imagined. We disregarded the fictitious narratives during the analyses.

Respondents were asked to describe the two situations in detail. They were then asked to list reasons why they had wanted to engage in sexual intercourse or sexual activity, reasons why they had not wanted to engage in sexual intercourse or activity (if any), and whether these reasons had changed over time. They were asked why they had said "no" when they meant "yes." Other questions involved their and their partner's feelings immediately after the situation and currently, long-term effects on their relationship, whether they would do anything differently if they could replay the situation, whether they had been using alcohol or drugs, and if so what effect they thought this had had. All the questions were open-ended.

Results

Frequency of Token Resistance

Contrary to the stereotype, women were not more likely than men to report token resistance; in fact, there was a trend in which more men (82.5 percent) than women (67.7 percent) reported having engaged in token resistance in at least one situation. Significantly more men than women reported having engaged in token resistance in situations involving sexual intercourse (Situations A and/or B). Broken down by situation, significantly more men than women endorsed Situation A (sexual intercourse

with a new partner); there was a similar trend for Situation C (any type of sexual activity). The only situation not endorsed more often by men than by women was Situation B (sexual intercourse with a previous partner).

Qualitative Descriptions: Evidence of Misinterpretation

Respondents' qualitative descriptions of their experiences cast doubt on the percentages reported in the previous section. Respondents' narratives often indicated that they had misinterpreted our questions.

Confusion about desires and intentions. Many respondents described situations in which they wanted to engage in sexual intercourse or other sexual activity but did not intend to do so; they indicated no and meant no. They seemed to have disregarded the phrase "you had every intention to and were willing to engage in sexual intercourse/sexual activity." For example, one woman wrote the following:

> I met a fellow at an amusement park. I ended up spending most of the day with him. At the end of the day he wanted to have sex in the woods. During the day we had kissed and hugged—it was the romance of it! Anyhow that night I wanted to also. I like sex and I liked him but the whole thing wrong was that I really didn't know him or his sexual past. Those two things were too large of a negative and so although my body wanted him my mind knew better. Besides I feel that if you're going to have sex just because your body says it wants to—it won't be half as good as when your heart, soul, mind, and body say yes. By the way, we didn't have sex! (#209A)

A male respondent relayed the following:

> I was with a woman that I had a past relationship with several years ago. We had been intimate numerous times throughout the course of our relationship. We went out together on a date, "no strings attached" and with no obligations to each other. Late in the evening, after returning to her apartment she wanted to engage in sexual intercourse. I was feeling fairly aroused and decided it would be a pleasant experience except both her roommates were home in their separate rooms, she was obviously a bit intoxicated, as was I, and third, neither I, nor she, had any birth control device. Confusing because I had not been with her in a monogamous relationship for over two years, I was unsure about her sexual habits and decided not to "do the nasty." We slept together that night without engaging in intercourse. The following morning we both agreed it was the best thing not to have done it. (#130B)

One woman described a situation in which she was attracted to a man but said "no" to sexual intercourse. Her experience meets the legal definition of rape in Kansas:

> ... I was very sexually attracted to a guy in my senior class. We went to homecoming together. After the dance, we got plowed and one thing led to another. I can remember him being on top of me and hearing myself say "No." Then I remember saying, "We're really gonna do this, aren't we?" However, I did not put up any sort of fight. . . .
>
> *Why did you indicate no when you meant yes?* I'm not sure that I ever really meant yes, but I am sure that my no was pretty pathetic. If the guy can't understand a simple no, how would you convince him with a definite NO! (#224A)

All three of these respondents reported being attracted to the other person, but none of them intended to engage in intercourse. These narratives did not meet our definition because the respondents said "no" and meant no.

Confusion about indicating 'no' and meaning 'yes' simultaneously. Some respondents did not seem to understand that we were asking them about situations in which they indicated no and meant yes simultaneously. They reported indicating no while meaning no but changing their minds. For example:

> We had been dating for a month and on previous occasions I had not allowed intercourse to occur. I knew he wanted to, but something was holding me back. He wanted to talk about it, which I found difficult. When you're not for sure what you're thinking it is difficult to express to someone else. I told him I wasn't secure enough in our relationship and he asked what I meant by this. He wanted clarification on any vague answers I gave. He commented that women don't always express what they are thinking. He said he hated using the word "special," but felt this would be something special shared between us. It was the next progression in our relationship. I told him that for me if I agreed to sleep with him, it would be an exclusive relationship. He wondered if I wanted to date around or if I was seeing other people. I wanted to sleep with him, but I didn't know how he viewed the relationship. With an understanding that our relationship is exclusive, I felt more secure. I didn't really say "no" and mean yes, we both knew I wanted to say "yes" but couldn't. After our discussion I changed my mind. (#208A)

Confusion about what sexual activity was refused and what sexual activity was intended. In some cases the sexual activity that respondents indicated no to was not the same sexual activity that they intended to engage in. They may have said "no" to sexual activity in one situation while intending to engage in sexual activity in a different situation. One man reported the following:

> I had been after a girl in my math class since the beginning of the year. I liked her emotionally as well as sexually. I saw her at a party and we were both very drunk. After some small talk we went to a bedroom and started to mess around. She seemed very horny and I probably could have fucked her. But I thought if I fucked her now she would probably think I used her and would never talk to me again. So in order to start taking her out and fuck more often I didn't screw her that night. (#157A)

In this narrative, he reported indicating no to sexual intercourse on that night and intending to have sexual intercourse with her later. This did not meet our definition of token resistance.

Other misunderstandings of the definition. Respondents also misunderstood other aspects of our definition. In some cases, their partner had not wanted to engage in sexual activity:

> We had just got back from a bar. We went to this creek that had a 15-foot waterfall. We began kissing and caressing. She said she'd better stop because she was two years older than me. I indicated that I agreed when I didn't care how much older she was.
>
> *Why did you indicate no when you meant yes?* Because I didn't want to make her mad or force her to do any sexual activity. (#105C)

In other cases, the respondent had indicated "yes" and meant "yes" but felt reservations afterwards:

> One night stand—We were at my apartment and had been drinking. My roommate had brought back two women of which I had not met. We all got drunk and I started mashing with the girl. We later moved to the bedroom where she proceeded with fellatio. We never saw each other again. I loved it but felt kind of lost like I shouldn't have done it afterwards. (#104C)

Other misinterpretations involved indicating no and meaning no without ever wanting to engage in sex, indicating yes and meaning yes but being interrupted, indicating and feeling ambivalence, and having a partner misinterpret the respondent's behavior to mean no.

Raters' Coding of the Narratives

Because of the large number of women and men who misinterpreted our questions, we coded each narrative as to whether it met our definition of token resistance. Raters coded each narrative as token resistance or not token resistance according to the following criteria:

1. For a situation to be coded as token resistance, the respondent actually had to plan or intend to engage in sexual intercourse or other sexual activity.

2. For a narrative to be coded as token resistance, the act of indicating no and the intention to engage in sexual activity had to occur simultaneously.

3. The sexual activity that was refused and the sexual activity that a respondent intended to engage in had to be the same activity in the same situation.

4. For some of the criteria, we relied on the respondent's own interpretation of the situation.

Narratives were coded by two female and three male undergraduates, with each narrative being coded by one female and one male rater.

Of the 177 nonfictitious narratives respondents wrote as examples of token resistance, only 20 (11.3 percent) were coded as meeting our definition. For Situation A (heterosexual intercourse with a new partner), only 5.0 percent ($n = 1$) of the women's and 2.8 percent ($n = 1$) of the men's nonfictitious narratives met our definition. For Situation B (heterosexual intercourse with a previous partner), these percentages were 34.6 percent ($n = 9$) for women and 26.1 percent ($n = 6$) for men; for Situation C (any sexual activity with a new or previous partner of either gender), these percentages were 4.8 percent ($n = 1$) for women and 7.1 percent ($n = 2$) for men.

It was not possible to calculate the percentage of the entire sample who had actually engaged in token resistance to sex. Nevertheless, it is likely that the percentages of women and men who initially reported engaging in token resistance were extreme overestimates.

Themes Emerging From the Narratives

All the narratives that fit our definition of token resistance involved heterosexual interactions. We identified five major themes: moral concerns and discomfort about sex, adding interest to a relationship, wanting not to be taken for granted, testing a partner's response, and power and control over the other person.

Moral concerns and discomfort about sex. Two of the narratives, both written by women, reflected concerns about being "good." This example involved a new partner:

> I was with my boyfriend at my house, in my room, in the middle of the night. He had come over to my house and snuck in. He was there for a long time and we talked. Then we were kissing

and one thing just led to another. We had talked about sexual intercourse many times before but the topic of conversation didn't come up that night until I said "no." Once I said "no," he wouldn't engage in sexual intercourse. I thought and felt I should say "no" because I was unsure if it was the right thing to morally do, yet I had every intention of participating in sexual intercourse that night. After I said "no" we talked about our situation, the circumstances of the moment, and what we had been raised believing.

> *Why did you indicate no when you meant yes?* It was what a "good girl" would say. (#230A)

Adding interest to an ongoing relationship. Contrary to the stereotype, most of the narratives that met our definition of token resistance took place in the context of an ongoing sexual relationship. Five women and one man wrote about adding interest to an ongoing relationship. Most reported positive consequences, and most thought that their partner was aware of the game they were playing. One woman reported that both she and her boyfriend said "no" when meaning yes:

> The guy was a boyfriend of mine that I dated for two years. Throughout the relationship there were many times we would play around and joke about sex. I would say "no," even though I really wanted and intended to and he would either continue making advances or performing foreplay until I said "yes" or he would tease me by stopping any activity we were doing and would say he didn't want to fool around or have sex either. It was all in good fun. (#261B)

Thus, token resistance was sometimes used—successfully or unsuccessfully—to prevent a sexual encounter from becoming routine or to prevent sex from moving directly to intercourse.

Wanting not to be taken for granted. Token resistance in an ongoing relationship sometimes involved wanting not to be taken for granted. One woman described wanting to alter the routine in which she consented whenever her boyfriend initiated:

> This happened once or twice with my boyfriend—we've been dating for about two years. Sometimes I feel like he takes me for granted, that he has most of the control over where we go, what we do, etc., etc. We were in my room, looking for a certain record he needed right then. Before he had said he had to hurry, but suddenly he pulled me close to him and started kissing me. I laughed and felt happy but at the same time I'm thinking—before he was so rushed—he always gets his way. So when he pulled me to the floor I said "No! You don't have time and neither do I, besides my roommate will be home any minute."

But he knew I wanted him and I knew he would keep on trying to persuade me so I think it was more like a game—we both enjoyed it!

Why did you indicate no when you meant yes? I think I wanted it to be my decision not his. Mostly, he initiates and I consent. However sometimes that makes me feel like it's only his decision—he expects me to consent! (#234B)

Testing a partner's response.
Two respondents, one woman and one man, reported engaging in token resistance to test their partners. For example:

I have been seeing the same guy for almost three years. At times I have every intention of having intercourse with him and end up saying "no." I think some of the time I just want to see what his reaction will be. I start wondering what our relationship would be like without sex, so I feel guilty sometimes when we do. He has told me that it makes him feel as though he's making me do something I have no desire to do. This is not the case. I have the same intentions, but I want to be sure that he cares for me beyond sex.

Why did you indicate no when you meant yes? To test him. I wanted to see if he would take the time out to show a true interest in my feelings. (#212B)

Thus, this respondent wanted information about how her partner would react to her refusal and whether their relationship was based on more than sex.

Power and control over the other person.
Five narratives—four narratives written by three different men and one narrative written by a woman—reflected a desire for power over the other person. These narratives ranged from innocuous to manipulative and hostile. A woman wrote the following about an ongoing sexual relationship:

A guy who I was madly in lust for named _____ was my first. _____ and I didn't have a real relationship other than sexual and friendliness. He was always going out with other girls so when we had sex it was a big secret. I couldn't go out with him because he was my older brother's friend. Anyway it seems that _____ would always have to persuade me into having sex. I always wanted to be with him. Although the sex part was not really important. I knew when I would see him that we would end up together. Being in a room and having him there with me kissing and touching me, I knew I would be all over him. However, at times I would say "No _____" "No!" He would continue to persuade me. Sometimes he was unable. I think I said no because I like the fact that I was in control. I would tease him and that would make him want more and more.

Why did you indicate no when you meant yes? I think I said no to tease the guy so he would want more. (#213B)

Some of the narratives seemed more hostile. For example:

I met this girl at a bar. I didn't know who she was and I had never seen her before. When I met her we were both drunk it seemed. We started talking and then she wanted me to sit next to her. At this point I had a feeling that she wanted to get "fresh" with me. This turned me on and right away I thought about having sexual intercourse. As the night narrowed down I was thinking about how she really wants to "get busy." I wanted to just take her right away and do what a male and female do best—FUCK! Then I remembered about playing the role of the inexperienced one. One thing led to another, she agreed to come to my place for the night. Boom—I knew I had her then. Now all I had to do was pretend like I didn't want to for some kind of stupid reason. I always thought that would get a girl more anxious and ready for me. It's worked most of the time. When I'm fucking them I then let them feel the wrath of what I wanted from the beginning. (#101A)

Discussion

According to the stereotype, most women—and only women—engage in token resistance to sex, saying "no" when they mean yes. According to the stereotype, this occurs primarily in new sexual relationships because women do not want to appear "easy" or are playing "hard to get" (Muehlenhard, 1988; Muehlenhard & McCoy, 1991). The present study challenged all these assumptions. In the present study, more men than women initially reported engaging in token resistance, although most of the men's and women's narratives were coded as not meeting our definition. The percentages of women and men who wrote nonfictitious narratives meeting our definition did not differ significantly. Thus, based on the present study, it seems likely that, consistent with recent studies, men as well as women engage in token resistance to sex, but that, in this and other studies, many of the men as well as the women who report engaging in token resistance may have misunderstood the question.

The occurrence of token resistance in ongoing relationships also contradicts the stereotype that women play "hard to get" primarily with new partners. In fact, in a study of how token resistance relates to the sexual double standard, Muehlenhard and McCoy (1991) investigated only situations involving new partners. The present results suggest that individuals in ongoing relationships sometimes use token resistance for various reason.

Reasons for Saying 'No' When Meaning 'Yes'

Moral concerns and discomfort about sex. Two women mentioned such concerns. Even though both expressed intentions to engage in sexual activity, they expressed reservations. One mentioned that she had been "brought up [to think that sex] was wrong," and that she was "unsure if it was the right thing to morally do" (#230A); the other mentioned feeling "embarrassed" and "apprehensive" and trying to block out thoughts of her parents (#204B). Both mentioned wanting to behave like a "good girl." In some instances, token resistance may be a way to handle feelings of guilt. If this makes someone feel better, it may serve a useful function. These narratives seemed closest to the sexual script in which women "are not supposed to indicate directly their sexual interest or engage freely in sexuality" (Check & Malamuth, 1983, p. 344). These narratives, however, seem to reflect sincere reservations rather than concerns merely about appearing too eager.

In this study, no men mentioned moral concerns or discomfort. This might be because boys generally do not grow up internalizing "the complex of reluctances and ambivalences about sex that makes up that part of classical femininity" (A. Hunter, 1992, p. 377). Interestingly, several men mentioned not wanting to appear too eager for sex. Typically, these men expressed concern that the woman would think they were interested only in sex, when in fact they were interested in a relationship.

Adding interest to an ongoing relationship. Adding interest to an ongoing relationship was a common theme. "Apparently any continuously repetitious behavior will become boring, even sex" (Hendrick & Hendrick, 1992, p. 134). For some women saying "no" seemed to be a way to encourage sexual activity other than intercourse (sometimes called "foreplay"). For example, "I'd say no and he'd do things to me to make me say yes like kiss, fondle, or the things he knew drove me crazy" (#214B). Women are frequently dissatisfied with fast, goal-directed penile-vaginal intercourse (Crooks & Baur, 1993). Token resistance can be a way for some women to obtain sexual pleasure from sexual behaviors other than intercourse. It can be a way to resist "the dominant assumption that heterosexual intercourse (coitus) is synonymous with 'real' sex" (Gavey, 1992).

Men can be dissatisfied with goal-oriented sex as well (Zilbergeld, 1992). They may be less likely to use token resistance in such situations, however; to the extent that men "run the show," they are likely to

have other ways of getting the sexual behaviors they want.

Wanting not to be taken for granted. The traditional sexual script assigns the role of initiation to men and assigns the responsibility for regulating sexual activity to women (Crooks & Baur, 1993). "According to this script, males had positive control in a sexual encounter (using any available strategy to initiate sex), while females had negative control (using any available strategy to avoid having sex)" (McCormick, Brannigan, & LaPlante, 1984, p. 310). If a man makes a sexual advance, then a woman's only decision is whether to go along with it.

In this context, a woman's options are reduced to consenting or not consenting "in response to something that is *being done to her*" (Gavey, 1992, p. 337, italics in the original). If a woman in this situation always consents, she in effect has no control at all. Even if she has become sexually aroused, agreeing to have sex can be seen as being "had by someone who knows how to arouse the traitor body" (A. Hunter, 1992, p. 376). Not automatically agreeing whenever her partner makes an advance that arouses her can be a way for a woman to gain some control over a situation that she did not initiate. Refusing occasionally may give her some degree of control—even if she intends eventually to say "yes."

Conversely, the traditional sexual script dictates that men take advantage of every sexual opportunity, responding automatically to any sexual stimulus (Zilbergeld, 1992). This pressure can be a burden for men.

Testing a partner's response. Another theme involved testing a partner. One woman reported saying "no" to her partner "to see if he would take the time out to show a true interest in my feelings" (#212B). This is consistent with the stereotype of men's "being only after one thing" (Hunter, 1992). Many men espouse norms in which the goal is to obtain sex with many different women by lying, getting them intoxicated, or—if necessary—using physical coercion (Muehlenhard & Falcon, 1990). In this context, token resistance could allow a woman to evaluate whether her partner is interested in her for anything other than sex.

Power and control. "In our culture, male eroticism is wedded to power" (Griffin, 1971, p. 29). This culture perpetuates the idea that "sex would lose its sexiness if it no longer included the element of the 'hunt'" (Hunter, 1992, p. 376). Some theorists have described the "cultural and political meanings attached to penile penetration of women (being 'had,' 'possessed,' 'taken,' 'fucked')" [Kitzinger, Wilkinson, & Perkins, 1992, p. 313]. Consistent with this construction of heterosexual sex, several men described how they used token resistance to control women. Interestingly, despite the stereotype of the sly, manipulative woman, in this study the most consciously manipulative narratives were written by men. Only one woman wrote a narrative coded as reflecting power and control. She described teasing a man she "was madly in lust for" in order to "make him want more and more" (#213B).

In summary, respondents who reported token resistance seemed to have many motivations. Many of the narratives were understandable in the context of the traditional sexual script and the construction of sexuality in our society. However, others indicated that many people do not act in accordance with this traditional script.

Conceptual Issues in Defining Token Resistance

It was often difficult to judge whether a situation corresponded to our definition. One reason for this difficulty was that any one act may have multiple motivations. Another reason was that the concepts involved in the definition, such as wanting and intending, are themselves complex.

Researchers often ask whether someone did or did not want to engage in a particular sexual act. Conceptualizing sex as either wanted or unwanted is too simplistic in several ways. First, wanting is not an all-or-nothing state; there are degrees of wanting. Second, there are many dimensions along which a sexual act can be wanted or unwanted. This concept is exemplified by the statement, "although my body wanted him my mind knew better" (#209A). Physiological sexual arousal, emotional comfort, and so forth can be regarded as separate dimensions, with a sexual act being more or less wanted on each dimension. Third, sexual acts can have consequences. A person could want the sexual act but not want the consequences (e.g., disease, a reputation as "promiscuous"). Conversely, a person could not want the sexual act but want the consequences (e.g., pleasing the partner). Finally, all of the above can change over time as individuals become more or less sexually aroused, as they and their partner interact, and so forth. Thus, when researchers ask respondents to think of a situation in which they were with someone "who wanted to engage in sexual intercourse and you wanted to also," we are asking them to reduce a highly complex situation to a black-and-white decision about whether they did or did not want to engage in the behavior. Respondents often described ambivalence in which sexual behaviors were neither totally wanted with no reservations nor totally unwanted with no desire to engage in them.

Intentions are also complex. Intentions are partly a function of what a person wants, which is complex. Intentions vary over time. Sometimes people engage in behaviors spontaneously, without ever really intending to do so. Intentions are often contingent on circumstances. For example, if a man says to a woman, "I intend to have sex with you tonight," this might seem frightening to her, as if he intends to engage in sex with her regardless of her desires. When people speak of intentions to engage in sexual intercourse, these intentions are usually contingent on the other person's desires at the time, their own desires at the time, events occurring between the time of the intention and the time of the act, and so forth. When researchers ask people to think about situations in which "you had every intention to and were willing to engage in sexual intercourse," we are not asking about simple all-or-none phenomena.

Another conceptual question involves what is necessary for someone to indicate "no." According to the traditional sexual script, sex is something that men initiate; if men do not initiate, then nothing will happen (Gavey, 1992). This may result in gender asymmetry in the conceptualization of token resistance. A man might think—perhaps correctly—that nothing will happen unless he makes it happen. In this case, he might equate doing nothing with indicating that he did not want to engage in sex. In the present study, for example, when asked why he indicated no, one man wrote, "It really didn't come to that. I just didn't act on the situation. She was naked but I didn't act" (#106A). Conversely, a woman might think—perhaps correctly—that, even if she does nothing, the man may still initiate; he might interpret her lack of resistance as consent. Thus, for a man, doing nothing might be interpreted as indicating no, whereas for a woman, doing nothing might be interpreted as indicating yes. For a woman, indicating no might mean actively refusing—something that a man might find unnecessary.

An additional source of gender asymmetry in token resistance involves the component of the definition stating that the other person "wanted to engage in sexual intercourse." Given the script that women "are not supposed to indicate directly their sexual interest" (Check & Malamuth, 1983, p. 344), men are probably less likely than women to be in a situation in which their partner is openly expressing desire for sexual intercourse.

Methodological Issues in Defining Token Resistance

Compared with previous studies, in this study larger percentages of both men and women initially reported engaging in token resistance to sexual intercourse. These discrepancies may have occurred because, unlike previous studies, we asked respondents about two different situations involving sexual intercourse, one specifying a new partner and one specifying a previous partner, thus providing respondents with more memory cues. Consistent with this line of reasoning, in studies of child sexual abuse and rape, multiple screening questions asking about different circumstances to prompt respondents' memories generally elicit higher prevalence rates than do single, more general screening questions (Koss, 1993). In addition, rather than asking respondents whether they had been involved in various situations, we asked them how many times they had been involved in various situations, which might have had a normalizing effect.

In some studies (Muehlenhard & Hollabaugh, 1988; Shotland & Hunter, 1995), respondents were first asked whether they had ever indicated no to sex when they meant no, even though in a way they wanted to engage in sex; next they were asked whether they had said "no" when they meant maybe; finally they were asked whether they had said "no" when they meant yes. Asking questions in this sequence might help respondents distinguish between saying "no" and meaning yes and saying "no" and meaning no or maybe, thus decreasing the number of "false positives"—reports of token resistance based solely on confusion about the definition. In addition, in the present study follow-up questions such as "Why did you indicate no when you meant yes?" seemed helpful in clarifying whether respondents understood the definition.

Limitations

Our sample size, though adequate for a qualitative analysis, was too small to answer some questions, such as whether there are significant gender differences in token resistance. Additionally, percentages based on small samples are less stable than those based on larger samples. Our sample consisted of fairly young, mostly White/European American college students. Although this was similar to samples used in most previous studies and thus was appropriate for questioning the results of those studies, these results would not necessarily generalize to other groups.

Conclusions

Most women and most men initially reported having engaged in token resistance, although their narratives indicated that in most of these instances they had said "no" and meant no. The definition of token resistance specified on our questionnaire was identical or virtually identical to those used in other studies (Muehlenhard & McCoy, 1991; Shotland & Hunter, 1991; Sprecher et al., 1994); thus, it seems likely that many respondents in previous studies had also misunderstood the definition. Conse-

quently, it seems likely that the percentages reported in previous studies overestimated the actual prevalence of token resistance.

Although the definition of token resistance used in this and other studies seems clear to us, apparently it was unclear to respondents. Confusion between saying "no" and meaning yes versus saying "no" and meaning no even though in some ways one would like to say "yes" is likely to perpetuate the myth that women's refusals need not be taken seriously. Although both women and men sometimes engage in token resistance to sex, most do not. All refusals should be taken seriously. Engaging in sex with someone who does not consent is rape.

References

Alcott, L. M. (1968). *Little Women*. Boston: Little, Brown. (Original work published in 1868–1869.)

Austen, J. (1931). *Pride and Prejudice*. New York: Grossett & Dunlap. (Original work published in 1813.)

Check, J. V., & Malamuth, N. M. (1983). Sex role stereotyping and reactions to depictions of stranger versus acquaintance rape. *Journal of Personality and Social Psychology, 45,* 344–356.

Cowan, G., Lee, C., Levy, D., & Snyder, D. (1988). Dominance and inequality in X-rated videocassettes. *Psychology of Women Quarterly, 12,* 299–311.

Crooks, R., & Baur, K. (1993). *Our sexuality* (5th ed.). Redwood City, CA: Benjamin/Cummings.

Gavey, N. (1992). Technologies and effects of heterosexual coercion. *Feminism and Psychology, 2,* 325–351.

Griffin, S. (1971). Rape: The all-American crime. *Ramparts, 10,* 26–35.

Hendrick, S., & Hendrick, C. (1992). *Liking, loving, & relating*. Pacific Grove, CA: Brooks/Cole.

Hunter, A. (1992). Same door, different closet: A heterosexual sissy's coming-out party. *Feminism and Psychology, 2,* 367–385.

Hunter, B. A., & Shotland, R. L. (1994). *"Token resistance" and compliance to sexual intercourse: Similarities and differences in men's and women's behavior.* Manuscript submitted for publication.

Kitzinger, C., Wilkinson, S., & Perkins, R. (1992). Theorizing heterosexuality. *Feminism and Psychology, 2,* 293–324.

Koss, M. P. (1993). Detecting the scope of rape: A review of prevalence research methods. *Journal of Interpersonal Violence, 8,* 198–222.

McCormick, N. B., Brannigan, G. C., & LaPlante, M. N. (1984). Social desirability in the bedroom: Role of approval motivation in sexual relationships. *Sex Roles, 11,* 303–314.

Muehlenhard, C. L. (1988). "Nice women" don't say yes and "real men" don't say no: How miscommunication and the sexual double standard can cause sexual problems. *Women and Therapy, 7,* 95–108.

Muehlenhard, C. L., Andrews, S. L., & Beal, G. K. (1996). Beyond "just saying no": Dealing with men's unwanted sexual advances in heterosexual dating contexts. *Journal of Psychology and Human Sexuality, 8,* 141–168.

Muehlenhard, C. L., & Falcon, P. L. (1990). Men's heterosocial skill and attitudes toward women as predictors of verbal sexual coercion and forceful rape. *Sex Roles, 23,* 241–259.

Muehlenhard, C. L., & Hollabaugh, L. C. (1988). Do women sometimes say no when they mean yes? The prevalence and correlates of women's token resistance to sex. *Journal of Personality and Social Psychology, 54,* 872–879.

Muehlenhard, C. L., Linton, M. A., Felts, A. S., & Andrews, S. L. (1985, June). Men's attitudes toward the justifiability of date rape: Intervening variables and possible solutions. In E. R. Allgeier (Chair), *Sexual coercion: Political issues and empirical findings.* Presented at the Midcontinent Meeting of the Society for the Scientific Study of Sex, Chicago.

Muehlenhard, C. L., & McCoy, M. L. (1991). Double standard/double bind: The sexual double standard and women's communication about sex. *Psychology of Women Quarterly, 15,* 447–461.

O'Sullivan, L. F., & Allgeier, E. R. (1994). Dissembling a stereotype: Gender differences in the use of token resistance. *Journal of Applied Social Psychology, 24,* 1035–1055.

Shotland, R. L., & Hunter, B. A. (1995). Women's "token resistant" and compliant sexual behaviors are related to uncertain sexual intentions and rape. *Personality and Social Psychology Bulletin, 21,* 226–236.

Sprecher, S., Hatfield, E., Cortese, A., Potapova, E., & Levitskaya, A. (1994). Token resistance to sexual intercourse and consent to unwanted sexual intercourse: College students' dating experiences in three countries. *Journal of Sex Research, 31,* 125–132.

Warshaw, R. (1994). *I never called it rape* (2nd ed.). New York: Harper & Row.

Zilbergeld, B. (1992). *The new male sexuality.* New York: Bantam.

Chapter 35

Tactics of Sexual Coercion

When Men and Women Won't Take No for an Answer

Cindy J. Struckman-Johnson

David L. Struckman-Johnson

Peter B. Anderson

Some of you reading this chapter about tactics of sexual coercion may find yourself in the "been there done that" category. Perhaps you could even add your own scenarios to the firsthand accounts of the respondents' experiences with post-refusal sexual persistence: persistent attempts to have sexual contact with someone who has already refused, using pressure, alcohol or drugs, or force. But, things are changing in this respect.

Rape is but one result of coercive sexual behavior but it is a category in which a change of views seems almost as mercurial as the nightly news. In fact, new laws defining rape today are light years ahead of the public's perceptions of rape when your parents and grandparents were on university campuses or were already young adults in the world of work. As recently as the 1970s, rape was viewed as a sexual act in which a man had responded to a woman's sexual provocations. In 1971, MacDonald wrote, "[A] woman who accepts a ride home from a stranger, picks up a hitchhiker, sunbathes alone, or works in a garden in a two-piece bathing suit which exposes rather than conceals her anatomy invites rape" (1971, 311).

Then there were the years of terminological confusion. During the decade of the 1970s, feminist writers began to question the way that rape was commonly conceptualized. Brownmiller (1975) and Griffin (1971) began to depict rape as violence. Griffin characterized it as an act of aggression in which the victim is denied her "self-determination." Further, she em-

phasized that the fear of rape also limits women's freedom.

More recently, in the word game of terminology, more questions have been posed: Should the term "rape" be replaced with "sexual assault" in order to emphasize the violent nature of the act? Do we more correctly refer to "rape survivor" than to "rape victim," a less empowering word? Muehlenhard and Highby (1997) in their prolific writing on the subject concluded in the late 1990s that there was no clear consensus on these questions in law, popular media, research literature, or feminist writing.

But once again, the "order of the day" seems to be change, with troubling questions on the horizon about rape and consent. In January 2003, the California Supreme Court ruled that a man can be convicted of rape if a woman first consents, but later asks him to stop the sexual activity (Chiang 2003). In July 2003, a rape law was enacted in the State of Illinois that further clarified the issue of consent by emphasizing that people can change their mind while having sex. Simply stated, if a person in Illinois says "no," the act of sex becomes rape (McKinney 2003). In an Op-Ed column of the Boston Globe, Cathy Young (2003) characterized the broad scope of such actions as "hailed by some as a sign of progress and denounced by others as a sign of an anti-male witch-hunt" (p. A15). Young concluded that although there are many unresolved and troubling questions about force, consent, and credibility in rape cases, the principle is sound: forced sex is always rape. You may be amazed or amused at some of the archaic concepts of sexual assault and other forms of sexual coercion that have occurred over the years. As you somehow try to fit together the pieces of the puzzle, however, we hope your conscience will comprehend the seriousness of any kind of forced sexual activity.

Following this reading about sexual coercion, what changes on your campus could you suggest as prevention strategies for destructive sexual behaviors? Do any of them pertain to personal attitudes that need to be strengthened or modified? Could sharing these ideas with others in your social groups lead to broad social change about an important topic? Remember, when scrolling down the screen under the subject of sexual coercion, with a click of the mouse, anyone can instantly move from the virtual category of "problem" to "solution." By speaking up and adding your voice to the din about sexual coercion, however, you will move from the everyday category of "problem" to "solution." Your movement will not be as instantaneous as it would be online, but it will be more real and more life changing.

The Prevalence of Sexual Coercion

Sexually coercive behavior, defined in this paper as the act of using pressure, alcohol or drugs, or force to have sexual contact with someone against his or her will, has been studied among young adult populations for decades. From 1950 through the 1980s, the research focused on female victims and male perpetrators. One of the most influential studies was by Koss, Gidycz, and Wisniewski (1987), who found that 15 percent of the women in a national sample of over 6,000 college students had experienced rape. About 4 percent of the men indicated that they had perpetrated rape. In this survey, like many others conducted during this time period, only women were asked about being victims, and only men were asked about being perpetrators of coercive sexual behavior (Allgeier, 2002; Struckman-Johnson & Anderson, 1998).

In the late 1980s, a small number of investigators began to ask men as well as women about their experiences as victims of sexual coercion. Struckman-Johnson (1988) documented that 16 percent of men and 22 percent of women surveyed at a university reported being forced to have sexual intercourse while on a date. In the 1990s and early 2000s, at least a dozen more studies that included both male and female sexual victims appeared in the literature. For example, Lottes (1991) discovered that 24 percent of the men and 35 percent of the women in a classroom sample of college students reported that they had been coerced into sexual intercourse.

Tactics of Sexual Coercion

The present [chapter] is about gender differences in the tactics that are used in sexual coercion. In our review of the literature, we learned that men and women have been the victims of and have used a wide variety of coercive strategies for sexual contact. Most of the research has focused on the tactics men used to gain sexual access to women. Notably, Koss and her colleagues initiated a large body of research using the Sexual Experiences Survey (SES; Koss et al., 1987), which assessed a list of coercive tactics that men use to have sexual contact with women. For example, Koss et al. (1987) found that college women reported engaging in unwanted sexual intercourse because men had used verbal coercion (reported by 25 percent of the women), had threatened or used force (9 percent), had given the women alcohol or drugs (8 percent), and had misused authority (2 percent).

Anderson and Aymami (1993) measured college women's use of tactics for initiating sexual contact with men. One of the most commonly reported tactics was attempting to arouse the partner (cited by 79 percent of women). However, about *half* of the women reported initiating sex with a drunken man, 15 percent reported getting a man drunk or stoned, and 6 percent reported using physical force.

A few studies have explored male victims' perspectives on sexually coercive tactics used by female perpetrators. Struckman-Johnson and Struckman-Johnson (1998) found that 43 percent of college men had been subjected to at least one coercive sexual act with a woman since the age of 16. The most frequently cited tactics were verbal coercion (reported by 75 percent of male victims), being encouraged to get drunk (40 percent), and threats that the woman would withdraw her love (19 percent). Only 8 percent of male victims said that they were physically restrained by a woman. Surveying college men, Fiebert and Tucci (1998) documented that 70 percent reported being subjected to some form of sexual coercion perpetrated by a woman in the past 5 years. Most of the coercive activities fell into categories labeled mild (e.g., 17 percent to 39 percent experienced unwanted sexual touching and kissing) and moderate (e.g., 24 percent had unwanted sex with an insistent woman). Severe coercion involving a woman's threats or physical force was reported by only 1 percent to 3 percent of men.

Numerous studies have compared the coercive tactics experienced by male and female victims. In a classic work, Muehlenhard and Cook (1988) examined gender differences in reasons why college men and women engaged in unwanted sexual activity. The authors used factor analysis to create 13 categories of reasons for engaging in unwanted sexual activity, some of which reflected coercive tactics by the partner (e.g., verbal coercion by the partner) and some of which did not (e.g., peer pressure from the respondents' friends). Overall, they found that more women than men reported engaging in unwanted sexual activity because of the partner's verbal coercion (reported by 34 percent of the women and 27 percent of the men) and physical coercion (reported by 31 percent of the women and 24 percent of the men). None of the reasons for engaging in unwanted sexual activity were reported by more men than women.

Waldner-Haugrud and Magruder (1995) surveyed college students about unwanted sexual behavior in a dating context. According to self reports, more women than men were subjected to tactics of detainment, persistent touching, lies, and being held down. More men than women reported being victimized by the tactics of blackmail and use of a weapon. Larimer, Lydum, Anderson, and Turner (1999) used a gender-neutral version of the SES to assess sexual coercion among college students in

Greek organizations. Similar percentages of men and women reported having unwanted sexual intercourse because they were pressured by continual arguments and were given alcohol and drugs. However, for attempts at sexual intercourse, more women than men reported being given alcohol and drugs (17 percent vs. 9 percent) and being subjected to physical force (5 percent vs. 1 percent).

Finally, we found two studies that analyzed differences in tactics used by male and female perpetrators of sexual coercion. Hogben and Waterman (2000) measured the extent to which college men and women used a variety of tactics to engage in sex with someone against his or her will. They found that more men than women reported having engaged in the behaviors of touching above clothing, removal of clothing, and verbal attempts to obtain intercourse. However, men and women did not differ significantly in their reported use of violence or threats of violence. Zurbriggen (2000) found that similar percentages of men and women reported that they used tactics of complaining of sexual frustration, threatening to end a relationship, and getting a little drunk and forcing someone to have sex. However, more men than women said that they gave the silent treatment (40 percent vs. 16 percent, respectively), got someone purposefully drunk for sex (32 percent vs. 18 percent), or threatened that their feelings of affection would change (25 percent vs. 11 percent).

The preponderance of studies revealed that greater percentages of women than men had been subjected to the full range of tactics of sexual coercion from verbal pressure to physical force. The most commonly experienced tactics of sexual coercion, regardless of gender, appeared to be techniques of sexual arousal (e.g., persistent kissing and touching) and verbal pressure such as continual arguments. The least commonly experienced tactics were those involving physical force and harm. There is consistent evidence that more women than men were deceived for purposes of sexual access (e.g., Waldner-Haugrud & Magruder, 1996). There are contrasting findings for the tactic of taking advantage of intoxicated persons. Although at least one study indicates that more women than men were subjected to this tactic (Lottes & Weinberg, 1996), some studies found no gender difference (e.g., Lane & Gwartney-Gibbs, 1985). A majority of studies indicated that more women than men were subjected to tactics involving physical force, yet several studies found few differences or numbers of reports too small to analyze (e.g., Hogben & Waterman, 2000).

THE PRESENT STUDY

We designed the present research to study gender differences in the experience and use of tactics of sexual coercion using methods that would remedy many of these complications. Our first objective was to study tactics that could clearly be defined as sexually coercive, asking both women and men about both experiencing and using these tactics. We chose to study a behavior that we termed "post-refusal sexual persistence," defined as the act of pursuing sexual contact with a person after he or she has refused an initial advance. In our thinking, all acts of post-refusal sexual persistence are sexually coercive in that the receiver has already indicated that he or she does not consent to the action. While acts such as removing a receiver's clothing or making repeated requests would be considered noncoercive in an initial sexual advance, the same behaviors can be defined as coercive if the person continues to do them after the receiver has said no.

A second objective was to organize tactics that have been identified in past research into categories that reflect increasing levels of sexual exploitation. Based on our past research and a review of the literature, we proposed four levels of tactics.

Level 1 includes nonverbal sexual arousal tactics, such as persistent touching and kissing and clothing removal, that are intended to change the receiver's mind about saying no to sex. Because these tactics are normative acts of sexual seduction in consensual situations and do not involve verbal pressure or duplicity, use of drugs, or physical force, we considered them to be the least exploitative of sexually persistent acts.

Level 2 consists of tactics of emotional manipulation and lies. This category includes tactics that are typically termed verbal or psychological pressure, such as repeated requests, questions about a person's sexuality, threats of breaking up the relationship, deception, and blackmail. These tactics are exploitative in that they are intended to wear down the receiver's resistance, to take unfair advantage of the receiver's needs and desires for a relationship, and to deceive and trick the receiver into having sexual contact.

Level 3 includes tactics related to alcohol and drug intoxication, such as taking advantage of someone who is already drunk or purposely getting someone intoxicated to obtain sexual contact. We regard these tactics as a higher level of exploitation than manipulation or lies because the receivers may be too inebriated to consider requests, to give knowledgeable consent, to detect deception, or to physically escape the situation.

Level 4, tactics of physical force and harm, is the highest level of exploitation because the receiver is forced to engage in behaviors against her or his will. Injury and harm may occur. Depending upon the sexual outcome, behaviors in Levels 3 and 4 meet the legal definition of rape in many states.

A final objective of our study was to gain understanding of the dynamics of post-refusal sexual persistence by examining participants' descriptions of recent experiences. We used structured and open-ended questions to assess relationships between receivers and perpetrators, how the tactics were employed, and how participants were affected by the incidents.

Method

We distributed the survey to 656 college students: 213 men and 247 women from a Midwestern university and 62 men and 134 women from a Southern university. The average age was 21 years for men and 20 years for women. The survey was administered anonymously to students in general psychology, social psychology, sex roles, and human sexuality classes. This procedure prevents a problem in sexual coercion research in which men in classroom administrations tend to leave a large number of items blank (Senn, Verberg, Desmarais, & Wood, 2000). Over 95 percent of questionnaires were returned. A majority of the participants (82 percent) indicated on the questionnaire that they were Caucasian.

Measures

The post-refusal sexual persistence item read "Since the age of 16, how many times has a male [female; always the opposite sex from the participant] used any of the tactics on the list below to have sexual contact (genital touching, oral sex, or intercourse) with you after you have indicated 'no' to his [her] sexual advance?" Participants were further instructed to write in the space next to each tactic the number of times, to the best of their memory, that a male or female had used a tactic against them. Participants were then asked to answer questions about the most recent incident of sexual persistence they had experienced (if any). [They] were asked: "In your own words, please explain how this happened. What exactly did the male or female do when he or she tried to have sexual contact with you?" We then asked participants multiple-choice questions about their relationship with the perpetrator and what sexual activity took place. Participants rated the extent to which the incident affected them and their relationship with the perpetrator and wrote descriptions of these effects. We asked participants the same questions about their own use of post-refusal sexual persistence tactics since age 16 and in the most recent incident.

Results

Receivers of Post-refusal Sexual Persistence

Chi-square tests determined that the distributions of sexual persistence experiences for receivers did not differ between the two university samples, so the two samples were combined. The results revealed that 58 percent of the male sample and 78 percent of the female sample had been subjected to at least one tactic of sexual persistence.

Most frequently reported tactics across genders. The tactics category reported most frequently was sexual arousal, with 65 percent of all participants being subjected to at least one experience. Within this category, persistent kissing and touching was the most cited tactic. Emotional manipulation and deception was the next most frequently reported category, with 60 percent of participants being subjected to at least one experience. Within this category, participants cited the specific tactics of repeated requests and telling lies most often. Intoxication was the third most frequently reported category, with 38 percent of all participants being subjected to at least one tactic. More participants reported being taken advantage of while already intoxicated than being purposely intoxicated. The category with the lowest frequency of reports was physical force and harm, with 28 percent of participants being subjected to at least one tactic. The most frequently reported acts were having the retreat route blocked, being physically restrained, and being harmed. Less than 2 percent of participants reported that weapons were used against them.

Gender differences in receivers' experiences of tactics. Results revealed that more women than men reported being subjected to at least one sexual arousal tactic. Within this category, more women than men cited persistent kissing and touching. A greater percentage of women than men reported being subjected to at least one tactic of emotional manipulation or lies. Within this category, more women than men reported repeated requests and being told lies.

More women than men reported experiencing at least one intoxication tactic. This difference held for cases in which the participant was already intoxicated and for cases in which the perpetrator purposefully intoxicated the participant. There was no significant difference between the percentages of women and men who reported being subjected to at least one tactic of physical force and harm. However, within this category, a greater percentage of women than men reported being subjected to physical restraint and being threatened with harm.

Perpetrators of Post-refusal Sexual Persistence

Most frequently reported tactics across genders. As reported 43 percent of men and 26 percent of women reported having perpetrated at least one tactic of sexual persistence. Although there were fewer perpetrators than receivers, the two groups showed similar patterns for the most frequently occurring tactics. For perpetration of sexual persistence, the most frequently reported category was sexual arousal. Within the category, kissing and touching was the most used tactic. The second most frequently reported category was emotional manipulation and lies. Within this category, 20 percent reported using repeated requests, and 8 percent reported using lies. Only 8 percent of participants said that they had used at least one intoxication tactic, with 8 percent taking advantage of an intoxicated person and 3 percent using purposeful intoxication. Only 3 percent of participants reported using a tactic in the physical force and harm category.

Gender differences in use of tactics. More men than women reported using at least one tactic in the sexual arousal category (40 percent vs. 26 percent, respectively). Within this category, more men than women reported persistent kissing and touching and removing the receivers' clothing. More men than women also reported using at least one tactic of emotional manipulation and lies. Within this category, more men than women reported using repeated requests and lying.

For the category of intoxication, more men than women reported using at least one tactic. The difference held for taking advantage of an intoxicated person and for purposely getting someone intoxicated. There was no significant difference in the percentage of men and women who reported the use of at least one force tactic.

Variables Related to Most Recent Incidents

There were no gender differences for the relationship variable among the receivers or among the perpetrators. Half of the receivers reported being with an acquaintance, friend, or new date, and 38 percent reported being with a boyfriend, girlfriend, steady date, or fiance. A majority of perpetrators reported being with a steady partner, and 30 percent reported being with acquaintances or new partners. Fewer than 5 percent of all incidents occurred with strangers. There were no gender differences for sexual outcome of the most recent incident among the receivers or among the perpetrators. The most recent incident resulted in sexual intercourse for 48 percent of receivers and 55 percent of perpetrators.

Written Descriptions

Free response descriptions of most recent incidents were provided by 375 receivers (131 men and 244 women) and 174 perpetrators (95 men and 79 women). We sorted the descriptions according to the most exploitative tactics that were used in an incident. Our intent was not to conduct a systematic content analysis of the descriptions, but to record the variety of ways the tactics were carried out.

The tactics are illustrated with verbatim descriptions of incidents collected in the questionnaires. Spelling and grammar errors are left intact. We also summarize descriptions of the context and effects of the incidents.

Level 1: Sexual arousal. The incident usually began when the perpetrator either asked for sex or began touching and kissing the receiver. When the receiver expressed his or her refusal, the perpetrator usually responded first with persistent touching and kissing and removal of clothing. Leg, back, and genital massages were frequently mentioned in descriptions.

A woman wrote about what happened with a boyfriend. The outcome was sexual touching.

> We left a party & went to park. He was on top of me kissing me & stuff & trying to take all of my clothes off. He kept putting my hands down his pants & I kept pulling away. I made up some excuse for us to leave.

A man wrote about the following experience with a female acquaintance. Only sexual touching occurred. He reported that the incident hurt their friendship.

> We were at her parents house getting intoxicated. She went to "go take a shower," but came out of the bathroom with only a robe on. She removed it and was naked and tried to grope me.

Another man described what happened with a female friend. The outcome was sexual intercourse. He reported that the incident ruined their friendship.

> She asked me to bring her to the bank to get some money which was close to my house. Then she asked if I wanted something to eat I said yes, so we went to my apartment where she tried to kiss me. I told her to quit. She then grabbed my genitals and I quickly removed her hand. She then took off her clothes and said take me. I laughed at her. She asked why didn't I want her. I replied because I have a girlfriend. Then she kept pushing the issue until I gave in.

The perpetrator's perspective was given by a woman who said that she had persuaded reluctant men on many occasions. In this instance, the man was an acquaintance, and the outcome was sexual intercourse. She said that the incident had no bad effects on her.

> I told him how sexy he was & that he turned me on. And asked for sex. He refused. I retreated for a while but then continued to ask & say erotic things to him (putting ideas in his head) and every chance I could I would touch his genitals or buttox (sic).

Level 2: Emotional manipulation and lies. The most common form of emotional manipulation experienced by men and women was repeated requests. About twice as many men as women made repeated requests. One reason, we speculate, is that men are more practiced at verbalizing their desire in their role as sexual initiators. Perhaps women are not as comfortable as men with making direct sexual requests. Men and women often used repeated requests in conjunction with sexual arousal techniques.

According to descriptions, perpetrators often used deception when the tactics of sexual arousal and repeated requests failed to overcome the receivers' refusal. About twice as many women as men reported being lied to, and about five times as many men as women reported lying. Giving truth to an old stereotype (Zilbergeld, 1978), the lies told by men were usually false claims of love or affection. Another lie told by older men was that they were the same age as the college women. Presumably, this made the men seem more trustworthy. Men broke promises about not inserting their penises and told tales of "blue balls" and other peculiarities about their sexual anatomy and functioning.

A woman described being deceived by a male acquaintance. The outcome was sexual intercourse. She reported that the incident had no negative effects.

> He kissed and touched me in private places. He performed oral sex on me. He was begging and trying to trick me by saying it was his finger. It was his penis though. Afterwards, I threw him off of me.

Some women reported being manipulated emotionally by men who told them that they were "abnormal" to refuse because "everybody is doing it." Women were warned that their relationships with the men would end if they did not have sex. A few women were told that sex is what good friends do for each other or that sex with a new person is the best way to get over a breakup. Women were complimented by men, were told that they were the right kind of girl or the man's fantasy, or were told that they would be respected in the morning.

In the following description, a male perpetrator explained his manipulation tactic with a female acquaintance. The outcome was sexual touching.

> I first got her in my bed & started to kiss her, but after awhile she didn't want to so I stopped & then I told her exactly what she wanted to hear. (she asked me what I look for 'in a girl'). Then we started to kiss & she stopped my [first] attempt at her breast, & after I tried again she let me & after 3 attempts she let me in her pants.

He wrote that the woman hated him afterwards. He regretted his action and subsequently stopped trying when a woman said no.

Another man wrote about a lie that he did not mean to tell to a female acquaintance. The outcome was sexual intercourse.

> It was like this: She, before engaging in sex, asked me if it wasn't just a one-night stand. I told her no, it wasn't. At the time I thought I meant it but in the morning I didn't feel that way. Maybe the liquor?

The man said that they never spoke again. He added that he no longer started a relationship that he did not intend to finish.

Men were deceived by women who claimed to be in love with them or to care about them. Men's emotions were manipulated by women who complimented them, questioned their masculinity or heterosexuality, offered them sex as a perk of friendship, and asked them why they (the women) were not good enough or pretty enough or loved enough for sex.

In the excerpt below, a woman explained how she manipulated her boyfriend. The outcome was sexual intercourse.

> We were alone together and he didn't want to have sex cause he wanted it to be special. I felt rejected, telling him 'what it's not special enough that it's just you & me.' I started crying and basicly [sic] guilted him into having sex w/me.

The woman reported that their relationship was hurt. She said that much later she came to regret that she had hurt someone.

Several men were blackmailed by women. In the following case, a man had sexual intercourse with an ex-girlfriend:

> We had gone out for the previous two years and recently broken up. I had a new girlfriend of about four months, but cheated on her with my ex once before. My ex came over and tried to make out or have sex with me. I refused and she told me she would tell my girlfriend about last time if I didn't have sex with her. I gave in.

The man added that his ex-girlfriend told his current girlfriend about the incident and he never spoke to either one again.

Some men encountered threats of suicide and self-harm when they turned down women. One man wrote about his ex-girlfriend. The outcome was sexual touching. He said that the incident hurt their relationship.

> Entered my apt. to discuss recent break up, began to get real 'handsy.' Stated that if I didn't stop the pain by having sex with her she would find a way to 'end it all.' I could only assume she meant herself.

Level 3: Exploitation of the intoxicated. Of the respondents, 30 percent of the men and 42 percent of the women reported being sexually exploited when they were already intoxicated. According to written descriptions, receivers were often lured to an isolated area, such as a bedroom at a party house or outside away from the crowd. In numerous instances, the perpetrators simply waited for the receivers to pass out in a convenient bedroom. As documented, 19 percent of participants reported that they were purposefully intoxicated, with the percentage of female receivers being double that of male receivers. According to descriptions, perpetrators accomplished this by buying drink after drink for receivers, engaging the receivers in drinking games, and, rarely, drugging drinks.

Some exploited women were so drunk that they had little memory of what happened, as in the following case. The woman was with an acquaintance, and the outcome was sexual intercourse. She said that the incident had a very negative effect on her sex life.

> I was very intoxicated and I don't remember the details. He was just very pressuring; he kept trying to talk me into it and messing around until I didn't have the ability to resist anymore.

Another woman wrote about being purposely drugged by an acquaintance. The outcome was sexual intercourse. She reported that the incident had a very negative effect on her dating and sex life.

> He gave me a drink that had drugs in it. I passed out and awoke while he was on top of me having sex.

A common scenario for male receivers was being led to a bed or being joined in bed by a female perpetrator who tried to arouse him by removing his clothing or initiating oral sex. Sometimes, the woman got on top of an aroused man and inserted his penis. In some cases, inebriated men became so aroused that they became a willing participant in the sex. In the following case, a man described how an acquaintance took advantage of his intoxicated state. The outcome was sexual intercourse. He said that the incident had a negative effect on him.

> Alcohol was involved. She undressed me, tried to arouse me by touching my genitals, sex, and trying to force me inside of her.

Several men wrote that they were taken advantage of by women who were sometimes undesirable to them and who wanted to start a relationship with them. One female perpetrator reflected this motive in her description of sexually touching a drunken man:

> I liked this guy and I thought the only way we'd ever hook up is if we got drunk and fooled around.

The woman wrote that no relationship developed as a consequence. She added that she came to realize that a relationship should be based on more than just a drunken one night stand.

One man reported that he was purposefully intoxicated by a female acquaintance. He said that the incident did not have a negative effect on him.

> We were drunk and she kept buying me drinks. Later she grabbed my crotch & asked if it turned me on. Then unzipped my pants & proceeded with oral sex.

Another man described how a female stranger used multiple strategies, including purposeful intoxication, to have sex with him. Sexual intercourse was the outcome.

> At a party, she came up and began talking to me. I was already drinking some at the time. While playing cards, she talked me into finishing several of her drinks and beers. She said there was another party, and convinced me to go. I was too drunk to drive so she drove us. The 'party' seemed to lack other people. After about 1/2 hour of kissing/making out, I was tired and wanted to go home. She said no and told me she wanted to have sex. I said no, but she continued to kiss me and try to talk me into it. When she produced a condom, I gave in.

The man wrote that he was a virgin at the time and that he felt somewhat used afterwards.

Level 4: Physical force and harm. Similar percentages of men and women reported that someone tried to block their retreat, a minor form of physical force. According to participants' descriptions, the most common acts were when perpetrators stood in front of doors, locked doors, or locked car doors. About twice as many women as men reported being physically restrained, a more serious act.

In the following case, the woman was with an acquaintance whom she had turned down for sex when she was sober. She said that she ended the friendship after it happened.

> I was at a party and I was drunk but still knew what I was doing. He asked me to go for a walk

with him. I told him I would go but we were just going to walk down the street and back. He made sure my glass was full before we left. He talked me into jumping on a trampoline & he then pushed me down and pulled my pants down & forced his penis into me. Then told me that if I told anyone they won't believe me.

Another woman wrote how an acquaintance physically forced her into sexual intercourse. She said that she avoided him afterwards.

We were all drinking (I was with my older sister). This guy offered to bring me to go get cigarettes. Already being drunk I said yes. Trusting this guy. Well we never made it to the store. He brought me to the lake. That's when he brought himself on me. He was to strong. I couldn't get him off.

In the following case, a woman described how she was harmed by a stranger. The outcome was sexual intercourse.

Forced himself on me after a few drinks in a bar. When I tried to leave in my car (intoxicated) he climbed in and agressively [sic] attacked me sexually leaving numerous bruises on my backside. He kept slapping me on my ass, hurting me repeatedly.

The woman wrote that the man tried unsuccessfully to contact her again for a date. She added that she quit drinking.

The male perpetrators' descriptions of force tactics were sparse. Not many men reported using a force tactic, and those who did often left out descriptions, wrote about their regrets rather than about the incident, or cited memory loss due to intoxication. In the following example, the man was with a female acquaintance.

This girl and I occasionaly got together and had intercourse. Once when I was very drunk, she said we had anal intercourse when she wasn't willing. I don't remember this part of the night no matter how hard I try. Fortunatly [sic] I don't drink at all these days.

The man reported that their relationship was hurt. He added that the incident caused him to become more sensitive and passive when having sex with women.

Women were unlikely to use high levels of physical force with male receivers. Instead, they occasionally tried to grab and hold on to men, push them down on beds and sit or lay on them, and tie them up. Here is a description from a man who was physically restrained by a woman he had previously dated. He said that the incident had no effects on their limited relationship.

We had 'made out' the weekend before, but I didn't want to continue any further because I was al-

ready dating a different girl. She got drunk and so did I, she wanted to 'hook up again.' But I thought it was a bad idea. She pinned me down at one point (it was kind of thrilling) but I left.

In several instances, women bit, pinched, slapped, and hit male receivers. In some cases, a woman's harmful act appeared to be a means of persuasion; in others it seemed to be a way of "punishing" a man for refusing her.

I already had a girlfriend and she tried to have sex with me. I told her no and she kept kissing me and touching me. She kept asking and trying to make me have sex with her.

Female perpetrator descriptions of using force tactics were rare. In this example, the woman was with a male acquaintance. The outcome was sexual touching.

I locked the room door that we were in. I kissed and touched him. I removed his shirt and unzipped his pants. He asked me to stop. I didn't. Then, I sat on top of him. He had had two beers but wasn't drunk.

She wrote that the man refused to speak to her or get near her again after it happened.

DISCUSSION

A major finding of our study is that a form of sexual coercion that we call post-refusal sexual persistence is a fairly common experience among our college student sample. Nearly 70 percent of the participants had been subjected to at least one tactic of post-refusal sexual persistence since the age of 16. One-third of our participants said that they had used a tactic. We found that the most frequently reported tactics were sexual arousal and emotional manipulation and lies: categories that we consider to be less exploitative than intoxication and physical force. However, well over a third of our participants had been sexually exploited while intoxicated, and over one-fourth of our participants had been subjected to a tactic of physical force.

Our study is consistent with past research that has shown that women are more likely than men to report being sexually coerced (e.g., Byers & O'Sullivan, 1998). More women than men were subjected to at least one tactic of sexual arousal, emotional manipulation and lies, and exploitation due to intoxication. Although there was no difference in the percentage of men and women who had been subjected to at least one tactic categorized as physical force, a greater percentage of women than men had been subjected to the specific tactics of physical restraint and threats of harm.

Our study is also consistent with past research (e.g., Struckman-Johnson & Anderson, 1998) in finding that substantial percentages of men were subjected to the sexually persistent behavior of female perpetrators. Our study found that women generally used gentler or less exploitative tactics than men did when confronted with a sexual refusal. That is, women more than men appeared to restrict their behavior to tactics of sexual arousal and repeated requests. Still, moderate percentages of women reportedly engaged in deception, taking advantage of intoxicated men, and blocking men's retreat. However, reports of women engaging in serious acts of physical restraint or causing serious harm were uncommon.

In some respects, we found more similarities than differences in the ways that men and women were subjected to sexual persistence. Statistical tests revealed significant gender differences for only 7 of the 19 tactics. For example, approximately equal percentages of men and women were subjected to the tactics of having their clothes removed by a perpetrator, being threatened with a breakup, having their sexuality questioned, having their retreat blocked, and being physically harmed.

Our results are consistent with past research that indicates a strong relationship between drinking and sexual coercion (e.g., Larimer et al., 1999; Tewsbury & Mustaine, 2001). Nearly 40 percent of the participants in our study fell victim to sexual exploitation due to intoxication. We surmise that this tactic is used because it can be so easily accomplished by both men and women. Perpetrators do not have to worry about their attractiveness to the target, what to say, or how to prevent the target from leaving. One idea for future research would be to explore the motives of individuals who use specific tactics such as intoxication to gain sexual access to others.

Our research underscored the problems that result from sexually coercive behavior. We found that many of our victims of post-refusal sexual persistence reported long lasting negative effects from the incidents. In particular, we were struck by the number of respondents who reported in their written descriptions that romantic relationships and friendships were ruined by an incident of post-refusal sexual persistence.

One limitation of our research is that participants were asked to report incidents that had happened since the age of 16. It is possible that their recollections of postrefusal sexual persistence were influenced by the passage of time. In addition, some participants' memories of specific incidents may have been influenced by alcohol consumed at the time of the incident.

Another limitation is that our four categories of sexual exploitation may not be hierarchical as we propose. For example, one could argue that our *Level 1 tactic of sexually persistent touching* is equally or more exploitative than verbal coercion. This question could be investigated in future research by having respondents rate the perceived exploitation value of different tactics of sexual coercion.

Our study raises an interesting question about the disparity between the relatively large number of participants who reported being receivers of sexual persistence and the much smaller number who reported being perpetrators. To reiterate a question asked by many researchers in this area (e.g., Anderson & Sorensen, 1999; Lottes, 1991), who is committing the sexual persistence reported by our receivers? It could be that a small number of perpetrators are committing acts with numerous partners or that receivers are socializing with a population not included in our survey. It is also possible that participants did not report perpetration due to social undesirability of the acts. Our research method may have contributed to this effect: Respondents who were first asked to report having a tactic used against them may have been reluctant to then report that they had used such tactics.

Another explanation is that participants did not perceive their behaviors as tactics of sexual persistence. Many of our participant perpetrators qualified their behaviors as playful or beneficial, indicating that the behaviors were intended to improve their relationships. Numerous female perpetrators and some male perpetrators wrote that their partners changed their minds and were pleased to have sex. After reading so many receivers' complaints, we wonder if some of our perpetrators were unaware of the negative effects of their behavior. These speculations and others that may explain the receiver-perpetrator gap are ripe for future research.

Introduction References

Brownmiller, S. (1975). *Against Our Will: Men, Women, and Rape.* New York: Simon and Schuster.

Chiang, H. (2003, January 7). "Court Days Sex After Rescinded Consent Is Rape/State Justices Hear Case of 2 Teens." *San Francisco Chronicle*, p. A17.

Griffin, S. (1971). "Rape: The All-American Crime." *Ramparts*, 10, 26–35.

MacDonald, J. M. (1971). *Rape Offenders and Their Victims.* Springfield, IL: Thomas.

McKinney, D. (2003, July 29). "Clarifications of Rape Law Signed by Governor." *Chicago Sun-Times*, p. 6.

Muehlenhard, C., and Highby, B. J. "Sexual Assault and Rape." In R. T. Francoeur (Ed.), *The International En-*

cyclopedia of Sexuality, Vol. 3 (pp. 1546–1555). New York: Continuum.

Young, C. C. (2003, January, 20). "Troubling Questions About Rape and Consent." *Boston Globe*, p. A15.

References

Allgeier, E. R. (2002). Interpreting research results. In M. W. Wiederman & B. E. Whitley, Jr. (Eds.), *Handbook for conducting research on human sexuality* (pp. 371–392). Mahwah, NJ: Lawrence Erlbaum.

Anderson, P. B., & Aymami, R. (1993). Reports of female initiation of sexual contact: Male and female differences. *Archives of Sexual Behavior, 22,* 335–343.

Anderson, P. B., & Sorensen, W. (1999). Male and female differences in reports of women's heterosexual initiation and aggression. *Archives of Sexual Behavior, 28,* 243–253.

Byers, E. S., & O'Sullivan, L. F. (1998). Similar but different: Men's and women's experiences of sexual coercion. In P B. Anderson and C. Struckman-Johnson (Eds.), *Sexually aggressive women: Current perspectives and controversies* (pp. 144–168). New York: Guilford.

Fiebert, M. S., & Tucci, L. M. (1998). Sexual coercion: Men victimized by women. *Journal of Men's Studies, 6,* 127–133.

Hogben, M., & Waterman, C. K. (2000). Patterns of conflict resolution within relationships and coercive sexual behavior of men and women. *Sex Roles, 43,* 341–357.

Koss, M. P., Gidycz, C. A., & Wisniewski, N. (1987). The scope of rape: Incidence and prevalence of sexual aggression and victimization in a national sample of higher education students. *Journal of Consulting and Clinical Psychology, 55,* 162–170.

Lane, K., & Gwartney-Gibbs, P. (1985). Violence in the context of dating and sex. *Journal of Family Issues, 6,* 45–59.

Larimer, M. E., Lydum, A. R., Anderson, B. K., & Turner, A. P. (1999). Male and female recipients of unwanted sexual contact in a college sample: Prevalence rates, alcohol use, and depression symptoms. *Sex Roles, 40,* 295–308.

Lottes, I. I. (1991). The relationship between nontraditional gender roles and sexual coercion. *Journal of Psychology and Human Sexuality, 4,* 89–109.

Lottes, I. I., & Weinberg, M. (1996). Sexual coercion among university students: A comparison of the United States and Sweden. *The Journal of Sex Research, 34,* 67–76.

Muehlenhard, C. L., & Cook, S. (1988). Men's self-reports of unwanted sexual activity. *The Journal of Sex Research, 24,* 58–72.

Senn, C. Y., Verberg, N., Desmarais, S., & Wood, E. (2000). Sampling the reluctant participant: A random-sample response-rate study of men and sexual coercion. *Journal of Applied Psychology, 30,* 96–105.

Struckman-Johnson, C. J. (1988). Forced sex on dates: It happens to men, too. *The Journal of Sex Research, 24,* 234–240.

Struckman-Johnson, C., & Anderson, P. B. (1998). "Men do and women don't": Differences in researching sexually aggressive women. In P. B. Anderson and C. J. Struckman-Johnson (Eds.), *Sexually aggressive women: Current perspectives and controversies* (pp. 9–18). New York: Guiford.

Struckman-Johnson, C. J., & Struckman-Johnson, D. L. (1998). The dynamics and impact of sexual coercion of men by women. In P. B. Anderson and C. J. Struckman-Johnson (Eds.), *Sexually aggressive women: Current perspectives and controversies* (pp. 121–169). New York: Guiford.

Tewsbury, R., & Mustaine, E. E. (2001). Lifestyle factors associated with sexual assault of men: A routine activity theory analysis. *Journal of Men's Studies, 9,* 153–182.

Waldner-Haugrud, L. K., & Magruder, B. (1995). Male and female sexual victimization in dating relationships: Gender differences in coercion techniques and outcomes. *Violence and Victims, 10,* 203–215.

Zurbriggen, E. L. (2000). Social motives and cognitive power-sex associations: Predictors of aggressive sexual behavior. *Journal of Personality and Social Psychology, 78,* 1–23.

Chapter 36
Sexual Aggression Among Asian Americans

Gordon C. Nagayama Hall
Amy K. Windover
Gloria Gia Maramba

Some students may wonder why they need to read an article about sexual aggression among Asian Americans, because perpetration and victimization rates are lower for this group than all others. The answer is twofold. First, the unique patriarchal aspects of Asian cultures may place some of this population at more risk for sexual victimization or perpetration of sexually aggressive behavior than other groups. If so, special interventions that counteract these cultural aspects could further reduce that risk. Second, in setting the stage for their subject, the authors offer an excellent review of empirical findings concerning the risk factors for sexual aggression among both perpetrators and victims in the general population.

Touching on factors of childhood sexual abuse, peer influence, date rape, and re-victimization, this well-written piece enlightens readers who seek to determine if indeed there is a fine line or a vast chasm between normal and abnormal sexual behavior. The section on prevention and interventions with both women and men happens to focus on Asian Americans. But, in reality, it also casts a broader net, reviewing programs of risk reduction that appear to have positive results within the general population. An added bonus for students is the excellent list of references on the important topic of sexual aggression.

Existing research suggests that sexual aggression is a serious societal problem that affects as many as 1 in 4 Americans in terms of perpetration or victimization (Koss, Gidycz, & Wisniewski, 1987). Most of the available information on sexual aggression is applicable to European American populations.

However, there is some evidence of differential rates of sexual aggression in ethnic minority populations. Lower rates of sexual aggression in ethnic minority groups may suggest that there are protective factors against sexual aggression within these groups that may not exist in European American groups.

Sexually aggressive behavior is relatively infrequent among Asian Americans. This is a consistent finding in both official data and in anonymous self-report data among perpetrators and victims (Federal Bureau of Investigation [FBI], 1994; Koss et al., 1987). Yet the reasons for this low frequency of sexual aggression are poorly understood. Most sexual aggression involves male perpetrators and female victims, which are the focus of this article.

General Risk Factors for Sexual Aggression

Perpetrator Risk Factors

Past sexually aggressive behavior is the best single predictor of future sexually aggressive behavior (Quinsey, Rice, & Harris, 1995). For men who are not sexually aggressive, the appraised threats of sexual aggression, including legal or societal sanctions against it, constitute a threshold that prevents them from engaging in sexually aggressive behavior (Hall, 1996). However, men who are sexually aggressive violate this threshold because the appraised threats of sexual aggression do not outweigh its appraised benefits, such as power and sexual gratification. Men who have violated this threshold are at greater risk to become sexually aggressive again than men who have not violated the threshold, because this threshold is weakened.

Why do some men violate the threshold against sexually aggressive behavior? Sexually aggressive males may experience different developmental patterns than males who are not sexually aggressive. Some developmental risk factors include poverty, parental neglect, physical or sexual abuse, a family criminal history, academic difficulties, and interpersonal difficulties (Hall, 1996; Hall & Hirschman, 1991). These factors create a general risk for antisocial behavior. The developmental variables most specifically associated with sexually aggressive behavior involve heterosexual relationships. Sexually aggressive males tend to initiate coitus earlier than men who are not sexually aggressive (Malamuth, Linz, Heavey, Barnes, & Acker, 1995). Initiation of coitus before a person is developmentally capable of establishing the emotional relationships that provide a context for sex may increase a male's risk of perpetrating sexual aggression because he comes to view females as sex objects rather than as people (Hall, 1996).

Sexually aggressive males also tend to have more sexual partners than males who are not sexually aggressive (Malamuth et al., 1995). Promiscuous men often have an impersonal approach to sex in which the partner may be devalued and objectified (Malamuth et al., 1995). When the primary or sole purpose of sex is personal gratification, the needs of the partner are less relevant, and the likelihood of using coercion to meet personal needs may increase. Objectification of females may lead to short-lived sexual relationships and a failure to establish nonsexual friendships with peer females (Hall & Barongan, 1997).

What causes men who have been sexually aggressive once to persist in sexually aggressive behavior? Forced sexual intercourse is often accompanied by the perpetrator's physiological sexual arousal, which may be highly reinforcing. The more times this type of conditioning occurs, the greater the likelihood that a male will be sexually aroused by sexually aggressive behavior (Marshall & Barbaree, 1984). Another effect of perpetrating sexual aggression on multiple occasions is a desensitization to the negative effects of sexual aggression. For some men coercive behaviors may come to be viewed as necessary and excusable components of having sex with someone who refuses (Hall, 1996). Other males who have multiple shortlived sexual relationships with females may become angry toward women because these relationships tend to be neither lasting nor satisfying (Gold & Clegg, 1990). Sexual aggression is the behavior that becomes an expression of this anger (Malamuth et al., 1995).

Sexually aggressive men become sexually aggressive under certain circumstances but not under others (Hall, 1996). For example, 21 percent of a group of nonaggressive undergraduate men reported some likelihood that they would force a woman into sexual acts, and another 14 percent also reported some likelihood that they would rape if they could be assured of not being caught (Malamuth, 1988). Extreme reductions in sanctions against rape occasionally occur, such as in times of war, and some nonaggressive men do become sexually aggressive. However, sanctions against rape are generally weak relative to sanctions against other crimes (Koss, 1993). Thus, the relatively low likelihood of punishment for sexually aggressive behavior may disinhibit sexual aggression among some men. Another implication of Malamuth's (1988) data is that sanctions against sexual aggression deter most men from engaging in it.

Peers may have a greater influence over sexual behavior than other influences, e.g., parents, schools (Rodgers & Rowe, 1993). The availability of oppo-

site-gender peers who are willing to engage in sexual behavior creates the opportunity for sexual aggression to occur (Himelein, 1995), and the presence of sexually active same-gender peers, who may model the message that sexual activity is acceptable, is associated both with sexual activity and risk for sexual aggression (Vicary, Klingaman, & Harkness, 1995). Moreover, the presence of male peers who approve of sexually coercive behavior may increase a male's risk of engaging in sexually aggressive behavior (DeKeseredy & Kelly, 1995).

Sexually aggressive men often report that they used alcohol while they were sexually aggressive (Seto & Barbaree, 1995). However, alcohol may be used as an excuse for being sexually aggressive, and it is unlikely that alcohol use has a causal role in sexually aggressive behavior. More likely, alcohol use may disinhibit sexually aggressive impulses among some men (Seto & Barbaree, 1995).

In summary, a male's history of sexually aggressive behavior is associated with his likelihood of engaging in sexually aggressive behavior in the future. Developmental sexual factors, including early initiation of coitus and promiscuous sexual activity, may facilitate physiological, cognitive, and affective motivational factors for perpetrating sexually aggressive behavior. The likelihood that these motivational factors will influence a male to engage in sexually aggressive behavior may be mediated by situational factors. Among males who are motivated to become sexually aggressive, the likelihood of engaging in sexual aggression may be a function of perceived sanctions against sexually aggressive behavior, peer support for such behavior (i.e., availability of peer sexual partners, peer approval of sexual aggression), and alcohol use.

Victim Risk Factors

Victims of sexual aggression are not responsible for being sexually victimized. Most victims do not knowingly place themselves in situations in which they are likely to be sexually abused. However, potential victims' amount of contact with perpetrators comprises a risk factor for sexual victimization.

In a national sample of 32 colleges, Koss and Dinero (1989) found that the strongest predictors of sexual victimization among women were past sexual abuse, sexual activity, alcohol use, and sexual attitudes . . . [factors that] may appear to be under a woman's control. Thus women may appear to be responsible for these behaviors. However, many women who engage in behaviors associated with risk for being sexually victimized, such as having multiple sexual partners or drinking alcohol before engaging in sexual behavior, are not seeking to be sexually victimized. Moreover, such behaviors are risky only when they occur in the presence of a perpetrator. A woman who has multiple partners who are not perpetrators or who drinks on a date with a man who is not a perpetrator is not at increased risk for sexual victimization. Even when women engage in behaviors that may be associated with risk for sexual victimization, it is the perpetrator's decision to become sexually aggressive (Hall, 1996). Thus, women who happen to have sex with a perpetrator are not responsible for being sexually victimized.

A history of being sexually abused is associated with additional sexual victimization among females (Messman & Long, 1996). In a community sample, 21 percent of women who were not abused during childhood experienced sexual victimization involving physical contact during adulthood, whereas 56 percent of women who were sexually victimized during childhood experienced sexual victimization involving physical contact during adulthood (Wyatt, Guthrie, & Notgrass, 1992). Sexual victimization during childhood or adolescence is a risk factor for future sexual abuse insofar as the victim has come into contact with a pool of perpetrators, or at least one perpetrator from this pool, and is at risk for future sexual victimization any time she comes into contact with someone from this pool.

The increased risk of sexual re-victimization for victims of sexual abuse may exist in part because some women who have been previously sexually abused may begin to engage in indiscriminate sexual behavior in an effort to seek intimacy (Briere & Runtz, 1993). Sexual abuse of female children also may result in these victims' sexualized behaviors, including having an earlier first coitus, multiple sex partners, and brief sexual relationships that may place them at risk for additonal sexual abuse (Kendall-Tackett, Williams, & Finkelhor, 1993). Females who engage in indiscriminate sexual behavior may be perceived by perpetrators as more likely to engage in sex and may be targeted as potential victims more so than females who have more limited sexual contact (Himelein, 1995).

Data are conflicting on personality factors associated with risk for being sexually victimized once versus multiple times. Although there is evidence that single- and multiple-incident victims do not differ on personality characteristics (Wyatt et al., 1992), other evidence suggests that they do (Gidycz, Coble, Latham, & Layman, 1993). In a 9-month prospective study with a large sample of college women, a direct relationship was found between personality factors and additional sexual victimization among women who had been previously sexually victimized (Gidycz et al., 1993). Women who experienced greater levels of depression and anxiety after sexual victimization were more likely to be sexually re-victimized than were sexually victimized women who experienced less depression and anxiety (Gidycz et al., 1993). However, this association between victim personality factors and additional victimization was only partially supported in a follow-up study (Gidycz, Hanson, & Layman, 1995).

A second risk factor in Koss and Dinero's (1989) study for being sexually victimized was . . . [related to] sexual activity variables, including age at first coitus and number of sexual partners (Himelein, 1995; Vicary et al., 1995). Sexual activity is a situational variable that may increase contact with perpetrators. The greater the number of sexual partners, the greater the likelihood that a woman will come into contact with a perpetrator (Buss & Schmitt, 1993).

Although Koss and Dinero (1989) reported that sexual attitudes differentiated victims and nonvictims, three of the four items that composed Koss and Dinero's sexual attitudes variable involved questions about whether women had engaged in kissing, petting, and sexual intercourse. Thus, this variable appears to be more of a sexual behavior variable than an attitudinal one. Most rape victims and nonvictims do not differ on personality characteristics, including gender role attitudes and rape-supportive beliefs (Sorenson, Siegel, Golding, & Stein, 1991).

Alcohol use by females has been consistently associated with sexual victimization (Abbey, Ross, McDuffie, & McAuslan, 1996). It is possible that some victims may blame their victimization on their drinking behavior in a manner similar to the way perpetrators blame alcohol for their sexually aggressive behavior. However, the primary risk of female alcohol use may be that it is perceived by perpetrators as an excuse for becoming sexually aggressive (Koss & Dinero, 1989).

In summary, developmental factors that increase the likelihood of contact with peer or nonpeer perpetrators, including amount of sexual activity (e.g., early initiation of coitus, multiple sex partners) and sexual victimization, increase risk for sexual victimization during adulthood. The likelihood of adult sexual victimization is mediated by situational variables, including number of sexual partners and alcohol use, that may activate a perpetrator's cognitive distortions about the justifiability of becoming sexually aggressive. There do not appear to be specific personality characteristics of attitudes associated with women's risk for sexual victimization.

Risk and Protective Factors Among Asian Americans

Risk Factors

Women often have a subordinate status in Asian cultures (Ho, 1990). Some Asian American women may view themselves as responsible for being sexually victimized (Yoshihama, Parekh, & Boyington, 1991), and women who believe that women are to blame for rape may be at risk for being sexually victimized themselves (Muehlenhard & MacNaughton, 1988). Asian American women may be viewed by perpetrators as particularly vulnerable for these reasons. Moreover, stereotypes of Asian American women held by Asians and non-Asians are that they are exotic, sexual creatures. Some Asian American women may not want to report abuse to authorities because they blame themselves for what happened, feel that they will bring disgrace to their families, or fear that they or the perpetrator will face discriminatory or even brutal treatment by social service agencies when the perpetrator is Asian American (Yoshihama et al., 1991). Moreover, the Asian American community may also ostracize the woman if she reports being sexually victimized. Asian American women are less likely to report dating violence to police than are Latina and African American women, although Asian American women are not less likely to report dating violence to police than are European American women (Miller & Simpson, 1991).

Insofar as the percentage of non-Asian men who are sexually aggressive is greater than the percentage of Asian American men who are sexually aggressive (Koss et al., 1987), Asian American women who date non-Asian men may be at increased risk for being sexually victimized. Asian American women who date non-Asians may be more sexually active than Asian American women who exclusively date Asian American men (Huang & Uba, 1992). Opportunities for sexual behavior also create opportunities for sexually aggressive behavior. Some non-Asian men may deliberately choose to sexually victimize Asian American women because of their perceived vulnerability and relatively low likelihood of reporting sexual aggression. Immigrant women and those who have limited English language skills may be particularly vulnerable. However, because surveys typically have not assessed the ethnicity of perpetrator and victim (Cochran, Mays, & Leung, 1991; Koss et al., 1987), the prevalence of interracial sexual aggression among Asian Americans is unknown.

In summary, the patriarchal aspects of Asian cultures may create a risk for sexual aggression. Because they are often subordinated, some Asian American women may submit to sexually aggressive behavior and may be unwilling to report it to authorities. The perceived vulnerability of Asian American women may be attractive to perpetrators. Asian American men may be at risk to be sexually aggressive against those who appear to be members of out-groups. Nevertheless, very few Asian American men perpetrate sexual aggression, and very few Asian American women are sexually victimized. The reasons for this infrequency of sexual aggression among Asian Americans are unknown.

Protective Factors

Unlike the emphasis on individualism in mainstream American culture, American cultures having non-Western origins often emphasize collective values (Hill, Soriano, Chen, & LaFromboise, 1994). Whereas there tends to be a consensus about cultural norms and sanctions against violating these norms in collectivist cultures, there are often multiple, sometimes conflicting, cultural norms for which violation is often not punished in individualist cultures. Interpersonal conflict and violence tend to be minimal in cultures with collectivist orientations, because individual goals are subordinated to those of the group, social support is high, and competitiveness is low. Crime levels and collectivist influences are inversely associated (Triandis, 1995). In the United States, arrest rates for violent crimes perpetrated by Asian Americans are about one-third the rate of the numbers of Asian Americans in the population (American Psychological Association Commission on Violence and Youth, 1993).

The largest and most representative national survey of sexually aggressive behavior, in which participants' identities were anonymous, suggests differences in prevalence rates of sexual aggression across ethnic groups during adulthood (Koss et al., 1987). Prevalence rates of rape in Koss et al.'s (1987) study were significantly lower for Asian American women (7 percent) than for women in other groups (European American = 16 percent, Asian American = 10 percent, Latina = 12 percent, Native American = 40 percent). These findings are consistent with other multi-ethnic studies of self-reported rates of rape among college women (Urquiza & Goodlin-Jones, 1994: European American = 26 percent, Native American = 38 percent, Latina = 18 percent, Asian American = 11 percent). Moreover, few Asian American men perpetrate rape relative to most other groups.

It is possible that Asian Americans have narrower definitions of rape and other sexually aggressive behaviors than do other non-Asian groups (Mori, Bernat, Glenn, Selle, & Zarate, 1995). For example, a narrow definition would define rape as occurring only when physical force is involved. Such a definition would exclude rapes in which threats (e.g., with a weapon) or psychological coercion are involved. Koss et al.'s (1987) study avoided such definitional problems to some extent with the use of specific descriptions of sexually aggressive behaviors instead of terms such as *rape* or *sexual aggression*.

It is possible that the lower reporting of sexually aggressive behavior among Asian Americans is a function of social desirability (Urquiza & Goodlin-Jones, 1994). Russell (1984) suggested that Asian women may be less likely than non-Asian women to disclose intimate information. Nevertheless, among Asian Americans who were sexually active, there were no significant differences in sexual behaviors between those who were U.S. born and foreign born (Cochran et al., 1991). Moreover, there were also few differences between Asian Americans who were sexually active and members of other ethnic groups who were sexually active (Cochran et al., 1991). It is possible that social desirability is less influential for the responses of sexually active people than it is for those who are not sexually active.

Perhaps there are specific aspects of Asian American culture that serve as protective factors against sexually aggressive behavior (Hall & Barongan, 1997). The high value placed on self-control among Asian Americans (Uba, 1994) may prevent the development of the impulse dyscontrol associated with sexually aggressive behavior (Baumeister, Smart, & Boden, 1996). In Asian cultures, in which the self is not separate from others, any behavior that upsets group interdependence is not approved of (Markus & Kitayama, 1994). Deviant behavior may result in loss of face or the threat of loss of one's social integrity (Sue & Morishima, 1982). Loss of face may be a more important mediator of behavior among Asian Americans than among European Americans.

In collectivist cultures, the most important relationships are vertical, e.g., parent-child (Triandis, Bontempo, Villateal, Asai, & Lucca, 1988). Thus, parents may have more influence over their children's behavior than peers have. Age at first coitus is delayed among adolescents who perceive their parents as more influential than peers (Wyatt, 1989). Delaying coitus may limit opportunities to become a perpetrator or victim of sexual aggression.

Other-focused emotions, including empathy, tend to be more common in collectivist cultures than in individualistic cultures, in which ego-focused emotions, including anger, may be more common. The cognitions of collectivists tend to be directed toward the needs of the in-group, whereas cognitions among individualists tend to be directed toward personal needs (Triandis, 1995). Thus, sexual aggression by Asian Americans against other Asian Americans would be deterred by empathy, which may reduce the likelihood of the development of cognitive distortions about victims (Hall, 1996).

In a multi-ethnic sample of college students, 47 percent of Asian Americans were sexually active versus 72 percent of European Americans, 84 percent of African Americans, and 59 percent of Latinos (Cochran et al., 1991). These percentages are consistent with the percentages of sexually active college students by ethnic group in other samples (Huang & Uba, 1992). In some traditional Asian families, dating for females may be unacceptable until a certain age or until their education is completed (Yoshihama et al., 1991). Thus, some Asian American women may have limited contact with men, particularly in situations in which sexual aggression is likely to occur (e.g., dating, sexual situations). Huang and Uba (1992) speculated that Chinese Americans may delay sexual intercourse because they want to wait until they are certain that there is adequate emotional commitment, which also was found to be the primary reason for maintaining virginity among European Americans (Sprecher & Regan, 1996).

The collectivist aspects of Asian cultures may also contribute to lower rates of sexual activities among Asian Americans. Romantic relationships for Asian Americans may occur within the context of interconnectedness of larger social networks (Dion & Dion, 1993). Thus, relational aspects of romance may be emphasized over sexual aspects. Indeed, Asians tend to be more friendship oriented in their romantic relationships than do people of European ancestry (Dion & Dion, 1993).

Unlike non-Asian American groups, in which males tend to be more sexually experienced than females (Rodgers & Rowe, 1993), there is evidence to suggest that Asian American men have less sexual experience than Asian American women (Huang & Uba, 1992). The absence of opportunities for having sex may deter Asian American men from being sexually active more than it deters Asian American women (Huang & Uba, 1992). Stereotypes of Asian men are generally negative (Huang & Uba, 1992). Many Asian Americans may perceive themselves as unassertive and socially unskilled (Zane, Sue, Hu, & Kwon, 1991). Self-perceptions of shyness have also been found to be associated with virginity among European American males (Sprecher & Regan, 1996). Peer norms may also influence Asian Americans' behavior. The majority of Asian American college students are virgins (Huang & Uba, 1992). This may create less peer pressure toward compulsory heterosexual behavior among Asian Americans (Hall, 1996).

Having non-Asian sexual partners also affects Asian Americans' sexual behavior. Whereas approximately one third of Chinese Americans who dated only Asians and Asian Americans had experienced coitus, nearly two thirds of those who dated European Americans had done so (Huang & Uba, 1992). The greater sexual activity of Asian American females relative to Asian American males may be a function of Asian American females' greater sexual access to non-Asians. Greater contact among Asian American women with non-Asian men who may be more sexually aggressive than Asian American men may place these women at greater risk for becoming sexually victimized.

Alcohol use in dating situations is associated with risk for becoming a perpetrator or victim of sexual aggression. There is consistent evidence of lower rates of alcohol and drug use among Asian American men and women (Gillmore et al., 1991), which may reduce risk for sexual aggression in dating situations.

In summary, Asian Americans may have less involvement as perpetrators and victims of sexual aggression because of cultural influences. A cultural emphasis on impulse control may limit Asian Americans' sexual behavior. Limited sexual behavior decreases opportunities for sexual aggression to occur during development or adulthood. This emphasis on impulse control may make Asian American males unlikely to develop physiological, cognitive, and affective motivations to become sexually aggressive. Asian American peer support for promiscuous sexual behavior and for sexual aggression may be very limited. Alcohol use, which is a risk factor for sexual aggression, is relatively limited among Asian Americans.

Preventive Interventions

Interventions With Women

Most interventions for victims of sexual aggression have focused on the traumatic effects of victimization. For example, the diagnosis and treatment of posttraumatic stress in sexual assault victims has been extensively examined (Foa, Rothbaum, & Steketee, 1993). However, ameliorating the effects of sexual victimization does not necessarily reduce the likelihood of being re-victimized.

One effective method of preventing additional sexual aggression is the incarceration of men who have previously been sexually aggressive and are at the highest risk to become sexually aggressive again. Incarceration of sexually aggressive men is contingent on these men being reported to authorities. Unfortunately, Asian American women may be less likely to report incidents of sexual aggression to authorities than are non-Asians because of a tendency not to identify sexually aggressive acts as such (Mills & Granoff, 1992). Moreover, more than European Americans, Asian Americans tend to view victims as being more responsible for the sexual aggression and generally tend to hold negative attitudes toward victims (Mori et al., 1995). Thus, preventive interventions with Asian American women should emphasize that any violation of consent constitutes sexual aggression and that perpetrators are solely responsible for engaging in sexually aggressive acts.

Non-Asian men tend to be more sexually active and more sexually aggressive than Asian American men (Huang & Uba, 1992; Koss et al., 1987). Asian American women may benefit from knowing that non-Asian men may have differing expectations of sexual behavior in a relationship than they may have. Moreover, an awareness of stereotypes of Asian women as both sexual and submissive may help Asian American women to avoid or confront Asian and non-Asian men who believe these stereotypes.

There is empirical evidence that women can reduce their risk of being sexually victimized by becoming aware of risk factors and by changing their behavior. Hanson and Gidycz (1993) designed a program for college women to (a) increase awareness of sexual assault, (b) dispel common myths about rape, (c) educate participants about social forces that foster a rape-supportive environment, (d) teach practical strategies for preventing rape, (e) change dating behaviors associated with acquaintance rape (alcohol consumption while on a date), and (f) foster effective sexual communication. Only 6 percent of college women who participated in an acquaintance-rape prevention program were sexually victimized over a 9-week period following the program, whereas 14 percent of college women who did not participate in the program were sexually victimized (Hanson & Gidycz, 1993). However, sexual victimization rates among college women who had previously been sexually victimized did not significantly differ between women who did and did not participate in the program, with re-victimization rates ranging from 10 percent to 44 percent.

It is unclear why Hanson and Gidycz's (1993) program did not reduce the sexual victimization rates of women who had been previously sexually victimized. It is possible that these women did not have the resources to make changes in their behaviors and lifestyles that would prevent further victimization. It also is possible that perpetrators may perceive women who have been previously sexually victimized as more vulnerable than nonvictimized women.

Primary prevention with women who have not been sexually victimized may be more effective than tertiary prevention involving sexually victimized women. Moreover, many sexually victimized women, including Asian Americans, do not receive interventions because of their unwillingness to disclose their victimization to authorities or to mental health professionals (Koss, 1993). Thus, prevention programs that broadly target women may reach victims who would not otherwise receive interventions.

Interventions With Men

Perpetrators are responsible for sexually aggressive behavior, and effective prevention methods targeted at perpetrators or potential perpetrators would reduce the necessity of victim intervention programs (Hall, 1996; Hanson & Gidycz, 1993). Asian American men appear to be at lower risk than other groups for perpetrating sexual aggression (Koss et al., 1987; Mills & Granoff, 1992). However, Asian American men who perceive women as an out-group or who perceive women's role as being subservient to men may be at risk to become sexually aggressive. Thus, modifying cognitive distortions about women may be important in prevention programs for Asian American men.

There exists empirical evidence that men's attitudes concerning sexual aggression can be modified by means of primary and secondary prevention. Programs to enhance victim empathy that involve participation have been demonstrated to reduce cognitive distortions about sexual aggression (Gilbert, Heesacker, & Gannon, 1991; Schewe & O'Donohue, 1993). In one study, men who participated in a prevention program reported that they were less likely to commit rape than were men who did not participate in the program (Schewe & O'Donohue, 1993). However, the effectiveness of primary prevention programs in reducing actual sexually aggressive behavior is unknown.

Conclusion

Rates of perpetration of sexual aggression and sexual victimization are lower among Asian Americans than among other groups. These lower rates may be associated with a lower prevalence of risk factors among Asian Americans that are associated with perpetration and victimization. Moreover, Asian cultural restraints on sexual and impulsive behavior may serve as protective factors. However, there have not been empirical investigations of the role of culture in the low rates of Asian American

sexual aggression. Research is necessary to determine the relative contributions of cultural, developmental, motivational, and situational factors in perpetration and victimization among Asian Americans.

References

Abbey, A., Ross, L. T., McDuffie, D., & McAuslan, P. (1996). Alcohol and dating risk factors for sexual assault among college women. *Psychology of Women Quarterly, 20,* 147–169.

American Psychological Association Commission on Violence and Youth. (1993). *Violence and youth: Psychology's response.* Washington, DC: American Psychological Association.

Baumeister, R. F., Smart, L., & Boden, J. M. (1996). Relation of threatened egotism to violence and aggression: The dark side of high self-esteem. *Psychological Review, 103,* 5–33.

Briere, J., & Runtz, M. (1993). Childhood sexual abuse: Long-term sequelae and implications for psychological assessment. *Journal of Interpersonal Violence, 8,* 312–330.

Buss, D. M., & Schmitt, D. P. (1993). Sexual strategies theory: A contextual evolutionary analysis of human mating. *Psychological Review, 100,* 204–232.

Cochran, S. D., Mays, V. M., & Leung, L. (1991). Sexual practices of heterosexual Asian American young adults. Implications for risk of HIV infection. *Archives of Sexual Behavior, 20,* 381–391.

DeKeseredy, W. S., & Kelly, K. (1995). Sexual abuse in Canadian university and college dating relationships: The contribution of male peer support. *Journal of Family Violence, 10,* 41–53.

Dion, K. L., & Dion, K. K. (1993). Gender and ethnocultural comparisons in styles of love. *Psychology of Women Quarterly, 17,* 463–473.

Federal Bureau of Investigation. (1994). *Uniform crime reports for the United States, 1993.* Washington, DC: U.S. Government Printing Office.

Foa, E. B., Rothbaum, B. O., & Steketee, G. S. (1993). Treatment of rape victims. *Journal of Interpersonal Violence, 8,* 256–276.

Gidycz, C. A., Coble, C. N., Latham, L., & Layman, M. J. (1993). Sexual assault experience in adulthood and prior victimization experiences. *Psychology of Women Quarterly, 17,* 151–168.

Gidycz, C. A., Hanson, K., & Layman, M. J. (1995). A prospective analysis of the relationships among sexual assault experiences: An extension of previous findings. *Psychology of Women Quarterly, 19,* 5–29.

Gilbert, B. J., Heesacker, M., & Gannon, L. J. (1991). Changing the sexual aggression-supportive attitudes of men: A psychoeducational intervention. *Journal of Counseling Psychology, 38,* 197–203.

Gillmore, M. R., Hawkins, J. D., Catalano, R. F., Day, L. E., Moore, M., & Abbott, R. (1991). Structure of problem behaviors in preadolescence. *Journal of Consulting and Clinical Psychology, 59,* 499–506.

Gold, S. R., & Clegg, C. L. (1990). Sexual fantasies of college students with coercive experiences and coercive attitudes. *Journal of Interpersonal Violence, 5,* 464–473.

Hall, G. C. N. (1996). *Theory-based assessment, treatment, and prevention of sexual aggression.* New York: Oxford University Press.

Hall, G. C. N., & Barongan, C. (1997). Prevention of sexual aggression: Sociocultural risk and protective factors. *American Psychologist, 52,* 5–14.

Hall, G. C. N., & Hirschman, R. (1991). Toward a theory of sexual aggression: A quadripartite model. *Journal of Consulting and Clinical Psychology, 59,* 662–669.

Hanson, K. A., & Gidycz, C. A. (1993). Evaluation of a sexual assault prevention program. *Journal of Consulting and Clinical Psychology, 61,* 1046–1052.

Hill, H. M., Soriano, F. I., Chen, S. A., & LaFromboise, T. D. (1994). Sociocultural factors in the etiology and prevention of violence among ethnic minority youth. In L. D. Eron, J. H. Gentry, & P. Schlegel (Eds.), *Reason to hope: A psychosocial perspective on violence and youth* (pp. 59–97). Washington, DC: American Psychological Association.

Himelein, M. J. (1995). Risk factors for sexual victimization in dating: A longitudinal study of college women. *Psychology of Women Quarterly, 19,* 31–48.

Ho, C. K. (1990). An analysis of domestic violence in Asian American communities: A multicultural approach to counseling. *Women and Therapy, 9,* 129–150.

Huang, K., & Uba, L. (1992). Premarital sexual behavior among Chinese college students in the United States. *Archives of Sexual Behavior, 21,* 227–240.

Kendall-Tackett, K. A., Williams, L. M., & Finkelhor, D. (1993). Impact of sexual abuse on children: A review and synthesis of recent empirical studies. *Psychological Bulletin, 113,* 164–180.

Koss, M. P. (1993). Rape: Scope, impact, interventions, and public policy responses. *American Psychologist, 48,* 1062–1069.

Koss, M. P., & Dinero, T. E. (1989). Discriminant analysis of risk factors for sexual victimization among a national sample of college women. *Journal of Consulting and Clinical Psychology, 57,* 242–250.

Koss, M. P., Gidycz, C. A., & Wisniewski, N. (1987). The scope of rape: Incidence and prevalence of sexual aggression and victimization in a national sample of higher education students. *Journal of Consulting and Clinical Psychology, 55,* 162–170.

Malamuth, N. M. (1988). A multidimensional approach to sexual aggression: Combining measures of past behavior and present likelihood. In R. A. Prentky & V. L. Quinsey (Eds.), *Human sexual aggression: Current perspectives* (pp. 123–132). New York: New York Academy of Sciences.

Malamuth, N. M., Linz, D., Heavey, C. L., Barnes, G., & Acker, M. (1995). Using the confluence model of sexual aggression to predict men's conflict with women: A 10-year follow-up study. *Journal of Personality and Social Psychology, 69,* 353–369.

Markus, H. R., & Kitayama, S. (1994). The cultural construction of self and emotion: Implications for social behavior. In S. Kitayama & H. R. Markus (Eds.), *Emotion and culture: Empirical studies of mutual influence* (pp. 89–130). Washington, DC: American Psychological Association.

Marshall, W. L., & Barbaree, H. E. (1984). A behavioral view of rape. *International Journal of Law and Psychiatry, 7,* 51–77.

Messman, T. L., & Long, P. J. (1996). Child sexual abuse and its relationship to revictimization in adult women: A review. *Clinical Psychology Review, 16,* 397–420.

Miller, S. L., & Simpson, S. S. (1991). Courtship violence and social control: Does gender matter? *Law and Society Review, 25,* 335–365.

Mills, C. S., & Granoff, B. J. (1992). Date and acquaintance rape among a sample of college students. *Social Work, 37,* 504–509.

Mori, L., Bernat, J. A., Glenn, P. A., Selle, L. L., & Zarate, M. G. (1995). Attitudes toward rape: Gender and ethnic differences across Asian and Caucasian college students. *Sex Roles, 32,* 457–467.

Muehlenhard, C. L., & MacNaughton, J. S. (1988). Women's beliefs about women who "lead men on." *Journal of Social and Clinical Psychology, 7,* 65–79.

Quinsey, V. L., Rice, M. E., & Harris, G. T. (1995). Actuarial prediction of sexual recidivism. *Journal of Interpersonal Violence, 10,* 85–105.

Rodgers, J. L., & Rowe, D. C. (1993). Social contagion and adolescent sexual behavior: A developmental EMOSA model. *Psychological Review, 100,* 479–510.

Russell, D. E. H. (1984). *Sexual exploitation: Rape, child sexual abuse, and workplace harassment.* Beverly Hills, CA: Sage.

Schewe, P., & O'Donohue, W. (1993). Rape prevention: Methodological problems and new directions. *Clinical Psychology Review, 13,* 667–682.

Seto, M. C., & Barbaree, H. E. (1995). The role of alcohol in sexual aggression. *Clinical Psychology Review, 15,* 545–566.

Sorenson, S. B., Siegel, J. M., Golding, J. M., & Stein, J. A. (1991). Repeated sexual victimization. *Violence and Victims, 6,* 299–308.

Sprecher, S., & Regan, P. C. (1996). College virgins: How men and women perceive their sexual status. *Journal of Sex Research, 33,* 3–15.

Sue, D. W., & Sue, D. (1990). *Counseling the culturally different: Theory and practice* (2nd ed.). New York: Wiley.

Sue, S., & Morishima, J. (1982). *The mental health of Asian Americans.* San Francisco: Jossey-Bass.

Triandis, H. C. (1995). *Individualism and collectivism.* Boulder, CO: Westview.

Triandis, H. C., Bontempo, R., Villareal, M. J., Asai, M., & Lucca, N. (1988). Individualism and collectivism: Cross-cultural perspectives on self-ingroup relationships. *Journal of Personality and Social Psychology, 54,* 323–338.

Uba, L. (1994). *Asian Americans: Personality patterns, identity, and mental health.* New York: Guilford Press.

Urquiza, A. J., & Goodlin-Jones, B. L. (1994). Child sexual abuse and adult re-victimization with women of color. *Violence and Victims, 9,* 223–232.

Vicary, J. R., Klingaman, L. R., & Harkness, W. L. (1995). Risk factors associated with date rape and sexual assault of adolescent girls. *Journal of Adolescence, 18,* 289–306.

Wyatt, G. E. (1989). Reexamining factors predicting Afro-American and White American women's age at first coitus. *Archives of Sexual Behavior, 18,* 271–298.

Wyatt, G. E., Guthrie, D., & Notgrass, C. M. (1992). Differential effects of women's child sexual abuse and subsequent sexual revictimization. *Journal of Consulting and Clinical Psychology, 60,* 167–173.

Yoshihama, M., Parekh, A. L., & Boyington, D. (1991). Dating violence in Asian/Pacific communities. In B. Levy (Ed.), *Dating violence: Young women at risk* (pp. 184–195). Seattle: Seal Press.

Zane, N. W. S., Sue, S., Hu, L., & Kwon, J. (1991). Asian-American assertion: A social learning analysis of cultural differences. *Journal of Counseling Psychology, 38,* 63–70.

Chapter 37
Effects of Cybersex Addiction on the Family
Results of a Survey

Jennifer P. Schneider

What are anonymous, convenient, and readily available to potential partners, making them a major conduit for unhappiness in many marriages? Cybersex and Internet affairs (Schnarch and Morehouse 2002). Relatively "new kids on the block," interpersonal relationships in cyberspace were unheard of before the past decade. In fact, few persons other than professionals in research laboratories and universities had even used the Internet. By 2003, there were an estimated 135 million Internet users, with the numbers expected to continue to grow (Nielson/NetRatings 2003). Jennifer Schneider used e-mail to survey persons identified by therapists as dealing with cybersex problems in the family, illustrating the dramatic difference a decade can make, even in research methods.

The most frequently searched topic on the Internet today is a three-letter word, spelled "sex" (Freeman-Longo and Blanchard 1998). And, the statistics are daunting. In a survey by MSNBC, over nine million users were found to visit adult entertainment websites, and of these, 23 percent of the women and 50 percent of the men surfed for visual erotica (Cooper, McLoughlin, and Campbell 2000). The use of cybersex on the Internet occupies, on average, 11 hours per week for the compulsive user (Cooper, Putnam, Planchon, and Boies 1999). But, herein may lie another problem of terminological confusion. Of 7,000 persons surveyed by MSNBC, over 60 percent did not consider cybersex with another person to be marital infidelity (Cooper et al. 2000). It was considered instead to be more like pornography and less like a real relationship.

David Schnarch and Ruth Morehouse (2002), Co-Directors of the Marriage and Family Health Center in Evergreen, Colorado, have helped to clarify the confu-

sion by defining three related concepts from their perspectives as therapists:

- Cybersex involves the use of computerized text, images, or sound files for sexual stimulation;

- Cyber infidelity occurs when a partner in a committed relationship uses a computer to violate agreements of sexual exclusivity; and

- Internet affairs involve the use of interactive computer chat rooms to create exchanges to sexually arouse self or others as well as creating shared sexual excitement, often culminating in simultaneous masturbation (p. 15).

Giving cybersex addiction a psychological spin, Schnarch and Morehouse contend that many people are so afraid of rejection, or so inexperienced at initiating novel sexual experiences, that they prefer to express their sexuality in the obscurity of the Internet. The therapists believe there are predictable, progressive steps in the development of Internet affairs:

- Conducting nonsexually explicit flirting;

- Using sexual innuendos and explicit repartee;

- Scheduling sex-laced chats;

- Discussing sexual preferences and fantasies;

- Engaging in simultaneous masturbation online; and

- Planning face-to-face meetings for physical contact (Schnarch and Morehouse 2002, 15).

Even though it is far too early to predict the extent of cybersex addiction or its effects on the family of the twenty-first century, this reading will at least acquaint you with the concept and the inherent conundrums surrounding the issue. After reading Schneider's work, you will be better able to agree or disagree with the definitions and opinions of Schnarch and Morehouse concerning cybersex. Regardless of varying opinions about terminology, researchers (including sociologists, psychologists, and family therapists), are currently involved in gathering data about destructive sexual behaviors, many of which are related to the Internet. Soon, we should know more about the warning signs of compulsive sexual behavior on the Internet, which would enable earlier intervention. Eventually, we will get to the "how" and the "why" factors. When we understand more about the cause and not just the effect, what then? Then parents, schools, churches, media, and all of the social institutions that influence a child's healthy sexuality will share in the responsibility to ensure its development.

It felt like there was another woman or a "something" there that was competing for his attention. I felt like he was choosing between me and "it," and "it" usually won. I felt that I should have been first in his heart, but "it" was. I guess that I was a co-addict, as I considered sex and love as the same, and when he was choosing the computer, he was rejecting me. When I was home nights, and he would finally come to bed, then say he was too tired, I would try to interest him, and when I was unsuccessful, I would go into the living room and cry for hours.

He said that the computer was only a small part of the sex addiction, that pornography and meeting other people was a greater part, but the computer was an object that I could see, and, I guess, hate. When he was away from home, he could make up excuses for what he was doing, but when he was sitting in front of the computer and conversing for hours, there was no doubt what he was doing.

The kids knew what was going on, to an extent. My son says there is no way that he can trust his dad, but my son also has been visiting porn sites, until we found out and talked to him about it.

I resented the computer for years, until I finally accepted the fact that it was the user, not the machine that was causing the problem.

—41-year-old woman, married 23 years

I knew my husband was masturbating all the time, but I thought it was my fault. When I found the computer disk going back five years, everything made sense. I had been in denial about how much I knew, and how much my life was out of control. I feel very used and violated because of this behavior, and I have lost my trust.

My husband would blame me when I would catch him masturbating at the computer. He would not do any chores when I was out; when I returned, he would throw the blinds and turn off the light really fast. He would keep looking at his pants to see if I could tell he had an erection. He would run out of the bedroom like he was just changing. He would call me and say he was coming right home at 4:00, and not show up until 7:00. He would say he was working really hard and not to give him a hard time.

I knew he would be masturbating if I left the house. I never said no to sex unless he was wasted drunk, I was not feeling well, or I was working. I believed that if I had sex more often, or if I were better at sex, he would not masturbate as much. I surveyed my friends to see if they'd caught their husbands masturbating, to see how often they thought it was normal to masturbate, to see what kind of sex they had with their husbands and how often.

I thought I was not good enough because I did not look like the girls in the pictures. I thought that if I dressed and looked good it would keep him interested. I would give up competing with his masturbating and not want to have sex with him. I would not walk into the room at night because I did not want to walk in on him.

If the kids and I were coming home from somewhere and his car was there, I would run into the house first and be loud so the kids would not walk in on him. I found semen on my office chair and pubic hair on my mouse. I would get dressed fast so I would not have to have sex with him. I stopped making dinner because I would not know when he would be coming home. I would have to mentally prepare myself for sex. I tried to talk with him about masturbation and how often he wanted to have sex. I was in denial about how unhappy I was.

My husband does not believe he has an addiction. He doesn't think it's a big deal because he says he was never with anyone else. He thinks all he needs is a more loving wife.

—38-year-old woman, married 15 years, divorcing

When I know that my husband has masturbated to cyberporn, I don't want him to touch me. I feel like I am leftovers, not first-run as I should be. My self-esteem is damaged beyond belief. To be honest, our sex life is pretty incredible—we are not prudes by any means. I just don't understand. How can it be soooo good for both of us but still not enough for him?

—31-year-old woman, married one year

The growth of the Internet has been phenomenal. Before 1993 the Internet was used by only a few persons in laboratories and universities. [Today, an] increasing number of people are drawn into using Internet access to obtain sexual satisfaction. Most of these people are "recreational users," analogous to recreational drinkers or gamblers, but a significant proportion have preexisting sexual compulsions and addictions that are now finding a new outlet. For others, with no such history, cybersex is the first expression of an addictive sexual disorder, one that lends itself to rapid progression, similar to the effect of crack cocaine on the previously occasional cocaine user.

In contrast to pornographic bookstores and theaters, involvement with prostitutes, exhibitionism and voyeurism on the street, purchase of pornographic magazines, and anonymous sex in hotels and parks, the Internet has several characteristics ment (Cooper, Putnam, Planchon, & Boies, 1999). It is widely accessible, inexpensive, legal, available in the privacy of one's own home, anonymous, and does not put the user at direct risk of contracting a sexually transmitted disease. It is also ideal for hiding the activities from the spouse or significant other (SO), because it does not leave obvious evidence of the sexual encounter. It takes some computer savvy on the part of the spouse to retrace the user's online adventures.

METHODS

To learn more about the effects of cybersex on the SO and family of the user, I employed the same qualitative research method used in previous studies of the effect of sex addiction on couples (Schneider, Corley, & Irons, 1998). The only difference was that the research was done entirely via e-mail, as I assumed that the target population would have access to a computer. A cover letter was sent to approximately 20 therapists who treat sex addicts, and they were asked to forward the letter to any persons they knew who were dealing with cybersex involvement in the family. The letter explained the nature of the research and invited the client to e-mail me to obtain a brief survey.

The survey asked questions both about the adverse effects of cybersex use on the partners and about their efforts at resolution of the problems, either individually or as a couple. When reading the overwhelmingly pained, discouraged, and negative comments of the SOs, it is helpful to know that many of the same writers later describe recovery from their codependency and their pain, whether or not they are still in the relationship. In a number of cases, the cybersex user is taking major positive steps toward recovery from the addiction, and the couple relationship has changed significantly for the better.

This survey of partners of cybersex users did not attempt to formally diagnose sex addiction in the (mostly) men described by the respondents, and by its nature represents only the perspective of the respondents. Any addictive disorder comprises loss of control (i.e., compulsive behavior), continuation despite adverse consequences, and obsession or preoccupation with the activity. It is likely that the vast majority of the cybersex users fulfill these criteria and indeed have an addictive sexual disorder. However, this study was not designed to ascertain this. Therefore, use of the term "cybersex addict" in this article is informal and should not be construed as a definitive medical diagnosis.

RESULTS

Demographics

Responses were obtained from 94 persons whose spouse or partner was heavily involved in cybersex activities. The 94 SOS comprised 91 women and 3 men. One woman and 2 men reported being in a homosexual relationship. The 94 cybersex addicts were 92 men and 2 women. The mean age of the 94 respondents was 38.0 years, with a range of 24–57 [years]. They had been in the relationship for a mean of 12.6 years and a range of 0.5–39 years. In response to the question, "Are you still in the relationship?" 78.7 percent replied yes, 9.6 percent no, and 11.7 percent were separated. That is, 21.5 percent were living apart. Several partners who were still living with the spouse stated that the marriage was essentially over and that they were planning to divorce.

The cybersex involvement had been a problem for the partners for a mean of 2.4 years and a range of 1 month to 8.5 years. Several, however, commented that although they had learned about the behavior very recently, they now recognized that it had been going on for a long time and was probably responsible for problems in the relationship whose nature they had not understood before.

What Partners Told About the Cybersex Addicts

Sexual Activities

When asked about the addict's sexual activities, all responses included viewing and/or downloading pornography along with masturbation. Other behaviors were reading and writing sexually explicit letters and stories, e-mailing to set up personal meetings with someone, placing ads to meet sexual partners, visiting sexually oriented chat rooms, and engaging in interactive online affairs with same- or opposite-sex people, which included real-time viewing of each other's bodies using electronic cameras connected to the computer. Related activities included phone sex with people met online, and online affairs that progressed to real affairs. Several SOs knew that the addict was participating in unacceptable or illegal online activities such as sadomasochism and domination/bondage, bestiality, viewing child pornography and pornographic pictures of teenagers, and having sex with underage persons. One man reportedly signed on as a teenage girl and solicited lesbian sex, and another man posed as a teenage boy in teen chat rooms.

Live or Offline Sexual Activities

One might hypothesize that offline or live sexual encounters would be more problematic for a relationship than virtual encounters. Compared with the 57 people who had reportedly not had offline affairs, the 28 who did have live affairs were on the average older and had been in the relationship longer.

Online Sex Is a Continuation of a Preexisting Addictive Sexual Disorder

In 30.9 percent [of the reports], the cybersex activities were said to be a continuation of other compulsive sexual behaviors. Because some SOs may not have known about other behaviors, or may not have thought to mention them, this figure is likely to be an underestimate. Behaviors included phone sex, voyeurism, seeing prostitutes, and going to massage parlors. Most common was heavy involvement with pornography (magazines, videos, movies, etc.), often since the teen years.

Progression, Including Live Sex With Others

A well-known characteristic of addictions is tolerance, which is the need to do more and more to get the same results. This may involve an increase in the quantity of the drug or behavior, or an escalation in the type of activity. For sex addicts, this may mean more hours on the Internet, a larger number of partners, or more bizarre or riskier activities, or going from vitual to actual sexual encounters.

> Cybersex really accelerated ,the addiction on his part. It went from just magazines and movies to spending hours on end on the computer looking at images to hours on end chatting with anyone who would 'talk.' It took only 3 months to go from simple e-mail to all this, and he said it would have only been a matter of time before he did start to meet women in person had I not found the disk. [30-year-old woman who found a porn disk in the drive]

Their partner's cybersex activities [17.6 percent] had indeed progressed to live encounters with other people. In some cases these were people they met online in chat rooms, via e-mail, etc. In other cases, the computer sexual activity triggered other addictive behaviors which involved other people. For example, a gay man wrote that his partner's bathhouse activities with other people had increased. Women wrote that their husbands had begun new activities such as a sexual massage parlor, visits with prostitutes, the first real affair, or an additional affair.

Denial, Minimization, and Blame

Some SOs wrote that their spouses were now attending 12-step meetings for sex addicts and/or going to counseling. Many others, however, explained that their spouses did not believe they had a problem or, even if they did recognize this, were not motivated to do anything about it. Several SOs had separated, divorced, or were planning to leave because of their spouse's refusal to recognize the problem, go to counseling, or seek other help.

Effect of Addict's Cybersex Involvement on Partners

On the Partner's Emotions

Most SOs described some combination of devastation, hurt, betrayal, loss of self-esteem, mistrust, suspicion, fear, and a lack of intimacy in their relationship. Other responses were extreme anger or rage, feeling sexually inadequate or feeling unattractive and even ugly, doubt one's judgment and even sanity, severe depression, and, in two cases, hospitalization for suicidality.

> This behavior has left me feeling alone, isolated, rejected, and 'less than.' Masturbation hangs a sign on the door that says 'You are not needed, I can take care of myself thank you very much.' I have threatened, manipulated, tried to control, cried, gave him the cold shoulder, yelled, tried to be understanding, and even tried to ignore it. Denial and codependence are my character defects. [55-year-old woman, married 36 years]

Trust was a major casualty of the secrecy of cybersex addiction. Many SOs felt that this was at least as harmful to the relationship as the sexual activities themselves. Partners reported losing all trust in their mate and in anything he/she told them. Many reported that despite the addict's promises, "behavior has continued, but he has learned to be much more secretive about it." A common theme was, "The lies he told me concerning his whereabouts, while he looked me straight in the eye, have hurt worse than his having sex with them."

Three women reported having engaged in extramarital affairs or encounters, either to shore up their own self-esteem or else to get revenge on their spouses.

Effect on the Sexual Relationship

A 34-year-old woman who had learned of her husband's cybersex involvement only weeks earlier, described the effects on the couple's sexual relationship:

I realize now that many of the things he most liked and requested when we made love were recreations of downloaded images. He is unable to be intimate, he objectifies me, he objectifies women and girls on the streets, he fantasizes when we're together. I feel humiliated, used, and betrayed, as well as lied to and misled. It's almost impossible for me to let him touch me without feeling really yucky and/or crying. I tried to continue being sexual with him initially (and in fact, being 'more' sexual, trying to fix it by being sexier, better than the porn girls), and I couldn't do it. We have now been consensually abstinent for 3 weeks.

This description contains various themes that were brought up recurrently by survey respondents: a feeling of being objectified, comparing herself with the cybersex women, initial attempt to increase the quantity and/or variety of sexual activities, and a decreased desire to have sexual relations with the addict. This woman did not experience the most common complaint: Loss of interest by the addict in having sex with the partner.

Two-thirds of respondents (68.1 percent) described sexual problems in the couple relationship that were generally related to the cybersex addict's sexual activities. In some cases these problems had resulted in decreased interest by the cybersex user in relational sex. In others it was the SO who had lost interest, and in some cases both partners had a decreased interest. In only 31.9 percent [of] coupleships were both partners still interested in sex with each other.

When asked about the effect of cybersex on their sexual relationship, fully half (52.1 percent) said that their husbands were not interested, or hardly interested in sex with them. Note that 65.3 percent of those who had decreased sexual interest stated that they now have less sex than they want. The remaining 18.1 percent reported that they too had shut down sexually, so that the lack of sexual activity at the same time of reporting was mutual in 17 couples.

In summary, 34 percent of the SOs complained that they were feeling deprived of relational sex, and another 16 percent of SOs reported that it was only the cybersex user who was unhappy with the lack of relational sex. Twice as many SOs as cybersex users wanted more sex with their relational partner than they were getting.

The SOs who were not interested in sex with the cybersex addict attributed their loss of interest primarily to their negative reaction to the Internet user's sexual activities with cybersex, phone sex, live encounters, etc. In total, half of the cybersex addicts and one third of the partners were no longer interested in marital sexual relations. This was re-

portedly not a problem for the addicts, who had substituted cybersex for sex with SO, but was definitely a problem for the partners, who felt angry, hurt, rejected, and often sexually unfulfilled.

Respondents who reported that the cybersex addict had been sexually compulsive (paper pornography, phone sex, etc.) even before the Internet came on the scene often stated that the couple's sexual relationship had been infrequent in those days as well. Some added that the problems in the sexual relationship had intensified since the cybersex activities began.

Cybersex Addict Alone Has Lost Interest in Couple Sex

[Although] 34 percent reported that they still wanted a sexual relationship, the cybersex addict had withdrawn his sexual (and general) attention from the partner and family and devoted his (or her) time and energy instead to computer sex. Recurrent themes here follow:

- The partner felt hurt, angry, sexually rejected, inadequate, and unable to compete with cyber images and sexy online women (or men) who were willing to do anything.
- The addict made excuses to avoid sex with the partner (not in the mood, too tired, has already climaxed and doesn't want sex, the children might hear).
- During relational sex, the addict appeared distant, emotionally detached, and interested only in his/her own pleasure.
- The partner ended up doing most or all of the initiating, either to get her/ his own needs met, or else in an attempt to get the addict to decrease the online activities.
- The addict blamed the partner for their sexual problems.
- The addict wanted the partner to participate in sexual activities which she/he found objectionable.

Since my husband was living in a fantasy world of Internet porn, I was the only one who initiated sex. I thought if I didn't we would never have sex and this would cause him to go elsewhere. He would respond but always seemed to be in another world during sex. When confronted with why he was not interested in sex, he said that "it was not as important to him as it is to other men." [28-year-old woman, married 8 years]

Partner Alone Has Lost Interest in Couple Sex

In 15 cases, the cybersex addict maintained his/ her desire for sex with the SO, but the partner was less interested. In some cases the partner refused to have sex; in others, the partner didn't want to but continued out of fear of driving the addict further into online activities. Major themes reported follow:

- The partner's initial response in some cases was to increase the sexual activities in order to "win back" the addict. This early response was only temporary.
- The partner felt repelled and disgusted by the addict's online or real sexual activities and no longer wanted to have relationship sex. The partner could no longer tolerate the addict's detachment and lack of emotional connection during sex.
- The partner's anger over the addict's denial of the problem interfered with her/his sexual interest.
- In reply to pressure or requests by the addict to dress in certain ways or perform new sexual acts, the partner felt angry, repelled, used, objectified, or like a prostitute.
- Partner fears sex with the addict because the partner fears catching a disease from the addict, or has already caught one.

At first we had sex more than ever as I desperately tried to prove myself, then sex with her made me sick. I get strong pictures of what she did and lusted after, and I get repelled and feel bad. I used to see sex as a very intimate loving thing. We always had a lot of sex and I thought we were intimate. Now that I found out my wife was not on the same page, I can't be intimate or vulnerable-sex is now more recreational or just out of need. [44-year-old man, married 26 years]

Both Partners Have Lost Interest in Couple Sex

In 18.1 percent, loss of interest by both partners put a virtual end to sexual relations between them. Typical dynamics were a man who was more interested in sex with the computer than with the wife, and a woman who felt rejected, angry, and unable to compete—i.e., a combination of the individual themes.

Comparison With Online Sexual Partners

The knowledge that the addict's head is full of cybersex images inevitably produces in the SO a comparison between the spouse and the fantasy woman in terms of appearance, desirability, and repertory of sexual behaviors. Both addicts and partners were reported to make such comparisons. The SO feels she/he is competing with the computer images and people. ("If only I were perfect like his porn, then he would want the real thing and love me.") The result is often confusion—on the one

hand, desire to emulate and better the cyberwoman (or man), on the other [hand] revulsion at the lack of intimacy and mechanical nature of the sex. Survey respondents reported vacillating between these two polarities.

He's never been physically unfaithful, but he has had experiences with others. I feel cheated. I never know who or what he is thinking of when we are intimate. How can I compete with hundreds of anonymous others who are now in our bed, in his head? By chatting sex, he and others made up fantasies and pretended. How can reality ever satisfy him now? When he says something sexual to me in bed, I wonder if he has said it to others, or if it is even his original thought. Now our bed is crowded with countless faceless strangers, where once we were intimate. With all this deception, how do I know he has quit, or isn't moving into other behaviors? [34-year old woman, married 14 years to a minister]

Partner Increases Sexual Activities to Combat the Problem

Some partners attempted a sexual solution to the cybersex addiction problem, typically either increasing the frequency of sexual activities with the addict, or else joining with the addict in his preferred activities:

My husband is a minister who was stationed overseas for a year. We chatted daily, but never sexually. Then I learned about his cybersex activities, and felt cheated. Why wouldn't he ask me to have cybersex? I wasn't comfortable with this, but I thought I could 'rescue' him. So we began a cybeysex relationship. But much to my horror, he never quit with all the anonymous partners. So he lumped me together with all the online whores. When he returned, he continued his cybeysex even though we were reunited. [34year-old woman, still in a long-term marriage]

What's the Big Deal About Online Sex?

This is the most common question that is asked by persons who focus on the absence of skin-to-skin contact during cybersex activities, and cannot understand why marriages actually break up over this issue. This question elicited the most emotional and eloquent responses of the survey.

CONCERN ABOUT ESCALATION. Tolerance—the need to do more to get the same results—is a common feature of addictive disorders. Online viewing, which begins as harmless recreation, can become an all-consuming activity and can also lead to real sexual encounters, either with sexual partners met online or escalation of the sex addiction in general. Even when the sex involves only the computer, there is often escalation of conflict in the relationship.

> I might say to those who say, 'it's only cyber[sex]' that it's so easy to go on to more from there! I never thought the cyber addiction would be so hard to control, and I nearly went on to meet individual men myself. If I had, I think I would be dead right now because I was becoming so lackadaisical in personal protection issues. [51-year-old woman who is herself recovering from sex addiction and is married to a sex addict]

IT'S STILL CHEATING/A MENTAL AFFAIR/ADULTERY. Thirty respondents explained why they consider online sex activities the same as adultery. The most important reasons are:

1. Having interactive sex with another person is adultery, whether or not they have skin-to-skin contact.

2. Cybersex results in lying, hiding one's activities, and covering up, and the lies are often the most painful part of the affair.

3. The spouse feels betrayed, devalued, deceived, "less than," abandoned—same as with a real affair.

4. Cybersex takes away from the sexual relationship of the couple.

5. A real-life person cannot compete with fantasy. The cybersex addict loses interest in his spouse because he has "ideal" relationships where there is no hassle.

6. Cybersex takes the addict away from his partner—in terms of time and emotions. It results in emotional detachment from the marriage.

EFFECT ON SELF-ESTEEM. The reason some respondents gave for why cybersex is so destructive is the adverse effect on their self-esteem.

> True, you don't have the risk of the diseases, but it is still an emotional thing. It's hard to think that the sex addict wants to do it without the actual touch-how can it be better for them? Especially since they have to do all the work themselves! It really hurts your self-esteem, and most of us don't have a very good self-esteem as it is. [37-year-old woman, married 17 years]

I CAN'T COMPETE WITH FANTASY/CAN'T MEASURE UP. Cybersex taps into partners' deepest insecurities about their ability to measure up. The need to compete with interactive sex online pressures them into unwanted sexual activities. "Sex with the fantasy leaves practically nothing left to be desired when compared with the all-too human and flawed spouse," explained one woman.

On the Internet it is possible to find groups of people who are interested in all kinds of unusual or even deviant sexual practices. Interacting with these people desensitizes the user to these activities and "normalizes" them. Some cybersex users eventually come to blame their partners for being unwilling to engage in these behaviors.

IT HAS ADVERSELY AFFECTED OUR RELATIONSHIP. Some SOs focused not on the adultery aspect of cybersex, but rather on the overall effect on the couple relationship:

> Not everyone who looks at pornography is an addict, some are merely curious. But when the addict never admits to viewing pornography, when he lies about his use of pornography to the marriage counselor he's agreed to go to because he wants to save his marriage, that's when it becomes a problem. I tell them I knew something was wrong in our intimate relationship and I always wondered who he was making love to, because it never was me. [39-year-old woman, divorced after an 8-year marriage]

Partners Who Have Experienced Both

Several partners who had dealt with both cyber-affairs and live affairs said they hurt the same.

> They should try it for themselves one time, and see how it feels to be less important to their partner than a picture on a computer screen! They should see what it feels like to lie in bed and know their partner is on the computer and what he is doing with it. It's not going to do much for the self-esteem. My husband has actually cheated on me and it FEELS NO DIFFERENT. The online 'safe' cheating has just as dirty, filthy a feel to it as does the 'real-life' cheating. [38-year-old woman, married 18 years]

Effects on the Children

The most commonly reported adverse consequence was that one or both parents were unavailable to spend time or pay attention to the children. Respondents complained of the addict's unavailability to the children, and failure to fulfill family responsibilities: "One afternoon he was so caught up in the computer that he failed to meet my daughter coming off the school bus. I told my husband that the only way the kids recognize him is by the back of his head." The other parent may also be unavailable because of preoccupation with the addict. SOs who got divorced or were separated mentioned that their children had lost their two-parent home.

Even if children did not see the online sexual images, they observed arguments and stress in the home; this was the second most commonly mentioned adverse effect. Two women wrote of the children witnessing episodes of domestic violence. Thirty percent of those with children believed that their young children, and adult children who were out of the home, were not significantly affected by the family problems related to online sex addiction.

Other adverse effects were related to viewing pornography (and occasionally masturbation) and to exposure to the cybersex addict's objectification of women. Some SOs reported that their children had found pornography that had been left on the computer, had walked in when the cyberaddict was chatting in a chat room, had overheard the addict having phone sex, or had observed the addict having interactive sex online. As a result, one woman wrote, "One daughter became promiscuous, the other wants me to leave him. My son now thinks that hurting women is normal." Other consequences were that the children became "horrified, ashamed, and embarrassed," got angry at the father and/or lost respect for him. Teenage children began viewing online pornography themselves. Others began selling it: "My son found old porn movies I was told had been disposed of, and he and a friend copied them and were selling them at school. My 14-year-old baby had a porn ring going!"

Several mothers were worried because their husbands surfed the Internet while supposedly watching younger children, who got to view the pornography and sometimes the masturbation.

> My daughter caught him masturbating once and told me about it. I felt sick. I am scared that someday, when she gets to the age of the women that he likes to look at, that he will hurt her. I am confused about how to talk to my children about love, sex, and masturbation. [27-year-old woman, married 3 years and still in the relationship]

When Both Partners Are Cybersex Users

There are many legitimate dating services on the Internet which have facilitated single people meeting each other. The risks and advantages of meeting in this way have been discussed before (Cooper & Sportolari, 1997). However, when two people meet online specifically for sex, then later attempt to convert the relationship to a more traditional one, there are predictable risks. A 46-year-old woman met a man online in a sexually oriented chat room. They participated in cybersex for many months, then finally met in person.

> I met him online five years ago. I thought he was "faithful" to our online relationship. I found out a few months ago that he has been nonmonogamous from almost the very first time we met in person. He was into porn extensively, and into meeting 'swingers.' I assumed he was honest

with me, but I found out otherwise. We had an amazing, exciting, and satisfying sexual relationship until he disclosed to me a few months ago. Then it turned sour. . . . I met him on online, and now I know . . . it is no different than meeting someone in 3D. People are people, and sickness and addictions are everywhere.

She reports that currently she is experiencing major depression, related to the sense of betrayal and the ending of the relationship.

Both men and women, many of them sexually compulsive, engage in online sexual activities. Not surprisingly, a sexually addicted couple can get drawn into cybersex activities. One of the survey respondents wrote that she and her husband had both been actively involved in cybersex activities with other people. Her marriage is in trouble because she is now sexually sober but her spouse is still acting out on the computer. If one member of such a couple bottoms out and seeks recovery before the other, the relationship will become destabilized.

Discussion

In planning this survey, I was very concerned with issues of anonymity and privacy. It was surprising to me, therefore, that only 3 of the 94 respondents returned the survey by regular mail, thereby remaining completely anonymous. In some cases their willingness to e-mail me was situational—several commented in their survey that they were familiar with my writings. I would hypothesize that the comfort of other respondents with e-mail reflected the ease of use of the computer and sense of anonymity of the internet culture.

One-third of respondents volunteered the information that their partner's online sexual activities had been preceded by years of other compulsive sexual behaviors. As stated earlier, the actual numbers are likely to be significantly higher. Cooper, Delmonico, and Burg (2000) reported that 4.6 percent of a large sample of cybersex participants were sexually compulsive, as determined by their scores on a sexual compulsivity scale. The present sample, in contrast to Cooper's cohort, was selected specifically because the cybersex use had caused significant problems for the partner. It is likely that the majority of the remaining cybersex users in the present study belonged to the "at-risk" group, those with prior vulnerability to compulsive Internet involvement.

Divorce and separation were two other consequences of cybersex addiction which were common in this survey. We may speculate that more couples get divorced over cybersex addiction than over excessive time spent on the Internet in general. Also, it is probable that workers who use company time to access the Internet are more likely to get fired if the content of their Internet activity was sexual than if it was not.

The Stages of Prerecovery of the Cybersex Coaddict

In this study, SOs were aware of the cybersex addict's online activities for time periods ranging from eight years to just a month or two. It is possible to infer from the survey responses the time course of responses by the partner to the cyberaddict's ongoing involvement with online sex.

Stage 1: Ignorance/Denial

The partner recognizes there is a problem in the relationship but is unaware of the contribution of cybersex to the problem. ("I knew something was wrong the first two years of our marriage, but I could not identify it.") The SO believes the addict's denials, explanations, and promises. She tends to ignore and explain away her own concerns, and may blame herself for the sexual problems. When cybersex addiction is present, a frequent problem is lack of interest by the addict in marital sex; in response the SO may try to enhance her own attractiveness to the addict. Self-esteem is likely to suffer, but the partner is unlikely to seek help at this point.

Late in this stage, suspicions may increase and "detective behaviors" begin. However, snooping or detective behaviors are accentuated at a later stage.

Stage 2: Shock/Discovery of the Cybersex Activities

At some point the partner learns of the cybersex addict's activities. In some cases this occurs accidentally, either because the partner comes upon the addict in the midst of the activities, or because the SO turns on the computer and discovers a cache of pornographic pictures. In other cases, the discovery is the result of deliberate investigations by the SO. No matter how the discovery occurs, the result is that the partner's ignorance and denial are over.

Discovery often leads to strong emotions of shock, betrayal, anger, pain, hopelessness, confusion, and shame. Because the pull of the computer is so strong and its availability in the home and at work is so great, there is a great tendency for the addict to return to cybersex activities even after discovery by the spouse, no matter how sincere the initial intention to quit. The result is that many respondents described a cycle of discoveries, promises made and broken, and additional discoveries and promises.

Feelings of shame, self-blame, and embarrassment often accompany the early days of dealing with a partner's cybersex addiction. These feelings may prevent the SO from talking with others and appealing for help, and the resultant isolation worsens the situation. Covering up for the addict is part of this stage.

> We have only told our therapists about this problem. It's so hard to go to family events and everyone thinks we're doing great. I don't want to tell them because I don't want this to be all that they think of when they think of my husband. And we don't feel like we can trust any of our friends with our 'secret.' So we're dealing with this alone and that hurts. [25-year-old woman, married 2 years, just recently discovered the cybersex addiction]

Stage 3: Problem-Solving Attempts

The partner is now energized to take action to resolve the problem, which is perceived as the cybersex behaviors. At this stage the classic sexual coaddictive behaviors peak-snooping, bargaining, controlling access to the computer, giving ultimatums, asking for full disclosure after every episode, obtaining information for the addict on sex addiction and addiction recovery, and (early in this stage) increasing the frequency and repertory of sexual activities with the addict in hopes of decreasing his desire for cybersex.

> The breaking point became his willingness to lie to me to cover his activities and his shame. We both knew this would not work and I especially would spiral downhill when I would find out he had broken his promises. At some point I had asked that if he acted out that he tell me right away so that we could work with it. My preference of course was that he come to me when he felt like acting out, but that didn't happen. I could deal with the addiction if it were out in the open, because we would both begin to gain insights into the why's of this complicated issue. [38-year-old woman, married 8 year]

This type of agreement rarely works for long. It provides a measure of comfort for the wife to know what is going on and gives her the illusion of control. But the result establishes a parent-child dynamic between the couple, engenders resentment in the addict, and typically ends up in continued lying.

A sexual solution to the sexual problem seems to make sense in this stage. SOs may agree to sexual practices with which they are not comfortable, have sex even when tired, and think about improving their appearance by undergoing breast enhancement surgery or liposuction. For the cybersex user, none of these methods are likely to diminish the lure of the Internet.

The partner believes that additional information will enhance her or his ability to manage the situation. This leads to "snooping" or "detective" behaviors. Co-addicts who are computer savvy learn how to trace the addict's activities, and in some cases may even try to entice him by logging on into the same chat rooms themselves.

When the cybersex activities come to light, the couple tries to come to some agreement to try to limit the addict's use of the computer. This may consist simply of promises not to use it, or to restrict usage to legitimate needs. Often, the SO, with the addict's agreement or at least knowledge, assumes control of the access. In addition, the SO or the couple may purchase filtering software (e.g., Net Nanny) which prevents access to sexually-oriented sites. None of these "negative" methods tend to be successful for long if they are not accompanied by "positive" recovery-oriented activities.

The above three stages—ignorance/denial, shock/discovery of the cybersex, and problem-solving attempts—are specific applications of the phases of prerecovery of sexual co-addicts described by Milrad (1999). She found that the prerecovery stage, lasting approximately 4–8 years, was divided into two phases—a denial phase, when partners recognize there is a problem but remain in denial about its cause, and a more active phase, when they come out of denial about the addict's problem and seek active solutions, but remain in denial as to their own issues.

The findings of this survey support Milrad's phases. As she observed in her study, the end of the prerecovery phase and the beginning of recovery is an awareness by sexual co-addicts that they are in crisis and need help. In the present study, SOs entered the crisis stage when they realized that their problem-solving efforts were unsuccessful and when the costs of remaining in the status quo became intolerable—depressive symptoms, isolation, loss of libido, a "dead" marriage, their own dysfunctional behaviors in some cases (affairs, excessive drinking, violence), and awareness of the effects on the children of the family dysfunction. This is the stage when the SO seeks help for herself/himself rather than in order to fix the addict, and learns that she/he did not cause the problem and cannot solve it. Once the SO is in therapy and getting help, the chances increase that the marriage or relationship will end unless the cybersex addict too becomes committed to recovery.

Limitations of This Study

The chief limitation of this study is that it includes only a self-selected population of people who have experienced significant adverse consequences as a result of their partner's cybersex addiction. It can provide no information about (a) the nature of the consequences, if any, to families of recreational or occasional cybersex users or (b) the prevalence among all cybersex users of significant consequences to the family. A random sample of partners of all cybersex users would be needed to provide such information.

Introduction References

Cooper, A., Putnam, D. A., Planchon, L. A., and Boies, S. C. (1999). "Online Sexual Compulsivity: Getting Tangled in the Net." *Sexual Addiction & Compulsivity*, 6, 79–104.

Cooper, A., McLoughlin, I. P., and Campbell, K. M. (2000). "Sexuality in Cyberspace: Updates for the 21st Century." *CyberPsychology & Behavior*, 3, 521–536.

Freeman-Longo, I. B., and Blanchard, G. (1998). *Sexual Abuse in America: Epidemic of the 21st Century*. Brandon, VT: Safer Society Press.

Nielson/NetRatings. (2003, October 21). "Kids Account for One Out of Five Internet Surfers in the United States." New York: NetRatings.

Schnarch, D., and Morehouse, R. (2002, September-October). "Online Sex: Dyadic Crises, and Pitfalls for MFTs." *Family Therapy Magazine*, pp. 14–19.

References

Cooper, A., Delmonico, D. L., & Burg, R. (2000). Cybersex users, abusers, and compulsives: New findings and implications. *Sexual Addiction & Compulsivity*, 7, 5–29.

Cooper, A., Putnam, D. A., Planchon, L. A., & Boies, S. C. (1999). Online sexual compulsivity: Getting tangled in the Net. *Sexual Addiction & Compulsivity*, 6, 79–104.

Milrad, R., (1999). Coaddictive recovery: Early recovery issues for spouses of sex addicts. *Sexual Addiction & Compulsivity*, 6, 125–136.

Schneider, J. P., Corley, M. D., & Irons, R. R., (1998). Surviving disclosure of infidelity: Results of an international survey of 164 recovering sex addicts and partners. *Sexual Addiction & Compulsivity*, 5, 189–218.

Chapter 38

"What's a Nice Girl Like You Doing in a Place Like This?"

Pathways to a Career in Stripping

Nova D. Sweet
Richard Tewksbury

Some of your more unenlightened friends may think that they invented sex. Not so. They might be amazed to learn that their great-grandparents and grandparents who lived in the 1930s and the 1950s were living in the two "golden ages" of stripping in the United States (Boles 2001). During the depression years of the 1930s, burlesque shows were revived as thousands of young women moved to large cities, desperately looking for work. During this time, stripping was "invented" by two dancers, named Hinda Wassau and Carrie Fennel (Corio 1968). Supposedly, history was made when Wassau danced the "shimmy" as her dress gradually slid to the floor. Fennel, afraid of having her act cancelled, told the audience she would remove one item of clothing a week as long as her act was held over. She remained on stage for 52 weeks (Corio 1968).

Nudity and semi-nudity have long been features of the theater. In 1866, the Black Crook was the first entertainment on the American stage where female nudity made its appearance (Zeidman 1967). Before World War I, in England, female and male nakedness was allowed on the stage if the nudes did not move. Producers staged historical events or famous works of art in nude tableaus of characters, frozen in position (Boles 2001). Eventually, a more lively form of entertainment evolved called burlesque. In the 1930s and 1940s, when stripping became the cornerstone of burlesque, names like Gypsy Rose Lee and Lily St. Cyr lit the marquees. Today, the traditional strip clubs are being replaced by "nude" bars, often called "Gentlemen's Clubs" (Boles 2001).

Despite the growing popularity of exotic dancing by women today, American culture continues to look down on this behavior as a deviant, somewhat disrespectable occupation. Dancers are often categorized as deviants: drug addicts, prostitutes, exhibitionists, and sex addicts. They are often referred to as "sluts," "whores," "sleazes," and "druggies." As a result of such labeling, those who are associated with, or who participate in, stripping as part of the sex industry are often alienated from reputable society (Sweet and Tewksbury 2000).

The strength of the following Sweet and Tewksbury study is that it does add an unusual experiential twist in the form of tidbits from the life stories of twenty (20) experienced strippers, revealed in their own words. All of the interviews were conducted by Nova Sweet, one of the researchers. The fact that the information was collected in the course of her work, dancing in strip clubs across America, is an obviously unique feature. The title alone is intriguing. And, the length of the chapter makes it a quick read; but, the poignant vignettes portrayed in the words of these young women are guaranteed to linger long after the pages of the book are closed.

Among the most "deviant" occupational and career options available in contemporary society are jobs in the illicit drug economy, politics, and the sex industry. However, within each of these occupational fields the specific jobs available vary widely in both their degree of acceptability and their income potential. Within the sex industry, there are a number of occupational choices one may choose: prostitution, performing in pornographic movies, erotic writing, and stripping. This research is concerned with the stripping aspect of the sex industry and the characteristics that are associated with women who choose to enter the industry.

Despite being a part of the sex industry, stripping is widely considered a rather impersonal occupation. Those involved do not know each other, yet they understand one another's needs and implicitly accept the nature and structure of involved transactions. Thus, the "deviant act" becomes much easier to perform for the dancer, becomes more acceptable for patrons, and becomes something that can be engaged in and then forgotten by both customer and dancer as soon as it is over. Notwithstanding the acceptance of strippers by the customer-participants, strippers are widely viewed as "bad" by nonparticipants (and sometimes even by participants) because they challenge all social decorum by removing their clothes (McCaghy and Skipper

1969; Thompson and Harred 1992; Bell, Sloan, and Strickling 1998).

Although investigation of stripping is a relatively fresh area of research, there have been a number of researchers who have developed insightful and informative findings about female strippers and the industry. Researchers have outlined motivational factors (McCaghy and Skipper 1969; Boles and Garbin 1974; Barron 1989; Reid, Epstein and Benson 1995), means by which interactions with customers are experienced and managed (Forsyth and Deshotels 1997; Sijuwade 1995), as well as occupational and organizational norms of strippers (Boles and Garbin 1974; Forsyth and Deshotels 1997; Bell et al. 1998). On the basis of these studies there is an understanding of who strippers are and how and why they perform their jobs. However, gaps remain in our understanding; the present research sought to add to our base of understanding regarding the backgrounds and developmental characteristics of women who work in the stripping industry.

Several common background factors have been identified among strippers. Factors associated with women's eventual entrance into stripping include early physical maturity and early sexual experiences, early independence and departure from home, absence of the father from the home prior to adolescence, average educational levels, and a relationship between exhibitionistic behavior and previous job experience (Skipper and McCaghy 1970; Ronai and Ellis 1989; Peretti and O'Connor 1989; Thompson and Harred 1992).

The majority of strippers reach puberty at an early age, and this is accompanied by a significant degree of emotional and social stress. Early physical maturity also tends to bring about heightened sexual attractiveness. Consequently, when these women later become adults they are accustomed to using these attributes to get special and/or extra attention. As long as strippers can remember, their bodies have been objects for talk, staring, and sexual passes. Even though these experiences are often humiliating, these women come to the conclusion—usually at some point in their teens—that because their bodies attract men, their bodies can bring them money (Skipper and McCaghy 1970; Ronai and Ellis 1989; Thompson and Harred 1992).

In addition, strippers' backgrounds often show a relationship with their ordinal position in the family. Patterns appear consistent: Firstborn women often seek the company of others outside the family to meet their need for affection; nevertheless, there is no evidence of causal linkage between stripping and ordinal position. However, strippers who were firstborn tend to have experienced broken family ties by age 18 and to have been raised in broken and unstable homes where they received little attention and affection (Peretti and O'Connor 1989; Thompson and Harred 1992). The absence of a male figure appears related to the willingness of women to participate in stripping; such work allows for "special" male attention. If a stripper did have a father present in her childhood home, he typically had a disintegrating influence on family relationships (Skipper and McCaghy 1970). Although firstborn women tend to demonstrate independent qualities and to have experienced broken family ties, and strippers have customarily encountered similar circumstances, this is not to imply that firstborn girls without a father in the home are destined to become strippers.

Women who strip are often thought of as being uneducated and "stupid" (Ronai and Ellis 1989; Reid et al. 1995). Therefore, the educational background of strippers has been, and still is, a relevant arena of inquiry. Research conducted in the 1960s and 1970s suggested that strippers had, on average, an educational level of only Grade 7 or 8. More recent research (Reid et al. 1995), however, has indicated that strippers in the 1990s have significantly more education; strippers are typically high school graduates, often with some college experience.

The literature has also suggested congruence between the content of previous jobs and stripping. Strippers have frequently held previous jobs in which the display of their physical attributes was an integral part of job success. These jobs included work as singers, models, actresses, and waitress-barmaids (Ronai and Ellis 1989; Thompson and Harred 1992). Thus, a pattern of exhibitionism is apparent in the strippers' career choices. Although this does not suggest that stripping is the next logical step in a career trajectory, it does suggest that when an opportunity to strip arises, such past job experiences may facilitate women's perceiving stripping as an acceptable occupational alternative.

Although prior research has identified numerous common factors in the backgrounds of strippers—including prior jobs that include the display of one's body and early physical maturity—it remains unknown whether one factor is more influential than another or how these factors are related. Discussions in numerous studies have attributed the lack of attention and/or absence of a father figure in these women's lives as the foundation for detrimental behaviors and attitudes, including low self-worth, low self-concept, and early sexual experiences. Regardless of what is at the core, it is rather clear that childhood and adolescent experiences, and characteristics of young adulthood, facilitate or attract women to the deviant career of stripping. Although informative, the existing literature is, nonetheless, incomplete. The present study sought to add to this body of knowledge by further assessing both these and additional childhood and young adult experiences of female strippers.

METHOD

Sample

The present research is based on in-depth, qualitative interviews conducted with a sample of women currently employed as strippers. The 20 women in this sample were, for the most part, experienced strippers. Only 15 percent of the interviewees had been dancing for less than 1 year, 70 percent had between 1 to 4 years of experience, and 15 percent had more than 4 years experience. These women lived and worked in a variety of cities, including Chicago, Boston, Atlanta, Las Vegas, New York, Tampa, Orlando, St. Louis, Phoenix, San Francisco, Charlotte, Houston, and Louisville. A few women worked in several cities, traveling on a weekly basis; however, most of the sample worked in only one city. The sample ranged in age from 18 to 34 years old. The majority of the sample was Caucasian (60 percent), and the other 40 percent of the sample was identified as African American, Asian, Hispanic, or mixed race.

Of the 20 women interviewed, 50 percent were mothers; 60 percent of these women became mothers during their teenage years. At the time of this study, most of the sample were in some kind of relationship; 60 percent reported having a steady boyfriend, 20 percent reported being single or never married, 10 percent had a steady girlfriend, 5 percent were married, and the other 5 percent were divorced.

Research Process

All interviews were conducted by Nova Sweet, who solicited interviews through the course of her work dancing in strip clubs throughout the continental United States. No requests for interviews were denied, although several women who initially volunteered were unable to schedule time. Interviews were conducted in hotel rooms, homes, and automobiles and by telephone; scheduling constraints and privacy considerations guided the choice of locale. Interviews ranged from 1 to 2 hours in length. A semistructured format was used, all interviews were audiotaped, and analysis was based on verbatim transcripts.

All interviewees were guaranteed confidentiality; all interview tapes were identified by first name only and were destroyed at the conclusion of the project. All names used are pseudonyms.

FINDINGS

Overall, this study supported the general patterns, norms, characteristics, and motivations regarding female strippers currently available in the literature. More important, in combination with these factors, we found four additional common issues in the backgrounds and experiences of strippers. We offer four additional issues common to the background of female strippers: athletic background, entertainment background, childhood abuse, and the "ugly duckling syndrome."

Previously Established Factors

Prior researchers have established that women who work as strippers generally both begin sexual activity and physically mature at an early age. Among the women in this sample, two thirds reported their first sexual experience at age 15 or younger, one in three at age 13 or younger. Elaine remembered when she lost her virginity and what a relief it was to her: "I was like 11, in the cornfield with Brian. What's so funny is that he actually said afterwards, 'Well at least I know you're not gay.' And I was thinking, 'yeah, oh God, thank God.'" Most strippers who became sexually active this early did not recall their early sexual experiences as positive, however. In fact, two of the women reported their early-in-life, first sexual experiences as rape. Monica recalled that

> My first sexual experience was when I was 15. I was volunteering at a hospital, and my boyfriend at the time brought me down to the basement, which was where his office was located; he forced me into a dark cluttered storage room, and that's where I involuntarily lost my virginity.

On the issue of early physical maturity, our data were somewhat less conclusive. Nearly one-half of the women reported having physically matured faster than other girls. It appears safe to conclude that women who strip share patterns of engaging in sexual experiences at an early age; however, they do not necessarily identify as having physically matured at an early age.

Other researchers (Ronai and Ellis 1989; Thompson and Harred 1992) have suggested that because many strippers physically mature at an early age they begin to unconsciously use their bodies and looks to get what they want from people. This behavior typically develops into early sexual experiences for these women. However, the existence of such a relationship was not strongly supported by this sample. Although the majority of these women had early sexual experiences, these did not appear to be directly connected to their physical maturity. The fact is, many of the women in our study experienced sex at an early age, before having fully matured physically.

Previous research has also suggested important commonalties among strippers regarding their ordinal family position, early independence from home, and the absence of a father figure from the home prior to adolescence. On these issues, we found strong support for a relationship with work as a stripper during young adulthood. The majority of women in this research were either firstborn (50 percent) or only children (10 percent). Of the firstborns, nearly all reported early independence from or in home, between 14 to 16 years of age. These women were either teenage mothers; had to join the workforce to help a single parent with bills; suffered from sexual, mental, or physical abuse and left home; or were left at home unsupervised to do as they pleased. Among those women who reported being only children, early independence from home was not reported but rather was primarily focused inside the home. As Brenda, an only child, reflected on her childhood, she recalled that

> My mom was putting herself through med school when I was growing up; I was an only child at that time, and she wasn't home a lot. I took care of myself; I was old enough to stay home by myself for a few hours, so she wasn't there a lot. Med school took up a lot of her time. I strongly feel that somewhere in my childhood I invented this story that I wasn't an okay person, and ever since then I've been doing things to try to prove to myself that I was okay, and dancing was one of those ways.

Sara's situation as a firstborn child was very different, but nonetheless focused on early independence. Sara left home at a young age and explained her reasoning as: "I ran away from home when I was 14 because I was bored with life. When I turned 15, I met a guy and got pregnant. I told my parents; they asked me if I was going to get married. I was like 'I'll just stay with him.' So I did, and I had my baby." Early independence, not ordinal family position, appears to be the more influential factor related with a subsequent career in stripping. Where this becomes most clear is in the fact that for all women (only children, firstborns, and "others"), early independence from home—usually between 12 to 15 years of age—was very common. Women with siblings reported the most traumatic reasons for independence. All of these women indicated they received absolutely no parental guidance, stability, or

guidelines during adolescence. Common issues in their stories included deadbeat parents; alcoholic and drug-abusing parents; physical, mental, and sexual abuse by parents, relatives, or friends of parents; being frequently moved from one home environment to another; teenage pregnancy; and being homeless. Early independence for these women, then, can be seen as essentially inevitable. For some women, early independence was essentially forced on them. Jessica reflected on her entry to stripping, pointing out that it was less of a choice than it was the only way she perceived being able to survive: "It was a week before my 18th birthday when I started dancing. I was homeless, I had a 1-year-old son, and I needed to survive. I've been dancing for 4 years now . . . I only want to dance long enough to go back to school. I'm thinking I'll be done in about 2 more years." Or, as Sable recalled, her family problems revolved around a lack of authority and guidance: "I moved into an aunt's house for a few months; I actually kind of moved around a lot, I was never really welcomed and secure in one spot for very long, and I was given way too much freedom."

Eight of the strippers reported either that their parents were still married or that at least one or both parents had died;. most commonly, strippers reported their parents had divorced and been remarried. For these women, coming from a broken home created important, often detrimental, consequences beyond pushing them into early independence. Depending on which parent was present and/or active in their lives, developing issues revolved around competition for the attention, affection, acceptance, and praise of the parental figure who was not in the picture. Brenda reflected on the consequences of being raised by a single mother and its effects on her: "I didn't see my mother have very many healthy relationships with men when I was growing up. She's been married four times; my father's been married five times." Of the women who reported growing up in single-parent homes, most were raised by their mothers. Those strippers whose mothers were not their primary caregiver indicated their mothers were not around, not active, or completely uninvolved when it came to their childhood. According to Sara, money, not love, was the reason her father kept custody. Of the women who were raised by their mothers, the majority reported some kind of ongoing contact with their father. However, although contact may have been maintained, most often these relationships were negatively affected by drug and alcohol abuse and/or mental, physical, or sexual abuse. As Phoebie explained, when her stepfather came into her life everything changed:

My whole life changed when my stepdad came in the picture. He was very abusive mentally, physically, he beat on my mother and my sister and I, and he would never touch my brother. That's what really deterred me from being at home. He wouldn't let us be children; I went from a straight-A student up 'til high school. All of a sudden my sophomore year I started making Fs. I was scared to go home, that's how bad it was.

Although Victoria's father did not sexually abuse her, she recalled a painful childhood:

My father was both mentally and physically abusive. As long as he never touched my little brother it seemed all right because that's how I was raised. When I was 16 he about hit my brother, but I stepped in the way and stood up to him. Instead of hitting me, his punishment was inviting my uncle to the house the next day. I had told him that my uncle tried to molest me, but he didn't care.

Alcohol and drug abuse by parents was one of the most common themes in these strippers' childhoods. Fifteen of the 20 strippers reported one or both of their parents abused alcohol and 10 had at least one parent who abused drugs. Deidra remembered her father's involvement with drugs and his abuse toward her: "My father has done drugs, he used to deal them. I hate him; he's a piece of shit that doesn't deserve to be able to speak to me. He's done a lot of mean things to me, every abuse possible." As Veronica recalled her mother, she expressed the strong belief that her mother's lifestyle was a significant influence on her life: "My mother was an alcoholic; she was also a dancer. I think that had a lot to do with how I turned out."

Tying these issues together, the absence of a responsible and caring male figure in a young girl's life coupled with parents who abused both substances and their daughters sets up the scenario from which women moved to employment in the sex industry. Stripping allows for, and facilitates, the pursuit of special attention, especially attention from men.

A second typical characteristic found in the literature on strippers is that strippers have very low levels of education (Prus and Irini 1980; Ronai and Ellis 1989). More recent research (Reid et al. 1995) has challenged this finding, showing that a majority of strippers in the 1990s are high school graduates, and some have college experience. Our findings parallel this challenge; all but one of the women in this research had graduated from high school. In fact, the slight majority of the women in this sample had some college education. However, only one woman actually held a college degree; most of these

women did, however, indicate an intention or desire to return to college.

A third pattern reported in previous research is the association between exhibitionistic behavior and previous jobs held. The literature (Ronai and Ellis 1989; Peretti and O'Connor 1989; Thompson and Harred 1992) has suggested that women who strip have always been accustomed to using their bodies, good looks, sex appeal, and personalities in their everyday lives, especially in employment. The experiences of this sample reaffirmed this finding. The vast majority of these women identified themselves as having exhibitionist tendencies and enjoying being in the spotlight, showing off their bodies. Sophie explained her perspective on showing off: "If there's an opportunity and I'm around people, I'll probably take my clothes off. I like the shock value." In relation to prior employment, three-quarters of these women reported having been a waitress prior to stripping. Other jobs reported include professional career or management positions, retail, telemarketing, grocery store cashier, legal research, horseback riding instructor, and hospital volunteer. Hence, this sample was consistent with prior research samples in which prior jobs involved the use of their bodies, good looks, and personalities to be accepted and successful.

More interesting details about exhibitionistic behavior and employment were evident in the job aspirations reported by these women. The most common response to inquiries about childhood career aspirations was a desire to be a model. In American society, modeling is associated with beauty, popularity, fame, acceptance, praise, and money. There are clear similarities and overlap between aspirations to model and the fact that these women strip for a living. Basically, stripping offers everything modeling offers, except for societal acceptance. Interesting as well is that only one-half of these women stated they had a desire to become a dancer when they were young (although for them this did not mean stripping). Rather, these women dreamed of dancing in ballet companies and music videos and for backup groups. Only two women stated that stripping was somewhat glamorized in their lives so they had thought about it specifically. Marty is one of these women; as a little girl: stripping was glamorized, and she was perhaps guided toward stripping. "When I was little, my grandmother used to come in the room with just her towel and dance around, it was glamorized to me. She used to tell me when I turned 18 that I could go see male strippers, it was always glamorized to me."

Many women also aspired to own their own businesses. Some envisioned operating an adult entertainment club; others desired more mainstream businesses (beauty salon, or some kind of shop [novelty, coffee, or clothing]). A few women had other aspirations for professional careers (medicine, law, or psychology) or other skilled occupations (glass blowing, graphic arts, massage therapist, commercial acting, police officer, or motherhood).

In summary, there is significant evidence offered in this study that supports prior research findings regarding a congruence between the content of previous jobs and stripping. It is true of this sample that most of the women held previous jobs or participated in activities that required the display and use of their physical attributes and personalities. The question remains, then, what other factors may be common in the characteristics and backgrounds of female strippers? It is to this issue that our discussion turns next.

Previously Unidentified Factors in Strippers' Backgrounds

In addition to issues previously identified in the literature as relevant, we also assessed qualities we presumed to be prevalent among exhibitionist women, factors we suspected would be related to sex industry employment. These qualities include being outgoing, independent, creative, motivated, and competitive. With these in mind, we hypothesized what other common activities would encourage such behavior. As a result, questions pertaining to a stripper's prior involvement in athletics and mainstream entertainment, as well as histories of abuse, were included in interviews. These areas of inquiry, somewhat surprisingly, have not been thoroughly discussed in previous research.

Both athletic and entertainment backgrounds were common in the lives of the women in this sample. Among these strippers, 75 percent had participated in athletics. Athletic backgrounds in order of most to least frequent included track/cross country, cheerleading, gymnastics, softball, dance (ballet or dance team), volleyball, swimming, soccer, basketball, tennis, Tai Kwon Do, and saddle-breaking horses; one woman performed as a college mascot.

Also, a majority of the sample indicated previous involvement in the entertainment industry. Here the most frequently reported areas of involvement were participation in theater arts, followed closely by modeling, then singing, dancing, and, last, work as an artist. Taken together, these factors suggest something about women who strip and commonalities of earlier life experiences. Generally speaking, these women tend to be very outgoing, independent, creative, motivated, and competitive. These qualities are a necessity when it comes to athletics

and entertainment, as well as critical to success as a stripper.

Therefore, the question arises, Did these women, especially as teenagers, become so accustomed to using their bodies for achievement, or being outgoing in different activities, that when the option and opportunity of stripping was presented, it seemed "natural" to participate? Or, were these women so desperate for attention, affection, and acceptance that when stripping was an option the attraction is irresistible? This study suggests the answers are between these extremes. An athletic or entertainment background is good for building confidence, attitude, and independence, which are all excellent qualities for a dancer. However, these women's personalities have been shaped by experiences that create deeper issues regarding attention and affection. Together, these characteristics facilitate entry into the life of stripping: Illustrating this point, Monica explained that ever since she could remember, she wanted to be a model and believed a modeling career would give her attention and proclaim her beauty: "I love having my picture taken. I don't think I was that pretty when I was a little girl and I didn't play with make-up, or Barbie dolls, and I didn't watch Miss America. I didn't think of doing anything like that, I just wanted to model, I wanted the attention."

A second issue not (directly) addressed in the literature is the frequently implied relationship between childhood abuse victimization and subsequent sex industry employment. However, as our research shows, it is not abuse in and of itself that correlates with stripping. Rather, it is abuse victimization and the consequential lowering of self-esteem that is critical. In recollections of childhood and adolescence, two of the strippers' most common themes centered on some sort of mental, physical, or sexual abuse and self-descriptions emphasizing a lack of self-confidence, self-worth, or self-esteem. On the basis of our initial contacts—and previous involvements with strippers—we queried these women in detail about their childhoods, looking for indications of all three forms of abuse as well as issues pertaining to self-esteem. What we quickly discovered was that our initial impressions were substantiated and that strippers experienced a particular variety of low self-esteem, which they repeatedly referred to as the "the ugly duckling syndrome."

Sexual abuse or molestation as a child was reported by one-third of the sample; however, an additional one-third indicated they had suffered from what they labeled mental and/or physical abuse, rape, and forms of self-inflicted sexual abuse (being promiscuous or sleeping around for love and acceptance). These negative experiences were, at least in the minds of these women, directly related to later decisions to enter into stripping. Victoria remembers the negative reinforcement of being unsatisfactory in her father's eyes:

> I think I get my low self-esteem from my childhood. My father and I never had a good relationship at all. I haven't spoken to my dad in 5 years. Everyday it was like you're not pretty enough, you're not smart enough, and you're not skinny enough. I was never good enough. When you're dancing, everyone thinks you're pretty. You get all kinds of compliments.

The sexual abuse reported by women most often involved molestation by a family member, usually an older male relative (father, stepfather, uncle, or mother's boyfriend); when the abuser was not a family member, these women reported their molesters as a male neighbor. In most cases, the sexual abuse took place between the ages of 7 to 10, although for some it began as early as age 4 or as late as age 13. Melanie, whose experiences were highly representative of women in this sample, reflected on her recurring molestation experiences as a child:

> The first time I was about 7, and then again when I was about 9. It was different people, family, friends, neighbors, and other people's parents. When I was 7 I had a friend, and his dad, who was a teacher, sent him outside to play; I didn't know. I never told my mom until several years later. There's probably been at least three other times it happened during my childhood. I wasn't much for telling people because it was embarrassing to me.

Or, as Veronica recalled,

> My first sexual experience was not by choice. It was with an old man who was about 60; I was 11. It was actually one of my mother's clients, she was on drugs at the time, and so she sent me to sleep with this guy so she could get money. I knew what was going on, and I did have sex with the guy, but I ran away afterwards, and I never did that again.

Finally, clearly showing her belief in the connection between sexual abuse victimization and her current work as a stripper, Brenda recalled her childhood:

> I had no self-esteem when I was growing up. My stepfather sexually molested me, and I had a lot of bad issues with my mom, and her entire family. I just didn't like myself, I didn't think very highly of myself; I didn't think I was an okay person. I didn't have any self-esteem until dancing. You take your clothes off for money, and men look at you like you're a goddess, they tell you

how beautiful you are, and it's like a temporary fix for your own inferior issues.

What about those women who did not suffer abuse, but grew up with little self-esteem or a false sense of self-confidence? How did they develop low self-esteem, and in what areas of their lives was it focused? The ugly duckling syndrome illustrates childhood struggles among women who at some point while they were growing up felt awkward, ugly, uncoordinated, or "geeky." As children, many of these women did not feel especially feminine or attractive. One in four indicated that they grew up as tomboys, and four of every five believed that they suffered from the ugly duckling syndrome.

A young woman who feels ugly may turn to stripping for personal validation and confirmation that she has grown to be a beautiful and sexy woman. Ferrah recalls her childhood as extremely unpleasant, largely because of others' reactions to her size. "When I was in high school I was so chubby, I was wicked unpopular. They used to call me Horse Lady because I was so chunky. I was tall and 140 pounds." Sophie explained her struggle with a memorable childhood experience where she felt taken advantage of:

> I fall into that percentage of dancers who've had some sort of sexual issues, not necessarily abuse. I think the biggest reason I became a dancer was because there was this boy in high school and he got me at my junior prom. I sweared no guy would ever break my heart, and I would be the queen of knowing what men want, and I would use my sexual power to get what I wanted.

Jessica also reported a childhood that had a disintegrating influence on her self-esteem. However, Jessica's lack of confidence in herself, especially her femininity, was related to her appearance and choice of activities rather than to sexual issues: "I was pretty much a tomboy my whole younger years. Not hard core, but all my friends were boys. I played soccer, softball; I was on the swim team for several years. I do remember being geeky and awkward when I was in elementary school."

During adolescent years, negative reinforcement by parental figures and peer groups left these women with low self-esteem and a strong sense of not being physically appealing. For these ugly ducklings beauty was simply an unattainable dream. Hence, with maturity and age these girls worked to develop into beautiful women who desired to have their appearances accepted and they found an arena—the strip bar—that would allow for the ultimate praise and worship.

Unfortunately, childhood experiences, such as sexual, mental, or physical abuse as well as being a tomboy or feeling like an ugly duckling, touched the lives of over three-quarters of the women in this sample. The women who suffered due to these factors were deeply scarred. As children they were oppressed; their role models and peers constantly denigrated them; they were told they were not good enough; they were taught they were not appealing physically; their families and peers exposed them to adult behaviors (sex, drugs, and alcohol); and they were generally socialized to believe they were flawed or less valuable than others. When these girls became adult women, their feelings of being less than adequate did not go away; their feelings were not expressed; and these women did what felt natural. They sought out the acceptance of others, especially men. The strip club provided them with the ultimate stadium of acceptance. Strippers never run out of customers who show their approval in so many ways.

CONCLUSION

Nobody grows up consciously wanting to be an outcast from the mainstream. People enjoy and strive for acceptance and approval from their peers and society. A stripper does not make a carefully thought-out decision to enter a world in which she will be bombarded by negative judgments, disgust, negative attitudes, shame, disgrace, and stereotypes. Rather, these women's backgrounds and experiences facilitate their initiation into a career in the sex industry by providing them with negatively imbued statuses and self-perceptions.

As this analysis of women in the stripping industry showed, there are identifiable, specific characteristics associated with women who pursue stripping as an occupation. As shown in our data, the factors that influence and facilitate a woman's decision to become a stripper include:

- early physical maturity and early sexual experiences
- order position, absence of a father in the home, early independence from or in home
- average educational levels
- a relationship between exhibitionistic behavior and previous job experience
- athletic or entertainment backgrounds
- childhood abuse
- the ugly duckling syndrome

These findings clearly add to the body of literature that identifies and summarizes characteristics among women who choose to strip for a living (Forsyth and Deshotels 1997; Lewis 1998; Reid et al.

1995). Most important, however, the present research advances our understanding by adding to the list of previously identified shared qualities.

What stands as the apparently most influential predisposing factors that lead one to stripping include the absence of a father figure during adolescence; a link between exhibitionist behavior, prior job experience, and athletic or entertainment backgrounds; childhood abuse; and the ugly duckling syndrome. These factors all share a common link to women's self-esteem and self-confidence. Contrary to common assumptions, strippers are not necessarily strong and confident individuals with high self-esteem. These qualities are typically present in dancers, but they are not qualities that lead women into stripping.

Introduction References

Boles, J. (2001). "Stripping." In N. Davis and G. Geis (Vol. Eds.). *Encyclopedia of Criminal and Deviant Behavior*, Vol. 3. Sexual Deviance (pp. 399–401). Philadelphia, PA: Taylor & Francis.

Corio, A. (1968). *This Was Burlesque*. New York: Grossett & Dunlop.

Sweet, N., and Tewksbury, R. (2000). "'What's a Nice Girl Like You Doing in a Place Like This?': Pathways to a career in stripping." *Sociological Spectrum*, 20, 325–343.

Zeidman, I. (1967). *The American Burlesque Show*. New York: Hawthorne.

References

Barron, Kate. 1989. "Strippers: The Undressing of an Occupation." University of Kansas. Unpublished manuscript.

Bell, Holly, Lacey Sloan, and Chris Strickling. 1998. "Exploiter and Exploited: Topless Dancers Reflect on Their Experiences." *Affilia*, 13: 352–368.

Boles, Jacqueline and A. P. Garbin. 1974. "The Strip Club and Stripper-Customer Patterns of Interaction." *Sociology and Social Research*, 58: 136–144.

Forsyth, Craig and Tina Deshotels. 1997. "The Occupational Milieu of the Nude Dancer." *Deviant Behavior*, 18: 125–142.

Lewis, Jacqueline. 1998. "Learning to Strip: The Socialization Experiences of Exotic Dancers.ö *The Canadian Journal of Human Sexuality*, 7: 51–66.

McCaghy, Charles and James Skipper. 1969. "Lesbian Behavior as an Adaptation to the Occupation of Stripping." *Social Problems*, 17: 262–270.

Peretti, Peter O. and Patrick O'Connor. 1989. "Effects of Incongruence Between the Perceived Self and the Ideal Self on Emotional Stability of Stripteasers." *Social Behavior and Personality*, 17: 81–92.

Prus, Robert and Styllianoss Irini. 1980. *Hookers, Rounders, and Desk Clerks*. Salem, WI: Sheffield.

Reid, Scott A., Jonathon A. Epstein, and D. E. Benson. 1995. "Does Exotic Dancing Pay Well But Cost Dearly?" Pp. 284–288 in *Readings in Deviant Behavior*, edited by Alex Thio and Thomas Calhoun. New York: Harper Collins College Publishers.

Ronai, Carol Rambo and Carolyn Ellis. 1989. "Turn-ons For Money: Interactional Strategies of a Table Dancer." *Journal of Contemporary Ethnography*, *18*(3): 271–298.

Salutin, Marilyn. 1971. "Stripper Morality." *Transactions, 8*: 12–22.

Sijuwade, Philip O. 1995. "Counterfeit Intimacy: A Dramaturgical Analysis of an Erotic Performance." *Social Behavior and Personality, 23*: 369–376.

Skipper, James and Charles McCaghy. 1970. "Stripteasers: The Anatomy and Career Contingencies of a Deviant Occupation." *Social Problems, 17*: 391–404.

Thompson, William E. and Jackie L. Harred.1992. "Topless Dancers: Managing Stigma in a Deviant Occupation." *Deviant Behavior, 13*: 291–311.

Part IX

Sexuality and Society: Law, Economics, Religion, and Education

With changes in technology making pornography "easier to order into the home than pizza" and court decisions that offer broad legal protection to vendors, selling sex has become a $10 billion industry in the United States (Egan 2000). Meanwhile, the "crazy aunt in the attic" phenomenon has been spawned: "everyone knows she is there, but no one is talking about her!" It seems that legal issues about sexuality and money have become silent partners. American Telephone and Telegraph, Time Warner, General Motors, Marriot International, and the Hilton Corporation are all corporations with a big financial stake in the adult video film market, but all remain low-key about pornography profits. With market players of such magnitude, it is logical to question the relationship of economic factors to laws that have been or could be effected, especially those pertaining to sexual behavior and sexual exploitation. Part IX flushes out significant sociological questions related to legal, economic, religious, and educational issues surrounding sexuality.

Legal issues are critically related to the sexual health of Americans. To understand how legal issues influence sexuality, one must be somewhat knowledgeable about legislative and legal processes. Basically, the levels of jurisdiction throughout the country begin at local levels, progressing from city, to county, to state, and, finally, to federal government, each with its own legal code. Additionally, even the military has a legal code of its own. All laws are subject to the provisions of the Constitution of the United States and, likewise, laws governing sexuality at any level cannot be inconsistent with the next highest level of governance.

The law charts included in the Daley, Orenstein, and Wong article will intrigue students curious about their state sexuality laws and how such laws compare with those in other states.

The report that looks at sexuality laws and the sexual rights of citizens has been compiled by the public policy arm of the Sexuality Information and Education Council of the United States (SIECUS). A nonprofit voluntary health organization, SIECUS was founded in 1964 to help people understand, appreciate, and use their sexuality in a responsible and informed manner (LeVay and Valente 2003). This interdisciplinary organization, the brainchild of a lawyer, a sociologist, a family life educator, and a physician, is the premier sexuality information center in the United States. Mary Calderone, the first female physician in the state of New York, was a cofounder and the first executive director. It is of note that prior to the founding of SIECUS, two female physicians were also the driving forces in similar health education movements in their own countries, one in Sweden and one in Denmark (Moore 1986). Before the early 1950s, when Agentha Braestrup, M.D., spearheaded the establishment of the Danish system of sexuality education and family planning, a medical prescription was required to purchase a condom at the corner drugstore. Indeed, the Danes have come a long way.

New to Part IX, "Sexuality and Society," the Lyons selection is about both interrelationships and juxtapositions of the sacred and the secular: religion and the law. Labeled as the "Tort Battle," the subject of this chapter happens to be the legal issues surrounding the sexual abuse scandal shaking the very foundation of the Catholic Church. But, adversarial relationships between these two venerable social institutions could just as easily have been inferred from public reaction to other recent headlines, i.e., the U.S. Supreme Court's decision about the sexual act of sodomy or the Massachusetts Supreme Judicial Court's decision that same-sex marriages were constitutionally permissible and must be legalized.

"It is like warfare." In this chapter, students will encounter these sentiments of Saint Thomas University Law Professor Patrick Schlitz, who has defended religious organizations in more than five-hundred (500) sexual abuse lawsuits. On the basis of his experience, Schlitz believes that we are in the second of three planned attacks by lawyers in the Tort Battle. *Phase One* was for plaintiff lawyers to maximize bad publicity and to destroy the credibility of the Church. *Phase Two* is for them to use that publicity to push for legislative changes. And, *Phase Three* will be the pay off, in which the lawyers collect. The problem, he says, is that fraudulent claims could get paid off along with legitimate ones.

Legal cases cited in the Lyons' selection address a phenomenon known as the "Memory Wars": recovered memory and the false memory syndrome. Various social movements and changes in the legal system have led to the upsurge in childhood memory cases experienced during the past two decades (Douglas-Brown, Goldstein, and Bjorklund 2000). Until recently, the concept of repressed memory was known only in the domains of psychiatry and psychology, but eventually, it became a household word. In the 1990s, media's focus on the false memory syndrome caused some to fear that the concept of repressed memory would be viewed as synonymous with false memory by the public (Broughton 1999).

Readers not only need to understand the difference between these two concepts but also that there are opposing professional opinions about these two perspectives as they relate to childhood sexual abuse. Most professionals in psychotherapy subscribe to the recovered memory theory, but most professionals in psychology take the position that the memories of events may be falsely induced through suggestions or hypnosis by unscrupulous or overzealous therapists (Loftus 1999). And, there are data weighing in on both sides of the argument. In the 1990s, the American Psychological Association (APA) commissioned a task force to study the issues of recovered memory and the false memory syndrome, searching for common ground that might lead to a consensus in the contentious debate. But, the dearth of information on the subject of memory hampered their ability to arrive at a definitive answer (Pope and Brown 1996). This selection is expected to raise different opinions among interested students, depending on their prior knowledge of the topic or personal experiences.

In any storyline, one first identifies the principal players. Frank Rich does a masterful job of this assignment in his *New York Times Magazine* article, "Naked Capitalists" in which both nakedness and capitalism are exposed. He flushes out the characters who are conducting an annual $10 to $14 billion business in the United States called the "Adult Industry" or the "Porn Business." Rich characterizes the business as "a mirror image of Hollywood," contending that the arrival of home video revolutionized pornography as much as sound had revolutionized Hollywood. And, his facts are staggering: Considering even the low-end $10 billion estimate, pornography is bigger business than professional football, basketball, and baseball combined. More money is spent for pornography than regular movie tickets or than all of the performing arts together.

The by-word for access to pornography today appears to be "no effort, no fear." In writing about pornography and sexual deviance, Bryant and Zillman (2001) contend that the benefits of living in the information age, with ready access to large quantities of information and communication options, can prove to be a proverbal two-edged sword: Not all access to mediated messages is beneficial or desirable. The negative social and psychological effects that appear to stem from repeatedly using hardcore pornography are cited as an example of the "dark side" of ready access to modern mediated communication.

College students likely represent a microcosm of varying opinions in the pornography debates: For example, about free speech versus censorship, issues that have created some unlikely allies. Antipornography feminist scholars find themselves allied with Christian evangelical leaders in antipornography debates, and law professors specializing in First Amendment issues are themselves defending the rights of publishers of the most graphically explicit materials in anticensorship litigation (Carroll 2005).

But, the issue of pornography nowhere has been more divisive than among feminists themselves. Antipornography feminist leaders Catherine MacKinnon and Andrea Dworkin contend that pornography is less about sex than power over women. They claim that it reinforces male dominance and increases sexual and physical abuse against women (LeVay and Valente 2003). Anticensorship feminists, such as Camille Paglia (1994) and Nadine Strossen (1995), argue that censorship of sexual materials will be used to suppress feminist writings about erotica, endangering women's rights and freedom of expression. Extensive arguments on both sides of the censorship issue are so compelling that readers are often left with feeling that the answer to the question "Are you for or against censorship of pornography?" is "yes."

Putting a face on the women and men who are in this multibillion dollar business, Rich reveals how they feel about their work, why they got into the adult industry, and, interesting trivia, such as whether they themselves watch pornography. Understanding their motives, missions, and misgivings will provide students with a better knowledge base from which to formulate their own opinions about pornography and the women and men who promote it. Historian Vern L. Bullough has advanced a convincing argument that society itself plays a key role in promoting the sex industry. In writing from a historical perspective about prostitution, a largely illegal (except in Nevada) form of deviate sexual behavior, he proposes that the prostitute herself is the traditional woman in a specialized occupation. Bullough argues that as women become more assertive, the prostitute herself will change. He observes, "to label a woman sick for what all women have been acculturated to do is ahistorical" (Bullough 1979, 93).

Readers will find this offering different from most of those on pornography. It is neither a moral brief nor a passionate defense of pornography. Although Rich does not sift through the large body of research on the topic, he does inform students about many of the pertinent facts surrounding the Adult Industry. And, all of this is accomplished through the eyes of women and men who are leaders in the industry. As their human interest stories unfold, stereotypes are guaranteed to be dispelled.

In the thirteenth century, St. Thomas Aquinas developed a standard for sexual intercourse. For sexual activity to be deemed morally acceptable, only heterosexual genital intercourse was allowed; sexual activity had to serve a strictly procreative function; and sexual intercourse was sanctioned only within the confines of the marital institution (Reiss 1990). Such religious influence upon human sexual interactions still persists in much of the thinking and feelings toward sexuality today (Curran 1992). This presumption is illustrated by the stigma attached to the subject of human sexuality that often moves it beyond the realm of honest, open discussion. But, there is good news on the horizon. Recently, some adults, parents, and others in schools, churches, and social service agencies have begun approaching the important topic of human sexuality as a source of health and pleasure, and less as a punitive matter, surrounded by stigma and mystery.

Nevertheless, guilt and sexuality are historically rooted. And, as with all social issues, their linkages may be slow to change. Some still question, is sexuality inherently a guilt-laden phenomenon? David-

son and Moore argue no; it is socially constructed and, as such, it may be religiously reinforced. But, by any measure, sexual guilt has the unfortunate potential to preclude a healthy sexual script, making this topic vitally important for sexuality students. The present study is based on the premise that religiosity, measured by varying degrees of attendance at religious services, leads to greater or lesser exposure to church doctrine that may, in turn, influence a person's beliefs and attitudes toward sexuality and affect one's sexual behavior. The social science literature of the last two decades generally substantiates that, indeed, a relationship does exist between sexual behavior and religion. For example, research on widely divergent populations, one, an earlier study of professional nurses with a mean age of 33 years (Davidson, Darling, and Norton 1993), and the other, a recent study of adolescents (Meier 2003), have each confirmed that religiosity does affect the timing of first sexual intercourse. As Davidson and Moore re-examine the relationship between religiosity and sexual attitudes and behavior, they ask additional questions from the perspective of guilt and sexual responsibility.

Recalling Kierkegaard's philosophy that potentialities do not become actualities without anxiety, Rollo May elucidates: "The potentiality for sexual intercourse, which takes a decisive leap ahead at puberty, brings excitement and joy but also the anxiety associated with new relationships and responsibilities" (May 1972, 122). Students of sexuality have a responsibility to promote a safer, healthier sexual landscape because, in many instances, they are among the growing number of young people postponing committed relationships well beyond the years of sexual maturity. As educated adults in other present or future roles (such as parents, teachers, researchers, religious leaders, or simply concerned citizens), they hold the key to problems surrounding sexuality. And, it seems to be labeled *responsibility*. Solution-oriented readers of this chapter are challenged to do some critical thinking about the following questions:

- If sexual guilt and religiosity are related, age-old questions again must be asked. Is guilt a by-product of behavior or does guilt play a role in determining behavior?

- Based on the premise that at least a moderate degree of guilt is a part of the normal development and, therefore, crucial to the process of socialization, is guilt within the context of sexuality desirable or undesirable?

- What other sociological and psychological factors pertaining to sexual guilt should be factored into the equation, since religion itself is only one intervening variable?

Finally, students may wish to reflect on how important the opinions of friends and family were in arriving at their answers to these timeless questions. Which, of course, lands them back in square one, a space clearly marked *values*.

Responding to an embarrassed 21-year-old whose girlfriend had joked about the size of his penis, Drew Pinsky, M.D., a.k.a. Dr. Love, the key player on *Loveline*—a former Los Angeles-based MTV television show during the late 1990s—clarified that size is not a crucial factor in sexual satisfaction for women. But, the caller on this nighttime call-in program was not only reassured, he was also admonished to reframe the issue by recognizing the fact that he was in a relationship with an abusive partner. Dr. Drew's chief mission on *Loveline* was to change what he viewed as the culture of "broken down interpersonal relationships" that lack intimacy (Barovick 1998). A long-time veteran of an alternative approach to sexuality education, Pinsky is still countering what he has termed the "abdication of parenting ethos" of the 1970s. He viewed his show as a "sheep in wolf's clothing," discouraging sexual activity and encouraging responsibility and connection, a stark contrast to the rest of the media force, which often depicts sex as a simple physical act without an emotional component. In what some see as a "bad news" milieu, Pinsky's good news is that young teens today are more inquisitive and realistic about sexuality than their predecessors. Such good news is long overdue. Stodghill's exposé of teen sexual behavior, circa 2000, which realistically describes how America's youth really do learn about sex is an important piece of the sexuality puzzle.

The Terrance Olson chapter on sexuality education is new to this Edition of *Speaking of Sexuality*. The author was assigned a difficult task when he was asked to review the research literature about sexuality education and attempt a rational analysis of the realities reflected in the current situation, within philosophical and practical parameters. Because this work is not an exercise in technical writing but, instead, one that often finds itself embedded in the midst of deepest values, it would be a challenge for any scholar undertaking such a project to maintain a professional detachment, permitting a value-free approach to the process. This chapter is one person's Olympian effort to do just that. Yet, as we read, it is important to remember, "anything approaching impersonality of experimental science will only succeed in purifying the subject out of its actual existence in the world of human affairs" (Kovel 1976, xiii).

Although sexuality education is moored in ideology, it is expressed in real practice. This author conducts an inquiry into the inner assumptions that guide the practice of sexuality education, grounds his findings with philosophy, and, best of all, does not pretend that "the observer stands separate from the observed" (Kovel 1976, xiii). Well-equipped to do this project, Olson has been engaged in the field of family science for a number of years, developing and evaluating sexuality education programs as well as training teachers throughout the United States and abroad.

But, sexuality education is an ideological debate. As in all ideological warfare, when like-minded people band together, they are probably not going to hear both sides of the story. In remarks about the two major political parties, the Republicans and the Democrats, Robert Baron, a social psychologist at the University of Iowa, offered this commentary, "The discussion will be twisted and biased, emphasizing those things that support the dominant form and disparing or questioning the credibility of things that contradict" (Bishop 2004, A1). Our hope is that the English poet Robert Blake (1757–1827) was correct in his assertion: "Without contraries [there] is no progression" (Kovel 1976, xiii). If this admonition is true, we seem to be making significant progress in the field of sexuality education today, with our numerous "contraries" much in evidence. This chapter must be read to see that Olson does accomplish his assignment without undue polemics. That he gives ample space to the actual contradictions in the political and moral landscapes is hopeful.

After reading the chapters in Part IX, readers will be more aware of the effect of social problems pertaining to sexuality in this new millennium and certain that they cannot be adequately solved with archaic strategies. Pouring "new wine into old wineskins" will not work. But, neither can workable solutions be secured without some form of wineskins. Whether these are called norms, mores, or values, a judicious mix of old and new is required: As always, change must be balanced with continuity.

References

Barovick, H. (1998, June 15). "Dr. Drew, Afterhours Guru." *Time*, p. 59.

Bishop, B. (2004, April 8). "The Growing Cost of Political Uniformity." *Austin American-Statesman*, pp. A1, A6.

Broughton, F. (1995). "The Memory Debate in Perspective: And Some Future Directions." *Psychiatry, Psychology, and Law*, 2, 91–96.

Bryant, J., and Zillman D. (2001). "Pornography, Models of Effects of Sexual Deviancy." In N. Davis and G. Geis (Vol. Eds.), *Encyclopedia of Criminal and Sexual Deviance*, Vol. 3., Sexual Deviance (pp. 241–244). Philadelphia, PA: Taylor and Francis.

Bullough, V. L. (1979). "Prostitution, Psychiatry, and History." In V. L. Bullough (Ed.), *The Frontiers of Sex Research (pp. 87–96). Buffalo, NY: Prometheus.*

Carroll, J. L. (2005). *Sexuality Now: Embracing Diversity.* Belmont, CA: Wadsworth.

Curran, C. E. (1992). "Sexual Ethics in the Roman Catholic Tradition." In R. M. Green (Ed.), *Religion and Sexual Health* (pp. 17–35). Boston: Kluver.

Davidson, J. K., Sr., Darling, C. A., and Norton, L. (1995). "Religiosity and the Sexuality of Women: Sexual Behaviors and Sexual Satisfaction Revisited." *The Journal of Sex Research*, 32, 235–243.

Douglas-Brown, R., Goldstein, E., and Bjorklund, D. F. (2000). "The History and Xeitgeist of the Repressed-False-Memory Debate: Scientific and Sociological Perspectives on Suggestibility and Childhood Memory." In D. F. Bjorklund, (Ed.), *False Memory Creation in Children and Adults: Theory, Research, and Implications (pp. 1–30). Mahwah, NJ: Lawrence Erlbaum.*

Egan, T. (2000, October 23). "U.S. Corporations Finding Sex Sells." *Austin American-Statesman*, pp. A1, A8.

Kovel, J. (1976). *A Complete Guide to Therapy From Psychoanalysis to Behavioral Modification. New York: Pantheon.*

LeVay, S., and Valente, S. M. (2003). *Human Sexuality.* Sunderland, MA: Sinauer Associates.

Loftus, E. F. (1999). "Lost in the Mall: Misrepresentations and Misunderstandings." *Ethics and Behavior*, 9, 51–60.

May, R. (1972). *Power and Innocence: A Search for the Sources of Violence. New York: Norton.*

Meier, A. M. (2003). "Adolescents' Transition to First Intercourse, Religiosity, and Attitudes About Sex." *Social Forces*, 81, 1031–1052.

Moore, N. B. (1986). "Cross-Cultural Perspectives: Family Life Education as a Forum for Strengthening Families." In M. B. Sussman (Ed.), *Charybdis Complex* (pp. 91–115). New York: Haworth.

Paglia, C. (1994). *Vamps and Tramps.* New York: Vintage.

Pope, K. S., and Brown, L. S. (1996). *Recovered Memories of Abuse: Assessment, Therapy, Forensics.* Washington, DC: American Psychological Association.

Reiss, I. L. (1990). *An End to Shame: Shaping Our Next Sexual Revolution. Buffalo, NY: Prometheus.* ✦

Chapter 39

SIECUS Looks at States' Sexuality Laws and the Sexual Rights of Citizens

Daniel Daley

Susie Orenstein

Vivian Wong

Should the government be in the bedroom of consenting adults? What is the appropriate role for the legal system to play in supporting the sexual health and sexual rights of citizens? Questions such as these have sparked controversy for well over a century since the United States Congress passed an anti-obscenity bill, the first law of its kind. Not as amorphous today, queries are less philosophical and more pragmatic. Where do individual rights (i.e., the rights of a woman to an abortion) intersect with the rights of a fetus? Or, do we violate individual rights (i.e., of parents) if sexuality education is mandated by states? What about release time for "nonbelievers of sexuality education"?

The SIECUS Public Policy Staff has assembled an excellent accounting of current sexuality laws in American culture. In charts especially prepared for this anthology, seven areas of sexuality are compared on a state-by-state basis: sexuality education, contraceptive services, abortion services, HIV/AIDS infection, sexual orientation, sexual behaviors, and sexual exploitation. A perusal of these analyses will confirm that these United States are far from united about the topic of sexuality. This is a short treatment of the subject, but vital information for anyone concerned about promoting sexual health for self and others.

A basic tenet of our nation is that all Americans are equal under the law. But state laws vary. An American in one state enjoys different rights and privileges than an American in another state a mile

away. So reality has a dash of George Orwell's *Animal Farm*—some citizens are more equal than others. Unfortunately, this is also true of laws governing intimate issues such as sexuality.

Most Americans don't give much consideration to the government's decision making concerning their sexual lives. They generally agree that sexual behavior is private and that what they do in their bedrooms is their own business. They may even think that sexuality-related laws are enacted for other people—not themselves. As a result, most Americans don't consider a state's laws on sexuality and sexual rights when deciding where to live or visit. Perhaps if they saw how the patchwork of laws come together to describe sexual rights in their state, they would.

SIECUS advocates for the right of individuals to make responsible sexual choices. This broader right is composed of a variety of specific rights—the right to information, the right to sexual health services, the right to engage in sexual behaviors in private with another consenting adult, the right to live according to one's sexual orientation, and the right to obtain and use materials that have a sexual theme or content. SIECUS believes that it is important to look at states' sexuality-related laws in total rather than by a single issue. SIECUS has, therefore, compiled information on state laws on a variety of sexuality-related topics. This is the first in an ongoing effort. Current research and analysis on the laws of each of the 50 states is broad and somewhat limited. Not every law in every state has been recently researched or interpreted. Not every issue has been addressed by state legislatures. SIECUS will continue to look at sexuality-related laws and will keep you informed of its findings.

Analysis of Categories

For this analysis, SIECUS is designating states' laws as (1) supportive of sexual health and sexual rights ("S"); (2) unsupportive of sexual health and sexual rights ("U"); or (3) neither supportive nor unsupportive of sexual health and sexual rights, [i.e., neutral] ("N"). These designations were determined by comparing the content of laws with SIECUS' position on the issue. In some cases, the absence of a state law is designated with an "NL" for no law. In other cases, the absence of a state law was interpreted as supportive or unsupportive depending on its impact on sexual rights.

In determining a state's overall supportiveness of sexual health and sexual rights, SIECUS counted each "S" as one point, each "U" as minus one point, and each "N" as no point. If a state's point total was positive, SIECUS termed it supportive or S; if it was negative, SIECUS termed it unsupportive or U; if it was zero, SIECUS termed it N for neither supportive nor unsupportive. NLs did not affect a score.

Sexuality Education

SIECUS believes that all people have the right to comprehensive sexuality education that addresses the biological, sociocultural, psychological, and spiritual dimensions of sexuality. Comprehensive school-based sexuality education that is appropriate to a student's age, developmental level, and cultural background is an important part of preparing young people for adulthood and is a critical component in promoting sexual health.

Opponents of comprehensive sexuality education once attempted to ban sexuality education outright. When that strategy proved unsuccessful, they tried to restrict the content and scope of such education. Even so, many states continue to mandate comprehensive sexuality education and HIV/AIDS education for their students. While these mandates provide a legal basis for program implementation, they do not necessarily result in programs in every school. The enforcement of such mandates has not been determined or evaluated.

SIECUS believes that state mandates are supportive of sexual health and sexual rights (S); and that the absence of a state mandate is unsupportive of sexual health and sexual rights (U). As for content requirements, states that only require the teaching of abstinence without information about contraception and disease prevention were assigned unsupportive (U) status. States that require the teaching of abstinence with the inclusion of contraception and disease prevention information were assigned a supportive (S) status (see Table 39.1).

Overall, the majority of states and the District of Columbia are supportive of educating young people about sexuality issues. But there are some significant caveats. States are likely to focus on HIV/STD-prevention education rather than on overall sexuality education. They are also likely to remain silent on contraceptive and disease prevention information other than abstinence.[1]

Contraceptive Services

SIECUS believes that all people should have ready access to comprehensive contraceptive information, education, and services, regardless of age, gender, or income. While parents should be involved in their children's contraceptive decisions, each person has the right to confidentiality and privacy when receiving such information, counseling and services. SIECUS supports adolescent access to low-cost prescription and nonprescription methods through public funding and private insurance coverage.

SIECUS examined information on laws concerning insurance coverage for contraceptive services and parental consent or notice or minors' access to contraceptive services. SIECUS also included information on state funds for contraceptive services, and considered states that used any amount of state funds as supportive (S).

SIECUS believes states that require coverage for contraceptive services in private insurance are supportive of sexual health and sexual rights (S) because it removes financial barriers. Two states—Montana and West Virginia—stand alone in requiring health maintenance organizations to provide, as a part of preventative services, voluntary family planning (see Table 39.2).

Studies have confirmed that adolescents are likely to delay or avoid seeking care when parental consent or notice is mandated for family planning services. SIECUS considers such mandates as unsupportive of sexual health and sexual rights (U). States that have no law explicitly authorizing minors' ability to consent for contraceptive services are designated as having no law (NL). States that explicitly authorize the minor to make contraceptive decisions were considered supportive of sexual health and sexual rights (S).[2]

Abortion Services

SIECUS believes that every woman, regardless of age or income, should have the right to obtain an abortion under safe, legal, confidential, and dignified conditions as well as at a reasonable cost. She should also have full knowledge of alternatives, and should be able to obtain complete, unbiased information and counseling on the nature, consequences, and risks associated with abortion, pregnancy, and childbirth.

SIECUS believes in public funding and mandated insurance coverage for abortion services. It also believes that parental consent laws, late-term bans, and waiting periods have a negative impact on reproductive health and rights. Clinic anti-violence and harassment laws promote safer access to such services and help to eliminate unconscionable attempts to undermine women's reproductive health rights.

For this issue, SIECUS examined a wide variety of topics because abortion is heavily legislated. These subjects included public funding, mandated insurance, parental consent, waiting periods, abortion procedure bans, and violence against abortion service providers. In many cases, states have placed

Table 39.1
Sexuality Education

	AL	AK	AZ	AR	CA	CO	CT	DE	DC	FL	GA	HI	ID	IL	IN	IA	KS	KY	LA	ME	MD	MA	MI	MN	MS	MO
Sexuality Education Mandate	S	U	S	S	U	U	U	S	S	U	S	S	S	S	U	S	S	U	U	U	U	U	U	U	U	U
STD/HIV Education Mandate	S	U	S	U	S	U	S	S	S	S	S	S	S	U	U	S	S	U	U	S	S	S	S	S	U	S
Mandate Includes Contraception	NL	U	U	NL	S	NL	NL	NL	NL	NL	S	NL	U	U	U	NL	NL	U	NL	NL	NL	NL	U	NL	NL	NL
Mandate Includes Disease Prevention	S	NL	NL	S	NL	NL	S	NL	NL	S	S	NL	S	U	S	NL	NL	NL	NL	NL	NL	S	S	NL	NL	NL
Composite Score	S	U	S	U	N	N	S	S	S	S	S	S	N	S	U	S	S	U	U	U	S	U	N	S	N	N

	MT	NE	NV	NH	NJ	NM	NY	NC	ND	OH	OK	OR	PA	RI	SC	SD	TN	TX	UT	VT	VA	WA	WV	WI	WY
Sexuality Education Mandate	U	U	S	U	S	U	U	S	U	U	U	S	S	S	S	U	S	S	S	S	S	S	S	S	U
STD/HIV Education Mandate	U	U	S	S	S	S	S	S	S	U	S	S	S	S	S	S	S	U	S	S	U	S	S	S	U
Mandate Includes Contraception	NL	NL	NL	NL	S	NL	NL	NL	NL	NL	S	NL	NL	NL	NL	U	NL	NL	S	S	S	S	NL	NL	NL
Mandate Includes Disease Prevention	NL	NL	NL	NL	S	S	S	S	S	S	S	S	NL	S	S	NL	S	S	S	S	S	NL	NL	NL	NL
Composite Score	U	U	S	S	S	S	S	S	N	N	S	S	S	S	S	N	S	S	S	S	N	S	N	N	U

Source: National Abortion and Reproductive Rights Action League, *A State-by-State Review of Abortion and Reproductive Rights* (NARAL Foundation, Washington, DC, January 1998).

KEY
S = Supportive
U = Unsupportive
NL = No Law
N = Neutral

TOTALS
Sexuality Education Mandate: S = 20; U = 31
STD/HIV Education Mandate: S = 36; U = 15
Mandate Includes Contraception: S = 13; U = 10; NL = 28
Mandate Includes Disease Prevention: S = 22; U = 3; NL = 26
Composite Score: S = 27; U = 14; N = 10

Table 39.2
Contraceptive Services

	AL	AK	AZ	AR	CA	CO	CT	DE	DC	FL	GA	HI	ID	IL	IN	IA	KS	KY	LA	ME	MD	MA	MI	MN	MS	MO
State Funding	S	S	S	U	S	S	S	NL	S	S	NL	S	U	S	S	S	S	S	S	S	S	S	S	S	S	S
Insurance Coverage	U	U	U	U	U	U	U	U	U	U	U	U	U	U	U	U	U	U	U	U	U	U	U	U	U	U
Parental Consent/Notice	NL	S	NL	S	S	NL	NL	S	S	S	NL	S	S	NL	S	S	S	NL	S	S	NL	NL	NL	NL	S	NL
Composite Score	N	S	N	S	S	N	N	S	S	N	N	S	N	N	S	S	S	N	S	S	N	N	N	N	S	N

	MT	NE	NV	NH	NJ	NM	NY	NC	ND	OH	OK	OR	PA	RI	SC	SD	TN	TX	UT	VT	VA	WA	WV	WI	WY
State Funding	S	S	U	S	S	S	S	S	NL	S	S	S	S	S	S	NL	S	S	S	S	S	S	N	S	U
Insurance Coverage	U	U	U	U	U	U	U	U	U	U	U	U	U	U	U	U	U	U	U	U	U	U	U	U	U
Parental Consent/Notice	NL	NL	NL	S	S	NL	NL	NL	NL	NL	NL	NL	NL	NL	S	S	NL	NL	NL	S	NL	NL	NL	NL	S
Composite Score	U	N	U	S	S	N	N	N	U	S	S	S	U	U	S	N	U	U	U	S	N	S	N	S	U

Source: "Teenagers' Right to Consent to Reproductive Health Care," *Issues in Brief* (Alan Guttmacher Institute, New York, 1997); "Public Funding for Contraceptive Sterilization and Abortion Services, 1994." *Family Planning Perspectives*, 28(4), July–August 1996.

KEY
S = Supportive
U = Unsupportive
NL = No Law
N = Neutral

TOTALS
State Funding: S = 37; U = 10; NL = 4
Insurance Coverage: S = 2; U = 49
Parental Consent/Notice: S = 24; NL = 27
Composite Score: S = 21; U = 13; N = 17

a variety of conditions upon abortion services (see Table 39.3).

While the U.S. Supreme Court ruled in Roe versus Wade that a woman has a fundamental right to terminate a pregnancy, opponents of the procedure have sought to limit access. SIECUS rated states which have enacted laws to limit such access as unsupportive of sexual health and sexual rights (U).

Public funding for abortion. The patchwork of state laws concerning public funding for abortion services is complex. As a result of the Hyde Amendment, the use of federal Medicaid funds for abortion is prohibited except in cases where the woman's life is in danger. The amendment was expanded in 1993 to include situations where the pregnancy resulted from rape or incest. Each state establishes its own abortion funding policy related to state revenues. Fifteen states fund abortion in their state medical assistance programs in all or most circumstances, [and] SIECUS termed them supportive (S). States which fund abortions only in highly restricted situations, such as life endangerment, rape, or incest, or those that do not fund abortions at all, were termed as unsupportive (U).

Private insurance coverage. SIECUS termed unsupportive (U) those states that ban insurance coverage for abortion unless women pay an extra premium. It gave the same rating to states that prevent access to insurance coverage for abortion in some circumstances in which public funds are used or public employees are insured. SIECUS termed states that mandated insurance coverage as supportive (S) and states that didn't have laws as no law (NL).

Abortion procedure bans. States are now considering bans on abortion procedures carried out in the second and third trimesters called "Dilation and Extraction" (D&E) and dubbed by opponents as a "partial-birth abortion." These bans prevent a physician from exercising discretion to determine the most appropriate procedure. Some courts have held that such bans are unconstitutional because they fail to provide an exception to the ban when protecting a woman's health. SIECUS rated states where abortion procedure bans are in effect, are scheduled to go into effect, or are partially in effect as unsupportive (U). States with no bans are indicated with no law (NL).

Provider violence and harassment. A nationwide campaign of blockades, harassment, and violence has impeded women's access to abortion services. SIECUS rated states which have enacted laws to protect medical personnel and women seeking services as supportive of sexual rights (S). States not offering these protections are rated unsupportive (U).

When examined as a whole, state-level protection for abortion rights reflects the public ambivalence about abortion. SIECUS found many states unsupportive because of public funding and restrictions on late-term abortions. This is troublesome because these issues address the most vulnerable populations. Also troubling is the lack of state efforts to protect its citizens from harassment and violence at legal medical facilities. Only 15 states and the District of Columbia do so.[3]

HIV / AIDS Infection

SIECUS believes that HIV testing should occur only with informed consent and that case reporting should utilize unique or coded identifiers to insure the privacy and confidentiality of the individual. Every state should provide anonymous testing. SIECUS compiled information on state laws related to HIV testing options and HIV infection reporting (see Table 39.4). Name-reporting is currently a contentious issue and many state legislatures may soon consider it.

SIECUS assigned an unsupportive (U) rating to states that use a names-based reporting system because it compromises confidentiality and is, in turn, a disincentive to testing. States that have a system of reporting that is not names-based were designated as supportive (S). States with no reporting requirements were assigned no law (NL). States offering anonymous and confidential testing sites were considered supportive (S), whereas states offering only confidential sites were termed neither (N) supportive or unsupportive, [i.e., neutral].

It appears that states are not aggressively pursuing HIV/AIDS policies that protect the privacy of individuals. States are relatively evenly divided among supportive, unsupportive, and neither. SIECUS acknowledges, however, that these two issues are in transition, and that other indicators, such as state appropriations, may prove a more definitive indication of support for HIV/AIDS prevention and treatment.[4]

Sexual Orientation

SIECUS believes that individuals have the right to accept, acknowledge, and live in accordance with their sexual orientation, whether bisexual, heterosexual, gay, or lesbian. The legal system should guarantee everyone's civil rights and protection. Prejudice and discrimination based on sexual orientation is unconscionable. SIECUS has reviewed state statutes relating to sexual orientation in such areas as workplace discrimination, public school discrimination, and the adoption of children by same-sex partners (see Table 39.5).

Table 39.3
Abortion Services

	AL	AK	AZ	AR	CA	CO	CT	DE	DC	FL	GA	HI	ID	IL	IN	IA	KS	KY	LA	ME	MD	MA	MI	MN	MS	MO
Public Funding	U	U²	U²	S	U²	U²	S	S	S	U	U²	S	U	U	U²	U³	U²	U²	U²	U²	S	U²	S	U	U¹	U²
Mandated Insurance	NL	NL	NL	U	NL	NL	NL	NL	NL	U	NL	NL	NL	NL	NL	NL	U	NL	NL	NL	NL	NL	U	NL	U	U
Parental Consent	U	S	U	U	S	U	S	U	NL	U	U	U	U	S	U	U	U	U	U	S	S	S	U	U	U	U
Waiting Periods	S	S	S	S	S	S	S	S	NL	S	S	S	U	S	U	NL	U	U	U⁵	S	S	S	S	S	U	U
Procedure Bans	U⁶	U⁷	U⁷	U⁷	NL	NL	NL	NL	NL	U⁵	U⁶	NL	U⁷	NL	U⁷	NL	U⁷	U⁷	U⁷	NL	NL	NL	U⁷	NL	U	NL
Anti-Violence Laws	NL	NL	NL	S	S	NL	S	NL	S	NL	NL	S	NL	S	S	S	NL	NL	S	S	S	S	S	S	NL	NL
Composite Score	U	U	U	U	S	U	S	U	N	U	U	S	U	U	U	U	U	U	U	U	S	S	U	U	NL	U

	MT	NE	NV	NH	NJ	NM	NY	NC	ND	OH	OK	OR	PA	RI	SC	SD	TN	TX	UT	VT	VA	WA	WV	WI	WY
Public Funding	S	U²	U²	S	U³	S	U²	U²	U	U²	U²	S	U²	U²	U¹	U²	U²	U²	S	U³	S	S	U	U²	U²
Mandated Insurance	NL	U	NL	NL	NL	U	NL	NL	NL	U	NL	NL	NL	U	NL	U	NL	NL	U	NL	NL	NL	NL	NL	NL
Parental Consent	S	U	S	U	NL	U	NL	U	U	U	U	U	U	NL	U	U	U	U	S	NL	NL	NL	U	U	NL
Waiting Periods	S	U	S	S	NL	S	NL	S	U	U	U	U	S	NL	U	U¹	U	S	U	NL	U	NL	U	NL	NL
Procedure Bans	U⁷	NL	NL	U⁷	NL	NL	NL	U⁷	U⁷	U⁷	U⁷	NL	U⁷	NL	U⁷	NL	NL	U⁴	NL	NL	NL	NL	U⁵	S	NL
Anti-Violence Laws	NL	NL	S	NL	S	NL	S	NL	NL	NL	NL	S	NL	S	NL	NL	NL	NL	S	S	S	S	NL	S	NL
Composite Score	S	U	S	S	S	S	S	U	U	U	U	S	U	S	U	U	U	U	U	N	U	S	U	S	U

Source: National Abortion and Reproductive Rights Action League, *A State-by-State Review of Abortion and Reproductive Rights* (NARAL Foundation, Washington, DC, January 1998).

1. Provide funding for abortions only when the woman's life is endangered.
2. Cover abortions for life endangerment, rape, and incest.
3. Cover abortions for life endangerment, rape, incest, and certain health circumstances.
4. "Partial-birth" abortion bans are in effect. *
5. "Partial-birth" abortion bans are scheduled to go into effect. *
6. "Partial-birth" abortion bans are partially in effect. *
7. "Partial-birth" abortion bans are blocked by state or federal court. *
* Information current as of 1998.

TOTALS
Public Funding: S = 15; U = 36
Mandated Insurance: U = 11; NL = 40
Parental Consent: S = 19, U = 31; NL = 1
Waiting Periods: S = 37; U = 14
Procedure Bans: U = 26; NL = 25
Anti-Violence Laws: S = 16; NL = 35
Composite Score: S = 21; U = 26, N = 4

KEY	
S	= Supportive
U	= Unsupportive
NL	= No Law
N	= Neutral

Table 39.4
HIV / AIDS

	AL	AK	AZ	AR	CA	CO	CT	DE	DC	FL	GA	HI	ID	IL	IN	IA	KS	KY	LA	ME	MD	MA	MI	MN	MS	MO
HIV Infection Surveillance	U	NL	U	NL	U	U	U¹	NL	NL	U	S	NL	U	S	U	S	S	U	S	U	U⁴	NL	U	U	U	U
HIV Testing Options	NL	S	S	S	S	S	S	S	S	S	S	NL	S	S	S	S	S	S	S	S	S	S	S	S	NL	S
Composite Score	U	S	N	N	N	N	N	S	S	N	N	U	S	N	N	N	N	N	N	N	N	N	N	N	N	N

	MT	NE	NV	NH	NJ	NM	NY	NC	ND	OH	OK	OR	PA	RI	SC	SD	TN	TX	UT	VT	VA	WA	WV	WI	WY
HIV Infection Surveillance	S	U	S	U	U	NL	U	S	U	U	U	U²	N	S	S	NL	NL	N	U³	U	NL	U⁴	U	U	U
HIV Testing Options	U	S	NL	S	S	S	S	S	NL	S	NL	S	NL	S	S	NL	NL	S	.S	S	S	S	S	NL	NL
Composite Score	S	N	U	N	N	N	N	N	U	N	U	N	U	N	N	U	U	U	U	N	N	N	N	N	U

Source: *Guide to Information and Resources on HIV Testing Document B053* (U.S. Centers for Disease Control and Prevention, National AIDS Clearinghouse, Atlanta, May 1997); "HIV Infection Surveillance," *AIDS Action Alerts* (U.S. Centers for Disease Control and Prevention, National AIDS Clearinghouse, Atlanta, February 1998).

1. Requires reports of HIV in children under 13 years of age by names; reports of HIV infections not required for adults/adolescents 13 years of age or older
2. Requires reports of HIV infection in children under six years of age.
3. Requires reports of HIV in children under 13 years of age by name; requires anonymous reports for adults/adolescents 13 years of age or older.
4. Requires named reporting of symptomatic HIV infection and AIDS.

TOTALS
HIV Infection Surveillance: S = 9; U = 33; NL = 9
HIV Testing Options: S = 41; NL = 10
Composite Score: S = 18; U = 10; N = 23

KEY
S = Supportive
U = Unsupportive
NL = No Law
N = Neutral

Table 39.5
Sexual Orientation

	AL	AK	AZ	AR	CA	CO	CT	DE	DC	FL	GA	HI	ID	IL	IN	IA	KS	KY	LA	ME	MD	MA	MI	MN	MS	MO
Workplace Discrimination	U	U	U	U	S	S	S	U	S	U	U	U	U	U	U	U	U	U	U	S	S	S	U	S	U	U
Public School Discrimination	NL	NL	NL	NL	U	NL	U	NL	U	NL	NL	NL	NL	NL	NL	NL	NL	NL	NL	U	NL	U	NL	U	NL	NL
Family Formation	NL	NL	NL	NL	NL	NL	NL	NL	NL	NL	NL	NL	NL	NL	NL	NL	NL	NL	NL	NL	NL	NL	NL	NL	NL	NL
Composite Score	U	U	U	U	S	U	S	U	S	U	U	U	U	U	N	U	U	U	U	S	U	S	U	S	U	U

	MT	NE	NV	NH	NJ	NM	NY	NC	ND	OH	OK	OR	PA	RI	SC	SD	TN	TX	UT	VT	VA	WA	WV	WI	WY
Workplace Discrimination	U	U	S	S	S	U	S	U	U	U	U	U	U	U	U	U	U	U	U	S	U	S	U	S	U
Public School Discrimination	NL	U	NL	NL	NL	NL	NL	NL	NL	NL	U¹	NL	NL	NL	NL	NL	NL	U¹	NL	NL	NL	NL	NL	NL	NL
Family Formation	NL	NL	NL	NL	U	NL	U	NL	NL	NL	NL	NL	NL	NL	NL	NL	NL	U	NL	NL	NL	NL	NL	NL	NL
Composite Score	U	U	U	U	U	U	U	U	U	U	U	U	U	U	U	U	U	U	U	N	U	S	U	S	U

Source: *State and Local Laws Protecting Lesbians and Gay Men Against Workplace Discrimination, Overview of Lesbian and Gay Parenting* (American Civil Liberties Union, New York, 1998).

1. Laws passed to prohibit gay student organizations from meeting on school campuses. These laws are being challenged in the courts (as of 1998).

TOTALS
Workplace Discrimination: S = 11; U = 40
Public School Discrimination: S = 2; U = 49
Family Formation: U = 2; NL = 49
Composite Score: S = 3; U = 40; N = 8

KEY	
S	= Supportive
U	= Unsupportive
NL	= No Law
N	= Neutral

Table 39.6
Sexual Behaviors

	AL	AK	AZ	AR	CA	CO	CT	DE	DC	FL	GA	HI	ID	IL	IN	IA	KS	KY	LA	ME	MD	MA	MI	MN	MS	MO
Sodomy Laws	U	S	U	U	S	S	S	S	S	U	U	S	U	S	S	S	U	S	U	S	U	U	U	U	U	U

	MT	NE	NV	NH	NJ	NM	NY	NC	ND	OH	OK	OR	PA	RI	SC	SD	TN	TX	UT	VT	VA	WA	WV	WI	WY
Sodomy Laws	S	S	S	S	S	S	S	U	S	S	U	S	S	U	U	S	S	U	U	S	U	S	S	S	S

Source: *Status of U.S. Sodomy Laws* (American Civil Liberties Union, New York, NY, 1998).

Key
S = Supportive
U = Unsupportive

TOTALS
Sodomy Laws: S = 30; U = 21

SIECUS rated states as supportive of sexual health and sexual rights if they ban discrimination on the basis of sexual orientation in the workplace and in the public school setting. It rated states without such laws as unsupportive (U) because there are no current federal protections to offset the lack of state law. It also rated states that restrict the family formation of same-sex couples as unsupportive (U).

It is clear that state laws addressing sexual orientation are the most unsupportive of sexual health and sexual rights of any covered in this article. In fact, it is the only category in which most states received unsupportive ratings.[5]

Sexual Behaviors

Sodomy laws were first initiated by religious institutions as "crimes against nature" and were later enforced by English common law in the sixteenth century. While intended to forbid anal intercourse, the definition of sodomy has broadened to include contact between the mouth and genitals. The U.S. Supreme Court ruled in *Bowers versus Hardwick* in 1986 that the Constitution allows states to criminalize sodomy. Prosecution is almost entirely limited to sexual conduct in a public place and penalties range from $200 fines to 20 years imprisonment.

Sodomy laws are now in less than half of all the states (see Table 39.6). Six states ban these sexual acts exclusively between people of the same sex (AR, KS, MD, MO, OK, TX). Fifteen states ban these sexual acts between gays and heterosexuals alike (AL, AZ, FL, GA, ID, LA, MI, MA, MN, MS, NC, RI, SC, UT, VA). All other states currently have no sodomy laws.[6]

SIECUS rated states with a sodomy law as unsupportive (U) and those with no sodomy law as supportive (S) of sexual health and sexual rights, because, in most cases, these states have taken legislative action to repeal archaic sodomy laws.

Sexual Exploitation

SIECUS believes that sexual relationships should be consensual between partners who are developmentally, physically, and emotionally capable of understanding the relationship. It believes that coerced and exploitative sexual acts and behaviors—such as rape, incest, sexual relations between adults and children, sexual abuse, and sexual harassment—are always reprehensible and should be outlawed.

SIECUS has examined laws addressing sexual exploitation through rape and sexual assault; child pornography; child prostitution; and sexual harassment in the schools. SIECUS also gathered information on state laws regarding the use of computers to exploit children and proliferate child pornography (see Table 39.7).

Sexual assault and rape. Sexual assault is any nonconsensual sexual act forced by one or more individuals upon another. The legal term *sexual assault* encompasses rape (forced vaginal intercourse), sodomy (forced anal or oral intercourse), incest, molestation, sexual battery or any unwanted touching of the sexual parts of the body. It is a felony in every state to engage in sexual penetration/intercourse where the offender causes the victim's submission through physical force. Most states also consider it a felony if the victim is incapable of consent due to physical or mental incapacitation. States prohibiting sexual assault and rape were assigned a supportive (S) rating.

Child pornography. Virtually all states have statutes on the solicitation, promotion, dissemination, or displaying of obscene matter containing a visual representation of a minor. These states legislate that sexual exploitation is committed if the child is induced to engage in any explicit sexual conduct for a commercial purpose. The definition of a minor ranges from 16 to 18 years of age depending on the state. Penalties for such crimes range from felonies to misdemeanors. States that have laws prohibiting child pornography were assigned a supportive (S) rating while states without child pornography laws were viewed as unsupportive (U).

Child prostitution. Child prostitution statutes address the inducing or employing of a child to work as a prostitute. The crime generally involves the persuasion, arrangement, or coercion of a minor for the exchange of money to provide acts such as sexual intercourse or sodomy. Most states categorize prostitution as a felony, with prison terms of three to 10 years, plus fines. While the severity of the penalties vary, states with laws prohibiting child prostitution received a supportive (S) rating and those states without child prostitution laws received an unsupportive (U) rating.

Computer-related exploitation of children. Individuals have used computers to disseminate child pornography and to meet children to solicit sexual acts. Many states have passed laws to forbid the transmission, production, and possession of computerized child pornography. Such laws make it unlawful to photograph, display, distribute, or sell pictures of minors engaged in sexual conduct via computers. Some states have also criminalized the dissemination of a minor's name for the purposes of soliciting sexual conduct. States that have passed such legislation have received a supportive (S) rating, and because of the seriousness of the issue,

states without such legislation were assigned an unsupportive (U) rating rather than no law (NL).

Sexual harassment. Sexual harassment is generally an issue decided by the courts rather than state legislatures. There is currently no compilation of states' statutes on sexual harassment, in general, or in the workplace. However, state laws on sexual harassment and discrimination in schools include statutes that address unwanted sexual advances or inappropriate sexual conduct. Many states require schools to adopt policies that prohibit sexual harassment in elementary, secondary, and post-secondary schools. SIECUS views such states as supportive (S) and states that do not have such laws as unsupportive (U).

More than in any other sexuality-related category of law, a clear majority of states determined that sexual exploitation is serious enough to merit government intervention, especially when it concerns children.[7]

Conclusion: Work Ahead

When the seven categories in this article are viewed collectively, most states were supportive of sexual rights and sexual health. Specifically: 28 states and the District of Columbia were supportive, 17 states were unsupportive of sexual rights in general, and five were somewhere between supportive and unsupportive in their policies (see Table 39.8). No state demonstrated support in every category. On the other hand, no state had exclusively unsupportive laws. There is no definitive regional trend, although states along the West Coast and in the Northeast create small pockets of overall support.

In many ways, the overview of state sexuality-related laws reflects the broad ambivalence about sexuality in America's culture. State laws are generally more focused on putting restrictions or stipulations on sexual decisions than on affirming sexual rights and healthy sexual decision making. From the perspective of state laws, sexuality is still something from which the citizens must be protected.

States have a clear consensus on protecting citizens from sexual harm. Nearly every state makes activities such as rape, child pornography, and child prostitution illegal. For other issues, states have no consensus even though some have enacted laws. For issues such as abortion and sexuality education, state laws articulate a wide variety of views. For these issues in particular, sexual rights are often governed by political considerations rather than public health and civil liberties concerns. Still, in many cases, the absence of laws speaks loudly. For sensitive and emerging issues, such as discrimination based on sexual orientation

Table 39.7
Sexual Exploitation

	AL	AK	AZ	AR	CA	CO	CT	DE	DC	FL	GA	HI	ID	IL	IN	IA	KS	KY	LA	ME	MD	MA	MI	MN	MS	MO
Rape and Sexual Assault	S	S	S	S	S	S	S	S	S	S	S	S	S	S	S	S	S	S	S	S	S	S	S	S	S	S
Child Pornography	S	S	S	S	S	S	S	S	U	S	S	S	S	S	S	S	S	S	S	S	S	S	S	S	S	S
Child Prostitution	S	S	S	S	S	S	S	U	U	S	S	S	S	S	S	S	S	U	S	U	U	S	S	S	S	S
Computer Crimes	U	U	U	U	S	U	U	U	U	S	U	U	U	U	S	U	U	U	U	S	U	U	U	S	U	U
Sexual Harassment in School Setting	U	U	U	U	U	U	U	U	U	U	U	U	U	U	U	U	U	U	U	U	U	S	S	S	U	U
Composite Score	S	S	S	S	S	S	S	S	U	S	S	S	S	S	S	S	S	S	S	S	S	S	S	S	S	S

	MT	NE	NV	NH	NJ	NM	NY	NC	ND	OH	OK	OR	PA	RI	SC	SD	TN	TX	UT	VT	VA	WA	WV	WI	WY
Rape and Sexual Assault	S	S	S	S	S	S	S	S	S	S	S	S	S	S	S	S	S	S	S	S	S	S	S	S	S
Child Pornography	S	S	S	S	S	S	S	S	S	S	S	S	S	S	S	S	S	S	U	S	S	S	S	S	U
Child Prostitution	S	S	S	S	U	S	S	S	S	S	S	S	S	S	S	U	S	S	U	U	S	S	S	S	S
Computer Crimes	U	U	U	U	U	U	U	U	U	U	S	U	U	U	U	U	U	U	U	U	U	U	U	U	U
Sexual Harassment in School Setting	U	U	U	U	U	U	U	U	U	U	U	U	U	U	U	U	U	U	U	U	U	U	U	U	U
Composite Score	S	S	S	S	S	S	S	S	S	S	S	S	S	S	S	S	S	S	S	S	S	S	S	S	S

Key

S = Supportive
U = Unsupportive

Source: *State Laws Prohibiting Sexual Harassment and Sexual Discrimination in Education* (National Organization of Women, Washington, 1996); *Child Abuse and Neglect State Statute Series, Volume V–Crime* (National Clearinghouse on Child Abuse and Neglect, Washington, DC, December 1996).

TOTALS
Rape and Sexual Assault: S = 51; U = 0
Child Pornography: S = 49; U = 2
Child Prostitution: S = 44; U = 7
Computer Crimes: S = 12; U = 39
Sexual Harassment in Schools: S = 8; U = 43
Composite Score: S = 48; U = 3

Table 39.8
Overview

	AL	AK	AZ	AR	CA	CO	CT	DE	DC	FL	GA	HI	ID	IL	IN	IA	KS	KY	LA	ME	MD	MA	MI	MN	MS	MO
Sexuality Education	S	U	U	U	S	S	U	S	S	N	U	S	U	U	U	U	U	S	U	S	S	S	U	S	N	N
Contraceptive Services	N	S	U	S	S	S	N	S	U	U	S	S	U	U	N	S	S	S	N	S	S	S	N	S	N	N
Abortion Services	U	U	S	U	S	S	S	N	S	N	S	S	U	N	N	S	S	S	N	U	S	S	N	S	U	N
HIV/AIDS	U	S	N	N	S	N	S	S	N	S	S	N	U	U	N	S	N	S	U	U	S	N	N	S	N	U
Sexual Orientation	U	U	U	U	S	N	N	N	U	U	N	U	U	U	U	U	S	U	U	S	U	U	U	S	U	U
Sexual Behaviors	U	U	U	S	S	U	S	U	S	U	U	U	U	U	U	U	U	U	U	S	U	S	U	U	U	U
Sexual Exploitation	S	S	S	S	S	S	S	S	U	S	S	S	U	U	S	S	S	S	S	U	S	S	U	S	S	U
Total Composite Score	U	U	U	U	S	S	S	S	U	N	U	S	U	U	N	S	S	S	N	U	S	S	N	S	N	N

	MT	NE	NV	NH	NJ	NM	NY	NC	ND	OH	OK	OR	PA	RI	SC	SD	TN	TX	UT	VT	VA	WA	WV	WI	WY
Sexuality Education	U	N	S	S	S	S	S	U	N	S	N	S	U	S	S	S	S	U	S	S	S	N	S	S	U
Contraceptive Services	S	U	N	S	S	U	S	N	S	S	S	U	N	U	S	U	U	U	S	S	N	S	N	S	U
Abortion Services	S	N	S	N	S	S	U	U	U	N	S	S	U	U	U	S	U	N	S	S	N	S	N	S	U
HIV/AIDS	N	S	N	S	U	N	U	N	N	S	S	U	U	S	U	N	U	N	S	N	N	U	N	U	U
Sexual Orientation	U	U	N	U	U	U	U	U	U	U	U	U	N	U	U	U	U	U	N	U	U	U	N	U	U
Sexual Behaviors	S	S	S	S	S	S	S	S	S	U	S	S	S	U	S	S	S	U	U	S	S	S	S	S	S
Sexual Exploitation	S	S	S	S	S	S	U	S	S	N	S	S	S	S	S	U	S	S	U	S	S	S	S	S	U
Total Composite Score	S	U	S	S	S	S	U	U	N	S	S	U	U	S	S	U	U	U	S	S	S	S	S	S	U

KEY

S = Supportive
U = Unsupportive
N = Neutral

and sexual harassment, states have yet to pass laws that would protect their citizens from harm.

Although this collection of state sexuality laws indicates that states generally support sexual health and sexual rights, even this preliminary overview attests that every state has work to do in developing state laws to support sexual rights and sexual health. SIECUS will continue to expand the scope and depth of information that it makes available on state laws and policies. This article is its preliminary examination of these issues. SIECUS will post these and subsequent findings on a state policy section of its Web page (www.siecus.org). Advocates of sexual rights will want to check it regularly as state laws change.

References

1. *A State-by-State Review of Abortion and Reproductive Rights,* National Abortion and Reproductive Rights Action League (NARAL Foundation, Washington, DC, January 1998).
2. T. Sollom, et al., "Public Funding for Contraceptive, Sterilization, and Abortion Services, 1994," *Family Planning Perspectives,* vol. 28, no. 4, July–August 1996; R. Posner and K. Silbaugh, *A Guide to America's Sex Laws* (Chicago, University of Chicago, 1996); *Teenagers' Right to Consent* (The Alan Guttmacher Institute, Washington, DC, 1997).
3. *A State-by-State Review of Abortion and Reproductive Rights. NARAL Foundation* (National Abortion and Reproductive Rights Action League, Washington, DC, January 1998); "Late Term Abortions: Legal Consideration," *Issues in Brief* (The Alan Guttmacher Institute, New York, NY, January 1997); "So-Called Partial Birth Abortions," *Issues in Brief* (The Alan Guttmacher Institute, New York, NY, April 1998); *The Appropriations Process and Discriminatory Abortion Funding Restriction* (National Abortion and Reproductive Rights Action League, Washington, DC, 1998); *Constitutional Analysis of H.R. 1122* (National Abortion and Reproductive Rights Action League, Washington, DC, 1998); *Mandatory Waiting Periods and the Freedom to Choose* (National Abortion and Reproductive Rights Action League, Washington, DC, 1998).
4. *HIV Surveillance and Name Reporting: A Public Health Case for Protecting Civil Liberties* (American Civil Liberties Union, New York, NY, 1997); "HIV Infection Surveillance," *AIDS Action Alerts* (AIDS Action Council, Washington, DC, February 1998); *Guide to Information and Resources on HIV Testing, Document #B053* (U.S. Centers for Disease Control and Prevention, National AIDS Clearinghouse, Atlanta, GA, May 1997).
5. *Hostile Climate: A State-by-State Report on Anti-Gay Activity* (People for the American Way, Washington, DC, 1997); *Measuring Up: Assessing State Policies to Promote Adolescent Sexual and Reproductive Health* (Advocates for Youth, Washington, DC, 1998); *Overview on Lesbian and Gay Parenting* (American Civil Liberties Union, New York, NY, May 1998); *State and Local Laws Protecting Lesbians and Gay Men Against Workplace Discrimination* (American Civil Liberties Union, New York, NY, November 1997).
6. *Status of U.S. Sodomy Laws* (American Civil Liberties Union, New York, NY, 1998).
7. *Child Abuse and Neglect State Statutes Series. Volume V—Crimes* (National Clearinghouse on Child Abuse and Neglect, Washington, DC, December 1996); *State Laws Prohibiting Sexual Harassment and Sexual Discrimination in Education* (National Organization for Women); R. Posner and K. Silbaugh, *A Guide to America's Sex Laws* (Chicago, University of Chicago, 1996).

Chapter 40
Sex, God, & Greed

Daniel Lyons

It is hard to imagine a more fascinating title for an article than "Sex, God, & Greed," or a thesis sentence more intriguing. Your assignment as a reader is to look for underlying meanings and connections in this fascinating piece by Daniel Lyons of Forbes. *In analyzing the religious, economic, and ethical issues that are raised, you may wonder if there are hidden motivations by the principal players? Are there personal agendas, or professional ones? Or, are there no underlying meanings? Did this Associate Editor do such a great job of writing and laying out the facts that you have no remaining questions about the subject? Hopefully not. Lyons himself would be disappointed were this the case. Perhaps the point of his article is that there are still "bigger than life" challenges about the relationships of these subjects to which you, as a young educated person in charge of the next generation, must respond.*

Following the publication of Lyons' article in February 2004, two anxiously awaited commissioned reports about priests in the Catholic Church who had been accused of sexual abuse were heralded in the print and broadcast media. One report was based on a survey of U.S. Catholic Dioceses conducted by the John Jay College of Criminal Justice to determine the number of abuse cases since 1950 and the action or inaction of the American Catholic Church hierarchy to them. The other report, developed by the 12-member National Review Board, a lay panel appointed by the U.S. Conference of Catholic Bishops, was concerned with the causes and context of the crisis itself (Cooperman and Murphy 2004).

Among the findings of the year-long John Jay survey was that 4 percent of all Catholic priests who have served in the United States since 1950 have been accused of sexually abusing minors, and that 81 percent of the victims were boys, with the majority being between the ages of 11 and 14 (Cooperman and Murphy 2004). The Review Board, in its report, reached two overarching conclusions. First, seminaries in the 1960s and 1970s failed to screen out psychologically immature and dysfunctional candidates for the priesthood. Second, seminaries failed to prepare priest candidates for a life of celibacy. The Review Board concluded that the requirement of celibacy

now in place was a subject for future study (Cooperman and Murphy 2004). These findings and conclusions were described as horrific and tragic by Andrew Greeley, a priest and sociologist, who himself has been writing about the evils of sexual abuse for two decades. But, Greeley then takes what may first appear to be a surprising turn by defending celibacy. In an op-ed article in the New York Times, *"For Priests, Celibacy Is Not Enough," he deftly reframes the issues with cogent arguments supporting his contentions that celibacy is not the problem driving sexual abuse by priests (Greeley 2004).*

This chapter must be considered thoughtfully in order to avoid missing the nuances and numerous pathways one could take in this clash of two time-honored societal institutions: law and religion. False memory syndrome, tort reform, the Catholic Church hierarchy: these are all possible destinations, but the skillful interweaving of such concepts by Lyons may lead to discoveries larger than the sum of these parts.

Asbestos, tobacco, guns, lead paint. What's the next jackpot for tort lawyers? It could be sex.

The focal point of this tort battle is the Catholic Church. The Church's legal problems are worse even than most people realize: $1 billion in damages already paid out for the victims of pedophile priests, indications that the total will approach $5 billion before the crisis is over. But this wave of litigation does not end here. Is there any reason to think that the priesthood has a monopoly on child molestation? The lawyers who are winning settlements from Catholic dioceses are already casting about for the next targets: schools, government agencies, daycare centers, police departments, Indian reservations, Hollywood. Plaintiff lawyer Roderick MacLeish Jr. and other litigators have parlayed the priest crisis into a billion-dollar money machine, fueled by lethal legal tactics, shrewd use of the media and public outrage so fierce that almost any claim, no matter how bizarre or dated, offers a shot at a windfall.

The lawyers are lobbying states to lift the statute of limitations on sex abuse cases, letting them dredge up complaints that date back decades. Last year California, responding to the outcry over the rash of priest cases, suspended its statute of limitations on sex abuse crimes for one year, opening the way for a deluge of new claims. A dozen other states are being pushed to loosen their laws.

"There is an absolute explosion of sexual abuse litigation, and there will continue to be. This is going to be a huge business," MacLeish, age 50, says. A Boston-based partner of the Miami law firm of Greenberg Traurig (2002 billings: $465 million), he has won upwards of $30 million in settlements for more than a hundred plaintiffs in lawsuits in the past decade. With a hit man's style and a gift for TV sound bites, he has played a key role in unearthing (and exploiting) the priest scandals of the past two years, prompting a nationwide cascade of similar reports.

In the resulting wave of lawsuits the majority of cases are legitimate, even officials of the Catholic Church concur. Dioceses will pay dearly for covering up the most abominable crimes and failing to prevent future offenses.

Overdue justice. But it could lead to a legal morass marked by extortion as much as fairness, in which a small cast of liars cashes in on the real suffering of victims. "Just think how this ripples out: daycare, babysitters, Boy Scouts, Girl Scouts, summer camps, study-abroad programs. You start thinking about it, and it boggles the mind," says Patrick Schiltz, Associate Dean of the Law School at the University of St. Thomas in Minneapolis, Minn. "There is impact in the tens of billions of dollars."

For Roderick MacLeish, sex litigation is a big business. MacLeish says he represents 240 people bringing abuse claims against the Roman Catholic Archdiocese of Boston. His most celebrated current case also is his most dubious one: three young men who tell lurid tales of being viciously and repeatedly assaulted in the 1980s by the Rev. Paul R. Shanley. Shanley, 72, has denied the charges but declines further comment. He makes an easy target. In 1994 the Archdiocese paid out settlements to an undisclosed number of people, including two clients represented by MacLeish, who said Shanley had molested them when they were teenagers. As part of the settlement Shanley had to be removed from ministry while he got treatment.

There's just one problem. MacLeish's three new clients were friends and former classmates, and all three claim they had blocked out all memory of these brutal anal rapes for more than a decade—what some psychologists call "repressed memory." Is it possible that the very notion is bunk?

Moreover, MacLeish's client, Gregory Ford, 25, of Newton, Mass., has spent time in 17 mental institutions and halfway houses and is on antipsychotic medication and unable to work, his parents say. In the past he has threatened to kill his father. Archdiocese lawyers believe Greg may previously have said he was molested by his father and a cousin; his parents deny it. Yet a Massachusetts Superior Court judge has allowed this case to proceed, which attests to MacLeish's considerable skills in court and in front of news cameras. "These are strong cases, and we are pushing them to trial," MacLeish insists. "We are going to pound and pound and pound."

Child sexual abuse litigation will probably not generate anything like the settlements for, say, asbestos claims ($54 billion to date). But, like asbestos litigation, it has the potential to snowball, with profits from early settlements financing the recruiting of an ever-widening ring of plaintiffs. Among the cases in this gold rush:

- In Florida, a lawyer who has filed numerous suits against Miami's Catholic Archdiocese filed a class suit on behalf of up to 100,000 Native Americans who allegedly were mentally, physically and sexually abused in government-run boarding schools. Attorney Jeffrey M. Herman says the suit, filed in April in the U.S. Court of Federal Claims in Washington, DC, asserts that damages could run as high as $25 billion. Canada faces a similar claim from up to 18,000 Native Americans and estimates it will spend $1.2 billion (U.S.) to settle it.

- In California, Beverly Hills lawyer Raymond Boucher, who has filed more than one hundred claims against various dioceses, recently filed a sex suit against the Elite Modeling Agency. His client is a former fashion model who claims Elite's founder, John Casablancas, impregnated her 15 years ago when she was a teenager. The Los Angeles Superior Court tossed out the claim against Casablancas because he doesn't live in California, but it let the case against Elite go ahead. Boucher says he has more claims coming against Elite, and that he may pursue cases involving Hollywood, where sexual abuse of children, he asserts, has been rampant for decades.

- In Los Angeles a man claiming recovered memory and exploiting the lifted statute of limitations has sued the Police Department and the Boy Scouts of America. He alleges that, 25 years ago in a Police Explorers program, he was molested by David Kalish, now the city's Deputy Police Chief. The city has suspended Kalish with pay. A grand jury is investigating. Meanwhile, the Los Angeles Archdiocese faces a claim based on an incident alleged to have occurred in 1931, though it says it has never heard of the priest named in the complaint. Last year a nun sued the diocese and charged that, 19 years ago, a priest raped her and fathered her son—in the Philippines. The case was tossed out.

- In Vernon Hills, Ill. two women sued a Children's World Day Care Center, accusing a staff member of molesting their two daughters, ages 5 and 11, and seeking $15 million each. Police dropped related criminal charges as unprovable—but the day care center settled civil claims for an undisclosed amount.

- Two Arizona women have sued the Tucson Diocese, alleging a priest molested their two brothers, causing the brothers to then molest them. In Louisville, Ky. a former topless dancer has sued the Church, claiming a priest kissed her 20 years ago. In Rockville Centre, N.Y. a lawyer seeks $1.6 billion from the diocese—on behalf of only 11 men, one of whom says he was molested once.

The frenzy stems from a decade-long campaign by plaintiff lawyers, says Schiltz of St. Thomas University, who has defended religious organizations in more than 500 sex abuse lawsuits. "It's like warfare," he says. "*Phase One* was for plaintiff lawyers to maximize bad publicity and destroy the credibility of the Church. *Phase Two* is to use that publicity to push for legislative changes. *Phase Three* will be to collect." The problem, he says, is that fraudulent claims could get paid off with legitimate ones. "Who's going to doubt them? I worry about the person who was an altar boy 30 years ago, and his life has been a disappointment, and now he realizes he has a lottery ticket in his pocket."

More than 500 cases are pending against the Boston Archdiocese, with at least a thousand more claims against Catholic dioceses nationwide. Some lawyers estimate as many as 20,000 people were molested by Catholic clergy in the United States in recent decades. And for every Catholic victim, Schiltz estimates even more may have been harmed by clergy of other faiths. These cases, moreover, MacLeish says, will prompt more victims of nonclergy abuse to come forward as people feel less stigmatized.

The lawyers help make that possible. In Los Angeles, Raymond Boucher has 220 clients and is trying to form a class action. His Web site boasts a list of priests who have been convicted or accused of sexual abuse and a "secure victim form" that lets visitors click their way to a confidential complaint. Boucher's office also provides space to a "victim advocate," who has been contacting hundreds of possible victims, though Boucher insists this is for outreach, not for recruiting.

In Minnesota, attorney Jeffrey Anderson, with more than 700 past clergy cases and 250 pending, aims to use the Racketeer Influenced & Corrupt Organization Act (RICO), arguing bishops conspired in a coverup. He also is trying to sue the Vatican, complete with a complaint he had translated into Latin.

Some of these cases are likely to bankrupt some Catholic dioceses, but this legal assault seeks even deeper pockets: big insurers. Put aside the pious talk about protecting kids, and the racket boils down to this: Plaintiff lawyers are going after old insurance policies written decades ago under entirely different circumstances. Boucher says he has found two insurers with big exposure in Los Angeles. Pacific Indemnity, a subsidiary of Chubb Group, wrote policies from the early 1950s to 1967 and could be on the hook for several hundred million, Boucher says. Chubb says any effect won't be material. Allianz Insurance Co., a U.S. subsidiary of Munich-based Allianz Group, wrote policies from 1979 to 1986 and could be responsible for more than $20 billion, Boucher insists. Allianz calls this estimate "grossly off-base."

Also at risk are the big companies that run daycare centers, such as KinderCare and Bright Horizons, both publicly held, and Children's World, which recently was acquired by Michael Milken's Knowledge Universe. These companies already are feeling the crunch: In some cases their insurance costs have risen by 20 percent to 30 percent, and a trickle of new abuse lawsuits has begun. The flow could quicken if more states lift their statutes of limitations, making it easier for repressed memory cases to proceed and all the harder for the accused to disprove allegations.

The False Memory Syndrome Foundation, a Philadelphia debunking group, says at least 100 clergy cases involve people who claim they were molested or raped, blocked it out for decades and now suddenly remember. "The notion that the mind protects itself by banishing the most disturbing, terrifying events is psychiatric folklore," declares Richard J. McNally, a Harvard Psychology Professor who has conducted a six-year study of abuse victims and has written a book, *Remembering Trauma*, to dispel myths of memory repression. "The more traumatic and stressful something is, the less likely someone is to forget it."

Yet in MacLeish's biggest case his three clients claim they recovered their memories only after the *Boston Globe* ran a long story on Jan. 31, 2002, describing other people's complaints against Shanley. He had been a popular "street priest" who wore jeans, grew his hair long and preached to street urchins and runaways. Ordained in 1960, he served in several parishes around Boston before moving in 1990 to California and working part-time as a priest in San Bernardino. He was dismissed in 1993 after the first charges surfaced in Boston.

The *Globe* story painted a plausible picture of a monstrous serial rapist who preyed on teenage boys, anally raping several victims and luring one to his bedroom for a game of strip poker. In Newton, Mass., Greg Ford's parents, Rodney and Paula Ford, read the article and immediately concluded that Shanley must have molested their son. For years they had wondered what had gone wrong with Greg, who they say was a healthy, normal boy until he was 13. Shanley had been a priest in their parish, St. Jean l'Evangeliste, from 1979 to 1990, by which time Greg was 12.

As his parents tell it, in years of therapy Greg had tried, unsuccessfully, to recall being molested by anyone. When his parents showed him the *Globe* article, he didn't remember Shanley or recognize his photograph. The Fords persisted, showing Greg a snapshot from his First Communion with Shanley. At last Greg collapsed, sobbing, and said that from age 6 to 11 he had been raped by the priest.

Later he estimated this happened 80 times. He alleged that Shanley took him from his one-hour Sunday school class, raped him, then returned him to his classmates. Verona Mazzei, who was Director of the Sunday school program, says she never saw Shanley take any kids from class. The Fords say Greg never exhibited any unusual behavior during these years. "As soon as it happened, each time he left that room, he forgot about it," Rodney Ford says. "The specialists he sees now are amazed that he could block this out, that he had such control."

When the Fords contacted MacLeish, he signed on. His first clergy killing came in 1992—a multi-million-dollar settlement on behalf of 101 clients in Fall River, Mass. A couple of years later he negotiated two settlements against Shanley, which were described in the *Globe* article. As MacLeish began to check out Ford's complaint, the case took an amazing twist: Two of Greg's friends also began to recover memories about Shanley assaults.

Paul Busa, 26, an Air Force policeman in Colorado, says that after hearing about the *Globe* story he, too, began to recover long-buried memories of being raped by the priest. Greg's parents said Busa called them. MacLeish says Busa called him too. Soon afterward MacLeish bought Busa a plane ticket to Boston, had him evaluated by a shrink, then took him on as a client.

In March 2002 MacLeish and Greg Ford met with Anthony Driscoll, also of Newton, Mass., and discussed a story Ford told about sitting on a pencil that Driscoll had placed on his chair in Sunday school class when they were 11 years old. Greg had received medical treatment, but now he claims that while he was waiting to go to the hospital, Shanley raped him. Doctors who treated the wound made no mention of sexual assault. "Even the doctors missed it," Rodney Ford says.

Driscoll confirmed the story—and asked MacLeish to recommend a psychologist because Driscoll, too, had been having flashbacks of being assaulted. One rape was punishment for the pencil prank, he later told Archdiocese lawyers in a deposition. He also recalls Shanley sitting naked to hear his confession, then forcing him to perform oral sex. In the same deposition Driscoll describes a past that includes an arrest for credit card fraud and juvenile charges of indecent assault. MacLeish referred Driscoll to a psychiatrist—and signed him up.

In April 2002 MacLeish and the Fords staged a press conference carried live on CNN, at which MacLeish released parts of Shanley's 800-page file and rocketed the Ford complaint to the forefront of cases nationwide. Rodney and Paula Ford appeared on *Good Morning America, Today, Dateline NBC, CNN,* and *Fox News*. They gave interviews to *Vanity Fair* and *USA Today*. Journalists were calling from around the world. "France, Australia, Sweden—the phone never stops ringing," says Rodney Ford, who has taken a leave of absence from his job as a cop at Boston College to become an advocate for sex abuse victims.

They also pursued criminal charges. Within weeks Shanley was arrested in California, extradited to Boston and arraigned. In July a grand jury indicted him on ten counts of child rape after hearing from Daniel Brown, a Boston psychologist who believes recovered memories may be valid, even when they involve far-out things like Satanic ritual abuse.

Since then MacLeish has outspun the Archdiocese at every turn. He has grilled bishops in videotaped depositions, obtained psychiatric evaluations and 45,000 pages of archdiocese memos and spoon-fed all of it to the press. He helpfully underscores the most lurid details. Yet he protested bitterly when the Archdiocese deposed shrinks who are treating his clients—standard procedure when someone claims emotional distress.

This lawyer relishes juicy cases. In 1995 he successfully defended Harvard Medical School psychiatrist John Mack, who was threatened with losing his tenure after he published a book arguing that alien abductions were real. He successfully defended Lars Bildman, disgraced chief executive of drugmaker Astra USA, against sexual harassment complaints. He also defended a Cape Cod high school teacher who got fired for making porno films in his spare time and he generated headlines when he sued the elderly wife of an alleged pedophile, collecting on her homeowner's policy.

In his assault on the Catholic Church, MacLeish uses the press to inflict pain and then pushes for a big settlement. But instead of retreating, the Boston Archdiocese has hired a killer litigator, Boston veteran Timothy O'Neill, 62, who for years has helped hospitals stave off medical malpractice lawsuits and also has defended priests against sexual abuse claims. In January O'Neill outraged victim advocates by deposing a therapist for Anthony Driscoll.

O'Neill now is pursuing half a dozen therapists who have treated Greg Ford in the past.

Archdiocese lawyers say Greg Ford's medical records and a deposition from his sister indicate he previously said others had molested him, including a cousin and his own father. MacLeish and the Fords say this is nonsense and held another press conference, where they complained about the tactics. The Fords are flabbergasted that the Archdiocese dares to challenge their claim. "Can you imagine the Archdiocese of Boston dragging the families of abuse victims into court? Are they nuts?" says Paula Ford.

O'Neill says the Church cannot operate like an ATM machine, dispensing cash to anyone who drives up with a claim. And he is eager to put Ford, Driscoll and Busa in front of a jury. "If you have a total recovered memory case, a jury is going to have trouble with that," O'Neill says.

The Boston Archdiocese—which has seen donations plunge 50 percent, is laying off workers and plans to sell 15 properties to raise cash—hopes to settle all 500-plus pending sex abuse claims in one group. MacLeish won't say how much money it would take for him to settle, but he insists that his three star clients won't take part in any group settlement.

MacLeish has three paralegals working on clergy cases and a database that tracks clergy sex abuse cases in the United States. Another tech marvel: an Optical Character Recognition system that lets MacLeish zoom through 45,000 pages of Boston Archdiocese records and pull up any page in the blink of an eye. "We're putting millions of dollars into this," he says. Even if the Shanley case falls apart, MacLeish will profit from it. In the discovery process he has dug up records on 139 other priests. He has gained a year of glowing free publicity, which has brought still more plaintiffs to his door.

MacLeish already is plotting his next career move. He says when the clergy cases end he will consult to businesses that want to protect themselves from sex abuse lawsuits. "This is now a hot-button issue. People will pay top dollar for experts with experience," he says. "I will spend a lot of time advising businesses on how they can avoid the experience of the Boston Archdiocese." His rate: $500 an hour.

Introduction References

Cooperman, A., and Murphy, C. (2004, February 29). "4% of Priests Accused of Sex Abuse, Panel Reports." *Washington Post*, p. A09.

Greeley, A. (2004, March 3). "For Priests, Celibacy Is Not Enough." *New York Times*, p. A23.

Chapter 41
Naked Capitalists

Frank Rich

In 1993, college student Marc Andreessen created the Mosaic Web Browser, the first tool that allowed ordinary people to easily explore the Internet. He then developed Netscape, a commercial version of Mosaic, and quickly became a "wealthy wunderkind" when two years later the company went public. Eventually, when he lost the browser war to Microsoft Corporation, Netscape became part of Time-Warner, Inc's AOL (Geewax 2004).

So, what is the relevance of this story? As you read Frank Rich's exposé, "Naked Capitalists," you may be reminded of the childhood fable of "Pandora's Box." If you remember, once Pandora's box was opened and the contents scattered, they could never be contained again. In the Netscape story, you may recognize Andreessen as a modern-day Pandora who opened the door to the sex industry as it is known today. The privacy provided by the technology that spawned the Internet, as well as cable television and VCRs, brought pornography to people who would never go to adult theaters or bookstores. This phenomenon, perhaps more than any other one factor, is responsible for the explosion of what is euphemistically called the "Adult Industry."

In this chapter, adapted from an article in the New York Times Magazine, you will find familiar concepts, but the context within which they are presented may be surprising. Rich has written about the astonishing relationship between pornography and capitalism with such verve that you seldom notice that the reading is an assignment. You may wonder, what are the names of Fortune 500 Corporations, such as Marriot, General Motors, AT & T, and AOL Time Warner doing in such a selection? If you stay tuned for the facts as they unfold, you may discover what most adults in the United States do not currently know. But, as you read, you may need to first lay aside your stereotypes, lest they be destroyed in the process. Then, prepare to be both entertained and informed by the author as he artfully uses the human interest approach to explore the business of adult entertainment.

Even though Rich focuses on the amazing partnership between our dollars and senses, his chapter may raise basic questions about pornography itself. Some readers may align themselves with those who wonder why pornography is allowed at all, but others may be more comfortable in the company of those who wonder, "What's the big deal? Why do some people even question its existence?" Do not expect all of your questions about pornography to be answered here. In spite of two Presidential commissioned reports on pornography, one in 1970 and the other, sixteen years later, in 1986, there still are many debatable issues about this explosive topic.

At the time the first investigation began, the greatest concern in the legal area was the interpretation of the word *obscene* (Neff 2001a). This struggle was apparent in a statement by Supreme Court Justice Potter Stewart concerning obscenity: "I shall not further attempt to define [obscenity], and perhaps I couldn't ever succeed in intelligibly doing so. But, I know it when I see it" (Jacobellis v. Ohio 1964). Previously, in 1957, the U.S. Supreme Court in Roth v. United States *had upheld laws against obscenity and found that obscene materials were not entitled to the protections accorded to "speech" in the First Amendment of the U.S. Constitution. However, during the first Commission's investigation, the Court, using* Stanley v. Georgia *(1969), modified the* Roth *decision and ruled that individuals have the right to read or view obscene materials in the privacy of their homes (Neff 2001a). Later, a legal ruling on the definition of obscenity occurred when in* Miller v. California *(1973), the U.S. Supreme Court imposed three new criteria that must be met for materials to be considered obscene:*

- *The average person, applying contemporary community standards, would find that the work, taken as a whole, appeals to the prurient interest.*

- *The work depicts/describes, in a patently offensive way, sexual conduct specifically defined by applicable state law.*

- *The work, taken as a whole, lacks serious literary, artistic, political, or scientific value.* (Miller v. California, 413 U.S. 15, 1973)

Both Presidential Commissions raised awareness levels about pornography and their findings resulted in much spirited public and professional debate. The 1970 Commission Report recommended that all legislation prohibiting the sale, exhibition, or distribution of sexual materials to consenting adults be repealed, but that legislation should prohibit such materials to children (Neff 2001a). A Minority Report was written with opposite conclusions by six dissenters, stating that pornography should be prohibited for adults. Although President Lyndon B. Johnson had commissioned the 1970 Commission Report, it was completed after President Richard B.

Nixon took office. President Nixon characterized the Report as "morally bankrupt," and the U.S. Senate voted 60 to 5 to reject and censure the Commission Report, as did other groups, such as the National Conference of Catholic Bishops (Neff 2001a).

The 1986 Report, prepared by the Meese Commission, reflected many of the same issues as did the 1970 Commission Report, except for the addition of child pornography. But, the results were dramatically different (Neff 2001b). Among the 92 recommendations of the Meese Report were conclusions such as these items:

- A linkage exists between the pornography industry and organized crime;
- A causal relationship exists between exposure to pornography and aggression toward women; and
- A need exists for criminal laws on pornography and obscenity (Neff 2001b).

The second Report received as much criticism as did the first one, but with a significant difference: while conservatives had criticized the 1970 Report for being too liberal, the liberals criticized the 1986 Report for being too conservative (Neff 2001b). The two female members of the Commission refused to sign the 1986 Report on the grounds that it was biased and did not consider all available facts. Neff concluded her excellent analysis of the Meese Commission Report by offering these observations:

> While sexually explicit materials wake strong sentiments and emotions in most people, there is no consensus on how society should respond to those beliefs. Expecting a small group of political appointees to make policy on such issues seems to only sharpen the divisions and conflicts that arise over such emotionally charged issues (Neff 2001b, 247).

Even if you were not already aware of the historical information about the two Presidential Commission Reports on pornography, as sexuality students, you probably do know more about the issues surrounding pornography than you do about the business side of the equation illuminated by Rich. As he reframes and interrelates the subjects of pornography and economics, you will be sometimes amazed, sometimes amused, but at all times informed.

In late January 1998, during the same week that America first heard the ribald tale of the President and the intern, *Variety* tucked [in] a business story that caused no stir whatsoever. Under a Hollywood dateline, the show-biz trade paper reported that the adult-video business "saw record revenues last year" of some $4.2 billion in rentals and sales. It soon became clear to me that these bicoastal stories, one from the nation's political capital and the other from its entertainment capital, were in some essential way the same story.

In the weeks that followed, Washington commentators repeatedly predicted that the public would be scandalized by the nonmissionary-position sex acts performed illicitly in the White House. But just as repeatedly, voters kept telling pollsters that they weren't blushing as brightly as, say, Cokie Roberts. The *Variety* story, I realized, may have in part explained why. An unseemly large percentage of Americans was routinely seeking out stories resembling that of the President and the intern—and raunchier ones—as daily entertainment fare.

The $4 billion that Americans spend on video pornography is larger than the annual revenue accrued by either the N.F.L., the N.B.A. or Major League Baseball. But that's literally not the half of it: the porn business is estimated to total between $10 billion and $14 billion annually in the United States when you toss in porn networks and pay-per-view movies on cable and satellite, Internet Web sites, in-room hotel movies, phone sex, sex toys and that archaic medium of my own occasionally misspent youth, magazines. Take even the low-end $10 billion estimate (from a 1998 study by Forrester Research in Cambridge, Mass.), and pornography is a bigger business than professional football, basketball and baseball put together. People pay more money for pornography in America in a year than they do on movie tickets, more than they do on all the performing arts combined. As one of the porn people I met in the industry's epicenter, the San Fernando Valley, put it, "We realized that when there are 700 million porn rentals a year, it can't just be a million perverts renting 700 videos each."

Yet in a culture where every movie gross and Nielsen rating is assessed ad infinitum in the media, the enormous branch of show business euphemistically called "adult" is covered as a backwater, not as the major industry it is. Often what coverage there is fixates disproportionately on Internet porn, which may well be the only Web business that keeps expanding after the dot-com collapse but still accounts for barely a fifth of American porn consumption. Occasionally a tony author—David Foster Wallace, George Plimpton and Martin Amis, most recently—will go slumming at a porn awards ceremony or visit a porn set to score easy laughs and even easier moral points. During sweeps weeks, local news broadcasts "investigate" adult businesses, mainly so they can display hard bodies in the guise of hard news. And of course, there is no shortage of academic literature and First Amendment debate about pornography, much of it snarled in the ideological divisions among feminists, from the antiporn absolutism of Catherine MacKinnon and Andrea Dworkin to the pro-porn revisionism of Sallie Tisdale and Susie Bright.

I'm a lifelong show-biz junkie, and what sparked my interest in the business was what I stumbled upon in *Variety*—its sheer hugeness. Size matters in the cultural marketplace. If the machinations of the mainstream TV, movie and music industries offer snapshots of the American character, doesn't this closeted entertainment behemoth tell us something as well? At $10 billion, porn is no longer a sideshow to the mainstream like, say, the $600 million Broadway theater industry—it *is* the mainstream.

And so I went to the San Fernando Valley, a.k.a. Silicone Valley, on the other side of the Hollywood Hills, to talk with the suits of the adult business. I did not see any porn scenes being shot. I did not talk to any antiporn crusaders or their civil-libertarian adversaries. I did not go to construct a moral brief. I wanted to find out how some of the top players conduct their business and how they viewed the Americans who gorge on their products.

Among other things, I learned that the adult industry is in many ways a mirror image of Hollywood. Porn movies come not only in all sexual flavors but also in all genres, from period costume dramas to sci-fi to comedy. Adult [film industry] has a fabled frontier past about which its veterans wax sentimental—the "Boogie Nights" 70s, when porn was still shot only on film and seen in adult movie theaters. (The arrival of home video revolutionized porn much as sound did Hollywood.) Adult also has its own *Variety* (*Adult Video News*), its own star-making machinery (the "girls" at Vivid and Wicked are promoted like bygone MGM contract players), its own prima donnas and cinéastes. It has (often silent) business partners in high places: two of the country's more prominent porn purveyors, Marriott (through in-room X-rated movies) and General Motors (though its ownership of the satellite giant DirecTV), were also major sponsors of the Bush-Cheney Inaugural. Porn even has its own Matt Drudge—a not-always-accurate Web industry gossip named Luke Ford, who shares his prototype's political conservatism and salacious obsessiveness yet is also, go figure, a rigorously devout convert to Judaism.

I didn't find any porn titans in gold chains, but I did meet Samantha Lewis, former real-estate saleswoman and current vice president of Digital Playground, whose best-selling "Virtual Sex" DVDs are, she says, "the Rolexes and Mercedeses of this business." I talked with Bill Asher, the head of Vivid, who is an alumnus of Dartmouth and U.S.C. (for his M.B.A.). I listened to the story of John Stagliano,

who was once a U.C.L.A. economics major with plans "to teach at the college level" but who instead followed his particular erotic obsession and became Buttman, the creator of hugely popular improvisational *cinema-vérité* porn videos that have been nicknamed "gonzo" in honor of the freewheeling literary spirit of Hunter S. Thompson. A political libertarian, [he] was for a while a big-time contributor to the Cato Institute.

If the people who make and sell pornography are this "normal"—and varied—might not the audience be, too? It can't be merely the uneducated and unemployed who shell out the $10 billion. Porn moguls describe a market as diverse as America. There's a college-age crowd that favors tattooed and pierced porn performers; there's an older, suburban audience that goes for "sweeter, nicer, cuter girls," as Bill Asher of Vivid Pictures puts it. There is geriatric porn and there's a popular video called "Fatter, Balder, Uglier." Oral sex sells particularly well in the Northeast, ethnic and interracial videos sell in cities (especially in the South), and the Sun Belt likes to see outdoor sex set by beaches and pools.

Yet such demographics are anecdotally not scientifically obtained. So few Americans fess up when asked if they are watching adult product, says Asher, "that you'd think there is no business." But in truth, there's no business like porn business. Porn is the one show that no one watches but that, miraculously, never closes.

"Porn doesn't have a demographic—it goes across all demographics," says Paul Fishbein, the compact and intense man who founded *Adult Video News*.

> There were 11,000 adult titles last year versus 400 releases in Hollywood. There are so many outlets that even if you spend just $15,000 and two days—and put in some plot and good-looking people and decent sex—you can get satellite and cable sales. There are so many companies, and they rarely go out of business. You have to be really stupid or greedy to fail.

He points me toward the larger producers whose videos top *AVNs* charts and have the widest TV distribution. There are many successful companies, but some of them cater to niche markets (like gay men) that as of yet haven't cracked the national mass market of TV, where pay-per-view pornographic movies, though priced two or three times higher and not promoted, often outsell the Hollywood hits competing head to head. In a business with no barrier to entry—anyone with a video camera can be a director or star—there are also countless bottom feeders selling nasty loops on used tape. Whatever the quality or origin of a product, it can at the very least be exhibited on one of the 70,000 adult pay Web sites, about a quarter of which are owned by a few privately held companies that slice and dice the same content under different brands.

Fishbein has a staff of 62 to track it all. He seems smart, sensible and mercurial—in other words, just like any other successful editor. And like almost everyone else I met in porn, he says he fell into it by accident. While a journalism student at Temple University in his hometown, Philadelphia, he managed a video store and found that customers kept asking him how to differentiate one adult tape from another. It was the early 80s, and the VCR was starting to conquer America, its popularity in large part driven by the easier and more anonymous access it offered to porn. Prior to home video, pornography had a far smaller audience, limited mainly to men willing to venture into the muck of a Pussycat Cinema—the "raincoaters," as the trade refers to that dying breed of paleo-consumer. The VCR took porn into America's bedrooms and living rooms—and, by happenstance, did so at the same time that the spread of AIDS began to give sexual adventurers a reason to stay home. There is no safer sex than porn.

As adult titles on tape proliferated, Fishbein started a newsletter to rate them. Other videostore owners, uncertain about which porn films to stock, took a look. Now, some 18 years later, Fishbein runs an empire that includes 10 Web sites and spinoff journals like *AVN Online*. He also stages trade shows and presents the *AVN* Awards in Vegas in January. An issue of *AVN* can run in excess of 350 slick pages, much of it advertising, in which a daunting number of reviews (some 400 a month) jostle for space with sober reportage like "For Adult, Ashcroft Signals Circle the Wagons Time." Fishbein has a soft spot for porn veterans like Al Goldstein, the 65-year-old paterfamilias of *Screw* magazine who writes a column for Fishbein's main Web site, *AVN.com*, in which Goldstein sometimes rails against the new corporate generation of pornographers who have no memory of the daring and sacrifice of their elders. "Al Goldstein took 19 arrests for this business," Fishbein says reverently.

Though he embodies the corporatization of porn, Fishbein exudes a certain swagger:

I'm here by accident, and now that I'm here, I'm proud of what I do, he says. My mother sits at my awards table each year when girls accept awards for oral sex. Sex sells and it drives the media, and it always has. Billboards, movies, ads, commercials. It's what we're thinking about at all times of the day. We're told it's bad, and it manifests itself as political debates.

Fishbein assures me that he has no "naked girls running through the office," and alas, he is right—though a staff member does wander in with a photo

to ask, "Was that the naked sushi party?" But there's a pleasant buzz and bustle about the place—one I associate with journalism. "This could be a magazine about pens and pencils," Fishbein says.

The browsers on the two computers behind his desk are kept on *CNN.com* and *AVN.com*, which is modeled on CNN's as a (porn) news portal. The décor of his large, meticulous office is mostly movie memorabilia. A film buff as well as a news junkie, Fishbein is a particular fan of the high-end comedies of Woody Allen, Albert Brooks and Preston Sturges, and he could be a highly articulate, slightly neurotic leading man out of one of them. He speaks glowingly of having just taken his 12-year-old stepdaughter to "Yi Yi." Does he watch the movies that *AVN* reviews? He flinches. "I haven't watched an adult movie without fast-forwarding since I saw one in a theater at 18. I watch them for business reasons. My wife and I don't watch them for entertainment. It is hard for me to look at it as more than product."

Many of the top porn producers are within blocks of Fishbein's office in the utterly anonymous town of Chatsworth—an unhurried, nondescript sprawl of faded strip malls, housing developments and low-slung (and usually unmarked) business complexes that look more like suburban orthodontic offices than porn factories. Everyone in the business seems to know one another. "There's a certain camaraderie among those who are on the fringe of society, a similarity to outlaws," Fishbein says. Yet he seems like anything but an outlaw; he was about to fly off to the Super Bowl and then a skiing vacation. I ask if organized crime is a factor in today's porn world. "When I got here, I heard there were mob companies," he answers. "But I've never even been approached by a criminal element. I've never been threatened or bribed. So if it ever existed, it's part of the history of the business." He almost sounds disappointed.

Russell Hampshire, who owns one of the biggest companies, VCA Pictures, did do time in jail—nine months in 1988 for shipping obscene videotapes across state lines to federal agents in Alabama. [He], who runs VCA with his wife of 10 years, Betty, has an Oscar Madison look—Hawaiian shirts, gym shorts and a baseball cap. I wouldn't want to get on his bad side. He's big and leathery and sounds like Lee Marvin as written by Damon Runyon. Asked why the sign outside says "Tray Tech" instead of VCA, he says he wants to stay "as innoculous as possible."

He has been in the business since 1978 and waxes nostalgic for the early video days, when you could transfer a prevideo Marilyn Chambers classic to cassette and sell it wholesale for up to a hundred bucks. Now his top movies wholesale for $18 or $19, sometimes lower. "There used to be only 10 to 12 titles to choose from in a video store," he says. "Now there are thousands of titles." A typical release may sell only 2,000 units or less—7,500 would be a modest hit—but thanks to TV and international sales, Hampshire says he makes money "on every title." Though the total income from a hit is pocket money by Hollywood standards, Hollywood should only have such profit margins. An adult film that brings in $250,000 may cost only $50,000 to make—five times the original investment. Production locations are often rented homes, shooting schedules run less than a week, and most projects are not shot on the costly medium of film. There are no unions or residuals. Marketing costs are tiny since quote ads run in *AVN* and skin magazines, not in national publications or on TV. Most economically of all, porn movies don't carry the huge expense of theatrical distribution: video killed off adult movie theaters far more effectively than it did regular movie theaters.

Still, Hampshire resents the lower overhead of porn's newcomers: "I have 80 employees. I have a 100 percent medical plan for everyone's family—dental and vision care too. Some of my guys have been working here 17 or 18 years. And I'm up against amateurs with $800 Handicams." He also grouses about the new administration in Washington, as many in the industry do, fearing there could be a replay of the war on porn during the Reagan years, when Attorney General Edwin Meese called for restrictions on live sex shows and the dissemination of pornographic materials. "I like the rest of Bush's cabinet—just not Ashcroft," Hampshire says.

With the company's in-house press rep, a former preschool teacher named Mischa Allen, in tow, Hampshire takes me on a tour of VCA's 40,000-square-foot operation, proudly showing off the state-of-the-art video-editing bays, the room containing 3,000 video-duplication decks (churning out 400,000 tapes a month) and the prop room in which I spot a neon sign for "Bada Boom" from the set of the recent "Sopornos 2." The mechanized assembly line on which the tapes are boxed and shrink-wrapped is as efficient as that for bottling Coke.

But more than anything, VCA resembles the corporate headquarters of a sports franchise. Only on close inspection do I realize that a towering glass case full of what look like trophies in the reception area in fact contains awards such as the 1996 Best Group Sex Scene, bestowed upon the "Staircase Orgy" from "New Wave Hookers 4." Hampshire, an avid golfer and bowler, has lined VCA's corridors with his collection of autographed sports jerseys, the latest from Tiger Woods. On one wall are plaques of appreciation from the Hampshires' philanthropic beneficiaries, including a local school to which they donate video equipment and free yearbook printing.

Hampshire's own office is spacious, outfitted with leather furniture, but—characteristically for the business—looks like a bunker. Above his desk is a console of TV screens tuned into the feeds from security cameras. Incongruously, this inner sanctum's walls are festooned with another variety of pompously framed "collectibles"—autographed letters and photographs from Anwar Sadat, Menachem Begin, Jimmy Carter and Richard Nixon. Hampshire says they're all copies, but he points to a melted-looking clock and says, "I've got Salvador Dalis all over the place—*authentic* Salvador Dalis." He also shows off a vintage group photo of Murder, Inc.

He almost never goes to a set, where the hurry-up-and-wait pace makes it as "boring as Hollywood." He ticks off his duties: "Dealing with distributors and OSHA rules and regulations. I have to write reviews of all my department heads and decide raises."

As I leave his office I notice still another framed artifact: a Bronze Star for "exceptionally valorous action on 12/8/67" while serving as a Company C rifleman in combat in Vietnam. The citation says that Hampshire "continually exposed himself to hostile fire" while saving the lives of his fellow soldiers. It's the only thing that seems to embarrass him. "I buried it for so long," he says. "When I first came out here, I was ashamed to say anything because people might say I'm a bad person."

Almost every adult company is pursuing innovative media, preparing for Internet broadband and interactive hotel-room TV. At Wicked Pictures' newly revamped Web site, for instance, a visitor can cross-index a particular porn star with a sexual activity, then watch (and pay for) just those scenes that match. Digital Playground's "Virtual Sex" DVDs resemble video games in how they allow the user to control and inject himself into the "action."

As in nonadult video, DVD is cutting into videocassette sales—even more so in adult, perhaps, because DVDs have the added virtue of being more easily camouflaged on a shelf than cassettes. Hampshire is particularly proud of VCA's DVD technology. With his vast catalog, he is following the model of Hollywood studios by rereleasing classics—"The Devil in Miss Jones 2," "The Opening of Misty Beethoven"—in "Collectors Editions," replete with aural commentaries from original stars like Jamie Gillis. As with Hollywood's DVD rereleases, they are pitched at nostalgic consumers in the "boomer-retro" market. "These aren't 'adult'—they're pop culture now," says Mischa Allen.

But VCA aims far higher than merely recycling golden oldies. In a windowless VCA office, I meet Wit Maverick, the head of its DVD production unit. He is 37, and with his blue Oxford shirt, goatee and glasses, he could be a professor somewhere—perhaps at Cal Arts, where he got a masters in film directing. He ended up at VCA, he says, because it was "the best opportunity to push the envelope of technology."

Maverick knocks mainstream studios for providing only a linear cinematic experience on their DVD's. "There's a great hubris in Hollywood," he says. "They think the way the director made the film is the only way the story can be told. We have a lot more humility. If a viewer wants something different, we give it to him." As an example he cites "Being With Juli Ashton," VCA's take on "Being John Malkovich." The viewer, Maverick says, "can go inside the head of the person having sex with Juli Ashton, male or female. He can choose which character to follow. He can re-edit the movie. Would James Cameron let anyone do that with 'Titanic'? I feel like filmmakers 100 years ago," Maverick continues. "It's a great technology, but we still don't know what to do with it. A hundred years from now I want grad students to read what I've done on DVD the way I read about D.W Griffith."

Wit Maverick collaborates on his DVDs at VCA with Veronica Hart, 44, one of the business's most prominent female executives and, before that, a leading porn star of the late 70s and early 80s. Universally known as Janie—her real name is Jane Hamilton—she is typical of the mostly likable people I met in the porn world. She combines hard-headed show-biz savvy and humor with an utter lack of pretension and even some actual candor—a combination unheard of on the other side of the hills.

"The difference between us and Hollywood," she elaborates, "is money and ego. We deal with thousands of dollars, not millions. In mainstream, people are more cutthroat and pumped up about themselves. We're just like regular people—it has to do with exposing yourself. If you show something this intimate, there isn't a lot you can hide behind. You're a little more down to earth. We're not curing cancer. We're providing entertainment."

Hart studied theater at the University of Nevada in her hometown, Las Vegas. After acting leads in plays by Pinter and García Lorca—as far east as Kennedy Center's annual college theater festival—she passed through the music business in England and worked as a secretary at *Psychology Today* magazine in New York before ending up in movies like "Wanda Whips Wall Street." While we are talking in her office she looks up Veronica Hart's 100-plus performing credits on the Internet, including some non-hard-core B movies with faded mainstream actors like Farley Granger and Linda Blair. "In this one I played a stripper," she says while scrolling down the list. "*That* was a real stretch."

She pulls back from the computer screen and sums up her career: "I was lucky enough to be a performer in the golden age of porn cinema. I'm no raving beauty, and I don't have the best body in the world, but I look approachable. And I've always really enjoyed sex." More recently, she played a cameo as a judge in "Boogie Nights," but she disputes that movie's historical accuracy about porn's prevideo age. "We never shot in L.A. back then, only in New York and San Francisco," she says. Indeed, adult exactly mimicked movie-industry history—beginning in New York, then moving west.

In 1982, at the top of her career, Hart fell in love and left the business. "AIDS had just started up, and I lost every gay person I knew," she says, listing close friends who worked on the production side of the straight-porn business. She had two sons and helped support her family in part by stripping. Though not intending to re-enter porn, eventually she did, as a producer and director.

Hart has been in adult longer than anyone I met and has done "everything" in it, she jokes, "including windows." She warns me that any blanket statement about the business is meaningless because it's so big that every conceivable type of person can be found in it:

> You'll find someone who's into it to provide spiritual uplift and educational self-help. . . . And if you want to find rotten, vicious, misogynistic bastards—you'll find them. You'll find everyone who fits the stereotype and everyone who goes against the stereotype. In the loop and disposable-porno section of our business, you'll find the carnival freak-show mentality. There has to be a geek show somewhere in our society. What ticks me off is that all of adult is classified according to the lowest that's out there. We've always been legal. Child molestation has never been in mainstream adult. We've always policed ourselves. There's no coerced sex. But there are little pipsqueaks who get their disgusting little videos out there. There's a trend in misogynistic porn, and it's upsetting. I've been in the business for more than 20 years, and I helped make it possible for these guys to make these kinds of movies. I don't believe that's what America wants to see.

As for her own movies, Hart, like many of her peers, is preoccupied with the industry's biggest growth market—women and couples. The female audience was thought to be nearly nil when consuming pornography required a visit to a theater, an adult book store or the curtained adult section of a video store. But now hard-core is available at chains like Tower (though not Blockbuster), through elaborate Web sites like *Adultdvdempire* that parallel Amazon and by clicking a pay-per-view movie on a TV menu (where the bill won't specify that an adult title was chosen).

The Valley's conventional wisdom has it that women prefer more romance, foreplay and story, as well as strong female characters who, says Bill Asher of Vivid, "are not only in charge of the sex but the rest of the plot." Hart isn't sure. "Just because women like romance doesn't mean we want soft sex," she says. "We want hot and dirty sex just like anybody else. For instance, many women love the fantasy of being taken—but how do you portray it without sending a message to some guys to abduct?"

Hart, who thought of herself as a sexual pioneer when she was a porn performer, finds that there is no shortage of women who want to appear in adult now. She never has to search for new talent; willing performers call her "from all over the country." The men? "They're props."

Today's porn stars can be as temperamental as their Hollywood counterparts, or more so. "I assume Sarah Jessica Parker and Kim Cattrall show up on the set on time," said Paul Fishbein rather tartly when I asked about Jenna Jameson, the industry's reigning It girl of recent years. Though he was trying to give her a free vacation as thanks for her work as host of the recent *AVN* awards, Jameson wasn't returning his calls. "In adult, they don't show up and don't care," Fishbein says. "Lots of girls in this business—and guys, too—are dysfunctional. The girls get here at 18 and aren't mature. They do it because they're rebels or exhibitionists or need money. They think they're making real movies and get really upset when they don't win awards or get good reviews."

Some porn directors have similar pretensions. They can receive grandiose billing—"A Brad Armstrong Motion Picture"—and are sometimes grudgingly indulged with a "big budget" project ($250,000 tops) made on film, even though sex scenes are far harder to shoot on film (with its trickier lighting and shot setups) than on video—and even though adult films are almost never projected on screens. "We have our own Brad Pitts wanting to make 'Seven Days in Tibet,'" said one executive. Performers are paid at fairly standardized rates—by the day or sex scene, as much as $1,000 per day for women, as little as $200 for men. The contract girls at Vivid and Wicked sign for $100,000 and up a year, in exchange for which they might make nine movies, with two sex scenes each, over that time, along with any number of brand-boosting promotional appearances at consumer conventions and video

stores. The top stars double or triple that figure by running their own subscription Web sites, marketing autographs and most lucratively, dancing in the nation's large circuit of strip clubs at fees that can top $10,000 a week.

But porn stars have an even shorter shelf life than Hollywood's female stars and fare worse in love. Though HIV and drug testing, as well as condom use, are rigorous at the top adult companies, one producer asks rhetorically, "Who wants to date a woman who's had sex with 60 people in two months?"

Since I've rarely found actors to be the most insightful observers of the movie business, I wasn't eager to sample the wisdom of porn stars. But I did seek out Sydnee Steele, a newly signed Wicked contract girl who is by many accounts a rarity in the business—she's happily married. Her husband is Michael Raven, a top adult director. They met in Dallas in the early 90s, when she was a jewelry saleswoman in a shopping mall and he was a car salesman who sold her a mariner blue Miata. Eventually they drifted into the local swingers' scene. (One porn worker would later tell me, "Texas, Florida and Arizona are where all the swingers and strippers come from, though no one knows why.")

"The industry looks up to our relationship," Raven says when I meet the couple, now married nine years, at Sin City, another production company in Chatsworth. Avid porn fans in Texas, they migrated to the Valley to turn their avocation into a livelihood. Like many of the directors and male performers in the business, Raven is a somewhat lumpy everyman, heading toward baldness and sporting a meticulous goatee. A Kandinsky poster decorates the Sin City office. "I've gotten jealous on occasion," Raven allows. "I'm not jealous of her because of sex in movies; I'm jealous when her work takes her away from me. I get lonely if she's gone two weeks on the road."

"Sometimes I'm too tired for my husband," Steele says. "We love what we do, but it's hard work—lots of 12-hour days." By now, I've watched some of what she does and find it hard to square the rapacious star of "Hell on Heels" with the woman before me, who is softer-spoken, prettier and considerably less animated than her screen persona. Maybe she can act.

The daughter of a college professor, Steele comes from what she calls a "'Leave It To Beaver' nuclear family," Raven from a religious one. "I've leaned toward the right in my politics," he says, "but I'm bothered by the Republicans' association with the religious right. I know from my experience of religious people that those who protest and scream the loudest usually have the biggest collection of adult under their bed." He wishes they'd protest violent entertainment instead: "In video games, you're supposed to destroy, maim and dismember an opponent. But if one person is giving pleasure to another in adult, that's evil. Sex on TV is more destructive than hard core. You can depict a rape on TV—we don't touch that subject."

Like his wife, Raven is increasingly recognized by strangers—largely because "Behind the Scenes" documentaries about his movies appear on DVDs and on cable erotic networks, much like *Backstory* features on American Movie Classics. But Raven no longer stays in contact with his own family. And Steele's parents, she says, "don't totally know what I'm doing and don't ask. We don't lie, but they've never really been told."

Bryn Pryor is the Director and a writer of "The Money Shot." He's an *AVN* staff member who arrived in the Valley after nine years in the theater, much of it children's theater, in Arizona. "Everyone at *AVN* writes under a pseudonym. We have people here who don't want anyone to know their real name." Variations on this theme were visible everywhere I went in the Valley. Receptionists at porn companies tend to answer the phone generically: "Production Company" or "Corporate Office."

Typifying this ambivalence is Steve Orenstein the owner of Wicked Pictures. He made his accidental entrance into the porn business through his mother—who got him a part-time job when she worked as a bookkeeper at an adult-book distributor and he was 18. But he does not seem eager to reveal his calling to his 9-year-old stepdaughter.

"Being in the business you walk that line all the time—do you say what you do or not?" he says. Orenstein has revealed his true profession to only a handful of people whom he and his wife have met on the PTA circuit. "I'm comfortable with what I do," he says, "but I don't want parents of our child's friends saying their kids can't play with her because of it." His stepdaughter has noticed the Wicked logo on his shirt. "She knows I make something only adults can see."

The Orensteins have spoken to a therapist about the inevitable day of reckoning with their child. "The counselors say don't tell her yet," he says, "don't overexplain." But surely she'll guess by adolescence? Orenstein, a slight, nervous man with a reputation as a worrier, merely shrugs. For the moment, he's more concerned about protecting the child from prime-time television, citing a recent episode of the sitcom "The King of Queens" on CBS. He recalls: "The guy's rolling off his wife, and my 9-year-old asks, 'What do they mean by that?' Should I be letting her watch it?"

Russell Hampshire's gambit is to tell strangers he's in "the video-duplication business." Allen Gold, a VCA executive with daughters ages 1 and 3, says he's "in the DVD business." Paul Fishbein doesn't bring either *AVN* or adult product[s] into his house. Michael Raven and Sydnee Steele have decided for now not to have children.

I ask Veronica Hart, whose two teenage sons are at magnet schools for the highly gifted, what they have made of her career. "It's horrible for them," she says.

> I'm their loving mommy, and nobody likes to think of their parents having sex and being famous for it. I'm not ashamed of what I do. I take responsibility for who I am. I chose. From the time they were kids, my stripping gear was washed and hanging in the bathtub. At the same time I apologize to my kids for how the choices in my life have affected them. They're well adjusted and can joke with me about it: 'I know I'm going to spend the rest of my life on the couch.'

No wonder the porn industry has its finger on the pulse of American tastes. Not only do its players have a lifestyle more middle class than that of their Beverly Hills counterparts, but in their desire to keep their porn careers camouflaged in a plain brown wrapper, they connect directly with their audience's shame and guilt. Still, the next generation of porn consumers and producers alike may break with that puritan mind-set. The teenagers who grew up with cable and the VCR "come to the table already saturated with sex," says Bryn Pryor. "They've never known a time without Calvin Klein ads and MTV. By the time they see porn, they've already seen so many naked people they're pre-jaded."

This may explain why Americans are clamoring for ever more explicit fare. In mainstream TV, sex is no longer sequestered on late-night public access shows like "Robin Byrd." At HBO, Sheila Nevins, the highly regarded executive in charge of its nonfiction programming, has been stunned by the success of sexual documentaries like "Real Sex," now in its 11th year, and "Taxicab Confessions." Focus groups complain to HBO that another hit series, "G-String Divas," doesn't go far enough. "They know what really happens in a strip club," Nevins says, and find HBO's version "too R-rated." Though HBO, known for its heavy promotions of "The Sopranos" and "Sex and the City," spends nothing to advertise its sex series, they always are among the network's most watched. "I can do all the shows I want about poverty in the Mississippi Delta," Nevins says, "but this is what hard-working Americans want to see. At first we were embarrassed by the sex shows, and producers didn't want their names on them. Now we have Academy Award producers, and their names can't be big enough."

At Playboy, Jim English, the head of its TV division, and his boss, Christie Hefner, have felt the heat. Its Playboy and Spice channels have been squeezed from both sides in the cable-satellite marketplace. The softer, if X-rated, cuts of hard-core movies that it runs are no longer much more explicit than regular cable programming at HBO, Showtime ("Queer as Folk") and MTV ("Spring Break"). Meanwhile, erotic networks like Hot and Ecstasy, which run XX films, are cannibalizing Playboy's audience from the other end of the erotic spectrum. The result: Playboy plans to start "Spice Platinum Live, " which edges toward XXX. (I'll leave the codified yet minute clinical distinctions separating X, XX and XXX to your imagination.)

Even in an economic downturn, everything's coming up porn. Newly unemployed dot-com techies who can't find jobs in Silicon Valley are heading to Silicone Valley, where the work force is expanding, not contracting. "Vivid overall has doubled, tripled revenues and profits in the past couple of years," says Bill Asher. While he says there's no such thing as a Hollywood-style "home run" in porn—unless another celebrity like Pamela Anderson turns up in a sex video, intentionally or not—he sees potentially "a tenfold jump" in profits as distribution increases through broadband and video-on-demand. "There are opportunities here that Paramount will never have in terms of growth," Asher says. "Our product travels well internationally and is evergreen. Five-year-old product is still interesting to someone; it's not yesterday's news like a five-year-old Hollywood blockbuster. Our costs are relatively fixed. As there's more distribution, 90 cents of a dollar hits the bottom line." The absence of adult retail stores in conservative pockets of the country is no longer a barrier. "You can get a dish relatively anywhere," Asher says, "and get whatever you want."

When Vivid took over and expanded the Hot Network in 1999, Asher says, "there was no outcry: We got thank-you letters and sales boomed. We put up two more channels in months. Cable companies were begging for them. It doesn't take a genius to do this. Literally the customers say, I like what you've got—give me some more of it." Entertainment-industry executives not directly involved in the adult business confirm its sunny future. Satellite and cable companies have found that the more explicit the offerings, the more the market grows. *AVN* reports that TV porn may actually be increasing video-store sales and rentals rather than cannibalizing them—by introducing new customers to the product. Though some cable companies say they don't want adult, only one of the country's eight major cable providers, Adelphia, forbids it. The others are too addicted to the cash flow to say no. The organized uproar that recently persuaded a teetering Yahoo to drop its adult Web store—but not its gateways into other adult sites—is the exception, not the rule.

And despite a rumor that one porn mogul keeps a Cessna waiting at Van Nuys airport to escape to Brazil if there's a government crackdown, the odds of that look slim. Too many Fortune 500 corporations with Washington clout, from AT & T to AOL Time Warner, make too much money on porn—whether through phone sex, chat rooms or adult video. At the local level, the Supreme Court's 1973 "community standard" for obscenity may be a non sequitur now that there's a XX national standard disseminated everywhere by satellite and the Web. A busted local video retailer in a conservative community can plead that his product is consistent with what the neighbors are watching on pay-per-view—as one such owner successfully did in Utah last fall.

Should John Ashcroft's Justice Department go after porn, smart betting has him pursuing shadowy purveyors of extreme porn on the Internet (though it's not clear that the actionable stuff originates in the United States) and child pornography, all of which is condemned by the professional adult industry. "No one in this business will complain if Ashcroft goes for the kid angle," Fishbein says.

Jim English of Playboy suggests that one way to meet the typical American porn audience en masse is to accompany him to a live broadcast of a hit Playboy show called "Night Calls 411." Fittingly, "Night Calls" is televised from a studio in Hollywood, right by the old Gower Gulch, where low-budget studios long ago churned out early features in bulk much as the adult business does now.

Two underclad hostesses, Crystal Knight and Flower, intersperse wisecracks and sex tips with viewers' phone calls. Though only a few callers get on the air, as many as 100,000 try to get through, with still more deluging the show with "Miss Lonelyhearts" e-mail. It's not "Larry King Live," but in some ways it could be an adult version of the "Today" show, whose fans cross the country with the hope of being in view as the camera pans Rockefeller Center. The "Night Calls" devotees go further: many of them are engaging in sex when they call. "Having sex is not enough of a turn-on in America—you have to be on TV too," jokes English. The callers often ask that the hosts talk them through to what *The Starr Report* called completion, and the women oblige—hoping for slam-bam speed so they can move on to the next caller. I'm struck by how much the male and female callers alike mimic porn performers, with their clichéd sex talk and over-the-top orgasmic shrieks. The adult audience apes its entertainers as slavishly as teenagers do rock idols.

By now, I've become intimately familiar with the conventions of adult entertainment, having asked those I met in the business to steer me to their best products. I've watched Wicked's "Double Feature," a multiple winner of *AVN* awards, among them "Best Comedy," and found it full of erudite cinematic references, including a campy spoof of Ed Wood films. I've seen Vivid's new "Artemesia," a costume drama set in sixteenth-century Italy and given *AVN's* highest rating; it is laced with high-flown ruminations on the meaning of art, somewhat compromised by the tattoos on the performers. From Video Team, a company specializing in interracial porn, there is a thriller called "Westside" with a social conscience reminiscent of "West Side Story" soundtrack that features music by Aaron Copland and a take on the drug wars that wouldn't be out of place in "Traffic."

It's no wonder, though, that Stagliano's gonzo, in which the performers just get it on, has such a following. All the plot and costuming and set decoration and arty cinematography—why bother? The acting—who needs it? (In "Flashpoint," Jenna Jameson, cast as a female firefighter, sounds the same when sobbing over a colleague's death as she does in coital ecstasy.) The films are tedious, and I'm as tempted to fast-forward through the sex scenes as the nonsex scenes. No matter what the period or setting, no matter what the genre, every video comes to the same dead halt as the performers drop whatever characters they're supposed to be assuming and repeat the same sex acts, in almost exactly the same way, at the same intervals, in every film. At a certain point, the Kabuki-like ritualization of these sequences becomes unintentionally farcical, like the musical numbers in a 30s Hollywood musical or the stylized acrobatics in a martial-arts film. Farcical, but not exactly funny. All the artful *mise-en-scene* in the world cannot, for me anyway, make merchandised sex entertaining or erotic.

I tell Bryn Pryor of *AVN* and "The Money Shot" my reaction. He's a professional porn critic. Is this the best that adult has to offer? "The top of the heap in porn is the bottom in mainstream," he says.

> The sad fact is that while consumers are more aware than they've ever been, nobody cares if it's a good movie, and we all know that. They care if

it's hot in whatever subjective way it's hot to them. Most porn directors don't even watch the sex; they just direct the dialogue. They tell the camera people they want three positions and then go off and eat.

He continues: "Porn is not a creative medium. Everyone in the porn industry says he's on the way to something else, like waiters and bartenders, but it may be that most of us belong here. If we were really good, we'd be doing something else." Pryor envisions a day when adult and Hollywood will converge, but in a sense that's already the case. If much of porn ranges from silly to degrading, what's the alternative offered on the other side of the hills? The viewer who isn't watching a mediocre porn product is watching what? "Temptation Island"? WWF?

Moralists like to see in pornography a decline in our standards, but in truth it's an all-too-ringing affirmation of them. Porn is no more or less imaginative than much of the junk in the entertainment mainstream—though unlike much of that junk, it does have an undeniable practical use. In that regard, anyway, there may be no other product in the entire cultural marketplace that is more explicitly American.

Introduction References

Geewax, M. (2004, March 29). "Extolling the Virtues of Hiring Oversees." *Austin American-Statesman*, p. 1E.

Jacobellis v. Ohio, 378 U.S. 184 (1964).

Miller v. California, 413 U.S. 15 (1973).

Neff, J. L. (2001a). "Pornography—First Presidential Commissions Report." In N. Davis and G. Geis (Vol. Eds), *Encyclopedia of Criminal and Deviant Behavior*, Vol. 3, Sexual Deviance (pp. 238–240). Philadelphia, PA: Taylor and Francis.

——. (2001b). "Pornography—Second Presidential Commissions Report. In. N. Davis and G. Geis (Vol. Eds.), *Encyclopedia of Criminal and Deviant Behavior*, Vol. 3, Sexual Deviance (pp. 245–247). Philadelphia, PA: Taylor and Francis.

Stanley v. Georgia, 394 U.S. 557 (1969).

Chapter 42
Religiosity and Sexual Responsibility
Relationships of Choice

J. Kenneth Davidson, Sr.
Nelwyn B. Moore
Kristen Marie Ullstrup

Crossing the great divide from the adult industry to religious institutions may be a precipitous journey in sexuality. Questions raised in the Davidson and Moore chapter on religiosity and sexual responsibility indicate that the distance between sex and religion may be less than imagined. Historically, society and cultural norms have been lenses through which we view sexual standards. Religion and sexuality became polarized when, in ancient Greece, dualism divided women and men into two realms—the bodily and the spiritual. Tied to the earth with their reproductive capabilities, women occupied the bodily realm, while men, who experienced neither menstruation nor childbirth, were of the spiritual, godly realm. At the end of the fourth century, sexual activity was declared by St. Augustine to be a display of animal lust, in which logic and reason were lost to passion (Nelson 1978).

Judeo-Christian dogma has long asserted that any nonprocreative sexual activity is sinful. This denial of sexual pleasure, historically rooted in religion, has permeated and often compromised the contemporary view of healthy sexuality. The Universal Catechism of the Roman Catholic Church, *published in 1992, reinforced many of the earlier teachings such as abstinence or the rhythm method are the only acceptable forms of contraception; homosexuality, although not chosen, is an ordeal in which homosexuals are intrinsically "disordered" and so, ordered to remain chaste; and lastly, women are denied the right to become priests or to have an abortion (Catechism 1993).*

Though religion may adversely affect the sexual views of both sexes, it is woman who has been sys-

tematically portrayed as evil, trying to thwart man's spiritual advancement by luring him into the bodily realm of sexuality and lust. Judith Daniluk (1993) scrutinized the role of religion in shaping the construct of female sexuality: "Dichotomous images of the Madonna/Whore left little room for any notion of healthy female sexuality—the emotional legacy of such anti-woman indoctrination was experienced . . . in the form of shame, guilt, fear, and self-blame" (p. 59).

We know that today we have come a long way from the archaic thinking of St. Augustine. But, this Davidson and Moore selection asks, How far? How far have we come in the twentieth century? When the answer is from Sigmund Freud to Sex in the City, *it is obvious that dramatic changes in our understanding of sexuality have occurred since the days of your ancestors. As you peruse the events revealed in this sexuality timeline, consider these questions. When on the timeline were your parents, grandparents, and great-grandparents young adults? How many of these changes resulted from scientific discoveries? Or from legal decisions? How large a role has been played by the print and broadcast media in promoting these*

Twentieth-Century Sexuality Timeline

- **1905** Sigmund Freud's *Three Essays on Sexuality* misinforms about female orgasm.

- **1934** Henry Miller's *Tropic of Cancer* banned in United States.

- **1952** Lucille Ball, the first pregnant woman to play a mother-to-be in a sitcom on TV, was not allowed to say the word pregnancy.

- **1953** Alfred Kinsey's *Sexual Behavior in the Human Female* was published.

- **1953** Marilyn Monroe takes it all off in the first issue of *Playboy.*

- **1960** The Food and Drug Administration approved the birth control pill.

- **1966** William Masters and Virginia Johnson's *Human Sexual Response* was published.

- **1973** In *Roe v. Wade*, the U.S. Supreme Court gave women the right to an abortion.

- **1984** Researchers isolated the virus causing AIDS.

- **1993** Lorena Bobbit cut off her husband's penis with a kitchen knife.

- **2004** The final year of HBO's *Sex in the City,* which candidly chronicled the love lives of four single, professional women in New York City (Brewster, 2003).

changes? And, finally, what is the relationship of these changes to religion, the subject of this chapter?

The cultural norms of a society are lenses through which sexual behavior is viewed, the roots of which are firmly intertwined with centuries of religious tradition. For example, in the thirteenth century, St. Thomas Aquinas set morally acceptable standards for sexual intercourse: only heterosexual genital intercourse that served a procreative function was allowed, and then only when it occurred within the confines of church regulated marriage.[1] These principles of St. Thomas were reiterated in the latter twentieth century in published moral teachings from the Vatican.[2] Runkel[3] postulates that sexual pleasure today is still considered immoral or sinful in many Christian religions.

Past research has found a relationship between church attendance and sexual attitudes and behavior.[4,5] Among college students, women report higher levels of religiosity than men do[6] and also that their degree of religiosity is more likely to influence their premarital sexual behavior.[7] This investigation sought to examine the current influence of women's religiosity upon their sexual behavior and attitudes, including any feelings of guilt.

Sexual Attitudes

As a state of mind,[8] attitudes reflect judgments that may be based on facts or feelings, or both, complicating attempts to quantify them. This is particularly true when measuring sexual attitudes whose geneses are highly speculative.[9] An individual's sexual attitudes are a composite of the life-long lessons learned about their sexuality from many sources. Sex therapists suggest that negative societal and parental messages children receive about their sexuality can lead to feelings of sexual guilt or anxiety in adulthood.[10] Further, most sexually dysfunctional patients are "woefully ignorant of both basic biology and effective sexual techniques" (p 3).[10]

Sexuality Education

Today's youth learn about sexuality primarily by word of mouth via friends,[11] from the media,[12] or from mothers,[13] findings that may help explain both educational deficits and distortion of attitudes. Regrettably, friends and the media are often unreliable sources of important information on topics such as protected sexual intercourse, transmission of HIV, or contraception. Unfortunately, inadequate or inaccurate information about sexuality not only pro-

motes unnecessary risk taking in sexual scenarios, but it can also lead to decreased physiological and psychological sexual satisfaction.[14] Although schools are not the main source of sexuality education for students, when they are, they appear to promote responsible sexuality: The use of some form of contraception at first intercourse and the use of a latex condom.[15] Therefore, the risk is less for unwanted pregnancy and exposure to and transmission of sexually transmitted diseases (STDs), including HIV.[16]

Sexual Behavior

Masturbation

Although masturbation is believed to be a normal, healthy way to explore one's sexual response system and orgasmic capabilities[17] many religions discourage engaging in masturbation.[6] The higher the degree of religiosity among college women, the less positive their reaction to masturbatory behavior and the greater likelihood of guilt feelings about their participation.[17] Women reporting "no religion" and liberal Protestant women (e.g., Episcopal and Presbyterian, USA) masturbate more frequently and more often experience orgasm during masturbation than do conservative Protestant (e.g., Baptist and Assembly of God) and Catholic women.[18]

Oral-Genital Contact

Because the practice of oral-genital sex is nonprocreative, typically it has not been viewed by religious institutions as an approved sexual activity. Thus, women with high degrees of religiosity are found to have less experience with oral-genital stimulation.[19] Women indicating "no religion" and liberal Protestant women are more likely to have both given and received oral-genital stimulation than are conservative Protestant women.[18] Catholicism now sanctions oral-genital stimulation as a form of marital foreplay, but only if it culminates in penile-vaginal intercourse.[20]

Sexual Intercourse

Most Fundamentalist Protestants who attend religious services believe that sexual intercourse before marriage is wrong.[21] Although 75 percent[22] to 81 percent[23] of unmarried college women have experienced sexual intercourse, only 40 percent of those who rate themselves as very religious have done so.[24] Not only is church attendance linked with virgin status among college women,[25] but higher rates of attendance and participation in religious services are also associated with less frequent sexual activity.[26] Among Protestants, Fundamentalists are least likely to engage in premarital sexual intercourse,[27] and those with higher levels of religiosity have fewer lifetime sexual partners.[28] Further, nonreligiously affiliated college women are 2.8 times more likely than Jewish women and 1.8 times more likely than Catholic women to have engaged in sexual intercourse.[24]

Anal Intercourse

No significant differences are found between the more and less religious college women who had ever engaged in anal intercourse.[29] However, in a noncollege sample, women indicating "no religion" and liberal Protestant women were more likely than conservative Protestant women to have experienced anal intercourse.[18]

Contraceptive Usage

Jews and mainline Protestants are more likely to use a contraceptive at first intercourse[28] than are Roman Catholics and Fundamentalist Protestants.[27] Jews use condoms more than oral contraceptives, whereas Protestants use withdrawal, but, regardless of denomination, respondents with the highest level of religiosity are most likely to use less effective methods of contraception.[24] Research findings concerning religiosity and specifically condom use have been inconsistent. Although Zaleski and Schiaffino[26] recently found that college women with higher levels of religiosity are less likely to use condoms, an earlier metaanalysis of 121 studies found no significant differences in condom use and degree of religiosity.[30] Nonuse of contraception and engaging in risk-taking behaviors such as consuming alcohol or taking other drugs are correlated,[31] but women with high levels of religiosity are less likely to engage in binge drinking, more likely to consume less alcohol, and less likely to engage in risky sexual behavior.[32]

Guilt and Sexuality

The realization that one has violated an ethical, moral, or religious principle produces feelings of guilt believed to be associated with lowered self-esteem.[8] Both an emotional and behavioral reaction, sexual guilt, which manifests itself by encouraging some sexual behaviors and discouraging others, leads to both avoidance and nonuse of contraceptives.[33, 34] Gender is correlated with guilt feelings, with significantly more women than men experiencing guilt with first sexual intercourse. Women also report guilt as the primary reason that their first sexual intercourse was not psychologically satisfying.[35] Guilt is a pervasive problem as it relates

not only to oral-genital sex and coitus, but also to masturbation.[36] Shame is reported by 30 percent of women as a leading factor in avoiding masturbation[37] and 50 percent of college women who masturbate report feelings of guilt and shame.[18]

Methodology

An anonymous questionnaire was administered to a sample consisting of 683 never-married, undergraduate women from a Midwestern residential university. In the interest of creating a more homogeneous sample, those individuals who indicated their sexual orientation as bisexual or lesbian or who failed to respond to the inquiry about sexual orientation were omitted from the data analyses. Further, those respondents under age 18 and over age 23 were excluded from the sample as well as respondents who reported "never" attending religious services or who did not answer the question about frequency of attendance at religious services. The Beck et al[38] typology of religious denominations was used to classify the religious backgrounds of the respondents. Because of small Ns, all categories other than mainline Protestant or Catholic (Baptist, Institutional Sect, Fundamentalist, and Non-Christian) were also declared as missing values. The final subsample of 535 never-married women included 41.1 percent–freshmen, 33.3 percent–sophomores, 18.7 percent–juniors, and 6.9 percent–seniors.

Results

Profile of Religiosity

Because single-item measures of religiosity have been found to be not only adequate, but also less confusing for respondents than multiple-item scales,[39] the frequency of attendance at religious services was used as the measure of religiosity in this study. Of the respondents, 21.7 percent reported weekly attendance, 41.7 percent–monthly attendance, and 36.6. percent–yearly attendance. For ease of reporting the remaining data analyses, 3 respondent categories were established: *W Group* (weekly attendance at religious services), *M Group* (monthly attendance at religious services), and *Y Group* (yearly attendance at religious services).

A significant relationship was found between attendance at religious services and self-reported perception of religiosity: W Group women were more likely to view themselves as more religious than other persons of the same religious denomination whereas M Group women and Y Group women reported being less religious than others. The yearly mean for attending religious services was 53.3 times for W Group women, 22.0 times for M Group women, and 5.2 times for Y Group women.

Sexuality Education

There were no differences in the mean age for receiving first information about sexuality: W Group women, M = 10.5 years; M Group women, M = 10.3 years; Y Group women, M = 10.3 years. Regarding the source of first information about sexuality, parents were cited most often: W Group = 50.9 percent; M Group = 44.1 percent; Y Group = 38.8 percent, whereas peers were cited least often: W Group = 20.9 percent; M Group = 25.6 percent; Y Group = 34.4 percent. There were no significant differences between respondent groups concerning how often they discussed sexually related topics with their mothers or fathers.

Respondents received their first contraceptive information approximately 3 years after having received their initial sexuality information: W Group women, M = 13.5 years; M Group women, M = 13.3 years; Y Group women, M = 13.6 years. Teachers, not parents, were most often reported as the source of first contraceptive information by all groups: M Group women = 63.4 percent; W Group women = 60.0 percent; Y Group women = 53.7 percent. Parents were cited least often by all groups: W Group = 16.2 percent; Y Group = 14.1 percent; M Group = 12.9 percent.

Sexual Attitudes

To determine the degree to which religiosity affects one's attitudes toward specific sexual behaviors and/or practices, a number of variables were examined, some of which were significant. W Group women were more likely than other respondents to agree that couples should refrain from oral-genital sex and from anal intercourse, even when choosing to use a condom. M Group and Y Group women held more liberal attitudes than W Group women towards abortion within the first trimester of pregnancy, and W Group women were more likely to cite love as a prerequisite for sexual intercourse, to desire to marry a virgin, and to want to marry someone with whom only they had had sexual intercourse. Interaction effects were found between the variables "marry someone who had intercourse with only you" and "source of first information about sexuality," with W Group women placing the most importance on a partner with limited sexual experience if parents were their first source of sexuality information. Interaction effects were also found for the variable "no sexual intercourse without love," with W Group women placing the most importance on love as a prerequisite for

sexual intercourse if parents were their first source of sexuality information. Conversely, Y Group women whose peers were their first source of sexuality information placed the least importance on love as a prerequisite.

Love did play an important role in the decision about whether or not to engage in sexual intercourse as illustrated by all 3 groups of women who cited "didn't love potential partner" as the most important reason not to have sexual intercourse. However, W Group women, more than other women, cited both "wrong before marriage" and "religious reasons" as important reasons not to have sexual intercourse, whereas "fear of pregnancy" and "lack of opportunity" were cited by M Group and Y Group women, respectively.

A slight majority of all women cited "against personal beliefs" as the most important reason not to engage in masturbation. However, more W Group women than other respondents reported "against religious beliefs" as a reason for abstaining from masturbation, whereas more M and Y Group women cited "feel uncomfortable."

Sexual Behavior

Masturbation. As for the practice of masturbation, 59.6 percent of W Group women, 43.2 percent of M Group women, and 53.4 percent of Y Group women had engaged in this behavior. The mean ages at first masturbation were M = 15.9 years, W Group women; M = 16.0 years, M Group women; and M = 14.7 years, Y Group women. Of those who had masturbated during the past year, there were no significant differences for mean number of times: W Group women, M = 29.8 times; M Group women, M = 30.2 times; and Y Group women, M = 39.9 times.

Sexual intercourse. Significant differences were revealed between respondent groups with regard to having experienced sexual intercourse: 55.2 percent of W Group women, 72.9 percent of M Group women, and 83.1 percent of Y Group women. Differences were also suggested for the mean number of times per year for sexual intercourse: M = 68.4 times, W Group women; M = 96.5 times, M Group women; and M = 101.7 times, Y Group women. However, using two Likert-Scale variables, no significant differences were found between respondent groups for current levels of physiological sexual satisfaction: M = 3.892, W Group; M = 3.945, M Group; and M = 4.048, Y Group or psychological sexual satisfaction: M = 3.901, W Group; M = 3.940, M Group; M = 4.042, Y Group.

First coitus. No significant differences were found among respondent groups for age at first sexual intercourse nor age of first sexual intercourse partner. There were also no significant differences between respondent groups for the following variables: under influence of alcohol or other drugs at first intercourse, used contraception/first intercourse, or type of contraceptive used/first intercourse. Significant differences were found for reasons contraceptive was not used at first sexual intercourse, with most M Group and Y Group women indicating "contraceptive unavailable" and W Group women indicating "too naive or dumb." No significant differences between groups surfaced for physiological or psychological sexual satisfaction with their first sexual intercourse experience.

High-risk sexual behavior. No significant differences were found between respondent groups for the high-risk behaviors "anal intercourse" and "sexual intercourse with person just met while under influence of alcohol/drugs." Y Group women did report significantly more sexual partners during their lifetime and during the past year than did the other women. However, Y Group women were significantly more likely to have planned their most recent sexual intercourse experience and to have used a condom while engaging in oral-genital sex than were the others. No significant differences were found between respondent groups for the variables "told new sexual partner total number of lifetime partners" and "type of contraceptive used during most recent sexual intercourse." Finally, all respondent groups only irregularly asked their latest sex partner if he was infected with a sexually transmitted disease.

Guilt and Sexuality

There were no significant differences between respondent groups for the variable, "embarrassed to admit to close friend/masturbate." However, W Group women were more likely than M Group and Y Group women to feel guilty about engaging in masturbation, petting, first sexual intercourse experience, and currently engaging in sexual intercourse, but W Group women were less likely to feel guilty if an orgasm was not experienced during sexual intercourse than were either M Group or Y Group women. When the variables "experience orgasm during sexual intercourse" and "first source of information about sexuality" were tested for interaction effects, Y Group women who received their first information on sexuality from their parents were most likely to experience orgasm during sexual intercourse. Conversely, W Group women who received their first sexuality information from parents were least likely to experience orgasm while engaging in sexual intercourse.

Discussion

To better understand respondents' sexual attitudes, it is helpful to first address their education about sexuality. Our data suggest that these respondents are atypical concerning source of first sexuality information. Much of the previous research found peers to be the adolescent's first, though often misleading, source.[12] These findings that parents were cited more often than peers agree with those of Moore and Davidson,[13] leading us to the tentative conclusion that parents may be more willing now than in previous years to discuss sexually related topics. Nevertheless, parents still may not be comfortable in discussing all aspects of sexuality as was demonstrated by the fact that teachers most often were the first source of contraceptive information. Perhaps parents are in denial about their daughter's eventually becoming sexually active, or they may believe the myth that teaching about contraception and safer sexual techniques promotes promiscuity.

Sexual Attitudes

Differences in attitudes towards sexuality between W Group, M Group, and Y Group women were especially apparent regarding the non-procreative activities of oral-genital sex and anal intercourse. The fact that these sexual activities are engaged in strictly to derive sexual pleasure raises questions that may not be fully addressed until the process by which attendance at religious services affects women's enjoyment of their sexuality is further clarified.[4] Traditional attitudes of "saving oneself" for a partner considered to be worthy of marriage were evidenced by W Group women, who also valued virginity, wanted to marry a partner who had engaged in sexual intercourse with only them, and did not believe in sexual intercourse without love; but this study did not attempt to determine the nature of the relationship of such behaviors to these traditional attitudes. Not only did M Group and Y Group women tend to de-emphasize traditional attitudes towards sexuality, but both groups also held more liberal attitudes towards abortion. Although these findings suggest that more frequent attendance at religious services does reinforce more traditional attitudes towards sexuality, many unanswered questions remain about how or if sexual attitudes are actually played out in sexual behavior.

Sexual Experience

The researchers are puzzled as to why the most religious women (W Group) who indicated the most guilt about masturbation were significantly more likely to have engaged in the behavior than were either M or Y Group women. Less likely to engage in sexual intercourse and to approve of oral-genital sex, perhaps masturbation was the only sexual outlet for W Group women. In spite of this unexpected finding, neither age at first masturbation nor mean number of times masturbated per year differed significantly. The conclusions of others[25] were confirmed when M Group women and Y Group women were found to be more likely to have engaged in sexual intercourse than were W Group women. Although not significant, group differences were implied for the mean number of times for sexual intercourse during past year, with Y Group women being the most sexually active, as in the research of Zaleski and Schiaffino.[26]

First coitus. Brewster et al[27] and Zaleski and Schiaffino[26] found that high levels of religiosity among college women were associated with inconsistent condom use. Conversely, this study suggests that the more religious women were more likely to use a contraceptive at first coitus than were the less religious ones. Given their greater degree of religiosity, perhaps the W Group women perceived greater consequences if they should contract an STD or have an unintentional pregnancy. Unexpectedly, it was M Group and Y Group women who gave as their two primary reasons for noncontraceptive use "sexual activity unplanned" and "no contraceptive available," suggesting that they, more than W Group women, were driven by the "passion of the moment." The fact that all women who were contracepted at first coitus overwhelmingly chose to use a condom confirms the meta-analysis of Sheeran et al[30] who found no significant differences in condom use related to degree of religiosity. Finally, that there were no significant group differences in the levels of physiological or psychological sexual satisfaction for first coitus suggests that the similarities between respondent groups in both sexual attitudes and behavior may outweigh the differences.

High-Risk Sexual Behavior

The fact that the majority of all women were likely to voluntarily tell a partner about their own sexual history raises the issue of sexual scripts. Could such behavior be fulfilling gender-role scripts in the belief that volunteering one's own personal information may, in turn, spur one's partner to do the same without directly being asked? Unfortunately, all women irregularly asked new sexual partners if they had an STD, lending credence to the argument of the female gender script of passivity. Another plausible explanation for failing to ask about partner's sexual history may be this age group's perception of personal invulnerability. Or

these women may feel that the sexual partners they choose are "not the type" to have an STD, therefore posing no threat to their health. Finally, some may believe they should not be assertive in asking a potential sexual partner about his sexual history in order to maintain the "nice girl" image.

The fact that Y Group women had significantly more lifetime sexual partners than did either M Group or W Group women is consistent with the findings of Ratliff-Crain et al[28] that high levels of religiosity are associated with fewer sexual partners. This may be attributed, in part, to Y Group women's placing less importance on love as a prerequisite for sexual intercourse than W Group or M Group women. That M Group women who engaged in more types of sexual behavior were more likely to use condoms during oral-genital sex may indicate a trend towards safer sex practices in the age of AIDS. Of course, it is possible that W Group women, because of the social groups to which they belonged, believed that they were unlikely to contract an STD, especially if their partners were from the same social group. It is likely that women who attend weekly religious services socialize with people who have similar levels of religiosity, and thus, they may have a false sense of trust.

Guilt and Sexual Expression

Determining how often guilt feelings are experienced after engaging in masturbation, petting, and sexual intercourse can illustrate the degree to which religiosity affects one's sexuality. Significant differences between respondent groups were found for several guilt variables: engaging in solitary masturbation, first coital experience, current sexual intercourse, and engaging in sexual intercourse without orgasm occurring. Although all women appeared to be embarrassed about admitting they engaged in masturbation, W Group women reported the most guilt. These findings are consistent with those of Clark and Wiederman[6] and Davidson and Moore,[33] who found that the higher degree of religiosity among college women, the greater the likelihood of guilt feelings associated with masturbation.

What does it mean that Y Group and M Group women are more likely than those in the W Group to report feelings of guilt if no orgasm was experienced during sexual intercourse? Loos et al[40] chronicled the high value placed on coital orgasm by college women. Perhaps experience breeds expectation. Are the more sexually experienced Y and M Group women more accustomed to experiencing orgasm during coitus, and therefore, do they expect to do so? Thus when orgasm is absent, do anxiety levels increase, which in turn elicit guilt feelings? Is the guilt for Y Group and M Group women derived not from the behavior of engaging in the act of sexual intercourse, but from the fact that they did not sufficiently exhibit pleasure to their partner as demonstrated by having an orgasm? If so, gender-role scripting would be suspected. These findings would appear to support those of Davidson and Moore,[33] who found that those college women who were more likely to report guilt feelings if they did not experience an orgasm during sexual intercourse were also more likely to have their moral values determined by others.

W Group women felt the most guilt about engaging in both first and current sexual intercourse, although they were the most discriminating, deciding against participating in sexual intercourse if they did not love their potential sexual partner. The fact that the more religious W Group women reported the most guilt feelings surrounding the act of sexual intercourse confirms the other recent findings.[28, 29] Frequency of attendance at religious services seemingly served to reinforce moral teachings and potentially contributed to guilt feelings surrounding sexual behavior that transgresses societal mores.

Conclusion

It has been demonstrated in this study of unmarried college women that positive attitudes towards nonprocreative, pleasurable sexual practices differ based on levels of religiosity of respondent groups. That women who attended church more frequently held more conservative attitudes towards oral-genital sex, vaginal-penile intercourse, and anal intercourse and felt more guilt about their sexual behavior suggests that sexual guilt may be socially and religiously constructed.

If sexuality is not inherently a guilt-laden phenomenon, why is the "Liberated Victorian," as characterized by Reiss,[1] still very much a reality today? Some may wonder if guilt and sexuality among women are so historically intertwined that they are impossible to separate. In trying to answer these questions, therapists, researchers, and sexuality educators must work together to understand what promotes and what constrains sexual problems. In so doing, they must gather all of the pieces of the puzzle in order to form a composite whole. As important as religious influence is, it is only one variable in the equation. For example, this study suggests that there is also a need for more information concerning the important role of parents as their child's premier sexuality educator.

The good news is that sexuality educators and therapists are increasingly more vocal in stressing the valid and equally important topic of human sexuality as a source of pleasure, and less as a source of problems surrounded by social stigma and mystery. And, the puzzling fact that in this study perceived levels of physiological and psychological sexual satisfaction were found to be similar for respondent groups, regardless of religious experience, may help to reframe the issues. After all, except as a construct to researchers, even significant differences in the sexual attitudes and behavior of college women may be less than significant in the balance of life experiences.

Introduction References

Catechism of the Catholic Church. (1993). Rome, Italy: Liberia Editrice Vaticana.

Brewster, M. (2003, June 30). "Sex and the Century: A History." *Newsweek*, p. 44.

Daniluk, J. (1993). "The Meaning and Experience of Female Sexuality." *Psychology of Women Quarterly*, 17, 53–59.

Nelson, J. B. (1978). *Embodiment: An Approach to Sexuality and Christian Theology*. Minneapolis, MN: Augsberg.

References

1. Reiss IL. *An End to Shame: Shaping Our Next Sexual Revolution*. Buffalo: Prometheus. 1990:193–206.
2. Curran CE. Sexual ethics in the Roman Catholic tradition. In RM Green, (Ed). *Religion and Sexual Health*. Boston: Kluver. 1992:17–35.
3. Runkel G. Sexual morality of Christianity. *J Sex Marital Ther.* 1998; 24(2):103–122.
4. Meier AM. Adolescents' transition to first intercourse, religiosity, and attitudes about sex. *Soc Forces.* 2003; 81(3):1031–1052.
5. Knox D, Cooper C, Zusman ME. Sexual values of college students. *Coll Student J.* 2001; 35(1):24–27.
6. Clark DA, Wiederman MW. Gender and reactions to a hypothetical relationship partner's masturbation and use of sexually explicit media. *J Sex Res.* 2000; 37(2):133–141.
7. Bearman PS, Brucker H. Promising the future: Virginity pledges and first intercourse. *Am J Soc.* 2001; 106(4):859–912.
8. Hinsie LE, Campbell RJ. *Psychiatric Dictionary* (4th ed). New York: Oxford University Press, 1970:75–76.
9. Von Sadovszky V, Keller ML, McKinney K. College students' perceptions and practices of sexual activities in sexual encounters. *J Nurs Scholarship.* 2002; 34(2):133–138.
10. LoPiccolo J. Direct treatment of sexual function. In J LoPiccolo, L LoPiccolo, (Eds). *Handbook of Sex Therapy*. New York: Plenum, 1978:1–17.
11. Feigenbaum R, Weinstein E, Rosen E. College students' sexual attitudes and behaviors: implications

for sexuality education. *J Am Coll Health*. 1995; 44(3):112–118.

12. Ballard SM, Morris ML. Sources of sexuality information for university students. *J Sex Educ Ther*. 1998; 23(4):278–287.

13. Moore NB, Davidson JK Sr. Parents as first sexuality information sources: Do they make a difference in daughter's sexual attitudes and behavior? *J Sex Educ Ther*. 1999; 24(3):155–163.

14. Moore NB, Davidson JK Sr. Communicating with new sex partners: college women and questions that make a difference. *J Sex Marital Ther*. 2000; 26(3):215–230.

15. Wellings K, Wadsworth J, Johnson AM, et al. Provision of sex education and early sexual experience: the relation examined. *Br Med J*. 1995; 311(7002):417–420.

16. Buysse A. Adolescents, young adults, and AIDS: a study of actual knowledge vs. perceived need for additional information. *J Youth Adolesc*. 1996; 25(2):259–271.

17. Davidson JK Sr, Moore NB. Masturbation and premarital sexual intercourse among college women: making choices for sexual fulfillment. *J Sex Marital Ther*. 1994; 20(3):178–198.

18. Laumann EO, Gagnon JH, Michael RT, et al. *The Social Organization of Sexuality: Sexual Practices in the United States*. Chicago, University of Chicago Press, 1994:82–83.

19. Jensen L, Newell R, Holman T. Sexual behavior, church attendance, and permissive beliefs among unmarried young men and women. *J Sci Study Rel*. 1990; 29(1):113–117.

20. Janus S, Janus C. Janus. *Report on Sexual Behavior*. New York, Wiley, 1993:253.

21. Petersen LR, Donnenwerth GV. Secularization and the influence of religion on beliefs about premarital sex. *Soc Forces*. 1997; 75(3):1071–1089.

22. Page RM, Hammermeister JJ, Scanlon A. Everybody's not doing it: misperceptions of college students' sexual activity. *Am J Health Behav*. 2000; 24(5):387–394.

23. Voss J, Kogan L. Behavioral impact of a human sexuality course. *J Sex Educ Ther*. 2001; 26(2):122–132.

24. Pluhar E, Frongillo EA Jr, Stycos JM, et al. Understanding the relationship between religion and the sexual attitudes and behaviors of college students. *J Sex Educ Ther*. 1998; 23(4):288–296.

25. Woody JD, Russel R, D'Souza HJ, et al. Adolescent non-coital sexual activity: comparisons of virgins and non-virgins. *J Sex Educ Ther*. 2000; 25(4):261–268.

26. Zaleski EH, Schiaffino KM. Religiosity and sexual risk-taking behavior during the transition to college. *J Adolesc*. 2000; 23(2):223–227.

27. Brewster KL, Cooksey EC, Guilkey DK, et al. The changing impact of religion on the sexual and contraceptive behavior of adolescent women in the United States. *J Marr Fam*. 1998; 60(2):493–504.

28. Ratliff-Crain J, Donald KM, Dalton J. Knowledge, beliefs, peer norms, and past behaviors as correlates of risky sexual behaviors among college students. *Psychol Health*. 1999; 14(4):625–641.

29. Baldwin JI, Baldwin JD. Heterosexual anal intercourse: an understudied, high-risk sexual behavior. *Arch Sex Behav*. 2000; 29(4):357–373.

30. Sheeran P, Abraham C, Orbell S. Psychosocial correlates of heterosexual condom use: a meta-analysis. *Psychol Bull*. 1999; 125(1):90–132.

31. Cooper ML. Alcohol use and risky sexual behavior among college students and youth: evaluating the evidence. *J Stud Alcohol*. 2002; (Suppl 14):101–117.

32. Poulson RL, Eppler MA, Satterwhite TN, et al. Alcohol, consumption, strength of religious beliefs, and risky sexual behavior in college students. *J Am Coll Health*. 1998; 46(5):227–232.

33. Davidson JK Sr, Moore NB. Guilt and lack of orgasm during sexual intercourse: myth versus reality among college women. *J Sex Educ Ther*. 1994; 20(3):153–174.

34. Murray J, Harver SM, Beckman LJ. The importance of contraceptive attributes of college women. *J Appl Psychol*. 1989; 19(16):1327–1350.

35. Moore NB, Davidson JK Sr. Guilt about first intercourse: an antecedent of sexual dissatisfaction among college women. *J Sex Marital Ther*. 1997; 23(1):29–46.

36. Wyatt GE, Dunn KM. Examining predictors of sex guilt in a multiethnic sample of women. *Arch Sex Behav*. 1991; 20(3):471–485.

37. Atwood JD, Gagnon J. Masturbatory behavior in college youth. *J Sex Educ Ther*. 1987; 13(2):35–42.

38. Beck SH, Cole BS, Hammond JA. Religious heritage and premarital sex: Evidence from a national sample of young adults. *J Sci Study Rel*. 1991; 30(2):173–180.

39. VanWicklin JF. Conceiving and measuring ways of being religious. *J Psychol Christ*. 1990; 9(2):27–40.

40. Loos VE, Bridges CF, Critelli JW. Weiner's attribution theory and female orgasmic consistency. *J Sex Res*. 1997; 23(3):19–24, 41.

Chapter 43
Where'd You Learn That?

Ron Stodghill II

Stodghill addresses educational issues about sexuality and American youth who are in the middle of their own sexual revolution, a situation leaving many parents feeling confused and, perhaps, powerless. This exploration of the question, "How does young sexual experimentation begin?" is at once entertaining and alarming. It would be easy for readers to reminisce and say, "The more things change, the more they stay the same." But reality asserts otherwise. In a day when children and young persons, ages 6 to 18, spend more time watching television than they spend in the classroom, changing paradigms of sexuality education are in play.

Sources cited by the author from which teenagers today learn about sexuality are, in order, peers—45 percent, television—29 percent, parents—7 percent, and sexuality education—3 percent. Even with new sexuality paradigms, some things have not changed: teenagers are not always logical. The increasing use of oral sex and anal intercourse among teenagers to avoid an unintended pregnancy flies in the face of reason, ignoring the fact that these practices offer no protection against sexually transmitted diseases. And, even though growing numbers of teens are knowledgeable about the mechanics of sex, the author asks, "What about their emotional health and social behavior?" An engaging topic presented in a compelling manner, this is a selection that students will not want to miss.

The cute little couple looked as if they should be sauntering through Great Adventure or waiting in line for tokens at the local arcade. Instead, the 14-year-olds walked purposefully into the Teen Center in suburban Salt Lake City, Utah. They didn't mince words about their reason for stopping in. For quite some time, usually after school and on weekends, the boy and girl had tried to heighten their arousal during sex. Flustered yet determined, the pair wanted advice on the necessary steps that might lead them to a more fulfilling orgasm. His face showing all the desperation of a lost tourist, the boy spoke for both of them when he asked frankly, "How do we get to the G-spot?"

Whoa. Teen Center nurse Patti Towle admits she was taken aback by the inquiry. She couldn't exactly provide a road map. Even more, the destination was a bit scandalous for a couple of ninth-graders in the heart of Mormon country. But these kids had clearly already gone further sexually than many adults, so Towle didn't waste time preaching the gospel of abstinence. She gave her young adventurers some reading material on the subject, including the classic women's health book *Our Bodies, Ourselves*, to help bring them closer in bed. She also brought up the question of whether a G-spot even exists. As her visitors were leaving, Towle offered them more freebies: "I sent them out the door with a billion condoms."

G-spots. Orgasms. Condoms. We all know kids say and do the darndest things, but how they have changed! One teacher recalls a 10-year-old raising his hand to ask her to define oral sex. He was quickly followed by an 8-year-old girl behind him who asked, "Oh, yeah, and what's anal sex?" These are the easy questions. Rhonda Sheared, who teaches sex education in Pinellas County, Fla., was asked by middle school students about the sound *kweif*, which the kids say is the noise a vagina makes during or after sex. "And how do you keep it from making this noise?"

There is more troubling behavior in Denver. School officials were forced to institute a sexual-harassment policy owing to a sharp rise in lewd language, groping, pinching and bra-snapping incidents among sixth-, seventh-, and eighth-graders. Sex among kids in Pensacola, Fla., became so pervasive that students of a private Christian junior high school are now asked to sign cards vowing not to have sex until they marry. But the cards don't mean anything, says a 14-year-old boy at the school. "It's broken promises."

It's easy enough to blame everything on television and entertainment, even the news. At a Denver middle school, boys rationalize their actions this way: "If the President can do it, why can't we?" White House sex scandals are one thing, but how can anyone avoid Viagra and virility? Or public discussions of sexually transmitted diseases like AIDS and herpes? Young girls have lip-synched often enough to Alanis Morissette's big hit of a couple of years ago, "You Oughta Know," to have found the sex nestled in the lyric. But it's more than just movies and television and news. Adolescent curiosity about sex is fed by a pandemic openness about it—in the schoolyard, on the bus, at home when no adult is watching. Just eavesdrop at the mall one afternoon, and you'll hear enough pubescent sexcapades to pen the next few episodes of *Dawson's Creek*, the most explicit show on teen sexuality, on the *WB* network. Parents, always the last to keep up, are now almost totally pre-empted. Chris (not his real name), 13, says his parents talked to him about sex when he was 12 but he had been indoctrinated earlier by a 17-year-old cousin. In any case, he gets his full share of information from the tube. "You name the show, and I've heard about it. *Jerry Springer, MTV, Dawson's Creek, HBO After Midnight* . . ." Stephanie, 16, of North Lauderdale, Fla., who first had sex when she was 14, claims to have slept with five boyfriends and is considered a sex expert by her friends. She says, "You can learn a lot about sex from cable. It's all mad-sex stuff. If you're feeling steamy and hot, there's only one thing you want to do. As long as you're using a condom, what's wrong with it? Kids have hormones too."

In these steamy times, it is becoming largely irrelevant whether adults approve of kids' sowing their oats—or knowing so much about the technicalities of the dissemination. American adolescents are in the midst of their own kind of sexual revolution—one that has left many parents feeling confused, frightened and almost powerless. Parents can search all they want for common ground with today's kids, trying to draw parallels between contemporary carnal knowledge and an earlier generation's free-love crusades, but the two movements are quite different. A desire to break out of the old-fashioned strictures fueled the '60s movement, and its participants made sexual freedom a kind of new religion. That sort of reverence has been replaced by a more consumerist attitude. In a 1972 cover story, *Time* declared, "Teenagers generally are woefully ignorant about sex." Ignorance is no longer the rule. As a weary junior high counselor in Salt Lake City puts it, "Teens today are almost nonchalant about sex. It's like we've been to the moon too many times."

The good news about their precocious knowledge of the mechanics of sex is that a growing number of teens know how to protect themselves, at least physically. But what about their emotional health and social behavior? That's a more troublesome picture. Many parents and teachers—as well as some thoughtful teenagers—worry about the desecration of love and the subversion of mature relationships. Says Debra Haffner, President of the Sexuality Information and Education Council of the United States: "We should not confuse kids' pseudo-sophistication about sexuality and their ability to use the language with their understanding of who they are as sexual young people or their ability to make good decisions."

One ugly side effect is a presumption among many adolescent boys that sex is an entitlement—an attitude that fosters a breakdown of respect for oneself and others. Says a seventh-grade girl: "The guy will ask you up front. If you turn him down, you're a bitch. But if you do it, you're a ho. The guys are after us all the time, in the halls, everywhere. You scream, 'Don't touch me!' but it doesn't do any good." A Rhode Island Rape Center study of 1,700 sixth- and ninth-graders found 65 percent of boys and 57 percent of girls believing it acceptable for a male to force a female to have sex if they've been dating for six months.

Parents who are aware of this cultural revolution seem mostly torn between two approaches: preaching abstinence or suggesting prophylactics—and thus condoning sex. Says Cory Hollis, 37, a father of three in the Salt Lake City area: "I don't want to see my teenage son ruin his life. But if he's going to do it, I told him that I'd go out and get him the condoms myself." Most parents seem too squeamish to get into the subtleties of instilling sexual ethics. Nor are schools up to the job of moralizing. Kids say they accept their teachers' admonitions to have safe sex but tune out other stuff. "The personal-development classes are a joke," says Sarah, 16, of Pensacola. "Even the teacher looks uncomfortable. There is no way anybody is going to ask a serious question." Says Shana, a 13-year-old from Denver: "A lot of it is old and boring. They'll talk about not having sex before marriage, but no one listens."

Shana says she is glad "sex isn't so taboo now, I mean with all the teenage pregnancies." But she also says that "it's creepy and kind of scary that it seems to be happening so early, and all this talk about it." She adds, "Girls are jumping too quickly. They figure if they can fall in love in a month, then they can have sex in a month too." When she tried discouraging a classmate from having sex for the first time, the friend turned to her and said, "My God, Shana. It's just sex."

Three powerful forces have shaped today's child prodigies: a prosperous information age that increasingly promotes products and entertains audiences by titillation; aggressive public-policy initiatives that loudly preach sexual responsibility, further desensitizing kids to the subject; and the decline of two-parent households, which leaves adolescents with little supervision. Thus kids are not only bombarded with messages about sex—many of them contradictory—but also have more private time to engage in it than did previous generations. Today more than half of the females and three-quarters of the males ages 15 to 19 have experienced sexual intercourse, according to the Commission on Adolescent Sexual Health. And while the average age at first intercourse has come down only a year since 1970 (currently it's 17 for girls and 16 for boys), speed is of the essence for the new generation. Says Haffner: "If kids today are going to do more than kiss, they tend to move very quickly toward sexual intercourse."

The remarkable—and in ways lamentable—product of youthful promiscuity and higher sexual IQ is the degree to which kids learn to navigate the complex hypersexual world that reaches out seductively to them at every turn. One of the most positive results: the incidence of sexually transmitted diseases and of teenage pregnancy is declining. Over the past few years, kids have managed to chip away at the teenage birthrate, which in 1991 peaked at 62.1 births per 1,000 females. Since then the birthrate has dropped 12 percent, to 54.7. Surveys suggest that as many as two-thirds of teenagers now use condoms, a proportion that is three times as high as reported in the 1970s. "We're clearly starting to make progress," says Dr. John Santelli, a physician with the Centers for Disease Control and Prevention's Division of Adolescent and School Health. "And the key statistics bear that out." Even if they've had sex, many kids are learning to put off having more till later; they are also making condom use during intercourse nonnegotiable; and, remarkably, the fleeting pleasures of lust may even be wising up some of them to a greater appreciation of love.

For better or worse, sex-filled television helps shape young opinion. In Chicago, Ryan, an 11-year-old girl, intently watches a scene from one of her favorite TV dramas, *Dawson's Creek*. She listens as the character Jen, who lost her virginity at 12 while drunk, confesses to her new love, Dawson, "Sex doesn't equal happiness. I can't apologize for my past." Ryan is quick to defend Jen. "I think she was young, but if I were Dawson, I would believe she had changed. She acts totally different now." But Ryan is shocked by an episode of her other favorite show, *Buffy the Vampire Slayer*, in which Angel, a male vampire, "turned bad" after having sex with the 17-year-old Buffy. "That kinda annoyed me," says Ryan. "What would have happened if she had had a baby? Her whole life would have been thrown out the window." As for the fallen Angel: "I am so mad! I'm going to take all my pictures of him down now."

And then there's real-life television. MTV's *Loveline*, an hour-long Q-and-A show featuring sex guru Drew Pinsky, is drawing raves among teens for its informative sexual content. Pinsky seems to be almost idolized by some youths. "Dr. Drew has some excellent advice," says Keri, an eighth-grader in Denver. "It's not just sex, its real life. Society makes you say you've got to look at shows like *Baywatch*, but I'm sick of blond bimbos."

With so much talk of sex in the air, the extinction of the hapless, sexually naive kid seems an inevitability. Indeed, kids today as young as seven to ten are picking up the first details of sex even in Saturday-morning cartoons. Brett, a 14-year-old in Denver, says it doesn't matter to him whether his parents chat with him about sex or not because he gets so much from TV. Whenever he's curious about something sexual, he channel surfs his way to certainty. "If you watch TV, they've got everything you want to know," he says. "That's how I learned to kiss, when I was eight. And the girl told me, 'Oh, you sure know how to do it.'"

Even if kids don't watch certain television shows, they know the programs exist and are bedazzled by the forbidden. From schoolyard word of mouth, eight-year-old Jeff in Chicago has heard all about the foul-mouthed kids in the raunchily plotted *South Park*, and even though he has never seen the show, he can describe certain episodes in detail. (He is also familiar with the AIDS theme of the musical *Rent* because he's heard the CD over and over.) Argentina, 16, in Detroit, says, "TV makes sex look like this big game." Her friend Michael, 17, adds, "They make sex look like Monopoly or something. You have to do it in order to get to the next level."

Child experts say that by the time many kids hit adolescence, they have reached a point where they aren't particularly obsessed with sex but have grown to accept the notion that solid courtships—or at least strong physical attractions—potentially lead to sexual intercourse. Instead of denying it they get an early start preparing for it—and playing and perceiving the roles prescribed for them. In Nashville, 10-year-old Brantley whispers about a classmate, "There's this girl I know, she's nine years old, and she already shaves her legs and plucks her eyebrows, and I've heard she's had sex. She even has bigger boobs than my mom!"

The playacting can eventually lead to discipline problems at school. Alan Skriloff, Assistant Superintendent of Personnel and Curriculum for New Jersey's North Brunswick School System, notes that there has been an increase in mock-sexual behavior in buses carrying students to school. He insists there have been no incidents of sexual assault but, he says, "we've dealt with kids simulating sexual intercourse and simulating masturbation. It's very disturbing to the other children and to the parents, obviously." Though Skriloff says that girls are often the initiators of such conduct, in most school districts the aggressors are usually boys.

Nan Stein, a senior researcher at the Wesley College Center for Research on Women, believes sexual violence and harassment is on the rise in schools, and she says, "It's happening between kids who are dating or want to be dating or used to date." Linda

Osmundson, Executive Director of the Center Against Spouse Abuse in St. Petersburg, Fla., notes that "it seems to be coming down to younger and younger girls who feel that if they don't pair up with these guys, they'll have no position in their lives. They are pressured into lots of sexual activity." In this process of socialization, "no" is becoming less and less an option.

In such a world, schools focus on teaching scientific realism rather than virginity. Sex-ed teachers tread lightly on the moral questions of sexual intimacy while going heavy on the risk of pregnancy or a sexually transmitted disease. Indeed, health educators in some school districts complain that teaching abstinence to kids today is getting to be a futile exercise. Using less final terms like "postpone" or "delay" helps draw some kids in, but semantics often isn't the problem. In a Florida survey, the state found that 75 percent of kids had experienced sexual intercourse by the time they reached 12th grade, with some 20 percent of the kids having had six or more sexual partners. Rick Colonno, father of a 16-year-old son and 14-year-old daughter in Arvada, Colo., views sex ed in schools as a necessary evil to fill the void that exists in many homes. Still, he's bothered by what he sees as a subliminal endorsement of sex by authorities. "What they're doing," he says, "is preparing you for sex and then saying, 'But don't have it.'"

With breathtaking pragmatism, kids look for ways to pursue their sex life while avoiding pregnancy or disease. Rhonda Sheared, the Florida sex-ed teacher, says a growing number of kids are asking questions about oral and anal sex because they've discovered that it allows them to be sexually active without risking pregnancy. As part of the Pinellas County program, students in middle and high school write questions anonymously, and, as Sheared says, "they're always looking for the loophole."

A verbatim sampling of some questions:

- "Can you get AIDS from fingering a girl if you have no cuts? Through your fingernails?"
- "Can you gets AIDS from '69'?"
- "If you shave your vagina or penis, can that get rid of crabs?"
- "If yellowish stuff comes out of a girl, does it mean you have herpes, or can it just happen if your period is due, along with abdominal pains?"
- "When sperm hits the air, does it die or stay alive for 10 days?"

Ideally, most kids say, they would prefer their parents do the tutoring, but they realize that's unlikely. For years psychologists and sociologists have warned about a new generation gap, one created not so much by different morals and social outlooks as by career-driven parents, the economic necessity of two incomes leaving parents little time for talks with their children. Recent studies indicate that many teens think parents are the most accurate source of information and would like to talk to them more about sex and sexual ethics but can't get their attention long enough. Shana sees the conundrum this way: "Parents haven't set boundaries, but they are expecting them."

Some parents are working harder to counsel their kids on sex. Cathy Wolf, 29, of North Wales, Pa., says she grew up learning about sex largely from her friends and from reading controversial books. Open-minded and proactive, she says she has returned to a book she once sought out for advice, Judy Blume's novel *Are You There God? It's Me, Margaret*, and is reading it to her two boys, 8 and 11. The novel discusses the awkwardness of adolescence, including sexual stirrings. "That book was forbidden to me as a kid," Wolf says. "I'm hoping to give them a different perspective about sex, to expose them to this kind of subject matter before they find out about it themselves." Movies and television are a prod and a challenge to Wolf. In *Grease*, which is rated PG and was recently re-released, the character Rizzo "says something about 'sloppy seconds,' you know, the fact that a guy wouldn't want to do it with a girl who had just done it with another guy. There's also another point where they talk about condoms."

Most kids, though, lament that their parents aren't much help at all on sexual matters. They either avoid the subject, miss the mark by starting the discussion too long before or after the sexual encounter, or just plain stonewall them. "I was nine when I asked my mother the Big Question," says Michael, in Detroit. "I'll never forget. She took out her driver's license and pointed to the line about male or female. 'That is sex,' she said." Laurel, a 17-year-old in Murfreesboro, Tenn., wishes her parents had taken more time with her to shed light on the subject. When she was six and her sister was nine, "my mom sat us down, and we had the sex talk," Laurel says. "But when I was 10, we moved in with my dad, and he never talked about it. He would leave the room if a commercial for a feminine product came on TV." And when her sister finally had sex, at 16, even her mother's vaunted openness crumbled. "She talked to my mom about it and ended up feeling like a whore because even though my mom always said we could talk to her about anything, she didn't want to hear that her daughter had slept with a boy."

Part of the problem for many adults is that they aren't quite sure how they feel about teenage sex. A third of adults think adolescent sexual activity is wrong, while a majority of adults think it's O.K. and, under certain conditions, normal, healthy behavior, according to the Alan Guttmacher Institute, a non-profit, reproductive-health research group. In one breath, parents say they perceive it as a public-health issue and want more information about sexual behavior and its consequences, easier access to contraceptives, and more material in the media about responsible human and sexual interaction. And in the next breath, they claim it's a moral issue to be resolved through preaching abstinence and the virtues of virginity and getting the trash off TV. "You start out talking about condoms in this country, and you end up fighting about the future of the American family," says Sarah Brown, Director of the Campaign Against Teen Pregnancy. "Teens just end up frozen like a deer in headlights."

Not all kids are happy with television's usurping the role of village griot. Many say they've become bored by—and even resent—sexual themes that seem pointless and even a distraction from the information or entertainment they're seeking. "It's like everywhere," says Ryan, a 13-year-old seventh-grader in Denver, "even in *Skateboarding* [magazine]. It's become so normal it doesn't even affect you. On TV, out of nowhere, they'll begin talking about masturbation." Another Ryan, 13, in the eighth grade at the same school, agrees: "There's sex in the cartoons and messed-up people on the talk shows—'My lover sleeping with my best friend.' I can remember the jumping condom ads. There's just too much of it all."

Many kids are torn between living up to a moral code espoused by their church and parents and try-ing to stay true to the swirling laissez-faire. Experience is making many sadder but wiser. The shame, anger or even indifference stirred by early sex can lead to prolonged abstinence. Chandra, a 17-year-old in Detroit, says she had sex with a boyfriend of two years for the first time at 15 despite her mother's constant pleas against it. She says she wishes she had heeded her mother's advice. "One day I just decided to do it," she says. "Afterward, I was kind of mad that I let it happen. And I was sad because I knew my mother wouldn't have approved." Chandra stopped dating the boy more than a year ago and hasn't had sex since. "It would have to be someone I really cared about," she says. "I've had sex before, but I'm not a slut."

With little guidance from grownups, teens have had to discover for themselves that the ubiquitous sexual messages must be tempered with caution and responsibility. It is quite clear, even to the most sexually experienced youngsters, just how dangerous a little information can be. Stephanie in North Lauderdale, who lost her virginity two years ago, watches with concern as her seven-year-old sister moves beyond fuzzy thoughts of romance inspired by *Cinderella* or *Aladdin* into sexual curiosity. "She's always talking about pee-pees, and she sees somebody on TV kissing and hugging or something, and she says, 'Oh, they had sex.' I think she's going to find out about this stuff before I did." She pauses. "We don't tell my sister anything," she says, "but she's not a naive child."

Chapter 44

Sexuality Education

Philosophies and Practices in Search of a Meaningful Difference

Terrance D. Olson

The lines of the polarized debate between advocates of a conservative approach to sexuality education and a more liberal one may be blurring, as indicated by a national survey conducted by the Alan Guttmacher Institute. Of all school districts, 23 percent currently require schools to teach abstinence until marriage and discuss contraception only in the context of its shortcomings. But, even among the one-third of parents who say schools should teach abstinence until marriage, a substantial number also want schools to arm their children with information about obtaining and using condoms, contraception, and abortion, in case they do become sexually active (Schemo 2000). Is it any wonder that educators in the trenches often characterize our culture as sexually schizophrenic?

This great American ambivalence is illustrated in the different approaches to sexuality education at the beginning of the AIDS epidemic by the usually considered "conservative" Britons and the "liberal" Americans. The British inaugurated the nationwide "Don't Die of Ignorance" campaign after England had diagnosed only a few cases of AIDS. In the United States, it took six years and thousands of cases of AIDS before the President even uttered the word in public. One professional offered this analysis:

> . . . [W]hile the British aim earnestly to protect their young from ignorance, we misguided Americans have [enlisted ignorance] in the fight! While the British motto might well be 'Just Say Know!,' we offer, in place of the power of knowledge, 'Just Say No.' And who are the 'we'? We are the same adult community who can be seen saying 'yes' all day long in those endless television images, contradicting ourselves in the eyes of our young with every change of channels. (Roffman 1992, 7)

Straight talk is urged by experts in the field of sexuality education as an antidote to such adult "double-speak." Roffman continues,

> Taking our cue from the sensible British, we might say: We love you and want you to be safe. The best way to do that is to abstain [from] any potentially risky behavior. Next best is to protect yourself and others as best you can. Here's how. . . . (1992, 7)

The Terrance Olson chapter about sexuality education will not spell out nor recommend specific programs and practices. It will offer a philosophical perspective with which you can reframe this perennially controversial topic yourself.

The New England Journal of Medicine published this observation about a sex education approach in the United States Army:
"A recent release from the Office of the Surgeon General reports a remarkable drop in the incidence of venereal disease [in the military]."

> . . . For the Army as a whole, the decrease amounted to 40 percent; for soldiers stationed in the United States, it was more than 50 percent. This is an encouraging note in view of the trend toward increased [the] rate in the civilian population as recently reported. The Surgeon General credits this accomplishment to a new approach on the part of the Army, based on 'an intelligent appeal to the higher moral sense of the individual,' with 'moral, spiritual, psychological, as well as objective factors.' In this program the reasons for good conduct are stressed through group and individual education and conferences. . . . This approach has supplanted prior concepts, which emphasized the aspects of prevention, with the implication that the soldier was not remiss so long as his illicit relations did not result in infection. Training films . . . have been replaced by new films reflecting the current trend, dramatizing 'The rewards of good conduct as well as the effect of social diseases on an individual's future health and happiness.' (1948: 784)

At some point in the above paragraph, it may have become obvious that this is historical commentary over 50 years old. The tip-off might have been how the program was described approvingly and that the writer used judgmental terms, such as "illicit" relations. But more to the point, the quote reveals that over two generations ago, at least two approaches to the consequences of sexual relations among the unmarried were being implemented—at least by the U.S. Army. This observation by the Surgeon General of the United States is just one example in the ongoing public debate regarding what the societal, public response to various sexual activities in the population, especially the adolescent population, ought to be. As soon as the debate centers on what kind of intervention—or what kind of education—should be initiated and delivered as a prevention for, or solution to, the consequences of sexual activity (presumably not including such activity in marriage), the issue becomes a matter of moral philosophy as well as social science, or public policy, or both.

It is proposed that anytime the social sciences spawn intervention programs that the motivation of the clinicians and practitioners so engaged is similar: to improve the quality of the human condition. Of course, if the issue is the quality of human experience, then judgments have to be made regarding the nature/characteristics of quality living. Making those judgments is a moral enterprise. Interventionists (such as therapists and family life educators) are inescapably addressing and drawing conclusions about what is moral or what is ethical, for they have purposes that promote certain outcomes deemed to be of quality, rather than over outcomes deemed to be less beneficial or even destructive.

Some have argued that the moral domain is inherent in the study of human experience and does not appear just only when intervention is the issue. Regarding the case of psychology, Williams and Gantt (2002) have defined the moral very broadly: ". . . we will understand as moral anything—or more appropriately, any event—that has some meaningful implication or consequence in the lives of human beings. In other words, the moral is that which makes a meaningful difference to a human person in a given human context" (2002:11). Counselors and educators—and, perhaps, especially sex educators, given the sensitive and central nature of their task, purpose, and topics—are seeking to make a meaningful difference in the lives of those exposed to sex education. It is assumed that the meaningful difference is in the quality of lives lived by those who are so educated.

Occasionally, researchers and theorists reflect, in a meta-theoretical way, on the assumptions or theories that guide their practices and their intervention efforts. Back (1983), for example, was, perhaps, stating the obvious when he noted that, in efforts to decrease adolescent pregnancy rates, the scientist might focus on the two dimensions that generate the rates in the first place: the level of sexual activity among the adolescent population and the level of contraception use in the same population. But Back indicated that up to the mid-1980s, this was not what had happened: " . . . we are struck by the preponderance of research and application on the second factor—the use of contraceptives, to the virtual exclusion of the first, the increase of teenage, nonmarital intercourse" (1983:2).

Now, twenty years later, the debate has altered somewhat because research has been carried forth addressing both factors. Each group of researchers is not only committed to getting to the core of the problem, but both groups also bring a philosophy of what kind of sexuality education would make "a meaningful difference"—to refer back to the description of moral activity made by Williams and Gantt (2002). The conclusions are conflicting regarding the value and pragmatic benefits of the content and delivery of various programs. Deciding how to respond to these conflicting views is not a simple issue for those committed to intervention. Even the target behaviors or contexts to address are not identified unanimously by researchers or practitioners, but a source of understanding the conflicting starting points of intervention could be to grant that empirical work in social science is also guided by various philosophies of science (Slife & Williams, 1995).

To illustrate, social scientists in recent years have become explicit about the reality and value of the moral domain in drawing conclusions about what kinds of interventions are most valuable (see Doherty, 1995; Coles, 1988). In moral philosophy, many models of normative ethics (identifying what principles are invoked to espouse what is good or right) have been presented. One integrated model offered back in the late 1970s is still a valid summary of the conceptual possibilities (Boyce & Jensen, 1978). At least the questions about normative ethics have remained the same: In deciding what is "good" or quality human experience, do I take an instrumentalist view (Nothing is intrinsically good; all things are means, there are no ends) or an intrinsic view (There are intrinsically good things. There are goods that are good in and of themselves)? The latter view is a bit more complicated, because then a variety of intrinsic goods can be proposed: pleasure; something other than pleasure; pleasure plus something(s) other than pleasure—all are possibilities. In addition, once a concept of the good has been identified, the means to promoting that good must be decided. The possibilities involve taking only consequences into account (teleological positions), or taking only the nature of the action itself into account, or taking the nature of the act itself and the consequences into account (deontological positions) (Boyce & Jensen, 1978).

It may be that interventionists do not see themselves as engaged in a moral enterprise, but it is likely that even if they have not been explicit about what is good or what will bring to pass the good in which they believe, they are offering a moral possibility to their audiences—or, at the least, a possibility they believe is moral. This is because the moral dimension of intervention is inescapable, and intervention efforts, whether acknowledged as such by their creators, are addressing moral realities of our culture. Even if interventionists have not been explicit about the good they are seeking to bring about, their efforts can be categorized somewhere in the intellectual frameworks provided by moral philosophy. The only way intervention efforts could be considered not a moral activity is if they described themselves as not intending to make any meaningful difference. Such a description would make intervention efforts nonsensical.

Thus, sexuality education is a controversial topic, not because science is conflicting with the values of nonscientist consumers of the sex education product—although sometimes the debates are characterized that way—but because of conflicting philosophies of what is good and right regarding human sexuality. Neither scientists nor consumers have exclusive claim to beliefs and systems of thought on that subject. And though it is important to be fair and straightforward in interpreting research results, such interpretations use data on issues and outcome variables already deemed to be worthwhile (both relevant and moral) by those who constructed the research efforts. In any event, the reality of disagreement regarding quality, regarding the ethical and the moral, and regarding how to achieve or produce quality outcomes in the lives of adolescents is what generates the debate central to all sex education efforts.

If we are to deliver sex education as a means of promoting the quality of life, we must decide what kind of knowledge is most appropriate, what practices we wish to promote, what contexts of conduct are most beneficial, and what practices are to be discouraged. For example, if we are to engage in prevention, exactly what are we to prevent and why? Adolescent pregnancy prevention is deemed a worthwhile and realistic goal of sex education (SIECUS, 1996; Planned Parenthood, 1984, Abstinence Clearinghouse, 2002; Kirby, 2001; Abstinence Clearinghouse, 2003; Richard, 1990). Two "brands" or categories of sex education seem to describe most intervention efforts. Comprehensive sex education is described as providing accurate information, exploring sexual attitudes and values, developing interpersonal skills and exercising responsibility regarding sexual relationships (SIECUS, 2003). Abstinence education is described as promoting appreciation for and practice of sexual abstinence until marriage through distribution of age-appropriate, factual and medically accurate materials (Abstinence Clearinghouse, 2003). These approaches, in addition to offering knowledge about the biology and physiology of human sexual-

ity, address the two factors contributing to adolescent pregnancy as noted by Back (1983): the level of use of contraception among participating teens and the number of unmarried teens who participate in intercourse at all.

The most widespread prevention efforts seem to be of the comprehensive type (the SIECUS and Planned Parenthood websites offer lists of comprehensive curricula), although a greater variety of abstinence-based programs now seem to be available (Abstinence Clearing House, 2003; Richard, 1990). Although both types of intervention are now generating empirical research, the types of studies and the meanings of the variety of results generate continued debate. Back (1983), before numerous evaluation efforts were being reported extensively in the literature, attributed the disparity in types of prevention efforts not to how realistic a given approach may or may not be (to convince teens either to use condoms or to abstain altogether), but to ideology among social scientists who have already decided where the prevention line is to be drawn. A greater array of research results is now available, but the debate as to what best creates a meaningful difference is as intense as ever.

Sexuality education begins in philosophy, not in curricula or research efforts. The latter two activities are symptoms or expressions of philosophical starting points. The Sex Information and Education Council of the United States (SIECUS) subscribes to the idea that early sexual involvement by teenagers is undesirable. The work of this counsel articulates guidelines and values within those guidelines. It is in the SIECUS statements of values that their philosophy of human sexuality and of prevention is revealed:

1. Sexuality is a natural and healthy part of living.

2. All persons are sexual.

3. Sexuality includes physical, ethical, social, spiritual, psychological, and emotional dimensions.

4. Every person has dignity and self-worth.

5. Young people should view themselves as unique and worthwhile individuals within the context of their cultural heritage.

6. Individuals express their sexuality in varied ways.

7. Parents should be the primary sexuality educators of their children.

8. Families provide children's first education about sexuality.

9. Families share their values about sexuality with their children.

10. In a pluralistic society, people should respect and accept the diversity of values and beliefs about sexuality that exist in a community.

11. Sexual relationships should never be coercive or exploitative.

12. All children should be loved and cared for.

13. All sexual decisions have effects or consequences.

14. All persons have the right and the obligation to make responsible sexual choices.

15. Individuals, families, and society benefit when children are able to discuss sexuality with their parents, or other trusted adults, or both.

16. Young people develop their values about sexuality as part of becoming adults.

17. Young people explore their sexuality as a natural process of achieving sexual maturity.

18. Premature involvement in sexual behaviors poses risks.

19. Abstaining from sexual intercourse is the most effective method of preventing pregnancy and STDs/HIV.

20. Young people who are involved in sexual relationships need access to information about health care services (adapted from SIECUS, 2003).

The starting point of the SIECUS philosophy is to see individuals as sexual beings who are to express their sexuality in responsible, knowledgeable ways. Responsible parents who are open and involved in providing sexual knowledge preferably begin sexuality education. This parental involvement is to include the transmission or discussion of parental values and beliefs regarding human sexuality.

Embedded in the philosophy of comprehensive sex education (SIECUS, 2003) also are threads of relativism (all sexual values are to be respected and accepted—Point 10) and of individualism (young people develop their values about sexuality and explore sexuality as a natural process of becoming adults—(Points 16–17). In addition, these guidelines suggest that all people are valuable and should attend to their cultural heritage (Point 5) and that parent-child discussions of sexual values and behavior are beneficial.

The Abstinence Clearinghouse also identifies guidelines for sex education and includes in the definition of what is responsible, knowledgeable sexual expression the idea that sexuality is restricted to marriage. Thus, this view of sex education is that it ". . . promotes the appreciation for and practice of sexual abstinence (purity) through the distribution of age-appropriate, factual and medically-accurate materials" (Abstinence Clearinghouse, 2003:1). The organization supports a variety of curricula that promote, in various ways, the abstinence-until-marriage message.

At the general level of analysis, these two organizations already reveal differing viewpoints in the philosophy that guides their sex education efforts. For SIECUS, the fundamental issue is that humans are sexual beings and should express their sexuality responsibly in a wide variety of possible practices and contexts. For the Abstinence Clearinghouse, humans are sexual beings whose responsible sexual practices are to be reserved for marriage. Both organizations affirm the destructiveness of manipulative, coercive sexual involvement, and both thus take a moral stand on sexual conduct on the basis of consequences. However, Abstinence Clearinghouse and most abstinence curricula extend a moral stance to include the context of the sexual involvement, and not just the conduct. This difference in philosophies is grounded in differing philosophies of the human being and human sexuality and precedes any empirical work on these two distinct approaches to sexuality education. Comprehensive sex education (as presented by SIECUS and others) is extensive in addressing values, beliefs, practices, consequences, and sexual expression as a natural feature of being a human being. Abstinence curricula typically emphasize knowledge, consequences, beliefs, and values and the context of marriage as the appropriate domain of practice.

With the exception of acknowledging that sexual practices be mutual (noncoercive or exploitive), comprehensive sex education seems to be philosophically "acontextual" (the practices are the concern, irrespective of relationship contexts), and the moral-guidelines focus on whether sexual practices manage to avoid destructive consequences. These consequences are most often thought of as physical (avoiding pregnancy, STDs, HIV, etc.), but theoretically they include social-emotional outcomes as well. The values and beliefs associated with sexual participation grant the possibility of being unique to the individual. In this view, sexual practices are portable across a myriad of contexts, as long as the practices are mutual, freely chosen, and nondestructive. When practices and behaviors are the targeted focus of sexuality education, the philosophy leans toward defining, presenting, and promoting certain behaviors and practices without prime attention to the contexts in which those practices might be carried out. Thus, such curricula could be categorized as behavioral rather than contextual. In fact, they are philosophically acontextual, with minimal attention paid to the relationship context in which sexual activity takes place.

Given that the comprehensive guidelines also indicate such relativistic values as "Individuals express their sexuality in varied ways" (SIECUS, 2003, Point 6) and "In a pluralistic society, people should respect and accept the diversity of values and beliefs about sexuality that exists in a community" (SIECUS, 2003, Point 10) the potential exists for great conflict between what parents may teach is acceptable sexual behavior and what the comprehensive curricula may teach. For example, for parents and students to "respect" sexual practices or contexts that some parents find morally reprehensible is unlikely, let alone to expect students to "accept" them. An alternative description that more parents might respond to positively would be a statement such as the following: "In a pluralistic society, some sexual practices might be promoted, some might be protected, and some might be prohibited. Individually, we have the right and obligation to declare our stance on such matters, and to view with compassionate tolerance those who disagree" (Focus on the Family, 2001:8). Such a statement acknowledges that a philosophy of relativism need not be a feature of either approach to sex education, and that it is possible to acknowledge and support parental moral boundaries without justifying destructive attitudes toward those who differ—either in their moral arguments or in their sexual practices. The practical degree of parental involvement in comprehensive sex education may not always be extensive, as challenged by some abstinence educators (Focus on the Family, 2001:8). Of course, reasoned dialogue regarding these issues is to be carried out with compassionate tolerance, not through dictatorial or arrogant contention and certainly not in a way that is dismissive of others' stances.

Abstinence education seems to be more attentive to contextual realities; and its moral guideline is that sexual participation is only legitimate in a context of marriage. The exclusion of other sexual options for adolescents is no different from the context approved for adults. Both mutual consent and marriage are the essential contexts within which sexual activity is to take place. This stance places sexual activity in a relational context—a person-centered context—thus relegating a focus on sexual practices to secondary status. Abstinence educators are standing on ground that restricts adolescents, many of whom are, of course, also legal minors, from nonmarital sexual access. They are drawing the moral boundary more restrictively than the limits drawn by the philosophy that underlies comprehensive sex education in which mutual consent and nondestructive consequences are the prime moral boundaries.

In fact, at a more fundamental level, the differing philosophies of sex education illustrate different views of what attitudes and behaviors in a society are legitimate—or at least preferred. Abstinence educators see a society in which sexuality is expressed in marriage and not as a matter of mere individual, noncoercive preference. Both philosophies of sex education acknowledge abstinence as the best way to avoid a host of destructive consequences, but abstinence educators opt to teach that philosophy as preferred; however, comprehensive sex educators see the marriage requirement as only one of many options and seem to suggest a moral equality to almost any noncoercive sexual involvement. Thus, their vision of society is of a sexually-participating adolescent and adult population who has every (moral) right to sexually express itself, on the assumption, of course, that coercion or manipulation are not features of the activity. Observers of sexuality education may sometimes see abstinence education as teaching the way they believe society ought to be, but comprehensive education is teaching the way society actually is. Of course, because society consists of individuals who believe and behave according to each philosophy we have discussed, abstinence education is, in fact, an expression of the beliefs and behaviors of one constituency in society, and comprehensive education is an expression of another constituency. If the values, beliefs, and even behaviors of an audience were assessed in advance, the content could be configured to benefit that specific group within specific moral boundaries—that is, within the concept of what content will make a meaningful difference. But our culture's approach to sex education is generally to fit the audience to the already constructed curriculum.

The differences in the philosophies of sexuality that deem what kinds of sex education are appropriate are not resolved in the research arena. Various programs from a variety of philosophies have achieved statistically significant results in the intended direction of the intervention curricula, but they also have produced failures to change behavior significantly. The specific outcomes identified, the methods of measurement, and the interpretations of results do not dissolve the philosophical debate (see Franklin et al., 1997 for a review of numerous programs).

Empirical Studies

A few studies and results are illustrative of the philosophical division in the research community and especially among those intervening to make a meaningful difference. Two types of studies can be examined: studies that provide background data on relevant factors describing the adolescent population and direct intervention studies designed to make a meaningful difference.

An early survey study by Hanson, Myers, and Ginsburg (1987) of 10,000 never-married females, completed during their sophomore year of high school and coupled with 3 years of follow-up surveys, found the following factors not related to the likelihood of a black or white student having an out-of-wedlock birth as a teenager: (1) Having had a school sex education course, and (2) birth control knowledge. In other words, those two factors simply did not make a difference in the likelihood of a student in later years having an out-of-wedlock birth. However, the authors also report the factors related to reducing the likelihood of an out-of-wedlock birth. Specifically, (1) when adolescents and their parents mutually endorse values and live by behaviors that stress responsibility; (2) when young women hold high educational expectations; (3) when parents show concern about their adolescents' activities (including monitoring homework and whereabouts); (4) when adolescents behave in school responsibly and with self-discipline; (5) when adolescents avoid going steady; (6) for whites, when adolescents attribute success to their own initiative; (7) for whites, when parents hold high educational expectations for their child; and (8) for blacks, not reporting that they would consider having a child out-of-wedlock (adapted from Hanson et al., 1987:250–251).

First of all, it is evident that the significant factors here are related to personal beliefs and values as well as the contexts, relationships, families, and communities where such commitments were nurtured (or not). Parental concern, expectations and monitoring contribute to self-discipline and responsibility. Hanson et al. reported an attitudinal connection regarding teenagers' responses to sex education and contraceptive knowledge: "...taking a sex education course and having greater knowledge of birth control increase the chances that a black teenager will consider giving birth while unmarried. Birth control knowledge, but not sex education, increases these chances for whites" (1987:251). Behaviorally, moreover, and for those most at risk, the knowledge was not a factor in changing their behavior. Notably, no data were reported regarding participation rates in sexual intercourse, or pregnancy rates, or abortion rates. Thus, it is not possible to draw conclusions regarding those factors that may or may not contribute to other problems of adolescent sexual involvement (including the contracting of STDs, for example, or of differential abortion rates in the categories analyzed). This is a common feature, both of background and inter-vention studies. The big picture of understanding statistically significant results is obscured by the telescopic focus on a few outcomes. Nevertheless, such studies give family life educators starting points of understanding the issues, even though definitive conclusions regarding the overall problem must be held in abeyance.

Perhaps knowledge and skills are incorporated into a culture when they are compatible with it, but ignored when counter to it. Generically speaking, sexuality education may not address the subcultures of students, neither those most or least at risk for adolescent pregnancy. A significant feature of adolescents in subcultures, however, is the relationship they have with their parents, and both comprehensive sex education and abstinence education articulate values that include—at the theoretical level anyway—parental values and involvement. However, intervention efforts often fall short, for whatever reasons, of following through on the declared philosophies of both groups regarding parents. Even the conclusions of Hanson and colleagues (1987) in this background study seem misaligned with the authors' results. Having just noted that beliefs, values, and parental relationships are the significant antecedent conditions for lower rates of adolescent childbirth, more salient even than sex education or birth control knowledge, what did the authors recommend but more knowledge. In fairness, the authors called for school programs to include values and attitudes along with the technical knowledge, granting that parental values and influence are crucial to reducing rates of out-of-wedlock pregnancies. This approach could be a key to obtaining more positive outcomes.

Another early study funded by the Ford Foundation is the evaluation of a systematic and longitudinal treatment program for an extremely high-risk population with respect to adolescent pregnancy. The treatment group consisted of adolescent women age 17 or younger who were pregnant or had already borne a child out-of-wedlock. The purpose of the program was to help the women avoid a repeat pregnancy and redirect them to "a path of economic self-sufficiency" (Polit & Kahn, 1985). Since this truly comprehensive program targeted economic self-sufficiency in the young women, an array of counseling services (counseling, employment training, networking with service providers) was made available.

Four cities with groups of teens receiving the treatment program were matched for social and economic characteristics with four other cities geographically similar. For 12 months, the treatment group was nurtured with an array of services, including employment training, contraceptive instruction, and so forth. At the end of one year, the repeat pregnancy rate of the targeted group was 14 percent as compared with 22 percent for the comparison group. This difference of 8 percent was statistically significant. In the following year, neither group received treatment. At the end of 24 months, the repeat pregnancy rate of the treatment group had increased to match that of the comparison group (45 percent and 49 percent), so that by the final interviews, no statistical difference in pregnancy rates was evident (Polit & Kahn, 1985).

This study is strong in its thoroughness of research evaluation, although the reporting includes some odd omissions of information very relevant if the concern were with the meaning or context of repeat pregnancies. For example, almost 3 times as many of the comparison teens were married as were the project teens (3.3 percent vs. 8.9 percent), although the former's percentage of the total sample was small (Polit & Kahn, 1985). Economically disadvantaged or not, a repeat pregnancy, or contraception, or employment, or school status might have a different meaning for a married teenager than an unmarried one.

Yet, the conceptual significance of the study is the discouraging fact that the group targeted for the most extensive interventions did as well (or poorly) on the target variables as the groups who received no services or more limited intervention. One plausible explanation would require examining the community connections of the various groups.

Commendably, Polit (1989) revisited the sample in a 5-year follow-up study. At this point, the statistically significant results included favorable improvements for the Redirection group in contrast to the Comparison group. The Redirection women reported a higher percentage of having held jobs, of working a greater number of hours per week, and of receiving a smaller percentage of AFDC help; fewer mean number of abortions (.3 vs. .5); and a greater number of live births. No differences in aspects of contraceptive use were noted between the groups (p.166).

Again, relevant contextual differences in the groups were not examined statistically. For example, 24 percent of women in the 5-year follow-up were married, and about one-third of the women were living with a male partner at the time of the most recent interview (Polit, 1989). Thus, contextual factors might be relevant regarding such issues as contraceptive use, the context of repeat pregnancies, mean number of live births, accessibility to the workplace, and so forth. When the issue is how best to intervene, the more we know about contextual factors, the better we can focus our efforts.

In a more recent and thorough review article of family factors associated with reducing risk of adolescent pregnancy, Miller, Benson, and Galbraith (2001) noted several variables that public schools might be able to build upon if the desire is to reduce the risk of pregnancy among its targeted school population. As paraphrased, the following points are made:

1. Parent/child connectedness, defined as support, closeness, and warmth, is related to lower adolescent pregnancy risk, and ". . . is greatest for this effect through delaying and reducing adolescent sexual intercourse" (2001:24).

2. Parental supervision and monitoring generally are related to lower adolescent pregnancy risk.

3. Parental attitudes and values that disapprove of either sexual intercourse or unprotected intercourse and pregnancy are related to lower adolescent pregnancy risk.

4. Although the direct effects of parent/child communication are noted as inconclusive, parent/child communication, linked with parental values and closeness of the parent/child relationship, ". . . have important interactive effects on adolescent pregnancy risk through reducing sexual intercourse and/or increasing contraceptive use" (2001:25).

These variables are highlighted because they are the kinds of contextual factors that could be subject to the influence or support of school sex education curricula. When sexuality educators take into account variables that contribute to reduced risk, such as family variables, and include discussions of family issues in the classroom, they are addressing that portion of the audience whose family variables are relevant to prevention. Although much sex education addresses the "most at risk" portion of a student audience, it may be wise, relevant, and possible to structure components of a course that acknowledge the heterogeneous reality of any given class and deliver content designed to strengthen those students who already are less at risk, either because of their own beliefs and behavior or because they are products of family variables that statistically reduce risk.

Regarding contextual factors, parental influence ranks first or second, including influence regarding adolescents' sexual values, beliefs, and behavior (Miller, Benson, & Galbraith, 2001). But contextual factors, though attended to in nonexperimental studies (such as Hanson et al. and many of the articles reviewed by Miller, Benson, & Galbraith) are typically not a prime feature of sexuality education curricula.

In Search of Meaning

Perhaps the realities of intervention in human affairs are so complex that it is simultaneously laudable and yet naïve to create sexuality education programs that cannot possibly deliver the dramatic results their creators, and society itself, might hope for. As Sarah Brown noted in the Foreword to a summary of pregnancy prevention efforts as compiled by the National Campaign to Prevent Teen Pregnancy (National Campaign, 2001),

> Although we believe that having accurate, research-based information can only help communities make good decisions about preventing teen pregnancy, the National Campaign recognizes that communities choose to develop particular prevention programs for many reasons other than research—including, for example, compatibility with religious traditions, available resources, community standards, and the personal values and beliefs of the leaders in charge. In this context, I would add that it is crucial for such leaders to understand that community-based programs are only part of the solution to the teen pregnancy challenge and that no single effort can be expected to solve this problem by itself. Teen pregnancy is, after all, a very complex problem, influenced by many factors, including individual biology, parents and family, peers, schools and other social institutions, religion and faith communities, the media, and the list goes on. In an ideal world, we would mount efforts to engage the help of all these forces, particularly popular culture, schools, faith communities, parents and other adults. But we are a long way from doing so, and many communities mistakenly believe that modest community programs can do this single-handedly. In many instances, these programs are fragile and poorly funded; even apparently "effective" programs often achieve only modest results; and not all teens at risk of pregnancy are enrolled in programs. The simple point is that no single approach can solve this problem alone, whether it is a national media campaign, a new move in faith communities to address this problem, or a well-designed community program. Advocates of any single approach . . . should therefore be modest in both their promises and their expectations. (2001:iii)

This is a sobering assessment indeed. Summarizing results from the diversity of programs designed to reduce adolescent pregnancy or sexual activity is difficult. Not only is there a diversity of methods, programs, and audiences, but there is also additional research, all of which makes the task of arriving at definitive conclusions about the elusive situation somewhat like trying to pinpoint a moving ship at sea. Nevertheless, Kirby's (2001) work,

though acknowledging we have a long way to go in intervention efforts, is representative of the issues, the outcomes, and the possibilities. For example, Kirby (2001) has noted ten common characteristics of effective sex and HIV Education Programs:

1. Focus on reducing one or more sexual behaviors that lead to unintended pregnancy or HIV/STD infection.

2. Use theoretical approaches that have been demonstrated to influence other health-related behavior and identify specific important sexual antecedents to be targeted.

3. Deliver and consistently reinforce a clear message about abstaining from sexual activity and/or using condoms or other forms of contraception. This appears to be one of the most important characteristics that distinguishes effective from ineffective programs.

4. Provide basic, accurate information about the risks of teen sexual activity and about ways to avoid intercourse or use methods of protection against pregnancy and STDs.

5. Include activities that address social pressures that influence sexual behaviors.

6. Provide examples of and practice with communication, negotiation, and refusal skills.

7. Employ teaching methods designed to involve participants and have them personalize the information.

8. Incorporate behavioral goals, teaching methods, and materials that are appropriate to the age, sexual experience, and culture of the students.

9. Last a sufficient length of time (i.e., more than a few hours).

10. Select teachers or peer leaders who believe in the program and then provide them with adequate training. (2001:10)

The ten characteristics, not surprisingly, focus on content, behaviors, and methods of delivery. Yet, not all the empirical possibilities gleaned from background studies are attended to. Possible additions would include such factors as parental interest and involvement, discussion with parents about sexual values and beliefs, parental support, connectedness, monitoring, disapproval of premarital sexual involvement, adolescent definitions of the future, adolescent beliefs, and so on (Miller et al., 2001; Franklin et al., 1997).

As difficult as it may seem, figuring out ways to highlight contextual factors and the kinds of beliefs and values that contribute to behavior change would improve the efforts. Sexuality education that focuses only on behaviors and skills is delivering information in a contextual vacuum. It is a bit like teaching an airplane mechanic how to use a special tool without knowing under what conditions the tool is to be used to advantage or benefit.

Moreover, research measuring the effects of sexuality education is always more limited in scope than is desirable, when one considers the total number of effects that could be measured. A truly comprehensive evaluation of sexuality education would have to take into account all relevant effects: sexual activity, contraceptive use, adolescent pregnancy, STD transmission (which ones, how frequently, how severe, etc.), social-emotional influences, economic well-being, parenting practices, and so on. Incremental improvement in prevention efforts may be insufficient to make a significant reduction in the problem without some kind of upheaval in other culturewide factors that seem to inhibit or foster the problems sexuality education is trying to solve or the benefits sexuality education is trying to produce (see Flinn & Hauser, 1998).

In other words, the larger culture also is a feature of whether a meaningful difference is likely to occur in the adolescent population. Family background factors, cultural patterns of belief and behavior, media philosophies and images relevant to sexual issues, peer group boundaries, individual responses to calls to responsible behavior—these are inescapable contexts in which all prevention efforts operate, and they inevitably include major influences that a mere curriculum can hardly control. These reminders illustrate the problem with prevention that Brown noted (Kirby, 2001): We cannot do everything. School curricula alone will not create benefits and help students avoid liabilities.

Perhaps all school, agency, or government-based sexuality education is a compromise grounded in the idea that if parents are not going to do this, somebody has to. Sexuality education becomes a backup or replacement for parental neglect or inadequacy. The goal is to help children and adolescents protect themselves from self-destruction due to irresponsible or risky sexual involvement. But a neglected factor in the choosing of both the content and delivery of sex education is to examine the nature of the audience receiving the program. It may not be wise to assume that the audience for sex education efforts is a homogeneous group of adolescents with similar at-risk backgrounds and contextual factors. Sex education is delivered to heterogeneous audiences, but the nature of sex education is hardly ever structured for specific subgroups of those audiences.

Public sexuality education, perhaps of necessity, is delivered as if the receiving audience were homogeneous. That is, everyone is assumed to be equally at risk; the same knowledge, facts, and philosophy are assumed to be relevant to all; and whatever factors might insulate or reduce the risk for many in the audience are rarely addressed. This need not be so. Comprehensive sexuality education could move toward more bold affirmations of abstinence as being the best way to avoid a myriad of problems (National Campaign, 2001), but would need to do so while simultaneously acknowledging the philosophical realities that underlie such a viewpoint. Similarly, we need to hear from the proponents of the philosophy guiding the notion of responsible participation in sexual activity outside of marriage which would also need to be articulated.

Sexuality education programs need to be evaluated both empirically and philosophically. It is not typical for such programs to be examined for their philosophical underpinnings, but it may be that a program's philosophy—as well as the beliefs and values of the targeted audiences—could contribute to the effectiveness of the program. At the very least, it would allow the possibility of matching curricula and content to audiences and their values and beliefs to curriculum content.

Citizenship and Sexuality

One unique starting point of considering how philosophy of behavior might relate to or affect that behavior is to consider the idea of sexual behavior as a matter of citizenship responsibility. This would legitimize and highlight the recognition from both the abstinence and comprehensive sexuality educators that a quality community needs to attend to the sexual nature of human experience and foster those attitudes and behaviors that are nondestructive of human well-being. Sexuality is a matter of concern for the community. That is one reason why sexual practices and contexts are a concern of government. Community may be essential to understanding the solutions to social problems, including sexual problems.

Community is neither public nor private. It is an expression of a shared commitment or understanding or willingness to be connected. It has to do with the quality of those connections. As Berry (1992) summarized,

> Community life is by definition a life of cooperation and responsibility. Private life and public life, without the disciplines of community interest, necessarily gravitate toward competition and exploitation. As private life casts off all com-

munity restraints in the interest of economic exploitation or ambition or self-realization or whatever, the communal supports of public life also and by the same stroke are undercut, and public life becomes simply the arena of unrestrained private ambition and greed. (1992:120)

The current climate in the United States is too often that schools are publics rather than communities. Thus, their attempts to solve various social problems include debates about private and public interests, usually ending in deference to the idea that private behavior cannot be attended to by the public school. This suggests that few brands of sex education will be very successful. Whether such programs encourage abstinence or promote condom distribution, whether they achieve statistically significant results that affect a small proportion of the sample studied, they will generally fail overall because they work within a paradigm that fails to make sexuality an issue of community. If we were to address sexual involvement as a matter neither fully private nor wholly public, it could then be discussed as an act in which the community has an interest, and not as private behavior solely based on free choice. But has community interest been deleted by the categories of public or private? If the notion of community is excluded in advance from prevention efforts, no conversations about citizenship, responsibility, morality, or acting in behalf of the next generation are appropriate, however practically or conceptually or relationally relevant they may be. In fact, perhaps the meaning of the current few, but recurring, positive results of sexuality education obtained for some students from a variety of programs could be reexamined. Perhaps the results may best be understood according to the culture or sense of community the students already hold. Those cultures either help prevent or produce the problems the programs are trying to solve. If students already have a sense of community, then either abstinence-based or comprehensive programs are more likely to succeed. If students have already lost a sense of community and have adopted the public-private argument as their own, then they may defend their privacy without understanding its relationship to community. Strictly behavioral approaches seem not to have an effect in the aggregate, that is, although some programs report an increase in contraceptive use among the audiences for their programs, or a slight decrease in premarital pregnancies, this outcome is not quite sufficient to offset the attending increase in sexual activity (see Franklin et al., 1997 for a review of 32 programs).

Responsible citizenship, of course, is deeper and broader than responsible behavior, the latter being a matter of individual choice, and the former a matter of community. A matter in which individual behavior could threaten the well-being of the community is the business of the community. Community concern about sexuality is a matter of citizenship, because it portends consequences far beyond the private acts of individuals. Public schools could cast sexuality education efforts in an unabashed context of citizenship and community obligation, where that education would nurture the idea that even in (or especially in) the sexual domain, we must act as good citizens, in each others' best interests and in ways that do not threaten community. This suggestion is a possibility to be considered, and the operative word for implementation is could.

Recommendations

Given the multi-faceted approaches and divergent philosophies attending sexuality education efforts, there is no common vision regarding next steps. Nevertheless, the profession has progressed in the task of evaluating sexuality education programs during the past two decades. These empirical evaluations suggest directions future interventions might take and have also revealed limitations in the way we go about evaluating outcomes. In addition, admitting that all empirical efforts are guided by theoretical assumptions and beliefs—philosophies of science—would enable sexuality educators to understand their starting points of agreement and disagreement regarding how to proceed. The following are possibilities:

1. Perhaps being more explicit about the philosophy of science and of human sexuality guiding any given program would help consumers understand the risks and benefits of sexuality education. Acknowledge that every intervention program is grounded in a guiding philosophy and that the implications for what to teach, how to intervene, and where to draw the line of moral responsibility are often incompatible across philosophies. Moreover, in the debate over what programs or philosophies or interventions are most effective, the distinction between statistical significance and practical significance is important. Targeted behaviors and outcomes are achieved for what percentage of the audience?

2. Perhaps taking into account the developmental level of the recipients (moral, social, intellectual) could result in the content of curricula being developmentally appropriate. For example, the media culture may present sexually-related programming targeted to an older audience than it is watched by. This heightens the need for curricula to become not more sexually so-

phisticated, but more developmentally sensitive, and it needs to be straightforward about the meaning of various contexts. Some curricula seem to grant individual autonomy in decision-making very early, violating both developmental principles and the meaning of accountable decision-making by legal minors.

3. Perhaps the parental dimension should be addressed more extensively in content and delivery contexts, because research repeatedly acknowledges that parental influence and involvement in the lives of adolescents acts as an insulator against many risk-taking sexual behaviors (Miller, Benson, & Galbraith, 2001). This focus would grant a space for parental voices and involvement. Any curricula, at the least, could provoke parental involvement, even if only through joint parent-adolescent homework assignments and discussions. Greater effort to harness these community and family resources could enhance the meaningful difference made by public curricula efforts.

4. Perhaps acknowledging that audiences are not homogeneous in values, beliefs, practices, cultural patterns, and family circumstances, and that people respond to the same content in different ways, could temper the way concepts are delivered. Audience response to curricula is not uniform, and care should be taken not to make the philosophy and content of public sex education programs a Procrustean bed into which the differing shapes and sizes of the values and beliefs of the students must be made to fit. Either a curriculum that addresses the common ground an audience might share, or tailor-made curricula for different audiences should be considered. Logistically, this could be taxing on schools, but it would enhance the possibility of making meaningful differences to heterogeneous audiences.

5. Perhaps examining the specific contexts of changes and outcomes could lead to refinement of both content and delivery of sexuality education. What is the response of subgroups in our audiences? Does a given curriculum serve blacks or whites better? Who responds most positively to parental involvement? How successful is a curricula with those with abstinent beliefs versus those without such beliefs, with those sexually involved and those abstaining? The more we know about which audiences a given curriculum is reaching, the better we can improve our efforts. And the more we attend to specific characteristics of an audience the more multidimensional a picture of the

consumers of family life education we will have, and the better we can use programs to make a meaningful difference in their futures.

6. Perhaps addressing the moral domain—especially regarding what it means to seek others' best interests—would temper the content delivered. We admit that intervention designed to make a meaningful difference is a moral enterprise. This does not mean somebody's "values" are being imposed on someone else. If we claim we are totally value-free, or just providing knowledge, we are naïve regarding the moral philosophy that attends such positions. It is just as legitimate to make a reasoned moral case for an approach to a problem as to make a (supposedly) purely pragmatic or empirical argument. The latter two arguments, however, always reveal a philosophical position as well (Slife & Williams, 1995). Pragmatism is governed by moral limits as are all other positions designed to make a difference. Our intent, as family life educators, is to make a difference that helps adolescents avoid choices that undermine their own or others' best interests. As has been shown, this stance places us inescapably in moral territory. All philosophies of sex education seem to grant the immoral and irresponsible nature of coercion, manipulation, and placing oneself or others at risk. Philosophies diverge, just by the fact that some curricula focus on individual autonomy in decision making about practices, and others focus also on which contexts of sexual activity are practically tied to a quality future.

7. Perhaps considering the possibility that the ideal curricula have not yet been created would spawn surprising approaches that might include new starting points altogether. One possibility is to reaffirm or transform schools from publics to communities, where, though personal rights are granted without discrimination, privileges of citizenship are earned and supportive of the common interests of families in the community. Make citizenship education a schoolwide enterprise. Place the understanding of human sexuality back in the domain of good citizenship, where the quality of relational and familial connections across time and across generations is acknowledged.

8. Perhaps acknowledging that sexuality education programs are only one factor among many that would foster more positive approaches to sexual expression. Reaffirming the limitations of the concept of a school curriculum being the major influence on sexual decision making of

adolescents could better address destructive influences in the broader culture and could be the beginning of a broader philosophical debate. In the absence of consensus, dialogue invites everyone to consider new possibilities.

Introduction References

Roffman, D. M. (1992). "Common Sense and Nonsense About Sex Education." *Family Life Matters*, pp. 2, 7.

Schemo, D. J. (2000, October 4). "Survey Finds Parents Favor More Detailed Sex Education." *New York Times*, pp. 1A, 23A.

References

Abstinence Clearinghouse. (2003). Mission.

Back, K. (1983). Teenage pregnancy: Science and ideology in applied social psychology. In R. F. Kidd, & M. J. Saks, (Eds.), *Advances in applied social psychology* (pp. 1–17). Hillsdale, NJ: Lawrence Erlbaum.

Berry, W. (1992). *Sex, economy, freedom, and community*. New York: Pantheon.

Boyce, W. D., & Jensen, L. C. (1978). *Moral reasoning: A psychological-philosophical integration*. Lincoln, NE: University of Nebraska Press.

Coles, R. (1988). *Harvard diary: Reflections on the sacred and the secular*. New York: Crossroad.

Doherty, W. J. (1995). *Soul searching: Why psychotherapy must promote moral responsibility*. New York: Basic Books.

Flinn, S. K., & Hauser, D. (1998). *Teenage pregnancy: The case for prevention: An analysis of recent trends and federal expenditures associated with teenage pregnancy*. Washington, DC: Advocates for Youth.

Focus on the Family. (2001). *Take twelve: The truth about abstinence education*. Colorado Springs, CO: Author.

Franklin, D., Grant, D., Corcoran, J., Miller, P., & Bultman, L. (1997). Effectiveness of prevention programs for adolescent pregnancy: A meta-analysis. *Journal of Marriage and the Family, 59*, 551–567.

Hanson, S. L., Myers, D. E., & Ginsburg, A. L. (1987). The role of responsibility and knowledge in reducing teenage out-of-wedlock childbearing. *Journal of Marriage and the Family, 49*, 241–256.

Kirby, D. (2001). *Emerging answers: Research findings on programs to reduce teen pregnancy* (Summary). Washington, DC: National Campaign to Prevent Teen Pregnancy.

——. (2002). *Do abstinence-only programs delay the initiation of sex among young people and reduce teen pregnancy?* Washington, DC: National Campaign to Prevent Teen Pregnancy.

Miller, B. C., Benson, B., & Galbraith, K. A. (2001). Family relationships and adolescent pregnancy risk: A research synthesis. *Developmental Review, 21*, 1–38.

National Campaign to Prevent Teen Pregnancy. (2001). *Halfway there: A prescription for continued progress in preventing teen pregnancy*. Washington, DC: Author.

Planned Parenthood Federation of America. (1994). *Mission Statement and Policy Statement on Sexuality Education*. New York: Author.

Polit, D. F., & Kahn, J. R. (1985). Project redirection: Evaluation of a comprehensive program for disadvantaged teenage mothers. *Family Planning Perspectives, 17*, 150–155.

Polit, D. F. (1989). Effects of a comprehensive program for teenage parents: Five years after Project Redirection. *Family Planning Perspectives, 21*, 164–169, 187.

Richard, D. (1990). *Has sex education failed our teenagers? A research report*. Colorado Springs, CO: Focus on the Family Publishing.

SIECUS. (1996). *Guidelines for comprehensive sexuality education*. New York: Author.

SIECUS. (2003). *Sexuality education: Values inherent in the guidelines*. New York: Author.

Slife, B. D., & Williams, R. N. (1995). *What's behind the research? Discovering hidden assumptions in the behavioral sciences*. Thousand Oaks, CA: Sage.

U. S. Army. (1947). Army venereal disease rate drops as a result of new program. *The New England Journal of Medicine, 238*, 784.

Whitehead, B. D., Wilcox, B. L., Rostosky, S. S., Randall, B., & Wright, M. L. C. (2001). *Keeping the faith: The role of religion and faith communities in preventing teen pregnancy*. Washington, DC: National Campaign to Prevent Teen Pregnancy.

Williams, R. N., & Gantt, E. E. (2002). Pursuing psychology as the science of the ethical: Contributions of the work of Emmanuel Levinas. In E. E. Gantt & R. N. Williams (Eds.), *Psychology for the other: Levinas, ethics, and the practice of psychology* (p.11). Pittsburgh, PA: Duquesne University Press.

From Terrance D. Olson (2003). "Sexuality Education: Philosophies and Practices in Search of a Meaningful Difference." Unpublished manuscript, Brigham Young University. ✦